MANAGEMENT
CONCEPTS & PRACTICES

SECOND EDITION

Tim Hannagan

Former Principal and
Chief Executive of Uxbridge College

With contributions from

Roger Bennett	Mike Harry
Ruth Boaden	Len Holden
Andrew Brown	Kate Prescott
Leslie Chadwick	Richard Welford
Dominic Cooper	Mik Wisniewski

FINANCIAL TIMES
PITMAN PUBLISHING

FINANCIAL TIMES

MANAGEMENT

LONDON · SAN FRANCISCO ·
KUALA LUMPUR · JOHANNESBURG

*Financial Times Management delivers the knowledge,
skills and understanding that enables students,
managers and organisations to achieve their ambitions,
whatever their needs, wherever they are.*

London Office:
128 Long Acre, London WC2E 9AN
Tel: +44 (0)171 447 2000
Fax: +44 (0)171 240 5771
Website: www.ftmanagement.com

An imprint of Pearson Education Limited

First published in Great Britain 1995
Second edition published 1998

© Chapters 1–8 & 20, Tim Hannagan 1998
© Chapters 17 & 18, Richard Welford 1998
© Chapter 9, Andrew Brown 1998
© Chapter 10, Len Holden 1998
© Chapter 11, Roger Bennett 1998
© Chapter 12, Dominic Cooper 1998
© Chapter 13, Mik Wisniewski 1998
© Chapter 14, Ruth Boaden 1998
© Chapter 15, Mike Harry 1998
© Chapter 16, Leslie Chadwick 1998
© Chapter 19, Kate Prescott 1998

British Library Cataloguing in Publication Data
A CIP catalogue record for this book is available on request from the British Library.

ISBN 0–273–63103–9

10 9 8 7 6 5 4 3 2

Typeset by Pantek Arts, Maidstone, Kent.
Printed and bound in Great Britain by Clays Ltd, St Ives plc.

The Publishers' policy is to use paper manufactured from sustainable forests.

CONTENTS

SECTION B · POLICY AND PLANNING

SECTION C · ORGANISING

LIST OF CONTRIBUTORS

Dr Roger Bennett, Reader, London Guildhall University (*Chapter 11*)

Dr Ruth Boaden, Lecturer in Operations Management, Manchester School of Management, UMIST (*Chapter 14*)

Dr Andrew D Brown, Lecturer, The Judge Institute of Management Studies, University of Cambridge (*Chapter 9*)

Dr Leslie Chadwick, Lecturer in Financial Management, Bradford University Management Centre (*Chapter 16*)

Dr Dominic Cooper, Chartered Psychologist and Management Consultant, Applied Behavioural Sciences Ltd, Hull (*Chapter 12*)

Dr Mike Harry, Senior Visiting Fellow in Management and Information Systems, University of Bradford Management Centre (*Chapter 15*)

Dr Len Holden, Principal Lecturer, Department of Human Resource Management, Leicester Business School, De Montfort University (*Chapter 10*)

Kate Prescott, Lecturer in International Business, University of Bradford Management Centre (*Chapter 19*)

Richard Welford, Professor of Business Economics, University of Huddersfield (*Chapters 17 and 18*)

Mik Wisniewski, Senior Manager, Accounts Commission for Scotland (*Chapter 13*)

PREFACE

Managers are facing increasingly rapid change in the technology, culture and environment in which they work. Rapid developments in the application of information technology are matched by equally rapid changes in the structure of organisations, in the role of managers and in the economy and society in which they operate. This puts pressure on management which helps to emphasise the importance of understanding both the concepts and practices involved.

The objective of this book is to analyse these concepts and practices in all areas of management in order to provide an understanding of the way organisations are managed and an appreciation of the most recent developments in management theory and practice. This analysis is based on a consideration of past developments as well as looking towards those likely to take place in the future.

The book is intended for teachers and students on management programmes such as the Certificate in Management, Diploma in Management and MBA, first degree programmes, Higher National Programmes, and professional courses such as marketing, personnel and accounting. This general introduction to management is also important in engineering, building and construction, and project management as well as in many other areas of study and work.

This new edition brings the information in this book up to date and includes the very latest ideas on management development. For example, the chapter on information systems management introduces a section on communications and the Internet and includes a discussion of the World Wide Web and moves towards global computerisation, while the chapter on human resources management discusses recent legislation on equal opportunities and includes sections on sexual harassment in the workplace and on ageism.

All the chapters begin with a list of objectives and give a summary of the main features covered in the chapter. Each chapter ends with questions for review and discussion. Case studies are included in the text and at the end of every chapter and provide a basis for further discussion and comment. This edition includes many new case studies, including extracts from the *Financial Times*. These extracts are the copyright of the *Financial Times*, which has kindly given permission to reproduce them in this book. References to books and articles for further reading are provided for each chapter. The content of this book and the examples used in it are designed to provide both a European and international perspective. It has been produced to be user-friendly, and to appeal to undergraduates as well as graduates and post-experience managers on business, management and related professional programmes and courses. An *Instructor's Manual* including questions on the case studies, answer points and additional materials is available free of charge to tutors and lecturers upon application to the publishers.

It is argued that the basic function of managers in the modern economy, and in the future, is the management of change. This is the underlying theme of the book, which also contains an international perspective on the role of managers. Chapters have been contributed by experts in their fields, while the whole book takes an integrated approach to management in order to establish the manager's role and a sense of direction for the organisation. In dealing with these issues, the book is divided into five main sections focusing on the major functions of management – which can be summarised as organising, controlling and planning – and on management at a time of change, looking forward also to those management issues which will be particularly important in the future.

The challenge of management is considered in terms of leadership, the importance of the customer, and in maintaining a competitive edge through marketing. Strategic management is considered from the viewpoint of both policy and implementation, combined with ensuring high-quality development and control. The organising function is seen to involve working within a corporate culture to provide good communications and effective human resource management in order to motivate employees. In controlling the organisation, there is a focus on making management decisions, and on operations management, information management and financial management. Current issues in management which are given prominence include corporate responsibility and management ethics, environmental issues, multinational management and the role of the manager in the twenty-first century. The international dimension is a major theme and these issues help to highlight the importance of this wider perspective.

The importance of corporate culture is increasingly recognised as a factor in management and is strongly linked to business ethics and 'green' issues. Multinational factors play an essential part in the life of many managers with the opening up of the European market, developments in international trade and investment, and the use of the information superhighway. With all these developments taking place, the changes occurring for managers establishing a career path are recognised and the effect of those changes in the future are considered.

Organisational restructuring has meant that the career expectations of managers has changed dramatically. Managers now have to take control of their own careers to an extent unknown in the past. This provides a personal challenge as well as a challenge in working with other people. It is argued that this is a dynamic factor in a situation where, more than ever, effective and efficient management can make and is making a real difference in all types of organisation. Managers make a difference in private companies, in public sector institutions and in voluntary organisations, because of changes in technology, the pressure of competition, the problems of understanding customer needs, added to cultural developments and environmental challenges. The role of the manager has never been more rewarding or challenging and it has never been more important to understand this role.

Tim Hannagan

ACKNOWLEDGEMENTS

A number of people have contributed to the production of this book. I would like to thank the contributors from a range of University Business Schools and Management Centres, who have used their expertise to provide chapters in their specialist fields; Penelope Woolf, Elizabeth Tarrant and Simon Lake at Financial Times Management for their considerable support; Helen Gardiner for her typographical and processing skills; Yvonne, my wife, for providing me with the time to work on the book; and the many other people who have supported the project.

Every effort has been made to trace and acknowledge ownership of copyright. The Publishers will be pleased to make suitable arrangements with any copyright holders whom it has not been possible to contact.

MANAGEMENT AT A TIME OF CHANGE

1 THE CHALLENGE OF MANAGEMENT

Tim Hannagan

OBJECTIVES

The objectives of this chapter are to:

◆ identify the manager's role in a time of change

◆ analyse different theories of management

◆ consider the levels of management responsibility

◆ apply an understanding of the management role and responsibility to the management of change

MANAGEMENT

The manager's role

It can be argued that, in the environment in which managers work, change is the natural order of things and the most important management skill is the management of change. This arises from the fact that the really skilful part of a manager's job is setting up the method of working in the first place.

At first glance a manager's role is to organise, supervise and control people so that there is a productive outcome to work. Organisations of one type or another are essential for productive work because they bring people together with raw materials and equipment in order to achieve a variety of goals. By combining people's talents and energy with resources, very often more can be achieved than by individuals working on their own. Organisations, whether they are companies, educational institutions, hospitals or football teams, will all have objectives. They will all have a purpose for being in existence and for continuing their work. These objectives or goals may be expressed in terms of profits, market share, educational achievements, health or winning games. Every organisation will have a plan to achieve these objectives in order to make sure that they have the right people doing the right jobs with the best possible equipment at the right time.

Managers are the people responsible for helping organisations to achieve their objectives and for creating and implementing their plans. They are responsible for:

> *'the process of planning, organising, leading and controlling the efforts of organisation members and of using all organisational resources to achieve stated organisational goals.'*
>
> (Mescon, Albert and Khedouri, 1985)

This definition helps to describe what managers do, while the skill of management can be described as:

> *'getting things done by other people.'*   (Mary Parker Follett, 1941)

This definition emphasises the fact that managers achieve organisational objectives by arranging for other people to perform whatever tasks are required, and do not necessarily carry out these tasks themselves. This is obviously essential in a football team where even a player–manager must have other people to help the team to win. In industry one-person businesses can succeed by specialising in one aspect of the process, but major products and services are supplied by larger organisations because one-person businesses cannot produce a sufficient quantity of goods and services to meet consumer demand. It is a characteristic of developing economies that as the market for goods and services grows the importance of the one-person business declines relative to larger forms of organisation.

It can be argued that management is:

> *'the process of optimising human, material, and financial contributions for the achievement of organisational goals.'*
>
> (Pearce and Robinson, 1989)

This definition begins to move the idea of the role of the manager into a more dynamic and up-to-date relationship with the organisation. The relatively 'old-fashioned' definitions emphasise the running of an organisation in terms of administration and control, which represents what can be described as an operational view of management. The more modern and dynamic view of management has been expressed by Professor Sir Roland Smith in stating that management should be based on 'innovation, marketing and risk'. This view suggests that people are imprisoned by their own experience and that in order to remain dynamic an organisation needs to change its structure frequently. The emphasis is not on running the organisation so much as planning, developing and changing it. In Fig 1.1 all managers may be involved with the operational aspects of management, but as they are promoted and develop, their role becomes increasingly one of planning, innovation and leadership.

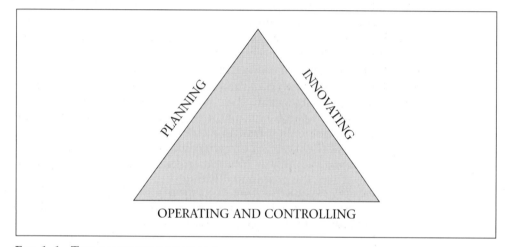

FIG 1.1 THE MANAGEMENT ROLE

When technological progress is slow and other aspects of organisations remain the same for many years, perhaps a major part of a working lifetime, the important skills are supervisory and administrative in order to make sure that the established process continues. Under these circumstances operating and controlling are paramount, but when working methods and processes change every few years or more or less constantly, managing change becomes the most important management attribute. As well as constant change in working methods, managers are now faced with increasingly complex organisations and a rapidly changing economic and social environment, which again makes the older definitions of management, in terms of running the business, inadequate and inappropriate descriptions of the role.

The management challenge

The management challenge is to maintain control over the processes of an organisation while at the same time leading, inspiring, directing and making decisions on all sorts of matters. The challenge for modern managers is to deal with this tension between operating the present systems, structures and processes and the need to change in order to survive.

'Management as it has been systematised and professionalised, has developed many axioms over the past century. But in the past twenty years, the stable conditions (large scale mass-production) that led to the slow emergence of these universals have blown apart.'

(Tom Peters, 1987)

Organisations, whether they are commercial companies or non-profit institutions, have to meet customer demands if they are to succeed. This is obvious with motor car companies and high street shops, but is now also true in the non-profit sector for organisations such as schools, universities, hospitals, museums and state-owned zoos. As customer needs alter, so the business must change by anticipating customer wants, leading these where appropriate as well as responding to them. The emphasis today is on a focus on the customer so that all managers are concerned with leading their organisation, section, unit or team to enable work to be carried out successfully in response to the needs of their market. As society and the economy develop and as managers are promoted from junior to middle and senior levels, the requirement to be flexible, creative, innovative and able to absorb and communicate new ideas becomes of increasing importance.

This view of modern management suggests that it is about change because in order to meet their objectives, organisations need to focus on their customers through a marketing culture. This is as true of a professional football team as of a multinational company, a hospital trust or a small business. Management of a kind is required in the smallest task; in a one-person business, that one person will have to combine all the qualities of management as well as working at an operational level. Above all, in one way or another, the individual running a one-person business must satisfy the customers through the quality of the work and the service provided. The larger an organisation the more specialised management can become, while at the highest level there will need again to be a convergence of skills, although on a different plane (*see* Fig 1.2).

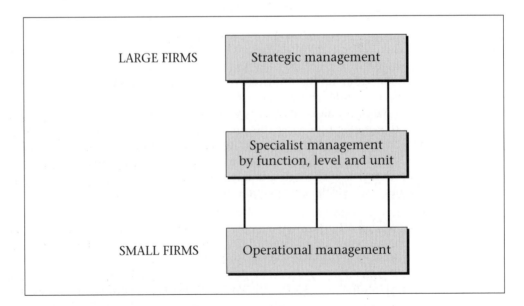

FIG 1.2 LEVELS OF MANAGEMENT

Management as a science

The science of management is based today on the view that 'what can't be measured isn't worth doing'. This is a view supported by Professor Sir Roland Smith, but even this apparently 'up-to-date' theory has been described by John Harvey-Jones as out of date. This is partly because of the echoes thrown forward from the 1960s when there was a management view that everything could be measured and that success would follow improvements in systems of measurement, particularly accountancy. The modern version of this theory has been greatly encouraged by developments in information technology which has vastly increased the potential for measurement. Although all managers have to accept the need for business accounts and the application of statistics in making decisions, at the same time managers must consider the derivation and accuracy of the numbers presented to them. At times it may be sensible to override all the facts and figures that are available; for example, Sony produced the Walkman against the evidence of market research which suggested that the product would not be successful. This example does not invalidate market research, but puts it in its place as one of a number of factors in the management decision-making process.

Managers have to operate in the situation in which they find themselves:

> *'The difficulty is that there can never be any single correct solution to any management problem, or any all-embracing system which will carry one through a particular situation or period of time.'*
>
> (John Harvey-Jones, 1993)

The fact is that over the years management styles and fashions change and business environments alter. As a subject of study and analysis management can be seen as a mongrel form of social science, borrowing as necessary from other social sciences, and because it is concerned with people and their behaviour there is an element of unpredictability about the whole process.

THE SCIENCE OF MANAGEMENT

Background

The various quotations included so far illustrate that there are, of course, different views about management, some of which have attempted to create the concept of a single approach to management problems. There have always been a variety of theories about management and they have been particularly important since the industrial revolution of the eighteenth and nineteenth centuries. This produced the need for a systematic approach to management because of the development of new technologies and the concentration of great quantities of raw materials and large numbers of workers in one place. Workshops and then factories produced goods in large quantities which had to be distributed widely. The move from a self-sufficient economy to one based on the division of labour created a need for co-ordination which called attention to the question of management. The development of economic theories based on the factors of production developed by Adam Smith in *The Wealth of Nations* emphasised the relationship between the separate elements of labour, capital, raw materials and enterprise. These theories were allied to those concerning the division of labour based on people specialising in one task and developing a limited range of skills.

The production line was a clear example of this. The view developed that it was possible to analyse each operation in the production process so that the various skills involved could be isolated. Charles Babbage, an English mathematics professor, became convinced in the early years of the nineteenth century that the application of scientific principles to work processes would both increase productivity and lower costs. Each factory operation would be analysed so that the various skills involved could be isolated. His view was that the constant repetition of each operation would improve these skills and therefore the efficiency of the workers. This was the basis of 'scientific management', developed in order to achieve increases in productivity and remaining today, in one form or another, as one of the driving forces behind change.

Management theory was a relatively new phenomenon in the nineteenth century, so that Henry R Towne's assertion in 1886 that management was a field of study equal in importance to engineering was a radical new approach. He was the co-founder and president of the Yale and Towne Manufacturing Company in the USA and he expressed these views to the American Society of Mechanical Engineers. His observation was that the management of work was disorganised and largely intuitive without any basis of principle or theory. The development of the so-called classical school of management theory was an answer to Towne's view and can be seen most clearly in the work of Frederick Taylor and Henri Fayol. Their opinions were based on Adam Smith's idea of the 'rational man', the idea that people tend to choose a course of action that maximises their personal gain. Founded on this 'rational' approach, Taylor and Fayol believed that the control of human behaviour could be obtained by putting a logical structure into place.

Scientific management

At the end of the nineteenth century skilled workers were in short supply in the USA, and in order to meet demand, productivity needed to be expanded by increasing the efficiency of the workers who were available. In order to do this, Frederick W Taylor (1856–1915) developed a body of principles which came to be known as 'Taylorism'. He based his managerial system on production-line time studies. He analysed each job by breaking it down into its component parts and then designed the quickest and best methods of operation for each part. By doing this he was able to establish how much workers should be able to do with the equipment and materials available, and how far pay could be related to levels of productivity.

This process developed into a 'differential rate system' based on greater pay for greater productivity which in turn, it was argued, would lead to greater profits. The higher payments would continue, Taylor thought, because they were 'scientifically correct' rates set at a level that was best for the company and the worker. Increased profits would encourage companies to expand and ensure continued employment for those workers able to meet the required productivity standards. Those who did not meet these standards would easily find work, in his opinion, because of the shortage of skilled workers. This process is what might be referred to now as a form of performance-related pay, and it is interesting to note that Taylor decided to put his ideas into effect as a private consultant as early as 1893.

One well-documented example of his work as a consultant management engineer was with the Simonds Rolling Machine Company. In one operation, 120 women inspected bicycle ball bearings. Taylor's approach was to study and time the movements of the best workers; he then trained the rest of the workers in the methods of their more effective colleagues and transferred or laid off the poorest performers. He introduced rest periods during the working day and a differential pay rate system. The results were increases in productivity, quality, earnings and morale and a fall in costs (*see* Fig 1.3).

- **Monitor, study, time the best workers**
- **Train the other workers to the same standard**
- **Introduce changes such as differential pay rates in order to increase productivity**

FIG 1.3 THE TAYLOR PROCESS

The problem with Taylor's approach was that it did lead to lay-offs, and there was the fear that increased productivity would mean that the available work would be completed even sooner, causing more lay-offs. By 1912 opposition to Taylorism led to strikes and to hostile members of Congress asking for explanations of his ideas and methods. Taylor stated that his philosophy rested on a few basic principles:

- The development of a true science of management, so that the best method for performing each task could be determined.
- The scientific selection of workers so that each worker would be given responsibility for the task for which he or she was best suited.
- The scientific education and development of the worker.
- Intimate, friendly co-operation between management and labourer.

Taylor's views are summarised in his book *Scientific Management*. He believed that for these principles to succeed there needed to be a change in working attitudes and practices, 'a complete mental revolution' on the part of management and employees. He felt that the concentration of effort should not be on profit, but that both management and labour should concentrate on increased production, which he believed would mean that profits would rise to an extent where management and labour would no longer have to compete for them.

This need for change was at the heart of the problem with the Taylor approach, because changing attitudes is notoriously harder than changing practices; although the new technology was adopted by management, Taylor's philosophy was not.

Increases in productivity in fact often led to lay-offs or changes in pay rates that left workers producing more output for the same income. The proponents of scientific management did not sufficiently take into account the actual needs of people at work. They assumed that the prime motivation for work was pay, and that provided there was an increase in their pay workers would be happy. In fact, modern views suggest that workers wanted then, as they do now, to have satisfaction in their work, to have good working conditions and to feel they have a say in matters which directly affect them. As summarised in Fig 1.4, modern management practices are based on consulting people and giving them responsibility for their work, while scientific management was based on telling people how to increase their earnings, training them and then expecting them to go ahead and do it.

ARGUMENTS FOR:	PROBLEMS WITH:
Use of technology	Attitudes
Productivity increases	Lay-offs
Motivation: pay	Motivation: satisfaction, working conditions, control
Telling employees	Consulting employees
Long-term benefits	Focus on work design Training

FIG 1.4 'TAYLORISM'

Contributors to scientific management extended Taylor's work. For example, Henry L Gantt (1861–1919) reconsidered and developed his incentive system and produced the 'Gantt' chart to record a worker's progress. Frank B Gilbreth (1868–1925) extended Taylor's research on time and motion problems, and his wife Lillian M Gilbreth (1878–1972) focused on the scientific selection, training and placing of employees to provide the precursor to present-day human resource management. Lillian Gilbreth in particular developed as well as extended scientific management. However, the basic theory remained the concept of the division of labour and the belief that, by specialising in certain tasks, a team of people can out-produce the same number of people each performing all the tasks. The highly productive modern assembly line is a direct descendant of these ideas. The ideas of efficiency propounded by scientific management, such as time and motion studies, promoted awareness of the equipment and physical movement involved in a task, while the emphasis on the training of workers recognised the importance of ability and its development in increasing productivity. The focus on work design has encouraged managers to have a fresh look at the way a job is done and has pointed the way towards the idea of the professional manager.

Administrative management

Of course Frederick Taylor was concerned largely with the detail of organisational functions and how they could be managed to provide benefits for the whole company. Other contemporary ideas were based on the whole organisation and the influence of the management of this on company functions and effectiveness.

In classical organisation theory it was believed that managerial practice fell into certain patterns that could be identified and analysed. Henri Fayol (1841–1925), for example, was a contemporary of Taylor, but was interested in the management of large groups of people rather than organisational functions. Fayol believed that 'with scientific forecasting and proper methods of management, satisfactory results were inevitable'. He insisted that management was a skill like any other so that managers were not born, but made. Once the underlying principles were understood and a general theory of management formulated, management could be taught. This was a major change in views of leadership as well as management and forms the basis of many modern attitudes.

Fayol divided business operations into units which he described as technical, commercial, financial, security, accounting and managerial, all of which were closely dependent on one another. His primary focus was on the management of the operational areas which he defined in terms of five functions:

- **planning** – a course of action for the organisation to meet its goals;

- **organising** – to ensure the availability and co-ordination of the material and human resources of the organisation to put the plans into effect;

- **commanding** – to provide direction to employees;

- **co-ordinating** – to ensure that the resources and activities of the organisation work together to achieve the desired goals;

- **controlling** – to monitor the plans and ensure they are being achieved.

Compared with Taylor, Fayol had a comprehensive view of management very similar to modern ideas. This comprehensive view was being developed at much the same time by Max Weber (1864–1920) in Germany. His ideas were based on the structure of the organisation, or the 'bureaucracy', which was characterised by:

- **a clear definition of authority and responsibility;**

- **a chain of command;**

- **selection based on qualifications, training and examination;**

- **appointed officials working for fixed salaries;**

- **strict rules, disciplines and controls.**

Weber wanted to depersonalise management in order to promote a uniformity which would provide for the fair and equal treatment of all workers. His 'bureaucracy' was designed to provide stability and certainty in an organisation and his model of management has contributed to organisational thinking over the last 100 years, particularly in large national and multinational companies.

BEHAVIOURAL THEORY

Organisation of people

Some of the classical theories of management appear inappropriate for consideration today, but they developed when organisations were relatively stable and existed in relatively predictable environments. As working situations have changed and become more unsettled, classical theories have become less relevant but have still left their mark on management thinking. The administrative approach shifted the emphasis of management thought towards considering the organisation as a whole. This was followed by more people-oriented ideas and a human relations approach which is more in tune with present-day ideas on styles of management.

Early contributors to this included Mary Parker Follett (1868–1933), who asserted that the hierarchical distinction between managers and subordinates was artificial and obscured a natural partnership between labour and management. In her view they shared a common purpose as members of the same organisation, and she stressed the interdependence among their activities and functions. She considered that leadership should not be based on authority but on the superior knowledge and ability of the manager.

Other managers such as Chester I Barnard (1886–1961) carried these ideas further. He became president of New Jersey Bell in 1927 and through his experience as a manager and his reading he developed the view that an organisation could operate efficiently only when its goals and the aims of the individuals working for it were kept in balance. He put an emphasis on both the individual worker as the strategic factor in organisations and the importance of individuals working in groups. This was a clear statement of the behavioural view that 'the organisation is people'.

While management theories and styles have altered over the years, the basic management problems have remained the same. One of these is to increase productivity in order to increase output and to compete successfully. The scientific management approach was to consider this mainly as an engineering problem, while the behavioural management approach considered it to be concerned more with people. The latter rediscovered the views of Robert Owen who in the early 1800s managed several cotton mills in New Lanark in Scotland. In the new factories that had developed as a result of the Industrial Revolution, working conditions for employees were very poor and Owen saw the manager's role as one of reform. He built better housing for his workers, opened schools for their children and reduced the number of hours in the standard working day. He believed that by improving conditions there would be increased productivity and profits, so that while other managers concentrated on technical improvements he stressed that the manager's best investment was in the workers. In fact, his methods did work in that his factories were profitable, but it took a long time for people to apply these ideas more generally.

The Hawthorne effect

In the late 1920s and early 1930s, American researchers such as Elton Mayo (1880–1949) emphasised the concept of 'social man' to complement the classical concept of 'rational man'. Although it was recognised that personal economic needs remained an important source of motivation, it was emphasised that social needs, such as job satisfaction and work group pressures, were also very important. These social factors placed a heavy emphasis on management style, on how managers operated as well as what they did. Elton Mayo was involved in the famous 'Hawthorne experiments' which were an important study in human behaviour at work and are still influential today. They were a series of experiments carried out mainly at Weston Electric's Hawthorne plant near Chicago. The early studies were carried out by company engineers in collaboration with the National Academy of Sciences, with problems posed by this initial research then investigated by a team of researchers led by Elton Mayo, F J Roethlisberger and W J Dickson of Harvard in the period between 1927 and 1932.

The research was to examine the effects of changes in lighting on the productivity of workers. These were divided into two groups so that the control group could be exposed to a consistently well-lit workplace, while the experimental group worked under varied lighting conditions. The results of the experiment were ambiguous because although the productivity improved when the test group's lighting conditions were improved, the increases were erratic. There was also a tendency for productivity to continue to increase when lighting conditions were made worse. To add to the confusion, the control group's productivity also rose as the test group's lighting conditions were changed, even though there was no change in the lighting. Similar results were achieved in a new set of experiments which varied wages, rest periods and the length of working days and weeks for the test group. Mayo and his associates decided that financial and other incentives and changes were not causing productivity improvements. They believed that a complex chain of attitudes was involved in the productivity increases, with the main factor arising from the situation that the groups had been singled out for special attention, so that a group pride developed which motivated them to better performance. (*See also* Chapter 12.)

The phenomenon known as the 'Hawthorne effect' suggests that employees work harder when they believe management is concerned about their welfare and when managers pay special attention to them. It was also concluded that the social environment of workers and their informal work groups had a positive influence on productivity. Many employees found their work dull and meaningless, but their social links with co-workers imparted some meaning to their working lives. This reinforced Mayo's concept of the 'social man' motivated by social needs and responding more to work group pressures than to management control. The Hawthorne experiments have exerted a profound influence on the way managers approach their jobs in that they have focused attention on the development of people-management skills. In terms of motivation, follow-up experiments only served to illustrate the complexity of the issue. Attention is now given to working conditions and to motivation, and while the experiments did not solve any problems they did highlight relatively neglected areas where management could have an important influence.

MANAGEMENT SYSTEMS

Operations management

These examples of approaches to management in the nineteenth century and the first half of the twentieth century indicate that management problems have not particularly changed, while styles and approaches have. These are very much dependent on the circumstances of the time, so that although managers may feel they have a better approach than their predecessors, in fact it is a different approach which may be better or worse, according to the needs of the particular time. Operations research is a good example of this, developing out of the necessity in the UK to solve complex technical problems during the Second World War. At that time groups of mathematicians, scientists and engineers were brought together to solve such problems. The result was that significant technological and tactical breakthroughs were achieved by this approach, and after the war they were quickly applied to industry.

This management science approach has been characterised by solving problems through mixed teams of specialists from relevant disciplines who analyse the problem and suggest courses of action. Its main contribution to modern management has been in the development of models to help managers analyse complex statistical data in order to obtain a greater understanding of a problem. It has produced an emphasis on decision making, on the use of quantitative models in planning and the evaluation of the effectiveness of decisions which has been greatly encouraged in the second half of the twentieth century by the development of computers.

Modern management practice

All these approaches plus off-shoots and mixtures of them can be identified in modern management practice. John Harvey-Jones (1993) has written that:

> *'when I first started in industry in the fifties, attractions of work measurement and method study as a means of improving productivity seemed almost like a philosopher's stone.'*

During the 1960s 'there seemed to be a common belief that everything could be measured', while the '1970s were the period when we discovered that concentrating on method and systems somehow didn't seem to make the expected breakthroughs' and 'social science came back in fashion'. He has noted the optimism of the 1980s in contrast to the pessimism of the 1990s, and has found it fascinating that 'management fashions seem to spread across the world with the speed of light, whereas transferring technology appears to be an extraordinarily difficult task to achieve'.

An example of the rapid spread of management fashions is the emphasis on quality management in the late 1980s and early 1990s, which can be seen as another way of dressing up old ideas in new clothing. It can be argued that like other management theories, quality management has been around a long time but it has to be discovered again by each new group of managers. In the same way, modern theories have included attempts to view the organisation as a single, integrated system, either through a systems approach or through a contingency approach, and these ideas are important in the understanding of modern management thinking and the role of managers.

The systems approach

The systems approach is based on the view that managers should focus on the role each part of an organisation plays in the whole organisation, rather than dealing separately with each part. It takes into account the different needs of various functional management areas, such as production, marketing and finance. For example, the marketing department might want to be able to sell a large variety of products, while the production unit would prefer to have long production runs of a few items, and financial managers might be mainly concerned with keeping costs as low as possible.

The systems approach means that managers have to discuss their various requirements in terms of the needs of the whole organisation. Production scheduling, for example, would only be completed once marketing and finance were in agreement with the plans. This interaction requires a high degree of communication and the breaking down of barriers between the various departments and functions of an organisation. The emphasis is on management awareness of:

- **Subsystems**, which are the individual parts that make up the whole organisation, for example, a unit, department, company, industry.

- **Synergy**, which emphasises the interrelationships between all the parts of an organisation, reflecting the concept that the whole is greater than the sum of its parts. This suggests that departments and units in a business are more productive when they work together than when they operate separately.

- **Open and closed systems**, which reflect the extent to which an organisation interacts with its environment. Companies providing services to the public will normally be open systems, while those working within a larger organisation such as component part manufacturers will be more closed.

- **Boundaries**, which in a closed system will tend to be more rigid than those in an open system, where boundaries with the outside environments are constantly changing.

- **Flows** of information, materials and human energy which move through a system and are transformed in the process into goods and services.

- **Feedback**, which is the process of monitoring information about systems in order to evaluate their operation.

This approach implies that management at all levels needs to be sensitive to the complexity of the organisation and accept a system which enables the organisation to work efficiently.

THE CONTINGENCY APPROACH

The pragmatic view

This can be described as the 'golf club approach'. Like picking out the right golf club for a particular shot at a specific time on a particular day, the contingency approach to management problems suggests that different problems and situations require different solutions. Much depends on managers' experience with this approach, and it is understood that what might work well in one situation may not work in another. The task of management is to identify which technique will work in particular circumstances. In one case the solution to creating greater productivity is to motivate employees by giving them greater responsibility; in another case, if the employees are relatively unskilled for example, it may be better to provide extra training and supervision as at least a preliminary step.

The contingency approach has developed through attempts to apply concepts drawn from the major schools of management thought. In applying these to solve management problems, advocates of this approach take the pragmatic view that no one approach is universally applicable. For example, on the one hand techniques used in scientific management, such as time study, may be used to investigate a particular problem; on the other hand, the ideas of the behavioural school may be involved in an inquiry into workers' motivation, perhaps followed by a quantitative analysis of the results.

The internal and external environment

Like a golfer selecting a club with full regard to all the variables such as distance, obstacles to be avoided as well as wind direction and other conditions, so will a manager need to consider the objectives of a particular action, the people involved, the equipment available, and the internal and external conditions which prevail. The internal environment is the way the organisation works, its corporate culture, management structure and communication systems. Although golfers need to know their own capabilities and temperament in order to make a good start, they do not usually play as a team. A manager needs to take into account the abilities and temperament of his colleagues as well as his own. The external environment consists of the social, political and economic factors that affect an organisation, and a manager has to judge such matters as the movement of exchange rates and their effect on the international prices of company raw materials and finished products. Ethical considerations or green issues may play a part in the organisation's market and the manager will need to consider the effect of such issues when making decisions on products and their marketing.

Managers also need to be aware of the relationship between the internal and external environments. Green issues may cause problems for the design and production departments, but may be too important to ignore. For example, the move to unleaded petrol in the UK saw a major turnaround in the design of car engines and in the allocation of petrol pumps on service station forecourts.

At the same time there are internal constraints existing within every organisation that managers must take into account in making decisions. These include:

- **Technological constraints** which derive from the equipment required by a company in order to produce its goods and services. Steel plants, for example, require expensive capital equipment and it is difficult for them to change technology quickly to meet new demands. Car manufacturers need to have reasonable runs on their production lines in order to receive a profitable return on their investment. Small-scale engineering companies can use less specific capital equipment to produce special and individualised orders.

- **Task constraints** arise from the nature of the jobs performed and the skills of the workers involved. Assembly line workers may be able to move to a different assembly line with a minimum of training, while finding it more difficult to take on more varied work.

- **Human constraints** reflect the competence of the people employed by an organisation and their motivation. A competent, well-trained and motivated workforce will exert fewer constraints on a manager than a less competent and poorly motivated workforce.

THE ART OF MANAGEMENT

A synthesis

The management challenge is to answer the questions 'What are we doing?', 'How do we do it?' and 'What do we do next?' This is against the background of a rapidly changing external environment and has in the foreground an increasingly well-trained and educated workforce. The answer given by the contingency approach to these questions is, 'it all depends'. Each situation is examined to determine its unique attribute before a management decision is made. This contrasts with earlier approaches that tended to deal in universal principles which could be applied in every situation. The modern management approach is to analyse the situation and then to draw on the various schools of management thought in order to decide on the most appropriate combination. This contingency approach helps managers to be aware of the complexity in every situation and to take an active role in trying to determine what would work best in each case. It calls for a bringing together or synthesis of approaches, and this throws a strong element of responsibility onto management. On the one hand managers are not encouraged to eliminate unpredictable circumstances, and on the other hand they are encouraged to consider all contingencies and to be sufficiently flexible to take all possibilities into account.

Managers are now encouraged to recognise the ability of the people they manage and to push decision making as near as possible to the point of action. This process can develop 'flexibility by empowerment' (Tom Peters, 1987) and it carries the contingency approach to what might be considered its logical conclusion. This suggests that the people who have to implement a decision should make it, by analysing the situation and deciding on a course of action. Tom Peters believes that the empowering of people 'can most effectively be tapped when people are gathered in human scale groupings, that is, teams, or more precisely, self-managed teams'. This move to self-managed teams and decision making at the point of action makes it necessary for the integrative approach to management to come to terms with human-relations management. The integrated approach developed through systems management and contingency management, which between them view the organisation as a single integrated body and at the same time include the diversity of self-managed teams.

The integrated approach

In the 1980s, William Ouchi (1981) observed that many of the most successful American companies displayed organisational behaviour similar to practices common in Japanese organisations. This included the emphasis on collective decision making and group responsibilities, on quality control based on periodic on-site meetings, and on the lifetime commitment to an organisation. On the other hand, he observed that the Japanese managerial style was borrowed from Western models of scientific management. He felt that an integration of these approaches would lead to management success. Scientific work methods could be incorporated into an integrative management theory and combined with human relations management. He felt that organisational goals could be achieved by making decision making a participatory activity for a greater number of employees, so that responsibility becomes a collaborative function as the product of group or team processes.

The corporate culture

If management can be seen as a synthesis of ideas, culminating in choices made in the end intuitively, then it can be described as an art. In golf, club selection may be based on scientific measurement, observation and experience, but there is also an intuitive element which can turn a good professional shot into a great one. In spite of all the information the golfer may have, the very skilful golfer may have an immediate insight into the club and shot required in the circumstances which overrules the rational information available. This is the skill or art of the professional golfer, and this skill or 'feel' for a situation plays a part in the work of the professional manager and is set against the background of the management theories summarised in Fig 1.5.

Modern management is essentially about managing people as well as processes, in a rapidly changing environment. There is a mass of information available to most managers in terms of costs, prices, market conditions, but in the end decisions may be based on 'hunch' or intuition. This is where experience and a 'feel' for the particular process and people involved becomes essential, and can be helped by the corporate culture of the organisation. Culture is an important factor in the art of management, because for any organisation to operate effectively it must, to some extent, have a generally accepted set of beliefs and assumptions. These will usually have evolved over time and represent a collective experience without which managers would have to start from scratch each time they made a decision. This collective experience will be influenced by wider cultural perspectives so that managers have to be aware of the social, economic and political context they are working in, whether it is a region of the UK or an organisation in another country.

The art of management can be characterised as reflection in action, so that managers' experience and understanding of the context in which they operate can be

Scientific management:	
ADAM SMITH – BABBAGE – TOWNE – TAYLOR	1800–1914
Administrative management:	
FAYOL – WEBER	1900–1925
Behavioural theories:	
FOLLETT – BARNARD – MAYO	1900–1940
Management systems:	
OPERATIONS MANAGEMENT	
SYSTEMS MANAGEMENT	1940+
Contingency theories:	
PRAGMATIC MANAGEMENT – SITUATION THEORIES	1980+
Art of management:	
SYNTHESIS – INTEGRATION – ORGANISATIONAL CULTURE	1980+

FIG 1.5 MANAGEMENT THEORIES

applied to the particular situations they face. They need to have a similar view to their colleagues of the nature of the organisation and the internal and external environment in which it operates. It is this organisational view of the world which helps interpret the changes facing the organisation and the individuals within it. Changes tend to develop incrementally, decisions building one upon another, so that past decisions mould future strategy. It is the management task to steer this process in the right direction, as well as being prepared to deal with the less frequent but more fundamental changes of direction that occur from time to time.

LEVELS OF MANAGEMENT

Junior, middle and senior management roles

The art of management applies to all levels. Just as any job can be carried out well or badly, so can management at any level. While intuition is particularly important at the strategic level, applied experience is essential in the management of the most mundane task. An alert junior supervisor will quickly learn that there are a number of ways of achieving the same results from his or her subordinates. Although in any organisation managers can be distinguished by their functions and by their level of responsibility, the management skills they apply will depend on their actual role in the organisation. Attempts to produce flatter management structures may have reduced the number of stages in the hierarchy but have not greatly changed the underlying situation in most organisations. This remains a pyramid with a relatively small number of senior managers at the top, a larger number of middle managers at the centre, and an even larger group of junior managers supervising the majority of employees who are non-managerial (*see* Fig 1.6).

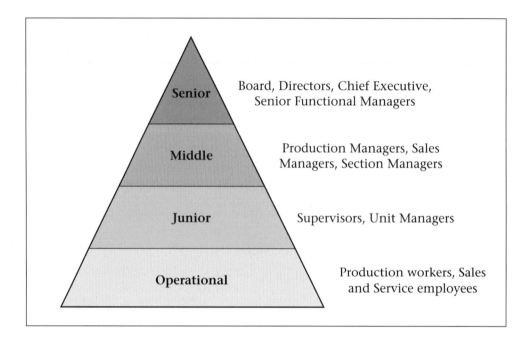

FIG 1.6 MANAGEMENT LEVELS

The 'typical' junior manager will be a supervisor of a unit or the senior member of a team. They are working at or very close to the operational level and may have titles such as foreman, team leader, co-ordinator, operational manager or, of course, supervisor. Their role is to co-ordinate the work of non-managerial employees and to have direct responsibility for machinery and materials. Junior managers are expected to be skilled at both overseeing work and doing it. They are able to supervise and to fill in when and where needed in order to maintain the smooth operation of the system. They are the non-commissioned officers of management who become immensely experienced in their area of work.

Middle managers are usually accountable for the work of junior managers and they in turn report to senior management. They will have a wider remit than the supervisors reporting to them and spend much more of their time on management functions rather than in an operational role. They may step into an operational role from time to time but they may be managing areas of expertise in which they have some knowledge but not at an operational level. The manager of a large store may be able to take over from sales, at the till or in filling shelves, but not necessarily in wordprocessing or in maintaining refrigerated units. At the same time, middle managers will have limits to their responsibilities, so that the store manager may not control pricing policy, advertising or training but may be involved in making sure that these policies are implemented.

Senior managers are the executives, at the highest level of the organisation, responsible for its overall direction and co-ordination and for directing its major activities. Senior managers are responsible for company-wide planning, organising, directing and controlling, and for providing strategic leadership to the company. They are also concerned with the demands imposed on the organisation by outside influences such as customers and suppliers. Above all they are responsible for the overall direction and success or failure of the organisation.

Within these three layers of management there may be numerous intermediate stages, particularly in middle management. Figure 1.7 shows a simplified management organisation chart.

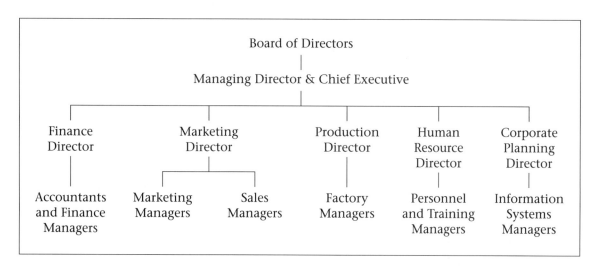

FIG 1.7 MANAGEMENT ORGANISATION CHART

Line management and functional management

The chart in Fig 1.7 depicts the formal, line-management relationship between members of an organisation, but does not attempt to show their functional relationship. In practice, there will be more or less formal networks of people on a functional basis, in some cases forming project committees, in other cases communicating across management lines in order to progress the work of the organisation. Some companies have developed matrix structures to facilitate these communication networks, but in fact networks can create an informal matrix in any organisation.

Matrix structures usually involve managers being responsible to more than one senior manager, so that for one part of their work they will be line managed by one manager, and for another part by another. For example, the allocation of resources may be separated from the production process, so that a middle-ranking plant manager may be responsible to a marketing manager for the output and to a production manager for new materials. There may be responsibility to a third manager, say a

21

human resource manager, for control of staff. It can be argued that this approach provides greater expertise in the various areas of work, but it lacks the simplicity and certainties of a hierarchical structure where the plant manager reports on all matters to, say, the production manager. As illustrated in Fig 1.8, matrix structures are usually based on a division between a functional management role, such as marketing, or a project role, such as the production of a particular commodity.

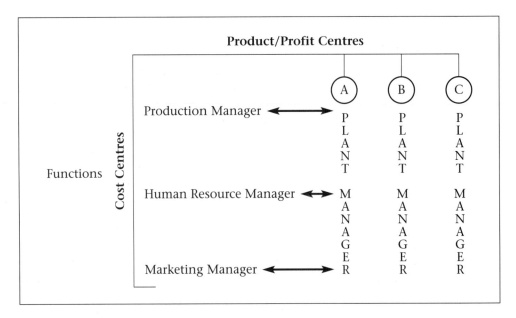

FIG 1.8 MATRIX STRUCTURES

Flatter management structures aim at reducing the layers of control and approval or veto over decision making. Peter Drucker (1988) has suggested that the ultimate flat structure is the factory manager in Nebraska who has himself as manager and 120 operatives on the production line without any intermediate managers. In large and complex organisations this very simple approach may be difficult to implement while retaining control and co-ordination, but the move towards fewer layers of management can help speed up decision making and push the point of decision nearer the point of action. For example, companies can achieve one layer of senior management, one of middle and one of junior management, each with its own sphere of responsibility and decision making.

At every level, managers may have functional responsibilities or may be general managers responsible for a range of functions. Managers responsible for all the activities of the organisation or a complex part of it can be considered to be general managers. Most factory managers and shop/store managers are of this kind. They will line-manage people with a variety of skills and roles and will have some involvement in most of the organisational functions, such as finance, production, marketing, human relations. On the other hand, functional managers will be responsible for one activity within the organisation, such as marketing or finance. They will be responsible for line-managing staff within the same function. The marketing manager, for example, will be responsible for staff in sales, in promotions, advertising and public relations, and in market research. The market research manager will line-manage staff in data collection, statistics and information. In order to remain competitive, organisations have to find the structures which work best for them and reform these structures as necessary.

MANAGEMENT ROLES

What managers do

It may be reasonably clear in an organisation who the managers are and the types and levels of responsibility they hold, but the question remains as to what they actually do. The theories of management provide some clues to what people in the past have considered to be the management job, while the level at which managers work also plays a part in what they do. Figure 1.1 indicated that managers move from a more operational role to one of planning and innovation as they move from junior to middle and senior management. Junior managers are likely to spend a large proportion of their time doing an operational job, whether it is production or sales. Depending on their exact role and the size of the unit they are managing, a greater or lesser proportion of their time will be spent on supervision, training and involvement with networks of other managers in the organisation. They may need to attend training sessions themselves in order to keep up to date, or they may be on a quality assurance committee or have regular briefing meetings with their line manager. A limited time will be spent planning and this will tend to be about specific projects.

The middle manager will have much less of an operational role and will spend most of the time on management. This will include much more co-ordination and monitoring than supervision, although this is likely to remain an important part of the job. Organising, controlling and some planning are likely to be the main elements of the work. The large branch store manager will spend some time planning and preparing for the next day or week or month, a large proportion of time monitoring and supervising junior managers, and the rest of the time as a general manager involved in finance, purchasing, marketing, staffing matters and dealing with outside providers. His junior managers in charge of particular sections of the store will spend much more time tied down to their sections and supervising all aspects of them.

Senior managers spend much of their time planning, organising and dealing with outside factors, including customers and suppliers. Henry Mintzberg, in a study on *The Nature of Managerial Work* (1980), found that senior managers all in one way or another have three independent roles:

- interpersonal roles;

- informational roles;

- decisional roles.

How these roles are performed depends on the structure and type of organisation and on the personality of the manager. Interpersonal roles arise from the managers' position in their particular company and from the extent to which they appear as a figurehead or in terms of leadership and liaison. At times they will represent the company either internally or externally, at presentations and with other companies, and at other times they will initiate more productive links between other managers and teams through liaison with them.

Senior managers will have an informational role because they become the focal point for receiving and sending information within the organisation and outside it. They monitor developments within the organisation, such as performance, as well as opportunities and threats outside the organisation, such as customer behaviour. They disseminate information in order to influence the actions of other people in the organisation, and they act as spokespeople and publicisers in representing the organisation to outside agencies. In decision making, managers strive to allocate resources in the most productive way, to encourage innovation and change, and to negotiate with other managers and groups within the organisation in order to develop it further. The way in which decisions are made in an organisation is an important indicator of the way it functions, whether it is relatively autocratic or democratic, and this in turn depends on the leadership role of senior managers and the resultant corporate culture (*see* Chapters 2 and 9).

How managers spend their time

As a clearer indication of what managers do, there have been surveys of how they spend their time. These show that at senior and middle levels, at least, time is spent in a range of activities, depending very much on the nature of the organisation and the character of the individual. Figure 1.9 is a list of these activities in rank order. It needs to be remembered, however, that because a particular function does not

- **Controlling**
- **Solving problems**
- **Planning**
- **Communicating informally and formally**
- **Communicating upwards**
- **Communicating downwards**
- **Attending meetings**
- **Reading**
- **Writing memos and letters**
- **Representing the company**

FIG 1.9 HOW MANAGERS SPEND THEIR TIME

appear on the list does not necessarily mean that it does not happen. For example, Management By Walking About (MBWA) may not exist in some managers' time allocation, but was stressed by Tom Peters and Robert Waterman in *In Search of Excellence* (1982) as an essential element in managerial success. Any list will not represent the full range of activities of an individual manager.

A 1997 survey of 258 chief executives carried out for the *Sunday Times* found that 79 per cent of those surveyed thought that the business social and economic environment had created a culture in which cost cutting was the driving force for managers, instead of the development of the rounded skills needed to manage growth, expansion and innovation. Asked to name the most important management skills from a list of 11, the chief executives put leadership first, followed by vision, people management, communications and financial literacy. Although they said that a lack of management skills in their organisation had already prevented them from fully exploiting commercial opportunities, they were optimistic about the future because they thought that future managers would be better educated and trained and more aware of competition.

Managing change

'The way we do things around here'

Descriptions of what managers do and how they spend their time provide only a partial view of a manager's actual role. Almost by definition, managers are a small minority of people in the employment of any organisation and therefore most people do not have experience of being a manager. Whereas managers have usually been through the operational stage and can to some extent transfer this type of experience to any operational area, it is more difficult for operators who have never been managers to understand the management viewpoint. On the other hand, of course, most people have some understanding of management processes, because their work involves some of these processes, they have to manage their personal lives and their homes, and because they will experience the results of different management actions, approaches and styles. At a simple structural level there is often an understanding that work has to be managed, that someone has to make major decisions, and that the organisation and individual jobs within it depend on management functions being performed.

The management of change in an organisation is an area of potential conflict because of these inherent issues of understanding and communication. Management actions to facilitate change can easily be misunderstood because the procedures and processes already in existence appear to be perfectly good. These days the management of change is the most important management skill because it can be seen as a constant process of setting up working methods to meet changing circumstances. These 'changing circumstances' need to be understood by everyone. John Harvey-Jones (1993) has stated that change is easier to manage when there is an element of danger present in an organisation and there is an obvious need for change:

> *'It is impossible to change organisations which do not accept the dangers of their present way of doing things.'*

Although the decision to implement change may be considered to be largely conceptual in nature, it takes effect in action and behaviour. Managing change is essentially about people and not concepts and ideas, while the results of change will be seen most clearly by most people in matters of detail. Faced with pressure for change, managers are likely to deal with the situation in ways which coincide with the culture of the organisation. This raises a particular challenge to management when the action required is outside the assumptions and beliefs of members of the organisation. Much change is incremental in that one change leads to another, and the main challenge to modern management is that the incremental steps are closer together than in the past. However, it is this increasing frequency of change which challenges the underlying culture of organisations: 'the way we do things around here'. For example, technological change may mean the gradual introduction of wordprocessors to replace typewriters, or the introduction of an automated assembly line with robots replacing the assembly line jobs all at the same time. In the first case, a few people will be left behind who are unable to make the change from typewriters to computers. In the second case, all or most jobs will disappear, with perhaps a few new ones appearing in the form of maintenance or quality control. As a result of technological and scientific development 'the way we do things around here' may be altered overnight, but even in the most extreme cases the manager's role is to anticipate the change and prepare for it.

All change involves people and their working patterns and it can be argued that organisations can only change at the speed at which people in them are willing and able to change. Fundamental changes in attitudes take years rather than months, and the first part of the process is a clear understanding that the status quo is no longer possible. This may be through dissatisfaction with the present position or fear of the consequences of adhering to it. For example, if competitors are clearly affecting the viability of the company, the present position can be seen as a threat and the need for change will be easily appreciated.

Uncertainty

When faced with change in their organisation, it has been observed that people will often attempt to deal with the situation by searching for areas of change they can understand and cope with in terms of the existing culture. They will attempt to minimise the extent to which they are faced with uncertainty by looking for what is familiar. This will usually be as true of managers as of anybody else. Faced with change, managers will first seek a means of improving the implementation of existing strategy. They may start by tightening existing controls and making minor adjustments to the organisation. If this is not effective, they may move onto further changes in line with the existing procedures.

The problem with this approach is that it is backward-looking. For example, managers may consider price changes or attempt to reduce the costs of production. These may be the right policies arrived at almost by chance rather than by considering the fundamental reason for change, which may be, for example, alterations in the expectations of customers and the need to alter the products and services provided for them. It may be that changes in price and reduction in costs are the correct decisions, but it may be that the company is producing the wrong product range or has not concentrated sufficiently on staff training in order to provide high quality customer service.

Change should be forward-looking, otherwise the organisation will gradually, perhaps imperceptibly, become more and more at odds with the environment in which it operates. Managers have to consider the type and quality of products or services that should be produced to meet the needs of their customers, and the level of service and back-up required to encourage customers to make use of them. At the strategic level at least, managers need to look forward towards the changes that are necessary for the success of the organisation and then start to prepare people in the organisation to meet these changes. Major changes in the market-place may occur as a result of competitors altering their policies and practices in one way or another; there may be a change in fashion among consumers or there may be a sudden shortage of materials. Managers can make piecemeal modifications in the operations of the organisation to meet the changes if they can be predicted to some extent. These may be sufficient in the short term, but for more permanent change managers need to flag up situations in order to create a climate suited to more fundamental questioning of what is taken for granted. For example, this can be done by emphasising downturns in performance or putting a spotlight on external threats and, at the same time, the need for change can be signalled by making internal organisational changes.

Forces for change

Organisations have both influences encouraging change and other influences acting to keep the organisation in a state of equilibrium. Those forces which oppose change can also be seen to be supporting stability and the status quo. In forcefield theory, any behaviour can be seen as the result of an equilibrium between driving and restraining forces, with the driving forces pushing one way, the restraining forces the other. It can be argued that the performance that emerges is a reconciliation between these two sets of forces. For example, an increase in driving forces, say an autocratic style of management, may increase the level of active restraining forces, say distrust and resistance. This can mean that if managers attempt to initiate change by a series of orders and commands, this is likely to be met by either active resistance or more passive avoidance. It is not always easy entirely to avoid taking action which creates a strong counter-reaction. The extreme example is the closing down of a company, which can be accomplished while minimising disruption and hardship but particularly in times of recession may come very suddenly. Opposition to a sudden closure may take the form of some type of strike or legal action. However, these can be considered to be exceptional circumstances and most change within an organisation can be managed in such a way that restraining forces are minimised. This process has been highlighted by Kurt Lewin (1951) in his work on forcefield theory (*see also* Chapter 13). He has identified multiple causes of behaviour which are summarised in Fig 1.10. Programmes of planned change can have the objective of weakening the restraining forces and supporting the driving forces in order to create a high level of performance.

New technology, changes in raw materials supply and competition are among the factors which create a need for change, but these driving factors can also be seen in slightly different terms:

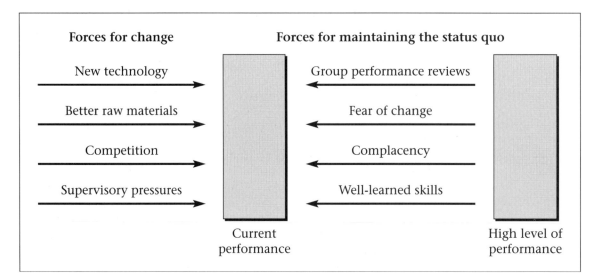

Fig 1.10 Forcefield diagram

- **time**
- **turbulence**
- **interdependence**
- **technology.**

These terms summarise the reasons for change, so that, for example, the *time span* for the communication of information has been radically reduced as the capability of IT has grown. Peter Drucker (1988) has referred to:

> *'a shift from the command and control organisation, to the information based organisation – the organisation of the knowledge specialists . . . it is the management challenge of the future.'*

The development of communication technologies and the power of the computer has enabled information-based tasks to be carried out more productively and more quickly and has necessitated considerable changes in business processes.

At the same time *turbulence* has been caused by rapid changes in politics, culture and society. Even in the most politically stable countries there are changes in policy, often as a result of economic pressures, necessitating considerable change in commercial and other organisations. Changes in exchange rates, trade regulations and educational and social policy will influence many organisations to a greater or lesser extent. At the same time there are cultural changes occurring, alternatives in tastes and fashions which can create forces for change. For example, the fluctuations in oil prices since 1974 have had an economic consequence on many companies, while government policies on interest rates have affected the cost of borrowing and the return on investment. The growing number of 'dependants' as against productive workers in the UK has led to the consideration of major changes in social policy.

Interdependence has increased with growing specialisation and attempts to improve productivity. Many companies have moved away from the idea of controlling all the sources of supply or sale they require or all the services they might need. The 'outsourcing' of services has meant that a company may buy in functions such as training or legal advice and rely increasingly on consultants. The company can then specialise on what it can do best, leaving other specialists to provide raw materials or sales outlets. For example, many companies 'outsource' their cleaning and catering requirements as well as other specialist activities, such as information technology, premises management and aspects of personnel management.

Technology has altered whole areas of work making some skills redundant while developing new areas. For example, automation has meant that some factories require more skills in terms of maintenance and quality control than in machine operation. The typing pool has been replaced by wordprocessors, photocopiers, fax machines and electronic mail. The need for quick responses, personally addressed correspondence and other forms of multiple or individual communication has been taken over by office machinery.

As a result of these forces, organisations require a dynamism which may be missing in the traditional culture, so that successful modern organisations do not simply respond to change, they see it coming and exploit the opportunities it creates. This requires a clearly articulated vision of the direction of the organisation and a strategy for change. It requires an ability to manage change and be able to intercept and respond to what is to come in the future. The challenge to management is to position an organisation so that it can move from its current state to its desired future state and be able to do this again and again.

The process of change

It is possible to recognise certain characteristics in the process of change. These include uncertainty about the causes and effects of change, unwillingness to give up existing practices, and awareness of problems in the change process. These characteristics arise from a natural reaction to deny that the change is necessary, to resist any change whatever its merits and, if necessary, to avoid changes when they are introduced.

Managers have to determine the actual causes of resistance to change and remain flexible enough in their approach to overcome them in an appropriate manner. There is a considerable degree of interaction between interdependent elements in any organisation, and this has to be recognised. The structure of the organisation, the technology which is applied and the people working in it are highly interdependent and all three have to be involved in the change process. The task of the manager is to direct energy away from feelings of powerlessness and looking backwards and towards seeing the opportunities for the future.

This is particularly important because in the process of change, people feel that they are threatened by the future while they need to recognise the danger in the present position and the opportunity in the new one. The process may involve denial of the need to change and resistance to it, until the change is able to be explored when opportunities may be discussed and commitment created.

Figure 1.11 illustrates the transition that can take place in the change process, from denial and resistance to exploration and commitment. The challenge for managers is to help people through the process. People move from the familiar to the unknown and often experience a feeling of loss when they struggle to accept a new direction. This experience of loss can take a variety of forms:

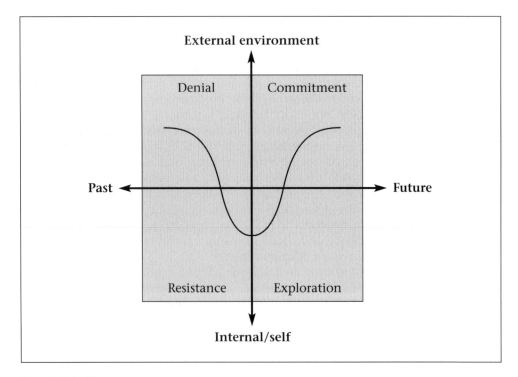

FIG 1.11 TRANSITION

- **Security** – people feel unsure of their position in the organisation and how it will change; 'we don't know where we stand'.

- **Competence** – they become worried about their ability to carry out new tasks; 'we don't know what to do'.

- **Relationships** – they may feel that familiar contacts will be lost with other employees, with managers and teams and groups; 'we don't know who we report to'.

- **Territory** – they may feel uncertain about their work space or job responsibility; 'we don't know where we work or whether we can do this or not'.

- **Direction** – they lose a clear view of where they are going; 'why are we doing this?'

These feelings of loss are a normal part of the transition process. The management task is to acknowledge these feelings and attempt to allay them. This involves more than providing information because people in organisations will not necessarily alter their behaviour simply by being told. For example, many people have continued to smoke in spite of health warnings. People need support and encouragement and there is an important leadership role in the change process in creating a trusting and supportive relationship. This requires considerable management skill and can place managers in an exposed position.

Managing change

The purpose of change is to move an organisation from its present point to a different one which is more desirable in meeting its objectives. In managing this process the gap between the starting point and the desirable conclusion needs to be identified. The usual steps are:

- **Vision** – a process of reminding everybody and clarifying to everybody the direction of the organisation; 'where we are going'.

- **Strategy** – outlining how this is to be achieved through the development of objectives and goals; 'how we are going to get there'.

- **Monitoring change** – progress is measured in order to observe and encourage change; 'this is how far we are now'.

Different stages of changes require different strategies. At the denial stage, information has to be provided, time given in order to explain this information and suggest action. At the resistance stage, managers have to have an acceptance of people's responses and encourage support. If people tell managers how they feel, the manager can be helped to respond effectively. In the exploration stage there can be a concentration on priorities, training can be provided and planning take place. There is then a commitment stage where long-term goals can be established with a concentration on team building.

The curve in Fig 1.12 can indicate the time taken by most people to move from one stage to the next. A deep curve can indicate a lengthy period of resistance and exploration before there is a commitment. At one extreme there may be an

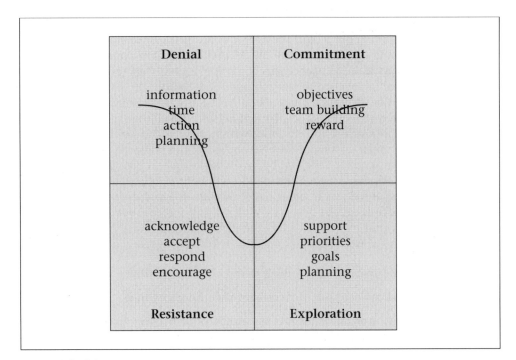

FIG 1.12 MANAGING CHANGE

intense period of denial and resistance, with people becoming angry or anxious, depressed and frustrated, and a concentration on the impact the change will have on them personally.

Stress may appear during the exploration stage, with the expressed concern that the new system will be chaotic. Exploring new responsibilities and ways of doing things can mean that an understanding of a new system begins to emerge. Some people may experience what has been referred to as a 'Tarzan swing' in that they believe they have jumped to the final stage of commitment by swinging straight over resistance and exploration. This may be the result of a very persuasive manager or arise by concentrating on only one aspect of the change, perhaps particularly favourable to the individual. It may only be a short-term conversion which fades away over time and leaves long-term doubts. It may be better to work more slowly through the stages by developing a programme for change in order to establish long-term commitments.

The programme for change will include:

- **leadership** – a person who provides a clear statement of the vision and objectives;

- **coherence** – agreement on the operational tasks and goals consistent with the strategic view;

- **communication** – the provision of clear and appropriate information to the relevant people about what is happening and why it is happening;

- **timing** – decisions on when to take action;

- **structure** – a structured approach which moves logically through an understanding of the forces for change to the agreement on the management of the change process.

This programme will inevitably contain traps for managers. Ignoring resistance to change or attempting to block it will tend to encourage resistance being felt more deeply and lasting longer. It can be argued that resistance should be sought out, taken seriously and the reasons for it should be discussed. Pushing too hard, too soon on structural change or a change such as increasing productivity may prove to be counter-productive. Time to absorb the change needs to be provided in order to enable short-term responses, which may be emotional and negative, to fade and be overtaken by a more rational and positive approach.

This process is helped by involving people in planning for change and monitoring its progress. Active participation will help people to understand how the change will affect them and to come to terms with it. Employees need to be helped to say 'good goodbyes' to old practices, and resistance to change can be taken by managers as a sign that people have left the denial stage and are moving on. In this process it is essential that managers are clear about objectives, and that these are SMART:

S   specific about what is to be accomplished

M   measurable differences must be identified

A   attainable targets should be established

R   result output oriented change is desirable

T   time limits should be established

There should also be a reward system for people attempting as well as accomplishing change. The rewards may be in the form of pay if this is appropriate, as for example if there is a change in contracts or job description, or in the form of status or recognition. A reward system can provide motivation, but that can also be developed through leadership and encouraging involvement. People need to be part of the process which makes change work, for example by being a member of a team which decides on the detail of the change and by participation in task forces and quality circles.

Continuous change

People in organisations are often unwilling or unable to alter long-established attitudes and behaviour. A change in management style or attitude or a change in working practices may be seen as a violation of people's self-image or an indication of inadequacy. It is difficult to introduce change without suggesting a criticism of previous styles and methods. If it is suggested to a work unit that they should do things in a different way, they will immediately wonder what is wrong with their present operating method. There is an implied criticism, however diplomatically the suggestion is worded. If change can be perceived as a continuous process it may be possible to avoid this problem, because it will become part of working practices.

If change is seen to be a short-term process, after a brief period of doing things differently people may return to their earlier practices. In order to avoid this a three-step model can be applied to the change process:

- **Unfreezing**: the need for change is made so obvious that individuals and teams can easily recognise and accept it.

- **Leadership**: managers foster new values, attitudes and behaviour through the process of identification and internalisation.

- **Refreezing**: the new practices are locked into place by supporting and reinforcing mechanisms so that they become the new norm.

This process can be used to improve an organisation's response to continuous change. This can be seen as:

> *'a top management-supported, long-range effort to improve an organisation's problem solving and renewal processes, particularly through a more effective and collaborative diagnosis and management of organisation culture.'* (French and Ball, 1984)

This involves consultation right across the organisation, and one part of the change process is decentralising management by transferring ownership of the problem to the lowest possible level. Decentralisation, flatter management organisation and decisions taken at the point of action can increase both the ability to change and the speed with which change can be accomplished. Managers have to look at every way in which an organisation conducts itself in order to find the most productive and efficient processes.

Through this approach it is possible to institutionalise change so that it becomes a continuous process instead of a set piece every five years. This is the modern management view based on observation of Japanese management practices. For example, the concept of 'just-in-time' production involves close and flexible working between manufacturer, supplier and purchaser. Japanese car manufacturers can be seen as specifiers and assemblers rather than manufacturers in the old sense, whereas General Motors in the USA has aimed at a high degree of vertical integration, controlling the manufacturing process from raw material to final product and customers. The 'just-in-time' process recreates the producer/customer relationship at every stage so that there is an urgency at each point. This may be a difficult feeling to transfer to departments and sections of a large organisation.

The Japanese have been determined to have continuous incremental development and believe that this is most likely where there is a direct link with the customer. In an organisation which is managed vertically, that is with a chain of control running from the raw material to the retail outlet, there is a vast amount of capital invested before the person nearest to the ultimate customer is reached. However strong the links may be in this chain, the final and crucial link with the consumer may not be sufficiently strong to control the weight of expectations of the rest of the company. In large, vertically controlled companies, the people nearest to the ultimate customer may have difficulty in controlling everything that stands behind them. Rigidities tend to build up and pressures generate the wrong way. The 'just-in-time' philosophy may operate effectively in this type of organisation, but only if managers encourage close working between supplier and customer at every level and then leave them to resolve all the day-to-day problems, rather than pushing decisions up the line to others who will not feel the urgency of the situation.

CONCLUSION

The Japanese approach is based on a need continuously to improve productivity faster than the competition. This can be seen as the challenge for all management in both the private and public sectors. In the public sector the challenge may be measured in different ways to those used in the private sector. Profit may not play a part, but measurement of activity against costs may replace monitoring of the return on capital invested. Income is now often linked to output and outcomes, while expenditure is firmly controlled and audited. Public sector managers are increasingly being asked to manage their organisations in a more commercial and effective way, exposed to competition and without any guarantee of survival. In many areas, public sector management is little different from that in the private sector, with the same urgencies and pressures. This is exemplified by the increasing frequency of movement of managers between the two sectors.

It is apparent that management theories apply to all managers. The contingency or 'golf club' approach may be used by any manager facing a difficult decision. The skills required of managers may be differently applied, but are basically the same whether they are working in a profit-making company, a non-profit charity, or a hospital trust or grant-maintained school. There have been, in the past, considerable differences in the sense of 'urgency' in different organisations, so that government agencies and non-profit organisations have been epitomised as lacking in this area because their survival is guaranteed. In the private sector too, the sense of 'urgency' is felt more strongly at the point of contact with the customer than further back in the company, while some companies have drawn this into their culture at every point and level to an extent not present in other companies. The meeting of customer demands means that it is here more than anywhere else in the management of change that managers have to apply their full abilities. Theories and examples of good practice can help in this matter as in many other situations, but in the end managers are judged on the success and effectiveness of their actions, on how well they adapt their organisations in order to satisfy customer demands.

SUMMARY

■ The manager's role is greater than the process of organising people in order to achieve particular outcomes. While it includes this process, the real challenge is to manage change by leading and inspiring people.

■ Change has become a central factor because in order to meet their objectives organisations need to focus on their customers and the changing requirements of these customers.

■ Past and present theories of management provide ideas about the practice and process of management in order to decide on questions of organisation, control and planning.

■ Management skills are required at a variety of different levels, in different organisational structures and functional responsibilities, and these skills are clearly necessary for dealing with the complexities involved in the management of change.

REVIEW AND DISCUSSION QUESTIONS

1   Are the most important management skills organising and controlling or are they planning and leading?

2   What are the main challenges a manager has to face these days?

3   Is management a science or an art?

4   What is the importance of the 'Hawthorne effect' in the management of change?

5   How do the behavioural and contingency theories of management compare and contrast with scientific management?

6   Are the same management skills required at different levels of management?

7   How far does forcefield theory help to explain the main influences for change in organisations?

8   Are managers in the public sector faced with different challenges to those which face managers in the private sector?

CASE STUDY: WHY BAD MANAGEMENT IS ALL IN THE GENES [FT]

Are you oblivious to other people's feelings? Slow to realise that your colleagues are upset or angry? Unreasonable? Always interrupting conversations? Do you have difficulty following commands?

If you answer yes to much of the above, there is no need to feel bad. The chances are that you are a bloke, and that you can't help yourself. Thanks to scientists at the Institute of Child Health, we find that there may be a special gene that controls 'social cognition' – which is switched on in females and switched off in males.

If there is any truth in this, it seems that they may have inadvertently stumbled on the management gene. The unfortunate behaviours outlined above, found to be more common among boys than girls, are almost exactly the same ones that trendy management books argue are most likely to ruin a manager's career. What the scientists call 'social cognition' is similar to what Daniel Goleman has famously labelled 'emotional intelligence'. It is supposed to be precisely what is needed if you want to succeed.

This presents a puzzle. If these skills are the crucial ones, and if they are more common in females than males, one wonders why it is the males who are at the top. It is possible that these traits are only recently in such demand. In the old days of grand hierarchies they may have even been a handicap. On this argument it is no coincidence that women are now catching up. According to a survey published today by the Institute of Management, the numbers of women in management are rising at all levels, and their pay is going up too. But when you look at these women, doubts arise. They seem no better at 'social cognition' than men in similar positions.

This leads to an interesting reversal. We used to think that men and women were born the same, but that society taught the girls to be sensitive and intuitive. Now it seems that women may be born with an advantage, but that those who climb the greasy pole – erected by males in the days of male dominance – unlearn the very skills that they will need if they plan to stay at the top. ■

Source: *Financial Times*, 16 June 1997. Reprinted with permission.

REFERENCES FOR FURTHER READING

Barnard, Chester I (1938) *The Functions of the Executive*, Cambridge, Mass: Harvard University Press.

Drucker, Peter (1988) 'The coming of the new organization', *Harvard Business Review*, Jan./Feb.

Fayol, Henri (1930) *Industrial and General Administration*, Geneva International Management Institute.

French, W L and Ball, C H (1984) *Organization Development: Behavioral Science Interventions for Organization Improvement*, Englewood Cliffs, New Jersey: Prentice-Hall.

Gilbreth, Lillian M (1914) *The Psychology of Management*, New York: Stangus & Walter.

Harvey-Jones, John (1993) *Managing to Survive*, London: Heinemann.

Lewin, Kurt (1951) *Field Theory in Social Science*, New York: Harper & Brothers.

Mayo, Elton (1953) *The Human Problems of an Industrial Civilization*, New York: Macmillan.

Mayo, Elton, Roethlisberger, F J and Dickson, W J (1939) *Management and the Worker*, Cambridge, Mass: Harvard University Press.

Mescon, Michael H, Albert, Michael and Khedouri, Franklin (1985) *Management: Individual and Organizational Effectiveness*, New York: Harper & Row.

Mintzberg, Henry (1980) *The Nature of Managerial Work*, Englewood Cliffs, New Jersey: Prentice-Hall.

Ouchi, William (1981) *Theory Z: How American Business Can Meet the Japanese Challenge*, Reading, Mass: Addison-Wesley.

Parker Follett, Mary (1941) *Collected Works*, New York: Harper & Brothers.

Pearce, John A and Robinson, Richard B Jr (1989) *Management*, New York: McGraw-Hill.

Peters, Tom (1987) *Thriving on Chaos*, London: Macmillan.

Peters, Tom and Waterman, Robert (1982) *In Search of Excellence*, New York: Harper & Row.

Smith, Professor Sir Roland (1993) 'Windsor Business Forum', Cable Telecom.

Taylor, Frederick W (1947) *Scientific Management*, New York: Harper & Brothers.

Weber, Max (1947) *The Theory of Social and Economic Organizations*, New York: Free Press.

2 LEADERSHIP

Tim Hannagan

OBJECTIVES

The objectives of this chapter are to:

◆ describe leadership and identify the relationship between leadership and management

◆ analyse different theories of leadership as they apply to management

◆ examine styles of leadership and their impact on organisations

◆ consider the question of leadership power and control

WHAT IS LEADERSHIP?

Definition

Leadership is the process of motivating other people to act in particular ways in order to achieve specific goals. The motivation of other people may be achieved in a variety of ways which affect leadership styles, and the way a person exercises leadership can be identified as a series of actions which are directed towards a particular objective. The emphasis is on action because, although leaders may exert influence through inspirational speeches, they are judged on what they do.

> *'Not the cry but the flight of the wild duck leads the flock to fly and to follow.'* (Chinese proverb quoted by John Adair, 1989)

The word leader derives from words meaning a path or road and suggests the importance of guidance on a journey. Both the word itself and the role of leader are about looking forward, identifying the way ahead or steering others towards agreed objectives. This process means that leaders need to have followers and to share common goals with their followers. People following leaders give up, temporarily at least, their ideas of the direction they should be going, in favour of the leader's ideas on this; they accede to the preferences of the leader in exchange for the rewards that they expect to receive as a result. The role of the leader is to convince them that this exchange is worthwhile; the greater the conviction, the higher the level of motivation there is likely to be and the more likely the common objectives will be attained.

Leadership involves other people, who by the degree of their willingness to accept direction help to define the leader's status. Leadership involves authority and responsibility, in terms of deciding the way ahead and being held responsible for the success or failure of achieving the agreed objectives. Although leadership is most clearly seen at times of high drama, it can arise in all sorts of situations when an individual takes charge and decides what to do next. It can be argued that people can exhibit 'qualities of leadership' in a variety of circumstances. These qualities are usually seen to be in the taking of decisions and communicating them to other people in such a way that action is taken. At the same time people are sometimes referred to as 'born leaders', as though leadership is an inherent or even inherited quality. On the other hand, if leadership is seen as a process which can be analysed, and a series of actions which can be identified, then it can be learned, at least to some extent.

John Adair in *Great Leaders* (1989) suggests that:

> *'The common sense conclusion of this book is that leadership potential can be developed, but it does have to be there in the first place.'*

The delegation of decision making in organisations means that it is essential for many people at all levels of management to have and to develop some potential for leadership.

THE MANAGER AS LEADER

Management implies leadership, and in fact the success or failure of managers can be judged on their leadership qualities. If the manager's role is to achieve organisational goals, then these are reached by showing people the way forward to find solutions and overcome obstacles. In a constantly changing social, economic and technological environment, leadership has become a more important attribute of management than in the past. In a more static environment, controlling and organising might be seen as more important than leadership for most managers, but this has changed. It is not just senior managers who need to look forward in order to foresee the changes which are coming and to act accordingly. Team managers and supervisors also have to implement change at their own level, to understand it and to take their working colleagues and subordinates along with them.

Leadership can be seen as a subset of management in the sense that management is broader in scope as it is concerned with behavioural as well as non-behavioural matters. It can be argued (*see* Massie and Douglas, 1977) that managers are concerned with bringing together resources, developing strategies, organising and controlling activities in order to achieve agreed objectives. At the same time managers, as leaders, have to select the goals and objectives of an organisation, decide what is to be done and motivate people to do it. Leadership can be seen as performing the influencing function of management, largely involved with establishing goals and motivating people to help achieve them. Looked at in this way, leaders decide 'where we are going' and influence people to take that particular direction, rather than describe 'how we are going to get there'. The debate on the role of the manager against that of the leader is perhaps more a question of definition than substance, although inspired leaders are not necessarily good organisers and excellent managers may appear to be rather mundane in terms of leadership. In practice the most effective managers are also leaders and the quality of leadership has become an increasingly important part of management ability.

THEORIES X AND Y

One of the greatest contributions to the understanding of leadership has been the work of Douglas McGregor (1960) in developing Theories X and Y. He described the potential for leadership in terms of two opposing sets of assumptions that managers might hold about their subordinates. For the sake of simplicity these assumptions have been labelled Theory X and Theory Y to represent two extremes at opposite ends of a continuum.

Theory X

Theory X managers tend to believe that people have an inherent dislike of work, regarding it as necessary for survival, and will avoid it wherever possible. Furthermore these managers believe that people are lazy, prefer to be directed, want to avoid responsibility and are relatively unambitious. They have to be coerced, controlled and directed to make them work towards organisational goals. Above all, those managers who subscribe to Theory X believe that people want security. This means that these managers will be very directive in their approach to leadership and very strict and authoritarian with their subordinates. Organisational goals will not be agreed, they will be established, passed down from above and pushed through.

Theory Y

At the opposite end of the spectrum is Theory Y, which represents a much more optimistic view of human nature. Theory Y managers believe that people see work as a natural phenomenon, that they accept responsibility and in fact seek it. Furthermore, Theory Y managers believe that under the right circumstances people can derive satisfaction from their work and will work hard. They will help to achieve organisational objectives provided that they both understand them and are rewarded for their efforts. This means that these managers will work co-operatively with subordinates in order to decide work objectives and the methods of achieving them. They will encourage the development of self-managed teams and the delegation of decisions towards the point of action. These managers believe in participative management and that the organisational structure as well as its culture can bring out the best in its employees by encouraging personal development and creativity.

Historically there has been a shift towards Theory Y approaches to leadership (*see* Fig 2.1). These developments remain patchy, with companies using different approaches in practice, sometimes at odds with their declared policy. Within an organisation there may be differences as well, so that attempts by the senior managers to lead in a participative way may be partly thwarted by middle or junior managers who implement this policy in an autocratic way. On the other hand, junior managers may attempt to encourage their subordinates to work as a self-managed team setting its own objectives and work schedules, while a dictatorial senior management may insist on particular objectives and work practices. In order to achieve a well-organised, efficient Theory Y working environment, subordinates need to become accustomed to this kind of leadership, so that they learn to take responsibility and make decisions.

	MODERN		TRADITIONAL	
Theory Y	Participation	Control		**Theory X**
	Co-operation	Direction		
Work is natural	Communication	Orders		*Work is a necessity*
	Creativity	Security		

FIG 2.1 MANAGEMENT MODELS

It can be argued that in organisations where the workers are professionals, such as in teaching or in a science-based company, there is a good response to Theory Y leadership, while workers in unskilled jobs tend to work better under a more supervised Theory X approach. The reduction in unskilled work in recent years, added to the expansion of participation through self-managed teams and quality circles, belies this differentiation. There is now the view that many people have in the past left their creativity and responsibility at the factory or office door and leaders now want them to use these qualities and abilities as far as possible in the workplace.

The self-fulfilling prophecy

McGregor's research revealed that there was a self-fulfilling prophecy in leaders' views of their followers. His work showed that, to a large extent, subordinates behaved as their leaders and managers expected them to behave. This could mean that managers were good predictors of behaviour or that employees responded to their managers' expectations. His research illustrated that when managers believed their workers would perform well, objective controls showed that they did; and when workers were expected to perform poorly, they did. This situation arises because leaders themselves behave in accordance with their expectations about their subordinates. When they thought their subordinates would perform well, they supervised them, often without realising it, in a way that enhanced the likelihood of high performance. If leaders or managers have low expectations then they tend to behave in ways which inhibit the performance of subordinates and demotivate them.

This can be seen very clearly when a new leader takes over a situation. When General Montgomery assumed command of the British Eighth Army in North Africa in 1942 during the Second World War, he found a dispirited army and senior officers who had little confidence in a new commander, their fourth within a year. He had to change this situation quickly and decided to alter the way that the officers were thinking. Instead of considering the next position to which the army could fall back, he encouraged a positive attitude which did not allow for retreat:

> *'We will stand and fight here. If we can't stay here alive, then let us stay here dead.'* (General Montgomery, quoted in John Adair, 1989)

This was an uncompromising position, but it worked. When a new chief executive takes over a company he or she may be able to turn its fortunes around by an approach to leadership as much as by taking particular decisions. 'This is the way we will work' may be as important as 'this is what we will do'.

DECISION MAKING

One of the most important tasks of a leader is to make decisions. Effective leadership requires the decisions to be both sound and practical, whether they are about the direction the organisation should take, or the means by which it will make its way there. Just as there are Theory X and Theory Y leaders, so there are relatively autocratic or relatively democratic ways of making decisions. Some leaders will not tolerate any opposition to their decisions or the process by which they arrive at them. Other leaders will reach a decision by a process of consultation and discussion so that a consensus opinion emerges (*see* Fig 2.3).

To some extent these differences will depend on the personality and experience of the leader. Leaders' decision making will also depend on the confidence they have in their subordinate's development. Some leaders prefer to have absolute certainty about a decision, others can tolerate a degree of ambiguity. In delegating decision making to others a leader has to expect some uncertainty about how problems will be solved. In modern management situations, the role of managers as leaders will tend increasingly to be to encourage others to reach decisions on a wide range of issues.

THEORIES OF LEADERSHIP

There are a number of approaches to understanding leadership, ranging from the traditional view that leaders are born and not made, to the relatively recent view that leadership is more to do with the situation than to any universally desirable set of attributes.

Trait theories

The first systematic effort by researchers to understand leadership was the attempt to identify the personal characteristics of leaders. It can be argued that there is a pre-disposition to consider leaders as naturally braver, more aggressive, more decisive and more articulate than other people, so that they stand out in terms of physical characteristics, personality and intelligence. One popular myth is that natural leaders are tall and stand above the crowd like Charles De Gaulle or Abraham Lincoln.

Alexander the Great was of medium height at a time when physical height was associated with superiority. When he first sat on the throne of Cyrus the Great, it is reported that his servants had to replace the footstool with a low table. When he met some Persian emissaries they initially made their addresses to one of Alexander's staff who was the tallest man in the royal party. Alexander had other physical attributes which compensated for his lack of height, and above all he could inspire and motivate his soldiers.

The opposite popular view also exists, that natural leaders are below average height, like Napoleon Bonaparte or Mahatma Gandhi, and that they become leaders because they have to be more assertive than others. In fact the results of studies on physical characteristics show that no physical traits clearly distinguish leaders from non-leaders. Some studies have shown that leaders as a group have been brighter, more extrovert and self-confident than non-leaders. However, although millions of people have these traits, few of them will attain positions of leadership. It is also possible that we are back again in the self-fulfilling prophecy situation, where individuals become more assertive and confident once they occupy a position of leadership, so that this trait may be the result rather than the cause of leadership ability.

Edwin Ghiselli researched the question of leadership personality traits for many years, while Fred Fiedler studied personality and intelligence traits. These researchers confirm the general conclusion that there are certain desirable traits in leaders, but the fact that an individual has some of them does not determine success. Ghiselli (1971) felt that the ability to supervise other people was important along with intelligence and decisiveness. Fiedler (1971) concluded that successful leaders were more perceptive than their subordinates and more psychologically distant.

A complicating factor in this trait theory is the question of cultural bias. If there is a bias towards tall leaders, then most leaders will be tall because they are the ones who will be chosen. In the same way, the so-called 'glass ceiling' prevents women from becoming senior managers in some companies and therefore they do not emerge as leaders. When women do become senior managers, research shows that they can be just as effective leaders as men. Even though an increasing number of people believe in equality of ability and opportunity, persistent, often unconscious social stereotyping can still continue to be an obstacle in the recognition of women as leaders. Research has also shown that male and female managers are judged to be equally effective by their subordinates (Donnell and Hall, 1980).

The research into personality traits, or a set of qualities that can be used to discriminate leaders from non-leaders, has failed to produce any consistent position. It appears that no trait or combination of traits guarantees that a leader will be successful.

The behavioural approach to leadership

When it became evident that effective leaders did not apparently have any distinguishing traits or qualities, researchers tried to understand how successful and unsuccessful managers behave differently. Instead of trying to find out what effective leaders were, research turned to trying to determine what effective leaders did. The questions asked in these studies were about how leaders communicated to their subordinates, how they attempted to motivate them, how they made decisions and so on. It was felt that if the effective behaviours could be identified, then prospective managers who behaved in the more effective ways could be hired and current managers could be trained in such a way as to increase organisational productivity. The importance of arriving at this conclusion is that it meant the correct actions and behaviour could be learned and training could be provided for leadership.

Research by Ralph Stogdill (1957) and others at Ohio State University during the 1940s concluded that there were two principal dimensions to leader behaviour. On the one hand there was a concern for people, and on the other a concern for production:

- **A concern for people:** this behaviour involves a manager's concern for developing mutual trust with subordinates. This was seen as an employee-oriented approach characterised by managers' concern for their employees. The manager's behaviour encourages mutual trust and two-way communication.

- **A concern for the task:** this behaviour involves managers' concern for directing subordinates in order to achieve production targets. It is a task-oriented approach, where managers tend to be highly directive and emphasise completing a task according to plan.

The research discovered, as might be expected, that employee turnover rates were lowest and employee satisfaction highest under leaders who were rated high in consideration for people. Conversely, high grievance rates and high turnover were associated with leaders who were rated low in consideration for people and high in task orientation. However, it was not, of course, quite as simple as this. The researchers found that subordinates' ratings of their leaders' effectiveness depended not so much on the particular style of the leader as on the situation on which the style was used. For example, managers who worked in manufacturing and who exhibited high concern for task completion and low concern for people were rated by their supervisors as more proficient than more employee-centred managers. In service organisations, including hospitals and restaurants, the reverse was true, so that these most highly rated managers were those with a high concern for people and a lower concern for task completion.

The management grid

The research into leadership behaviour has shown that it is multidimensional. The management grid identifies a range of management behaviours based on various ways that task-oriented and employee-oriented styles can interact with each other (*see* Fig 2.2). There are 81 possible interactions, but to attempt to define every one would not be productive so the researchers have described five extreme positions. Managers can then decide how close to any of these is their form of leadership.

- **Country club management** scores high on concern for people and low on concern for production. This management style may be based on a belief that the most important leadership activity is to secure the voluntary co-operation

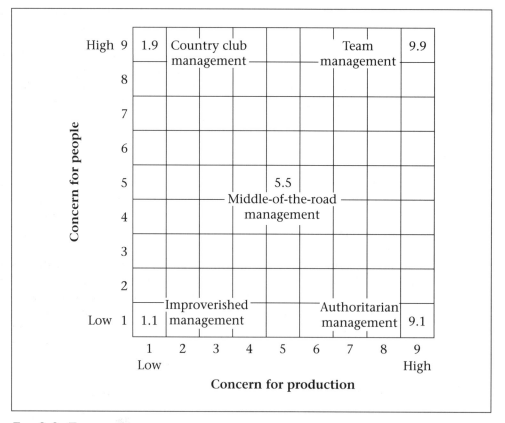

FIG 2.2 THE MANAGEMENT GRID

Source: R R Blake and J S Mouton (1985) *New Management Grid: The Key to Leadership Excellence*, Houston: Gulf Publishing Co. Adapted from Robert R Blake, Jane S Mouton, Louis B Barnes and Larry E Greiner (1964) 'Breakthrough in Organizational Development', *Harvard Business Review*, November–December, p 136. Copyright © 1973 by the President and Fellows of Harvard College; all rights reserved.

of group members in order to obtain high levels of productivity. Subordinates of these managers report generally high levels of satisfaction, but managers may be considered too easy going and unable to make decisions.

- **Authoritarian management** scores a high concern for production and efficiency and a low concern for people. This management style is task oriented and stresses the quality of the decision over the wishes of subordinates. Such managers believe that group-centred action may achieve mediocre results. They can be conscientious, loyal and personally capable, but can become alienated from their subordinates who may do only enough to keep themselves out of trouble.

- **Impoverished management** scores a low concern for both people and production. This management style does not provide leadership in a positive sense but believes in a 'laissez-faire' approach, relying on previous practice to keep the organisation going.

- **Middle-of-the-road management** scores a moderate amount of concern for both people and production. Managers applying this management style believe in compromise, so that decisions are taken but only if endorsed by subordinates. These managers may be dependable and support the status quo, but are not likely to be dynamic leaders and may have difficulty facing up to innovation and change.

- **Team management** scores high on concern for both people and production. Blake and Mouton argue that this management style provides the most effective leadership. These managers believe that concern for people and for tasks are compatible. They believe that tasks need to be carefully explained and decisions agreed with subordinates to achieve a high level of commitment.

The contingency approach

Research into trait and behavioural approaches to effective leadership shows that it depends on many variables, in terms of individual personality, management style, corporate culture and the nature of the tasks to be performed. There is not one trait or approach which is effective in all situations. The contingency approach focuses on the situational factors which influence leadership.

Robert Tannenbaum and Warner Schmidt (1973) were among the first researchers to describe various factors which influenced a manager's choice of leadership style. They took into account the manager's need to consider certain practical considerations before deciding how to manage. Also they recognised that managers had to distinguish between types of problems they should handle by themselves and those they should resolve jointly with their subordinates. They concluded that there were three main 'forces' on a manager in deciding a leadership style:

- **personal forces** – the managers' own background, experience, confidence and leadership inclinations;

- **the characteristics of subordinates** – the managers' need to consider subordinates' relative willingness or unwillingness to accept responsibility and take decisions;

- **the situation** – the managers' need to recognise the situation in which they find themselves, in terms of corporate culture, their colleagues' style of work, the nature of the tasks to be performed and time pressures.

Tannenbaum and Schmidt combined these 'forces' into a leadership continuum (Fig 2.3).

This continuum suggests that a manager should consider a full range of options before deciding how to act, from a very autocratic leadership style to a very democratic one. Some problems, those for example which involve everybody, may be best dealt with through laissez-faire leadership. If all employees are accountable and influential in the decision-making process, the best role for the leader may be to follow a 'hands-off' approach.

The discussion of management style demonstrates another self-fulfilling prophecy, in the sense that people will often react to a management style in such a way that managers will feel justified in their choice. For example, a leader may manage subordinates in an authoritarian style believing them to be low performers. This style may demotivate them, so that they do become low performers. A more democratic style may have encouraged greater initiative and high performance. This can affect the whole organisation because lower-level managers will model themselves on their superiors and attempt to manage in a similar way. E A Fleishman (1953) found that superiors who learned about new management styles in a human relations programme tended to change their actual behaviour if this was not consistent with their line manager's leadership style, and this was in spite of anything they learned on the programme.

The pressures to adopt a particular leadership style are also seen through the effects of corporate culture and peer expectations. Organisations have particular ways of doing things or place an emphasis on a particular measure of performance. For example, an advertising company may be fairly relaxed about working methods as long as the results are achieved. Leaders in this type of company may not be too concerned about how or when their employees work, provided that their outcomes and results are successful. On the other hand, a finance company may want to ensure strict accountability at every stage of its operation, so that there is close supervision of subordinates by senior managers. The opinions, attitudes and behaviour of managers' peers can also affect leadership style in making managers either more cautious than they would be otherwise or more confident. If managers feel they may be criticised for an employee-based approach, they may become more autocratic, whereas if they know that their peers favour the employee-based approach, they may adopt this approach.

The point about leadership style is that it shifts the focus from the individual leader to the functions that leaders perform within an organisation. In order for any group to operate effectively, both tasks and problem-solving functions have to be performed and, at the same time, group-maintenance or 'social' functions. It can be argued that any group of people needs to have leadership in both functions, so that, on the one hand, decisions are made and, on the other hand, the ideas and feeling of the whole group are considered. The social functions can develop the cohesion of the group and may be carried out by encouragement and support, and by recognising the importance of all members of the group to its smooth operation.

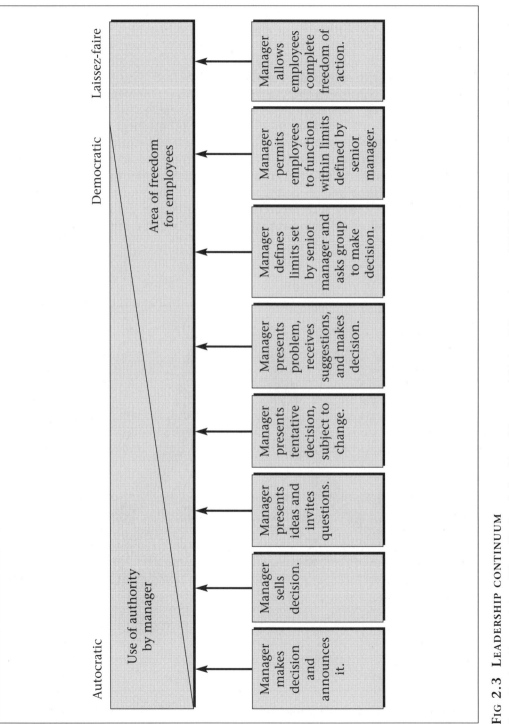

Fɪɢ 2.3 LEADERSHIP CONTINUUM

Source: Reprinted by permission of *Harvard Business Review*. Adapted from an exhibit from R Tannenbaum and W H Schmidt, 'How to choose a leadership pattern', *Harvard Business Review*, May–June 1973. Copyright © 1973 by the President and Fellows of Harvard College; all rights reserved.

The situational theory of leadership

Hersey and Blanchard (1982) developed the view that leadership approaches depended very much on the 'maturity' of their subordinates. They defined 'maturity' as a desire for achievement and willingness to accept responsibility. They developed the theory that the relationship between leaders and followers moves through phases as subordinates 'mature', and that managers need to vary their leadership style with each phase (*see* Fig 2.4).

Hersey (1998) considered that, in the initial phase, when employees first join an organisation, a high task orientation is most appropriate (Fig 2.4, 1). New employees have to be instructed in their tasks and in the organisation's rules and procedures. At this stage a non-directive manager can cause anxiety in the new employee and confusion about what is to be done. As new employees become familiar with tasks and procedures, a more employee-oriented style can be introduced (2). As employees become familiar with the work and culture of the organisation they may seek greater responsibility and the leadership style can become participatory (3). A point may be reached when a high level of delegation can be achieved (4).

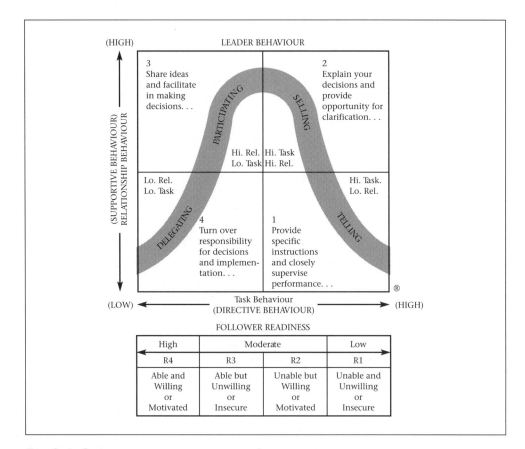

FIG 2.4 SELECTING APPROPRIATE STYLES

Source: Paul Hersey (1998) *The Situational Leader*. Reprinted by permission of the Center for Leadership Studies, Escondido, California.

The idea that the situation plays an important part in leadership style provides a dynamic and flexible view of leadership rather than a static one, which suits the modern approach to management and corporate culture.

On the one hand, the manager can develop and encourage employees to take responsibility and become more 'mature'; on the other hand, the employees' willingness and ability to take decisions and manage themselves affect the leadership style a manager can adopt. Situational theory does depend on managers' ability to be flexible in their leadership style. If they can be flexible then they can be effective in a range of situations. If not, then they can only be effective in a situation which matches their particular style. This argument emphasises the importance of the 'followers' to leadership, and the fact that the employees are an important influence on the style of leadership adopted in an organisation; they can be said to limit the power of a manager. The most effective followers or employees have characteristics which help the organisation to be successful. In a modern context this means that ideally they will be well behaved, responsible, energetic, committed and flexible. They will make sensible decisions in their sphere of control, and they will focus their energies. All this, of course, means that they may well succeed without strong leadership.

Research carried out by Fiedler (1971) was based on the view that managers have difficulty in altering the style which has helped them to achieve success, and that in fact they are not very flexible. It followed from this that trying to change a manager's style to fit the situation may be both useless and inefficient and, therefore, effective group performance could best be achieved by matching the manager to the situation or by changing the situation to match the manager. For example, an authoritarian manager can be selected to fill a post that requires directive leadership, or the job could be changed to give an authoritarian manager more formal authority over employees.

Fiedler argued that successful and effective leadership depended on three factors:

- **Leader–member relations** – this is the most important factor in leader effectiveness. The degree to which leaders have the acceptance, confidence, support and loyalty of subordinates is an essential feature of leader effectiveness. When these relations are strong the leader has a firm base from which to influence the behaviour of subordinates. When the leader–subordinate relation is weak, the influence of the leaders is only through the impersonal authority provided by their position in the organisation.

- **Task structure** – this is measured by the complexity or simplicity of the job to be carried out in an organisation. Managers have considerable power where the work of employees is highly structured and routine, because it is possible in these circumstances to establish very specific criteria to enforce a desired level of performance. Managers will usually need to adopt a democratic, consultative leadership style if the work of an organisation is complex and employees have problem-solving responsibilities which are not routine.

- **Leaders' position power** – the extent of formal or informal power which a manager is able to exert may be conferred on them by the organisation in which they work and the position they hold in it. The chief executives or managing directors of a company will have a great deal of authority because of their position in a commercial organisation. People in these positions can exert an autocratic style of leadership. Managers lower down the hierarchy of a company may have to be more democratic or laissez-faire.

The leadership styles contrasted by Fiedler are similar to the employee-centred and task-oriented approaches; Fiedler's model, however, uses a simple scale to measure leadership style to indicate 'the degree to which a man described favourably or unfavourably his least preferred co-worker'. This was the employee with whom the person could work least well. Fiedler's theory was that managers who described their least preferred co-worker or LPC in favourable terms were managers who had great concern for human relations. These are described as relationship-oriented leaders who are relatively permissive and considerate of the feelings of employees. On the other hand, it is argued that managers who describe their LPC in an unfavourable manner tend to be task-oriented leaders who are less concerned with human relations and are relatively autocratic in their leadership style. These low-LPC managers want to achieve the completion of a task, and the reaction of subordinates to their leadership style is of lower priority to them than the need to maintain production. This approach is a method of measuring the location of managers on the leadership style continuum.

In Fig 2.5 combinations 1, 2, 3 and 8 are most likely to prove successful for task-motivated leaders. The situation in combination 1 is very favourable to the leader, and followers will accept directives in order to maintain their good standing with the leader. Although the leader's organisation power is diminished in combination 2, the strength of the leader's personal power, combined with the limited discretion allowed by a structured task, provide considerable opportunities for the task-oriented manager. In combination 3, the strength of the leader's personal and

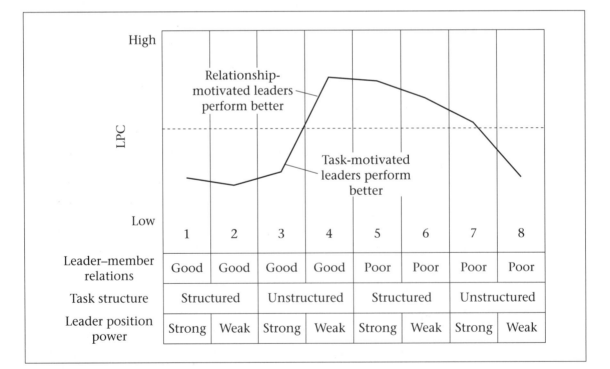

	1	2	3	4	5	6	7	8
Leader–member relations	Good	Good	Good	Good	Poor	Poor	Poor	Poor
Task structure	Structured		Unstructured		Structured		Unstructured	
Leader position power	Strong	Weak	Strong	Weak	Strong	Weak	Strong	Weak

FIG 2.5 SITUATIONAL DETERMINANTS OF EFFECTIVE LEADERSHIP

Source: F E Fiedler and M M Chemers (1974), *Leadership and Effective Management*, p.80, Copyright © John Wiley & Sons, Inc. 1974. Reprinted with permission of John Wiley & Sons, Inc, New York.

organisational power makes forceful leadership possible. In combination 8, the situation facing the leader is so unfavourable that a forceful, directive approach offers the most promising option.

In the other four combinations (4, 5, 6 and 7) a relationship-oriented style is likely to be most effective. These situations require a wide variety of skills and knowledge that can only be provided by encouraging the abilities of a number of people.

The path–goal theory of leadership

This theory was developed by Robert House (1971) and others as an approach to understanding and predicting leadership effectiveness in different situations. The theory focuses on the leader as a source of rewards and attempts to predict how different types of rewards and different leadership styles affect the performance of subordinates, based on the view that an individual's motivation depends both on the expectation and the attractiveness of the rewards available. The manager identifies the 'goals' and rewards which are available and the 'paths' to be taken to reach them.

In this process an effective leader:

- identifies and communicates to subordinates the path they should follow in order to achieve personal and organisational objectives;

- helps subordinates along this path;

- helps to remove obstacles on the path that might prevent the achievement of these objectives.

The manager's leadership style will influence the perception of the rewards available and what has to be achieved to earn them. An employee-centred manager will offer a wide range of rewards and also be sensitive to individual needs. The rewards may be in terms of pay and promotion, but will also include support, encouragement and recognition. On the other hand, a task-oriented manager will offer a more limited set of rewards which will be less concerned with individual needs. However, people working for this type of manager will know precisely what they have to do in order to obtain the particular rewards available. For example, extra pay may be obtained for a clearly defined increase in productivity. It follows from the expectancy model of motivation that the 'best' leadership style for particular employees depends on the type of rewards they want.

So the path–goal theory suggests that the most effective leadership style will depend on the personal characteristics of employees and on the situation in the workplace. For example:

- Employees who believe they have some control over their work situation and who are highly skilled may favour a participatory form of leadership which supports and encourages them and may resent an authoritarian approach.

- Employees who believe they have little control over 'how things are done' and who are less skilled may prefer more directive leadership, so that they can complete their tasks effectively and earn any bonus that is on offer.

51

This suggests that managers need to consider the characteristics of their employees and the work to be carried out, before deciding on their leadership style. Vroom and Jago (1988) have criticised the path–goal theory as incomplete because it fails to take into account the characteristics of the type of decision with which they are faced and the situation in which the decision is being made. This can be seen as a further theory of leadership based on the level of participation between managers and employees. (*See also* Chapter 12.)

The participatory theory of leadership

Vroom and Yetton (1973) developed a model of situational leadership in order to help managers decide when and to what extent they should involve employees in solving a particular problem. They suggested that managers needed to ask themselves a number of questions before deciding on an appropriate leadership style:

- Is it necessary to make an objective decision with which employees may disagree?

- Do the managers have sufficient information or skill to solve the problem on their own?

- Is the problem structured?

- Is the acceptance of the employees critical for the success of the decision?

- If the decision was made by management, would it be accepted by the employees?

- Is there likely to be conflict among employees about the best solution?

- Do employees share the achievement of the same objectives in solving the problem?

Once these questions have been answered, it is then possible to select a leadership style, although there may be further choices to be made. Vroom and Yetton defined five leadership styles in terms of the degree of participation by subordinates in the decision-making process:

- **Autocratic I (AI)** – managers solve the problem or make the decisions themselves, using available information.

- **Autocratic II (AII)** – managers obtain information from subordinates before making a decision, and then decide on the solution to the problem themselves. The role of subordinates is to provide information for decision making, and they may or may not have been told what the information is for or what the problem is that needs to be solved.

- **Consultative I (CI)** – managers share the problem with the relevant subordinates individually and obtain their ideas and information. Managers then make the decision, which may or may not be influenced by the subordinate's opinions.

- **Consultative II (CII)** – managers share the problem with the relevant subordinates as a group and obtain their ideas and information. These may or may not be used in decision making.

- **Group Participation (G)** – managers share a problem with subordinates as a group. The managers and subordinates together analyse the problem and consider alternative solutions. Managers act as co-ordinators in order to enable the group to reach a consensus, which is then accepted and implemented.

Depending on the nature of the problem, more than one leadership style may be appropriate because, once managers have answered the questions they need to ask themselves, the quality of the decision, and its acceptance have been taken into account. Vroom and Yetton developed a 'tree diagram' or flow chart (Fig 2.6) to provide a guide to the process of arriving at an appropriate leadership style. Their research has shown that decisions consistent with this model have tended to be

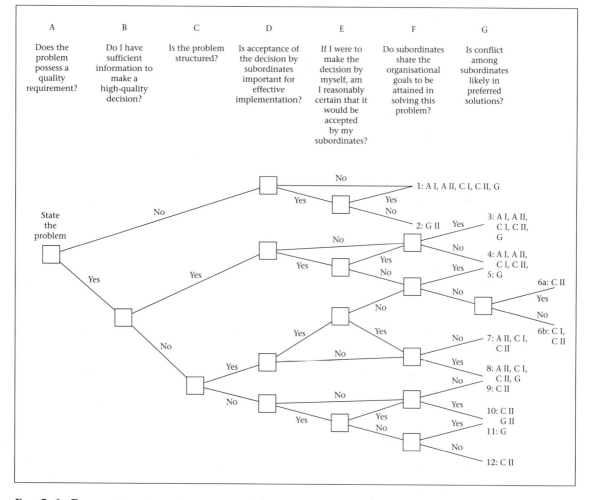

FIG 2.6 PARTICIPATIVE DECISION MODEL

Source: Reprinted from *Leadership and Decision Making*, by Victor H Vroom and Philip W Yetton, by permission of the University of Pittsburgh Press. Copyright © 1973 by University of Pittsburgh Press.

successful, while those that are inconsistent will tend to be unsuccessful. This research has been taken further to suggest that subordinates prefer their managers to make decisions consistent with this model.

When decisions have to be made quickly because of limited time and the managers have sufficient information to make a decision, an autocratic style may in fact satisfy everybody. On the other hand, if there are important problems to be solved in a situation where the subordinates have most of the information and it is important that they accept the choice of solution, then a participatory style of leadership is likely to be the most effective. In an emergency, a leader makes quick decisions often within an established framework or policy, while on long-term strategy the achievement of consensus may be more important, with the leader's role being concerned with maintaining a focus on the problem and co-ordination of the process of arriving at a solution.

It can be argued that the effectiveness of decisions may depend on:

- **the quality of the decisions;**

- **the commitment made to the decision;**

- **the time taken to make a decision.**

There is a cost factor, certainly in terms of time, in making effective decisions which has to be balanced against the time lag between identifying a problem and solving it. Equally taking a reasonable amount of time may help to develop the ability of other people to analyse problems and arrive at solutions. With fundamental and important decisions it is usually essential, in order to obtain the best results, for the people responsible for implementing the decision to feel that they have participated in arriving at it. Even if the final decision is not quite the one some people would have chosen, if they have been consulted they may still be able to give it their full support.

By working through the questions A to G in Fig 2.6, managers can arrive at the appropriate level at which to involve their subordinates in the decision under consideration. For example, if managers are attempting to decide about buying a new piece of equipment they may answer 'No' to question B, 'Yes' to D, 'No' to E and 'No' to F. This means that the managers do not have sufficient information to make a high-quality decision; the acceptance of the decision by subordinates is important for effective implementation; if managers make the decision by themselves it would not necessarily be accepted by subordinates (perhaps because they have to operate the new equipment); and the subordinates do not necessarily share the organisational goals to be attained in solving the problem. The conclusion is that the suggested management approach is to share the problem with subordinates as a group, and together the group will generate and evaluate alternatives before trying to reach a consensus decision.

CHARISMATIC LEADERSHIP

Charismatic leaders are able, through their personal vision and energy, to inspire followers and have a major impact on an organisation. This is all that matters in some views of leadership. Leadership qualities and abilities are not something to analyse, train and develop; from this point of view, either a person is a leader or not. This view of leadership suggests that it is a quality which is both mysterious and powerful and can act for either good or evil. Charismatic leaders can be identified in politics, war and industry, although whether they are charismatic or not is perhaps a matter of opinion. What Alexander the Great, Napoleon, Churchill, Hitler, Gandhi, Lee Iacocca and Jim Jones had in common was their vision and their ability to persuade people to follow it. To their followers, charismatic leaders transform their lives in one way or another and they often do not want to ask too many questions about how this is achieved. More objective analysis of their achievements usually identifies that the leaders had 'clay feet' and that there were a variety of complex factors combining to help them shine brightly for a time. In spite of these arguments the fact remains that some leaders are able to exert great charisma and considerable influence.

Max Weber, in the early part of the twentieth century, identified three forms of authority: traditional, charismatic and bureaucratic. According to Weber (1947), charisma is 'a certain quality of an individual personality by virtue of which he is considered extraordinary and treated as endowed with supernatural or exceptional forces or qualities'. In this sense, charisma is a quality which is generated from inside a person, and it derives from the capacity of particular people to arouse and maintain belief in themselves as the source of knowledge and authority. A tragic example of this was Jim Jones (Fig 2.7), who for a short time in the 1970s created a group of followers with blind faith in his leadership.

A more recent example with some similarities to this was the leadership of David Koresh which led to hundreds of his followers dying at Waco in Texas in 1992.

Napoleon Bonaparte was considered to be a charismatic leader by the French nation of his day. Although the generals close to him recognised the mundane side of his character, they still considered that he possessed a magnetic attraction. Marshal Lannes was reported to have stated that 'I have always been the victim of my attachment to him', and Marshal Marmont wrote 'we marched surrounded by a kind of radiance whose warmth I can still feel as I did fifty years ago' (quoted in *Great Leaders* by John Adair, 1989).

In the early 1970s a pastor in the United States, Jim Jones, created a devoted following in San Francisco called the People's Temple Sect. As a result of unwelcome interest in his activities in the USA, in 1974 Jones moved his sect to Guyana where he established a commune. Complaints of oppression within the commune led to a visit by a US congressman, who was shot along with his companions.

As the investigation into this shooting closed in on him, Jones gathered together his followers and invited them to participate in a mass suicide. Most of them obeyed him without question, including parents who administered cyanide to their children: 914 people died in this tragedy, including over 240 children.

FIG 2.7 JIM JONES

The focus on leadership theory has moved from the attempt to identify the inborn traits of leaders, through the study of the roles and behaviour of leaders, to the analysis of the leadership situation, work tasks and followers. The concentration on the individual leader has shifted. Although some charismatic leaders have personal characteristics which do make a difference in their organisations, the fact is that exceptional leaders are rare, by definition. Not every organisation can have one, but where they do exist they can be a powerful amplifier of organisational energy and performance. These qualities are not fully taken into account in the theories that have been so far considered. Perhaps it is a question of 'place and time', as suggested by the former British Prime Minister in Fig 2.8.

In analysing the concept of transformational leadership, Bernard Bass (1985) contrasted two types of leadership: transactional and transformational. Transactional leaders determine what subordinates need to do to achieve their own and organisational objectives, then classify these requirements and help subordinates become confident that they can reach their objectives. In contrast, transformational leaders motivate people to do better than they would have expected by raising motivation and the importance of the value of people's tasks within the organisation. These leaders go beyond transactional leadership by using their personal vision and energy to inspire their followers.

> 'Great leadership comes in many different forms. From the steady determination and emotional appeal of a Winston Churchill to the gentler consensual style of a Stanley Baldwin. Both gave strong leadership, but they were leaders for different times and different circumstances. The British people needed a Churchill in War Years, but looked elsewhere when peace returned. As Carlyle observed, great leaders both lead and reflect the age in which they live.
>
> It's the same in business. At one end of the scale is the colourful visionary with little taste for detail. At the other, the brilliant accountant, head full of figures, always looking at the costs and the fine point. Both have their place and their time.
>
> But in my mind, there are two qualifications above all which I consider to be vital to good leadership. First, good leaders have the courage of their principles and clear, long-term objectives and goals. Second, good leaders never forget the people who work for them. The difference between passive obedience and active loyalty can make the difference between success and failure. From manager to messenger – they are all individuals with their own hopes, their own self-esteem and their own interest. A good leader remembers that and behaves accordingly.'

FIG 2.8 LEADERSHIP

Source: John Major, British Prime Minister 1992–97 (*Management Today*, November 1993).

Richard Boyd (1987) has proposed that there are new skills required of leaders:

- **anticipatory skills** in order to provide foresight into a constantly changing situation;

- **vision skills** in order to lead the organisation towards the leader's or the general objectives;

- **value skills** in order to be in touch with employees' needs, both physical and spiritual, so that shared values and goals can be encouraged;

- **empowerment skills**, so that power is shared;

- **self-understanding** in order for leaders to understand their own needs and those of their employees.

The question then arises of, how far these skills can be taught? Peter Drucker (1992) has stated that:

> *'more leaders have been made by accidental circumstances, sheer grit, or will, than have been made by all the leadership courses put together.'*

He suggests that heredity and early childhood experience may be the most important factors in leadership activity. Robert House (1971) considers that charismatic leaders communicate the imagination and energies of their followers. He suggests that they create an image of success and competence and set examples of the values they support through their own behaviour. They have high expectations of their followers and help to create the confidence that they can achieve high levels of performance.

Charismatic leaders of this kind provide for a need to find meaning in a common cause. This can be said to reflect a desire for certainty in a commercial world which has become more complex over the years.

Peter Drucker (1992) has written that leadership has little to do with leadership qualities and even less to do with charisma:

> *'Leadership is not by itself good or desirable. Leadership is a means. Leadership to what end is the crucial question. History knows no more charismatic leaders than this century's triad of Stalin, Hitler, and Mao – the misleaders who inflicted as much evil and suffering on humanity as have ever been recorded.'*

The feature which distinguishes what Drucker terms the misleaders from the leaders is their goals. In this, charisma can become the undoing of leaders. He argues that it makes them inflexible, convinced of their own infallibility and unable to change, so that charisma does not in itself guarantee effectiveness as a leader. Drucker gives the example of John F Kennedy as perhaps the most charismatic person ever to occupy the White House, but who in fact achieved very little.

The power of leaders

The power of managers over employees can be described as 'social power' because it is derived from the social interaction of leaders and their followers. This can be understood better by analysing this social power in more detail:

57

- **Coercive power** is a form of power that is often the main consideration in a general discussion on the subject. It is based on subordinates' fear of the leader and on punishment and threats, and is linked to the most extreme form of autocratic leadership.

- **Expert power** is based on the leader's possession of expertise, skill or knowledge, and the recognition of this by others provides the leader with the power to make decisions.

- **Legitimate power** is based on the hierarchy of the organisation and the perception of subordinates that they should obey the orders of senior managers. On this basis, the more senior the managers are, the more legitimate power they have.

- **Referent power** is based on the charismatic power of leaders. People will accede to these leaders because they admire them and want to increase identification with them.

- **Reward power** is based on the leader's ability to provide rewards for followers. Subordinates support these leaders because of positive rewards such as pay, promotion and recognition.

- **Connection power** is based on a leader's relationships with influential partners, both inside and outside the organisation. Followers may want to remain on good terms with this leader.

- **Information power** is based on the leader's access to information that is valuable to other people. Followers want to share this access or to be involved with somebody who has such access.

Studies by Pearce and Robinson (1987), for example, have shown that the most effective managers today rely more on expert, referent and connection power than on coercive, legitimate, reward or information power. Leaders now tend to use personal power rather than positional power as management structures have become flatter and management practice more open. Information is now more widely shared and management is seen as a form of partnership in order to achieve agreed objectives. There are still, of course, organisations which base their power on coercion and reward, and individual leaders who rely on these as the foundation of their power.

Is leadership necessary?

It can be argued that leaders only emerge in response to a perceived need by followers. At the same time the development of participative management and self-managed work groups may have reduced the need for leadership in the old sense. Manz and Sims (1987) have suggested that, although organisations provide individual employees with certain attitudes and values, people have their own value systems. Organisational control systems direct the behaviour of individual employees, but the influence is indirect because it is on the self-control systems and values that individuals bring to an organisation. This is illustrated in Fig 2.9.

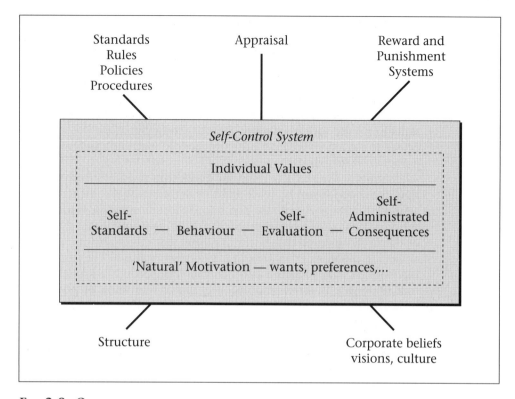

Standards Appraisal Reward and
Rules Punishment
Policies Systems
Procedures

Self-Control System

Individual Values

Self- Self-
Self- Administrated
Standards — Behaviour — Evaluation — Consequences

'Natural' Motivation — wants, preferences,...

Structure Corporate beliefs
visions, culture

FIG 2.9 ORGANISATIONAL CONTROL SYSTEM

Source: Reprinted by permission of *Academy of Management Review*. A figure from 'Self-leadership: Toward an expanded theory of self-influence processes in organizations', by Charles C Manz (Vol II, No 3, 1986). Copyright © 1986; all rights reserved.

Manz and Sims argue that the new leadership roles that emerge with the development of self-managed groups are more effective than the more formal and traditional roles. They defined 'self-leadership' as the ability of workers to motivate themselves to perform tasks which are naturally appealing to them and those that are necessary but are not particularly attractive. They also suggest that this type of leadership encourages employee development and behaviour which does not deviate significantly from the organisation's behavioural standards. The creation of self-managed teams and groups requires the nurturing of a particular organisational culture which enables this process to work. It can be argued that leadership is still required to establish this situation and to provide the support necessary for this culture.

According to Charles Handy (1991), the modern organisation requires us:

> *'To learn new ways and new habits, to live with more uncertainty, but more trust, less control, but more creativity.'*

He argues that leadership remains as difficult to pin down as ever, and it has to be seen in action to be recognised:

> *'The studies agree on very little but what they do agree on is probably at the heart of things. It is this: "A leader shapes and shares a vision which gives point to the work of others".'*

The conclusion is that leadership is necessary, but new organisations in new situations need to be run in new ways. Flatter organisations mean that the traditional idea of constant upward movement by promotion into leadership positions with ever-increasing responsibility is no longer valid. There are fewer promotional posts and ambitious managers have to look at the horizontal rather than the vertical fast track. This means that they have a succession of different jobs at the same level, which gives them a wide view of the organisation and an opportunity to test their skills in a wide variety of roles. This has to be based on the view that a horizontal career is a good thing and prepares people well for the few senior management posts which do exist.

The questioning of the need for leadership puts an emphasis on the argument that leadership is not by itself good or desirable; it is a means to an end, that is to achieving certain objectives. The foundation of effective leadership can be seen as thinking through an organisation's mission, defining it and establishing it. The role of the leader is to establish the goals and objectives and monitor progress towards achieving them. As Peter Drucker (1992) has written, 'The leader's first task is to be the trumpet that sounds a clear sound.' The second task of the leader is to accept that leadership is about responsibility rather than rank or privilege. Leaders accept responsibility for what happens in their organisations – in the words of Henry Truman, 'the buck stops here' – while allowing their subordinates to make mistakes and enjoy success. Peter Drucker argues that the third requirement of effective leadership is to earn trust. Without trust there are not any followers and there is, therefore, not a leader. Trust is belief in the vision of leaders and the conviction that they mean what they say.

It can be argued that leadership has little to do with charisma and much more to do with very hard work and being consistent. As Peters and Waterman (1982) have described it:

> *'Leadership is many things. It is patient, usually boring coalition building. It is the purposeful seeking of cabals that one hopes will result in the appropriate ferment in the bowels of the organisation. It is meticulously shifting the attention of the institution through the mundane language of management systems. It is altering agendas so that new priorities get enough attention. It is being visible when things are going awry, and invisible when they are working well. It is building a loyal team at the top that speaks more or less with one voice. It is listening carefully much of the time, frequently speaking with encouragement, and reinforcing with believable action.'*

Peters and Waterman believe that in almost every excellent company there is somewhere in its history an example of transforming leadership, most likely when the company was relatively small.

Sir Graham Day goes further than this in stating that a world-class firm will have a world-class leader (*see* Fig 2.10). He argues that leadership addresses the questions of motivation, the objectives of working and the improvement of organisations.

In *Thriving on Chaos* (1987), Tom Peters argues that the leader at any level in an organisation must become an empiricist:

> *'That is, the firm must become a hotbed of tests of the unconventional. It must become an experimenting (and learning), adaptive change-seeking organisation.'*

'I am very attracted by the words of Professor Abraham Zaleznik: "Leadership is made of substance, humanity and morality and we are painfully short of all three qualities in our collective lives."

There's the John Wayne, gung ho, follow-me attitude – but if there is no perceived reality or no human touch then it is unlikely to touch the constituents you want to lead. And without morality you may as well be Adolf Hitler. Leadership is the ability to change compelled performers into willing participants. If you only have a mandatory leadership, you have three negatives: pressure without motivation; process without substance; organisation without improvement. True leadership addresses those negatives. The attributes which ultimately matter are the abilities to communicate and inspire.

A world-class firm, regardless of size, will have a world-class leader. The CEO's ability and confidence in communicating his or her vision to all levels of the corporate hierarchy, and also to the community, will set him or her apart as an exceptional leader.'

FIG 2.10 WORLD-CLASS LEADERS

Source: Sir Graham Day, *Management Today*, November 1993. Reprinted with permission.

The organisation, it is argued, must ceaselessly send its people out to visit other interesting organisations of all kinds. The objective is for people to learn more and to learn faster so that they can deal proactively with change. 'The organisation learns from the past, swipes from the best, adapts, tests, risks, fails, and adjusts – over and over.' Peters suggests that the core paradox is that all leaders at all levels must contend with creating and fostering internal stability in order to encourage the pursuit of constant change. He argues that this dichotomous task has not been imposed on leaders before. They must on the one hand insist on a clear vision, a way forward, and on the other hand, insist upon the constant testing of this vision so that it is expanded, contracted and eventually destroyed and replaced with a new vision. In this sense, the role of the leader is simultaneously to promote stability and instability in the organisation.

So discussion and argument on leadership continue. Warren Bennis and Burt Nanus (1986) wrote that leadership remains the most studied and least understood topic in all the social sciences. They argue that, like beauty or love, we know it when we see it but we cannot easily define it or produce it on demand. They conclude that:

> 'Leaders articulate and define what has previously remained implicit or unsaid; they invent images, metaphors and models that provide a focus for new attention. By so doing, they consolidate a challenge provoking wisdom. In short, an essential factor in leadership is the capacity to influence and organise meaning for the members of the organisation.'

In looking at the relationship between management and leadership, Bennis and Nanus suggest that:

> *'Managers are people who do things right and leaders are people who do the right thing. The difference may be summarised as activities of vision and judgement – effectiveness versus activities of mastering routine efficiency.'*

It is difficult to avoid military metaphors when discussing leadership, because of the clear need for leadership in a military crisis. The link between the military and other spheres has been well summed up by General Sir Peter Inge in discussing his own views of the essential qualities of leadership (*see* the Case study on pages 63–4). His list includes many of the qualities explored by other writers on the subject: personality, character, courage, willpower, knowledge and initiative.

SUMMARY

■ It can be argued that management is largely concerned with leadership, because managers need to establish a sense of direction and to motivate people to move in that direction.

■ The understanding of theories of leadership provides a basis for analysing leadership and management styles. This understanding is also a factor in the process of making decisions.

■ The consideration of charismatic leadership helps to illustrate the power of leaders. Discussion of the need for leadership highlights the management tasks and objectives which are involved.

REVIEW AND DISCUSSION QUESTIONS

1   What is the connection between leadership and management?

2   How relevant are Theories X and Y to modern management?

3   Analyse the main considerations leaders need to take into account in making decisions.

4   Should the situation and the circumstances in which leadership is being exercised make a difference to the style of leadership?

5   What provides the power of leaders over their followers?

6   Is there a need for leadership?

CASE STUDY: THE QUALITIES OF LEADERSHIP

The definition of a leader makes leadership sound simple: 'A person or thing that leads or a person followed by others.' In fact, the more one exercises leadership or is led, the more one realises that the fundamental nature of leadership is very personal and is not susceptible to clear scientific analysis. A study of great leaders shows an enormous diversity in their style of leadership, personalities and in their ethos. This variety of personality, character and style leads me to believe that leadership is an art and not a science.

We, of course, have to recognise that leadership is not always inherently good and, indeed, many evil men have been very effective leaders. I will concentrate on good leadership in a democracy and, in particular, leadership within armed forces.

In this context, good leadership is perhaps best described as getting others to do often difficult and sometimes dangerous tasks willingly. However, leadership is required in all walks of life and, although the way that leadership is exercised and emphasis given to particular qualities may vary, I believe many of the essentials are similar. It was Field Marshal The Viscount Slim who said, 'When talking about leadership, one always comes back to the same basic principles.' I have to declare my hand and admit that he is one of my military heroes and his analysis of leadership and the way he exercised it are second to none. I lean on him very heavily in the points which follow.

Before turning to some specific qualities in a successful leader I would like to make one general point. I believe that it is fundamentally important for a leader to have a credo or belief in what he stands for and in the organisation, formation or body in which he is a leader. I suspect everyone has his own list of the essential qualities necessary in a leader. Here are mine:

Personality and Character. Great leaders have the strength of character and personality to inspire confidence and to gain the trust of others. Clearly this is a personal thing but it can be developed by experience and training. I would emphasise that leaders do not have to be roaring extroverts to be successful. Some very charismatic leaders have been just quietly confident, although they had the ability to communicate.

Courage. Field Marshal Slim said, 'Courage is the greatest of all virtues for without it there are no other virtues.' Although he was talking about both physical and moral courage, it was moral courage on which he laid the greatest emphasis. Indeed, I believe that moral courage is the single most important quality for a successful leader. It is the courage to do what you believe to be right without bothering about the consequences for yourself. The funny thing is that the more you use your moral courage on small issues, the easier it becomes to use it on big issues. Physical courage is, of course, the reverse and is more like a bank account. The more you use it the more likely it is to become overdrawn.

Willpower. A leader has to learn to dominate events and never allow these events to get the better of him and this determination or willpower concerns not only rival organisations or, in the case of armed forces, the enemy, but equally colleagues and allies.

Knowledge. This means knowledge not only of your profession but equally knowledge of the men under your command. Knowing them well and being known to them is vital if you are to gain their confidence. As a newly-joined platoon commander, after every one of my first few muster parades, the company sergeant major always asked me about a particular soldier. I was never able to answer him satisfactorily. Eventually, I plucked up courage to ask him what he meant and why he was asking me these questions. He said, 'I watch you on muster parade, Sir, and you inspect the men very thoroughly, their belts, their boots and their weapons, but you don't look them in the eye. Every morning you must look your soldiers in the eye and that will tell you how they feel and if they have a problem.' It was outstanding advice and done in a way that made me never forget it. Quite a psychologist.

Initiative. This is, of course, a fundamentally important quality in any walk of life but nowhere more so than on the battlefield. I can do no better in this context than to quote Field Marshal Slim: 'Here one comes up against a conflict between determination, fixity of purpose and flexibility. There is always the danger that determination becomes plain obstinacy and flexibility, mere vacillation. If you can hold within yourself the balance between these two – strength of will and flexibility of mind – you will be well on the road to becoming a leader in a big way.'

In conclusion, I would add two final qualities. They are unselfishness and showing that you enjoy being a leader. In summary, to quote General Sir John Hackett: 'Successful military leadership is impossible without the leader's total engagement in the task in hand and to the group committed to his care for its discharge.' For all I know, this may be so not only in the military but in other spheres as well. ∎

Source: General Sir Peter Inge, *Management Today*, November 1993. Reprinted with permission.

REFERENCES FOR FURTHER READING

Adair, John (1989) *Great Leaders*, Guildford: Talbot Adair Press.

Bass, Bernard M (1985) 'Leadership: Good, Better, Best', *Organizational Dynamics*, No 3.

Bennis, Warren and Nanus, Burt (1986) *Leaders*, New York: Harper & Row.

Blake, R R and Mouton, J S (1985) *New Management Grid III: The Key to Leadership Excellence*, Houston: Gulf Publishing Co.

Boyd, Richard (1987) 'Corporate Leadership Skills: A New Synthesis', *Organizational Dynamics*, No 1.

Donnell, S and Hall, J (1980) 'Men and Women as Managers: A Significant Case of No Significant Difference', *Organizational Dynamics*, Spring.

Drucker, Peter (1992) *Managing for the Future*, Oxford: Butterworth-Heinemann.

Fiedler, Fred (1968) 'The Leader's Psychological Distance and Group Effectiveness', in D Cartwright and A Zander, *'Group Dynamics'*, New York: Harper & Row.

Fiedler, Fred (1971) 'A Theory of Leadership Effectiveness', *Administrative Science Quarterly*, September.

Fleishman, E A (1953) 'Leadership Climate, Human Relations Training Behaviour', *Personnel Psychology*, No 2.

Ghiselli, Edwin (1971) *Explorations in Managerial Talents*, Santa Monica, California: Goodyear.

Handy, Charles (1991) *The Age of Unreason*, London: Century.

Hersey, P and Blanchard, K (1982) *Management of Organizational Behaviour: Utilising Human Resources*, Englewood Cliffs, New Jersey: Prentice-Hall.

House, R (1971) 'A Path Goal Theory of Leadership Effectiveness', *Administrative Science Quarterly*, September.

House, R and Mitchell, T (1974) 'Path–Goal Theory of Leadership', *Journal of Contemporary Business*, Autumn.

McGregor, Douglas (1960) *The Human Side of Enterprise*, New York: McGraw-Hill.

Management Today (1993) 'Present Bearers of the Leadership Mantle . . .', November.

Manz, Charles (1978) 'Self-Leadership: Towards an Expanded Theory of Self-Influence Processes in Organizations', *Academy of Management Review*, 3.

Manz, Charles and Sims, Harry (1987) 'Leading Workers to Lead Themselves: The External Leadership of Self-Managing Work Teams', *Administrative Science Quarterly*, No 32.

Massie, Joseph L and Douglas, John (1977) *Managing: A Contemporary Introduction*, Englewood Cliffs, New Jersey: Prentice-Hall.

Pearce, J and Robinson, R (1987) 'A Measure of CEO Social Power in Strategic Decision Making', *Strategic Management Journal*, May/June.

Peters, Tom (1987) *Thriving on Chaos*, London: Macmillan.

Peters, Tom and Waterman, Robert Jr (1982) *In Search of Excellence*, New York: Harper & Row.

Ricie, R, Instone, D. and Adams, J (1984) 'Leader Sex, Leader Success and Leadership Process: Two Field Studies', *Journal of Applied Psychology*, February.

Stogdill, R and Coons, A (1957) *Leader Behaviour: Its Description and Measurement*, Columbus: Ohio State University, Bureau of Business Research.

Tannenbaum, Robert and Schmidt, Warner (1973) 'How to Choose a Leadership Pattern', *Harvard Business Review*, May–June.

Vroom, V H and Jago, A G (1988) *The New Leadership: Managing Participation in Organizations*, Englewood Cliffs, New Jersey: Prentice-Hall.

Vroom, V H and Yetton, P W (1973) *Leadership and Decision Making*, Pittsburgh: University of Pittsburgh Press.

Weber, Max (1947) *The Theory of Social and Economic Organizations*, New York: Free Press.

3 FOCUS ON THE CUSTOMER

Tim Hannagan

OBJECTIVES

The objectives of this chapter are to:

◆ focus on the importance of customer service

◆ stress the importance of flexibility in management structures in order to be able to meet customer needs

◆ analyse the strategies required to meet customer needs and to maintain a competitive edge

◆ consider the effects of the focus on the customer on the qualities and skills required in management

◆ help understand new forms of organisational structure designed to meet customer needs

THE CUSTOMER COMES FIRST

Organisations have changed and are changing as a result of a focus on the customer. It is now recognised that meeting customer needs is the foundation of any successful organisation, and that the customers come first, second and third. Customers have, of course, always been important; what has changed is the priority given to them and the urgency with which their needs are considered. It can be argued that customer service is now the only factor which distinguishes one organisation from another in the same business. At the same time, the customers have changed, they have become more demanding and they have more choice. It is these changes which have made imperative a change in the role of managers. For most organisations their customers' perceptions are formed by contact with people representing the organisation. In order to provide an excellent service, these representatives have to have the power to make decisions without constantly conferring with a line manager. Employees have become responsible for a range of decisions which would have previously required management approval.

This change was heralded by the so-called 'death of bureaucracy' identified by Warren Bennis (1966), among others. He argued that every age develops the organisational form appropriate to its time and that bureaucracy was appropriate to the first two-thirds of the twentieth century but not beyond that. His view was that the order, precision and impersonal nature of bureaucracy were a reaction to the personal and capricious nature of management in the nineteenth century, remnants of which survived well into the twentieth century. Bennis recognised that there were new conditions developing in the last third of the twentieth century which had major implications for management. There was rapid and unexpected change in the position of most organisations, with increasing diversity which created a need for flexibility and new and specialised skills. This changing world was predicted by Alvin Toffler in *Future Shock* (1970), a book which produced as much interest in its time as *In Search of Excellence* more than a decade later. At the same time, the human relations approach to organisational management had emphasised the importance of leadership and communication, intrinsic job motivation, and practices which facilitated flexibility and involvement.

The changes recognised by Bennis and Toffler have encouraged the view that there is no one best way to manage an organisation and that the appropriate method depends on the particular situation. This contingency approach has developed and expanded since the 1960s in response to competition and technology. W R Scott (1987) pointed out:

> *'that previous definitions tend to view the organization as a closed system, separate from its environment and comprising a set of stable and easily identified participants. However, organizations are not closed systems, sealed off from their environments but are open to and dependent on flows of personnel and resources from outside.'*

Open organisations are characterised by uncertainty over the actions of others, such as customers, which leads them constantly to monitor these actions. They are also uncertain about the development of influences outside the organisation, for which they produce contingency plans. At the same time there are wide variations in the use of technology within organisations, even by those producing similar products or services, and in the speed of change and innovation. Organisations are also of different sizes and this has an effect on their management style. Some of the characteristics of open organisations and factors influencing their style are summarised in Fig 3.1.

Work at the University of Aston in the 1960s (Pugh and Hickson, 1976) found that size was the most important predictor of management style, so that the larger the organisation, the more likely it was to adopt bureaucratic structures, while the smaller the organisation the more likely it was to adopt flexible structures. The increasing emphasis on the customer now points to the need for all organisations, large or small, to have a high degree of flexibility.

Uncertainty over matters and events outside the organisation including:

- the actions of others;
- the inability ever to understand and control events fully;
- the uncertainty of forecasts;
- the dependence on outside events (such as the changes in Eastern Europe in the 1990s);
- the uncertainty created by other people's forecasts (such as views about the depth and duration of the recession in the UK and other developed economies of the early 1990s, and in the Far Eastern economies in the late 1990s);
- the behaviour of customers and suppliers.

Development and innovations in technology:

- the use of different technologies by organisations producing different products and services;
- the use of different technologies by organisations producing similar products and services;
- the constant changes in technology owing to innovation.

Difference in size between organisations:

- it has become recognised that the structure and practices for the efficient organisation of large institutions may not be those most suitable for smaller ones;
- as organisations grow in size, more decentralised and impersonal structures may become appropriate.

FIG 3.1 OPEN ORGANISATIONS

Contingency theories have moved a long way towards suggesting that management needs to be flexible and to apply the appropriate techniques to factors such as the size and situation of an organisation. Even so, it can be argued that the contingency approach does not provide a convincing explanation of how organisations do and should operate. It may be considered that organisational culture is not sufficiently taken into account and that it has become increasingly important for members of an organisation to take control of their structure and decision-making processes. Peters and Waterman (1982), for example, attempted to predict the way firms would need to organise and operate in the future based on what the best companies were doing at the moment or planning to do in the future.

IN SEARCH OF EXCELLENCE

Peters and Waterman carried out a study for management consultants McKinsey and Company of the 62 most successful companies in the USA. They were able to identify eight key attributes which organisations needed to manifest in order to achieve excellence. It can be argued that every one of these attributes is about people, and most of them focus directly or indirectly on the customer. Peters and Waterman argue that these attributes are largely opposed to the rational theories of management which have been so popular in the past, whether they have been based on scientific management, bureaucratic control, human resource theories or a contingency approach. They argue that these rational approaches produced 'paralysis through analysis' to an extent where action stops and planning runs riot. Analysis may reach a point where it attempts to be precise about matters which are inherently uncertain, and at the same time the analysis of situations can become so complex that it becomes unwieldy. They suggest that a problem may arise where a 'correct' answer to a problem is identified irrespective of its application to the situation in question.

Peters and Waterman argue that past management techniques should be used as an aid to, but not a substitute for, human judgement. They suggest that it is the freedom given to managers and employees to innovate and experiment with different solutions which distinguishes excellent companies from the less successful ones. In their study, they identified the attributes which characterised most closely the distinct features of excellent, innovative companies, which are summarised in Fig 3.2.

In Peters and Waterman's view, these core values may be concerned with such matters as the quality of customer service, or the importance of reliability. For example, they quote the McDonald's food franchise slogan, QSCV: Quality, Service, Cleanliness and Value. Excellent companies really do get close to their customers, while others just talk about it. The best organisations take customer service to extreme lengths in order to achieve quality, service and reliability. They listen to their customers by observing the customer view on product, quantity, quality and service, and they claim to receive their best ideas for new products from listening intently and regularly to their customers. The excellent companies are:

'driven by their direct orientation to the customers rather than by technology or by a desire to be the low-cost producer. They seem to focus more on the revenue-generation side of their service.'

- A bias for action, rather than too much planning or waiting for something to happen

- Keeping close to the customer by learning from the people they serve and providing a high quality and reliable service

- Fostering autonomy and entrepreneurship through encouraging the development of leaders and innovators throughout the organisation and supporting creativity and risk taking

- Developing productivity through people by recognising that the main productivity gains could be achieved by employees rather than through capital investment

- Practising a hands-on, value-driven approach, by concentrating on achievements rather than technological or economic resources or organisational structure

- 'Sticking to the knitting' by staying close to businesses that are already known and by following the approach that a company should never acquire a business it does not know how to run

- Organising a 'simple form' and 'lean staff' structure, so that the organisation remains uncomplicated with relatively few top-level staff

- Maintaining simultaneous loose–tight properties: both centralised and decentralised, with autonomy pushed down to the shopfloor and product development team, and centralisation around the core values

FIG 3.2 EXCELLENT COMPANIES

Rosabeth Moss Kanter (1989) has attempted to define what organisations need to be like in the future if they are to be successful. She believes that today's corporate elephants need to learn to dance as nimbly and speedily as mice if they are to survive in an increasingly competitive and rapidly changing world:

> *'If the main game of business is indeed like Alice in Wonderland croquet, then running it requires faster action, more creative manoeuvring, more flexibility and closer partnerships with employees and customers than was typical in the traditional corporate bureaucracy. It requires more agile, livelier management that pursues opportunity without being bogged down by cumbersome structures or weighty procedures that impede action. Corporate giants, in short, must learn how to dance.'*

Companies must be constantly alert and keep abreast of their competitors' intentions and their customers' needs, Kanter argues, and they must open themselves up to form alliances.

MANAGER 2000

This theme of co-operation and collaboration has been developed by Robert Heller:

> *'Manager 2000 will practice co-operation and collaboration with everybody, inside and outside the firm, from colleagues and subordinates to customers and suppliers.'*
> (Robert Heller, 'The Manager's Dilemma', *Management Today*, January 1994)

He argues that managers of the future have to be tolerant team players, putting the objectives of the team above the ambitions of an individual. This approach is encouraged by the devolution of power and delegation of decision making to self-managed teams at the point of production or customer service. Managers will work in organisations where the hierarchical pyramid is inverted, placing top management at the base and the customer at the summit (*see* Fig 3.3).

In this situation the manager's role is to support individuals and teams producing goods or supplying services directly to the customer. In placing the customer at the top of this pyramid, the objective is to provide the best in quality and service and through this process to find a competitive advantage. This in fact means 'keeping close to the customer' and finding out from them what they want in terms of quality and reliability.

'Managers 2000', at all levels, will have to be involved in developing the potential of everybody around them. Hierarchical bureaucratic systems provided a framework for establishing and keeping the rules of an organisation, whether these were openly established or part of an accepted corporate culture. Heller argues that the horizontal principle is displacing the vertical principle in everything, from organisational structure to markets. The outcomes of business processes are all important and innovation has become a necessity. The development of self-managed teams is perhaps less about 'empowerment', which suggests giving people the ability to manage work more effectively, as about 'enablement' by ceasing to stop them from organising work effectively. In Rank Xerox, for example, the managing director is subjected to twice-yearly feedback from the 15 people who report

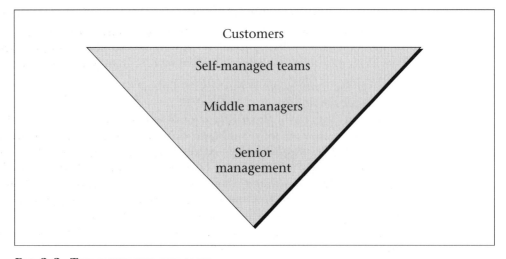

FIG 3.3 THE INVERTED PYRAMID

directly to him, and the same applies to each of them and throughout the organisation. Everybody knows specifically what is expected of them and everybody is involved in deciding what they have to do.

It can be argued that organisations will be judged on their outcomes, and these will depend on looking at customer requirements with totally fresh eyes and reshaping the entire corporation in order to meet the redefined customer need:

> *'The "virtual corporation" seeks to meet customer needs in the shortest possible time by continual adaptation.'*
> (Robert Heller, 'Customer Focus Means Commitment to Constant Change',
> *Management Today*, January 1994)

As a result of this, Managers 2000 will not expect their jobs to be static, because the business process will determine what is expected at any given time. They will advance in prestige and pay by moving from one successful assignment to the next, not by exchanging one title for another.

SYNERGY

Synergy occurs when the whole adds up to more than the sum of the parts, so that every part of an organisation adds value to the whole. A priority for managers is to ensure that this is what actually happens in the business. In essence this means identifying and concentrating on the core business areas and removing all obstacles to their efficient and effective operation. Non-core activities are eliminated and concentration is focused towards the top of the inverted triangle, at the point of contact with the customer.

The result of this 'search for synergy' is to create flatter, more responsive and less complex organisations. Non-core activities are 'hived off' and their functions contracted out, 'outsourced', or taken over by technology or by individual business units. For example, the company payroll may be computerised or contracted out to a specialised company and catering services may be 'outsourced' to a national catering company or to a separate business unit. The objective is to increase productivity, flexibility and cost control by concentrating effort on the core business and making sure that all parts of this business are adding value to the whole organisation. One of the results of this has been a change in employment patterns:

> *'The job for life is a thing of the past, part-time and flexible work patterns and fixed-term contracts are becoming the norm. Managers must recognise this. To keep their options open, they need to grasp every available training opportunity.'*
> (Roger Young, Director General of the Institute of Management, 1993)

In a survey of long-term employment strategies carried out in 1993 by the Institute of Management and Manpower plc, a move towards flexible working was identified. Over the previous five years it was found that 90 per cent of the UK's largest organisations had restructured and for 86 per cent this had resulted in job losses at all levels. Nearly 40 per cent expected to restructure again in the following year and 66 per cent over the next four years. As well as shedding permanent jobs, it was noted that employers were introducing greater flexibility into the working patterns of the staff who remained: 75 per cent of the companies predicted an increase in contracting out over the next few years.

This process of change has led to a flattening of hierarchies and a shrinkage in chains of command. In most organisations the terms of employment and the business itself are no longer disconnected. There is not sufficient slack in the economy to allow this. The new reality draws a very close connection between a person's job and the success or failure of their organisation.

THE ECONOMIC FOCUS

At a basic level there are two agents involved in any transaction, a consumer and a producer. In economic terms the consumers attempt to maximise their 'utility' or 'satisfaction' by purchasing goods and services which give the greatest value relative to the price charged for them. On the other hand, the producer attempts to maximise profits by charging the highest price consumers will pay. In order to increase their profits, producers have two choices. Either they produce goods and services which deliver better value to customers than those offered by competitors and thereby expand volume and sales, or they can reduce their costs in order to enhance the margin for profit on each unit of a commodity or service sold. The competitive element will, in economic terms, keep the market in equilibrium. If the price is too high relative to the cost of producing particular goods and services, other producers will find it profitable to enter the market in order to take advantage of the high profit margin. This will have the effect of lowering prices, as the supply of the goods and services increases relative to the demand for them. If the price is too low, production will be reduced because profits are not high enough, and as supply falls below demand, prices will rise.

These basic economic laws of supply and demand mean that for companies to be successful they need to provide goods and services that customers want, and to do so better and/or at a lower cost than their competitors. Unless an organisation has some form of monopoly position, it will have to meet customer requirements better than its competitors in order to make a sale. Consumers will normally buy from a producer whose mix of product, price and service provides more value or satisfaction than that of its competitors. The only occasion when this will not be the case will be when consumers do not know what the competitors are offering or where there is no real choice. This lack of choice may be due to a monopoly position, where for example railways provide the only viable form of transport, or where there is a factor such as location, where for example there is only one major store within travelling distance, which in practice limits consumer choice.

CASE STUDY: PRODUCED TO PRICE   **FT**

I wrote an article in 1980 which explained why a contraction of manufacturing industry was an inevitable consequence of the growth of British North Sea oil production. This was my first encounter with manufacturing fetishists.

The article proved to be very controversial – it was, incidentally, right. Few critics focused on technical weaknesses in the argument. They said instead that what I was saying ought not to be true or, if true, ought not to be said.

I started to understand that for many people the role of manufacturing industry was an emotional issue rather than an economic one. 'Surely you don't think that an economy can survive on hairdressing and hamburger bars?' No, I did not, any more than I thought it could survive on steel and car production. But because I was not in favour of manufacturing industry, I was regarded as being against it.

It seems that it is impossible to be a disinterested observer of the share of manufacturing in national income – any more than it is possible to be a disinterested observer of Eric Cantona, or a test match between England and Australia.

The origins of manufacturing fetishism might be better explored by a psychologist or an anthropologist, but let me have a go.

Thousands of years ago people hunted, fished and made primitive implements. If a man was good at these things, his wife and children prospered; if not, they died. From this we have inherited the notion of a hierarchy of needs – food and shelter running ahead of chartered accountancy and cosmetic surgery. With it comes a notion of a hierarchy of importance for economic activities – agriculture and basic manufacturing running ahead of hairdressing and television programming.

All this ceased to have economic relevance, however, once technology advanced enough for it to be unnecessary to hunt and fish all day to get enough to eat – a state of affairs reached many years ago. Once primitive tribes achieved this, they started to add discretionary activities to the fulfilment of their basic needs.

The services that came into production then remain representative of the services we buy today. There was the priest, who warded off evil; the bureaucrat, who ruled over the tribe; the repair man, who sharpened the stones and the knives – and eventually the insurance agent, who organised a scheme of mutual support for unlucky villagers whose cow died or whose house burnt down.

With the rise of a market economy came Adam Smith's division of labour. Specialist tasks were assigned to those best qualified to fulfil them. As Smith noted, the division of labour was limited by the extent of the market, and the growth in the geographical scope of markets has steadily increased the division of labour. But even in the early stages of discretionary expenditure, rewards became divorced from the place activities enjoyed in the hierarchy of needs.

You got paid only for goods that people wanted, but it soon became apparent that insurance and priestly services were among the things they did want. Given that what you produced was wanted, earnings reflected the scarcity of the talents needed to produce them, and your position in the power structure of the tribe. The first explains why the insurance and repair men did well, and the second accounted for the prosperity of the bureaucrat and the priest.

Those who are lucky enough to have that power or these rare talents have often felt embarrassed by earning more than those who work to satisfy more basic elements in the hierarchy of needs. Often, they also enjoy occupations that are less arduous and more fun. The embarrassment is rarely very great, and does seem to have diminished recently, but emphasising the importance we attach to these other supposedly more necessary, but less well-remunerated activities, is a means of assuaging it.

Whatever the truth of all this, none of it should provide a basis for economic policy or industrial strategy.

There is a slightly more persuasive version of the intellectual confusion that tends to the view that manufacturing is special. This suggests that manufacturing output is more important than services because manufacturing, unlike services, is sold to foreigners. Of course, many services are sold to foreigners and many manufactures are not, but there is some truth in the stereotype.

But the real weakness in this argument points the way to the correct answer to the valuation of different activities. If what matters is the tradeability of output, then why draw the line around the nation state? Why not draw it more broadly, or more narrowly? After all, neither the City of London nor a steelworks could survive on its own. You cannot drink derivatives or eat steel. They survive and are valuable because – and only because – they can persuade people outside their boundaries to value their output. The output is valuable, not because it can be sold to foreigners, but because it can be sold.

So the economic significance of an activity is not measured by its place in some objective hierarchy of needs. It is measured by what someone, other than the producer, thinks it is worth. ■

Source: Kay, J, *Financial Times*, 13 June 1997. Reprinted with permission.

Strategic management can be said to be the understanding, planning and implementation of business policies based on these basic economic principles. It involves companies taking actions to direct their efforts towards the areas where customer value and competitive advantage can be achieved. It is in fact difficult for a company to decide how and where it should focus its efforts. Its marketing intelligence will help to do this, but this does involve answering complex questions about customer requirements, competitive response and relative cost position. Managers' decisions are likely to be based on a mixture of market research, forward planning, political and cultural forces and what can be referred to as 'hunch' or even as 'vision'. Managers need to understand the criteria by which their existing and potential customers choose to purchase their company's products or services, and how they decide from which company to make their purchases. Within a company different groups of people may have a variety of ideas about customer needs and may emphasise different factors in relation to their products, such as technical quality, lower prices, prompt delivery, packaging or advertising.

CUSTOMER STRATEGY

Managers need to understand their customers in order to meet those customers' needs better. From an economic point of view, customer demand will depend on a range of factors to do with costs, prices, preferences and competitive advantage (Fig 3.4).

To meet customer needs better:

- at lower cost

- at maximum customer satisfaction

- with competitive advantages

FIG 3.4 CUSTOMER STRATEGY

Organisations need to know the specific requirements of each customer and whether these requirements can be segmented. If there are well-defined customer segments, this can have important implications for both product design and marketing. Companies will attempt to segment customer requirements in an attempt both to satisfy as many people as possible on the one hand, and on the other hand in order not to have to tailor-make every item for each individual customer. In the production of a tailor-made suit, for example, there is an attempt to make it fit an individual customer 'perfectly', while 'off-the-peg' suits are produced in large quantities to fit a range of people segmented by such means as height, waist and chest measurements.

'Getting to know the customer' also involves being aware of how many different people are involved in the purchasing decision and the different kinds of requirements they may have. Even in a family the purchase of a suit for one of their members may give rise to sharp differences of opinion. In a company, purchasing may be viewed very differently by the product, finance and marketing managers. The finance manager, for example, may be particularly concerned about costs in terms of cost saving, while the marketing manager may consider costs in a rather different way, perhaps largely by comparison with competitors.

At the same time, people will have different priorities in terms of the qualities they require in a product or service. These will include design, technical preferences, reliability and availability as well as price. The producers need to know how important these factors are to customers before they can decide which aspect to concentrate on improving. Without this knowledge it is very difficult for a manager to develop a strategy to obtain competitive advantage.

> *'The key element which distinguishes strategy from marketing is the explicit consideration of competitive advantage.'*
> (David Faulkner and Gerry Johnson, 1992)

Faulkner and Johnson, in their book in the Cranfield Management Research Series, argue that it is critical to know customer purchase criteria, and equally critical to understand how well a company meets these needs relative to those of its competitors. It is through an interaction of customer needs with competitor offering that determines who will make the sale, and it is the company which meets customer needs better than its competitors which is likely to grow and be successful.

In order to monitor this competitive success, a company's products and services have to be based on a fundamental advantage in cost or skills. It is critical for managers to understand what the company costs are and what skills it has compared to competing companies. The skills available to an organisation will depend very heavily on its structure and organisation, its recruitment and retention policy and on staff training and development. Cost differences may arise because of the level of investment in equipment linked to the skill and productivity of employees. The scale of the operation may influence costs and the efficiency of management. Any structural skills or cost differences which are difficult for a competitor to replicate can be the basis of a competitive advantage if they result in an organisation being able to service customer needs better and at a lower cost.

It follows from this that organisations, in order to be successful, need to concentrate their efforts or activities in areas in which they have or can develop and maintain a competitive advantage in terms of cost and skills. It can be argued, for example, that the British motorcycle industry collapsed in the 1960s and 1970s because it failed to keep up with competitor improvements in terms of costs and customer needs, and the success of the Japanese motorcycle industry was as a result of concentrating on both these factors.

THE 'NEW' MANAGER

It can be argued that Theory Y will dominate management in the twenty-first century as organisations attempt to gain competitive advantage through developing employees' own motivation. As we saw in Chapter 2, Theory Y is based on the optimistic view of human nature that employees will help to achieve organisational objectives. This theory views the manager's role as working co-operatively with other employees in order to decide work objectives and methods of achieving them. Managers will encourage the development of self-managed teams and the delegation of decisions towards the point of action, and they will seek to develop people's own motivation by involvement in the organisation. In this process the 'soft' values, such as shared corporate objectives, become more important than the 'hard' values of control and direction (*see* Fig 3.5).

The manager of the future has to 'live the vision' as well as being accountable for the performance of the organisation. The 'new' manager does less planning, organising and controlling and much more advising, enabling and encouraging. Jack Welch, the Chief Executive of General Electric in the USA, has been quoted as saying that the twenty-first century commercial wars are going to be won 'on our ideas, not by whips and chains'. Honeywell UK has developed self-managed manufacturing cells with full responsibility for product lines. The role of the manager in these circumstances is to advise self-managed groups, to ensure that they have the necessary resources and to encourage ideas and initiatives.

In an article entitled 'Survival skills for a new breed' (1993), Karen Clarke (the winner of a competition called 'Managing for Tomorrow') argues that:

> *'The manager as we know him or her – decision maker, expert, boss, director – is extinct. The "new" manager has three roles – leader, coach and facilitator.'*

She argues that managerial success will be determined to an increasing extent by the ability to develop and position the organisation strategically and will be measured by staff performance. This means that managers have to accept the fact that they will no longer be the focus of attention but that they will be part of a team. It follows from this that rewards for managers will be based on the performance of the team. As a leader, managers will be looking at the wider picture, how the team fits into the plans for the whole organisation, and how well it is meeting customer needs.

In these circumstances managers are responsible for establishing the boundaries and the culture in which people can work successfully and creatively. One of the 'new' management roles is to act as 'coach'. In this role, managers help employees to be successful and creative by ensuring that they understand the boundaries of their responsibilities and the resources available to them. The 'coach' helps to build up confidence and trust and supports training and development to add to the skills of the team. Successful outcomes are then recorded, and as individuals and teams increase in expertise they are given more freedom to organise their own work.

- **We put our customer first**
- **We are professional**
- **We respect each other**
- **We work as a team**
- **We are committed to continuous improvement**

FIG 3.5 BRITISH TELECOM'S 'SOFT' VALUES

The 'new' manager is also a facilitator in the sense of encouraging new ideas and helping to carry them forward. There can always be a gap between plans and initiatives and their implementation:

> *'If words were deeds, the remaining 1990s would be the Years of the Customer – and 2000 would usher in a whole century of customer worship. But management science is the study of the gap between verbiage and action: the more lip-service the customer receives, the wider the gap is liable to grow.'*
>
> (Robert Heller, 'Customer Focus Means Commitment to Constant Change,' *Management Today*, January 1994)

The manager has to act as a facilitator in closing this gap, so that customers receive the benefits they want and come back for more. It has been estimated (by David Perkins of Loyalty Marketing Service) that typically it costs 80 per cent of the gross margin on an existing customer to obtain a new one. The manager has to make sure that the product or service is right first time and to research the scale and causes of customer loss. The manager as 'facilitator' has to recognise that although 'customers pay the bills, they do not pay the wages'. In other words, individuals and teams in organisations look inwards at colleagues as well as outwards at customers. Decisions on pay and promotion are made internally and it is essential that the correct organisational culture exists in order to enable confidence and trust to grow.

THE 'NEW' CULTURE

The rapid changes in the international marketplace have led to alterations in the corporate culture of even the organisations slowest to respond to culture change. Companies such as Delta Airlines and IBM, for example, had more or less official no-redundancy policies, but the increase in international competition and the worldwide recession changed this, so that in the early 1990s there were layoffs at Delta and considerable 'downsizing' at IBM. For managers as much as any other employees the idea of a 'job for life' has disappeared and the new contracts between many employers and their managers have become short term and based on mutual benefits. Apple Computer and General Electric, for example, have moved towards 'contractor charters' and away from the old-style long-term employment contracts (Gerard Egar, 1994).

These charters contract the services of a manager as long as the relationship is mutually beneficial. When forces outside the direct control of the company, such as the economy or competition, create difficulty for the company, then the future of the contract may become open to question. There is an emphasis on the employee as a 'contributor' rather than only a player, which means that the manager must find ways of adding value to the business, and grow and develop. The manager must become a 'learning person' within a 'learning organisation' which constantly changes, develops and grows. This form of 'contract' or 'charter' complements flatter organisational structures where promotions are scarce and movement is more likely to be horizontal than vertical. These horizontal moves are into positions which add value to the organisation and provide opportunity for the individual to develop. Rewards tend to be based on performance outcomes rather than on factors such as age or length of service. This type of charter is based on a view that the organisation provides opportunities for individuals to develop and be rewarded as long as this process is adding value to the organisation.

This approach to working life tends to appeal only to flexible, enterprising self-starters and not to managers and employees who are looking for a 'job for life'. The meaning of such words as 'commitment' and 'loyalty' is altered in these circumstances. People are committed to the organisation by adding value to its product and their loyalty is to the particular organisation which at a particular time provides them with the opportunity to develop and be rewarded for this. Under these conditions individuals have to take responsibility for their own development and career paths; they cannot expect this necessarily to be mapped out by the company for which they are working (*see* Chapter 20).

> *'What people are increasingly working to acquire is the capital of their own individual reputation instead of the organisational capital that comes from learning one system well and meeting its idiosyncratic requirements. For many managers, it might be more important, for example, to acquire or demonstrate a talent that a future employer or financial advisor might value than to get to know the right people several layers above in the corporation where they currently work.'* (Rosabeth Moss Kanter, 1989)

The 'new' culture promotes the idea of a 'shared destiny' that develops collaboration and 'alliances' and what could be described as 'enlightened self-interest'. In its most developed form this approach brings together all the 'stakeholders' in an area of activity in a mutually beneficial alliance. Competitors can prosper together by increasing the overall size of the market, while managers, employees, shareholders, suppliers and customers can collaborate in obtaining the required levels of service and value. The original Rover and Honda collaboration contained elements of this approach in the same way as did the alliance between IBM and Apple Computers. The takeover of Rover by BMW in 1994 could be seen as not only a commercial development, but also as the ending of the previous mutually beneficial alliance.

The obvious stakeholders in this form of alliance are shareholders, managers and employees who will share in the creation and distribution of wealth (*see* Fig 3.6). The customer can be a 'stakeholder' of such an alliance by being involved in the quality of the product or service. There is a need for two-way communication through customer surveys, complaints procedures, open meetings and the development of a 'consumer charter' expressing the level of quality and service customers should be able to expect. It is the role of the 'Manager 2000' to ensure that there is a high level of co-operation and collaboration with customers so that the latter can be involved in product and service development.

NEW FORMS OF ORGANISATION

Charles Handy has argued in *The Age of Unreason* (1989) that there are fundamental changes taking place in organisational life. He suggests that companies are moving away from the labour-intensive organisations of the past to new knowledge-based structures. They will increasingly receive added value from their knowledge and creativity, and this is reflected in changing organisational structures. He acknow-

Stakeholders in an alliance need to:

- create wealth and then distribute it

- replace 'loyalty' with commitment to the creation of wealth

- play an active part in wealth creation

- invest in the future through technological and employee development

- provide opportunities for managerial and employee development

- take account of the realities of the marketplace

- be prepared to accept change

- help employees at a mutually beneficial time to return to the marketplace with transferable skills

- encourage employees to accept responsibility for their development and their future

FIG 3.6 ALLIANCES

ledges that companies are moving at different speeds and that the process is an evolutionary one, where they may take on some of the characteristics of a 'shamrock' organisation, which may or not be or become part of a 'federation' and will slowly evolve into a 'Triple I' type of organisation.

The shamrock organisation

Handy suggests that this form of organisation, like the plant after which it is named, has three interlocking leaves, in the sense that it is composed of three distinct groups of workers who are treated differently and have different expectations (*see* Fig 3.7).

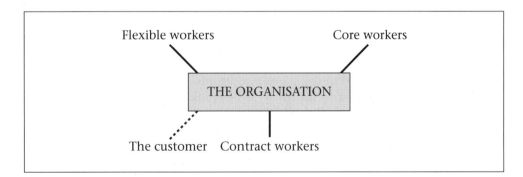

FIG 3.7 THE SHAMROCK ORGANISATION

79

CORE WORKERS

A small group of specialist 'core' workers form the first leaf. They are the nerve centre of the organisation in the sense that they are essential to its work and success. They are both specialists and generalists who run the organisation and control the technology which has replaced, to a large extent, much of the labour force.

The core workers are expected to be loyal to the organisation, and to be flexible in meeting the challenge of constant change in both competitors and customer requirements. Core workers operate as colleagues and partners in the organisation as opposed to superiors and subordinates. They are stakeholders in the company and in many ways they *are* the company. They expect to be rewarded for their achievements, rather than for any position they might occupy in the hierarchy. The role of the manager in this situation is one of coach, adviser and facilitator. There is considerable pressure on the core workers, 'a pressure which could be summed up by a new equation of half the people, paid twice as much, working three times as effectively' (Handy, 1989).

The shamrock organisation is small compared to its output. This is achieved by the use of technology on the one hand, and the contracting out, to individuals and other organisations, of work which was previously carried out by core employees.

> *'To get that three times improvement the smart organisation will equip their people with all the technological aids they need . . . It will also expect those people to be smart, to be dedicated to their work (none of the leisure age here) and to be prepared to invest enough time and energy to keep ahead of the game, to go on learning, in other words, in order that they can go on thinking.'* (Handy, 1989)

THE CONTRACTUAL FRINGE

The second leaf, the contractual fringe, may or may not work exclusively for the company. They are contracted to carry out certain tasks for which they are paid a fee based on results, rather than based on the time taken. The advantages of this arrangement are that it is cost effective because companies only pay for what they receive, it makes management easier because fewer people are on the payroll, and when demand is reduced it is the contractor who faces the problems rather than the company.

> *'Those organisations, although often smaller than the main organisation will have their own shamrocks, their own cores and their own subcontractors. It is a chinese box type of world. The individuals will be self-employed professionals or technicians, many of them past employees of the central organisation who ran out of roles in the core or who preferred the freedom of self-employment.'* (Handy, 1989)

THE FLEXIBLE LABOUR FORCE

The third leaf of the shamrock organisation comprises a pool of part-time workers who are available for use by the organisation. These are people with relevant skills who are not in need of, or who cannot obtain, full-time employment, but who are prepared to work on a part-time basis. They may be housewives who combine part-time work with raising a family, people who have retired early, or people who prefer to have a variety of part-time jobs. They do not have the commitment to the company that core workers do, but they enable the organisation to respond flexibly to changes in demand for their product or service.

The shamrock organisation can have a large output, while being small in terms of direct employees. It can be organised with little bureaucracy and modern management practices. It can be extremely flexible in order to react to or anticipate 'ups and downs' in customer demands. Core employees in particular can keep close to their customers and make sure that they satisfy their needs.

> *'The shamrock organisation, always there in embryo, has flourished because organisations have realised that you do not have to employ all the people all the time to get the work done.'* (Handy, 1989)

They are also going further and realising that they do not need necessarily to locate everybody in one place. The development of technology enables an increasing number of people to work at a distance so that 'the early morning crush in the commuter train will one day be a thing of the past or at least a twice weekly chore'.

A FOURTH LEAF: THE CUSTOMER

There is another form of 'subcontracting' which Handy suggests could be a 'fourth leaf' on the shamrock. This is the strong trend towards allowing the customer to do the work. This process is disguised as improving services whether it actually does so or not, while it creates a situation where the customer does work previously carried out by paid employees. Examples of this process include self-service in supermarkets, self-assembly furniture, cashpoints, carveries and buffet-style restaurants, self-service petrol stations which may include payment at the pump, and so on.

These examples all have in common self-service by customers. This saves the organisations vast amounts of money in terms of wages for staff to provide these services. The services can then be provided at an extra charge so that it is no longer part of the core of the organisation but is part of the contractual fringe. Self-service is marketed as a benefit to customers when in fact its main advantage may be to the organisation.

The federal organisation

The federal organisation consists of a variety of individual organisations or groups of organisations allied together by a common approach and mutual interest. It provides a way for relatively small companies based on core workers to obtain the advantages of large companies

> *'It allows individuals to work in organisation villages with the advantage of big city facilities.'* (Handy, 1989)

This enables organisations to enjoy the advantages of small, lean structures with the resources and power of big corporations. The drive and energy come from the parts of the federation rather than the centre:

> *'Federalism implies a variety of individual groups allied together under a common flag with some shared identity. Federalism seeks to make it big by keeping it small, or at least independent, by combining autocracy with co-operation. It is the method which businesses are slowly and powerfully evolving for getting the best of both worlds – the size which gives them clout in the market place and in the financial centres, as well as some economies of scale and the small unit size which gives them the flexibility which they need, as well as the sense of community for which individuals increasingly hanker.'*
> (Handy, 1989)

Shamrock organisations will retain their own autonomy in this system, while the federation provides a common platform for the integration of their activities. The federal organisation will be concerned mainly with the future, in order to keep its members ahead of the competition. It seeks to maximise the innovative and creative potential of its members by specifying the central vision and quality standards and then encouraging innovation and initiative.

The management role in this situation is to provide an overall direction and then to develop opportunities for growth. At the same time the relatively small shamrock organisation members are able to maintain close links and alliances with their customers. Handy argues that:

> *'Organisational cities no longer work unless they are broken down into villages. In their big city mode they cannot cope with the variety needed in their products, their processes and their people. On the other hand, the villages on their own have not the resources nor the imagination to grow. Some villages, of course, will be content to survive, happy in their niche, but global markets need global products and large confederations to make them or do them.'*

The Triple I organisation

Both the idea of the shamrock organisation and the federation can develop into what Handy refers to as the Triple I organisation. This is one based on Intelligence, Information and Ideas which form the intellectual capital represented by the core workers. The three Is equal added value because as well as intelligence they need good information to work with and ideas to build on if value is to be made from knowledge. These core workers will be:

> *'expected to have not only the expertise appropriate to his or her particular role, but also be required to know and understand business, to have the technical skills of analysis and the human skills and the conceptual skills to keep them up-to-date.'* (Handy, 1989)

These are learning organisations, serving their customers as a result of their employees remaining at the leading edge of knowledge and skills. It is these types of organisations which require the changes in role of the manager, concerned with performance more than formalities and acting as a coach, adviser and facilitator. There will still be mundane jobs in the organisation, but its heart will be a Triple I operation otherwise value will not be added to pay for the support services. The specialists and professionals involved cannot be managed in the old ways, they have to be managed by consent and not by command, and they are obsessed with the pursuit of learning in order to keep up with the pace of change of quality because that produces long-term success. This concentration on quality is based on the organisation's customers and on providing them with the benefits they require.

THE INTERNATIONAL DIMENSION

Organisational change and alterations in the role of the manager are taking place across the world. David Kilburn (1994) has noted changes in Japan, for example. In many ways the Japanese style of management presents a paradox. The obsession on focus on the customer is one side of the equation, while the other side is what appears to be at least paternalistic if not autocratic forms of management. Japanese companies have been characterised by a strong loyalty to the company by employees; many employees join a company until retirement so that when they work with colleagues they are doing so on the basis that they will be working together most of their lives. Japanese society has been described as more group-oriented than the US or UK where the focus is more on individual achievement. The Japanese manager is essentially part of a team and will often not be able to hire or fire or restructure the team. The challenge to the Japanese manager is to motivate the team to achieve goals and to help them develop their abilities.

In the Japanese team many decisions are based on consensus and the manager's role is to lead the team towards this. This may take time, but once a decision has been made, everyone will be behind it so that implementation will be relatively smooth. Managers will tend to have paternalistic and deferential relationships with their superiors. Pay is related to the length of service rather than performance, with frequent on-the-job training in order to improve individual performance in achieving the strategic objectives of the company.

There are, however, signs that this traditional approach is changing. While it may still be true for the core workers, there is now greater mobility between jobs, more restructuring in companies, with a reduction in the workforce through voluntary retirement. Observers have noted that subsidiaries and affiliates are being used to a greater extent and that the softer corporate values are being emphasised now compared to the harder values, by concentrating more on staff training, developing skills and ensuring that all employees understand the organisation's values. Figure 3.8 illustrates the shift from the harder values of strategy, structure and systems to the softer ones of staff, skills and style.

At the same time the paradox does continue in that the central selection of staff and control of training and development are still based on structure and systems. The slow growth in the 1990s has led to a need for flexibility and this is having an effect on Japanese companies as well as those in other countries. In comparison to Japanese culture it is argued that in the USA, management styles are too individualistic for the changes taking place. The individualists have to be moulded into teams and the specialists have either to become generalists or be prepared to work with a range of people in these teams.

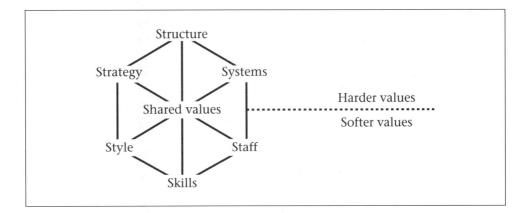

FIG 3.8 CORPORATE VALUES

As well as the theories of organisational change put forward by such management gurus as Charles Handy, there is also the view that many of the changes are pragmatic. Customer demands are changing and companies alter processes and services in order to meet these demands.

> *'Lofty strategic concepts are in the trash can of history. For example, the old idea that every corporation should have a "vision" has been shelved by Microsoft, IBM and Chrysler, to name a few, and in its place these companies are improving efficiency across a broad front.'*
>
> (John Thakray, 1994)

Peggy Salz-Trautman (1994) reports that it has been noted in Germany that tomorrow's manager will require broad-based skills and be able to work in teams. There are pressures on German companies to combine the solidity of industrial giants with the nimbleness of entrepreneurs. In other words, the giants have to 'learn to dance'. These pressures include cut-throat international competition, causing the restructuring of companies, and the expanding services sector based on meeting customer needs.

German managers have a long tradition of respect for technical expertise and attention to detail combined with a deep-seated respect for hierarchy and rank. Their managers of the future have to learn to be flexible and to embrace customer service in a wholehearted fashion. At the same time, companies such as Volkswagen AG recognise that the age of the charismatic individual leading the company is past and the role of the manager has shifted to one of being a coach, facilitator and team-worker. The technology-oriented German company based on 'hard' corporate values has had to shift towards the 'softer' values based on a customer focus.

The convergence of the world economy, brought about by vastly improved communication and seen in terms of both competition and co-operation, forces managers to adapt to new structures and fresh values or to see their organisations drown under a tidal wave of competition. In many companies, and large ones in particular, management teams are likely to include several nationalities. Just as American managers have top positions in European companies (such as Rank Xerox UK), so many European managers have top positions in US companies (such as General Motors). For the 'international' manager, boundaries between nations are no longer important. What is important is looking at customer requirements with fresh eyes and reshaping the organisation in order to meet customer need.

URGENCY

The objective of creating self-managed teams, concentrating on core workers and developing federations of relatively small companies is to keep an organisation close to its customer. The focus is an obsession with strategic innovation so that the company is different to its competitors and better fulfils customer needs. These processes help to create a sense of urgency throughout an organisation because most people can relate directly to customer needs. The flatter organisation means that there is not a hierarchy far removed from contact with customers and unable to relate to them.

The process of division of labour and the expansion of separate functional departments in manufacturing, marketing, sales and finance developed a structure of senior, middle and junior managers in every function and new departments, such as accountancy and MIS (management information systems), in order to manage them. Company time and effort was diverted into doing business with itself rather than with the outside customer. Re-engineering in the Michael Hammer approach (Michael Hammer and James Champy, 1993) means that instead of trying to improve co-ordination between departments organised into vertical functions, the organisation is structured into a collection of horizontal processes, each of which takes orders and delivers a product or service (*see* Fig 3.9).

This 'horizontal' principle shifts the focus of attention onto activities which are necessary to meet customer needs rather than on efforts to develop co-operation between internal departments. For many employees it leads to multiskilling and working in integrated teams which are 'empowered' to make a whole range of decisions about the way they work. Employers are 'involved' or experience 'job enrichment' so that their talents are used more effectively in order that the organisation becomes more competitive. Managers move away from the authoritarian image to one of leader, facilitator and coach.

At Forte's Harvester restaurant, for example, staff teams devise their own publicity, carry out their own recruitment and track their own sales targets. Supervisors have been eliminated and the branch manager's role has changed to one of facilitator. The company mission, menu and image remain central issues along with decor and uniforms. Rover, Lucas and Rank Xerox have all moved towards re-engineered self-managed teams. However, Hammer and Champy estimate that 70 per cent of all re-engineering efforts fail, because top managers do not, in the final analysis, support it, or middle managers subvert its implementation, or because the change is not communicated sufficiently well to employees.

This process of 're-engineering' develops a sense of urgency by promoting autonomy and entrepreneurship at the point of interface with the customer. It can be argued that in a fiercely competitive marketplace it is no longer enough simply to satisfy customers. It is now necessary to go beyond this in order to exceed customer

PRODUCTION	MARKETING	SALES	FINANCE		ORDERS	Dist/Mark/Sales/Fin	PRODUCT	SERVICE
P	M	S	F		O	Dist/Mark/Sales/Fin	P	S
R	A	A	I		R		R	E
O	R	L	N		D		O	R
D	K	E	A	RE-ENGINEERED	E		D	V
U	E	S	N		R		U	I
C	T		C		S		C	C
T	I		E				T	E
I	N							
O	G							
N								

FIG 3.9 RE-ENGINEERING

expectations time and again. The organisation, it can be argued, has to become customer driven, so that the entire company is saturated by the 'voice' of the customer. In this situation, the customer is the driving force behind the corporate vision and it is the customer who defines quality in products and services.

SUMMARY

■ This chapter is concerned with the changes in organisational structure brought about by a focus on the customer. Customer service has become a major issue in managing and organising companies and institutions. This has been highlighted by *In Search of Excellence* and other studies of successful organisations.

■ These developments have created the need for different qualities and skills in management. This has been emphasised by the 'search for synergy' in the move to flatter, less complex and more responsive organisations. The economic focus also emphasises the requirement to provide for customer needs.

■ Customer strategy involves achieving a competitive advantage in terms of cost and skills. The 'new' manager has to develop new roles in order to achieve and maintain this advantage as leader, coach and facilitator. Corporate culture has altered and become much more flexible so that managers face new challenges in their workplace and in their own careers. New forms of organisation have developed to reflect the increases in flexibility and the greater emphasis on customer service.

REVIEW AND DISCUSSION QUESTIONS

1   Is it possible for a manager to manage any type of organisation successfully, or is it necessary to have knowledge and experience of the area to be managed?

2   What are the most important skills a manager requires?

3   Do management careers follow a pattern, because of organisational, individual, or other factors?

4   How does the British manager compare to managers in other countries in terms of their development and training?

5   What qualities are required for managers to cope with the development of flatter organisations?

6   Of what use are management ideas and concepts in the practice of management?

CASE STUDY: A HALF CENTURY FREE OF 'FLUFF'

FT

House & Garden, the upmarket magazine which has specialised in bringing good design to a wider audience, marks its half century this month with a celebration of British design during the past 50 years.

In the 1940s, the magazine explains, it tried to be 'a stylish source of inspiration for coping with austerity' with a slant towards practicality and improvisation (although Cecil Beaton was featured 'at home' in his 1820s house).

By the early 1950s such well-known British designers as Terence Conran and David Hicks made their first appearances and in the 1960s John Fowles – 'doyen of the English country house interior' – rubbed shoulders with Michael Heseltine and his bride in their first home, David Hockney, Jean Muir, Mary Quant and Twiggy.

By the 1970s Jan Kaplicky and Richard Rogers were advocating their own brands of modernism at the same time as John Makepeace was spearheading a new age of craftsmanship in wood.

In the 1980s chintzes, toiles de Jouy, swags, tassels, stencilling, stippling, marbling, Biedermeier, candle-shades and Agas became 'best-sellers'.

In the present decade, *House & Garden* believes, the trends include simpler versions of the country-house look and 'beefed-up interpretations of Minimalism'.

The present editor Sue Crewe, who is only the fourth in the magazine's history, describes herself as the typical *House & Garden* reader. 'I am aware and passionate about how I live. I garden. I cook. I travel. I go to exhibitions and I am careful about what I pay for things.'

She came to magazine editing via running a dairy farm and later freelance writing. She was also in charge of Jennifer's Diary in *Harpers & Queen* magazine for a year.

Crewe insists that *House & Garden* is not a 'fluffy' magazine. 'We assume our readers are informed, not experts. But we don't protect them from the proper names of plants, for instance.'

The concept appears to be working rather well. Circulation – which was 150,000 when she took over – is now at a record 167,000. ■

Source: Ray Snoddy, *Financial Times*, 9 June 1997. Reprinted with permission.

REFERENCES FOR FURTHER READING

Bennis, Warren (1966) 'The Coming Death of Bureaucracy', *Think*, November/December.

Clarke, Karen (1993) 'Survival Skills for a New Breed', *Management Today*, December.

Egar, Gerard (1994) 'Hard Times Contracts', *Management Today*, January.

Faulkner, David and Johnson, Gerry (1992) *The Challenge of Strategic Management*, London: Kogan Page.

Hammer, Michael and Champy, James (1993) *Re-engineering the Corporate: A Manifesto for Business Revolution*, London: Nicholas Brealey.

Handy, Charles (1989) *The Age of Unreason*, London: Pan Books.

Heller, Robert (1994a) 'Customer Focus Means Commitment to Constant Change', *Management Today*, January.

Heller, Robert (1994b) 'The Manager's Dilemma', *Management Today*, January.

Kanter, Rosabeth Moss (1989) *When Giants Learn to Dance: Mastering the Challenges of Strategy, Management and Careers in the 1990s*, London: Unwin.

Kay, J (1997) 'Produced to price', *Financial Times*, 13 June.

Kilburn, David (1994) 'Japanese Management', *Management Today*, January.

Peters, Tom and Waterman, Robert (1982) *In Search of Excellence: Lessons from America's Best Run Companies*, London: Harper & Row.

Pugh, D S and Hickson, D J (1976) *Organisational Structure in its Context: The Aston Programme 1*, Farnborough: Saxon House.

Salz-Trautman, Peggy (1994) 'The Manager's Dilemma: Germany', *Management Today*, January.

Scott, W R (1987) *Organizations: Rational, National and Open Systems*, Englewood Cliffs, New Jersey: Prentice-Hall.

Snoddy, R (1997) 'A half century free of 'fluff', *Financial Times*, 9 June.

Thakray, John (1994) 'Strategic Concepts', *Management Today*, January.

Toffler, Alan (1970) *Future Shock*, New York: Random House.

Young, Roger (1993) 'Jobs for Life', *Professional Manager*, Institute of Management, November.

4 MARKETING

Tim Hannagan

OBJECTIVES

The objectives of this chapter are to:

◆ analyse the importance of marketing for all managers

◆ discuss the fundamental relevance of marketing in all organisations

◆ describe the basic principles and theories of marketing and methods applied in marketing

◆ promote an understanding of marketing concepts which can be applied to the formation of a marketing plan and strategy in all forms of organisation

MARKETING ORIENTATION

Organisational objectives have moved on from an overriding concern with technical excellence, costs and price to a consideration of customer service, quality and employee development. The development of the customer-oriented organisation has made marketing a central activity in most companies and public sector institutions. The importance of the customer is recognised in the Chartered Institute of Marketing's definition:

> *'Marketing is the management process responsible for identifying, anticipating and satisfying customer requirements profitably.'*

This consumer-centred view of economic activity can be traced back at least as far as Adam Smith's *Wealth of Nations*, published in 1776:

> *'Consumption is the role and purpose of all production; and the interest of the producer ought to be attended to only in so far as it may be necessary for promoting that of the consumer.'*

Much more recently, Peter Drucker has defined marketing as 'the whole business seen from the point of view of its final result, that is from the customer's point of view'. This illustrates the shift of marketing as a management function from a relatively low position in the order of priorities to a central one. Marketing has moved from being at best a second tier activity below production and finance, to being the integrating force represented at the top of organisational structures. Marketing is now a route to becoming a managing director or chief executive.

The position of the marketing function historically is often matched by the process by which companies raise the priority given to marketing. The nineteenth-century development of manufacturing industry was based on a product-orientation, with marketing hardly recognised as a separate activity. The early twentieth century saw the development of a sales-orientation based on the need to interest potential customers in the existing products and services which were increasingly threatened by competition. The second half of the twentieth century has seen the development of an increasing customer orientation in all areas of the economy and society, based on determining the needs and wants of the customers and satisfying them.

This developing position in the overall economy has been reflected in particular sections of it and in particular organisations. The computer boom in the 1970s and 1980s was based on the development of products and programs, and it was only when companies met competition and found that selling their products became difficult that they turned to marketing in the 1980s and 1990s. Similarly, travel companies which had been successfully founded and expanded through selling cheap packaged holidays have had to adjust to customer demand for higher quality, more expensive holidays. Travel companies who have not paid attention to marketing have found it difficult to adjust. In the 1990s public sector institutions in the health service and education have been faced with the need to market their services as a result of changes to their corporate status and funding mechanisms, with the objective of making them more consumer oriented.

MARKETING AND SELLING

A marketing orientation is not the same as a sales orientation; although the two overlap, they represent different approaches to management within a company. Marketing is the whole process directed at satisfying the needs and wants of people through exchange. Selling can be seen as the culmination of this process, the point at which an exchange is agreed between supplier and customer.

The marketing process comprises:

- **finding out what the customer wants;**

- **developing products/services to satisfy those wants;**

- **establishing a price consistent with the requirements of the supplier and the perceptions of the customer;**

- **distributing products/services to the customer;**

- **agreeing on the exchange – selling.**

At the point of sale, the objective is to persuade the customer to take the step from wanting a product or service to actually purchasing it. Some goods will 'sell themselves' and customers will actively seek them out, but in most circumstances this is not the case. The more closely the commodity or service matches the customer's needs, the easier it will be to close the sale. This is most likely to be the situation where the organisation is customer oriented.

The whole purpose of marketing is to provide a product/service that matches the customer's needs. In order to do this, managers have to understand that customers are not so much looking for particular products or services as for benefits. Consumers are looking for goods and services to satisfy their needs and there may be a variety of ways of doing this. A gardener who wants to remove a branch from a tree may immediately reach for a saw. If, however, the branch could be removed with a simple cut in the bark followed by an injection, the sale of saws could decline. Computer companies are well aware of this fact because many of them owe their development and success to having a solution to a particular business problem. When another company has found a cheaper or simpler solution to this problem, the demand for the original solution will decline sharply. In these examples the consumers' need is to remove the branch of a tree, not for a saw, and to solve a business problem, not for a particular computer program. In the same way, when a consumer buys a loaf of bread the basic need is not for bread but to satisfy hunger, and there are a variety of ways of doing this.

This view of consumer needs means that managers have to understand that they should be producing what can be sold rather than selling what can be made. This marketing concept changes the whole orientation of any organisation from one that produces what it is able to and then attempts to sell it, into one which produces what people want to buy. Managers have to determine the needs and wants of their target market and then deliver the desired satisfaction more effectively and efficiently than competitors. A selling orientation can easily concentrate on the needs of the seller, rather than the buyer, and the need to convert the company's product or service into cash. The selling concept starts with the company's existing product and looks for intense promotion to achieve profitable sales, while the marketing concept starts with the needs and wants of the company's target customers, and achieving profits through creating and maintaining customer satisfaction.

It can be argued that all managers are involved in marketing, even when they are far removed from the marketing function or where their organisation gives little attention to marketing. Product/service design, advertising and promotion or the provision of customer service are all aspects of marketing, just as all managers help to create and promote an image of their company in the way they carry out the job. The marketing-oriented manager will attempt to make selling as superfluous as possible by understanding the consumer so well that the product or service 'sells itself'. Ideally, marketing will result in a consumer who is ready to buy so that all that is needed to make a sale is for the product to be available (*see* Fig 4.1).

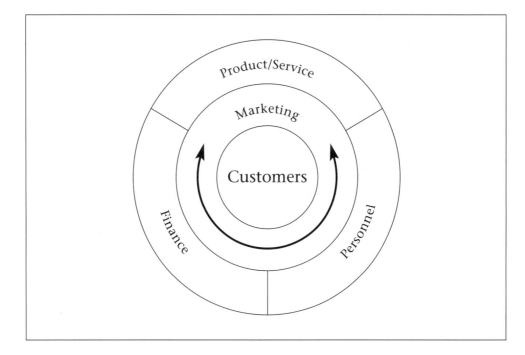

FIG 4.1 THE CUSTOMER-ORIENTED ORGANISATION

Managers and marketing

A fully integrated marketing orientation will permeate the whole structure of an organisation and will influence the thinking and the actions of every manager. Managers need to realise that while profits continue to be fundamental to business survival, they depend on the organisation satisfying the customer. This is the approach that provides a competitive edge.

It is essential for any organisation to identify its customers if it is to improve its customer services and provide what the customer needs. The customer is usually identified as the person who pays for the product or service. Where there is not a direct payment, such as in the public sector, the customer can be identified as the person who receives the service. There are different 'types' or 'levels' of customers, because wholesalers can be considered to be customers of manufacturers and retailers customers of wholesalers. The 'final' customer is the person who eventually uses the product. It is this role which makes marketing an integrative function involving all areas of an organisation and everybody working in it. The marketing department is responsible for the technical aspects of a marketing policy, but everybody is involved to a greater or lesser extent so that the whole corporate culture is affected, the image of the organisation and its strategic plan.

One of the greatest challenges for managers is to change the words of mission statements, visions and corporate strategies into deeds. As the needs of customers change, so the means of satisfying them have to change in response and adjust at least as quickly and where possible in anticipation.

KNOWING THE CUSTOMER

Managers have to decide about two fundamental marketing questions: What business are we in? Who is our customer?

What business are we in?

The answer to this may appear obvious and straightforward, but the examples of the saw manufacturer and the computer company illustrate the importance of arriving at a more fundamental answer. The computer company may describe its business in terms of information technology or computing or a software package, when it is in fact in the business of solving business problems through the application of technology. Once this is understood then the opportunities for the company open up and the meaning of 'sticking to the knitting' becomes clear.

It can be argued that when a company begins to ask what 'line of business' it is actually in, it is beginning to identify marketing as an important management function. The next step is to appreciate the fact that marketing needs to permeate every area of the company. The question 'What is our business?' has to be defined in terms of the underlying consumer need that the organisation is trying to serve. A large retail store on the outskirts of a town may be trying to serve the shopping needs of a wide area, limited only by the ability to travel to it by car, while the corner shop situated in a residential location will be trying to serve the shopping needs of customers in an area defined by the ability to walk to it. In order to serve their customers they may both aim to carry a very wide variety of goods and to be open 'all hours', although the supermarket will be organised for regular but infrequent major shopping at relatively low prices, while the local shop will be organised for more irregular and more frequent shopping at relatively high prices. They will both survive while they are able to serve the needs of the consumers better than competitors. The local shop cannot hope to compete with the supermarket on price or variety, but it may do so on its proximity to a group of consumers and its relative convenience.

Who is the customer?

The straightforward and obvious answer is that the customer is the person who pays for the product or service, and it is possible to define the customer in these terms (*see* Fig 4.2). In fact, of course, the situation is more complicated than this. Some purchases are made for other people as gifts and although the person paying for the commodity is still the customer, receiving the benefit of purchasing a present, the final consumer is the person receiving the present. In the public sector there may not be a direct payment for a service, although payment may be indirect, through the taxation and national insurance system. In this case the customer can be described as the person who receives the service, whether it is health, education or leisure. Where children are involved in receiving a commodity or service, whether there is direct payment or not, the parents are also customers in that they may play a part in the payment and in the choices of their children, who may be considered the 'primary' consumers.

Every organisation needs to know its customers, not only who they are but also what influences their purchasing decisions, the extent of their disposable income, the way they live, where they live and so on. Marketing depends on a detailed knowledge of customers and their needs so that the company or institution can meet these needs in the right place, at the right time and at the right price, and also anticipate fluctuations and changes in needs.

MARKET RESEARCH

After the acquisition of Hilton International by Ladbroke in 1987 there was concern that the Hilton name was being devalued in customer perceptions because it had been transplanted to other hotels. In 1988 an international market research survey was instigated under the direction of National Opinion Poll. The results were reassuring to the company, because Hilton scored higher than its international competitors for both spontaneous and prompted awareness and as the first-choice

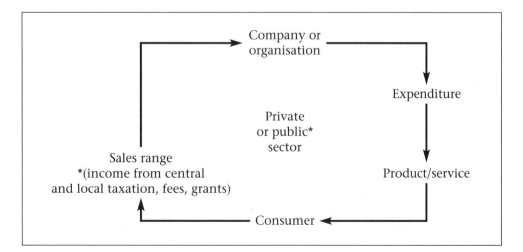

FIG 4.2 THE CONSUMER

chain of hotels. There were, however, some weaknesses identified by the research. The sub-brand Hilton National, created by Ladbroke from existing hotels, performed far less well in terms of awareness than the Hilton name; the Hilton International logo was the least well known of seven hotel logos tested; while although Hilton was noted number one in brand image, prestige, business orientation and efficiency, it was seen as unfriendly with a hint of traditionalism which was tinged with complacency.

This research was followed up by Ladbroke in a 'Take me to the Hilton' advertising campaign in 1989 which was translated into nine languages and seen by about 54 million people. Further research in 1991 showed that many of the problems remained, which led to the company reviewing its brand positioning so that the Hilton International concentrated on international business travellers and wealthy tourists, while the Hilton National offered 'the Hilton experience' at affordable prices. Hotels have been reassessed and the Hilton National logo developed to emphasise the 'Hilton' connection. The company has recognised that:

> *'far-reaching decisions can be taken by senior management on what to the outsider may seem like pure instinct. Research can be the necessary counter-balance. It offers the means to monitor the consequences of decisions and, when appropriate, it provides a mechanism for reviewing and refining the course of action selected.'*
>
> (*Marketing*, 28 January 1993, p. 26)

Market research is the planned, systematic collection, collation and analysis of data designed to help the management of an organisation to reach decisions about its operation and to monitor the results of these decisions. It can be said to provide, in the words of the British Market Research Society:

> *'information on people's preferences, attitudes, likes and needs, to help companies understand what consumers want.'*

Strictly speaking, market*ing* research is concerned with the marketing *process* while market research is concerned with the measurement and analysis of *markets*. In practice the two terms are often used synonymously, although facts about the market are 'neutral' and objective, while the attitudes and opinions of customers have to be interpreted in order to help managers to make decisions. Market analysis is undertaken to determine the opportunities existing in a particular market and is about defining the market, describing it and analysing it. In this sense, a market is the set of actual and potential consumers for particular goods and services. Managers are interested in:

- the size of the market for their products and services in terms of volume and value;
- the pattern of demand, including the economic, social, political and technical factors that might influence future demand and whether it is seasonal or cyclical;
- the market structure in terms of size and numbers of companies, income groups, sex and age distribution, and geographic location;
- the buying habits of people (both individuals as well as groups such as retailers and wholesalers) in the market;

- the market share of the company and how this compares with previous performance;

- past and future trends in areas such as population, national income;

- overseas markets that may present opportunities.

Managers need to be able to make predictions and decisions based on accurate information. While decisions can be made without very much information, a successful manager will want to have as many facts as possible before using judgement to make a decision. Market research enables decisions to be based on evidence and provides the basis for strategic planning and policy making.

The needs of customers in particular must be constantly monitored for managers to 'keep close to the customer'. It is important to know how satisfied customers are with products and services so that managers are able to introduce modifications or additions to satisfy customer needs more closely. The process will be a continuous one in order to keep up with or even ahead of changing needs (*see* Fig 4.3).

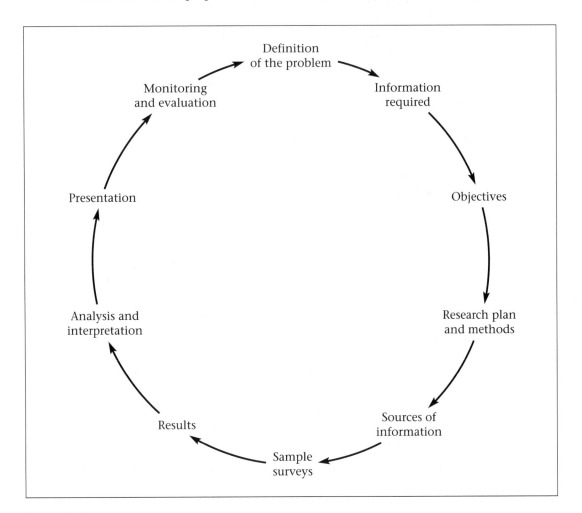

FIG 4.3 THE RESEARCH PROCESS

The questions to be answered to help managers make decisions have to be defined with as much clarity as possible about the information that is required. The objectives of the research need to be established so that there is agreement about the expected outcomes. If, for example, a company needs to know their customers' opinions of a new product, the objective of the market research will be to establish these opinions as clearly as possible so that the product can be modified to match them. A sample survey may be used for this research including a customer questionnaire and interviews. The results of this survey will be analysed and interpreted so that it can be presented to managers who will make decisions about the product. The research process will need to be monitored and as a result may be refined and the whole process will start again in order to see how well the modifications have been received by customers.

THE MARKETING PROCESS

Managers in any organisation must define the underlying need that it is trying to serve. This is reflected in the company mission statement or vision which describes the organisation's basic purpose. For example, a retail company may describe itself as offering customers a range of high quality, well designed and attractive merchandise at reasonable prices, while a computer company may want to emphasise the fact that it is not only about particular packages and products but that it concentrates on solving business problems. The corporate objectives will fill out the abstractions of the mission statements in more concrete terms, and lead to the operational detail that results in an action plan.

In a marketing-oriented company, much of this process is informed by marketing, on the grounds that there is no point in operating an organisation which is producing products or services which customers do not wish to buy. It can be argued that marketing analysis and planning begin and end with the customer. The starting point is to know about the organisation itself. This can be established through a marketing audit, which is a formal review of everything that has affected or may affect the organisation's marketing environment, internal marketing system and specific marketing activities.

The marketing audit

A company's marketing environment consists of all the factors that are external to its own marketing system and that impinge on a successful exchange process with its customers. These factors can be collected into categories, sometimes referred to as the STEP factors, which are:

- **Social**
- **Technological**
- **Economic**
- **Political**

Companies need to have a clear understanding of the population to which their products and services are directed. As well as the size of the potential market, there are questions of age distribution, sex distribution, income and education levels. As the population becomes wealthier or better educated, the range and quality of goods and services demanded may change and companies have to keep up with these changes. At the same time economic factors, such as levels of disposable income, will greatly influence consumer demand. For example, if disposable income falls, consumers will continue to buy necessities but will reduce spending on luxuries. In a recession, house prices will fall and families will move house less often so that demand for household goods will be reduced.

Managers should keep up to date with the legislation that affects their business. Health and safety regulations have to be met, pollution control may be a factor and the effects of taxation need to be considered. At the same time, technological changes can affect the competitive edge of a company and make it more or less cost effective compared to its competitors. The organisation needs to understand all these 'external' influences on its market and should know the market size, its likely growth or contraction and, of course, its own potential customers.

SWOT analysis

Equally as important as this external environment to a company's marketing plan is knowledge and understanding of its internal strengths and weaknesses. In marketing terms this process is known as a SWOT analysis:

- **Strengths**
- **Weaknesses**
- **Opportunities**
- **Threats**

The SWOT analysis helps managers to focus their attention on the key areas within a company that need to be taken into account in producing a marketing plan. It highlights internal strengths and weaknesses from the customers' point of view as they relate to external opportunities and threats.

The strengths of an organisation may be in terms of proximity to its customers, its expertise, its ability to produce high quality goods at low cost. Weaknesses will be the opposite of the strengths. A poor reputation, badly organised services and difficult communications may all be weaknesses of a company. The manager's role is to exploit the strengths of the company and to correct or compensate for the weaknesses.

The weaknesses of an organisation may give rise to opportunities, in the sense that the exposure of a weakness may be seen as an opportunity for development. A company that has been able to make a profit even though its customer care is poor can increase its profits and improve its position by taking the opportunity to improve its customer care. In terms of threats, competition is the most obvious for many companies and marketing is very much about maintaining a competitive edge. Other threats can be as a result of a fall in orders, increased import prices, changes in government regulations and changes in demand. The ability to meet and overcome these threats successfully is one of the strengths of a company and can separate those organisations which survive from those which do not.

THE MARKETING MIX

Once managers know the position of their organisation in relation to its market, understand its internal and external position, and have an idea of what their customers need, they can develop a marketing strategy. Managers have four major variables that can be controlled in order to arrive at their marketing strategy. These are the product or service produced by the organisation, its price, the way it is promoted, and the place or places through which it is made available to the consumers. These are the four 'Ps' which constitute the marketing mix:

- **Product**
- **Price**
- **Place**
- **Promotion**

The marketing mix is the appropriate combination, in a particular set of circumstances, of the four Ps. It consists of everything an organisation can do to influence the demand for its products and services. Management has to make sure that the balance between these four variables is maintained, or their marketing strategy will fail. What happens to one element in the marketing mix will have an effect on one or more of the others. For example, the quality of a product may be improved in order to meet customer demands, but this may increase the cost of production and the price. However, another possibility is that the improved quality increases demand so that sales rise, with the result that there are economies of scale and lower unit costs which can be reflected in the price.

An effective marketing strategy will bring the four variables together, in order to satisfy customer needs. To retain the competitive edge in a target market, managers have to develop and communicate the differences between their offering and those of competitors. The key to competitive positioning is to understand how members of the target market evaluate and choose between product brands. It may be on location, on price, or on the way the product is sold. Managers must choose a marketing mix that will support and reinforce their chosen competitive position at an expenditure level they can afford. By this process marketing managers seek to achieve the optimum marketing mix for their company, that is the least amount of money and effort required to make a profit. The process of achieving this optimum marketing mix can be summarised as APPEAL:

- **Assess the needs of consumers.**
- **Produce the right commodity or service.**
- **Price the commodity or service successfully.**
- **Ensure a high quality product and service.**
- **Advertise and promote the product/service effectively.**
- **Launch an efficient distribution system.**

Managers can manipulate and vary this process and the four Ps in order to improve the effectiveness of the marketing programme.

In terms of service marketing, it is possible to add three other Ps:

- **People**
- **Process**
- **Physical evidence**

1 Including people as a factor in the marketing mix emphasises the importance of all those involved in the transaction of a service, including the customer and the person (or people) providing the service. The success of the service will depend on the relationship between the customer and the provider. The customer will have certain expectations and, if these are not met by the provider, the service will not be a complete success. A holiday tour guide, for example, can provide minimal information to holiday-makers, or can suggest places to visit, arrange trips and provide support when problems arise. Some holiday-makers may be happy to be left alone, while others may want much more attention from the guide and be disappointed if they do not receive it.

2 The process is the interaction itself between all the people involved in the transaction. Training in service provision emphasises the importance of this interaction and the role of the provider in enabling the customer to recieve the service in an efficient and effective way.

3 Physical evidence can range from the location in which the service takes place to the ticket or voucher with which the customer is provided. A flight ticket is the physical evidence that the traveller has purchased a seat on an aeroplane flight between two designated places, while a voucher may be the physical evidence that the holiday-maker has purchased a place on a guided tour.

The inclusion of these three extra Ps suggests that marketing must take them into account, particularly in the service sector. They emphasise that transactions are between people, that there is a process involved in each transaction and that consideration should be given to all the other aspects of the transaction.

PRODUCTS AND SERVICES

> *'A product is anything that can be offered to a market for attention, acquisition, use or consumption that might satisfy a want or need. It includes physical objects, services, persons, places, organizations and ideas.'*
> (Philip Kotler, 1986)

This definition includes services and it is useful to realise both that they are 'products' in the broadest sense and that there are differences between them and physical commodities. Whereas a commodity is tangible and its sale involves a change in ownership, a service is essentially intangible and does not result in the exchange of ownership. When a car is bought and sold there is a change of ownership; when a holiday is bought and sold ownership of the travel company, airbus or hotel remains unchanged.

Managers can view all commodities and services as solving consumer problems, and marketing as selling benefits rather than features, but, of course, features may be important if they help to provide benefits. For example, car salespeople may concentrate their sales drive on the special features their car provides, while the ability of the car to provide a reliable form of transport is taken for granted. The features help to differentiate one car from another, but they will not serve any purpose unless the benefit of transport can be guaranteed. In fact, competition is often not so much about the product as about the value added to it in the form of packaging, services, customer advice, financing, delivery arrangements and so on. For example, Fig 4.4 illustrates the importance of packaging.

In considering their target market, managers need to take account of all aspects of it. These can be summarised by considering basic questions about the market which can be divided into the six 'O's:

- **Occupants** – which individuals constitute the market?

- **Object** – what do consumers wish to buy?

- **Occasions** – when do customers make purchases?

- **Organisations** – who is involved in the decision to purchase?

- **Objectives** – why do consumers buy particular commodities?

- **Operations** – how do consumers buy products and services?

Market research will help managers to understand their target markets so that their companies can produce the commodities and services wanted by the consumers in that particular market at a particular time. At the same time, managers need to base their decisions on who is involved in purchasing and how and where consumers make decisions on purchases.

In the run-up to Christmas 1993, Cadbury's decided to introduce a £5 million support package for 'Milk Tray'. This is one of the oldest and the best known mass-market brands and is the UK's biggest selling chocolate assortment brand. It had become squeezed by upmarket niche brands on one side and downmarket and own-label competitors on the other.

The support package was based on months of qualitative and quantitative research and was designed to increase the volume of sales by 20 per cent over 18 months. The revamp included the addition of two new flavours, truffle shell and praline fanfare – to reflect the company's view that consumers were being increasingly experimental in their tastes.

The big change was in the packaging for the chocolates, with a redesigned box to make it more upmarket with a cut-out lid, a separate choice card inside and a new tray design. The object was to make the product more 'feminine' and give it a more luxury feel.

FIG 4.4 MARKETING: VALUE ADDED

Making sure that the product or service is right for the consumer can be described as the single most important activity of marketing. If managers do not produce a commodity or service consumers want, no amount of promotion or price incentives will encourage them to buy it, at least not more than once. In fact, managers will be aiming to satisfy the consumer so that demand is likely to be repeated and other products or services of the company are also demanded. An important element of marketing is about reputation and recommendation. Personal recommendation is one of the most important ways in which a company's reputation and image are developed.

Ideally, managers will extend the features of the product or service so that they provide unique benefits not found in the competition. The concept of the 'unique selling proposition' includes the quality of design, style and service, reliability and cost. The successful development of this concept will help enhance customer loyalty. Loyal customers tend to be worth more to a company than new customers. The extra cost of replacing an existing customer with a new one can be as high as tenfold. Loyal customers are believed to spend more and have a higher purchase frequency, and a satisfied customer is the best possible walking advertisement for any company.

The increase of competition in the 1990s has been matched by rising customer sophistication, combined with price sensitivity, and has given impetus to consideration of 'relationship marketing' and customer loyalty.

> *'This more competitive environment will focus greater attention on the potential of existing customers. This will take two forms: an assessment of lifetime value and therefore the value of promoting loyalty; the possibilities of increasing the value of given customers through cross selling/upgrading programmes.'*
>
> (*Customer Loyalty*, report from The Henley Centre and Chartered Institute of Marketing, 1993)

1000 original customers, of which 800 are retained:

$$\frac{800}{1000} \times 100 = 80\% \text{ customer retention rate}$$

1000 original customers, of whom 200 are retained:

$$\frac{200}{1000} \times 100 = 20\% \text{ customer retention rate}$$

FIG 4.5 CUSTOMER RETENTION RATE

The link between customer defections, or 'promiscuity', and profit offers an explanation for a move away from a culture where 'closing the sale' is of overriding importance, to one where encouraging customer loyalty is paramount. Customer retention (*see* Fig 4.5) can be defined as:

'the number of customers present at the beginning of a period who remain as customers at the end of the period, divided by the number of those present at the beginning.'

Research from Bain and Company indicates that a business loses between 15 and 20 per cent of its customers each year (*Marketing*, 18 November 1993, p. 24). In any business, the more satisfied the customer, the higher the retention rate.

Long-term relationships with customers are more profitable because:

- the cost of acquiring new customers can be substantial – a higher retention rate means that less marketing expenditure needs to be allocated to targeting potential customers;

- loyal customers tend to spend more;

- regular customers tend to place frequent, consistent orders, therefore usually cost less to serve;

- satisfied customers are the best advertisement for any business and are likely to introduce new customers to the company through word-of-mouth recommendations;

- satisfied customers are often willing to pay premium prices to a supplier they know and trust;

- retaining customers makes gaining market entry or share gain difficult for competitors;

- the information collated and held on loyal customers through database management allows the company to communicate regularly with them.

Sales can be increased by introducing tactical promotion and reactivating lapsed customers with specially targeted offers. The development of Air Miles to encourage customer loyalty has been spread across a number of products and is similar to long-term promotions such as petrol tokens. The objective of these promotions is the same: to encourage customers to buy products or services where they can obtain the petrol tokens or Air Miles.

For example, in 1989 Newey & Eyre became an Air Miles client when it launched a customer loyalty programme. The national marketing manager stated, 'We felt that travel was still one of the most powerful motivators. We were also attracted by its flexibility and the fact that the perceived reward is greater than the cost.' Newey & Eyre are the largest electrical wholesaler in the UK and in spite of the recession they measured a growth in sales of 24 per cent in 1992. The company targeted a core group of customers from its more than 100 000 accounts and also provided Air Miles as an incentive for their own salesforce. The promotion was risk free in the sense that it secured incremental revenue. If the target was not reached the customer was not rewarded with Air Miles.

In 1993 the magazine *Marketing* noted an increasing range of customer-loyalty initiatives. Examples have included Vauxhall's GM card, Diners Club, Asda, American Express, Argos Premier Points, Sainsbury's Homebase and British Airways Air Miles.

LIFE-CYCLE ANALYSIS

Managers should understand the application of life-cycle analysis in terms of the products and services for which they are responsible. This analysis can also be applied to the general rise and fall of companies. All products and services have a life cycle in the sense that, after they are introduced, they often pass through periods of growth, then relative stability and finally decline. This process can be mirrored in the fate of companies who do not take or are unable to take sufficient notice of the life cycle. Many of the original 'excellent' companies from the early 1980s declined as their products and services were overtaken by others. IBM is a prime example of this (*see* Fig 4.6).

In the early 1980s IBM controlled the newest and fastest growing technology and its name was synonymous with computing. By 1992 the company had experienced the largest ever loss recorded by any company anywhere.

IBM was one of Peters and Waterman's 'excellent' companies:

> *'With one act . . . IBM simultaneously reaffirmed its heroic dimension (satisfying the individual's need to be part of something great) and its concern for individual self-expression (the need to stick it out).'*

In a period of ten years the company moved from being held up as an example of the success of capitalism to an example of its failings. It could be said that it was within its major strengths that IBM's weakness appeared. Its strength was based on an almost monopolistic position in the market for automated information. It was first with punch-cards and then with the mainframe and minicomputer.

As long as computers were the preserve of major corporations the IBM strategy worked, but with the development of the desktop personal computer this changed. IBM decided not to launch the desktop computer because they did not believe that anyone would want it, and it was left to Apple Computers and their competitors to move into this market. IBM quickly followed, but without time to develop its own components it bought in chips from Intel and software from Microsoft. The launch of the IBM PC legitimised the desktop for corporations, but also meant that other companies could produce IBM PC clones and Intel and Microsoft could sell their components to these companies. By 1994 there were 3000 clone manufacturers in Taiwan alone, helped in their success by the ability to network PCs to do much of the work of mainframes and minis.

In his book *The Fate of IBM* Robert Heller comments that IBM played a difficult hand badly, but in the end the new market was simply too big and the pace of change too fast for one company to remain in control.

FIG 4.6 THE DECLINE OF IBM

The performance of new products and services typically follows a pattern that includes four or five identifiable stages, each related to the passage of time and the levels of sales or demand (*see* Fig 4.7 below). The stages are:

- **introduction:** a period of slow growth as the product/service is introduced;

- **growth:** a period of rapid market acceptance;

- **maturity:** a period of slower growth because the product/service has been accepted by most of the potential buyers;

- **saturation:** a period when there are many competitors in the market which itself is no longer growing. This period can be combined with maturity;

- **decline:** a period when performance starts a strong downward drift.

Of course, not all products and services follow this exact pattern, and timescales can vary considerably, but careful analysis of the life cycle enables managers to focus on the appropriate marketing strategy for a particular stage in the life cycle of their products and service:

- **Introduction:** a new product or service may be a substitute for something else, either directly or indirectly. For a time, consumers may resist the new product while they consider that the old one still meets their needs. For this reason, and because the new product is not well known in the market, the demand will be slow in the introductory stage. The only exception to this is a fad or fashion which may make an immediate impact. The marketing strategy for most goods when they are introduced will be to target the groups of people who are likely to be most interested. Previous customers are an obvious target. Computer companies producing a new product or introducing a new service

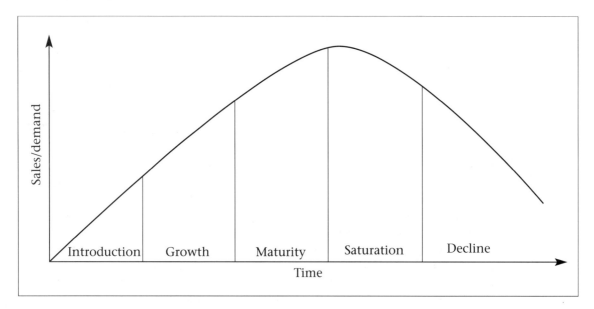

FIG 4.7 PRODUCT LIFE CYCLE

will send information to their previous customers in the first instance. They will also attempt to attract the attention of the 'innovators' who find out about new products without help and who do not need much persuasion.

- **Growth:** the benefit of the new product/service will have become accepted by this stage. Production difficulties will have been overcome and development costs covered, so that usually the price can be reduced. Marketing strategy will usually involve a wider promotion to target new customers. Competitors will begin to enter the market during this stage. They spend money on promoting their product, so the general awareness of it increases, helping to encourage further growth.

- **Maturity:** at this stage the product or service will have become widely accepted and competition will become the most important element for managers. Marketing may be aimed at an attempt to retain or assume the position of market leader or at challenging the leader by emphasising the advantages of the company's particular product.

- **Saturation:** sooner or later all the potential users of the product or service will have satisfied their demand for it, so that the market no longer grows. There will be plenty of suppliers competing in the market and this may lead to price wars. At the same time, managers will search for new products and services to replace the old ones.

- **Decline:** as newer products and services are introduced the demand for the old product or service will decline. Managers may decide to stop producing the commodity because it is felt to be better to invest in newer products. Advances in technology can cause the demand for a product to decline and changes in fashion or taste alter demand.

- **Recovery:** it is possible for companies to recover, so that after a period of decline and heavy losses (IBM lost $16 billion between 1991 and 1993 – *see* Fig 4.8) a company may introduce changes which are sufficient to bring it back to an early stage of the life cycle. This company renewal may involve new products, internal restructuring or a fresh approach to marketing and sales which result in the company starting new life cycle at the introduction or growth stage.

Life-cycle analysis is observed quite easily in the development and decline of a new model of a motor car. At introduction, the marketing strategy is likely to include heavy advertising to encourage all early demand. As the growth of sales develops promotion will be designed to establish market share. The reputation of the product will become more important than in the introduction stage when innovators and 'risk-takers' may be the main purchasers. Car manufacturers may emphasise matters such as reliability and security.

In maturity, the attempt will be made to retain market position against the competition, the emphasis may be on the quality of a well-established product and the features available in the car may play an important part in sales. Eventually the particular model of car will become relatively out of date compared with new models being introduced, and saturation will have been reached with a decline in sales. As

Although IBM had experienced record losses by 1993, by 1997 the company had achieved a remarkable recovery. The appointment of a new chief executive, Lou Gerstner, in 1993 brought about one of the most remarkable corporate turnarounds in US history. In 1997, for the first time in ten years, IBM's market value topped $100 billion and its shares were trading at record levels. Shipments of PCs rose 27 per cent in 1996 boosting IBM's market share from 8.1 to 8.9 per cent and the absorption of the software company, Lotus Development Corporation, in 1995 proved unexpectedly successful. One view was that the culture of the two companies would clash and that IBM's software division would not be revitalised, but Lotus sales rose 60 per cent in 1996 to $650 million.

It has been reported that Lou Gerstner had little knowledge of computers when he joined IBM, but he dismissed the idea that the company's problems were a lack of new products. His view was that the problem was in the company's management and one fundamental change he made was to instruct the company sales force to find out what customers really wanted, rather than believing that they knew best, and then giving it to them. At the same time the numbers of staff were being reduced from 300 000 to 215 000 and factories and research and development departments were closed. In 1997, two-thirds of IBM's revenue comes from PCs and services and although the use of an IBM scoring system at the Atlanta Olympics ran into difficulties, the defeat of Gary Kasparov, the world chess champion, for the first time by IBM's 'Deep Blue' computer was a successful publicity stunt.

FIG 4.8 THE RECOVERY OF IBM

demand declines, car manufacturers and showrooms may attempt to boost sales by producing 'special editions', or promotions which may involve price cuts. Some car manufacturers have followed a policy of replacing their models in a particular price range before a decline in demand is too obvious. This could be said, for example, of Ford's replacement of the Cortina by the Sierra and then the Mondeo.

MARKET SEGMENTATION

Where clear differences can be identified, it is possible to group customers into market segments for marketing and sales purposes. The reason for doing this is to find the most promising opportunities for a company's talents, so that its strengths are utilised and its weaknesses are not important. Car companies specialise in certain features or in producing, for example, off-road or commercial vehicles.

Segmentation is based on the characteristics of customers, such as:

- income;
- age;

- geography;

- life style.

This segmentation may lead to 'niche' marketing where a relatively small producer may find a particular segment of customer need which is not otherwise satisfied. A specialised car manufacturer such as Morgan is an example of this. One characteristic in the consideration of market segmentation is the 20/80 principle, sometimes described as the 'Pareto effect'. Managers may notice that, for example, 20 per cent of customers account for 80 per cent of demand. Some car producers sell 80 per cent of their cars to fleet or company buyers who may account for only 20 per cent of their individual customers, while for other producers it may be the other way around.

PRODUCT/SERVICE PORTFOLIO

Marketing is an essential factor in managers' decisions about the products and services a company will produce. As well as profits, managers are concerned with market share, because this is an indication of the extent to which a product can generate cash. In general terms, the larger the market share that a product obtains, the more cash it can generate. On the other hand, the greater the growth in the market, the more cash is used to support the expansion.

This situation can be summarised by a classification known as the 'Boston Matrix'. Figure 4.9 shows the main categories of products or services used in this classification, which are given distinctive names to indicate their prospects:

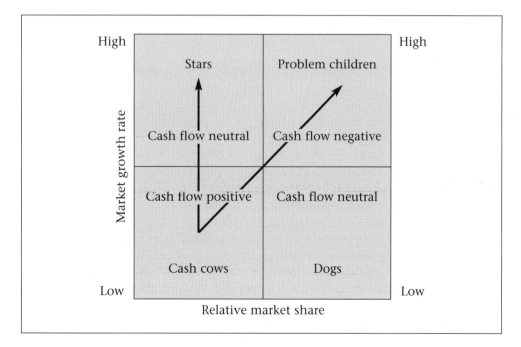

FIG 4.9 THE BOSTON MATRIX

- **A star** has a high market share and a high market growth rate. It will tend to generate as much cash as it uses and will be self-financing. In periods of economic expansion there will be a large number of stars, products and services which are in a growing market and have a large share of that market. Particular models of motor cars may fall into this category, along with household goods, popular holidays and so on.

- **A problem child** has a low market share but a high growth rate in a market that is itself growing. In order to increase market share, it may require investment and promotion and it will therefore use cash even though it is not generating very much. These products and services represent a problem because managers must decide whether to stop producing them or whether their potential growth makes an investment worthwhile. For example, a computer firm may decide that it is worth spending money on developing and promoting one of its software packages because, even though the sales are relatively small at the moment, there is considerable scope for expansion. It may be felt that the low sales are due to limited promotion and product development.

- **The cash cow** has a high market share and a low market growth in a reasonably stable market. As a result of its established position this type of product or service does not require developing or promoting and therefore cash is generated. A well-known brand of processed food may need little advertising, for example, and may still hold a large share of the market.

- **The dog** has a low market share and a low market growth, and in fact this type of product or service is likely to be a prime target for consideration for ending production. For example, a car model with poor and declining sales may cease to be manufactured, because the cost of the people and equipment employed in producing it may be considered a poor use of resources compared with the alternatives.

This analysis can provide managers with an indication of the type of policy they should follow for different products and services. The portfolio of the company would ideally include a range of products at different stages. Cash generated by cash cows could, for example, be invested by company managers in the stars or in selected problem children in order to make them into stars (the 'rising stars') as indicated by the arrows in Fig 4.9. The stars in turn could become cash cows as the need to promote and develop the product declines. Even some dogs can be saved from extinction by identifying segments of the market on which to concentrate, or by improving productivity in order to reduce costs. A car, for example, may retain a niche market even though its sales have fallen and with low production costs it may still be profitable. The British Leyland/Rover Mini is an example of this.

In considering marketing strategies managers will often be concerned with other aspects of the market, such as how far they are *penetrating* it in terms of reaching as many potential customers as possible, and how they can *extend* it in terms of opening new markets by finding new uses for the products or entirely new markets. Managers may also be concerned with *product development*, which means modifying or adding to the product or service in terms of quality and performance. They may want to *diversify* by both developing the product and extending the market (*see* Fig 4.10).

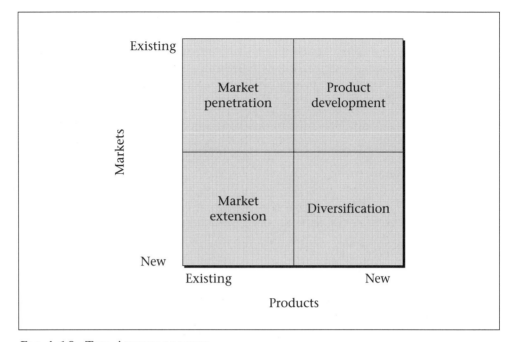

FIG 4.10 THE ANSOFF MATRIX

With existing products managers will attempt to achieve increased market penetration in existing markets and also attempt to find new markets. They will look for product development and help penetrate present markets, while aiming for new products or new uses for present products in order to diversify into new markets. Managers looking for market penetration and extension in the computer industry began to look towards the so-called SOHO market in the middle 1990s. The 'small office, home office' developed as a potentially fast-growing area as the divide between work and leisure applications became blurred. Car manufacturers have found it possible to extend their market for four-wheel-drive, off-road vehicles by developing more luxury products to sell as a fashionable vehicle to buyers who may never leave the tarmac road but who wish to enjoy a rugged, outdoor image.

Ideally, a company will produce a range of products which are at different stages of their life cycle, are stars and cash cows, and can be developed to further penetrate the market and extend it. It will do this by careful market research and developing new products to meet customer needs.

PRICE, PLACE AND PROMOTION

Price

An organisation will need to decide the price of its products and services based on marketing objectives. Price must be consistent with the total marketing strategy for a product. There is little point in charging a low price for a luxury item or a high price for a commodity to be sold in a mass market. In fact, price will depend very heavily on the supply and demand for the product (*see* Fig 4.11).

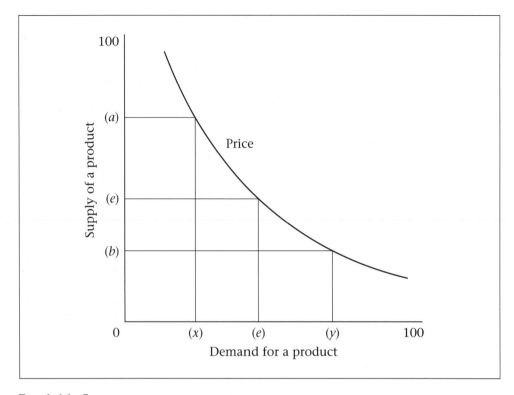

FIG 4.11 SUPPLY, DEMAND AND PRICE

If supply is high and so is price (say at point *a*), demand will be low (at *x*), while if supply is relatively low and so is the price (at point *b*), then demand will be high (at *y*). The equilibrium price (*e*) is where supply and demand are equal.

In practice managers will want to maintain prices as low as possible in order to encourage demand, while still retaining a high enough price to provide a good margin of profit on the sale of the product. In the introductory stage of the product life cycle the demand may grow very quickly and supply may be limited. At the same time, price may not be a very important factor in consumer decision making because they are anxious to be among the first to obtain the product. There is an opportunity for the organisation to charge relatively high prices to these 'innovators' and recover some of their research and development costs. The original personal computers, for example, were relatively expensive.

At the mature stage of the life cycle, the price of the product may be reduced in order to maintain or increase market share in what is likely to be an increasingly competitive market. At the saturation and decline stage, price will be manipulated depending on market share and sales volume. It may be raised in order to create a 'cash cow' within an established market, or lowered through sales 'promotions' in order to extend sales.

A company will often attempt to position itself in terms of the price of its products in one or other area of the market. A car manufacturer, for example, may see itself in the luxury area of the market and target products and prices accordingly, while another manufacturer may be aiming at wide coverage of the mass market and produce a range of cars to appeal to different segments. Although pricing policy may be a sophisticated process based on detailed market research and the consideration of a number of ratios, it is often based on a cost-plus process, on a consideration of competitors' prices, or on 'what the market will bear'. One factor in these approaches is that there is less uncertainty over costs than there is about demand, so that it is easy to arrive at a price by adding a percentage to costs. At the same time, it is not necessary to make frequent changes to price in response to changes in demand. 'Loss leaders' are often based on a price which covers fixed costs such as equipment, capital and overheads, while variable costs, such as labour, are subsidised for a limited time by other sources of income.

Prices may be fixed slightly above or below those of competitors. For example, petrol stations often follow this pattern. Or price may be based on what it is felt people will pay, 'what the market will bear'. In a relatively expensive area, where salaries are high, the price of food, petrol and other goods may be higher than the same goods bought in a cheaper area. However, the village shop may decide to charge high prices because it has a 'captive' market, while the city store may be cheaper because it is surrounded by competition. In practice, some products and services will have a far more price-sensitive market than others and managers need to take this into account in their pricing policy. At one extreme, a company may have a monopoly or near monopoly of the sale of a particular commodity. In these circumstances, the company can set whatever price it likes to match the desired level of demand. In more competitive markets, if a company puts a high price on its product, customers will not buy it because there are other suppliers. If an organisation lowers its price below that of other companies, competitors will lower their prices in order to compete.

Other things being equal, a high price will tend to reduce demand, while a low price will tend to increase demand. However, demand may be very responsive to changes in price (that is, elastic) or relatively unresponsive to changes in price (that is, inelastic). In a situation where managers have products which are not sensitive to price changes, they can use a price-skimming policy by charging a high initial price in order to recover development costs, and then lower prices as costs fall. When a product is more price sensitive, managers can introduce a low price to attract a large number of buyers and then raise prices to the normal level in the market, hoping to keep its market share. This will be helped by selling the product or service in the right place.

Place

In marketing terms the 'place' is where the final exchange occurs between the seller and customer. Managers have to make decisions about where this exchange takes place, and how, and channels of distribution. Bank services, for example, were at one time usually provided 'across the counter', but in recent years they have moved to cash points and increasingly telephone banking. A distribution channel is the process that brings together an organisation and its customers at a particular place and time for the purpose of exchange. This may be a shop, office, or via a computer link. Simple distribution channels between manufacturers, retailers and customers vary in length and breadth (*see* Fig 4.12).

Managers must decide how to organise their distribution channel, in terms of the number of outlets, whether to use middlemen and the preferences of their customers. Logistics management is about having the correct product or service in the right place at the right time.

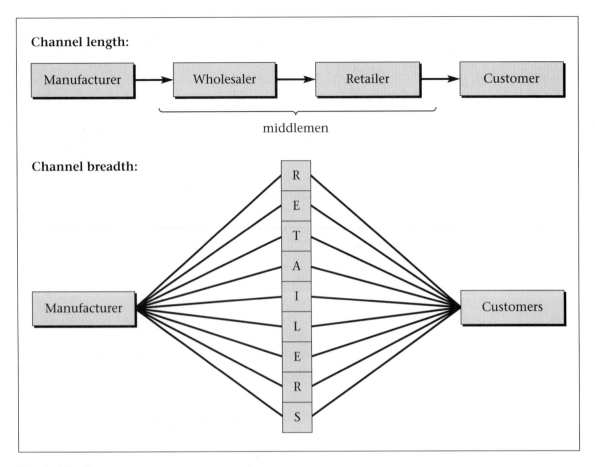

FIG 4.12 CHANNEL LENGTH AND BREADTH

Promotion

Promotion requires communication with customers and potential customers. Not only do customers have to be able to obtain a product or service, they also must have heard of it. They need information about the product in order to decide whether they want it or not. At the same time, most companies want to create a favourable image in order to maintain or increase levels of demand. This image will be developed through the nature of the product, the price, place and promotion. The image will be created by the marketing mix of those elements, and through publicity, public relations and advertising (*see* Fig 4.13).

This process of promotion will have the objective of encouraging consumers to reach a point where they 'demand' a product or service, that is 'the decision to buy'. The process of arriving at the final decision can be divided into awareness, knowledge, understanding, conviction and action. Consumers become aware of the fact that they have a need that must be satisfied, they discover that there are ways of satisfying it, consider the alternatives, make a decision and act on it by buying the product. This is the point at which customer requirements are satisfied and the marketing-oriented manager will have achieved a major objective. The image of the

In August 1994 the package holiday firm Owners Abroad decided to spend £5 million on a new image. This was widely reported in newspapers and marketing journals, and a change of name was proposed to First Choice Holidays.

The plan was to streamline overlapping brands and save cash by targeting three distinct sectors of the holiday market. Household names such as Enterprise, Falcon and Sunmed would give way to First Choice, Sovereign and Freespirit. The company was keen to boost its share of the £10 million UK holiday market in the summer of 1995.

It was expected that fierce competition between top tour operators Thomson and Airtours would launch a price war offering big discounts on 1995 packages. The company proposed to introduce a massive advertising campaign which should make sunseekers more aware of Owners' brands. The main new brand name, First Choice, would cover family package holidays, while the successful Sovereign label would be kept to cover more expensive and exotic trips. But a special Freespirit grouping would offer holidays for the young, free and single featuring adventure breaks. The company believed that up to £4 million holidays a year could be booked under this brand. It would aim to provide informal packages to childless adults who wanted more than a Club 18–30 break.

It was reported that Owners' new management was determined to build on the strong foundations which helped the firm defend itself from Airtours' hostile £290 million takeover bid in the previous year.

FIG 4.13 OWNERS ABROAD

company is essential in encouraging the customer to return to it rather than go to competitors, and the manager, whether selling or producing the product or controlling the process, has a prime role in establishing this image. The whole process of customer care within a marketing orientation is very important in the development of an excellent company and in its success. The 'best' or optimum combination of product, price, place and promotion can be developed by a manager into a marketing plan and strategy for the organisation (*see* Chapter 5).

SUMMARY

■ This chapter describes and analyses the importance of marketing in the management of organisations. The development of a focus on customer needs has created a position where marketing is a central and integrating activity in management.

■ The difference between marketing and selling is considered, as is the importance of market research as a foundation for meeting customer needs. The marketing process is essential for organisations to understand their position in relation to competitors.

■ The marketing mix is the combination of product or service, price, place and promotion which together can form a marketing strategy in order to meet customer needs and maintain a competitive edge.

REVIEW AND DISCUSSION QUESTIONS

1   Why is marketing such an important function for most organisations?

2   Is there any difference between marketing and selling, or are they the same activities described by different names?

3   What part can market research play in management decisions on product/service design?

4   How important is a marketing audit and SWOT analysis in the development of an organisation's marketing plan?

5   What is meant by a marketing strategy? Produce an outline strategy for a company, institution or club.

6   How is the price of a product or service determined? Is this an important element of an organisation's marketing strategy, or are promotion, advertising, location and product more important?

CASE STUDY: CHEESE MARKET   FT

When brothers Ian and David Skailes tuck into their Christmas lunch, the Stilton on their cheeseboard is likely to absorb more of their attention than usual. As specialist cheese-makers supplying London retailers Fortnum & Mason, Selfridges and Harrods, their priority is to produce the best cheese money can buy. But this year's deregulation of the milk market – accompanied by a surge in the cost of milk – has spurred them to find new ways of adding value to their cheeses.

'There's a strong market for jars of Stilton and presentation packs,' says Ian Skailes, production director of Cropwell Bishop Creamery, the family company based outside Nottingham. 'We do a lot of sales at airport shops. We're looking at new packaging and presentation and making sure quality is always at the top end of the market,' he says.

Since deregulation on 1 November, cheese-makers have had to pay up to 20 per cent more for their milk from Milk Marque, the dairy pro-

ducers' co-operative that replaced the statutory Milk Marketing Board and controls more than 65 per cent of supplies. Both specialist and mass producers are moving further upmarket in an attempt to maintain margins and market share.

Last month the Nottinghamshire creamery cut output of its lower value Cheddar and Leicester by 40 per cent. It is now making about 800 tonnes of Stilton and 500 tonnes of Cheddar and Leicester a year, a dramatic change from three years ago when the respective balance was 600 tonnes of Stilton to 1500 tonnes of 'hard-pressed' cheese. 'There's no money to be made out of Cheddar,' says Skailes. Milk represents 75–90 per cent of the cost of making Cheddar, but nearer 60 per cent of the cost of producing Stilton, which is more labour-intensive.

Cropwell Bishop hopes to pass on its increased costs to its customers in January in the form of a 10 per cent rise in prices.

Singleton's Dairy in Lancashire also foresaw an increase in milk prices as deregulation loomed. It decided to move away from its 60 per cent dependence on block Cheddar into higher-value cheeses. Last year, it launched Truckledown, a new cheese made from 'a mixture of a few of our old family recipes', says Bill Riding, director. This year it introduced Grandma Singleton's Strong Lancashire, matured for a record 9–10 months. 'We got a feeling the cheese market was looking towards more mature cheeses,' Riding explains. 'Cheese consumers are also becoming more cosmopolitan and trying more varieties.' The dairy is now building up its supplies of traditional farmhouse cheeses to supermarket delicatessen counters. Like Cropwell Bishop, it is also enjoying a growth in demand for its cheeses from the continent. At the mass end of the £1.2 bn cheese market, adding value is just as important, although the spur is the threat of imports rather than the promise of exports. The industry believes higher prices will draw in more imported cheese, which already accounts for 30 per cent of the market and is dominated by mild Cheddar, notably from Ireland.

The Cheese Company, Britain's biggest independent manufacturer, is busy trying to differentiate its product from such imports to hold on to its 24 per cent market share. It has adopted a marketing tactic known as 'sub-branding' – where the name of the creamery is carried on the label alongside that of the retailer. 'Our research has shown that way above the price and appearance of the cheese people like to know its origins,' says Sharon Rudd, product manager. The company has just launched a range of mostly mature cheeses from three of its five creameries – Taw Valley in Devon, Reece's in Cheshire and Castle Loch near Lockerbie in Scotland – in partnership with Marks & Spencer and Somerfield. The M&S labels provide a brief description of the cheese. Reece's Wensleydale is described as 'a young cheese with a clean, tangy flavour and a crumbly texture'.

This is one way for manufacturers to make inroads into a market that is 85 per cent dominated by retailers' own-label cheese. But does it amount to more than adding a few well-chosen words to a label? Roger Davenport, the Cheese Company's managing director, believes it does. 'We're making a contract with the consumer that cheese comes from where it says, and that the product is consistently delivering the expectations all the way through the year.' Although it has started with its most characterful, premium quality cheeses, the company hopes to pursue sub-branding throughout its range. It says other retailers are interested in the idea and aims to be in partnership with another leading multiple next year. ∎

Source: Maitland, A, *Financial Times*, 22 December 1994. Reprinted with permission.

REFERENCES FOR FURTHER READING

Drucker, Peter (1993) *Managing for the Future*, Oxford: Butterworth-Heinemann.

Hannagan, Tim (1986) *Mastering Statistics*, 2nd edn, London: Macmillan.

Hannagan, Tim (1990) *The Effective Use of Statistics: A Practical Guide for Managers*, London: Kogan Page.

Hannagan, Tim (1992) *Marketing for the Non-Profit Sector*, London: Macmillan.

Heller, Robert (1994) *The Fate of IBM*, New York: Little Brown.

Henley Centre and Chartered Institute of Marketing (1993) *Customer Loyalty*.

Kotler, Philip (1986) *Principle of Marketing*, 3rd edn, Englewood Cliffs, New Jersey: Prentice-Hall.

Maitland, A (1994) 'Cheese market', *Financial Times*, 22 December.

POLICY AND PLANNING

STRATEGIC MANAGEMENT

Tim Hannagan

OBJECTIVES

The objectives of this chapter are to:

◆ analyse the importance of strategic management

◆ consider the role of planning in management

◆ apply strategic management and planning to the process of developing corporate strategy

◆ identify the factors influencing the corporate portfolio

◆ analyse the competitive forces affecting corporate strategy

WHAT IS STRATEGIC MANAGEMENT?

At its simplest, strategic management can be described as a plan of action to enable an organisation to move from where it is now to where it wants to be at a future date. Managers need to have an idea about where they want the organisation to be in the future and the route it is going to follow to get there. If managers do not have a strategic plan, then the old cliché can apply: 'If you don't know where you are going, how will you know when you have arrived?'

Of course, managers may have a strategy without realising it. They may work on the basis that they do not have a plan, they simply continue to do what they are doing now. This is, of course, in its own way a plan. The problem with a 'passive' plan based on continuing to work as at present is that however successful this may have been in the past and is now, it may not be successful in the future. 'Other things' will not remain 'equal'. On the one hand the external environment will change in terms of economic factors and political policies as well as technological development; on the other hand competitors will be searching for ways to expand their share of the market.

This was a problem in the 1930s, for example, when the Ford Motor Company continued to produce its Model T in 'any colour the customer required as long as it was black', while their competitors produced more varied models which met customer requirements more closely. In the same way, in the 1980s many computer companies experienced similar problems when what they had always produced was superseded. For example, the computer games company Nintendo took an early lead in the video games market when it expanded in the late 1980s. The company developed its Gameboy hand-held 8-bit games console which made it a major force in this developing market. It was then beaten into the 16-bit market by Sega which introduced its Mega Drive. Market share of the UK's video games in 1994 was 55 per cent to Nintendo and 34 per cent to Sega, but Sega claimed 70 per cent of the 16-bit market and, at this time, Sega and other companies were developing 32-bit video games. Nintendo has struggled to keep up with these developments; rather than concentrate on the 32-bit market it decided to move on to develop a 64-bit machine, Project Reality, and to 'leapfrog' into a technological lead.

Given the pitfalls of not having a strategic plan or having a 'passive' one, managers need to have an 'active' strategy, a way forward on which to base their decisions. A past chief executive of Sears, the largest retailer of drug and soft goods in the USA, has stated that:

> *'Business is like a war in one respect, if its ground strategy is correct,*
> *any number of tactical errors can be made and yet the enterprise*
> *proves successful.'*
>
> (General Robert E Wood, quoted in Pearce and Robinson, 1989)

In this statement, it is being suggested that even if the detailed actions are wrong, they can be overcome where the overall strategy is effective. In other words, if travellers are on the correct road to their destination, a few diversions or stops may hold them up, but will not prevent them from arriving where they want to be. If they do not know their destination, or they are on the wrong road, their chances of arriving in the right place are very limited and in fact are a matter of chance. In this sense, strategy is a plan, a direction or a future course of action. It can also be seen as a pattern of behaviour over time, and it can be described as an organisation's way of doing things or, for that matter, what it actually does. Strategy, as applied to planning, is concerned with looking ahead.

> *'The maxim "managing means looking ahead" gives some idea of the importance attached to planning in the business world, and it is true that if foresight is not the whole of management at least it is an essential part of it.'*
> (Henri Fayol, 1949)

This means that the terms 'planning' and 'management' can almost be used synonymously. However, sometimes a division is made between 'planning' on the one hand and 'problem solving' on the other, while 'management' involves both. Strategic management is certainly about decision making and action based on plans, and it is clear that this process needs to be managed because plans can be seen as a drawing together of a set of independent decisions.

> *'Planning, of course, is not a separate, recognisable act . . . every management act, mental or physical is inexorably intertwined with planning. It is as much a part of every managerial act as breathing is to the living human.'*
> (C George, 1972)

In this way, planning can be seen as integrated decision making in the sense of bringing together a series of decisions so that they relate to each other and form a rational whole to establish the action to be taken.

WHAT IS THE PURPOSE OF PLANNING?

The major argument in favour of planning is in the co-ordination of decision making so that an organisation is moving in a well-focused direction. Without planning the efforts of the organisation may not be well co-ordinated and managers and staff may be heading in different directions. Planning also helps to ensure that the future is taken into account, so that the organisation can control the situation it finds itself in as far as possible and prepare for unexpected eventualities. Daily routines can lead to the future being forgotten if everybody is too busy to consider medium- or long-term problems. It can be argued also that planning is a rational form of management which enables organisations to acquire greater control over their future development.

In the past, scientific management, by emphasising the codification of routine tasks, encouraged the planning of operations. Mariann Jelinek (1979) argued that the equivalent of Taylor's work-study methods in terms of strategy is a system of planning and control to establish a pattern which is not overwhelmed by operational details. Corporate strategy has:

> *'made possible for the first time concerted co-ordination . . . and true policy for such organisations. So long as management is overwhelmed by the details of task performance, planning and policy will not occur . . . that is, until what is routine is systematised and performance replicable without extensive management attention, management attention will necessarily focus on the routine. By the time of Du Pont and General Motors, the specification of task had*

121

moved from codifying worker's routine activities to codifying managers' routine activities.' (Mariann Jelinek, 1979)

The argument used here is that planning is seen as the key to the formulation of strategy. As organisations have become more complex, the need for plans and systems has grown. At its extreme this argument suggests that it is not people so much as systems that create the strategies, because systems are reliable and consistent while people are relatively unreliable.

'It is the responsibility of planning to make sure that the entire organisation knows very well what its customers' requirements are, what is the direction in which customer needs and customer expectations are changing, how technology is moving and how competitors serve their customers.' (I A Marquanett, 1990)

This quotation by the head of planning for Bell & Howell states that responsibility is held by planning, rather than by planners. In his book on *The Rise and Fall of Strategic Planning* (1994), Henry Mintzberg seeks to demonstrate the fallaciousness of this approach. He argues that approaches based on formalisation, detachment and predetermination are not correct. The idea that a strategic plan can be translated into a system which accurately predicts the future is called into question. Forecasting is generally recognised as an uncertain science because all types of assumptions have to be made and a range of unpredictable forces may influence the outcomes. He quotes an earlier work in suggesting that:

'The pressure of the managerial environment does not encourage the development of reflective planners, the classical literature notwithstanding. The job breeds adaptive information-manipulators who prefer the live, concrete situation. The manager works in an environment of stimulus-response, and he develops in his work a clear preference for live action.' (Henry Mintzberg, 1973)

It is also the case that the less 'closed' the system, the more difficult accurate forecasting becomes. The Soviet Union attempted to create a closed and planned system under communism. This was of very limited success. Most managers work in much more 'open' systems where they are faced with the uncertainties of economic, social, political, technological and other change. Mintzberg concludes that too much planning may lead to chaos, but too little planning may also lead to chaos and more directly:

'Several decades of experience with strategic planning has taught us about the need to loosen up the process of strategy formation rather than try to seal it off through arbitrary formalisation.' (Henry Mintzberg, 1994)

It is of course an unwise organisation that insists on keeping to its plans in spite of changing circumstances. It can be argued that insistence on maintaining what had previously been a successful plan was the major cause of the collapse of the British motorcycle industry in the face of Japanese competition. This does not invalidate the whole planning process, but does illustrate its dangers. Planning may have benefits even where plans have to be changed from time to time, and these changes themselves may be able to be made against a background of relative 'planned' stability.

It is possible to identify behavioural benefits in organisations where planning is encouraged:

- managers are in a position to detect problems and how best to resolve them;

- alternative strategies can be considered in making decisions;

- employees gain a better understanding of their organisation's strategies and may become more committed to them;

- strategic planning can help clarify everyone's responsibilities;

- lower uncertainty about the future consequences of decisions can reduce resistance to change.

However, the dangers of a rigid adherence to planning need to be recognised. The plan may become inappropriate as factors such as competition and technology change, and a well-established plan may become so well accepted that it creates opposition to change.

Strategy as a grand plan

Strategic management is a method of defining the overall direction of an organisation, its objectives and how it expects to achieve them. In this process, organisations may develop a grand plan which describes the general actions to be taken to achieve long-term objectives. These plans are concerned with the overall intentions of an organisation, whether this is to retrench, remain stable or to grow.

Retrenchment

A company may decide to reduce its size in terms of employees, production, assets and other factors. This decision may arise from a decline in demand for its products, changes in competition, the introduction of new technology, or for some other reason. The retrenchment usually involves reducing business units, selling off parts of the business, or in the final analysis the liquidation of the entire organisation.

In the recession of the early 1990s, many companies reduced the size of their operation by using all these methods. 'Outsourcing' areas of activity was a common process, and enabled a company to relinquish ownership while retaining the service. 'Re-engineering' involves reducing the size of the labour force in order to reduce costs. Selling off parts of a company enables it to concentrate on what it considers to be its main core business. During this period Thorn-EMI, for example, reduced its training programme, sold off parts of its business and outsourced other areas. Rank Xerox UK decided to concentrate on its main business, photocopying and office documentation, and outsourced such areas as its information technology needs.

Stability

Stability involves a company attempting to remain the same size or grow in a very slow, controlled way. This 'pause strategy' often follows a period of rapid growth, when it is felt that time is needed to consolidate this expansion to make sure that it does not disappear.

Growth

Growth is often considered to be a company policy which will provide motivation and incentives to its employees and ensure its position in its markets. Increasing investment, product development, diversification into new markets and the acquisition of competitors are all processes for encouraging expansion.

Multinationalism

In order to grow, a company may decide to follow a multinational policy by expanding into foreign markets. Developments such as those in Europe with the dropping of customs barriers in 1992 have helped to encourage this type of growth. Car manufacturers such as Ford have on the one hand tried to produce models for particular markets such as North America and Europe, and on the other produced models for a worldwide market with models such as the Escort and the Mondeo.

When organisations become complex and diversified, such as is the case with major national and multinational companies, strategic planning is very much the role of top management because co-ordination of the organisation's functional areas becomes crucial. Planning at lower levels can be described as operational planning. While strategic planning concentrates on effectiveness, that is 'doing the right things', operational planning concentrates on efficiency, that is 'doing things right'. Strategic planning provides guidance and boundaries for operational management and the two overlap in providing organisational strategy and the operational activity to achieve it. The grand plan represents the top management view of the direction the organisation needs to take at any particular time. It provides a sense of direction which has to be implemented at all levels in the organisation if it is to succeed. This implementation requires a more 'operational' plan which ultimately arrives at a series of actions which need to be carried out in order to achieve it.

This 'operational' plan increasingly coincides with the organisation's marketing plan, because of the recognition that marketing provides the integration of organisational functions and that without customers to demand its products and services an organisation does not have a *raison d'être*. Meeting the needs of customers is the first priority for any organisation, whether it is in the private or the public sector. Therefore the strategic plan in practice coincides with the marketing plan. It is both informed by market research, in determining what should be done, and focuses on customer needs, in deciding how it is to be done. The development of an organisation's corporate strategy usually involves a series of stages moving from the relatively abstract to the very concrete, as outlined in Fig 5.1.

MISSION STATEMENT AND VISION

The grand plan provides an idea of the overall direction of a company, the way it is planning to develop if it is able to control matters. This may be particularly difficult with growth and multinationalism. However, even retrenchment and stability may be difficult to achieve in practice. In a recession, stability may prove to be an optimistic aim, while attempts to sell off part of the business may prove difficult in practice.

Increasingly organisations have attempted to encapsulate the purpose of their activity, as much as the direction they wish to take, in a single short statement.

Mission statement or vision	*What business are we in?*
Corporate objectives, goals and aims	*Where do we want to go and how do we get there?*
Market research	*Who are our customers and what are their needs?*
Audit of external environment	*What are the threats and opportunities we face?*
Analysis of resources	*What are our strengths and weaknesses?*
Marketing objectives	*How do we achieve our objectives in marketing terms?*
Strategic plan	*How do we match our objectives with our resources?*
Action plan	*What do we have to do to achieve our objectives?*

(A further stage can be added looping back to the beginning of the process in terms of monitoring and review.)

FIG 5.1 CORPORATE STRATEGY

This statement represents the 'vision' or 'mission' of the organisation, or 'what it is about'. For example, see the Ford Motor Company's Statement of Mission, Values and Guiding Principles in Fig 5.3 (pp 127–8).

The mission statements are changed by companies from time to time in order to reflect adjustments by the company to markets and competition. The examples of mission or vision statements in this chapter are provided to illustrate the form they take and may not be the ones in use by the companies now. The 'mission' might include the general direction the company is to take, but this may be expressed more clearly in the organisation's aims and objectives. In 1993 the airline British Midland described its mission in terms of improving service to meet customers' needs, 'allowing us to expand our business throughout Europe and, in doing so, generate the necessary profit to develop our company'.

The mission statement describes an organisation's basic purpose. A computer company, for example, may describe itself as providing low-cost, high quality solutions to business problems. A record company may describe itself as being in the entertainment business, a retail company may describe itself as offering customers a range of high quality, well designed and attractive merchandise at reasonable prices. Cadbury Schweppes has described its task as building on its tradition of quality and value to provide brands, products, financial results and management performance that meet the interest of its shareholders, consumers, employees, customers, suppliers and the communities in which it operates.

A characteristic of mission statements is that they are succinct, distinctive and wide in scope; they are 'short in numbers and long in rhetoric' in the sense that they identify the organisation without providing a very specific approach to dealing with a target market. The mission statement outlines the present view of the organisation's purpose without restricting future possible development (*see* Fig 5.2). The computer company may wish to emphasise its width of possible work: it is not simply concerned with computer hardware or solving problems in information technology, it is concerned with using computers to solve business problems. The retail company may want to emphasise that they offer high quality goods of all types at reasonable prices.

Mission statements focus on:

- **What business are we in?**

- **Who is to be served?**

- **What benefits are to be delivered?**

- **How are consumers to be satisfied?**

FIG 5.2 MISSION STATEMENTS

The mission statement of any organisation should answer the question 'What business are we in?' The National Children's Bureau, for example, has stated that it 'exists to promote and protect the welfare, interests and rights of all children in the UK, on the basis of research and knowledge'. An engineering consultancy has described its purpose to be 'a leading engineering consultancy engaged in the management and execution of projects requiring the effective application of engineering technologies and physical sciences'. There can be little doubt about what these two organisations do and what business they are in. The National Children's Bureau's purpose is to look after the interests of children, specifically in the UK, based on high-quality information. The Bureau is not concerned with the education or the health of children unless their welfare or rights need protecting in these areas. The management consultancy is clearly in engineering and not other areas of consultancy and the application of engineering technology. In the same way British Airways has attempted to produce a mission statement that supports its slogan 'The world's favourite airline' and has in the past declared its mission to be 'the best and most successful company in the airline business'. In support of this statement British Airways has emphasised the importance of safety and security, of financial strength, of the need to provide services and value, to anticipate and quickly respond to customer needs, to be a good employer and to be a good neighbour concerned for the community and the environment.

Ford Motor Company
Company mission, values and guiding principles

Mission

Ford Motor Company is a worldwide leader in automotive and financial products and services. Our mission is to improve continually our products and services to meet our customers' needs, allowing us to prosper as a business and to provide a reasonable return for our stockholders, the owners of our business.

Values

How we accomplish our mission is as important as the mission itself. Fundamental to success for the Company are these basic values:

▶ **People** – Our people are the source of our strength. They provide our corporate intelligence and determine our reputation and vitality. Involvement and teamwork are our core human values.

▶ **Products** – Our products are the end result of our efforts, and they should be the best in serving customers worldwide. As our products are viewed, so are we viewed.

▶ **Profits** – Profits are the ultimate measure of how efficiently we provide customers with the best products for their needs. Profits are required to survive and grow.

Guiding principles

▶ **Quality comes first** – To achieve customer satisfaction, the quality of our products and services must be our number one priority.

▶ **Customers are the focus of everything we do** – Our work must be done with our customers in mind, providing better products and services than our competition.

▶ **Continuous improvement is essential to our success** – We must strive for excellence in everything we do: in our products, in their safety and value – and in our services, our human relations, our competitiveness, and our profitability.

▶ **Employee involvement in our way of life** – We are a team. We must treat each other with trust and respect.

▶

FIG 5.3   FORD MOTOR COMPANY'S STATEMENT OF MISSION, VALUES AND GUIDING PRINCIPLES

Source: Copyright © Ford Motor Company 1996. Reprinted with permission.

> ▶ **Dealers and suppliers are our partners** – The Company must maintain mutually beneficial relationships with dealers, suppliers and our other business associates.
>
> ▶ **Integrity is never compromised** – The conduct of our Company worldwide must be pursued in a manner that is socially responsible and commands respect for its integrity and for its positive contributions to society. Our doors are open to men and women alike without discrimination and without regard to ethnic origin or personal beliefs.

FIG 5.3 CONTINUED

Once an organisation identifies what type of business it is in, it needs to answer the question 'What benefits do our customers seek?' Customers may be seeking the benefit of a solution to business problems which they want solved in the most cost-effective way possible. Whether this involves computers and information technology may not be important, provided that the solutions are effective. The question 'What is our business?' has to be defined in terms of the underlying need that the organisation is trying to serve. The engineering consultancy is offering the effective application of engineering technologies and the customers it serves will be looking for benefits in terms of these applications. The Ford Motor Company has made the quality of its products and services the number one priority (*see* Fig 5.3).

GOALS, AIMS AND OBJECTIVES

Once an organisation has decided on the business it is in, it can focus very clearly on its goals, aims and objectives. The corporate objectives of an organisation emphasise its direct aims, and in contrast to vision or mission statements, these are precise statements of intent. They must be capable of measurement, by one method or another, in order to confirm whether or not objectives have been achieved. It is possible to distinguish between objectives, which fill out the abstractions of the mission statement in more concrete terms, and corporate goals and aims, which provide the operational detail that can lead to an action plan. Organisational goals and aims are objectives restated in an operational and measurable form, and most of the time very little distinction is made in the use of these three terms. While the objectives may be expressed in terms of the grand plan, combined with the goals and aims they will provide a concrete idea of the direction of the organisation and how it will get there.

The computer company with a mission statement concerned with solving business problems may have corporate objectives which state that it aims at a particular level of profitability and that it intends to obtain a particular percentage share of its market. Objectives are often expressed in terms of profit, market share, growth, or all three. Therefore, while the mission statement is a relatively abstract statement of the organisation's purpose, the corporate objectives, aims and goals are a combination of the grand plan ('Where do we want to go?') and an idea of how to achieve it

('How do we get there?'). The objectives will not only express the fact that the organisation intends to grow but also by how much and perhaps the main market or markets to be penetrated. While in the BA example concrete financial targets are not set, a strong and consistent financial performance implies a healthy financial position. British Airways has emphasised the importance of financial strength, while DHL Worldwide Express has specified the aim to 'become the acknowledged global leader in the express delivery of documents and packages'. DHL has also declared that leadership would be achieved by establishing industry standards of excellence for quality service and by monitoring the lowest cost position relative to the company service commitment in all markets of the world. These can be seen as specific market aims, leadership position and costing policy. The example from DHL Worldwide Express is more specific in its market aims, leadership position and costing policy.

Corporate objectives can be seen either as primary or secondary objectives. *Primary objectives* are those which must be achieved if the organisation is to survive and succeed. These are often expressed in terms of profit, sales or market share, so that if a certain level of profit is not achieved the company will collapse. If certain levels of sales or market share are not attained the company will not succeed and again may be faced with the ultimate problem of survival. *Secondary objectives* are a measure of the efficiency of an organisation. They are critical for success, but may not affect survival for some time. They may be to do with customer care, product development, administrative efficiency, new office buildings and so on. In recent years many organisations, both in the private and public sectors, have raised the standing of such objectives as improving customer care from a secondary objective which is only considered to affect survival over a long period, to a primary objective which will have a much more direct effect on levels of activity, profits and therefore survival. Whatever the priority given to particular objectives, it is important that they are clearly expressed, measurable in one way or another and therefore realistic, with an assigned responsibility and a deadline for completion (*see* Fig 5.4).

S Specific: clearly and precisely expressed

M Measurable: so that there is confirmation of whether or not they are achieved

A Agreed: with those responsible for achieving them

R Realistic: so that they can be achieved

T Timed: with a deadline for achievement

FIG 5.4 **SMART** OBJECTIVES

Marketing Strategy

An organisation needs to base its objectives on market research which should enable it to understand the customer's needs. The information arising from market research helps the organisation to be customer oriented and to produce goods and services which meet customer needs. Market research will help to decide:

- **customer needs at present;**
- **customer location and characteristics;**
- **customer perceptions of the organisation's products and services;**
- **customer needs in the future;**
- **levels of customer satisfaction.**

Managers have to ensure that the entire organisation is customer oriented, otherwise one part of it may pull in a different direction. The mission statement, corporate objectives, goals and aims, and the marketing strategy need to interact so that they are all directed one way. At the same time, managers have to carry out an audit of the external environment. This 'environmental analysis' provides a systematic assessment of information about an organisation's strategic opportunities, as well as threats and problems which might prove to be obstacles to its development. This analysis enables managers to shape and evaluate strategic options and develop corporate strategy. In marketing terms, this is part of the SWOT (strengths, weaknesses, opportunities and threats) analysis. Opportunities may be discovered by revealing a part of the potential market that is relatively untouched. For example, a computer company may discover that while it has been concentrating on finding solutions to business problems in terms of products and finance there is a gap in terms of personnel and training functions. Clive Sinclair has invented products to fill perceived opportunities in the market such as portable computers, electric cars and powered bicycles, with more or less success.

Competition is the most obvious threat for most organisations. Market research identifies rival producers of goods and services. Most organisations are concerned with their market share and profitability and competing firms will have similar objectives. For example, McDonald's UK has described its purpose to be 'the United Kingdom's number one favourite quick service restaurant', led by the needs of its customers, committed to the welfare and development of its staff, with the provision of great tasting food in a relaxed, safe and consistent restaurant environment.

Matters such as competitors' product development and pricing policy will be taken into account in determining an organisation's own policies. For example, from time to time newspapers have entered into strong price competition. In 1994 *The Times*, in the UK, reduced its price to 20 pence while its rivals were priced at more than twice that level. This had a particular effect on *The Independent*, which attempted to counteract this pricing policy by reducing its own price to 30 pence.

Threats may also take the form of political, social, economic and technological changes. These may also represent opportunities, depending on how they affect the environment of the organisation. Tax changes, for example, may adversely affect a company or an industry. The changes in taxation on company cars in the UK, for example, have reduced their importance as a perk for managers and have altered the demand for particular cars. One change which illustrates this point was introduced in 1994. Instead of taxation being based on the cubic capacity of the car, it was based on its retail price. This enabled on the one hand larger-engined cars to be more widely sold to company car buyers, and on the other hand car companies had to look very carefully at their prices and margins and those of their competitors.

Changes in government regulation and European Union laws may affect companies, particularly in matters such as environmental control and human resource legislation. At the same time, the introduction of training grants and industrial development areas has provided opportunities for many companies. Social changes, such as the increase in leisure activities or the shifting age structure of the population, create opportunities for companies in the leisure business or for those who provide goods and services to pensioners, while presenting threats to companies producing goods for children. The development of technology presents opportunities to computer companies while representing a threat to companies having to keep pace with competitors. This highlights the organisation's strengths and weaknesses. Strengths may include location, product development, internal organisation, a skilled and dedicated labour force, good communications and image. Weaknesses may include the lack of financial resources, a small market share, a limited range of products and dilapidated premises. Of course many of the weaknesses represent opportunities for improvement and could therefore be turned into strengths.

The marketing strategy of an organisation will depend on the analysis of its market position, and an evaluation of its external threats and opportunities and its internal strengths and weaknesses. It will then hope to build on its strengths and opportunities so that it can meet its strategic objectives and achieve its vision. An example of this was IBM in the 1980s which considered its main strengths to be in the corporate market with the development of mainframes. It believed that its lack of direct retail experience with individual buyers constituted a weakness in terms of the new PC market. In comparing itself through market research with its competitors, it decided to enter the PC market by selling to business and corporate customers and gradually overcoming its weakness by licensing the sale of IBM PCs. At the time this appeared to be a sensible strategic marketing plan (*see* Fig 4.6 in Chapter 4).

THE STRATEGIC PLAN

The strategic plan of an organisation involves matching its corporate objectives and its available resources. In this development of corporate strategy managers are concerned with reconciling the business the organisation is in with the allocation of resources. The use of resources has to support the aims and goals agreed in the organisation and these in turn will determine the priorities in terms of resource use. If growth is a major element in the grand plan, then resources are likely to be allocated to marketing and product development, while if contraction or 'retrenchment' is the goal, then more resources may be given to paying for the costs of redundancy payments, early retirement and the negotiations and consultations involved. This allocation process is concerned with the general direction of an organisation, whether it is part of a so-called 'grand plan', the overall objectives or a 'strategy' designed to keep the organisation in business.

While the overall strategy may be determined at a senior level, the detail may be better left to those as close as possible to the organisation's customers. This view is supported by Tom Peters (1992) in terms of strategy:

> *'I don't believe top management should be in the business of strategy setting at all, except as creators of a general business mission. Strategies must be set from below. (No, not 'from' below. Set 'in' below – i.e. by the autonomous business units, for the autonomous business units).'*

Corporate strategy involves senior managers in establishing the overall purpose of the organisation and the objectives, aims and goals, while the question of tactics and approach to customers is decided at the level of individual business units. The strategic plan is the process of allocating resources in an organisation in order to achieve its strategic aims. This allocation will again be carried out at different levels, so that while resources may be allocated in a general way, detailed allocation will be left to business units or work teams. Of course, in many 'autonomous' business units the whole unit may prosper or fail depending on its relative success, and this will depend on its own strategic plan and the success of its implementation. However, it remains the situation that the overall purpose of an organisation, its vision and values remain the responsibility of senior management. Changing these is a slow process which requires the allocation of resources over a period of years.

Large companies such as British Airways have introduced staff training sessions, quality initiatives or corporate change programmes over many years in order to create different behavioural approaches in the company and to reinforce company values. They are usually, in the final analysis, about 'customer care', however they may be packaged. Resources are allocated centrally to these programmes in order to promote developments which match the mission and corporate objectives of the company. For example, in the 1980s British Airways developed 'Putting People First' and 'Managing People First' programmes in order to improve its service. It then evolved its mission statement ('to be the best and most successful company in the airline business') out of the purpose and success of its training programme (Fig 5.5).

THE ACTION PLAN

Once the strategic plan has been agreed, managers need to decide on particular courses of action in order to achieve corporate objectives with the resources available. Detailed guidelines have to be developed in order to initiate and control action. The purpose of an action plan is to ensure that people responsible for accomplishing short-term and long-term objectives have clear guidance on what they need to do and how they are to achieve these objectives. Action plans also provide a mechanism by which top managers can satisfy themselves that what is being implemented is consistent with the intention of the strategic plans.

Action plans are concerned with turning priorities and corporate plans into reality, and they are linked to the use of resources in the form of both physical and human resources. They may show how many people are to be involved with a particular activity, the numbers of people and their skills and qualifications. Action plans also take into account how much money is available for a particular activity and the amount and type of equipment and premises required. In reflecting the

In November 1983 British Airways introduced a training programme called 'Putting People First'. The aim was to put 12 000 customer contact people through a two-day course to improve their customer service skills. The programme consisted of a mixture of presentations, exercises and group discussions in which staff reviewed their personal experience as customers of other service organisations. They also examined the implications for British Airways and were pressed to identify what they would do about these implications. The response to the training programme was mixed – some were sceptical, some saw it as a harmonising exercise, some dropped out, and others were enthusiastic. But top management continued to support the programme, demonstrating their commitment to customer service. The non front-line staff began asking to be included and gradually the level of cynicism faded away. Staff began identifying the obstacles, confronting their managers with the fact that resources were insufficient to deliver the levels of customer care called for. The management responded to these issues and so encouraged staff to identify others.

Then in 1984, a programme for managers called 'Managing People First' was launched to change management styles. At the time, management style was perceived to be dominated by sales and procedures and the aim of the training programme was to replace this with something more open and dynamic.

Other changes were made to reinforce the training programmes. For example, quality assurance and performance related reward systems were introduced. The services being offered by the airline were also improved, demonstrating to staff that they would get the resources required to deliver better service.

It was only once the changes in behaviour were starting to show up as better service and greater customer satisfaction that mission statements were formulated in 1986.

FIG 5.5 BRITISH AIRWAYS

Source: Campbell, Devine and Young (1990).

organisation's strategic plan, action plans have a major impact on the successful implementation of these strategies in showing what actions are required and the timescale for completion.

At their simplest, action plans are lists of actions to be carried out by particular managers or operatives in order to achieve the requirements of the business unit. They are often the responsibility of operating managers in order to ensure that those responsible for implementing a strategic plan are also involved in developing it. They are usually accompanied by detailed budgets, which may act as a means of control as well as a means of communicating an action plan.

- **Functional plans** are produced to guide decisions and actions in the various functional areas of an organisation.

- **Project plans** are produced on a one-off basis in order to control specific programmes of work.

- **Long-term plans, policies or procedures** are used to establish guidelines for recurring activities.

These action plans can then be translated into detailed plans for individual employees or relatively small working units or teams. Corporate planning can mean that functional plans and policies become clear guidelines for individual action. In a sense, the working position can be seen as a series of projects each planned in order to control specific programmes of work and operating within policy guidelines. These project actions may be agreed by the self-managed team and the individuals within it, keeping within the policies established by corporate managers in order to achieve corporate objectives. For example, at its simplest the action plan of a salesperson may set out very clear actions and objectives in terms of the number of customers to be contacted, or the value of sales to be made in a particular period. The action plan may go further in establishing how the salesperson should function in terms of customer care, following up complaints and so on.

MONITORING AND REVIEW

The strategic planning process involves agreeing on a mission statement, deciding on corporate objectives, analysing markets and resources, auditing the internal and external environment, and arriving at an action plan. It is not, of course, a static process, and once the framework is in place and is working it needs to be reviewed in the light of any changes. Managers should review all aspects of the strategic plan at frequent intervals. At one extreme the action plan requires constant monitoring and adjustment, while at the other, the mission statement may need to be altered only rarely. This should reflect the fact that while the direction of the organisation should not be changing too frequently, the actions required to maintain that direction will entail frequent adjustment.

In reviewing the 'closeness of fit' between corporate actions and corporate direction and values alternative strategies may be considered. Managers look at existing strategies and can perform what is called 'gap analysis'. Here they simply attempt to determine whether a performance gap exists between what their existing strategy can realistically be expected to accomplish and the objectives that have been established. This can be in areas such as sales, productivity and profitability and also in areas such as staff training and development, customer care and in environmental issues. Where there is not a gap, then managers can assume that the current strategy is probably the appropriate one. Where serious gaps are found to exist, then managers will need to investigate these and look for alternative strategies. In extreme cases there may be a need for a significant change in the firm's strategic plan.

The monitoring and review process provides the loop back to all stages of corporate strategy and should provide a reminder that change and improvement are constant features of corporate life. The planning objective in general terms is an upward spiral of improved market information, better systems for competitor analysis, and more efficient and effective use of resources. In monitoring the strategic plan it can be matched against the corporate values and the guiding principles of the organisation. The review process can help to answer the question of how far the organisation's policies and actions coincide with and are supportive of its perceived values.

The values and guiding principles of an organisation are concerned with 'how it goes about its business'. As well as deciding what business it is in, what objectives it has and how it will achieve them, an organisation has to decide on its underlying values. These may be explicitly expressed (as in the case of the Ford Motor Company in Fig 5.3) or implied in the way in which business is conducted in an organisation. Usually this is expressed in terms of quality factors, customer care and employee development rather than in terms of corporate ethics, but social responsibility, equal opportunities and environmental issues may form an explicit part of the company 'philosophy'.

THE CORPORATE PORTFOLIO

Every organisation consists of at least one and usually many more products and services. Between them, these represent the 'business portfolio'. For example, in the case of automobile companies, there are different models of car and various services provided in relation to cars. With travel agents, their portfolio consists of a range of travel services which may include a number of different holidays. A company can be viewed as a 'portfolio' of business investments which managers must balance by expanding investment in some, while reducing investment in others. Decisions have to be made by managers on the investment of resources in the various areas of the portfolio and their contribution to the business in order to provide the company with a competitive advantage. Most companies like to have a balanced mix of business units which are at various points in their respective life cycles.

Growth-share matrix

One approach found to be useful in this process has been the Boston matrix (sometimes referred to as the Boston Consulting Group, or BCG, matrix or the growth-share matrix – *see* Chapter 4). The use of this for business units or product/service teams can help the corporation to define 'What business should we be in?', 'What is our basic mission?', 'How should we allocate corporate resources across the units and teams?' The matrix analyses businesses along two dimensions, business growth and market share. Business growth measures how rapidly the whole industry is increasing in size, while market share measures the share a business unit has of this market compared to competitors.

Once it has been decided what the growth rate is in a market and the particular product/service market share, it is possible to allocate each unit to one of four quadrants in the matrix (*see* Fig 5.6). The arrangement of business units that emerges within the matrix can provide managers with a means of establishing and describing corporate strategy. In terms of balance the desired grouping may be to have a number of units in each quadrant, because there would then be a number of products and services producing a cash flow, with others requiring an injection of cash to move them from being problems to stars and with other units on their way out. This means that units in the lower part of the matrix, the so-called 'cash cows'

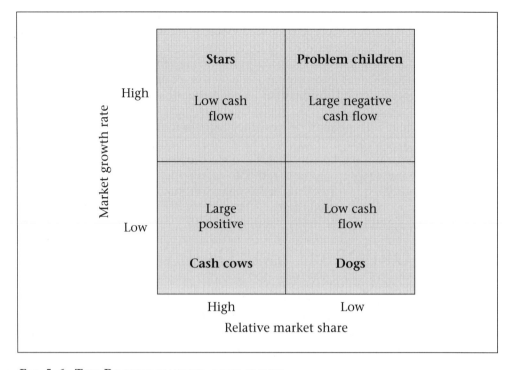

FIG 5.6 THE BOSTON MATRIX: CASH FLOWS

and 'dogs', could be used as a source of excess cash for investment in the 'problem children' (also referred to as 'question marks') and the 'stars' which represent the best opportunities for future growth and survival.

The allocation of individual business units to a particular position on the matrix helps managers to define strategic plans for the business with levels of activity consistent with corporate strategy. For example, 'cash cow' managers may be expected to produce relatively short-term profits, 'dog' managers may be expected to minimise expenditure and to reduce part of their operations to allow any available resources to be invested elsewhere, 'star' unit managers may be expected to increase market share with the help of investment in equipment and marketing, 'problem children' managers may be expected to review and evaluate the future potential of their business unit and to justify its continuation. It is, of course, crucial that a particular business unit is described accurately. For example, if a product or service has a low relative market share in a market with low growth, then it should be described as a 'dog' and therefore as a likely candidate for 'divestment' by the company so that its resources can be reinvested in another product or service.

The growth-share matrix approach has been criticised because of the difficulty of describing some products/services and business units sufficiently accurately. At the margin, the difference between a subject for 'divesting' and a 'problem child' with potential for growth and development into a 'star' may be very small. It may be based on an estimation of market growth and the potential for future growth. It can be argued that the approach oversimplifies the situation in many organisations and that the terminology used in the matrix encourages this oversimplification. It does, however, provide an excellent starting point for analysing the position of business units, and it would be an unwise corporation that did not use the portfolio approach in one way or another (*see* Fig 5.7). A range of variations on the Boston matrix have been developed, such as dividing the matrix into nine sections in order to define market share and market growth in more detail, but the basis of the process remains the same.

Gillette Company

Gillette has several cash cows in its corporate portfolio. The most famous is the shaving division, which accounts for two-thirds of the company's total profits and holds a large share of a stable market. This division sells Ultra, Trac II, the Sensor shaving system, Good News disposable and new Sensor razor for women. In 1992 the company captured major control of the largest major blade company in China and access to that nation's vast population pool. The Oral-B laboratories division is also a cash cow with its steady sales of toothbrushes and other dental hygiene products. The stationery products' division has star status. With a $560 million purchase of Parker Pen Holdings Limited, this division has become the world's largest marketer of writing instruments, which also includes Paper Mate, Flair, Erasemate, and Waterman, and it shows potential for rapid growth overseas. Gillette's question marks are in the personal care division. A line of women's toiletries aimed at the European market failed, and Gillette's success with other lines, for example, men's Right Guard deodorant and Foamy shaving cream – have enjoyed only cyclical success. A new line of men's toiletries featuring a gel-based deodorant and a gel shaving cream was recently launched. If this new line fails to generate sales and market share, it may be assigned to the dog category, to which the Cricket line of disposable lighters was relegated. The Bic disposable lighter dominated the Cricket line so completely that Cricket became a dog and was eventually put out of its misery through liquidation. Gillette continues to experiment with new products and question marks to ensure that its portfolio will include stars and cash cows in the future.

FIG 5.7 PORTFOLIO ANALYSIS

Source: Excerpt and Exhibit from *Management*, Third Edition, by Richard L Daft. Copyright © 1994 by The Dryden Press. Reprinted by permission of the publisher.

Life-cycle analysis

One of the frameworks used by managers in terms of portfolio strategy is life-cycle analysis. In this process business units' products/services are analysed and placed on a point against one of the four or five stages of the life cycle – introduction, growth, maturity (and saturation) and decline (*see* Fig 4.7). The typical situation is that managers are investing money in a product or service at the introductory stage, while expecting products at the mature stage to be cash cows and producing money for investment. Stars are likely to be seen in the growth stage, where the market is still growing and there is an expectation that the product will achieve an increased share of the market. Dogs will usually be in the decline stage, although they may be at another stage, such as introductory, but in fact be unsuccessful in terms of market share, or as a result of a lower than expected market growth.

Introductory stage strategies focus on confirming that market growth and market share do exist and that the product or service is meeting customer needs. At the same time, managers have to arrange for the financial support of the product at a time when investment significantly exceeds revenue. Growth stage strategy will focus on the size and potential of the market and opportunities to broaden the customer base. Managers need to strengthen the product/service's appeal by developing such areas as brand identification, distribution outlets and price. At the maturity stage, managers are faced with increasing competition and more resources may need to be invested in marketing, and searching for new sales opportunities. In the decline stage, managers will attempt either to monitor the business unit through a refocus of the customer base and cost cutting, or employ strategies to enable the organisation to move out of that particular product/service while retaining resources to reinvest elsewhere.

Competitive forces strategy

This strategy was developed in the 1980s by Michael Porter, a professor of economics and business strategy at Harvard Business School. He argued that five competitive forces exist in an organisation's environment (*see* Fig 5.8):

- Potential new entrants have more difficulty in setting up in a high capital-intensive industry (such as motor cars) than in a service industry (such as an estate agency). Capital requirements and the scale are both potential barriers to entry.

- The bargaining power of buyers increases as advertising and consumer information create a situation where customers know about the full range of price and product options available. This is especially true when a company sells mainly to a few customers, such as is the case where manufacturers are supplying one or two retailers.

- The bargaining power of suppliers depends on the availability of substitute suppliers. A sole supplier will have great power.

- The threat of substitute products is most powerful where there are alternatives and substitutes for a company's product. Changes in opinions about the environment, costs and so on may influence the demand for these products.

- Rivalry among competitors may appear in terms of advertising, price and product differentiation, such as appeared in the 'cola wars' between Pepsi-Cola and Coca-Cola.

Porter suggested that a company could find a competitive advantage against these competitive forces either through differentiation or cost leadership, or by combining policies focused on a particular strategic target. For example, the *differentiation strategy*

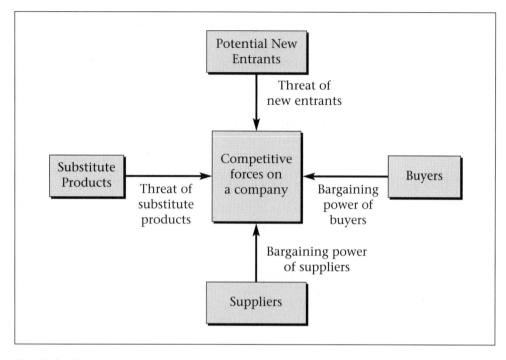

FIG 5.8 COMPETITIVE FORCES

Source: Adapted and reprinted with permission of The Free Press, a Division of Simon & Schuster from *Competitive Strategy: Techniques for Analyzing Industries and Competitors* by Michael E Porter. Copyright © 1980 by The Free Press.

involves an attempt to distinguish the company's products and services from others in the industry. Product differentiation may involve product branding, adding distinct features or providing extra services. If a product is felt by consumers to be different from its competitors they may be prepared to pay high prices. Chanel No. 5 perfume, Mercedes-Benz cars and Rolex watches are all examples of this approach.

A *cost leadership strategy* involves reducing costs in order to undercut competitors' prices while providing a similar quality product. Companies such as Tesco and Kwik-Fit have followed this policy, while the John Lewis stores chain claims not to be undercut on price. These companies are in a good position to withstand a price war: customers have difficulty in finding lower prices and buyers will have little scope for price negotiations with suppliers. The low price acts as a barrier against new entrants and substitute products. A *combined strategy* involves the company using a differentiation or low-cost approach concentrated on a narrow target market. For example some companies, such as Sun Alliance, have introduced low-cost insurance for the over-fifties.

Porter (1996) has argued (*see* the Case Study at the end of this chapter) that a sustainable strategic position requires trade-offs. Choosing a unique position is not enough to guarantee a sustainable advantage, because a valuable position will attract imitation either by matching the superior performance or by 'straddling'. The 'straddler' attempts to match the benefit of a successful position while maintaining its existing position, but a strategic position is not sustainable unless there are trade-offs with other positions. Trade-offs create the need for choice and a purposeful limitation on what a company offers. They deter straddling or repositioning because competitors that engage in these approaches undermine their strategies and degrade the value of their existing activities, and positions built on systems of activities are generally far more sustainable than those built on individual activities.

The managers' role is to create fit among a company's activities and to integrate them so that the company does many things well. This requires trade-offs in competing in order to achieve a sustainable advantage, so that managers have to decide what not to do as well as what to do.

STRATEGIC MANAGEMENT

In practice, many organisations apply a range of strategies depending on changes in circumstances. In order to remain competitive and survive managers need to be creative and innovative as well as using all the strategies available to them. Companies attempt to expand their markets by attracting new customers, and by moving into national or international markets. Organisations develop their products by adding features or modifying the design to remain ahead of the competition. This is a process adapted by car companies in updating their models by relatively small changes, adding features or producing special editions.

Organisations also use a number of other strategies in order to remain ahead of the competition. Vertical integration is a strategy with the aim of controlling channels of both supply and distribution. The company seeks to control its suppliers so that its supplies can be guaranteed at the lowest possible cost, and its distributors so that it is able to work closely with the final consumers. Horizontal integration is a strategy aimed at controlling competitors at the same level of production. A company may take over or merge with another company in order to acquire economies of scale, increased buying power and access to a wider range of consumers.

Diversification involves a strategy of spreading an organisation's activity beyond its main business. The main problem with this is that managers may find themselves working in areas where they do not have any expertise. Tom Peters has suggested that in fact managers should 'stick to the knitting', in the sense of diversifying only into areas where managers do have expertise. This needs to be an area to which they can transfer an already acquired skill. Manufacturers may move increasingly into a related service area in which they have already been working on a small scale. For example, motor companies have moved into car leasing and car hire services. Restructuring strategy can include a range of approaches designed to reorganise the company in order to meet new challenges. Periods of recession cause retrenchment and possibly liquidation when a company is sold for its tangible assets, not as a going concern. On the other hand 'retrenchment' and 're-engineering' are often approaches designed to concentrate on the main business of an organisation by 'outsourcing' or putting out to contract all those products or services which are not an essential part of the main business. Cleaning and catering services are among the most obvious of these, but others include car leasing, information technology and advertising.

Strategic management can be seen as a plan of action concerned with what an organisation should do in order to survive. Ralph Stacey (1993) has argued that the process is a highly complex one, involving, as it does, a whole range of networks and control systems within an organisation of any size, and given the many unpredictable elements with which managers have to contend. He suggests that 'one approach to strategy is based on the idea that successful organisations are pulled to an identified future point'. In this case the task of management is to maintain the status quo until the future point is reached. Stacey argues that this is an impossible approach in practice and if it is applied it will fail.

> *'To succeed managers must practice the other approach, the one based on the idea that successful organisations are driven from where they are now to a destination that they create and discover.'*

Hamel and Prahalad (1989) have questioned the idea of 'fit' and the view that successful organisations adapt to their environment. In their study of successful companies in the late 1980s (such as Honda, Komatsu and Canon) as against the less successful ones (General Motors, Caterpillar and Xerox), they found that a distinguishing factor was the different mental models of strategy guiding their respective actions. They observed that less successful companies followed the conventional approach to maintaining strategic fit, leading to a trimming of ambitions to those that could be met by available resources. Such companies were concerned mainly with product-market units rather than core competencies. Consistency was preserved through requiring conformity in behaviour and a focus on achieving financial objectives. On the other hand, the focus of successful companies was on leveraging resources, that is using what they had in new and innovative ways in order to reach new goals. The main concern of these companies was to use their resources in challenging and stretching ways to build up a number of core competencies. Consistency was maintained by all sharing a central strategic intent.

Hamel and Prahalad (1993) have supported the idea that organisational success arises from organisation-wide intention or strategic intent which is based on a challenging shared vision of the future leadership of the organisation. This is based on organisational learning, an obsession for winning, an understanding that competitive advantages are not inherently sustainable and that an organisation succeeds not by long-term planning but by achieving a broad, stretching and challenging intention to build core competencies. They argue that what distinguishes a small developing company from a larger developing one is not the smaller resource base, but the greater gap that exists between the resources base and the aspiration of the company. This gap they refer to as 'stretch', so that the problem of large, established companies is not a lack of resources but insufficient ambition, a lack of stretch in their aspirations. They suggest that companies such as NEC, CNN, Sony, Glaxo and Honda are more united by the unreasonableness of their ambitions and their creativity in obtaining the most from the least than from any cultural or institutional heritage. They suggest that creating stretch is the single most important task of senior management.

The strategic role of managers therefore is not so much to stake out the future of an organisation but to help to accelerate the acquisition of market and industry knowledge. Managers use the resources they have to create requirements of the environment which they can meet, they push to achieve stretching goals and they aim to continually renew and transform their organisation.

There is a sense of creative tension in strategic management because the development of a new direction and the concentration on stretch and leverage destroys the old certainties, and it is, therefore, at the forefront of the process of continuous change.

SUMMARY

■ Strategic management is concerned with looking ahead in order to establish the way forward for an organisation. This involves developing plans for strategic change.

■ The purpose of planning is to enable an organisation to achieve its objectives in a well organised and co-ordinated way. This is based on an effective understanding of customer needs and the integration of the marketing plan into the strategic plan in order to achieve the desired objectives.

■ Corporate strategy is the process by which the vision or mission of an organisation is converted into an action plan. The purpose of the action plan is to ensure that everybody in an organisation understands the objectives of the organisation, their responsibilities in relation to them, the achievement of stretch and leverage, and how to put these factors into action in order to achieve the desired results.

■ The action plan will include the formation of a corporate portfolio of products and services taking into account competitive forces. The whole process will need to be reviewed and monitored at regular intervals and then adjusted as necessary.

REVIEW AND DISCUSSION QUESTIONS

1 What is likely to be the result for an organisation of not developing a strategic plan?

2 Is the management of change an inevitable aspect of strategic management?

3 What processes can be used in developing a corporate plan from mission statement to action plan?

4 How important is competition as a factor in developing an organisation's corporate portfolio?

5 How should an organisation carry out the monitoring and review of its corporate strategy?

CASE STUDY: DARE TO BE DIFFERENT

If the theory of corporate strategy is a rising market, Michael Porter's stock has not quite kept pace. His reputation in the field, although immense, is based mainly on books published in the early 1980s. His best-known book, *The Competitive Advantage of Nations* (1990), is not primarily about corporations at all. But as professor of business administration at Harvard Business School, Porter is hardly out of touch. Nor, at 50, is he resting on his laurels. Much of his work lately has been on corporate strategy, and as he sees it, the discipline has taken some serious wrong turnings in the past decade. First, he says, the idea has grown up in some quarters that strategy is the same as operational efficiency. Companies need only employ modern techniques, such as total quality management or time-based competition, and the future will take care of itself. In reality, strategy and efficiency are fundamentally distinct. 'Operational improvement is doing the same thing better,' Porter says. Strategy, by contrast, involves choosing. 'Choice arises from doing things differently from the rival. And strategy is about trade-offs, where you decide to do this and not that.'

The essence of strategy, in fact, lies in deciding what not to do.

> 'That is the manifestation that you have a strategy. It also collides with many messages that managers have been assimilating for some time: be close to your customer, and be customer-responsive. Strategy is the deliberate choice not to respond to some customers, or choosing which customer needs you are going to respond to.'

At this point, Porter introduces the second part of his thesis. If strategy does not consist of operational improvement, neither does it consist of focusing on a few core competencies. Real sustainable advantage comes rather from the way the activities of a company fit together.

> 'Any individual thing that a company does can usually be imitated. The whole notion that you should rest your success on a few core competencies is an idea that invites destructive competition. Successful companies don't compete that way. They fit together the things they do in a way which is very hard to replicate. You have to match everything, or you've basically matched nothing.'

An example he gives is the car rental business.

> 'The companies your readers will be familiar with are Hertz and Avis, and National and Budget. Those will be seen as the "successful" companies because they have strong brand images, and people see them at the airport when they're travelling around. It turns out that none of those companies has been very profitable, ever. They are all locked into an operational effectiveness competition, offering the same kind of cars at the same kind of airports with the same kind of technology.'

Compare that with Enterprise, a family-run company. 'They do very little consumer advertising, and have no on-airport locations. Their whole strategy is to provide cars for people whose car is stuck in the repair shop, or who have wrecked their car and are waiting for a replacement.' Enterprise has a lot of smaller locations, and will often deliver the car to the customer. The cars are older and kept in the fleet longer. It hires more educated staff, who sell to car-service companies or insurance agents. 'They've chosen not just to try harder, like Avis, but to do almost everything differently. They've made clear trade-offs. They've walked away from the business travel market at airports, and from meeting a lot of needs that rental customers have,' says Porter.

For most companies, Porter argues, this kind of thinking presents immense problems. 'To put it simply, managers don't like to choose. There are tremendous organisational pressures towards imitation and matching what the competitor does. Over time, this slowly but surely undermines the uniqueness of the competitive position.' In part, he says, this comes from a

▶

curious notion which has grown up over the past decade: that there are no trade-offs any more. 'People have come to think that you can achieve low cost and the highest quality, or high service and the lowest cost. They confuse moving to the frontier with where you are on the frontier.' This is because when a company has been badly managed, it is often possible to improve quality and cost simultaneously. 'But once you get to good process designs, you have to make choices again. This notion that quality is free has caused many managers to believe not only that they don't have to make choices, but that they shouldn't.'

All this leads many companies to destroy their own strategies. 'They start out with a clear position, and over time they're drawn into a competitive convergence where they and their rivals are all basically doing the same thing. Those kind of competitions become stalemates.'

Porter used to believe, he says, that the hard thing about strategy was understanding the external environment.

'I've now become convinced an equally hard part is coping with the internal forces which work against making clear trade-offs and strategic choices. This has led me to a new interest in the role of leadership in strategy. Most often, it's to make the choices. Strategy can't be delegated. Nobody in the organisation will appreciate these trade-offs except the leader. Once a strategy has been established, most of what leaders do is essentially to say "no": to screen the constant barrage of ideas and opportunities against the strategy, and see if they fit.'

In some industries, he argues, the competitors are clones – companies so similar they cannot even conceive of a different way of competing. The task then is to decide whether the economics of the industry are such that there are no opportunities for trade-offs.

'That's usually the key question. What if I only did that; could I do it better? What if I chose this technology and not that, or this customer group and no others? If you can do terrifically well at X by giving up Y, that gives you the basis for a distinctive position. If there's basically only one dominant way of competing, then you're the hamster running around on the wheel. If you're in that kind of industry, you have to configure your organisation for that kind of world. You're just going to keep trying harder. I argue those industries are worth avoiding.'

Some would argue that in an era of global competition, all industries will come to look like that. Porter disagrees.

'I don't think we're moving towards a hyper-competitive world in which there are no trade-offs. We're probably moving in the other direction. There are more customer segments than ever before, more technological options, more distribution channels. That ought to create lots of opportunities for unique positions.'

Source: *Financial Times*, 19 June 1997. Reprinted with permission.

REFERENCES FOR FURTHER READING

Campbell, Andrew, Devine, Marion and Young, David (1990) *A Sense of Mission*, London: Hutchinson.

Daft, Richard L (1994) *Management*, Orlando, Florida, The Dryden Press.

Fayol, Henri (1949) *General and Industrial Management*, London: Pitman Publishing.

Foster, Timothy R V (1993) *101 Great Mission Statements*, London: Kogan Page.

George, C (1972) *The History of Management Thought*, London: Prentice-Hall.

Hamel, Gary and Prahalad, C K (1989) 'Do you really have a global strategy?', *Harvard Business Review*, July–August.

Hamel, Gary and Prahalad, C K (1993) 'Strategy as stretch and leverage', *Harvard Business Review*, March–April.

Jelinek, Mariann (1979) *Institutional Innovation*, New York: Praeger.

Marquanett, I A (1990) 'Corporate Planning Challenges', *Journal of Business Strategy*, June.

Mintzberg, Henry (1973) *The Nature of Managerial Work*, New York: Harper & Row.

Mintzberg, Henry (1994) *The Rise and Fall of Strategic Planning*, Hemel Hempstead: Prentice-Hall.

Pearce, John A and Robinson, Richard B Jr (1989) *Management*, New York: McGraw-Hill.

Peters, Tom (1992) *Liberation Management*, Basingstoke: Macmillan.

Porter, Michael E (1980) *Competitive Strategy: Techniques for Analysing Industries and Competition*, New York: Free Press.

Porter, Michael E (1996) 'What is strategy?', *Harvard Business Review*, November–December.

Stacey, Ralph D (1996) *Strategic Management and Organisational Dynamics*, London: Pitman Publishing.

THE IMPLEMENTATION OF STRATEGY

Tim Hannagan

OBJECTIVES

The objectives of this chapter are to:

◆ describe the actions managers take in order to implement corporate strategy

◆ analyse the processes of strategic planning to identify the functional role in achieving strategic objectives

◆ identify the barriers to planning and methods of overcoming these barriers

◆ consider the development of business plans and methods of forecasting future trends

◆ explain the importance of organisational development

FORMULATING A STRATEGIC PLAN

Modern managers are faced with a situation in which change is the only 'constant' on which they can 'rely'. One certainty in their lives is that things will not be the same in a year, three years or five years from now. The difficulty is to decide what these changes will be, and it can be argued that it is only by planning that the nature of the changes taking place can be fully charted and understood. In fact, managers take into account possible changes in deciding a course of action, in the form of contingency plans. This is part of the process of turning corporate strategic plans into detailed plans of action. While the strategic plan sets the expected, proposed and desired direction and the objectives to be achieved, this has to be translated into activity which can be implemented and controlled. Figure 6.1 illustrates the importance a company can put on the meeting of objectives, while behind this success lies detailed activity in meeting its 'tough objectives' to satisfy its 'customers, shareholders and employees'.

Automotive, Aerospace, Information, Innovation

Tomorrow is here: We used to say 'Tomorrow is Taking Shape at a Company called TRW'. While TRW has been helping to shape our world, we have also been working hard to streamline and strengthen our company.

We have set a course that aims to delight our three key constituent groups – customers, shareholders and employees – by providing each with superior performance. The facts demonstrated we are doing just that.

Several years ago, we set ourselves some tough objectives. We are meeting these objectives. Today, we are number one in our key markets. We are the world leader in occupant restraints, in steering systems, in certain automotive electronics markets, in advanced spacecraft technology, in defence communications and in consumer credit information, among others. We are also the world leader in complex systems integration.

Our businesses are in segments of industries that are outgrowing the markets themselves, and we are managing that growth for profit. Cost structures have been improved dramatically, and we are beginning to experience the benefits of our strategic investments over the past five years.

Further technology leadership, always a core TRW strength, is now helping to make us more competitive in all our businesses. Management is also stronger. Supporting a seasoned group of top managers, we have a highly qualified, energetic and experienced team around the globe.

What are our priorities? Delivering on our commitments to customers, shareholders and employees. We are positioned for sustainable, significant increases in both sales and earnings. We are doing what we say we will do, and we will continue to deliver our promises.

FIG 6.1 TRW INC OF CLEVELAND, OHIO

Source: TRW Annual Report, 1994.

Strategy has to be operationalised into small action plans to be carried out by employees so that taken together these actions should achieve the objectives established by the strategic plan. Much of this process is aimed at institutionalising the strategy so that it becomes part of the day-to-day work of the organisation; it has to become part of the culture of the organisation, 'the way we do things around here'. This process becomes overt and perhaps even obvious when an organisation is introducing major strategic change. For example, the British Airways customer service 'campaign' of the 1980s was designed to change the behaviour of its employees, so that in all their operations they put the customer first. This plan had the objective of creating major changes in behaviour. Many plans simply build on structures and accepted methods that already exist and are ingrained in the systems of the organisation.

One of the major changes in organisations in the 1990s has been the need for flexibility in the workforce, which means an ability to change as circumstances alter and not to expect that present working patterns will last for ever or even for very long. Technology has been a major factor in the pace of change and in the revolution in working methods and conditions for many people, and as a result of computerisation and information technology the working lives of many people have been completely altered. Managers often have difficulty in knowing how quickly these changes will take place and they may prove quicker or slower than expected. The demise of the manual and electric typewriter was predicted for many years until quite suddenly wordprocessors made a clean sweep in a matter of a year or two.

Where an organisation is on course in terms of its strategic plans, the manager's role may be to fine tune the situation by making relatively small decisions on a routine basis in response to problems that arise or in an attempt to improve a business unit's performance. Minor problems can be solved immediately by management intervention while ignoring the effect of the decisions being made on other parts of the organisation. In contrast to these small decisions and minor problems, serious problems may demand planned management interventions in more than one area of the organisation. Managers have to recognise the effect on the various parts of the organisation and arrange for appropriate actions to be taken to satisfy the various areas affected and to monitor progress on the strategic plan.

THE PLANNING PROCESS

Operational managers have to develop plans at the appropriate level in order to produce the actions required on a day-to-day basis to implement the strategic plan. Each functional area of the organisation will need a plan to guide its decisions and actions. If the strategic plan has the objective of growth in a particular market, then the sales and marketing division will have to decide how they are going to penetrate that market or expand in it if they are already present. This may involve market research into customer needs, pilot promotions to test customer response, and establishing outlets and channels of distribution. At the same time the production or service department will have to ensure that the product or service is adapted for the market and that suppliers will be available for the expected customer demand. The finance department will have to make sure that money is available to support an increase in output and increases in the marketing and sales expenditure. The personnel department will be involved in the appropriate recruitment of staff and the relocation of employees as necessary.

149

All the functional departmental plans have to be drawn together so that they operate smoothly in supporting each other. If the finance is not available at the right time or if the production department cannot meet sales orders, then all the functional plans and the overall strategic plan will have to be reviewed to avoid chaos. In large organisations the importance of this co-ordination is taken to the point of establishing a separate corporate planning unit whose role is to make sure that all the various plans do fit together and support each other both in operation and in time. Where there is not such a unit, corporate planning will usually be the responsibility of a senior manager.

It is in the operation of these functional plans that marketing has its integrating function in matching customer requirements to the product or service. The marketing department will be close to the point of sale and customer service on the one hand, and on the other hand close to the design and production department. In Fig 6.2 the strategic plan is translated into functional plans for marketing, sales, production, personnel and finance.

Other functional departments and divisions, such as sites and buildings, transport, purchasing and supplies, and administration will all need to have action plans which relate to the strategic plan and to the other functional plans. The sites and buildings department, for example, will need to discuss capital expenditure on new outlets for the company's products with the finance department. The finance

---

Strategic plan: growth in a new regional market

Functional plans:

Marketing: research into customer needs
establishing possible outlets
establishing channels of distribution
carrying out pilot studies

Sales: establishing contacts
preliminary advertising and sales promotion

Production: redesigning products as appropriate
organising expansion of production
arranging for increased supply of new materials
co-ordinating transport and distribution requirements

Personnel: recruiting new salespeople and administrators
relocating employees to the new regional staff

Finance: considering capital outlay
supporting investment in design and production
establishing cashflow plans
paying wages for staff in new region

FIG 6.2 FUNCTIONAL PLANS

department will be considering the financial control systems required by the new developments over purchasing and supplies, and any expansion in transport and distribution requirements.

Functional plans are usually developed to last for a relatively short period and they are then updated and possibly changed dramatically. However, they are designed over time. They can be distinguished in this way from project plans which are characterised by being designed for a one-off occasion which will not be repeated. This type of plan can be divided into programme plans and project plans, on the grounds that the programme plans are of greater complexity; however, it is often difficult to distinguish between these two types of activity. Whenever there is the need to plan for a one-off activity, whether it is to do with, say, health and safety training or building a new office block, it can be described as a project plan.

Project plans can be distinguished from functional plans in that they are established for a particular timeframe and they include more detail than is usually found in a functional plan. Once the plan has been implemented and the project is completed, the plans will be of little further use. Typical project plans are to build a new office block, design a one-off advertising campaign, or develop an employee sickness policy. Once the block is completed, the advertising campaign has taken place or the sickness policy has been established, these plans have achieved their objective and they are of little further direct use.

A plan to build a new office block will often be produced by a project team consisting of people seconded temporarily and on a part-time basis from the various functional departments. There will be representatives from sites and buildings, finance, personnel and administration. They will produce draft plans to be considered by senior management and from these they will produce a brief for the architects and surveyors to translate into the detail of drawings and specifications. They will produce a schedule of activities to be completed by certain dates and a flowchart to show the sequence of events that should lead to the completion of the project. All of this has to be set within the context of the capital funds available and also within the context of the company's strategic views on the appearance of the office and the way it should function (Fig 6.3). The retail company, Tesco, for example, build their stores to an established design both externally and internally, so that the project plans for the building of a new store have to include these designs whatever the shape or location of the site.

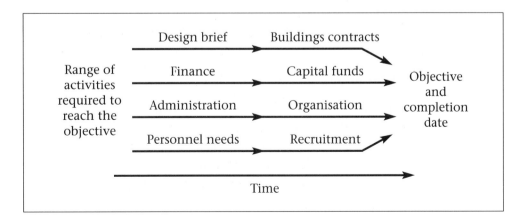

FIG 6.3 PROJECT PLANS: SIMPLE SCHEDULING AND FLOWCHARTS

151

Managers will also produce policies and procedures which establish the boundary lines for making recurring decisions. These policies provide a framework for action, a reference point for employees in their actions. Design policy in an organisation may influence plans, while plans concerned with factors such as employee training may become policies to be applied in all cases. For example, it may become company policy for all staff to receive training in customer care. Policies are created in order to meet the objectives of the organisation and should, with other plans, help in the implementation of the strategic plan.

BARRIERS TO PLANNING

Planning can be obstructed both by individuals establishing barriers to its success and as a result of the structure of the organisation.

Individual barriers

Managers may be more concerned with problem solving than planning and their focus is on day-to-day matters. This is more likely to be the case the closer managers are to the operations of an organisation, because their daily tasks involve an action-oriented approach, moving from one problem to the next. From their point of view, planning may be seen as an unnecessary luxury taking up valuable time which could be used to solve more problems and make more decisions. Individuals may also view planning as a threat in that it may 'put ideas into people's heads' by encouraging them to think ahead. Managers may feel that the process of planning raises the prospect of changing established methods and may raise more worries and concerns than it allays.

Planning also requires a commitment to specific objectives and results, which may be commitments managers are reluctant to make. This may be magnified by a lack of understanding about the purpose and process of planning by managers who have been promoted from the operational level without training in planning.

Organisational barriers

There may be little top management support for planning, or there may be support for strategic planning at senior management level but little support for this process being carried down to middle managers and the operational level. Even if there is support, the strategic plan may be too abstract or too statistical to be translated into operational terms. There is a danger that too much emphasis on planning will lead to very well-produced plans, expertly drafted but not in fact leading to implementation, so that operational activities ignore the plan and are based on the requirements of solving problems. Plans need to involve everybody concerned in both the process and in agreeing the objectives and the approach to implementation. Top management support is essential if middle management and operational teams are to allocate time and effort to planning and its implementation.

Environmental barriers

Complex and rapidly changing circumstances surrounding an organisation may discourage planning, because any plans will have to be hedged around with contingencies. Plans are produced provided that the economy remains stable, exchange rates do not change to any extent, supplies of new materials can be guaranteed, government policy does not drastically alter, and so on. Managers may feel that these factors, combined with increasing competition from rivals, make planning a useless activity and that they should concentrate on counteracting the threats and challenges the organisation faces. This is a 'passive' approach to the work of any organisation, allowing other rival organisations and events to dictate its activity. Against this approach, planning can be seen as a 'positive' and 'active' setting of unique objectives and directions for the organisation to follow and to be defended as far as possible from outside interference.

This is not to ignore the importance of external forces on an organisation. There is a danger of 'overplanning', that is spending too long on the planning process and sticking to plans that are no longer either viable or wise. Organisations at all levels require a sense of direction and require plans in order to keep up the momentum of moving in that direction, but they do not keep moving in a direction that proves to be a dead end (Fig 6.4).

Overcoming barriers to planning

Planning is part of every manager's role. Before managers can lead, organise or control a work situation, they must plan what needs to be done, when and how it needs to be done, and who will do it. Overcoming barriers to planning is an important part of this process.

Plans can:

- promote the uniform handling of similar issues;

- establish control over independent action by establishing clear policies;

- ensure quicker decisions by establishing a framework for decision making;

- offer a predetermined answer to routine problems;

- counteract further resistance to change once the plan has been agreed;

- avoid the making of hasty and ill-conceived decisions;

- establish a time horizon for monitoring progress on developments;

- establish long-term, medium-term and short-term patterns of activity.

FIG 6.4 EFFECTS OF PLANNING

153

TOP MANAGEMENT SUPPORT

Support is crucial to the success of planning. Senior managers must not only support plans but must be involved in them and be seen to be involved. Only then will middle managers and operational teams treat planning as a priority by allocating time to it.

The need for planning exists at all levels in an organisation, and this need is greatest at the top where it has the greatest potential impact on the organisation's success. Senior managers usually devote a majority of their time to planning and their skill in doing this and in making sure plans are implemented is how they earn their salaries. Even a small organisation needs to have a senior manager who plans, otherwise although day-to-day problems may be solved effectively events will catch up on the organisation for which it is not prepared.

Many barriers to planning can be overcome by senior manager support and any organisation which does not have this support is facing great difficulty. The solution to this is through management training, as managers are promoted through the organisation, in order to provide time to consider the role and guidance on it.

ALLOCATION OF RESPONSIBILITY

This is an essential element of the planning process. Someone has to be responsible for the successful completion of the plan, otherwise it will not be anybody's top priority to achieve it. The chief executive of an organisation will be responsible for the success of the strategic plan and the success or failure of the organisation, while other managers, at the appropriate level, need to be identified as responsible for specific plans designed to meet the overall objectives. Reporting and appraisal systems, management by objectives and other organisation and control systems are all designed to support this process.

CONSULTATION AND COMMUNICATION

Procedures in this area help to reduce barriers to planning by involving a wide range of people in the process. If managers and other employees have been consulted in the development of plans they will feel some responsibility for their success and 'ownership' of their implementation. At the least people in an organisation need to be able to obtain and understand information relevant to planning and any plan with which they are concerned.

TRAINING AND DEVELOPMENT

Training in planning skills and the implementation of the details of corporate plans encourage people to plan and use plans effectively. Individual barriers can be lowered by this process, particularly those associated with a lack of confidence in planning, fear of failure, and unwillingness to relinquish established systems.

SELF-MANAGED TEAMS

This form of organisational structure encourages planning at the operational level. Managers and teams can feel committed to plans they have produced themselves or have helped to shape. Teams will often be able to contribute to wider plans so that a two-way process can be developed, with strategic plans coming downwards and more detailed plans for implementation arising from the expertise and information of the self-managed teams. Their proximity to the organisation's customers and clients means that they are a valuable source of information in the development of a strategic plan, in monitoring it and in making adjustments to it.

REWARD AND ENCOURAGEMENT

Encouragement for individuals and teams can be attached to the outcome of plans. This may be by a system of managing by objectives or by a performance-related pay structure where individual and team rewards are linked to the accomplishment of objectives established in the planning process. These systems will increase the attention paid to planning and the commitment to it. Many reward systems have been organised more or less formally in this way, with a bonus, productivity pay or performance-related pay system attached to meeting planned objectives (*see* Chapters 8 and 12).

CONTINGENCY PLANNING

This consists of preparing an alternative course of action in case the preferred course either becomes impossible or no longer desirable. Contingency planning has become of increased importance as change and innovation have become a usual part of many organisations' environment. These plans provide a 'safety-valve' for individuals or groups of people who have doubts about the ability of plans to 'work'. They may be more prepared to try the plan when they see that there are alternative planned courses of action available.

The so-called 'worst-case' scenario is an extreme example of this process and can be based on taking 'what ifs' to their logical conclusion. For example, posing the question 'What if competitors reduce their prices significantly?' may lead to careful consideration of how costs could be contained, how long the organisation could sustain a price war, the importance of producing a quality product so that the price war could be ignored, and other possible courses of action. This approach can help to emphasise the importance of producing plans which are realistic and which clearly help to provide a competitive edge.

BUSINESS PLANS

As well as planning being 'a good idea' essential for the development of an organisation and for judging its progress, it is also a necessity in many circumstances, essential in order that an organisation can obtain financial support. In this more narrow sense, 'business plans' have developed over many years as a major component of investment decisions. A company seeking a loan or investment will be required by potential customers to produce a business plan in support of its application. This will be used to convince outsiders that managers have carefully thought out the direction the business will follow in the future, that given their present resources, and the proposed new investment, the company will be able to achieve its plans. Business plans may also be required in large organisations before a business unit can convince the 'parent' organisation to invest in it.

Many small organisations will have little more than a business plan with which to convince the bank manager that the banks should lend them enough money to start up or expand their business. The plan has to enable the bank manager or other investor to assess the degree of risk and the quality of the people involved. This plan can convert a 'bright idea' into a well-structured plan of action. A business plan can be seen simply as a more focused form of corporate plan:

> *'A Business Plan is a written statement setting out how the organisation making it intends to organise itself to satisfy the demands of its clients and thereby develop its business.'*
>
> (*Business Plans: A Move in the Right Direction*, Chartered Institute of Public Finance and Accountancy, 1992)

As well as a mission or vision, a statement of objectives and a clear view of strengths and weaknesses, opportunities and threats, a business plan must convince prospective investors that the planners have considered exactly who their customers are and what finance and resources are required in order to implement the plan. Customer needs can be ascertained by interviews and surveys which can determine the type of product or service they want and their views on the products or services available. This involves the production of qualitative information on customer views, expectations and perceptions, as much as quantitative information on how many customers buy a product or use a service. In terms of financial and resource planning, there will need to be an attempt to forecast the future budget and trading position and an analysis of the effects of inflation, taxation and other factors. This includes a risk analysis to consider how 'risky' the assumptions are that have been made in the plan, and a sensitivity analysis assessing how sensitive the plan is to change. This process involves the 'what if' approach – what if the assumptions prove wrong, or the environment changes – and will also need to assess how great will be the impact of the 'what if' factors on the plan.

A new business may assume a growth in sales of 20 per cent a year, based on their customer surveys, pilot sales schemes and the general growth of the market. What happens if the sales grow by only 10 per cent a year? Can the company survive on this or not? Similar questions can be asked about assumptions made on labour costs, raw material prices, changes in taxation, market growth rate, competitor activities and so on. While the usual barriers to planning exist with business plans, the fact that they are necessary in order to receive financial support removes

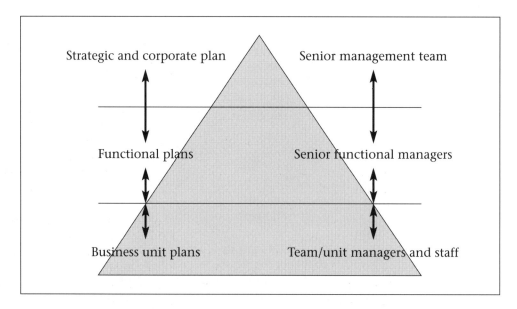

FIG 6.5 PLANNING LEVELS IN LARGE ORGANISATIONS

the most obvious obstacles in terms of the purpose of planning. In large organisations there will be a number of planning levels (Fig 6.5), with each unit, cost centre or self-managed team producing its own business plan, both to convince senior managers of their viability and also to help inform functional and corporate planning. In small organisations, the business plan may serve similar functions to the corporate and strategic plans of a large organisation.

PLANNING TECHNIQUES

Forecasting

All plans involve forecasting because, like planning, this is an attempt to predict what will happen in the future. The fact that forecasts are sometimes proved wrong does not mean that they are useless. Perhaps the most obvious and notorious use of forecasting is weather forecasting. In the UK people may plan to have a barbecue at the weekend because dry, warm weather is forecast, but they will have as a contingency plan the possibility of moving the barbecue inside if necessary. If it does rain on the night, this does not prove the uselessness of listening to weather forecasts, simply that not too much reliance should be put on them in a country with a volatile weather system. If the forecast had been for continuous heavy rain, it would have been unwise to plan for a barbecue in the first place.

In fact, most daily actions are based on some type of forecast which needs to be sufficiently accurate, sufficiently often to guide present actions in a valid and purposeful way. While not too much reliance is placed on weather forecasts in the UK, in countries with a more stable weather structure considerable reliance can be placed on forecasts. In fact, the most important use of forecasts is in order to arrive at the basic assumptions or premises on which the plan is based. The reliance that can be placed on any particular forecast is a matter of managerial judgement, and this is an area where a manager's experience can play an important part in business success. Forecasting is used, for example, in estimating market trends and then making business decisions based on them. A simple example is that if industrial and consumer surveys show that the market will grow in the next year, how does the organisation take advantage of this?

Forecasting is often based on *quantitative* data, for example that the market for packaged holidays will be 10 million holidaymakers next year. A common development of such data is to look at growth trends by taking past data and extrapolating it into the future. Not only can the general growth of packaged holidays be charted in this way, but also the growth or decline in the popularity of particular holiday destinations and the relative changes in different types of market, such as the family market and the singles market.

The extrapolating of past data is always open to variation and change as a result of altered circumstances and events. Where established data is not available or is unreliable, *qualitative* forecasting may be appropriate. This involves surveys, questionnaires and interviews asking for people's opinions and making judgements on the basis of the available information. Rating scales of various types can be used, for example asking consumers to note their views on a service on a scale between one and ten. Qualitative techniques are often used with new products because sales figures are unavailable and therefore potential consumers' opinions are particularly relevant. For example, once there are sales figures about the most popular colours for a product, marketing can be based on them, but with a new product a consumer survey can be used asking potential customers to note colours in order of preference. Other qualitative forecasting techniques include the so-called Delphi technique, where panels of experts are asked their opinions on a new product and the average of these groups of opinions are then used as a base for arriving at a judgement of the future of the product. Salesforce estimates are used by some organisations to predict the likely sales in each sales area and then to aggregate these for overall product forecasts. These and similar techniques all have the disadvantage of relying on subjective views, but they are usually very much better than not doing anything.

Quantitative techniques

These are statistical techniques which are usually considered to provide more reliable information on future trends than can be arrived at by subjective methods. Many statistics are already available to most organisations in terms of sales, turnover, marketing expenditure and so on. These can be analysed to produce ratios and trends which are very useful for planning.

Time-series analysis involves charting a variable, such as sales, over a period. The assumption is that the analysis of the past is a good predictor of the future. For example, if sales figures have risen over a series of months, then it may be assumed that this growth will continue. Trends such as seasonal variation in sales and the rate of growth can be analysed in order to plan production and marketing as well as cash flow for the company (Fig 6.6).

Figure 6.6 shows a 5-year moving average of sales against the annual sales figure. The moving average shows a trend of rising sales over a 10-year period with regular fluctuations between the troughs and peaks of sales occurring approximately every

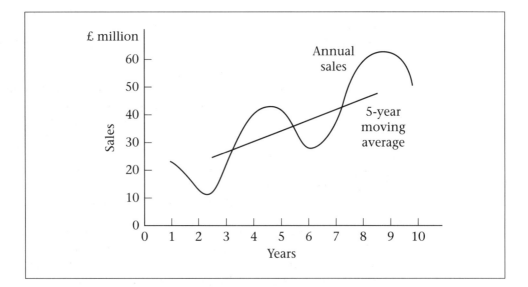

FIG 6.6 MOVING AVERAGE

three years. At the end of the 10-year period sales are beginning to fall again, and past trends would suggest that they will fall for a year or so before beginning to rise again. Past trends also suggest that the troughs will not be as deep as in years 2 and 6. In this extrapolation of the information, managers have to be very careful that they allow for the possibility that past trends will not be a good guide to the future, and do not become complacent in expecting these trends to occur in spite of any action they might take. In practice, managers need to try to prevent the downturn in years 9 and 10 and start to plan for this during the years of growth. For example, it may be possible to develop new products or to penetrate new markets in order to prevent what may appear to be an 'inevitable' fall in sales. A less optimistic strategy would be to prepare for the 'inevitable', by, for example, cutting costs so that the organisation could weather the period of relatively low sales and wait for the next period of growth.

Correlation and regression modelling may be used to consider the effects of different variables on each other. For example, organisations want to know the results of a marketing campaign on sales. Regression analysis is designed to estimate one variable (such as the sales volume) on the basis of one or more other variables (such as marketing expenditure) which are assumed to have some causal link with it. Correlation analysis compares two variables which are assumed to have an association with each other, so that a change in one will affect a change in the other. For example, an increase in advertising may be assumed to increase sales. While correlation shows whether there is an association between the two variables, the strength of this association and its direction, regression indicates the rate of change in one variable against the other. Between them it is possible to estimate, for example, whether increases in expenditure on advertising increase or decrease sales (i.e. the direction of association), as well as an indication of the amount of change in sales caused by a particular increase in advertising expenditure.

Linear trends can be shown by a straight line if there is in fact a linear relationship between the variables. A 'line of best fit' can be calculated, which is the line closest to the two variables. A simple method for producing this is illustrated in Fig 6.7, while more complex methods include regression lines which aim to minimise the total divergence of the variables' co-ordinates from the line. This is an objective mathematical approach rather than the more subjective approach used in the scatter diagram in Fig 6.7.

The scatter diagram is a simple matter of plotting sales revenue against advertising expenditure over a period of time and then drawing a straight line as close to the co-ordinates as possible. In Fig 6.7 there appears to be a positive correlation between sales and advertising, so that sales revenue rises as advertising expenditure rises and the relationship can be described as 'linear'. It is important to note, however, that correlation does not prove causality. In other words, the increased advertising expenditure may not have caused rising sales and vice versa. There may be a third ingredient which was of equal influence, such as a sudden growth in the market. The fact that there is a linear association between such variables does, however, provide a useful starting point for further investigation.

Linear programming is a more advanced statistical process used to determine the best combination of those resources and activities that are necessary to optimise an objective. For example, if the objective is to reduce costs, then the constraints in doing this have to be identified. These may be resources, capacity or the time available to accomplish the objective. Both the costs and the items that represent

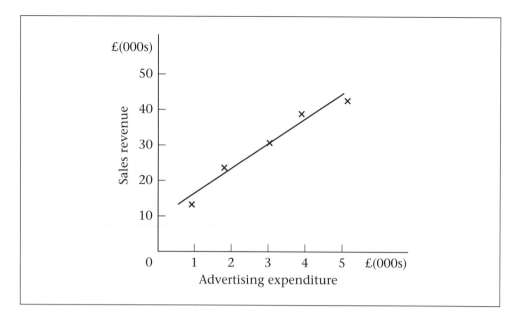

FIG 6.7 LINE OF BEST FIT

constraints then need to be expressed in linear terms either algebraically or in a graphical form, in order to provide a means for the manager to reach a 'solution'. The manager in this case will usually be the operations manager (*see* Chapter 14).

Scheduling techniques are designed to assist in the process of co-ordinating the activities of people and business units and the use of resources in order to achieve the completion of a specific task. For example, in the introduction of a new product the marketing manager needs to know exactly what customers want and the production manager needs to translate these demands into a design or a product. A schedule of a logical sequence of actions, and the co-ordination of people and resources are required to start the production of a successful product. A range of computer models are available as techniques to assist in the successful flow of activity to reach the desired aim. Operations management has developed into an important part of any large organisation's functions.

The basis of scheduling techniques is the ability to plan activities to achieve a desired end and to reveal discrepancies between planned and actual achievement as the project progresses. If a gap appears between planned progress and actual achievement, then managers can provide extra people and resources to fill this gap. Gantt charts have been used for many years as a means of control, with time charted on the horizontal axis and actions and tasks on the vertical axis (*see* Fig 6.8). Horizontal bars represent planned schedules and the time required for each task. In Fig 6.8 the filled bars show the actual progress against the outline bar which shows the time allotted. The use of colour coding can add to the complexity and the visual impact of such charts.

PERT (program evaluation review technique) is a long standing technique which helps managers schedule large-scale projects. It enables managers to create an accurate estimate of the time required to complete a project. All the activities necessary for completion are identified, with the events that indicate completion and the

Tasks	Time											
	J	F	M	A	M	J	J	A	S	O	N	D
Customer survey		▓	▓									
Design				▓	▓							
Setting up production line						▓						
Production staff							▓					
Raw materials								▓				

FIG 6.8 GANTT CHART

time required for each activity. This information is used to create a network diagram, which displays all the activities, events and times that are involved from the start to the end of the project. The PERT diagram is then used as a control and monitoring device. For example, in the building of a new office block, managers need to identify all the actions necessary to complete the project and construct a diagram to show the relationship between the different activities and events. A time is allocated for the completion of each activity and the sequence of activities is then tracked through to the completion of the project. Critical path analysis (CPA) is then applied to track the sequence of events which have to occur in a particular order, within a given time for the completion of the project on the due date. In the case of a new office block, the concept and design will be the first stage, along with the identification of finance and planning provision. Only when these factors have been identified and agreed can the building process actually start (*see* Fig 6.9).

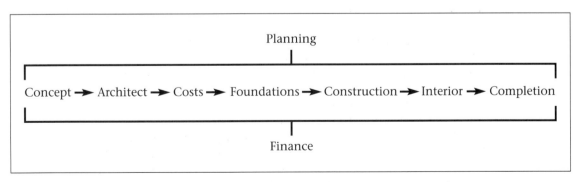

FIG 6.9 PERT

The critical path represents the least amount of time that a project can take from start to finish. This will be determined by such matters as the length of time required to obtain planning consent, the time required to lay foundations and so on. If an event on the critical path is delayed this will hold up the entire project. Both PERT and CPA are designed to save time and therefore save costs. They are based on actual time constraints as well as judgements about how long it takes to lay the foundations for a new office block, for example. They form the basis of a range of computer modelling techniques designed to assist managers in the planning process.

ORGANISATIONAL DEVELOPMENT

Managing an organisation's strategy is easier when it is consistent with the organisation's culture, that is the shared values, beliefs and attitudes that shape the behaviour of each member of the organisation (*see* Chapter 9). The priorities and attitudes of the strategy and culture need to coincide, and if this is not the case it becomes very difficult to implement the strategic plan. For example, where public sector organisations have been privatised, one of the main problems they have met is the market culture with which they are faced and the service culture to which the employees and consumers are accustomed. In these circumstances, managers have to seek to change the organisation's culture. This is a slow process because it does involve attitudes and 'how we do things around here'. British Airways did this in the 1980s with their 'Putting People First' programme.

Both the move to privatise UK public sector organisations and the effects of recession in the 1980s and 1990s have led to considerable discontinuities between strategy and culture in many areas. The old, cautious, traditional culture, based on 'jobs for life' and an established approach to clients and customers, has had to be replaced by a more aggressive competitive culture that promotes risk taking. Examples include British Airways, gas and electricity companies and hospital trusts in the public sector, and companies such as IBM in the private sector. In the 1990s IBM had to change their culture of a 'job for life' based on a strong organisational cultural identity, to a less certain job situation for employees and a more aggressive approach to meet competition.

In order to bring organisational strategy and culture closer together, managers responsible for the change process will have to concentrate on people and their attitudes, perceptions, behaviour and expectations. Organisational development (OD) is the skilled application of behavioural science to bringing about organisational change through people. It is a planned change, usually of the whole organisation, supported by senior managers. In large organisations it is an ongoing process which may be implemented through an OD manager and an OD department designed to improve internal relationships and to improve problem solving and with the ability to deal with environmental changes.

Organisational development can help managers to address a range of organisational problems. The most obvious of these are when two companies merge or one company is the subject of a takeover by another. In the process of merging the two companies, managers may concentrate on how well the products will fit together, or the marketing and management information systems, but fail to consider how closely they fit in terms of values, beliefs and practices. They may have quite different ways of 'doing things around here' which can greatly affect performance if it creates internal tensions. At the time of mergers and acquisitions managers may focus on finance rather than cultural differences, while in order to be sure of a smooth transition and integration, organisational development techniques need to be applied.

Another obvious source of potential behavioural problems in organisations is during a period of recession and decline. If the performance of the organisation leads to redundancies and reorganisation, tensions can develop which produce a lack of trust and also stress. The same may be true during a period of rapid change when people are asked to work in different ways or to increase their productivity. Although the strategy may be clear, its implementation may be held up by conflicts created by the speed of change. In fact conflicts may be a managerial problem at any time within a successful organisation. For example, there may be a conflict between the product designers and the marketing team, both perhaps believing that they know what the customer wants.

There are a range of activities which can be used in organisational development to help to solve the problem:

- **Training** is the most frequently used technique to bring about change. In the British Airways case, the whole organisation was involved because this was an attempt to change behaviour and not simply skills.

- **Team building** can enhance the cohesiveness of both units and the whole organisation. For example, cross-organisational teams can help employees from different departments and units to understand each other's problems and to co-operate with each other.

- **Communication** can be improved between various parts of the organisation and regarding strategic plans and their implementation. Understanding the reasons for changes in working practices and values can help employees come to terms with the changes. Consultation about the changes and their implementation can help both managers and other employees to understand and acquire ownership of the changes, particularly when they are as deep rooted as values and practices.

- **Survey–Feedback–Action** (SFA) techniques can be applied in order to encourage consultation and feedback. A questionnaire can be distributed to employees on such matters as working practices, values and organisation culture. After the survey is completed, an OD consultant can meet with groups of employees to provide feedback about their responses and the problems that have been identified, and to discuss the way forward. For example, British Airways used the slogan 'The World's Favourite Airline' to show the standards to which they aspired.

The process of achieving behavioural and attitudinal change involves unfreezing the situation, changing it and then refreezing it into the new mould (*see* Chapter 1). The unfreezing process requires a high level of communication and consultation in order to convince people that the changes are necessary. The immediate reaction of many people will be 'How does this affect me?' The so-called SARAH process will come into effect, with shock at the changes being proposed and anger at the apparent rejection of the present, well-tried and apparently successful working practices (Fig 6.10).

163

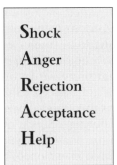

Fig 6.10 The change process

'Why do we need to change?' 'What is wrong with the present system?' 'Why are THEY proposing these changes?' These are the kind of questions produced by shock and anger. This period of change is often associated with a diagnosis of the present situation and why a new one needs to be developed. A 'change agent' can be involved at this stage, which may be an OD specialist who performs a systematic diagnosis of the organisation and identifies work-related problems. The role of the specialist is to gather and analyse information through personal interviews, questionnaires and by observing meetings. The diagnosis helps to determine the extent of organisational problems and helps managers to unfreeze by making them aware of problems in their behaviour. The 'change agent' may be an outsider who comes in as a consultant, or the OD unit within an organisation can perform this task.

As an ongoing process the survey–feedback–action technique can be used for 'upward feedback' by which managers assess the senior manager to whom they report. The managers complete a questionnaire and the overall results are then discussed by the OD specialist with the senior manager. A meeting is chaired by the OD specialist with the senior manager and the reporting managers in order for them to express their views about their boss. This process can produce surprises for senior managers about how they are viewed by the people who work directly for them. This process of 'reverse appraisal' can be applied throughout the organisation, starting at the top and working down to self-managed teams. In today's fast-changing work environment, managers need to update their diagnosis of the situation on a continuous basis, rather than only when 'major change' is taking place. It does, of course, have particular importance at sensitive times, such as when mergers, contraction or, for that matter, rapid expansion is taking place.

The changing stage occurs when people begin to experiment with new behaviour and learn new skills in the workforce. This process is assisted by the intervention of OD specialists and others, with specific plans for training and development of managers and employees. Training programmes will emphasise the new values and approaches, such as customer first programmes, quality developments and 'investors in people'. Team building is encouraged, consultation on work practices and symbolic leadership activities introduced. The rejection of change may be particularly vehement at the beginning of this stage, followed later by acceptance. Gradually, the people who have most strongly rejected the changes may be the ones who most wholeheartedly come to accept them.

The refreezing stage occurs when individuals acquire new attitudes, values and behaviours and are rewarded for them by the organisation. The OD specialist will provide help for everybody to change and an increasing number of people will look for help to adjust to the new values and approaches. The impact of new behaviours will be evaluated and reinforced. The reinforcement will be through training programmes, team meetings and the reward system.

The organisational development process suggests techniques which managers should apply continuously in organisations so that change is the accepted 'norm' rather than an occasional and rare phenomenon. In this sense, the use of terms such as unfreezing and refreezing suggests an end to the process before it starts again. In the altering of attitudes and behaviours it can be argued that in fact this is what often happens. While strategic change can be incremental, a step at a time, it is not always like this. The theory is that managers sense the changes required in the environment in which their organisations are working and gradually adapt to these changes through adjustment to the strategic plan and its implementation.

However, studies in the 1980s have suggested that managers resist change until a crisis occurs:

> *'Here managers resist changes that conflict with their predominant way of understanding their organisation and its environment, until some crisis makes it impossible to continue to do so.'* (Stacey, 1996)

This leads to strategic drift (Fig 6.11), because the organisation is carried forward by its own momentum, becoming more and more out of line with its environment. When this gap becomes too great, the organisation makes sudden adjustments.

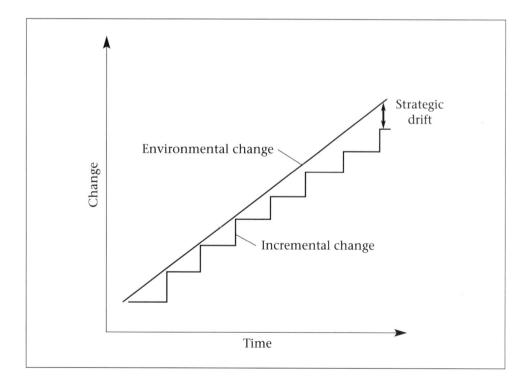

FIG 6.11 STRATEGIC DRIFT

Greiner (1972) has argued that strategic drift is virtually endemic in organisations in that they pass through a number of stages in order to sustain acceptable levels of performance. At each level they have to introduce major changes to the 'way they do things':

- **Growth through creativity** – the organisation grows through the creativity of a small group of people who manage in a highly personal style.

- **Growth through direction** – the organisation reaches a stage where it has to develop professional, functional management. This is often centrally directed and can develop into a restrictive hierarchy.

- **Growth through delegation** – delegation and decentralisation help to resolve the crisis of a rigid hierarchy, but may create divisions within the organisation.

- **Growth through co-ordination** – systems may be introduced to encourage co-ordination and co-operation, but this may produce a crisis of bureaucracy.

- **Growth through collaboration** – cultural change produces collaboration which is supported by teamwork.

Organisations may of course become stuck at one of these stages and not change their plans to grow further. The inability to change may stunt growth, and the processes of corporate planning and organisational development are essential to assist this process through encouraging consultation, communication, training and the constant re-evaluation of strategic planning.

ANNUAL OBJECTIVES

Central to the implementation of the strategic plan is the setting of annual objectives. They are important because they establish precisely what must be accomplished each year in order to achieve an organisation's plan. In the process they establish the targets and objectives for managers, units and teams throughout the organisation. The annual objectives help to clarify managers' tasks and their role in the process of achieving the strategy and plans, and they can provide a sense of purpose and motivation. They also provide a means of monitoring performance, and to do this they should be measurable.

The development of annual objectives can reflect shifts in the strategic plan and can provide for incremental growth. If an organisation is skilled in corporate planning and organisational development, it can perhaps avoid a 'crisis' change with dramatic alterations in direction or values. However, if external factors outside the control of the organisation alter dramatically, then it is difficult to avoid quite fundamental shifts in the corporate plan. The annual objectives can reflect this shift of position.

For example, government policy on the funding and governance of public sector institutions during the 1980s and 1990s has caused major changes in these institutions' ways of doing things and approach to the future. UK government policy encouraged the rapid expansion of higher education in the early years of the 1990s and then suddenly cut back on this expansion in 1994. In the same way, further education was encouraged to expand by 25 per cent in the period 1993–6 through the funding mechanism. Furthermore, the recession of the late 1980s and early 1990s caused private sector companies to re-evaluate their structures and organisation. Outsourcing of many services became common and there was a major shift to a group of core workers responsible for the core business of the company.

MANAGEMENT BY OBJECTIVES (MBO)

In order to implement annual objectives, managers have to develop a process to carry them through business units and to individuals. Management by objectives (MBO) was first proposed by Peter Drucker in *The Practice of Management* in 1955, and was very popular as a method of implementing strategic objectives in the 1960s and 1970s. Although it has fallen out of fashion as a system, many present-day methods are very similar to MBO in their approach and results.

MBO describes a set of procedures that begins with objective setting and continues through performance review. Each person's major areas of responsibility are clearly defined in terms of measurable results, so that they can be used by the employee in planning their work and by both employees and managers in monitoring progress. Performance reviews are conducted jointly over time and fresh objectives are established at appropriate intervals. The objectives identify the individual actions needed to fulfil the organisation's or business unit's strategy and annual objectives. Through this process, MBO provides a method of integrating and focusing the work of all the members of an organisation on the strategic plan.

While this process involves objective setting by managers in line with the corporate objectives, Drucker emphasised from the start the importance of participation by all employees. He supported the ideas and principles of Douglas McGregor's 'Theory Y' and felt that unless people were actually involved in their own objective setting, they could be half-hearted about the process. In more recent terminology, they need to feel 'ownership' of the objectives and the plans to meet them. This is of particular importance because of the autonomy usually provided in implementing plans. While it may be difficult to provide this autonomy for everybody in an organisation, managers, supervisors and team leaders are usually able to decide on the actions they need to carry out to achieve their objectives and those of the members of their team.

The essential elements of MBO have been carried forward into a range of company- and institution-based schemes of appraisal and performance, review and evaluation, which have been developed under a variety of names to match particular organisational needs. The development of increasing autonomy in business units and self-managed teams encouraged the setting of objectives at these levels, with a feedback mechanism within the unit and team as well as on an organisation-wide basis. The advantages are seen in terms of improvements on past performance, particularly when individuals determine their own objectives and when there is feedback on performance.

In the 1980s and 1990s the process of relating performance against objectives to the reward system has been extended through performance-related pay. However these systems have developed, the fundamental elements of MBO remain the focus on individual objectives and the feedback on their achievement. This focus has been considered to be a major motivator for many people in knowing what is expected of them and in their positive feeling of success when objectives are met. The participation of individuals in the process is essential in ensuring that the objectives which are established are realistic.

SUMMARY

■ Once an organisation has decided on a strategy, the managers have then to decide how to implement it. Overall action plans have to be operationalised into smaller plans and tasks for employees to carry out. The role of management is to make relatively small decisions in order to fine tune the situation to achieve the organisation's objectives.

■ The planning process includes the development of plans at appropriate levels to produce the actions required to implement the strategic plan. The plans and actions of functional departments need to be drawn together so that the organisation operates smoothly. Marketing is the integrating function in matching customer requirements to the final product or service.

■ There are individual, organisational and environmental barriers to planning which experienced management can overcome. Business plans establish how organisations intend to organise themselves to satisfy the demands of customers. This process is supported by forecasting techniques, both qualitative and quantitative.

■ Organisational development can help managers to deal with changes through staff training and development, team building and internal communication. If managers resist change or attempt to avoid implementing it, strategic drift can occur.

■ Strategic objectives can be implemented by processes such as management by objectives and performance-related pay. These systems focus on individual objectives and feedback on their achievement.

REVIEW AND DISCUSSION QUESTIONS

1   What are the main problems of implementing an organisation's strategic plan?

2   How are an organisation's plans translated into detailed actions?

3   When is it appropriate to establish a project team? How will its operation differ from a more functional approach?

4   Outline the main barriers to planning. How can managers overcome these barriers?

5   What techniques are used in the development of business plans?

6   How important are performance measures in attaining an organisation's strategic objectives?

CASE STUDY: KNOW YOUR PLACE

Standard Life and National Westminster are two businesses in the news. Each are organisations with a great past behind them. Each of them has a name which commands envy and respect. Each of them has well-publicised problems. And, although the businesses and problems are very different, there is an important sense in which the issues they face are the same.

The banks which were central to the British economy in the twentieth century are products of the nineteenth century. They came into existence in order to mobilise the small savings of individuals and lend them on to growing companies. Their effectiveness rested on the local knowledge of their managers. These managers were traditionally key figures in the local community. Their local knowledge gave confidence to depositors and allowed shrewd and informed assessments of the viability of the businesses the banks supported. There were some advantages to scale in banking. National coverage gave depositors confidence in the stability of the institutions which they trusted with their savings. An institution with branches from Carlisle to Camborne seemed likely still to be there when savers wanted their money back. The marble banking halls and grandiose head offices reinforced the sense of permanence.

And bigger banks were needed to handle bigger borrowers. By the 1920s the number of leading clearing banks in Britain was reduced to five. Midland, its roots in Britain's manufacturing heartland, was not just the largest bank in Britain; it was the largest bank in the world. Its rivals – Barclays, Lloyds, National Provincial and Westminster – were not too far behind. But around this time, the rationale for the banks' traditional collection of functions disappeared. Securities markets developed. That meant that you did not need to be a big financial services retailer to lend money to large corporations. And the skills involved in the two activities of retail deposit taking and business lending, once rather similar, had become quite distinct.

Nobody really noticed. As competitive pressures increased, the British banks followed the usual strategies of companies which do not really know what to do. They sought greater size by merger and internal expansion, and engaged in unfocused diversification into new businesses and new areas of the world. All of that was irrelevant, or worse. One final mega-merger created the National Westminster Bank, but the government blocked further concentration. Banks discovered that it is easy to meet targets for growing your balance sheet so long as you are not too bothered about getting your money back. And they lost a packet buying stockbrokers and American banks.

Standard Life, too, had a golden era of success. It pioneered the retailing of equities to a mass market. That was not what the business said it was doing; in fact, if it had, it would probably have been stopped. But by packaging equities as a life insurance product, it avoided restrictive regulation and secured effective distribution. There was not a long-term business there. It became easier, both legally and operationally, to sell shares more directly to individuals. And once that happened, there ceased to be a rationale for linking the three main things which Standard Life did: financial services retailing, investment management and the underwriting of risks.

Standard Life's response has been another standard recourse for those with no easy strategic options: if you are not doing well enough at what you are doing already, try something else. Become a bank, or an investment management house. But there do seem to be quite a lot of well capitalised banks and successful investment management houses around already. What National Westminster and Standard Life have in common is that each embraces a range of functions which were sensibly undertaken together at a particular point in history, but for which the rationale of combination has now disappeared.

And each business has found that when you unpick the individual things they do, most of them are performed better by someone else. The banks found that their retail deposit services were upstaged by building societies, that their merchant banking arms found it difficult to match the resources and professionalism of

▶

169

specialist investment banks, and that lending to very large corporate and sovereign borrowers was so competitive that no one has made any money out of it, or is ever likely to.

British insurers learnt that their retailing capabilities were very limited in competition with people who had branch networks – or a red telephone; that their investment skills were inferior to those of specialist fund managers; and that their underwriting was outstripped in professionalism by continental reinsurers.

So what should businesses faced with these kinds of strategic dilemmas do? The main requirement is to identify which of the many activities such a business will be engaged in are ones in which it has an ongoing competitive advantage. What can you do that others cannot readily do as well? Lloyds did this in the 1980s when it understood that its strengths were in retail financial services and lending to small businesses, and quit the more glamorous but less profitable activities which required it to compete with every other bank in the world.

But sometimes strategic dilemmas have no solution. This is difficult for executives to accept, but not all questions have answers. Sometimes the proper job of managers is to preside over an orderly transfer of the activities they control to other businesses. This does not often happen quickly or without the costs and uncertainties associated with the takeover process. Perhaps it should. ∎

Source: Kay, J, *Financial Times*, 27 June 1997. Reprinted with permission.

REFERENCES FOR FURTHER READING

Drucker, Peter (1955) *The Practice of Management*, London: Heinemann.

Drucker, Peter (1988) 'The Coming of the New Organization', *Harvard Business Review*, Jan.–Feb.

Faulkner, David and Johnson, Gerry (1992) *The Challenge of Strategic Management*, London: Kogan Page.

Greiner, L E (1972) 'Evolution and Devolution as Organizations Grow', *Harvard Business Review*, July–Aug.

Grundy, Tony (1992) *Corporate Strategy and Financial Decisions*, London: Kogan Page.

Grundy, Tony (1993) *Implementing Strategic Change*, London: Kogan Page.

Hannagan, Tim (1986) *Mastering Statistics*, 2nd edn, London: Macmillan.

Kay, J (1997) 'Know your place', *Financial Times*, 27 June.

McDonald, Malcolm (1992) *Strategic Marketing Planning*, London: Kogan Page.

Mintzberg, Henry (1994) *The Rise and Fall of Strategic Planning*, Hemel Hempstead: Prentice-Hall International.

Stacey, Ralph D (1996) *Strategic Management and Organisational Dynamics*, London: Pitman Publishing.

7

TOTAL QUALITY MANAGEMENT

Tim Hannagan

OBJECTIVES

The objective of this chapter is to introduce the concept of 'quality' in the management of organisations. Reading this chapter should enable a manager to understand:

◆ the concept of 'quality' applied to commerce and industry

◆ the application of this concept to all types of organisation

◆ how a quality system can be introduced and managed within an organisation

◆ the importance of focusing on the customer

◆ the link between total quality and the management of change

◆ the strategic importance of corporate objectives

◆ the use of performance management

◆ the differences between quality control and quality assurance

◆ techniques such as quality circles, 'right-first-time', 'just-in-time', BS 5750/ISO 9000, Investors in People and zero defects

◆ the way in which quality can inform the whole approach to management

WHAT IS 'QUALITY'?

> *'In today's competitive environment, ignoring the quality issue is tantamount to corporate suicide.'*
> (President of Hewlett-Packard, *Fortune,* October 1985)

In business and management terms there is an attempt to focus on a measurable concept of quality by concentrating on 'fitness for purpose'. A specification is supplied by the customer and the quality of the product is measured by how closely it conforms to this specification. It is based on the customer's perception of quality. In these terms quality can be defined as:

> *'continually meeting agreed customer needs' or 'what it takes to satisfy the customer', or simply 'fitness for purpose'.*

In more general terms, quality is an elusive concept and the usual dictionary definition does not help to make it less so: 'That which makes a thing what it is, its attributes, its characteristics'. The 'quality' of a person may be measured by certain characteristics, such as honesty and courage.

This approach involves values and judgements, while a statement such as 'the quality of a strawberry plant is that it bears strawberries' is value and judgement free – it is a statement of what the plant is. However, the fruit from different plants will be compared in size, colour and flavour and then may be graded into strawberries of different 'quality' in the more limited commercial sense.

Quality can be seen as an attribute of a product or service which ensures that it is attractive in the eyes of the customer. It is a relative property rather than an absolute one, in that a given product or service will be attractive to customers if it fulfils their expectations more fully than any other product or service under consideration. It means delivering the right product or service, which is fit for the purposes required by the customer, at the right price, and at the right time and place. A company that produces and delivers a beautiful-looking car to a customer will not be considered to produce quality goods if the car does not work well. Whatever the costs involved, the materials used, or the care taken in manufacture, the quality of the car will be considered poor if it is unreliable. A lawnmower that does not cut the lawn effectively is of no use to the customer whatever its price or however firmly the manufacturer describes it as a 'quality' or 'excellent' product.

FOCUS ON THE CUSTOMER

If it is accepted that high quality is a measure of excellence taken from the customer's point of view, then although producers may grade their goods in terms of quality, whether the producers' view of the grading is upheld will depend on customer perception. If customers like their strawberries to be large, firm, red and sweet, then fruit with those characteristics will be considered to be of the highest quality, and the producer of smaller, paler strawberries may not be able to convince customers of the high quality of their output, however sweet they may taste.

The focus on the customer means that quality is conceptualised in terms of the customer's perceptions. The organisation's objective is to identify customer requirements so that both the customer's and the organisation's needs are met. It is also the intention to meet these requirements first time and thus avoid the cost of sorting out problems. The process involves:

- **research;**

- **specification and planning;**

- **delivery;**

- **review.**

This process focuses on the customer at key points and returns constantly to research into changing customer needs (*see* Fig 7.1). When customer needs are identified, planning can take place into exactly what has to be delivered. The specifications and standards are determined so priorities can be established to ensure that the product or service delivered is what the customer needs and that it meets customer perceptions. Although costs and price play an important part in this, most customers will pay what is necessary in order to receive what in their view is good quality. This in turn will generate profits as customers demand this product or service above others.

A customer can be defined as anyone who receives a product or service. This approach has been extended by many companies beyond the satisfaction of the external consumer in order also to include the internal customer. One department in an organisation receives products or services from another department and passes these on to a third group. On an assembly line a commodity is passed along the line from one individual or team to another, each dependent on the other for the receipt of the commodity at the correct quality at the correct time, and aiming to pass it on with the correct added value and, again, on time.

The concept of the internal customer means that each process is viewed as a product so that evaluation takes place at once by the immediate customer or by the processor. This system will help to eliminate waste and reduce cost, while the overall objective will remain the satisfaction of the external customer. The product or service will be 'right first time' so that errors will be prevented through the need to satisfy the internal customer at each stage rather than through a final inspection.

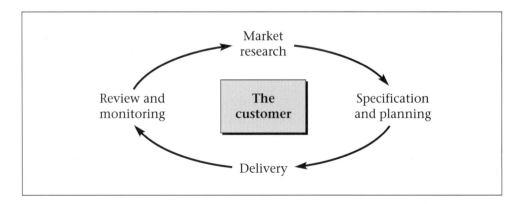

FIG 7.1 FOCUS ON THE CUSTOMER

TOTAL QUALITY MANAGEMENT

As companies have made a conscious effort to 'focus on the customer', total quality management (TQM) and other methods have been introduced to implement this. Total quality management is known by other names such as total quality improvement (TQI) or total quality control (TQC), or simply as total quality or as strategic quality management (SQM), and so on.

It is possible to identify differences between total quality management and titles such as strategic quality management. How important these are remains a matter of opinion. Total quality management is often described as a 'value-based' approach to quality management; it may be seen either as a goal which an organisation aims to achieve, or the idea of a goal of *total* quality may be considered unattainable. On the other hand, strategic quality management can be described as both systematic and value based. It can be seen to suggest that the reason for improving quality is that it will have maximum strategic impact on the future of the organisation. Strategic quality management is designed as a practical and pragmatic framework in which the drive towards quality improvement can be sustained while not making claims on *total* quality. A counter-argument to this is to consider the word 'total' in the context of total quality management to mean that every part of an organisation is involved.

The approach can be recognised, whatever its title, by its objectives. Total (or strategic) quality management can be defined as:

> *'an intensive, long-term effort to transform all parts of the organisation in order to produce the best product and service possible to meet customer needs.'*

In some Japanese companies there is no such thing as total or strategic quality management; it is simply the way they operate and it does not need a title in order to make sure it happens. The management at the Toyota plant in Japan has stated that:

> *'We estimate it will take you twenty years to be where we are now, and by the time we will have progressed further. We have moved from quality philosophy to measuring defects on an acceptable quality level basis to reducing our defect rate to below five to six parts per billion. Our last product recall was 1969 when we first started introducing what you know as Total Quality Management.'*

> (Atkinson, 1990)

Total quality management can be seen as a metaphor for the process and management of change, designed to realign the culture and working practices of an organisation for the pursuit of continued quality improvement. Initially the concept of quality tended to be considered in terms of narrow and specific techniques, such as quality circles or statistical process (or quality) control. The concept has developed into a pervasive one, touching every aspect of the organisation, including suppliers and customers.

In an organisation that practises total quality management, quality becomes the standard operating procedure and part of the culture. It is not simply a programme or project, but a way of life. It is proved by the quality of materials purchased from suppliers, the approach to defect control on the production line, the appearance of the building, the way problems are solved for customers, the way employees are organised and the organisation's internal communication system. This approach is founded on the premise that quality depends on individual effort and attitude. It is a rigorous, highly disciplined and skilled process which may challenge present practice and depends on a training programme throughout the organisation. Total quality management is predicated on a commitment to customer interests, needs, requirements and expectations, and on the commitment of everyone to the constant improvement of the quality of everything that the organisation does and provides for its customers.

TQM is a strategic approach within an organisation which can provide an 'umbrella' under which a number of quality initiatives can be managed (*see* Fig 7.2). These are all part of a quality culture. The philosophy that supported this culture and the practical application of it originated through the ideas of Dr W Edwards Deming, an American who provided the intellectual and practical drive behind Japan's post-war reconstruction. He encouraged Japanese companies to introduce total quality, and in particular to involve and consult with customers in an attempt to bring about continuous improvement of the product. J M Juran worked with Deming and concentrated on people-based management. He argued that in a normal situation, the general attitude was that maintaining and perpetuating current standards or levels of performance was good enough. He insisted that present performance in any function, at any level, can and should be improved, and that to achieve this improvement an organisation begins with identifying the internal obstacles that prevent people doing the best they can and then eliminates them.

Philip Crosby has been another important influence on total quality, again with a focus on the people responsible for improving quality. Peters and Waterman

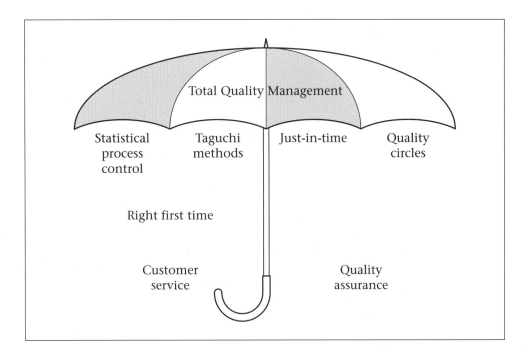

FIG 7.2 TOTAL QUALITY

expanded on these approaches in their book *In Search of Excellence* (1982). They found that many of the foremost 'excellent' companies were equally obsessed by quality and punctuality. They describe how the Caterpillar Tractor Company offers customers a 48-hour guaranteed parts delivery service anywhere in the world. If this guarantee is not met the customer receives the part free.

An article in *Fortune* magazine is quoted as stating:

> *'The company's operating principles are excellence of quality, reliability of performance, and loyalty in dealer relationships. Caterpillar has zealously pursued the goal of building a better, more efficient crawler tractor than anybody else in the world.'*
>
> (Peters and Waterman, 1982)

Another company highlighted by Peters and Waterman is McDonald's, whose theme is 'Quality, Service, Cleanliness and Value'. Founder Ray Kroc says, 'If I had a brick for every time I've repeated the phrase QSCV, I think I'd probably be able to bridge the Atlantic Ocean with them.' Quality is the priority because that is what McDonald's wants customers to enjoy every time they visit a McDonald's restaurant. All establishments are regularly monitored for QSCV and the results are linked to the manager's pay, while consistent failure to meet the McDonald's standards can lead to managers being sacked or the termination of the franchise. QSCV is not only applied to customer service but to all aspects of the business. The best ingredients are used in the food, and cleanliness is insisted upon. Peters and Waterman quote a former griddle tender as saying:

> *'There was never an idle moment, whenever there was a slack time in the store, we were cleaning something.'*

The computer company Hewlett-Packard has the same approach to quality. Routine systems in the company are made to reinforce the quality objectives. These are built into the management-by-objectives programme so that everyone receives the latest quality information as well as data on orders, sales and profits. There is a quality 'web' throughout the company, appropriately called the LACE (Lab Awareness of Customer Environment) programme, in which Hewlett-Packard customers make presentations to company engineers on their own needs and reactions to the products and services they receive.

> *'A Quality focus is ubiquitous in Hewlett-Packard because the employees don't seem to be able to separate it from anything else they are doing. If you ask them about personnel, they talk quality. If you ask them about field sales, they talk quality. If you ask them about management-by-objectives, they talk about quality-by-objectives.'* (Peters and Waterman, 1982)

Peters and Waterman found that quality and reliability were preferred by many leading companies to innovation, to being first in the field. Hewlett-Packard is quoted again:

> *'The company is seldom first into the market with its new products. The company's marketing strategy is normally that of a counter-puncher. A competitor's new product comes on the market and Hewlett-Packard engineers, when making service calls on Hewlett-*

> *Packard equipment ask the customers what they like or dislike about*
> *the new product, what features the customers would like to have . . .*
> *and pretty soon the Hewlett-Packard salesmen are calling on cus-*
> *tomers again with a new product that answers their needs and*
> *wants. The result: happy and loyal customers.'*

In these examples, and during the period of development of quality as the top priority for an organisation, it is apparent that total quality management involves the creation of an appropriate company culture, a climate based on 'never being satisfied' with the current quality of product and service in meeting customers' identified needs, requirements, interests and expectations. This search for opportunities for improvements can be referred to as total quality improvement. Not being satisfied with current inputs, processes, practices and outcomes encourages a system to be established covering research, analysis of needs, measurement of results, consideration of efficiency and effectiveness, in order to improve what is produced and how it is produced.

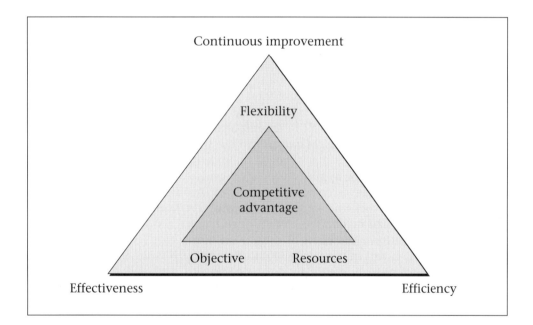

FIG 7.3 TOTAL QUALITY IMPROVEMENT

In Fig 7.3 a competitive edge is achieved by encouraging the best possible utilisation of resources by a highly adaptable workforce in order to achieve corporate quality objectives. Competitive advantage is achieved and maintained within a framework of efficiency and effectiveness and acceptance of a process of continuous improvement. TQM as a 'metaphor for the management of change' is a process for encouraging the attitude that change is the usual situation, because through this comes quality improvement and success.

177

The keys to total quality management can be summarised as:

- measuring quality;

- incorporating quality objectives into strategic planning;

- obtaining commitment of top management;

- forming teams in a structure of participative management;

- using resources efficiently and effectively;

- including suppliers and customers in quality improvement;

- building skills through training;

- developing an attitude which welcomes change.

IMPLICATIONS FOR MANAGEMENT

Total quality management impinges on every function in an organisation and will include marketing, product design, human resource development, financial resourcing, sites and buildings and estates management, and so on. The cultural change required in most organisations in order to introduce and maintain TQM has to be led by senior managers. They need to be aware of and understand the principles and practices of total quality and be prepared to support it at every level. Particularly important is the need to ensure monitoring, measurement and evaluation of progress in all functions, against identified and if possible quantified needs and specifications. Managers can use this evaluation in order to plan developments in TQM, as well as measuring the extent to which quality has been improved. The process can be applied inside an organisation as well as outside it, in the sense that everyone has a 'customer' and is a 'customer' inside the organisation, relying on others' work and service and passing on work and service to others. Factual evidence can be obtained by monitoring progress against agreed objectives, and this can inform the plans of each team in meeting its particular targets or objectives, which will in turn depend on other teams or individuals providing support in the form of high-quality goods or services.

TQM is implemented at the top of an organisation first because it is at this level that change can be initiated. Top managers require skills to enable them to change the way they work, so they can practise and promote quality management and then help others to acquire the necessary techniques and understanding.

The introduction of TQM through the whole organisation is a long-term strategy requiring a variety of approaches. For most organisations it is about the management of change and involves all aspects of human resource management, including leadership, problem solving, coaching, counselling, communication and team building. Training will be required at all levels, usually starting with those with a co-ordinating, supervisory or management role, but also concentrating on teams. Although TQM encourages consideration of factual information, it also encourages 'people-based' management.

This style of management is participative, designed to enable people at every level to share in management decisions and in responsibility for them. This means in one way or another devolving decision making to the closest possible point to where the effects of the decisions are felt. Decision making may be delegated to an individual or a team. People are encouraged to identify and 'own' problems and their solutions, rather than passing them up or around the organisation. At an early stage, teamwork becomes essential if problems are to be identified and addressed and not hidden away. This approach focuses on corporate goals, and teams identify with problems of specific relevance to their functions.

Teams need to know how their work relates to corporate goals and objectives so that they can understand the direction in which they are moving and can look for improvement opportunities. They need to have a clear idea of the resources at their disposal in order to achieve their particular objectives. It is then possible for the team to decide which members will carry out particular tasks, the methods to be employed, materials and equipment to use, and how and when to work. All of this puts great pressure on teamwork and on the team's responsibility for their own results (*see* Fig 7.4).

In the 1970s the Saab motor company broke away from the assembly-line system customarily used in car manufacturing and organised its workforce into teams working around each car. Teams could decide to rotate jobs and introduce other flexibilities into the way they worked, so long as they achieved their target output at the requisite cost and quality levels.

Black & Decker adopted a total quality plan in 1980 to include every aspect of the business. A 'People Plan' was formed in order to 'free the people for their fullest contribution to business success'. To implement total quality the company formed quality circles, and after four years there were 35 successful circles in operation. In 1984 this development was reviewed and considered to require rejuvenation. A new total customer service initiative was introduced which encompassed quality circles while focusing on 'excellence in everything we do'.

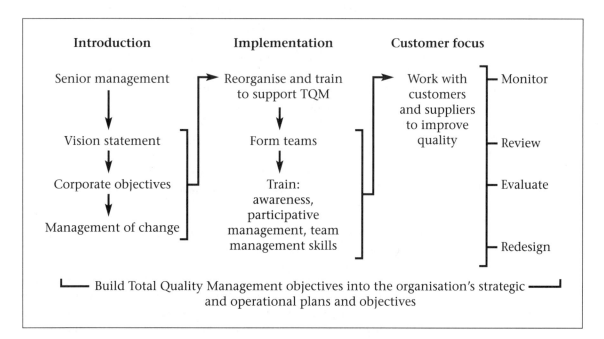

FIG 7.4 INTRODUCING TOTAL QUALITY MANAGEMENT

The Ciba Corning company also believes in total quality as a complete way of life affecting attitudes and commitments, 'a framework for bringing out the best in all employees'. The four principles underlying its approach are:

- **meeting the requirements of customers;**

- **error free work;**

- **managing by preventing errors rather than inspecting for error;**

- **measuring by cost of quality.**

These principles are delivered through a ten-point action plan which includes commitment from the top, communication, education and involvement for all employees. One approach to obtaining this involvement is the organisation of quality circles.

QUALITY CIRCLES

A quality circle is:

> *'a group who meet voluntarily and regularly to identify and solve their own work related problems and implement their solutions with management approval.'*   (Industrial Society)

Small groups of employees, usually from the same workplace and under the same supervisor, volunteer to meet to identify problems and find solutions. They look at the problems that occur in their work area and that affect their own job. The group itself applies the solutions if it has the authority; otherwise management is presented with recommendations and decides on implementation.

Membership of quality circles is usually voluntary, with a welcome for anyone who wishes to join and no official pressure for anyone to become a member. If the circle is successful, active and enthusiastic, it is expected that people will want to join. The supervisor of a work area will usually lead the circle. His or her role is to encourage volunteers to establish a group which he or she will chair because of previous experience and training in organising and running quality circles. The supervisor guides the circle in order to help it develop into a cohesive team and to focus on solving problems and improving quality. The circle will usually consist of between six and twelve members, large enough to generate a variety of ideas, small enough for everybody to be involved and have their say. If there are too many volunteers, either membership can be rotated or subgroups can be formed to consider particular tasks.

Management has to follow a 'hands-off' policy up to the point of implementation of a decision. Success depends on members of a quality circle being assured that it 'belongs to them' and has not been formed by management. Management can be supportive and may suggest topics for consideration by the circle, but if it is more 'heavy handed' the role of members will be restricted. The most important consideration for management is to ensure that actions do follow any ideas or decisions reached by a quality circle, or to provide good reasons for not following up such ideas or decisions.

Quality circles were originally an American idea but were first practised on a wide scale in Japan. In order to compete with other industrial nations, Japanese industry realised in the late 1940s and 1950s that old ideas of management had to be discarded and the initiative and skills of everybody on the workforce had to be harnessed. Emphasis was placed on training at shopfloor level and every effort was made to pass as much responsibility as possible to supervisors and operators. There was a particular emphasis on identifying quality problems at all levels and in all areas of companies.

In the late 1950s and through the 1960s Japanese companies introduced quality circles extensively, so that by 1980 it was estimated that over one million quality circles and ten million workers were involved. It is significant that the literal translation of the Japanese term for quality circles is:

'The gathering of the wisdom of the people.'

The concept of the quality circle coincides with the culture of Japanese companies and builds on loyalty to the company. The 'family company' approach of duty to the company by employees and responsibility by the company for the welfare of its employees is well developed, while there is also a well-nurtured culture of it being in everyone's interest for the company to succeed, combined with peer pressure to encourage the success of a voluntary approach. Professor Ishikawa has suggested (1984) that quality circles act as a 'focus of perception' to identify personal pride and self-esteem with corporate achievement.

Quality circles have been used across the world to draw on the expertise and knowledge of workers on the shopfloor in order to improve quality. They have been adapted by such companies as General Motors, Honeywell and Lockheed in the USA, and by Philips, Ford, Rolls-Royce and Marks & Spencer in the UK.

In many British companies, however, the culture has not been conducive to the development of quality circles. Where there is a strongly defended hierarchical structure, or sections and departments based on specialised expertise, the view that ideas from the shopfloor should be given priority is difficult to foster. At the same time the attitude that it is up to 'them' to solve problems may be strong at an operational level. Management/union dissension in the past has certainly discouraged the effective development of this kind of initiative.

It is clear that successful quality circles are not concerned with grumbles or complaints or irrelevant discussion of non-related subjects such as pay, personality conflicts or other grievances. The stress is on solving problems and producing action plans. For this approach to be understood and successful the culture of the company has to be one which encourages participative management. If the culture has bred suspicion and secrecy, grumbles and complaints may be at the top of the agenda. Quality circles are encouraged to discuss practicalities and not theories, so that positive results are produced rather than simply argument. One approach is to list problem areas and then to establish priorities and seek solutions by drawing on the skill and knowledge of the group. When problems are beyond solution by the group, specialists may be asked to join the circle for a number of meetings, or a subgroup may be established to investigate the problem in more detail.

Where the members of the quality circle have discretion to make a decision they will carry it out, while on matters where they do not have authority, they will make a presentation to the managers involved in the proposed change (*see* Fig 7.5). This may be a technical problem to do with the operation of machinery or equipment, it may be a staffing problem to do with skills or working times, it may be a question of the supply of materials, the purchase of spare parts, or it may be to do with

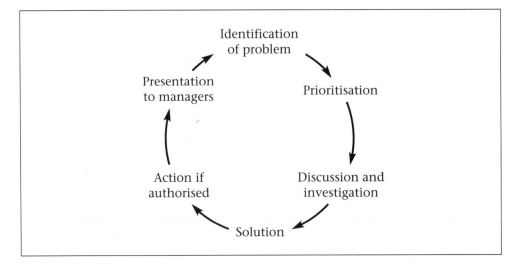

FIG 7.5 QUALITY CIRCLES

costs and finance. The managers must then decide to take action or explain in detail the reasons for not taking action at this time. Managers also have to make sure that people do not identify too strongly with their particular circle, when total quality has to be identified with the aims and objectives of the organisation as a whole. At the same time some problems need to be solved on the spot, rather than waiting for a quality circle meeting to sort them out.

An enterprising quality circle will, of course, anticipate as many problems as possible and solve them.

ITT has provided an example of a solution discovered by a quality circle:

> *'It was standard practice to completely remove capacitors from the metal handling equipment to check for correct nominal capacitance. After this operation the capacitors were discarded. By purchasing hand held capacitance meters it is possible to take the equipment to the work and simply applying one terminal lead, measure the nominal capacitance while the remaining terminal lead is retained on the handling strip. This enables the capacitor to continue with the batch through the finishing operations. This change will result in a saving of more than $10,000 when it is fully implemented.'*
>
> (*ITT Circle News*, March 1981)

Managers play an important part in the success of quality circles. There has to be a commitment to the system throughout the organisation, and one or two unsympathetic managers can ruin the whole process. Managers have to allow time and money for the circle meetings and for the preliminary training; they must be ready to attend presentations, to listen with an open mind to the proposals and to decide on their value on merit. Unions need also to be involved in the process so that their representatives understand what is happening. Unions will usually be supportive of the process because it involves the workforce more closely in the organisation and has the objective of improving job satisfaction. After all, quality circles have been described as 'a structured way of making management listen' (Industrial Society).

FOCUS ON TOTAL QUALITY

Whether it is quality circles or another method of providing a focus on quality, the pursuit of total quality must be led from the front, by the chief executive, otherwise it may be considered an afterthought. Deming put this another way:

> *'There is so much talk about involvement of employees, quality of work life, communications and other poetic words. What is needed is involvement of management: get the management involved. Employees will become involved, the quality of life will improve, once management takes on the job of restoring dignity to the hourly worker.'*
>
> (W Edwards Deming, *Quality, Productivity and Competitive Position*)

Combined with competitive pressures and the higher priority given to human resource management, the focus on quality has encouraged reorganisation in many companies in the 1980s and 1990s. These developments have been away from the single, giant pyramid structures consisting of many different layers of management and grades of operative, towards flatter structures often based on a total quality concept. Whole functions and levels have been eliminated in order to produce an organisation which is more flexible and speedier in response to market needs.

Waterman (1988) cites the Dana Company in the USA, which in the mid-1970s had 14 layers of management between the chief executive and the staff floor. By the mid-1980s these layers had been reduced to five:

> *'At the extreme the company has one plant in Nebraska that employs 120 people – the organisation structure there is simple: 120 people, one plant manager, nothing in between.'*

The key to this approach is often greater delegation. Many areas of decision making and accountability have been pushed down the organisation to be nearer the point where the decision takes effect. Senior management will adopt a more strategic role, setting broad objectives as a framework to ensure that all units are functioning effectively and working towards the corporate goals. The operational units are the closest group to their markets and they know best the requirements of the consumer. It is impossible for this level of delegation to work unless the practice and beliefs of management adapt to the new circumstances. There is a decline in supervision throughout the organisation as employees take on greater responsibility. The role of the manager is to initiate new ideas and policies, to facilitate the work of the operational units and to monitor their progress.

In order to introduce this level of involvement there has to be a clear recognition that the purpose of this strategy is to increase mutual understanding and to improve the individual's contribution. This is a policy of openness, of encouraging individual creativity and initiative in the interests of the organisation.

In order to achieve this level of delegation it is necessary to:

- make certain that each individual understands what is expected from them in terms of their time at work;

- set the limits of delegation so that everyone knows the extent of their responsibility;

- train individuals so that they understand the aims and objectives of the delegated system and are technically able to cope with it;

- communicate effectively the corporate business goals so that everyone understands how these relate to them;

- enable a reverse flow of information to take place, from the shopfloor upwards, so that each manager knows the attitudes and aspirations of each person reporting to him or her.

At the same time as this focus on the individual, there has to be a clear understanding of teamwork. In the introduction of total quality, teams are not the same as quality circles. The quality circle approach is based on voluntary groups of employees considering particular tasks. Total quality management teams include everybody working in a particular area or function or in a cross-functional role. Individuals cannot opt out of this team or of meetings to consider the working of the group, or fail to take responsibility for their work. The team will be responsible for making sure that everybody contributes to its success, and for discussing and implementing ways in which the whole team can improve performance. These teams may coincide with quality circles or the latter may form a separate system for considering quality – an alternative, perhaps task-oriented group. The usual process is for the functional team itself to become a type of quality circle on its own.

This process of delegating decision and responsibility to teams at the 'salt face' or 'firing line' is again not quite the same as a process popular in the 1980s known as 'team briefing'. These are meetings at regular intervals when leaders bring their teams together to communicate what is happening at the workplace. In the team briefing system, the priority is to achieve understanding of what people need to know because it affects their job; it is a systematic way of telling all employees about progress, policy, decisions, performance and future plans. It is not necessarily consultative and is not usually a method of encouraging two-way communication. Team briefing is a useful method of communication for management, but it should not be confused with the purposes behind setting up teams in a TQM system.

The same is true of consultative committees, which are structured meetings of management and employee representatives, with the purpose of discussing management matters of common interest. They are a way of seeking the views of employees before management decisions are finally made or before they are implemented. They may be used whenever decisions affect employees, but they are not about negotiation on such matters as pay, which requires once again a separate format of meetings. Consultative committees can play an important part in, for example, the management of change, and can be a way of informing discussion on quality teams when managers are considering the initiation of new policies.

The Confederation of British Industry in *The Will to Win* (1980) stated that 'the system of giving the line employee more responsibility increases his/her job satisfaction and involvement'. In contrast, the division of labour and scientific management or 'Taylorism' have encouraged the analysis of work into constituent activities and given particular tasks to individual workers. The close definition of the worker's specialist role has meant that at its extreme, workers respond by living up to the limited expectations of them by carrying out the tasks they have been given and no more or less.

Some organisations may have been paternalistic in their approach by not treating employees as adults; at the same time, other organisations do not regard their employees as the prime source of their prosperity. With a limited view of their job, employees substitute habit for understanding, and every change can, in Drucker's view, represent to the employee 'a challenge of the incomprehensible and . . . threatens his psychological security'. Drucker attacks scientific management for confusing analysis with action, for divorcing planning from doing. The successful companies 'hire a whole man or woman' and realise that 'with every pair of hands a mind comes free'. Ignoring the ideas of employees is epitomised by a General Motors' car worker in the USA whom Drucker (1968) quotes as saying:

> *'I guess I got laid off because I made poor quality cars. In 16 years not once was I ever asked for a suggestion as to how to do my job better. Not once.'*

In response to this, many successful companies have introduced suggestion schemes. In the USA, IBM has said that its suggestion plan yielded ideas from 30 000 employees during 1985 which resulted in savings of more than $125 million. The company was happy to pay the employees $18 million in cash awards for these suggestions. While these schemes can be very effective, they have to fit into the overall company policy because it may be difficult to run financial inducements for ideas alongside voluntary consultation and a delegated team approach. If the company ethos encourages everybody to think in terms of constant improvement and enables people to communicate ideas, a suggestion box may not be necessary (*see* Fig 7.6).

Strategies designed to maximise the potential and actual contribution of every employee have to give considerable emphasis to communication and involvement policies. The move away from an organisation based on command and authority from the top, with limited and routine tasks at the bottom, has created a re-evaluation of the way companies communicate internally. It is no longer a question of ensuring that instructions are passed to the relevant people and then monitoring what happens. Communication is now seen as a means of improving understanding, of

FIG 7.6 FOCUS ON QUALITY

securing involvement through a free flow of information in order to create cohesion and mutual commitment on the part of all members of the organisation.

Managers rely on the capabilities of those carrying out the various tasks allotted to them. Managers have to ensure effective teamwork and co-operation and are responsible for co-ordinating, planning and monitoring to make sure that more flexible and less authoritarian structures nevertheless meet their objectives. This requires the listening skills of a facilitator able to anticipate and solve problems, to treat individuals sympathetically and with respect, and to identify the relative strengths and weaknesses of everyone involved.

Managers need to communicate the corporate business goals effectively to every team or group so that they are understood in sufficient depth and related to the team and the individuals in it. This understanding must also include an appreciation of the external influences on the organisation, such as the nature of the competition, the impact of new technologies, the influence of government policy, and the importance of markets and customers. Managers have to assess the level of understanding of these matters by teams and individuals. Surveys, meetings and discussions can help to do this, and many organisations have found the most effective means of 'upward' communication to be a system of appraisal and performance review (*see* Chapters 6 and 8).

Measuring quality

The measurement of quality should not be thought of as a single and simple process, although in fact it can be if the one measurement that is used is profit. A simple indication such as profit growth, market share or the return on capital invested can be used to judge how well a quality management system has worked, and these certainly should be among the measures used. The problem is that taken on their own they do not indicate how they were achieved and, if successful, how they can be maintained. For this an analysis of the organisation is required with measurement taken at various levels.

At a strategic level, for example, in order to decide whether or not a performance management system has helped to put quality management into effect, it may be sensible to seek the answers to a number of questions:

- Is there a strategic plan supported by senior managers which establishes the organisation's direction?

- Is there a well-defined structure to support and develop a quality approach by managers, including a performance management system?

- Are skills and techniques for quality improvement part of the training for managers and supervisors?

- Are employees held accountable for on-the-job performance.

At the same time there has to be a decision about what is to be evaluated. This can be achieved by a clear statement of overall objectives, plus objectives for every unit and team as well as individuals. At the operational level this will mean detailed production or service targets. At a more strategic level managers may prefer non-routine activities and those of short duration; they may prefer to be problem solvers rather

PROBLEM SOLVERS	PLANNERS
Short-duration activities	Advance planning
Non-routine tasks	Agreed systems
Emphasis on decisive action	Systems and schedules
Informal interaction	Formal, regular sessions
Effectiveness through authority	Roles of coach and counsellor
Low priority given to personnel task	Human resource management

FIG 7.7 PLANNERS AND PROBLEM SOLVERS

than planners (*see* Fig 7.7). This tendency can be offset by a participative process for establishing objectives and forms of evaluation, so that managers can see the importance of longer-term objectives in establishing the context for detailed targets.

A manager needs to be both a problem solver and a planner and to be able to communicate the importance of medium- and long-term objectives to employees at all levels so as to support the attainment of objectives and targets and measure performance against these.

In *Thriving on Chaos* (1988) Tom Peters identifies 12 attributes of a quality system, which in themselves represent a checklist against which an organisation's management can assess the stage it has reached in the development of such a system:

- management is obsessed with quality;

- the company has a guiding system or ideology;

- quality is measured;

- quality is rewarded;

- everyone is trained in techniques for assessing quality;

- there is a shift of managerial philosophy from adversarial to co-operative;

- it is recognised that there is no such thing as an insignificant improvement;

- there is constant stimulation to improve quality;

- there is a structure within the company dedicated to quality improvement;

- everybody is involved in quality management, including suppliers, distributors, customers;

- it is understood that costs decline as quality increases;

- it is recognised that quality is relative and improvement is never ending.

QUALITY CONTROL AND QUALITY ASSURANCE

One of the 12 items on Peters' checklist suggests that quality improvement is never ending. It is a relative value compared with the competition as perceived through the customer's eyes. It is an elusive concept because customer perception is itself difficult to predict. Peters argues that if you own a car in which some major part goes wrong, you may have a better view of its quality than if a number of small things go wrong. If the carburettor stops working or the gear box collapses, you take the car to the garage and have the component repaired or replaced. If the service is efficient and problems do not recur, then you can forget about the problem.

If the radio crackles, the door squeaks, the window sticks and there are a number of other small problems, they may not, even cumulatively, be worth the trouble of taking the car to the garage until the next service. Meanwhile they remain a constant reminder of the poor quality of the car. All these problems can be seen as a problem of quality control, which can be defined as being:

> *'concerned with checking for errors during and after the process of manufacture.'*

Quality control often occurs at the end of the manufacturing process as a check to see if the commodity works. If it does not it is rejected and either scrapped or reworked. The problem with this approach is that there is heavy dependence on inspectors. This is expensive and obviously it is much better to identify the error at an earlier stage. Statistical process control (SPC) is a method of monitoring the conformity of a product to agreed specifications. By sampling units of the product, deviations from these specifications can be identified and adjustments made during the production process.

Modern control techniques are based on the idea of an 'error-free' or 'zero-defect' approach, or 'doing it right first time'. This concept arises because of the costs involved in correcting errors and the fact that the costs are usually greater the later they are identified. Under the TQM approach the team is made responsible for quality control, for reducing wastage and for ensuring that adjustments are made as soon as they are identified.

At a strategic level quality can be built into the planning of the product or service. Juran and Deming worked extensively with the Japanese to enhance product quality through statistical methods. The first stage is to ensure that the product conforms to design specifications. The next stage is the use of SQC (statistical quality control) or process-control procedures in order to monitor quality during the production of the commodity or rendering of the service. Work teams or quality circles can decide and be delegated the power to decide how to reduce errors and 'do it right first time', while management has to support this process at every stage.

The Ford Motor Company in the 1980s introduced a slogan, 'At Ford, Quality is Job One'. A programme of quality control was introduced along with a new policy of participative management. The emphasis on achieving quotas was changed so that the quality of the product came first. Employee groups were made an important element in the quality control process rather than relying on a separate team of inspectors. Ford's President Donald Peterson stated his commitment to quality:

> *'The principles by which we will live and die, is that once we can do something well, we have to figure out how to do it even better.'*
> (Quoted by Stoner and Freeman, 1989)

A concept which builds on quality control is the 'just-in-time' (JIT) principle. This is concerned with improving production efficiency and reducing waste. It is a technique for minimising storage through careful planning and purchasing to meet the exact requirements of the customer, internal or external, and this is only possible if the product does in fact meet agreed specifications and suppliers co-operate fully.

It is at the strategic management level that decisions are made about total quality management and systems of quality control. The strategic approach includes:

- analysis of current position;

- choice of an appropriate starting point;

- implementation of policy, deciding what will be done, how, by whom and by when.

Quality assurance (QA) provides a framework for quality control and quality improvement. Quality assurance supports teams of employees with systems, resources and discretion appropriate to their unique contribution to the organisation, to keep them in tune with progress of quality management and improvement. This aspect of management can help teams:

- understand quality characteristics;

- be realistic about the standards to be attained;

- undertake quality control through a measurement process, interpret the results and make or propose changes.

This process may be supported by a number of techniques such as QUEST (Quality in Every Single Task). This is the idea that everybody in an organisation is a 'customer' and 'supplier' and receives products and services from colleagues within the organisation.

The idea of service within the organisation enables each individual or group to undertake a QUEST analysis:

- Who are my customers?

- What do they demand from me?

- In what way do I meet these demands?

- How can I improve my service?

and

- Who are my suppliers?

- What service do I demand of them?

- In what way do they meet these demands?

- How can they improve their service?

KRA (key result areas) is a technique aimed at focusing on realistic outcomes for each team or individual. This may be by:

- identifying a range of quality characteristics for the team which are consistent with the company's strategy;

- agreeing realistic standards for each of these quality characteristics;

- devising a system which can be measured and monitored.

The Taguchi method is based on the ideas of Dr Genichi Taguchi who developed his approach to improve quality engineering at a low cost. It helps to quantify the loss due to lack of quality of a performance characteristic, with the objective of identifying the real cause of a problem. It concentrates on the design of products, reducing variation of performance against the target specification. The Taguchi method depends on a management culture committed to TQM and it has, therefore, developed most successfully in Japan and the USA.

The concentration on customer specification has produced approaches such as the British Standard 5750 registration mark and its international counterpart ISO 9000. These do not establish a level of excellence for a product or service, but they do provide:

'a way of describing the capability of a system to produce goods or services to a specification.'

Customers and potential customers should not expect BS 5750 to make a product the best available, and the registration mark is not a necessary prerequisite to total quality management. Quality is as much about 'doing the right thing' as 'doing things right', while BS 5750 is about 'doing things right'. It arises from the need in quality assurance to supply evidence to other organisations about a particular organisation's effectiveness.

These other organisations may be other companies, which are being supplied with the product or service, government agencies, consumer organisations or any other group which perceives, rightly or wrongly, that the possession of BS 5750 or ISO 9000 is a kitemark of effectiveness, efficiency or quality. Since the introduction of the BS 5750 series in 1979, approximately 10 000 organisations have been registered. The UK has been the leader in this process of certification since a Government White Paper in 1982 required BS 5750 registration for nationalised industries and for public sector procurement generally.

BS 5750 places great emphasis on written evidence, documented systems and procedures. It is based on the status quo rather than on continual improvement, which is the main goal of TQM. The British Standard is a procedural system for companies to follow in order to set up and document an organisation's operational systems. The approach is designed to control each step in a process so that products or services match the specification. This type of process originally developed in industries where safety was a critical factor, such as aerospace, nuclear power and defence. This background is what has provided its particular approach: a very careful, closely audited step-by-step control for procedures. The procedures are established to meet a particular specification and then audited to ensure they are being adhered to in detail. In the 1960s and 1970s the Ministry of Defence and the Central Electricity Board used their inspectors to visit potential suppliers to check that they could produce goods uniformly.

This is still the most important type of use for BS 5750, although some large companies (such as Ford and Marks & Spencer) 'inspect' potential suppliers and set their own operational and product quality standards which suppliers must meet. Some firms conduct their own auditing system in order to standardise procedures. None of these approaches should be confused with TQM.

INVESTORS IN PEOPLE

For many organisations people represent their largest cost, often 70 or 80 per cent of the total. In the UK, an initiative which recognises this fact and has the goal of attaining quality in organisations is 'Investors in People' (IIP). This rests on the premise that companies which have developed, or are developing, an awareness of quality acknowledge that people are the real key to achieving improvements. In a 'quality' culture, people take ownership of their work and responsibility for the quality of their work. IIP arises from 'gap analysis', particularly the gap identified by the Confederation of British Industry:

> *'The crucial importance of people to business success is now almost universally recognised by companies. But there is a huge gap between recognising this, and knowing exactly what to do about it.'*
> (Investors in People, *Briefing Document 1*, November 1990)

IIP is concerned with the contribution people can make to business success. By learning from the actions of those organisations which are already developing and using their people successfully, other organisations can adopt, and benefit from, an 'Investors in People' approach.

IIP arose from the 1988 UK Government White Paper *Employment for the 1990s* which launched a partnership between business and government. The National Training Task Force was established and the Training and Enterprise Councils and Local Enterprise Councils (in Scotland) were launched. A major priority of this initiative was to raise employer commitment to training, hence the IIP. The approach was to listen to businesses' ideas and needs, and look at the people factors which make one organisation more successful than another.

Organisations' own agendas are centred around:

- **productivity;**
- **quality;**
- **focus on the customer;**
- **flexibility.**

These priorities have given rise to operational and management practices such as TQM, and include customer care programmes, 'just-in-time' manufacturing and workplace teams. In all these practices, people are understood to be the key to achieving total quality, and there is an emphasis on teams and seeing colleagues as internal customers, while being genuinely motivated to develop existing skills, develop new ones, accept the devolution of responsibility, make the best use of current or new resources, and if required, acquire new managerial skills.

The Investors in People programme aims to help organisations improve performance through a planned approach to:

- **setting and communicating business goals;**

- **developing people to meet these goals;**

so that:

- **what people can do and are motivated to do;**

- **matches what the organisation needs them to do.**

This can be seen diagrammatically in Fig 7.8.

In order to encourage progress in this process, a national standard has been introduced to provide a focus and a discipline to an organisation's actions. This encourages organisations to think consistently of their people as an investment, not a cost, and act in a way which reflects this perspective. Organisations need to recognise people as a valuable business resource, which can be used to create, protect or waste assets; that there are investment costs as well as benefits in this process; that the benefits will be greater than the costs; and that organisations will only benefit fully from investing in people if they start with clearly defined objectives and actions.

The actions required to improve quality through the IIP process are based on four basic requirements:

An Investor in People makes a public commitment from the top to develop all employees to achieve its business objectives.

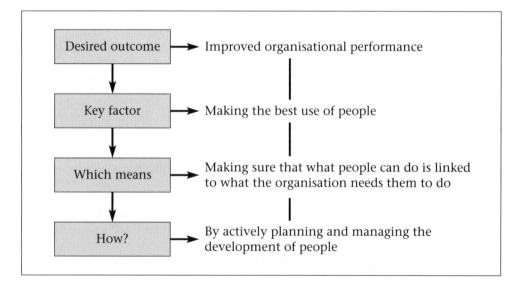

FIG 7.8 INVESTORS IN PEOPLE

- Every employer should have a written but flexible plan which sets out business goals and targets, considers how employees will contribute to achieving the plan and specifies how development needs in particular will be assessed and met.

- Management should develop and communicate to all employees a vision of where the organisation is going and the contribution employees will make to its success, involving employee representatives as appropriate.

An Investor in People regularly reviews the training and development needs of all employees.

- The resources for training and developing employees should be clearly identified in the business plan.

- Managers should be responsible for regularly agreeing training and developing needs with each employee in the context of business objectives, setting targets and standards linked, where appropriate, to the achievement of National Vocational Qualifications (or relevant units) and, in Scotland, Scottish Vocational Qualifications.

An Investor in People takes action to train and develop individuals on recruitment and throughout their employment.

- Action should focus on the training needs of all new recruits and continually developing and improving the skills of existing employees.

- All employees should be encouraged to contribute to identifying and meeting their own job-related development needs.

An Investor in People evaluates the investment in training and development to assess achievement and improve future effectiveness.

- The investment, the competence and commitment of employees, and the use made of skills learned should be reviewed at all levels against business goals and targets.

- The effectiveness of training and development should be reviewed at the top level and lead to renewed commitment and target setting.

Companies such as Ernest Ireland Construction, Radcliffe Catering Ltd, BICERI Ltd, Komatsu UK Ltd and Dow Corning Ltd have introduced this programme. They have recognised the crucial importance of people to their success and have bridged the gap between recognising this priority and doing something about it.

CONCLUSION

Improving productivity and effectiveness means not only raising the quantity of output per unit, it also involves improving quality. A key to understanding the importance of quality management is the conviction that costs decline as quality increases.

The opposite point of view is well rehearsed in all sorts of organisations and situations. A frequent approach centres on the point of view that 'of course we could improve the quality if we had more money and resources', and the idea that 'you get what you pay for', based on the premise that the more you pay the better the quality.

There is of course some truth in these ideas, and they may in fact describe the position very accurately in some situations. On the other hand, very often this is not the case. The increase in Japanese car sales in the 1980s and 1990s has been based on producing cars which are 'fit for the purpose'; they are designed to fulfil customer requirements, they are reliable and they are relatively cheap. Their success has been based on providing what people want at a price they can afford. At the extreme, it can be argued that a Rolls-Royce is a more carefully made car, which is reliable and of very high 'quality' or excellence, but the price puts it out of the reach of most people so that its quality will be compared with other 'hand-made' cars and not with the family saloon. Volvo has based the success of its cars on such factors as safety, reliability and longevity rather than price, because it believes that these are the qualities potential customers want. In fact the important feature of its cars is that they are different, and it is the difference in quality which the company relies on for its sales and profit.

If a company concentrates mainly on price, as for example cars produced by organisations in some Eastern European countries, then here there is a chance the relatively cheap car may not sell well because it does not have other qualities which customers require. The essential point is to produce goods which customers want at a price they can afford in a particular market, and the key to producing goods at a competitive price and with good quality is high productivity. The difference between the productivity of car manufacturers in Britain is considerable, with the most productive British worker employed by Japanese companies able to produce twice as many cars a year as the least productive British worker employed by British/American companies.

Differences between companies in terms of productivity arise as a result of greater investment in new equipment and technology, but as important as this are differences in management. The emphasis on quality, focusing of people's jobs, participative management, gaining the co-operation of unions, encouraging teamwork, setting clearly understood performance targets – these are all part of the difference. The lack of these aspects of management encourages expensive situations such as the rejection of products at the point of inspection or eventually by the customer, the waste of materials, unnecessary expense on 'troubleshooters', wasteful hold-ups on supply lines and the maintenance of large and costly inventories to replace rejected products or parts. At the same time, if too much energy is expended on fighting internal battles within the organisation, either between management and unions or between different sections and departments, there is a dissipation of the effort required to fight the real external competition. The competitive edge is achieved by creating a positive and productive internal organisation while focusing on beating external competitors.

A 'quality first', 'right first time' approach means that customers are satisfied and stocks of spare parts and replacements can be kept to a minimum. If performance targets are the responsibility of the individual and team and the internal customer approach is prevalent, there is little need for inspection of the end product, supervision can be reduced to a minimum and a comparatively 'flat' hierarchy can manage the company. All of this will save costs.

The TQM approach is based on the idea that managers are sure of their objectives within a broad vision, for everybody in the organisation to have both a clear focus on their aims and goals and an understanding of the context in which they are working, as well as taking responsibility for work over which they have control. Accountability then becomes a question of peer pressure for most people within the 'internal customer' framework. Quality improvement within an organisation structured in this way is not delegated or subcontracted, it is a responsibility that everyone actively shares.

Management has a responsibility for leading this approach by providing the structural framework and by presenting an example of hard, productive and effective work. The Japanese suggest that management is a way of life which is a progression towards self-enlightenment. They perceive the human skills of imagination, personality, leadership and creativity as just as important as management skills, so that managers are engaged in creating a vision or mission to motivate the workforce. Quality management is concerned with how managers see themselves, what standards they set for themselves and how they motivate others. Out of this analysis should arise the appropriate structure for the organisation.

TQM is a business management philosophy which recognises that customer needs and business goals are inseparable. It pervades an organisation's culture, inspires commitment and encourages communication in all directions, based on work teams and quality systems which utilise resources effectively (*see* Fig 7.9). At its best TQM can release a dynamic factor within an organisation which encourages success and profitability.

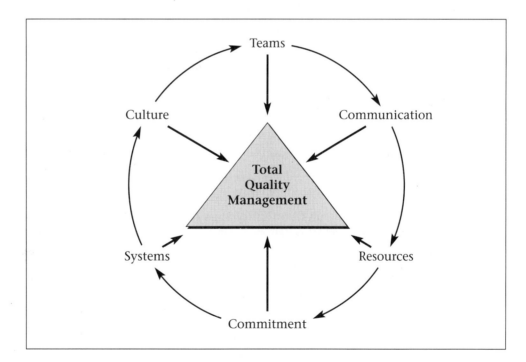

FIG 7.9 TQM

SUMMARY

■ The management of quality is an essential feature in any organisation for maintaining a competitive advantage. It has always been a feature of industry and commerce in one way or another, but since the 1940s it has become a priority interest of managers because of fierce competition in world markets. The Japanese needed to catch up and compete with the major industrial countries in the 1940s and 1950s, and by the 1960s they were doing this based on a total quality concept. UK managers in the 1980s and 1990s have been in a similar position, finding themselves outcompeted in world markets, so that total quality has become an essential feature of their fightback.

■ Underlying the quest for quality is the need to increase productivity by raising investment levels in high technology and by making the most of the workforce. This involves the delegation of decision making and responsibility in the process of achieving quality objectives. It also involves a concentration on training and development based on high expectations and increasing people's ability to deal with modern technology and participative management.

■ Actions to achieve quality include the introduction of TQM programmes, focus on the customer and the development of techniques such as 'right first time' and 'just in time'. Performance management programmes are another way of concentrating the attention of managers and everybody else in an organisation on the quality of their work and ultimately on the quality of products or services.

REVIEW AND DISCUSSION QUESTIONS

1   What is meant by strategic management? Is there an important difference between strategic and total quality management?

2   Consider an organisation that has a quality management programme. Summarise it. How does it compare with the examples outlined in this chapter?

3   How important is participative management for a total quality programme?

4   How do vision, mission statement and corporate objectives link to TQM?

5   What are the advantages and drawbacks of quality circles? What part can management play in quality circles?

6   What are the implications of total quality for the management structure of an organisation? How do your conclusions compare to the situation in your own organisation or one that you know?

7   How important is a performance management and appraisal system as a prerequisite for a total quality programme?

8   What are the differences between strategic quality management, quality assurance and quality control?

CASE STUDY: BRITISH AEROSPACE

The Airbus Division is part of British Aerospace commercial division which handles work arising from the company's 20 per cent stake in Airbus Industries. Approximately two-thirds of the Airbus Division's payroll of 9000 is engaged in producing Airbus wingsets, while the other activities include a maintenance contract for the US Air Force.

Quality assurance has been developed in the Airbus Division over the last 22 years. Quality managers have progressively been introduced to replace inspectors whose numbers have gradually fallen. A different philosophy of product quality has accompanied this change. Formerly, the aim was to produce 'engineering excellence' but now the goal is 'excellent engineering', a concept requiring a broader view of an item's function and with a higher priority for costs and the complexities of production. Essentially, the need is for excellent engineering at an affordable cost.

This has led to fresh approaches to all activities, from design onwards. Statistical quality control methods still have some applications, but not as many as in mass-production flowline operations. Training has been a high priority from apprentices through to management. Stress is placed on topics such as customer orientation, the awareness of suppliers and what constitutes an affordable cost. There is an approved firms list of suppliers, with inspections every two years. This has been found to work well with large suppliers but not so well with smaller suppliers, and those with a proven record of high quality have come to be valued.

It has been found that growth at British Aerospace has enhanced quality rather than caused a decline in it. This has been put down to the scale of investment, the long production lines with increased volume, and the concentration on quality as the top priority. Where amendments are made to production, a rule has been introduced that quality has to stay constant or improve. As a result, the larger the production lines, the more changes are made and the greater the number of quality improvements. This has been reinforced by the introduction of a total quality programme. ∎

REFERENCES FOR FURTHER READING

Atkinson, P E (1990) *Creating Culture Change: The Key to Successful Total Quality Management*, IFS Publications.

British Standards Institution (1987) *BS 5750: Quality Systems*, BSI.

Collard, R (1989) *Total Quality Success Through People*, IPM.

Confederation of British Industry (1990a) *Investors in People*, CBI.

Confederation of British Industry (1990b) *Working for Customers*, CBI.

Confederation of British Industry (1990c) *The Will to Win*, CBI.

Crosby, P B (1978) *Quality is Free,* McGraw-Hill.

Deming, W Edwards (1982) *Quality, Productivity and Competitive Position*, Cambridge, Mass: MIT.

Deming, W Edwards (1986) *Out of the Crisis*, Cambridge, Mass: MIT.

Department of Employment (1990a) *Managing Quality*, DOE.

Department of Employment (1990b) *Investors in People: The Context*, November, DOE.

Drucker, P F (1968) *The Practice of Management,* Pan.

International Standards Organisation (1987) *ISO 9000: Specification for Design/Development, Production, Installation and Servicing*, ISO.

Ishikawa, K (1984) *What is Total Quality Control the Japanese Way?*, Prentice-Hall.

Juran, J (1970) *Quality Planning and Analysis*, McGraw-Hill.

Martiboye, R J (1989) *Leadership & Quality Management: A Guide for Chief Executives*, Department of Trade and Industry.

Morland, J (1981) *Quality Circles*, The Industrial Society.

Oakland, J S (1986) *Total Quality Management*, Heinemann.

Peters, T J (1987) *Thriving on Chaos*, Macmillan.

Peters, T J and Waterman, R H (1982) *In Search of Excellence,* Harper & Row.

Schneier, C E, Beatty, R W and Baird, L S (1987) *The Performance Management Sourcebook*, Human Resource Development Press.

Stoner, J A F and Freeman, R E (1989) *Management*, Prentice-Hall.

Taguchi, G (1986) *Introduction to Quality Engineering*, Asian Productivity Organisation.

Waterman, R H (1988) *The Renewal Factor*, Barton.

Webb, I (1991) *Quest for Quality*, The Industrial Society.

MANAGEMENT CONTROL

Tim Hannagan

OBJECTIVES

The objectives of this chapter are to:

◆ describe the process of organising in an organisation

◆ analyse the structure of organisations

◆ discuss organisational functions and co-ordination

◆ consider the importance of division of work, delegation and authority

◆ analyse performance management and management control

ORGANISING

The work of all organisations has to be organised and controlled. The strategic plan and corporate objectives describe the direction to be taken, and the targets and the aims if the organisation is to be a success. Once the process of implementation and the action plan are agreed, managers have to organise the activities involved. *Organising* is the process of defining the tasks and activities to be carried out by a number of people to achieve particular objectives, while *management control* is the process of monitoring and adjusting these activities in order to achieve the greatest efficiency and effectiveness in meeting those objectives. In other words, organising is deciding what is to be done and who is to do it, while control is making sure that it is done and done well. These are fundamental areas of the manager's role at all levels, because it is through the process of organising and directing people and resources that the work of the organisation is accomplished. The control function loops back to the planning function as a review mechanism (Fig 8.1).

Organising and controlling include all management functions because of the need to organise all of them, allocate resources and integrate everybody's work. Organisation lies at the heart of all activities; without it, very little can be accomplished. It is, of course, possible to organise matters badly, so that people and resources do not work together effectively; the management role is to organise activities in such a way that the efficiency and quality of an organisation's output and work are improved. When this is achieved people working together can accomplish more than the sum of their individual efforts, just as a football team can play far better with a high level of teamwork than it can if team members play as individuals. The process of organisation involves the allocation of responsibilities so that everyone knows what their task is and what resources they have at their disposal in order to accomplish this within a particular timeframe. This promotes accountability so that employees know to whom they are responsible for the completion of tasks, and the structure of the organisation will establish these lines of responsibility.

The structure also establishes the formal communication system, but it must be recognised that informal networks may create quite different patterns. The

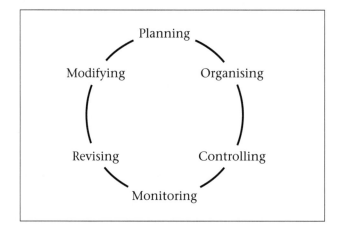

FIG 8.1 THE CONTROL LOOP

communication system should be efficient vertically, up and down, as well as horizontally across it, and the organisation structure can assist this process. It should also reflect the needs of the organisation in terms of accountability and control. The management of an organisation can be seen as a series of stages moving from original concepts to actual practice, so that managers at different levels have to:

- determine the essential actions and tasks required to achieve the organisation's aims;
- divide these actions and tasks into assignments which can be carried out by departments, units or teams;
- divide these actions into assignments for each individual person;
- decide who is responsible for each action and task;
- organise the co-ordination of the work of each team or group.

The second and third stages may be reversed, depending on whether the activities and tasks are grouped together before being subdivided into individual actions or afterwards. These stages describe the division of work within an organisation and the distribution of responsibility and authority (Fig 8.2). Their operation may be determined by the structure of an established organisation, or may help to determine the structure for a new organisation. In practice, companies should alter their structures to meet the needs of their customers, and if the gap widens between tasks and activities and the organisation's structure, tensions and inefficiencies are likely to arise. Therefore, if the work of a company changes to any extent, the structure has to be altered to reflect this. For example, if a company is organised so that there is a separate business unit for each main product, if one of the products declines, that unit may need to be closed down or merged with another unit. If this is difficult because units and departments have become too inflexible, this can lead to great inefficiencies.

STAGES	ORGANISATION OF
Determine essential actions and tasks	Division of work
Divide action and tasks between teams and units	Structure
Divide actions and tasks into assignments for each individual	Action plans
Decide on who is responsible for the completion of actions and tasks	Delegation
Arrange the co-ordination of the work of each team and department	Co-ordination

FIG 8.2 STAGES IN ORGANISING

ORGANISATIONAL DESIGN AND STRUCTURE

The outcome of a company's organising activities can be depicted in organisational design. The object of the design is to create an organisational structure which fits with its objectives, its resources and its environment, because the structure describes the relationship between different parts of the organisation and the people in it. It specifies the division of work, the hierarchy and authority structure, and the formal links that exist between people within the organisation. In practice, of course, there are cross-functional relationships, networks and informal links which are not described by a formal structure but may be of equal importance. A management or organisation chart is a diagram of an organisation's formal structure describing the functions, departments and position of people within the organisation and how they are related.

An organisation chart usually consists of a 'line' diagram showing the chain of command and official channels of communication. A hierarchical structure will usually be described in terms of the organisation of line management and reporting, while a matrix structure will be described more in terms of relationships between units and people and processes of co-ordination. In order both to describe company structure and reflect the company priorities other forms of diagram may be designed, or more than one diagram may be felt to be appropriate. For example, in order to focus on the importance of customers, a diagram such as an inverted triangle (*see* Fig 8.3) may be felt to be appropriate.

In Fig 8.3 the teams and employees closest to the organisation's customers are at the top of the triangle in order to emphasise the supporting role of functional departments and senior management (*see also* Fig 3.3). Of course, much greater detail can be included in this type of diagram and it can simply consist of an inverted management chart. Figure 8.4 shows a more traditional chart with senior managers at the top, middle managers below them and operational staff at the bottom. At the same time, the chart is divided into functional groupings with line

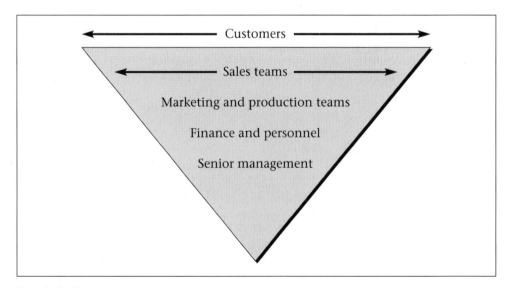

FIG 8.3 INVERTED TRIANGLE

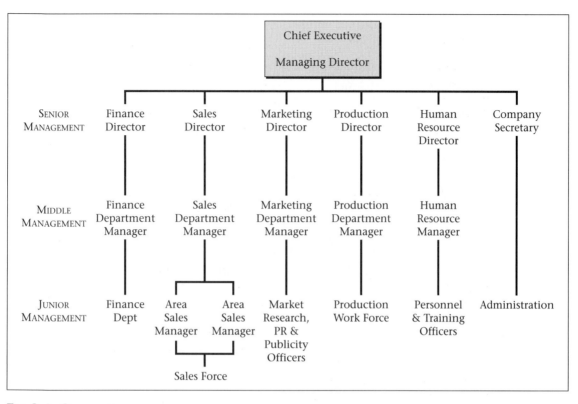

Fig 8.4 Organisational chart

management and responsibility flowing down the functions. It is difficult in this type of diagram to show functional links, co-ordination of projects and informal relationships. Some attempt can be made to do this by using dotted lines.

Functional structure

The functional structure illustrated in Fig 8.4 brings together all those engaged in related activities into one department. The production director and the production department are responsible for all the products manufactured by the company and the sales managers are responsible for all the sales of these products. This 'traditional' structure is often seen as the most 'logical' method for dividing up the work of the organisation. It is used in small and medium organisations and in an adapted form it may be used in large organisations. However, the disadvantage of this structure becomes more obvious as an organisation grows in size (Fig 8.5 summarises advantages and disadvantages).

This functional structure can bring together specialists and specialist equipment in order to develop high quality products and services from their particular department. The staff in these departments can provide support for each other and their teamwork can help innovation develop within their relatively narrow area. Line management control, leadership and authority are all very easily understood within this structure, and employees can develop considerable loyalty towards their department which may be more difficult to create for the whole company. This loy-

ADVANTAGES	DISADVANTAGES
Efficient use of specialised resources	Empire building and bureaucracy
Responsibility, authority and control are clear	Slow response to customer needs
Encourages specialised management expertise	Narrow perspective and limited innovation
Promotes employee loyalty to small unit	Obscures responsibility for overall tasks
Clear promotion path	Limits scope for development of general managers and employees to move into new areas
Good 'vertical' communication	Poor networks and 'horizontal' communication

FIG 8.5 FUNCTIONAL ORGANISATION

alty may develop into some suspicion and even antagonism towards other departments. Other departments may be blamed when things go wrong, or they may appear to be favoured by senior management and to receive more than their fair share of resources.

The advantages for managers and employees of a functional structure are that they can develop their expertise, they have a clear promotion path within the department, and they can communicate easily with other people with similar backgrounds and working on similar tasks. These departments can develop a paternalistic form of leadership and management which may favour some people at the expense of others. At the same time, the differences between the 'home' department and the others may be manifested in a variety of ways. Particular jargon may develop which makes it difficult for people from other departments to understand what is being said, stereotypes may be used to describe people working in other departments, company policies may be interpreted and put into practice differently in the various departments, and jealousies may develop over working space, equipment levels and so on.

Functional departments can encourage bureaucracy and empire building. The department may feel it is more important the greater resources it uses and the larger its staff. Managers and other staff may become reluctant to pass specialised information to people not in their department. There may be slow responses to changes in customer needs, particularly from those departments which have little contact with the final customer. Tasks which cut across departments may take a long time because they have to move sequentially from one department to another. This can be exacerbated by a lack of clear responsibility for such tasks, with each department able to lay blame for any delay on another department. For example, all employees may be taken on through the personnel department and if it is slow in this process, other departments may have a long wait for salespeople or production workers. Genuine conflicts may develop over priorities, so that, for example, new designs and innovation may not be seen as particularly important by the production department, whereas the marketing department considers that new designs are essential to meet customer needs.

As organisations grow in size, either by broadening their products and services or by expanding geographically, the disadvantages of a functional structure become apparent. It becomes more difficult to obtain quick decisions on actions because functional managers have to report to the central headquarters in order to have their decision endorsed. At the same time control over the departments becomes more difficult, and co-ordination may not be able to create a situation where the organisation's objectives can be achieved. These developments cause large organisations to consider other forms of structure to reflect their new requirements. The most extreme of these is the matrix structure.

Matrix structure

The usual matrix structure is designed to answer the main problems of the functional structure. It combines a vertical chain of command, through functions and departments or units, with a horizontal 'project', 'business unit' or 'product' team. The purpose of the matrix structure is to promote across company groupings of people and skills to provide a team in order to produce a product or service. This lateral structure is led by a project or group manager who is expert in the team's assigned area of specialisation. The individual therefore has two bosses, a functional manager and a project or group manager. This is the basis for the use of the term 'matrix' which in mathematics applies to an array of vertical columns and horizontal rows.

An example of a matrix structure is shown in Fig 8.6. Staff from production, marketing, sales, human resource and administration are divided into four project (or product/service) teams which consist of staff from all five functions under project managers who report to the chief executive. An individual employee in production, for instance, will be in a project team manufacturing a product and reporting to a project manager. The project manager is responsible for making sure that the team not only makes the product as specified but also markets it and sells it. Personnel, training or administrative staff may also be allocated to the team. The production employee will also report to the production manager of the company, who will be responsible for initially allocating the employee to this specific project and for the career of the employee in the organisation. The production manager is in fact the employee's line and functional manager, while the project manager is the task or activity manager.

In a similar way members of teams or units may have separate functional managers on a vertical scale, while the whole team moves together from one project to the next. Research teams in science and engineering will often work in this way, because the skills of the team may be complementary and essential for the completion of the task. At the same time, the functional managers provide the specialist support and career path which may not be available through the team. In this way the matrix structure is intended to combine the advantages of functional specialisa-

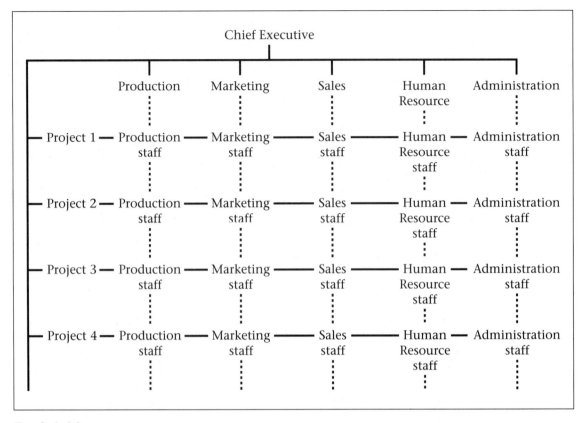

FIG 8.6 MATRIX STRUCTURE

tion with product or project specialisation. The matrix team work on relatively narrowly defined projects, while individuals retain the link with the functional structure of the organisation.

In some organisations a particular unit or section has a matrix structure, while the rest of the organisation has a functional structure. It has proved quite difficult in fact to organise on a full matrix in a large organisation, while small consultancies, research teams, advertising agencies and so on are able to work within this structure very easily. This is because an effective matrix structure requires a high degree of co-operation and flexibility from everybody at all levels. There needs to be open and direct lines of communication horizontally and vertically and a high level of confidence between managers and between employees. For these reasons matrix structures can work well where staff members have similar qualifications and share common goals, and where teamwork is more important than authority. Consultancies and research teams are good examples of this situation, and organisations such as advertising agencies may also operate in this way because everybody is working together on a variety of accounts.

The matrix structure can be an effective means of bringing together people with the diverse skills required to solve a complex problem, such as in research teams and consultancies. It throws the focus on the project to be completed. This provides a common purpose with a well-defined objective for which the whole team or group can be responsible, while the functional structure can too easily fragment the clarity of this aim. By working together, people from various functions can understand the demands placed on other people from different areas of work. For example, preconceptions by marketing personnel about engineers can be overcome in this way and vice versa. This understanding can produce a more realistic approach to each other's work. If the structure is sufficiently flexible and has not become rigid, it can help to keep down the costs of an organisation, because managers need only assign the number of people needed to complete a particular project (*see* Fig 8.7).

Although the matrix structure may be easy to design and appears to have great advantages over the functional structure, it may be difficult to implement. Problems can arise over shared responsibility, the use of resources in common and the question of priorities. One manager may be played off against another by employees, so that the project manager, for example, is told that the functional manager has decided to pull an individual out of the team to work elsewhere. If this happens without proper consultation it can cause great problems for the project team.

ADVANTAGES	DISADVANTAGES
Focuses on end product	Requires excellent communications
Stimulates creativity	Encourages power struggles
Provides challenges	Risks duplication of effort
Enables flexibility in an organisation	Confuses lines of responsibility
Improves communication and understanding	Requires high levels of interpersonal skills
	May lead to more discussion than action

FIG 8.7 ADVANTAGES AND DISADVANTAGES OF A MATRIX STRUCTURE

Product, market and geographical structures

As a company diversifies so that its products and services penetrate a range of markets and expands to cover broad geographical areas, its structure needs to reflect these changes. The functional structure is usually felt to be inadequate for these circumstances. Functional managers can find themselves responsible for the production or marketing of numerous and vastly different products and services, and senior managers can become responsible for co-ordinating areas which it is beyond their capacity to monitor and control. At the same time the matrix structure may not be suitable because it does not provide the necessary control over wide-ranging areas of work, and too many people of different qualifications, experiences and backgrounds will be involved.

There are a number of different approaches to the problem of finding a structure to match the requirements of a company in this situation, but the usual approach is to develop divisions or units which, unlike a functional department, resemble a separate business. There is a divisional head who is responsible for the operation of the division and may be accountable for its profitability; however, unlike a separate business, the division has to conform to the company requirements and is accountable to it.

The company may establish the rules and policies for its divisions in connection with such areas as finance, training, personnel, advertising and so on. Some 'divisions' are given a high degree of autonomy in, say, a geographical area, so that they become 'satellite companies' run as almost separate entities but owned by the parent company and responsible to it. For example, Rank Xerox UK plc is owned by the parent North American company, but enjoys a high degree of autonomy within the UK and Europe. The creation of a divisional structure has been advantageous in a geographically distinct area. The local company can produce products for its geographically local markets, it can develop marketing and sales techniques which are tailor-made for the local area, and it can develop a culture which is sympathetic to the locality. For example, Ford UK produces motor cars aimed specifically at the UK and European markets and adapts its marketing and sales techniques to the requirements of these markets. Through this process the UK can be treated as a distinct market requiring clear focus in the approach to it.

Of course, these factors are true also where there are clearly different markets for the same product or service, or where a company is producing clearly different products or services for the same market. For example, many publishers have an education division for publishing educational and training books and a general or fiction division for publishing novels. This may be subdivided by age group, so that a children's book division concentrates on that market. Some books will cross the divisional lines and may be sold as a children's book by one division, as an educational reader by another and as a general work of fiction by a third.

A divisional type structure (*see* Fig 8.8) has the advantage of combining all the activities, skills and expertise required to produce and market particular products or a product in a particular marketplace. The whole process can be easily co-ordinated and the speed of decision making can be increased, because divisional decisions are made relatively close to the point of implementation. Divisions are able to focus on

ADVANTAGES	DISADVANTAGES
Focus on a product/service/market	May develop a conflict of interests
Clearly defines responsibilities and accountability	Possibility of a drift in meeting corporate objectives
Provides autonomy to managers	May produce neglect of long-term priorities
Provides supporting services from the centre to divisions	Central control may stifle local innovation

FIG 8.8 DIVISIONAL STRUCTURE

the needs of their particular customers and managers have a degree of autonomy in meeting these needs. On the other hand, of course, there may be disadvantages to this structure. The interests of the division can be placed above those of the whole organisation. The division may not place organisational objectives in quite the same order of priority as the central organisation, and may place its short-term interests above the longer-term interests of the whole company.

Divisional structures can lead to a conflict of interest between divisions which develop different objectives and priorities, and it is the role of the central organisation to be responsible for co-ordinating the work of divisions. This is not the same as the federal organisation described in Chapter 3 (pp 81–2), where a number of separate organisations or companies come together out of mutual interest, although one of their objectives is to gain some of the advantages of a division of a large organisation in terms of support. Chapter 3 describes changes to organisational structure brought about by greater flexibility in the labour force, and this flexibility needs to be reflected in whichever management structure is chosen.

CO-ORDINATION

Co-ordination is the integration of the activities of individuals and units into a concerted effort that works towards a common objective. In order to achieve this managers have to make sure that people, teams, units and divisions all work together towards a common aim. This requires a well-understood chain of command and span of management. It has been considered an essential feature of a chain of command for there to be 'unity of command', that is, one person in charge. For example, Henri Fayol wrote in 1916 that:

> *'a body with two heads in the social as in the animal sphere is a monster and has difficulty surviving.'* (Quoted in Fayol, 1947)

One of the major weaknesses of a matrix structure is that each employee will have two bosses and strong co-ordination will be required to prevent conflict. On the other hand, it can be argued that strong command systems can be too rigid for the constant changes faced by organisations, and that managers require flexibility and excellent horizontal communication as well as the vertical communication promoted by a functional structure. The conflict arises, therefore, between unity of command on the one hand and the necessity to communicate between functions and other areas of expertise on the other. This has led to companies developing a variety of organisational designs, particularly in large and complex corporations.

As well as a clear 'boss', co-ordination requires a clear 'chain of command' in which authority is seen to start at the top and is scaled down through an organisation in an unbroken chain. In the traditional organisation chart (Fig 8.4) this means that most authority resides at the top of the pyramid and at successively lower levels it is dispensed among more people. This type of organisational design defines the formal lines of communication between subordinates and immediate superiors, and because there is absolute clarity about this it helps to reinforce the unity of command. For example, in Fig 8.4 a salesperson knows that his or her approach to the managing director will be through the area sales manager, the sales department manager and the sales director and, at the same time, directives will be passed down through this chain of command. It is of course essential that the salesperson can communicate with people in other functional areas without having to send a message up the sales chain of command and down the other functional chain of command. Discussion with, for example, a market researcher should be possible directly without involving the sales and marketing directors. This is the informal network that can be developed into cross-organisational project teams.

The span of command or span of management or span of control is the number of people or units for whom a manager is responsible. Choosing the correct span of control is important if an organisation's activities are to be successfully co-ordinated. If a manager is given too many subordinates to co-ordinate and control, the management of them may not be effective, while too few may not utilise the manager's abilities or may create a situation where there is very limited co-ordination. Attempts have been made to find an optimum span of management in terms of an ideal number of employees for a manager to control. The number recommended in recent times has often been around six, on the grounds that many more than this would mean the manager could not spend sufficient time with each subordinate to provide effective monitoring and control. However, it has become recognised that in practice the appropriate span of management depends on the work to be carried out.

It is now argued that the organisation's need to co-ordinate should dictate the most productive span of management. For example, a narrowly defined role in financial management may require an equally narrow span of management because the need to co-ordinate the work of the function is small, while a widely defined role in marketing may require an equally wide span of management to include area marketing and sales managers, market research staff, advertising, public relations and communications staff. Much will in fact depend on the work to be co-ordinated and controlled. Where the work is routine and procedures are standardised, it may be possible for a manager to have a very wide span of management. For example, store managers tend to control a fairly large number of people because their work is largely routine, while management information systems (MIS) managers may have a narrow span of management because this is a capital-intensive area of work with the need for innovative solutions to company requirements. Once these solutions become routine, the span of control of the MIS manager can be extended.

At the same time, managers vary in their ability to manage a number of people. Some managers are better at controlling a small team with a focus on a particular area of work, while others are able to cope with a general management role dealing with a variety of people and controlling a wide area of work. The amount of time a manager requires to co-ordinate the activities of workers is a factor in this, while the nature of the marketing situation will also be an important influence. Some managers are given a range of tasks to complete, while others have a fairly simple list of objectives. At the same time, the role of subordinates, their competence and ability to work on their own will have an effect on the optimum span of management. The proximity of employees to the manager and the effectiveness of communication can also be factors in the span of management. A manager will usually have more difficulty in co-ordinating workers in different locations than in a single location, but much will depend on the efficiency of internal communications (Fig 8.9).

Frequently as managers are promoted their span of control widens. They will take responsibility for more areas of work with more variety and complexity. In order to be effective in these areas, many of which might usually call for a narrow span of management, managers need to be of a high quality.

210

FACTORS INFLUENCING THE WIDTH OF CONTROL	RELATIONSHIP TO SPAN OF MANAGEMENT
Complexity of work activities	The more complex, the narrower the span
Variety of work activities	The greater the variety, the narrower the span
Quality of manager	The more talented the manager, the wider the span
Quality of subordinates	The more responsible and able, the wider the span

FIG 8.9 SPAN OF MANAGEMENT

ORGANISATIONAL DESIGN IN PRACTICE

Organisational design is the process of fitting the way an organisation works to its strategy in order to achieve the most successful possible performance. The way an organisation works includes a 'formal' structure, its informal attitudes and culture, the way decisions are made and the reward systems. These are not static factors and they change in organisations all the time. Organisational design has to change with them if discontinuity is to be avoided. The effect of not changing is strategic drift (*see* Chapter 6, pp 165–6), with an increasing gap appearing between the way the organisation works and its strategy. This can create tensions which will adversely affect performance. It is, therefore, important that:

- as an organisation grows in size, the design is increasingly decentralised and managers delegate decision making to those parts of the organisation best placed to make these particular decisions;

- as an organisation changes its strategy, the organisational design remains consistent with this change;

- as the priorities as well as the products and services of an organisation change over time, organisational design reflects these changes;

- as technology changes, so organisational design changes because of alterations to information requirements and decision making.

Large organisations develop divisional and unit structures, while the move to focus on the customer has given rise to the development of self-managed teams whose role is to meet customer needs. The structure behind these teams is designed to be supportive (*see* the inverted triangle in Fig 8.3). Grouping of staff in teams or units may change as a result of alterations to the product/service portfolio, so that

211

departmental barriers to people's or team's mobility have to be discouraged in order to retain flexibility. The introduction of new technology such as robotics, for example, has developed the need to consider the best form of structure in factories with fewer and perhaps more specialised staff.

Tension and discontinuity can arise because different parts of an organisation disagree over the purpose or direction of the organisation. The teams close to the customer, such as the sales teams, may be convinced that there is a need for a change in the design and packaging of the product, while the production team is convinced that the product is well made and to the specification required by consumers. Perhaps the salespeople view the company mission as being to 'serve the customer', while the production staff place much more emphasis on quality control and view the company mission in terms of 'producing a reliable, high quality product'. In an organisation in which people are unsure of their mission and objectives there is a communication problem which may be to do with organisational design. The design may need to be more sharply defined, with direction, purpose and responsibilities established very clearly.

The organisational design should set out the decision-making process so that a senior manager does not have to make decisions lower down the organisation except in a crisis. It should establish levels of responsibility and sphere of control. It should define the division of work, areas of responsibility and delegation. These should not be matters of conjecture and doubt if an organisation is to work smoothly. This definition may be on relatively 'mechanistic' lines so that the activities of the organisation are broken down into separate specialised tasks, with the objectives and authority for each individual unit precisely defined by senior managers. Or it may be more 'organic' in the sense that individuals work in groups, there is less emphasis on authority coming down the levels of management and more emphasis on communication across all levels of the organisation. In the constantly changing environment of modern management there is often an attempt to have a mixture of systems. The changes require flexibility and the ability of teams to react, while a feeling of stability may be promoted by a strong central system of delegation and overall objective setting.

DIVISION OF WORK

The division of work is the breaking down of tasks into component parts so that individuals are responsible for an activity or a limited set of activities instead of the whole task. The division of labour and specialisation have been recognised for a long time as an essential process of improving the productivity of an organisation.

For example, Adam Smith in *The Wealth of Nations,* published in 1776, described the vast increases in output which could be achieved by a division of work or division of labour. The illustration he used was in pin manufacturing. This relatively simple operation could be carried out by one person completing each individual pin or by a number of people working on parts of the production. He showed that 10 people working on their own produced 200 pins a day (20 each), while by dividing up the work they were able to produce 48 000 pins a day (4800 pins each). This remarkable difference was due to specialisation, according to Adam Smith. The task of producing pins was divided into drawing the wire, straightening it, cutting it, grinding the point and so on. Each person specialised in one of these operations and, because of this, they became expert in that particular operation. This enabled them to work much faster and more efficiently. They did not have to move from one operation to another and their skill in carrying out a single operation greatly increased.

This approach to the division of work was supported by Frederick Taylor and the supporters of scientific management (*see* Chapter 1). In practice, it was applied to the work of textile factories in the late eighteenth and nineteenth centuries and to other manufacturing processes during the industrial revolution of the nineteenth century. In the twentieth century the application has spread to service organisations such as McDonald's restaurants who have broken down the process of producing food into small steps. This process has considerable advantages, particularly in relation to efficiency and productivity:

- less skilled workers can be used, because the task has been simplified to a single operation or a few simple operations;
- training can be quick and relatively easy because each person can be trained on a particular task without the need to develop a wide range of skills;
- proficiency is gained very rapidly, because the specialised task is repetitive and the worker has a great deal of practice at it;
- there is an increase in efficiency because workers do not waste time moving between tasks;
- this increases the speed of operation;
- workers can choose or be assigned to the operation which best suits their aptitudes and preferences.

These advantages led to the assembly line based factories which have characterised manufacturing from early in the industrial revolution to the present. Specialisation and the breaking down of tasks into simple component parts have enabled the development of mechanisation and the use of robots to replace people in many operations. Machines have been invented to take over the work of assembly-line workers so that labour-intensive industries have become increasingly capital intensive. Computers have been developed to control the manufacturing process so that monitoring progress and quality has also become mechanised. A similar process has been taking place in service industries and in management itself with the development of information technology.

At the same time, this division of work and specialisation have given rise to problems and disadvantages as well as advantages:

- workers become skilled in only one operation and when that skill is no longer needed they have to be retrained;
- the mechanisation of many industrial operations has greatly reduced the demand for workers with limited skills and it is difficult to retrain workers to higher levels of skill if they do not have relatively high basic levels of education and training in the first place;
- constant repetition of a single operation is very boring and demotivating for many people;

- teamwork and creative innovation are not encouraged by this process;

- workers have to rely on a constant supply of products on which to carry out their particular operation and this may cause bottlenecks in production;

- workers are not motivated by a pride in the finished product or in the organisation because they perform such a small part of the overall production process.

In an attempt to overcome these disadvantages there have been a variety of schemes to establish different working systems to promote teamwork, pride in the product and quality. For example, the Saab Motor Company developed a system of producing its cars by teams of workers in the 1970s while other automobile manufacturers were using assembly-line processes. Each car was produced by a team working around an 'island' workstation, with the component parts being supplied to the island for the team to assemble the car. In this system, if any faults were detected the whole team was responsible for their correction. Teamwork was encouraged in order to raise productivity, the team assembled a finished product in which they could take pride, and they could carry out different tasks from day to day or week to week on the agreement of the team.

The traditional division of labour gave rise to the need for supervisors, progress chasers, foremen and quality control inspectors. The team process requires a team leader and the ability to access specialists such as maintenance engineers. Progress and quality will be controlled by the teams, particularly if rewards are linked to output. This structure does require flexibility and wide skills in that an individual may be called upon to carry out various tasks by the team. This can be described as 'job enlargement', where a number of routine jobs are within the worker's scope. The team approach also provides for job enrichment in that the team and each individual in it are given responsibility for deciding how the work is to be completed and how well it is carried out.

A central issue for managers is to determine the degree of specialisation appropriate to the effective completion of work. The 'narrower' the scope of the job and the 'shallower' it is, the greater the level of specialisation but the lower the employee's satisfaction may be. Work which is 'narrow' in scope will consist of one or a very limited number of operations. If it is also lacking 'depth', that is the worker has little control over it, it may be very boring. However, some people do prefer to have a limited, very predictable job which they can carry out without much thought. They know 'where they are' each day and do not have to face frequent changes. It can be argued that most people find this type of work boring and look for 'job enlargement' in terms of an increased number of activities related to their work, and job enrichment in terms of more autonomy over how they work.

Figure 8.10 provides a list of some of the characteristics of work which can help managers to decide on the content of individual tasks and to match the ability of individuals to particular areas of work. Work can be analysed in terms of the skill required to complete it, whether it can be divided into separate tasks or not, the degree to which an individual can decide on the job schedule, the extent to which the other people depend on the completion of the task, and the type of feedback to be given.

A highly specialised job on an assembly line, for example, may require limited skill, no autonomy, be a small part of the whole process and receive direct feedback in terms of the number of operations completed. Attaching an item such as door

Skill	the variety of talents required to complete a task; work that requires initiative and creativity tends to be more skilled than work which is operational and repetitive.
Autonomy	the extent to which the individual who performs a task has the freedom to plan and schedule the work programme.
Dimension	the work which involves completing a product may provide greater satisfaction and create a clearer job identity than that which is a small part of the overall process.
Significance	the extent to which work affects other people, either in terms of health and safety, or in terms of the dependence of other people on the completion of the tasks involved.
Feedback	the extent to which an individual receives information about the effectiveness of completed work.

FIG 8.10 WORK CHARACTERISTICS

handles on a motor car assembly line could have these work characteristics. The task would be very dependent on the supply of car bodies at the correct stage of readiness to work on and would in turn need to be carried out before the car is completed. On the other hand, a job such as product design requires a range of skills in matching the design to customer needs and company specifications, may have a high degree of autonomy in that the designer can schedule the work provided that deadlines are met, may at least involve seeing a product design through to completion, and be very significant in terms of the dependency of many people on the final design. Feedback would come in terms of the relative success of the design, perhaps measured by customer satisfaction.

Once the manager has decided on the nature of the work to be completed and has as far as possible matched this and the skills of the available workforce, he or she then has to group the operations and the work in such a way that they can be effectively managed. One way of doing this is to form teams of people with complementary talents so that a whole task can be completed. The team may have a high degree of autonomy and may only be dependent on others at the beginning and end of its process. Individuals and teams will normally be grouped into departments, divisions or units.

DEPARTMENTALISATION

Whatever the unit of management is called, the process of 'departmentalisation' is the grouping of jobs, tasks, processes and resources into logical units to perform an operation within an organisation. The term 'operation' is to some extent appropriate here, because in managing a medical operation a group of individuals are brought together to complete a particular task. They form a team dependent on each other while the operation is being performed. It is possible for managers to organise the people in these teams into a department, responsible for carrying out particular types of operation, or they can be organised into more specialised departments and brought together for a particular project. Departments can be function-, product- or market-based.

Functional

This is the grouping of jobs and resources within an organisation so that employees performing similar tasks are in the same department. In most organisations there are functional departments which will include production, finance, human resources, marketing. The individuals in the medical operating team may be in different functional departments, such as those concerned with surgery, anaesthetics, nursing, operating theatre management.

The purpose of this arrangement is to bring experts and specialists together so that they can further develop their expertise, while the departmental manager has to understand and co-ordinate only a relatively narrow range of skills. However, it is possible that members of the department may lose sight of the organisation's overall business because they are concentrating on their own department and expertise. A functional departmental structure may cause bottlenecks when work has to flow from one to another and when each functional area has to make its own separate decisions.

Product

This is the grouping of jobs and resources around the products and services offered by an organisation. Products or services may be grouped together in relation to their particular needs. This may be based on geographical location, on marketing or on some other division which is considered advantageous.

The product or products can become the central focus of the department and functions can adapt their roles to support it. Decision making can be facilitated by this focus and responsibilities can be clearly defined. However, each department will need its own functional specialists, which can be expensive, and the departments may concentrate on their own products or services at the expense of others produced in the organisation.

Market

This is the grouping of jobs and resources around the markets and customer groups identified by the organisation. The success of this form of departmentalisation depends on the ability to identify unique categories of customers and to focus on their particular requirements. One example of this exists in banks and other financial companies, who are able to distinguish between individual customers, small businesses and large corporations.

Departments based on markets are able to focus on the customers and to adjust rapidly to their needs. However, a high degree of co-ordination is required in order to make sure that this approach meets corporate objectives.

AUTHORITY AND DELEGATION

Authority is the power related to each position within the organisation. It involves the right to give orders, make decisions and spend resources. In an organisation authority provides a right to do these things supported by the structure of the organisation and understood by every employee when they join. The contract or job description will usually describe to whom the employees are responsible and for whom they are responsible. This means that employees accept orders and decisions and expect these to be carried out if they are agreed through the established structure.

Power is the ability to carry out an action, whereas authority can be seen as the right to do this. *Delegation* is the distribution of authority from a manager to a subordinate. Responsibility is an obligation to be liable for a task, decision or action. While authority can be delegated, responsibility cannot, so that a manager can provide a subordinate with the power to make a decision but still retains responsibility for it in the sense of being liable for the result. If the subordinate makes a decision which leads to a success, the manager can accept some of the praise; but if the decision leads to a problem, the manager is obliged to accept the blame. The managers are unable to simply pass all blame onto the subordinates, because they have been responsible for the delegation of authority and if this has led to a problem this can be traced back to their decision to delegate.

Delegation of authority can only be successful when the subordinate has the ability, information and willingness to perform a task or take a decision. This can be supported by the organisational structure where clear lines of management and communication can enable the process to operate without difficulty. The position of an individual in the organisation endows that person with a particular type of power, sometimes referred to as legitimate power. Both power and authority can be different to this, in that authority may arise, for example, out of respect for a person's expertise rather than their position, while power can arise from control over resources. An accountant, for example, may have the power to accumulate large amounts of clients' money without having the authority to do so. Managers may have the authority to make decisions in an organisation, but may not have the power to carry them out because their subordinates do not respect their decisions and find ways of ignoring them.

The classical theory of authority is based on the hierarchical principle that authority flows down from the top of an organisation and is also dependent on the position held. When removed from this position the individual no longer has the authority associated with it. The opposite to this view is the 'acceptance' theory proposed by Mary Parker Follett and Chester Barnard (*see* Chapter 1). In this theory managers' authority depends on their subordinates and whether these do or do not choose to accept the managers' orders. Subordinates have the power to deny authority or to accept it. A different approach to this suggests that circumstances decide who is in authority and this person will be different in different circumstances. For example, in an accident the first person on the scene may assume authority until the emergency services arrive, when the senior officer may take over. It follows on from this that it may be the most knowledgeable person in a given situation who has authority, so that, for example, the managing director of a company may exert authority over a senior management meeting, but will defer to the company accountant when there is a meeting on the financial accounts of the company or a meeting with the external auditors.

In practice authority is often a mixture of these theories in that, while managers' position in an organisation will greatly affect their range and depth of authority, it can only be exerted where it will be accepted. This acceptance may arise out of line management control, because subordinates will depend on their senior line managers for reports and promotion, or out of respect for the judgement and experience of a more senior manager or as a result of a consensus. It is in fact important to be aware how authority is exerted so that instructions are not confused, and so that as organisations become more democratic they increasingly arise from a consensus of what needs to be done.

Delegation arises because one manager cannot do all the work of the organisation. By delegating, the managers are able to extend their capability and capacity. They can take on new tasks while monitoring others delegated to subordinates. These more junior managers gain from the experience of taking on new tasks knowing that they can turn to the senior manager for help, and they can build up specialised knowledge and expertise. While responsibility for a task is given to subordinates, the ultimate responsibility remains with the manager; this cannot be delegated. Authority to make decisions and use resources can be delegated and will be necessary for a task to be accomplished. If a task is delegated without the necessary authority the subordinate will not be able to complete it. The subordinate will be accountable for the outcome of a delegated task to the manager who will be accountable to a more senior manager and so on. To an extent, authority flows upwards through an organisation.

Obstacles to delegation arise from managers' attitude towards it or subordinates' reluctance to accept it, or because of factors related to the organisation. Managers may not want to relinquish authority to a subordinate, or they may feel that 'if you want a job done properly, do it yourself'. They may have a concern either that to delegate may indicate they cannot carry out the job themselves, or that if it is carried out very well by the subordinates they will themselves appear to be less competent. Managers may feel that it is too time consuming to teach a subordinate how to carry out a task. Subordinates may lack confidence in their ability to complete a task and they may be afraid of failing in it. They may view delegation as simply giving them extra work, and they may not want to find out how to complete the task because it is easier to ask the manager. Some organisations are too small to provide much scope for delegation and in some it is not the 'corporate culture'. People may be assigned tasks which they are expected to carry out without recourse to delegation. The more centralised an organisation is the less delegation there is, because authority will not be widely distributed. In decentralised organisations, authority is widely delegated between business units, departments and teams, or between people.

PERFORMANCE MANAGEMENT

The process of managing organisations and control eventually comes down to the individual employee working in an organisation. Whatever the structure, the division of work, the level of co-ordination and the system of authority and delegation, the individuals have to know what they are to do and this has to be monitored.

Performance management systems are designed to establish individual objectives which assist the achievement of corporate objectives and monitor progress on accomplishing them. The term 'performance management' means different practices to different managers, but usually includes the following elements:

- the organisation has a shared vision of its objectives, or a mission statement or corporate objectives, which it communicates to its employees;

- individual performance management targets are set which are related to the organisational objectives;

- a regular, formal review is carried out to monitor progress toward these objectives;

- the review process is used to identify training needs, career development and possible rewards;

- the effectiveness of the whole process is evaluated against the overall performance of the organisation.

There is usually a strong emphasis on objective setting and formal appraisal and there is often a sequence of steps in the performance management cycle. Although these steps may be called by different names they include:

- agreement on the job description;

- establishing priorities;

- arriving at objectives;

- setting a time horizon;

- reviewing and monitoring.

This process results in the assessment of the individual's performance, and in 'coaching' in the sense of identifying means of improving performance through training and development and establishing career progression. Performance management can be defined as a method of improving business performance by focusing on key areas of activity.

Performance management can be thought of as an extension of management by objectives (MBO) (*see* Chapter 6). This system establishes objectives for an individual or a group and then judges performance on how well they have been achieved. This was a popular approach to management in the 1960s and 1970s. The main problems with it were that sometimes the objectives were established by more senior managers for their subordinates without any agreement, and that the 'coaching' and 'counselling' elements, felt to be so important in more recent approaches, were left out. Although the objectives were supported by senior management, they were in some cases seen to be imposed with little help forthcoming from above. In a well-organised MBO process managers were and still will be helped to appreciate the value of their personal efforts and the way these efforts are expected to fit into the contributions to be made by those above and below. This approach can lead to a fully integrated appreciation of the links to corporate objectives (Fig 8.11).

FIG 8.11 PERFORMANCE MANAGEMENT

MBO tended to be developed in a hierarchical structure where participative manage-ment was not the essential feature and target setting and control had a high priority. Modern performance management places a very high emphasis on participation and on 'coaching' at all levels. The emphasis is on progression and development rather than measurement and control. Increasingly, it is seen as a fundamental support for total quality management. The well thought-out MBO systems were the precursor of performance management linked to total quality. At its best only the terms have changed, and of course, to paraphrase the view of leading Japanese companies, 'who needs these terms anyway, it's the way we work'. Drucker (1955) outlines the story of the three stone-cutters to illustrate the point. When asked what they were doing:

> 'The first replied, "I am making a living."
> 'The second said, "I am doing the best job of stone-cutting in the
>   entire country."
> 'The third looked up and said, "I am building a cathedral."'

It can be argued that the first man knows what he wants from a day's work. He will give 'a fair day's work for a day's pay'. He will carry out his task but leave every-thing else to managers and supervisors. The second is a craftsman with his concentration on carrying out the best work possible within the limits of his craft. He will believe that he is accomplishing something useful by cutting and polishing stones expertly, but if, in fact, his work does not fit in with what is required for the building, then it is useless. Managers may often find themselves in this position, working with great expertise on a particular function and developing habits which concentrate on the performance of the function rather than the objective of the whole business. Managers, may for example, appraise their subordinates according to their craftsmanship and promote and reward them accordingly. The third stone-cutter does have a vision of the objectives of his work, of how his contribution fits in. He will not be content to carry out work which does not help to make progress in the building of the cathedral. He may suggest ways of improving the effective-ness of his work to ensure the objective is reached. For Drucker, the definition of a manager is that 'in what he does he takes responsibility for the whole – that in cutting stone, he builds the whole cathedral'.

This situation cannot be achieved by maintaining occasional drives or campaigns on particular issues. An economy drive, for example, will usually not lead to efficiencies across the company, but may lead to a cutback on staff and consumables where possible, which may not be in the most effective places for the company in the medium or long term. Managers need to take responsibility for their own work and to set objectives for themselves and their teams. They will take responsibility for their subordinates' performance in the same way that their line managers take responsibility for them.

In this form the MBO approach differs very little from modern performance management ideas: they both help to put into effect corporate objectives by directing attention to key areas of activity. One way or another managers need to assess their subordinates and to be assessed themselves by their supervisors (Fig 8.12). The appraisal process can judge people on:

- **what they achieve;**
- **what they do;**
- **what they are.**

In operating a performance management system, managers will start by appraising themselves. This process begins with outlining the main tasks of the post and from this establishing a description of the job. This job description can then be agreed with a manager's immediate boss, that is the line manager. The next stage is to agree on the main priorities of the job in particular time periods, say three months, six months and a year. The line manager will need to make sure that this fits in with company objectives. Then the manager's objectives can be arrived at, again by agreement, which is essential if the manager is to feel responsible for achieving the objectives. At the same time line managers will want to help to achieve these objectives in any way possible because they reflect their own objectives (Fig 8.13).

The objectives agreed by managers will take the form of actions to be completed within a certain period. They will be reviewed from time to time and may be altered in the light of changing circumstances by agreement between the manager

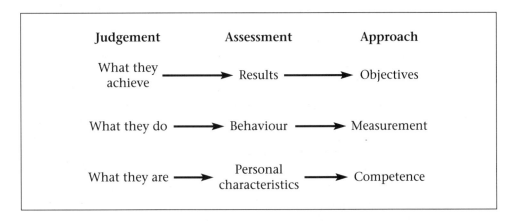

FIG 8.12 MANAGEMENT APPRAISAL

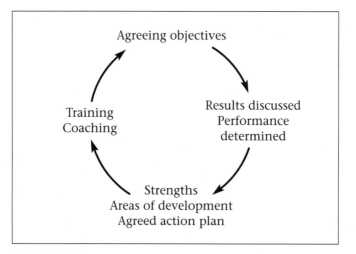

FIG 8.13 PERFORMANCE MANAGEMENT CYCLE

and line manager. The process is not one of appraising for weakness, but analysing the situation. If the manager and his or her boss can agree on an area for improvement, then this may be able to be helped through training. Alternatively, it may be possible to focus the job on the manager's strengths so that personal characteristics and behavioural patterns can assist in arriving at achievements.

The whole emphasis of this approach is on the future, not on the past. It is all about performance and help, or 'coaching' to achieve good performance. The personality of the manager is less of an issue in this system, while the company can provide financial support and time for training if problems are identified or it is considered important to develop particular management techniques. Many companies provide training in such subjects as time management, assertiveness and report writing. The performance management system provides leverage points for integration with total quality management by encouraging policies, procedures and values which promote performance and ongoing activities based on a set of skills which facilitate high performance.

This process may or may not be attached to a salary review and performance pay. It may be thought to be more effective if it is linked to a reward system; however, performance is not the only criterion used in determining salary increases and promotions, and in many cases may not be the main factor. The accountability of one manager for the work of another and the focus on particular activities in order to achieve corporate objectives are the essential features of this process. The approach can be applied throughout the organisation, with managers and supervisors responsible for their teams achieving objectives while the teams are, in turn, accountable to them. At a very operational level, where members of a team share or even interchange tasks, the team objectives and those of the individual may be indistinguishable.

A well-organised and sympathetically implemented performance management system can build trust and improve communication in all areas of an organisation, and this can promote similarity in the high level of performance expectations; it can promote equity and recognise quality through financial and non-financial rewards. While executive support is necessary for total quality management, executive action is critical and performance management can provide the focus for this action down to the most operational level. The strategic plan emphasises the direction a company must follow to take advantage of opportunities and to reach medium- and long-term objectives, while action plans make this a reality.

MANAGEMENT CONTROL

Management control is necessary in order to monitor what people are doing, how they are doing it and what they accomplish. *Operational* control is at the level where managers are concerned with using physical, financial and human resources to accomplish organisational objectives. *Strategic* control is at the level of factors which may affect the corporate strategy of the organisation. This involves monitoring customers, competitors, suppliers, government policies, changes in technology and developments in the community. Managers face constant changes, and this dynamic factor in the internal and external environment of organisations emphasises the importance of the link between planning and control. The time factor is important in this process because in the period between establishing objectives and accomplishing them changes can occur and will have to be taken on board. Well-designed controls enable managers to predict, monitor and adjust to changes. *Management* control can be seen as the process of monitoring and adjusting organisational activities in order to facilitate the accomplishment of organisational objectives. It is making something happen the way it was planned to happen.

The process of establishing objectives for individuals, teams and units through performance management helps to provide control, sometimes referred to as '*feedforward* control'. Performance management establishes what people are going to do and how they are going to do it. The attempt is made to predict problems and to consider ways of overcoming them in developing an action plan. '*Concurrent* control' is the process of controlling actions while they are being taken. The primary role of supervisors and foremen is to provide day-to-day, minute-to-minute control, making adjustments as a process is taking place. Team leaders, operational and junior managers control tasks and activities as they take place, watching daily, weekly and monthly results, making decisions, fine-tuning the process so that the objectives can be achieved. As a new office block or factory is built, the plans will need to be adjusted and adapted while sight is not lost of the overall objective. The plans are agreed, drawings of the completed building are presented and the actions required to reach this point are established. When the foundations are dug out it may be that an unexpected layer of rock is discovered and decisions will have to be made to adjust the plans to deal with this problem. '*Feedback* control' concentrates on the outcomes of action. It is at this point that judgements are made about the original plans and the actions taken to turn them into reality. Feedback is a process of evaluating the success of the tasks and activities, the work of individuals and teams, and plans made for future development. For example, questions can be asked and answered regarding how well the building was planned, how well it was built, what problems arose during the construction, and how well it is in fact suited to its purpose.

The process of control starts with establishing standards of desired outcomes. These may be in numerical terms, for example an assembly line will produce a thousand units a day, or in financial terms, such as a retail store being expected to create sales of £2000 a day, or in quality terms, in that a unit of production or a

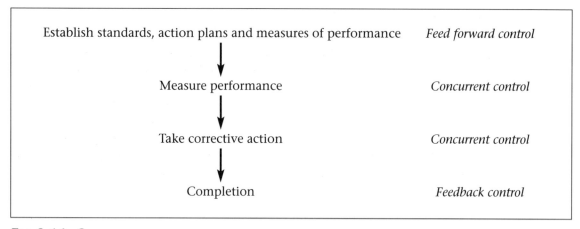

Establish standards, action plans and measures of performance   *Feed forward control*

Measure performance   *Concurrent control*

Take corrective action   *Concurrent control*

Completion   *Feedback control*

FIG 8.14 CONTROL PROCESS

building has to be fit for the purpose for which it is to be used and meets expectations. Standards may include a time factor and may be measured by customer satisfaction or by some other qualitative method.

Once standards have been established, the next stage is to monitor progress through quality control and observation. Points of reference may be fixed in order to check on progress. The manager has to compare outcomes to the established standards, decide how much deviation is acceptable and sort out any problems that may arise. This process of comparing performance to standards is followed by corrective action. Functional managers will have their own monitoring and control systems. Financial control will be provided by the organisation's financial management to ensure that any project remains within the planned limits. Production and premises managers will control physical plant and premises, supplies and energy. Human resource managers use performance appraisal systems to monitor people's work. Operations management, management information systems, the process of decision making and financial management are all aspects of this control process (*see* Fig 8.14).

These systems do not, of course, decide the performance of an organisation; they are an essential element in this performance and monitor and control it. Performance is as much to do with people as with the physical assets on which they work. In the division of labour between capital, labour, raw materials and enterprise, all four have to be present and working together for anything to be produced. What is produced and how it is produced will depend on the materials and money available and very heavily on the ability of the people who are available, their attitudes and creativity and on how well the whole process is managed.

SUMMARY

- The role of management is to organise and control the tasks and activities to be carried out in order to achieve the strategic objectives of a company or institution. Without organisation, actions will not be taken in order to achieve these objectives and to ensure the quality of products and services produced.

- There are a variety of organisational structures which help to achieve these actions and companies need to adapt their structures in order to support and facilitate their operations. In the process of deciding on the structure of an organisation, managers need to consider questions of co-ordination, delegation and authority.

■ Managers will have a particular span of control depending on the complexity of activities undertaken, the variety of work and the quality of managers and employees. Organisational design is the process of fitting the way an organisation works to its strategy in order to achieve the best possible performance.

■ Work has to be divided between people, and jobs and tasks grouped into units in order to perform operations. In the end, individuals in an organisation have to know their roles, and managers design performance measures in order both to establish individual objectives and monitor progress on accomplishing them. An appraisal process will assist this and enable management control to be focused at an individual level.

REVIEW AND DISCUSSION QUESTIONS

1 Why is management control important in any form of work? What purpose does it perform?

2 What is the function of organisational design?

3 What are the problems of a matrix structure as against a more functional design?

4 How does the span of management affect the role of a manager?

5 Is delegation an essential element of management or is it possible to manage without it?

6 Discuss the importance of management control and performance management.

CASE STUDY: IN SEARCH OF A MODERN STRUCTURE

Bertelsmann, the third largest media company in the world, is often held up as a model of corporate management in Germany. In spite of its size, however, it has always played up its origins as a small-town publisher and has maintained a decentralised structure.

The company has been one of the most noticeable examples of *Mittelstand* – small and medium-sized business – success. But now, principally as a result of sweeping change in the media sector, Bertelsmann is having to rethink its management structures, including the way in which its prized decentralisation works. Possible changes include the flotation of some of the group's businesses – a significant move for the privately owned company. Originally a printer of hymnals and bibles based in the Westfalian town of Gutersloh, the company was rebuilt after 1945 by Reinhard Mohn, who expanded successfully into book clubs and general publishing. The money earned from these activities financed the acquisition of the majority of Gruner & Jahr, the magazine and newspaper publisher. Other acquisitions, in the 1980s, included the US companies Doubleday, the publisher, and record label RCA.

While the company has long outgrown the *Mittelstand* and Gutersloh – last year it had sales of DM21.5 bn (£7.5 bn) and net profits of DM905 m – Mohn sought to keep Bertelsmann, in spirit at least, close to its roots. Rather than opting for a monolithic structure, a web of *Mittelstand*-like entities was created in which managers are encouraged to behave as if they were running their own companies.

While Mohn, who stood down as chief executive in the 1980s, sought to retain the vigour of *Mittelstand* culture, he also tried to resolve the issues of ownership and generational change which often plague *Mittelstand* companies. He created a charitable foundation which owns the majority of the shares in the company, creating a structure which appeared to offer the best of all worlds. While retaining *Mittelstand* character in the group's subsidiaries, it eliminated some of the risks that go with family ownership and avoided the pitfalls of going public.

Recently, however, the decentralised structure has been called into question. Mark Wossner, chief executive, engaged consultants to canvass the most senior managers. The results gave him a shock: rather than basking in the independence, the managers complained about the lack of synergies across the group. Says Wossner, who joined Bertelsmann nearly 30 years ago: 'Decentralisation brought all of us into this company. I would not have come here if I hadn't known I had the chance to run a company (profit centre) at a young age.' Wossner says the goal now is to create more 'cross-sections' in areas such as information technology within the group – without undermining the autonomy of managers. 'Back-office and infrastructure processes can be centralised. But the operational autonomy and the cultural and national approach in the different countries will be maintained,' he says.

For Wossner, the implementation of reforms also has a personal dimension, for he is due to stand down as chief executive next year. Before he goes he would like to leave his successor – thought most likely to be Thomas Middelhof, the board member responsible for the group's new media activities – with a reinvigorated structure. ■

Source: Studeman, F, *Financial Times*, 27 June 1997. Reprinted with permission.

REFERENCES FOR FURTHER READING

Drucker, Peter (1955) *The Practice of Management*, London: Heinemann.

Fayol, Henri (1947) *General and Industrial Administration*, London: Pitman Publishing.

Harvey-Jones, John (1993) *Managing to Survive*, London: Heinemann.

Studeman, Frederick (1997) 'In search of a modern structure', *Financial Times*, 27 June.

ORGANISING

ORGANISATIONAL CULTURE*

Andrew Brown

OBJECTIVES

The main objective of this chapter is to introduce the concept of organisational or corporate culture. Reading this chapter should give an understanding of:

◆ the concept of culture applied to the organisation

◆ the different definitions of organisational culture

◆ why it is important to be able to recognise the organisational characteristics that determine the culture

◆ the meaning of organisational stories, myths, ceremonies, rituals, heroes, symbols and language and their relation to organisational culture

◆ two different cultural typologies

◆ national cultural differences and how these impinge on the multinational organisation

◆ how changes in organisational culture are managed and some of the problems associated with such changes

◆ the connections between culture, strategy and performance

* This chapter is partly based on *Organisational Culture*, by Andrew Brown (1998, Financial Times Pitman Publishing). The section on consultation and negotiation has been contributed by Tim Hannagan, and Anne Benjamin, Lecturer in Business Policy and Marketing, Imperial College, and MBA course tutor, has also contributed to part of the chapter.

INTRODUCTION

Most people will experience employment in several organisations during their career. More and more of the working population find themselves working in more than one country. Indeed, as the marketplace becomes increasingly global, most organisations will have several different nationalities represented in the workforce. Being part of an organisation entails being part of its culture. It is important when entering an organisation to understand how it works, not just the formal procedures and systems, but also the attitudes and beliefs and values that underpin the working of the organisation as a whole. And, as the management environment becomes more international in outlook, it is equally important to understand how the different national attitudes, values and beliefs affect the workplace. In short, corporate and national culture are two of the variables that contribute to the diverse nature of the organisational environment. So, while this chapter is primarily concerned with corporate culture, some attention will be given to sources of variation attributable to national differences.

WHAT IS ORGANISATIONAL CULTURE?

It is difficult to define organisational culture because there seem to be many definitions given in the literature, indicating the diversity of views on what organisational culture really is. Some writers define culture as a metaphor. For instance:

> *'The culture metaphor points another means of creating organised activity: by influencing the language, norms, folklore, ceremonies, and other social practices that communicate the key ideologies, values, and beliefs guiding action.'* (Morgan, 1986)

Others will describe culture in more tangible terms using observable, but not necessarily measurable, organisation characteristics (*see*, for example, Fig 9.1 taken from Robbins, 1990).

These more overt aspects or characteristics of the organisation's culture are readily perceived by the employees, but other, covert aspects are harder to recognise – aspects such as the shared attitudes, behaviour, beliefs and values of the organisation.

Schein (1992) defines culture as:

> *'A pattern of shared basic assumptions that a group learned as it solved its problems of external adaptation and internal integration, that has worked well enough to be considered valid and, therefore, to be taught to new members as the correct way to perceive, think and feel in relation to those problems.'*

Culture can, therefore, be considered a complex mixture of tangibles, assumptions and behaviours, and such things as stories, myths, rituals, heroes, symbols and language of the organisation, all describing 'the way we do things here'.

Some suggested characteristics of organisational culture to be found in Robbins (1990) are:

- **individual initiative** – the degree of responsibility, freedom and independence that individuals have;

- **risk tolerance** – the degree to which employees are encouraged to be aggressive, innovative and risk taking;

- **direction** – the degree to which the organisation creates clear objectives and performance expectations;

- **integration** – the degree to which units within the organisation are encouraged to operate in a co-ordinated manner;

- **management contact** – the degree to which managers provide clear communication, assistance and support to their subordinates;

- **control** – the degree of rules and regulations, and the amount of direct supervision that are used to oversee and control employee behaviour;

- **identity** – the degree to which members identify with the organisation as a whole rather than with their particular work group or field of professional expertise;

- **reward system** – the degree to which reward allocations (i.e. salary increases, promotions) are based on employee performance criteria;

- **conflict tolerance** – the degree to which employees are encouraged to air conflicts and criticisms openly;

- **communication patterns** – the degree to which organisational communications are restricted to the formal line hierarchy of command.

FIG 9.1 CHARACTERISTICS DESCRIBING ORGANISATIONAL CULTURE

Source: Robbins, Stephen P, *Organization Theory: Structure, Design and Applications*, 3rd edn, © 1990, p 439. Reprinted by permission of Prentice Hall, Inc., Upper Saddle River, New Jersey.

The development of organisational culture

The employees can learn about their culture from different sources, by observing and absorbing these various indicators. So what are these sources exactly?

STORIES AND MYTHS

In most organisations stories will be passed on which illustrate and perpetuate the pervading culture. They keep the culture alive. A *story* is a narrative, based on actual events, that is frequently repeated and shared by the employees of the organisation. Eventually it will become a combination of truth and fiction as it is embellished with successive telling. Very often, these stories are about the organisation's founders, organisational crises, successes, failures and so on. They provide explanations and justification for current practices, anchoring the present in the past. *Myths* differ from stories in that they describe events that are wholly imaginary.

CEREMONIES AND RITUALS

A *ceremony* is a planned activity, usually in the form of a special event, and is conducted for the benefit of an audience, the audience being primarily employees of the organisation. These ceremonies, often dramatic examples of organisation values, are there to reinforce valued accomplishments and to create and strengthen bonds among employees. Examples of these can often be found in organisations which are concerned with personal selling. Staff who have achieved outstanding sales success will be fêted amidst often showy pomp and ceremony. These events act as motivators since successful and outstanding performance is publicly recognised and not infrequently materially rewarded.

Similarly, *rituals* are repeated sequences of collective activities that express and reinforce the key values and goals of the organisation. Business and departmental meetings, for example, can be held for apparently rational reasons but, in fact, are largely there for ritual purposes.

HEROES

Heroes provide role models for people to aspire to, and they are a means of providing a lasting influence within the organisation. Stories about heroes often survive long after they have left the organisation. Heroes are usually real people but have, on occasion, been symbolic, imaginary beings who have the characteristics which are highly valued by the culture. Writers such as Deal and Kennedy (1982) and Peters and Waterman (1982) identified the corporate hero and emphasised their importance to the ultimate success of the organisation. Many anecdotal examples can be found in these and the later writings, for example, of Peters.

The exploits of the heroes can be out of the ordinary, but not so far out as to be unattainable by other employees. In order to make it possible to develop new heroes for the ordinary employee, the organisation has to provide some vision of success which is within the potential of nearly all its members. Alternatively, many organisations have heroes who have challenged the way things are done in the organisation. This type of hero, sometimes seen by management to be an unreasonable man or woman, often signals areas where change is necessary in the organisation, or comes up with valuable innovatory ideas, simply because of their refusal to follow the rules. Many organisations actively try to eliminate unreasonable employees, thereby opting for a quieter life but perhaps missing out on some of their benefits. Other organisations have a strong enough culture to absorb unconventional employees and exploit them. Tom Peters has aptly quoted the following passage from George Bernard Shaw to illustrate the point:

> *'The reasonable man adapts himself to the world: the unreasonable one persists in trying to adapt the world to himself. Therefore all progress depends on the unreasonable man.'*

SYMBOLS

Cultural symbols are words, objects, acts or events that convey meanings to individuals and groups in the organisation. The jargon or words used by employees, the way they dress, corporate logos, the layout of offices and buildings, etc., are all examples of this cultural symbolism. This aspect of culture is possibly the most superficial and the most easily changed and adapted.

LANGUAGE

In a similar way, the language used by the organisation or sub-units of the organisation identifies members of a culture or sub-culture. By learning the language, employees confirm their acceptance of the culture and, by using it, help to reinforce it. The language may be specific terminology used by a certain profession, or acronyms relating the institutions and their structures – which are often unintelligible to the outsider.

Hofstede (1991) suggests that some of these aspects of culture can be subsumed under the term *practices*. They are visible to outside observers, but their cultural meaning is invisible – the way these practices are interpreted by the members (insiders) of the organisation determines the meaning. He also represents the culture as an 'onion', the central part of which contains the underlying *values* of the organisation; the 'practices' are the layers, having different levels of depth. 'Symbols' are the first layer of the onion to be revealed (*see* Fig 9.2).

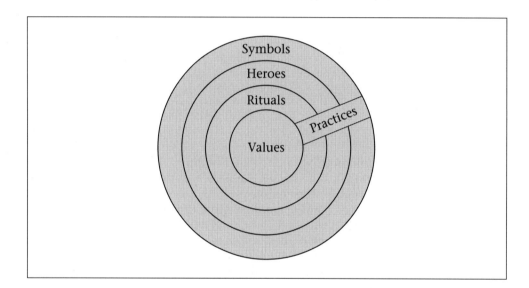

FIG 9.2 HOFSTEDE'S ONION DIAGRAM: MANIFESTATIONS OF CULTURE AT DIFFERENT LEVELS OF DEPTH

Source: Reprinted from Hofstede *et al.* (1990) by permission of *Administrative Science Quarterly*.

TYPOLOGIES OF ORGANISATIONAL CULTURE

Since the 1970s, several typologies or classifications of organisational cultures have been developed. While many organisations may not fit precisely into these classifications, they are nevertheless useful in illustrating some of the variations that exist between cultures. Two of the better known typologies will be discussed here, namely those of Harrison and Handy, and Deal and Kennedy.

The Harrison and Handy classification

Harrison (1972) proposed four types of organisation, namely *power, role, task* and *person.* These ideas were adapted by Handy (1978); he accompanies his description with a pictorial representation and by reference to the appropriate Greek gods as patrons (*see* Fig 9.3). Harrison and Handy's work provided a firm foundation for ideas on culture that were developed subsequently (*see also* Chapter 20).

POWER CULTURE

This culture, represented as a *web* (*see* Fig 9.3), has a central power source, with functional or specialist 'threads' of influence spreading from this pivot of power. The organisational effectiveness depends on trust and empathy, the emphasis being on personal communication. There is little bureaucracy in terms of rules and pre-scribed systems. The powerful centre exercises control through a group of key individuals and decisions are more often made as a result of political manoeuvring rather than by purely logical procedures. These cultures are able to react quickly, but whether they move in the right direction or not depends largely on the quality of the person or persons at the central source of power. One of the major power bases in this culture is *resource* power, with perhaps more *charismatic* power at the central core. The general atmosphere will be politically charged, power-oriented and with a general lack of concern for risk.

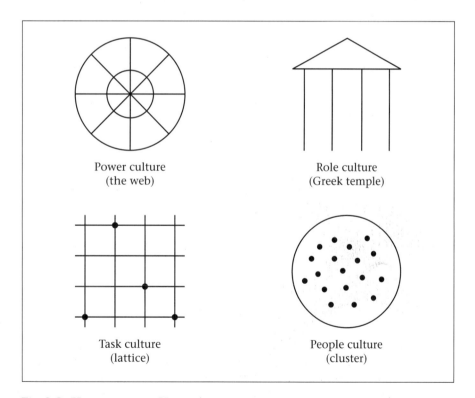

Power culture
(the web)

Role culture
(Greek temple)

Task culture
(lattice)

People culture
(cluster)

FIG 9.3 HARRISON AND HANDY'S TYPOLOGY OF CULTURE

Source: Adapted from Charles Handy (1993) *Understanding Organisations*, 4th edn, pp 183, 185, 187 and 190, London, Penguin Books Ltd. Copyright © Charles Handy 1993. Reproduced by permission of Penguin Books Ltd.

Just as a spider's web may break if extended too far, so this type of organisation may find itself with problems if it tries to extend its activities too widely. In this essentially tough, competitive atmosphere, there is more emphasis on the individual than the group. Employees are judged by end results rather than by how these results are achieved. However, there may be a problem with low morale and high turnover in the middle management layers because of the lack of desire to engage in 'competitive' activity. While a 'power' organisation can be strong and effective, it can also be deficient. And, if an appropriate succession for the central power position is not established, the organisation can become, as Handy puts it, 'a web without a spider' – an organisation with no strength.

Handy suggests Zeus, the all-powerful head of the ancient Greek gods, as the patron god of this culture.

ROLE CULTURE

This culture shares a number of characteristics in common with a bureaucracy. The culture works by logic and rationality. It is called a role culture because roles (or positions) in the organisation are given primacy over the individuals who hold them. The pictorial representation given by Handy is a Greek temple (*see* Fig 9.3). The 'pillars' are the functions or specialisms such as finance, marketing, production and so on. These are controlled by the 'pediment', a small group of senior management.

Roles and rules predominate in this culture. The rules cover job descriptions, recruitment, performance standards, definitions of hierarchy and authority. Promotion is based on the satisfactory attainment of the prescribed performance standards. The power bases which are important in this type of organisation are *position* power and to a lesser degree *expert* power. This sort of culture is more likely to succeed in a predictable and relatively stable environment. In an unchanging world, an organisation of this kind can become extremely efficient. The role culture is appropriate for organisations where, for instance, economies of scale are more important than innovation and flexibility. Individuals who favour predictability and security will be at home in such a culture. However, the current environment in which organisations operate is not so stable and the emphasis is on adaptability and innovation. The role culture finds it difficult to adapt to circumstances that are changing. Also, individuals who are ambitious and high achievers may find this culture stifling. The god suggested by Handy as a patron of this culture is Apollo, the god of reason.

TASK CULTURE

This culture has no single source of power defined by the hierarchy; power is based on expertise. This is because this culture is job or project-oriented. The pictorial representation is a *net*, with some strands appearing thicker and stronger than the others (*see* Fig 9.3). The main sources of power and influence are at the *knots* in the net, and generally power is more widely dispersed than in the previous two cultures. The culture is cross-functional, with project teams made up of individuals with different levels of expertise. The project team structure rather than the hierarchical authority structure is more important. Organisations with this culture often adopt a *matrix* structure. It is important that the right teams are formed, with the appropriate expertise, in order to achieve successful outcomes for the projects. Individuals who disrupt the team will damage the culture.

The advantage of this culture is that it is very flexible and adaptable; teams can be formed and disbanded according to the needs of the organisation. This culture is very appropriate in a frequently changing, competitive environment where short product life cycles and constant innovation exist. The disadvantage of this type of culture, however, is that it is difficult to produce economies of scale or any depth of technical knowledge, due to the short-term nature of the projects. If things go awry with the teams, it is hard to exert control without changing the culture from a task culture to the more conventional power or role culture. Where organisations require creativity, or quick reactions to changing circumstances, this may be the culture to adopt, e.g. organisations such as advertising agencies or management consultancies. Handy does not nominate a specific god for this culture, although he suggests that Athena, the warrior goddess, may fit the role best, since the emphasis is on getting the task done.

PERSON CULTURE

In this culture the individual is all-important. The organisation is there to serve the interests of the individuals within it. These individuals form a collective to gain the mutual support of like-minded people, and to take advantage of such benefits as a common administration, while developing their personal goals and ambitions. Groups of professionals, such as architects, lawyers or consultants, may organise themselves into this type of culture. The pictorial representation of an organisation like this is a *cluster* of individual dots, or 'a galaxy of stars' as Handy puts it (*see* Fig 9.3). Within a culture such as this, individuals will have almost complete autonomy and will make decisions on how their life is to be organised; their allegiance is to themselves rather than to the organisation. This culture will only exist by mutual agreement of the cluster, power being usually shared and based on expertise. Control and management of these talented individuals may be difficult, since the usual sources of power will have little impact on them. However, if the collective 'organisation' begins to drive out the individualism, a power or role culture may develop.

A person culture can be found as a subset of a larger role or power culture, for example specialist groups in universities or commercial businesses. The patron god of this culture is Dionysus, the god of the self-oriented individual.

The Deal and Kennedy classification

Another framework which is useful for classifying organisational culture is that developed by Deal and Kennedy (1982). After examination of many companies and their business environments, they came up with the following classification determined by considering two factors, namely 'the degree of risk associated with the company's activities, and the speed at which companies, and their employees, get feedback on whether decisions or strategies are successful' (*see* Fig 9.4).

Using these factors, corporate cultures can be classified into four distinct types:

- **the tough guy, macho culture;**
- **the work hard, play hard culture;**
- **the bet-your-company culture;**
- **the process culture.**

As with the previous typology, this framework presents a starting point for identifying a corporate culture, but Deal and Kennedy readily acknowledge that many companies will not fit *exactly* into any one of the cultures described.

	DEGREE OF RISK	
	High	**Low**
Rapid	Tough guy, macho culture	Work hard, play hard culture
Slow	Bet-your-company culture	Process culture

(SPEED OF FEEDBACK is the row label for Rapid/Slow)

FIG 9.4 DEAL AND KENNEDY'S CULTURE TYPOLOGY

Source: Terrence E Deal and Allen A Kennedy, *Corporate Cultures: The Rites and Rituals of Corporate Life* (adapted from pp 107–108). © 1982 Addison-Wesley Publishing Company, Inc. Reprinted by permission of the publishers.

TOUGH GUY, MACHO

This is an organisation made up of individuals (entrepreneurs) who are prepared to take high risks and get quick feedback on the actions they take and the decisions that they make. This is a high-pressure culture that, for the individual, can result not only in fast fortunes but equally fast losses. Many individuals in such a climate might suffer from 'burn out' – those who survive are tough risk-takers. People who flourish in this type of culture are not team players, but, as long as they are success-ful, temperamental and outlandish behaviour exhibited by these individuals is tolerated. Typical businesses where a culture like this might exist are advertising, entertainment, consultancy and construction – an example which aptly demon-strates this culture would be the derivatives market in the Far East. The requirement for quick feedback can be perceived as a weakness in this kind of organisation, since any long-term, persistent efforts are less likely to be noticed. 'Cooperation may be lacking and individuals who succeed may be immature and disruptive to the long-term maintenance of a strong culture' (Deal and Kennedy, 1982).

WORK HARD, PLAY HARD CULTURE

This again involves employees at a high level of activity. The feedback on the results of actions and decisions may be just as fast but the risks involved are much less. Risks to the individual are considered to be small since the odd failure will not make or break them. However, the high level of activity still means that there is a great deal of pressure on the employees. Sales organisations, estate agencies, mass consumer companies (such as fast food chains) and office equipment manufactur-ers represent this sort of culture. The successful people are usually those who are high achievers and who work well in a team – for example, the lead person in a sales team. Younger people who are attracted to the action will thrive in such a cli-mate, but it is often hard to retain senior staff. In this culture the emphasis is on high-volume sales, mass-produced goods and quick fix solutions which indicate the short-term focus on business. Shared cultural rituals manifest themselves in terms of sales conventions, contests and meetings.

BET-YOUR-COMPANY CULTURE

Here the organisation is involved in high-stake decisions but there will be a long wait for feedback. Typical of this sort of culture are oil companies, the aerospace industry, new ventures, research and development, and capital-intensive projects. Major decisions may risk the future survival of these organisations and, because of this, there is great attention paid to detail. Technical expertise is respected – the experts being promoted to decision-making roles as their careers develop. Individuals in this type of culture have the staying power and patience to wait and see the result of their actions. Many breakthrough inventions originate in these organisations, but the feedback is frustratingly slow. There is often a long wait of years to gain financial rewards from the investment, which all the time will be subject to the changing economic conditions.

PROCESS CULTURE

This type of culture gives very little feedback and involves low-risk, bureaucratic organisations such as government departments, insurance companies, some financial services and strictly regulated industries whose environments may be considered fairly stable. The emphasis here may be on rules and procedure, red-tape and record-keeping, job titles and the formal hierarchy. People in this type of culture tend to be rather 'protective' of their environment, keen on maintaining order and predictability. An organisation of this type will not be able to react quickly and adapt to changing circumstances, an ability which is becoming more important in the business environment of the 1990s.

Many companies may exhibit a mix of these cultures; for example, the accounts department could be a process culture; research and development could be a bet-your-company culture; and so on. However, if such a mix does exist, usually one culture will dominate. The two typologies described here are perhaps the better known of those devised. There are also those of Quinn and McGrath (1985), Scholz (1987), and Kerr and Slocum (1987). Some organisations will have mixed cultures where different sections/departments can be described differently.

THE EXTERNAL ENVIRONMENT OF ORGANISATIONS

One of the stronger influences on internal corporate culture is the external business environment of the organisation. In fact, Deal and Kennedy (1982) state that it is 'the single greatest influence in shaping a corporate culture'. The corporate culture of an organisation should include or absorb what is necessary to succeed in its business environment (*see also* Chapter 19). If the external environment expects extraordinary customer service, for instance, then the culture should be encouraging this. Similarly, any other requirement or expectation of the 'customer' should be reflected in the organisation's values.

In the discussion of the different typologies of culture, it was clear that culture would very much depend on the industry in which the organisation operated. Comparison of large and small companies, service and manufacturing companies, and public and private sector organisations will show different ways of operating and different patterns of development. The cultures of organisations operating in a very dynamic, highly competitive environment will be different to those of organisations from a more stable, more slowly changing environment.

Many factors in the business environment will have an influence. For instance, there will be a *political influence* inasmuch as the government will affect the cultures of organisations. Both public and private companies will be affected through regulation of monopolies and mergers, changes to the legal framework and management of the economy generally. Publicly-owned companies, in particular, can be very closely regulated and perhaps are more affected in the cultural sense by government policies.

The *sociological aspects* of the environment should also be considered. The changing views and values of society at large have to be monitored. Issues such as protection of the environment, equal opportunities for all and ethics in business have been taken on board by some organisations and have been absorbed into their cultures. Customers and shareholders are also influential to varying degrees. The 'quality culture' adopted by many companies is primarily customer driven. The shareholder influence has perhaps less impact. Cultures can also vary according to what types of profession are contained within an organisation – the professional institutions and associations will help to mould the culture with their influence on training and ethical standards.

In their study of more than 200 companies, the Harvard Business School researchers Kotter and Heskett (1992) found that some corporate cultures are good at adapting to changes while preserving the performance of the organisation, while others are not. They distinguished between 'adaptive' and 'unadaptive' corporate cultures and went on to define the core values and common behaviours in each kind of culture (*see* Fig 9.5).

	ADAPTIVE CORPORATE CULTURES	UNADAPTIVE CORPORATE CULTURES
Core values	Managers care deeply about customers, stockholders and employees. They also strongly value people and processes that can create useful change (e.g. leadership initiatives up and down the management hierarchy).	Managers care mainly about themselves, their immediate work group, or some product (or technology) associated with that work group. They value the orderly and risk-reducing management process much more highly than leadership initiatives.
Common behaviour	Managers pay close attention to all their constituencies, especially customers, and initiate change when needed to serve their legitimate interests, even if that entails taking some risks.	Managers tend to behave somewhat insularly, politically and bureaucratically. As a result, they do not change their strategies quickly to adjust to or take advantage of changes in their business environments.

FIG 9.5 ENVIRONMENTALLY ADAPTIVE VERSUS UNADAPTIVE CORPORATE CULTURES

Source: Adapted and reprinted with the permission of The Free Press, a Division of Simon & Schuster Inc. from *The Corporate Culture and Performance* by John P Kotter and James L Heskett. Copyright © 1990 by Kotter Associates Inc and James L Heskett.

INTERNATIONAL CULTURAL INFLUENCES

With the globalisation of business, and the fact that many organisations extend into many different countries, it is essential that the impact of national culture on organisations is understood. Most societies have become multicultural. Therefore, within the work context and also outside the work environment, people need to learn to deal with the various different values and ways of operating. International managers especially need to understand the culture in which they are working in order to avoid offending the people with whom they are dealing (*see also* Chapter 19).

What is national culture? Several different factors contribute to the overall cultural picture. Underlying values and attitudes, religion, language, education, the political and legal contexts will all contribute to the national cultural environment of organisations. All these elements will be affected by the history and beliefs held in each nation. There are differing views about the organisational similarities and differences that exist between countries. It is probably true that organisations across the globe are tending to show some similar characteristics in terms of structure, technology and hierarchies. It is also true that there still exist fundamental differences between certain nations. Individuals within the organisations will have different attitudes according to their national background. With increasing knowledge and understanding the differences can be allowed for in negotiations etc.

For example, there may be differences in terms of orientation towards time – some cultures have the view 'time is money' whereas other cultures have the attitude 'tomorrow will do'. Some cultures focus on the present or the immediate future, while others have a much more long-term view. Attitude to working will also differ in that some nationalities work at a frenetic pace and view work activity as all-important, while others work at a much slower pace and are more concerned with other aspects of life. Some cultures are inherently resistant to change; others are open to change. There are differing attitudes also to the accumulation of wealth, the basic nature of people and so on – the list is enormous; there are so many sources of diversity.

The language difference also can be a source of misunderstanding; the same language may be used by several nations but with subtle differences in meaning which can confuse issues, and, where translation is necessary, obviously more problems arise. Many organisations are now investing more in language training, which is essential in the international workplace. Political and legal systems are other sources of difference, as is religion. Religion is an important factor in many countries in the shaping of the individual, and the core values and beliefs of the major religions, where they are not understood, will cause confusion, or even major problems such as the loss of an important contract, in some situations.

Geert Hofstede (1983) completed a comprehensive analysis of cultural diversity in the 1970s. Hofstede surveyed 116 000 employees in more than 50 countries. All the employees worked for the same multinational company, IBM. The database eliminated any differences that might be attributable to varying practices and policies in different parts of IBM so that any variations between countries could be reliably attributed to national culture. The research found that national culture had a major impact on employees' work-related values and attitudes – more so than age, sex, position or profession. Hofstede found differences in four dimensions of national culture (*see* Fig 9.6).

---

1 Individualism versus collectivism

Individualism – the extent to which a society expects individuals to take care of themselves and their immediate families and the extent to which individuals believe they are masters of their own destiny.

Collectivism – refers to a tight social framework in which group members (relatives, clans, organisations) focus on the common welfare and feel loyalty to one another.

2 Power distance

Power distance – the socially determined, unequal distribution of power among individuals and institutions within a particular culture. If most individuals in a society support this unequal distribution, the 'nation' is ranked high on the power-distance dimension.

3 Uncertainty avoidance

Uncertainty avoidance – the way in which members of a society cope with uncertainty regarding the future. It is the extent to which people feel threatened by ambiguous and risky situations and attempt to avoid and reduce these situations.

4 Masculinity versus femininity

Masculinity – the relative importance of assertiveness, acquisition of money and things, as well as the degree of not caring for the quality of life and for other people.

Femininity – is the opposite end of the masculinity dimension, more of a nurturing and people orientation.

FIG 9.6 HOFSTEDE'S FOUR DIMENSIONS OF NATIONAL CULTURE

The four work-related value dimensions provide one way of understanding and predicting expectations and role relationships among employees, including managers, in the different national settings.

Hofstede's work has been much quoted in the literature and has been regarded by many as being a very valuable piece of research. However, some have criticised it on the grounds that it generalises, based on observations from one organisation, IBM. It could be argued that IBM attracts those people who are familiar with the language, customs and business practices of North American society. The values of these employees may not be typical of the values of the members of their own cultural society. Also, the findings were based on respondents from the marketing subsidiaries and did not include employees from the manufacturing subsidiaries. Working class groups were almost entirely excluded. The dimensions were also criticised for being too narrow. The measurement methods may not have been consistently followed. Despite these criticisms, the four work-related dimensions are seen in academic circles as important constructs in understanding cultural differences. The findings are interesting and worth looking into.

Managers and their families often have problems settling in foreign countries. These problems are different according to whether the person is in the work environment or is there as the accompanying spouse. In the work environment it can be very important to acknowledge the culture of the country with which the manager is dealing. As has already been mentioned, many a contract has been lost when a manager has inadvertently upset someone because of a failure to understand cultural elements. Some organisations pay special attention to the education of their international managers with respect to the cultures in which they will be operating. Special programmes are designed to prepare managers for the 'culture shock'. National culture, therefore, should be considered as one of the elements shaping the organisational culture.

MANAGING CHANGE IN CORPORATE CULTURE

The factors that contribute to the definition of an organisation's culture can usually be considered as being fairly stable. The culture has been developed and reinforced over many years. It is, therefore, difficult for the management to actually change the corporate culture (*see also* Chapter 1).

Employees are often strongly committed to the shared cultural values of the organisation. The way that the organisation functions may be determined by these values. For instance, the organisation usually makes some public pronouncement about its culture in the form of a mission statement or code of ethics, or a statement of aspirations. The buildings and physical workspace will give visible evidence of the culture. Organisational structure, management style, corporate rituals and procedures, and HR systems such as recruitment and promotion will all reflect the entrenched cultural values. Employees will have chosen to join and remain in the organisation because they actively support the practised culture and will therefore be extremely resistant to change. Similarly, senior management may choose to perpetuate the status quo by promoting managers who will continue the current culture. Promoting from within provides a stability and certainty which the majority of employees prefer. If a new chief executive is appointed from outside the organisation, he or she may attempt to change the culture to mirror his or her chosen philosophies and values. However, this may prove very difficult, and it is often the case that the chief executive may change and adapt to the existing culture, or there may be a gradual melding of the two sets of values.

There has been considerable debate concerning whether culture can actively be managed, much of the debate centring on the extent to which a culture can be modified to resemble a pre-stated ideal. The effective management of a culture, however, requires the ability both to introduce change and to maintain the status quo. It can be argued that cultures are not fundamentally static phenomena which managers can alter through various intervention strategies. Cultures are highly dynamic entities which are prone to change as a result of a variety of internal and external prompts. Thus, for it to be convincingly argued that managers can manage culture it must be shown that they can act to prevent change as well as to induce it.

Indeed, it could be argued that the ability to manage culture implies not just a capacity to change and maintain it, but to create, abandon and destroy it as well.

The differences between those who stress the ease and those who emphasise the difficulties of managing culture are of a relative rather than an absolute nature. Experience of the realities of culture management has in very recent times brought both sides of the debate even closer together. It is just not meaningful or helpful to state unequivocally that cultures can or cannot be managed or that their management is more or less difficult. There is a better case for changing the question from 'Can culture be managed?' to 'When and what aspects of culture can be managed?'

In addition to the whims of senior executives there are a vast range of factors currently operating on organisations to encourage them to change their cultures. These include rapid advances in technology, a tremendous expansion in the rate at which knowledge is being generated, increasingly rapid product obsolescence, demographic changes, a new-found interest in the quality of working life and new trade legislation. This list is by no means exhaustive. That many organisations are not constantly changing in response to these internal and external pressures is testament to the powerful inertial forces that act within them. These inertial forces may be identified at both the level of the individual and the organisation. Among the most common sources of individual resistance to change are:

- **Selective perception:** every individual has a unique view of how their organisation works and their role within it. Plans for change which seem to threaten some cherished element of this world view or which appear misguided or unfair are likely to be met with resistance.

- **Habit:** everyone has habits which allow them to deal quickly and easily with routine situations, and which therefore provide a degree of comfort and security. Proposed changes to employees' habits, especially where these are ingrained and appear reasonable and rational to people themselves, may well be resisted.

- **Security:** current working practices are often more familiar and thus less threatening to the psychological security of individuals than new methods and procedures. In extreme cases some individuals may even forgo promotions because their need for security is so great and fear of the unknown so intense.

- **Economic:** any change which might threaten an individual's basic pay, bonuses, pension, company car or other element in an employee's reward package may be resisted by that person.

- **Status and esteem:** changes which employees interpret as likely to lead to a reduction in their esteem and status may often be the cause of an individual's resistance to the proposed alterations.

Organisations, their various subsidiaries and departments are often as resistant to change as individuals. Most large organisations have a well-defined organisational structure and a variety of established rules and procedures which effectively consolidate the existing status quo. Such organisations have usually committed many of their scarce resources to projects (such as new product developments) which cannot easily be given up, and have entered into contracts with purchasers, suppliers and unions which cannot simply be disregarded. In addition, in any organisation there are those groups who perceive that they have power (over decisions, information or other resources), and they are rarely likely to concede their privileged position without a struggle. Perhaps the most pervasive force for resistance in large numbers of organisations, however, is their culture: prevailing dominant patterns of beliefs and values cannot generally be altered swiftly, while some have questioned whether basic assumptions can be changed at all (*see* Fig 9.7). An established organisational culture can, then, be a powerful block on the initiation of new cultural patterns.

THE ROLE OF HUMAN RESOURCE MANAGEMENT

It can be argued that human resource professionals are able to play a crucial role in managing key elements of culture, including symbols, rites and rituals, norms of behaviour, beliefs and values, and possibly even assumptions. The human resource function is often centrally involved in rituals and ceremonies such as office parties, staff meetings and award ceremonies. It also usually has a role in various organisational rites, especially rites of degradation like demotions and firings, rites of enhancement in the form of promotions and favourable transfers, and such rites of passage as induction programmes. In addition, norms can be influenced through codes of practice and rule books, beliefs and values may be shaped and conditioned by mission statements, and assumptions can be moulded over time by training programmes, the reward system and the performance appraisal process, all of which are (at least in large organisations) generally within the remit of the human resource department.

Human resource systems, policies and practices thus have great leverage over an organisation's culture. The precise nature of this leverage and dynamics of the interactions between a given system or procedure and any element of an organisation's culture is, though, likely to be highly complex. One consequence is that the results of any deliberate attempt to manage culture using the weapons in the human resource department's armoury may well be hard to predict. The human resource function can most effectively manage culture using what might be termed a *consistent cues approach*. The consistent cues approach states that all aspects of every human resource programme must unequivocally promote the desired state culture. The idea is that by consistently promoting certain norms, values and beliefs other cognitive and behavioural dispositions which the organisation has defined as 'deviant' will disappear. If the objective is to create a culture of highly competitive entrepreneurs, for example, then the reward system should reward competitive and entrepreneurial behaviours. If the objective is to value quality, then employees should be appraised according to their concern for quality.

While this strategy may sound simple and obvious, it is in fact neither. In the first place it is extremely difficult for organisations to correctly analyse the full implications of, for example, a particular reward system or promotions policy. This is partly because the full mechanics of any policy or system are often not worked out in sufficient detail, partly because those operating the systems and policies do not always follow procedures to the letter introducing unintended consequences, and partly because different employees (and whole sub-cultures) will tend to inter-

From their review of the culture management literature Hassard and Sharifi suggest the following general principles and guidelines:

- Organisations possess values and assumptions which define accepted and appropriate patterns of behaviour.
- Successful organisations tend to be those which possess assumptions and values which encourage behaviours consonant with the organisational strategy.
- Successful culture change may be difficult to achieve if the prevailing values and behaviour are incompatible with strategy.
- If an organisation is contemplating change it first needs to check to see whether the strategy demands a shift in values and assumptions or whether change can be achieved using other means.
- Senior management must understand the implications of the new culture for their own behaviour and be involved in all the main change phases.
- Culture change programmes must pay special attention to an organisation's 'opinion leaders'.
- Change programmes must also take an organisation's culture transmission mechanisms (such as management style, work systems and employment policies) into account.
- In order to create a change in culture, channels should be programmed with new messages and old contradictory ones eliminated.
- Every opportunity should be taken to reinforce the key messages of the new values and assumptions.

Qualifications
- The deeper the level of culture change required (artifacts being the most superficial and assumptions being the deepest), then the more difficult and time-consuming the culture change programme is likely to be.
- If there are multiple cultures and sub-cultures then this will make the change programme still more difficult and time-consuming.
- Some of the easiest changes to effect are alterations in behavioural norms.
- Managing the deepest layers of an organisational culture requires a participative approach.
- A top-down approach may work when there is only a single culture or when the focus is on changing norms rather than assumptions.
- Top-down approaches yield changes which may be difficult to sustain in the long term, because they produce overt compliance but not acceptance.
- Participative approaches are most likely to be successful and are the only real option if assumptions are to be altered. However, they are difficult to implement and extremely time-consuming to enact.

FIG 9.7 PRINCIPLES OF CULTURAL CHANGE

Source: Adapted from Hassard and Sharifi (1989).

pret the results according to their own often highly personal criteria. It is this variation of interpretation which massively complicates cultural life, especially attempts
to manage culture (*see* Fig 9.8).

Organisations tend to perpetuate their cultures through a variety of socialisation
mechanisms. While many of these means of socialisation are informal and beyond
the direct control of senior executives, others are susceptible to control and thus

---

Organisations are highly political entities, and political antagonisms can often cloud
rational economic judgements. Individuals' understandings of how their organisation
works are often incomplete or defective. Consultants brought in to advise on cultural
matters are often under pressure to perform quick and simple analyses in order to save
time and money. Thus the potential for error in cultural analyses may often be great.
In arriving at an understanding of an organisation's culture care should be taken that
the following do not occur:

- **Displacement:** suggesting that culture is the root cause of problems which are the
  result of, for instance, an inappropriate organisational structure, a failure to invest in
  new technology or poor financial control systems.

- **Whitewashing:** declaiming that senior executives are not to blame for problems,
  but that it is the mass of ordinary employees who require their cultural orientations
  to be altered.

- **Scapegoating:** identifying a particular group as culturally 'deviant' and blaming
  them for the organisation's ills.

- **Simplification:** taking the view that an organisation has a single unitary culture
  when in fact a number of sub-cultures are discernible.

- **Redefinition:** arguing that strong sub-cultures are a source of weakness, when they
  may in fact be contributing in a positive sense to the cultural identity of the organisation as a whole.

- **Missionary zeal:** believing that the employees in a complex and diverse organisation
  can be made to share a single purpose and vision that overrides sub-cultural interests.

- **Illusion:** failing to understand an organisation's culture, history and traditions and
  how they are linked to the organisation's environment.

These potential errors, derived from Anthony (1994), do not constitute an exhaustive
list, but they do give a valuable indication of the range of biases and prejudices that
afflict culture analyses.

FIG 9.8 SOME PROBLEMS ASSOCIATED WITH CULTURE ANALYSIS

Source: Adapted with permission from Peter Anthony (1994) *Managing Culture*, Open University Press, Buckingham.

represent a further tool for managing culture. In fact, one of the first opportunities to influence the enculturation process occurs in the selection phase of an employee's active organisational life. For example, the questions asked in the interview stage can be used to create an awareness of what issues are important to an organisation, while follow-up discussions can provide information to the applicant concerning what sorts of answers are considered most appropriate. In those instances where applicants progress through several rounds of interviews with managers of differing seniority and experience, this process of early attitudinal development can be particularly effective. Any organisation intent on managing its culture in this way must, of course, have decided on what sort of culture it wants to develop and thoroughly briefed its selection interviewers on what questions to ask and what responses to look for.

Individuals are at their most susceptible to new ideas and suggestions for new ways of behaving during the early stages of their employment with an organisation. In its weakest form attempts to manage socialisation take the form of chats or lectures about such things as fringe benefits, mission statements, rules and procedures. More progressive organisations such as Proctor & Gamble, IBM and 3M are far more opportunistic, and use their induction programmes to inculcate something of their history and philosophy. At organisations such as Intel and Tandem the president conducts the orientation in order to reinforce the significance of the cultural messages the induction programmes attempt to communicate.

PERFORMANCE APPRAISAL AND CULTURAL CHANGE

The introduction of a performance appraisal system into an organisation can generally be expected to have a profound effect on superior–subordinate relations (*see* Chapters 8 and 11), on interpersonal communication, on organisational politics, and on levels of morale and motivation. The precise nature of its impact will largely depend on the nature of the organisation's culture, and the sort of system introduced must often be sensitive to the existing culture as well as being geared to create the culture designed by senior executives.

In reaching a decision as to what an appraisal system should appraise, three basic options should be reviewed: the assessment of personal qualities or *traits* (such as intelligence, the ability to communicate effectively and the capacity to cope with change), the assessment of *behaviours* (what people have done) and the assessment of *results* (what people have achieved). An organisation that wants to develop a culture which values people for what they are might choose a trait-based appraisal system. Alternatively, an organisation that wishes to evolve a culture where people generally act in line with its rules for good behaviour may find a behaviour-based performance appraisal system more appropriate. Finally, an organisation wishing to create a culture where achievement is all-important will probably favour a results-based system. The fact that most appraisal systems focus on results is a good indication of the importance of achievement in work organisations.

In designing a performance appraisal system a fundamental choice has to be made whether to focus on the past behaviours and achievements of employees, their future potential, or both. While few organisations would deliberately set out to create a system that did not take account of the future potential of employees at all, as a matter of fact many existing systems make this omission. Moreover, although almost all organisations would probably wish to include an element of future orientation, there is still scope for considerable difference. Those organisations which wish to use the appraisal system in order to allocate performance-related rewards will usually develop historically focused systems. On the other hand those organisations that wish to develop a culture that is highly oriented towards the future and which value the personal development of their staff will be more likely to have a greater future orientation.

An organisation's reward system represents another powerful means for influencing its culture. The reward system specifies guidelines for what employees have to do in order to receive pay rises, bonuses, promotions and praise. An organisation's reward system, then, can be thought of as an unequivocal statement of its values beliefs and assumptions. One complication is that large diversified corporations often have multiple reward systems reflecting the demands of different business settings, product life cycles and competitive environments. Moreover multiple reward systems can serve to perpetuate multiple cultures, some of which may even be countercultures, by reinforcing natural divisions within an organisation. Managing culture through reward systems in large organisations is thus likely to be a highly complex matter.

Issues such as how large a proportion of total compensation bonuses should be, who decides who should receive a bonus, and whether the size of the bonus awarded should vary with length of service or seniority are important from the point of view of culture management. If bonuses represent only a small percentage of total compensation for individuals, then this is likely to dissuade people from engaging in behaviours which help their career at the expense of the organisation, though it may also lead to the development of a more cautious culture. If an employee's immediate superior decides whether or not he or she should receive a bonus, then this will reinforce the dependence of individuals on their line managers, perhaps resulting in a culture of conformity. If potential bonuses increase by level in the hierarchy, then this tends to emphasise the importance of long-term commitment to the organisation, leading to a culture in which loyalty is seen to be a central value.

The criteria used to decide who should get a pay rise and when are also important tools for culture management. Two of the most well-used criteria are length of service and performance as evaluated by senior managers. Where length of service is of overriding importance, then an organisation is likely to end up with large numbers of long-serving middle and senior managers, highly deferential to organisational norms, and possibly conservative and unadventurous. In those organisations where subjective perceptions of employee performance constitute the vital information on which salary decisions are made, then conflict in the form of personal and political antagonisms are often much in evidence. Where salary increases are determined by a rigid pay system, then order and predictability may tend to become ingrained within an organisation. Alternatively, where pay increases are a matter of discretion on the part of senior managers, then the building of close personal relationships, the formation of cliques and an upsurge in self-serving activity might develop.

The use of promotions may also influence culture. One basic choice to be made is whether to favour internal or external candidates for vacant positions. By adopting a policy of internal promotions values such as loyalty and consistency can be strengthened and basic assumptions are likely to remain unchallenged. Conversely, a policy of looking for external appointees is more likely to result in cultural diversity and can more easily lead to cultural change. Some organisations choose to use promotions to expose individuals to different functional areas and thus play a key role in their personal development. Such a policy can contribute to a tight, homogeneous organisation with a common language, experience and values, while also being a palpable indication of the organisation's commitment to its staff. In other organisations promotions are used in a political game to ensure that supporters of particular causes find positions of influence. While highly internally competitive organisations may find this acceptable others often try to eliminate such practices. Again, the argument being put forward here is that these sorts of issues should be actively considered and a coherent strategy formulated by any organisation attempting to mould and direct its culture.

CONSULTATION AND NEGOTIATION

Sound human resource management policies help to foster good industrial relations. The culture of an organisation will be reflected in its industrial relations policy. This policy defines the relationship between management and employees over such matters as pay and working conditions, selection and recruitment, health and safety. Personnel managers and industrial relations officers are specialists in consultation and negotiation and may take a lead in the communications involved in the process. All managers, however, have a role in consultation and negotiation (*see* Chapter 12), because of the importance of pay, working conditions, recruitment and redundancy in the process of change (*see* Chapter 1). Communication is an essential element of management and industrial relations, and consultation and negotiation are an important part of the work of all managers, because of the manager's authority, credibility, access to information and responsibility for the allocation of resources.

Negotiation means that two or more parties meet in an attempt to reach a solution systematically. It is a structural attempt at logical problem solving to identify and resolve a conflict or a potential conflict. Consultation is the process by which managers discuss matters of mutual interest with employees in an organisation. The actual purpose and process of consultation will depend on the culture of an organisation and the communication structures which have been developed in it. Levels of consultation will depend essentially on the prevailing management style (*see* Chapter 2). The 'leadership continuum' may tend to be autocratic, where managers rely on their authority, or democratic or laissez-faire, where there is much more freedom for employees' points of view. Consultation may provide:

- a communications channel in which management, having made a decision, simply informs employee representatives of the decision which has been made;

- a forum in which management seeks the views, feelings and ideas of employees prior to making a decision, while retaining the right to make that decision;

- a structure by which employees' views are made a part of a joint decision process.

In small organisations the process of consultation and/or negotiation can be on an informal basis between individuals and managers, with each person effectively carrying out their own pay and conditions bargaining. In large organisations, individual bargaining becomes impractical and systems are developed for classifying groups of employees into categories for pay and condition purposes. Changes in levels of pay or in working conditions within categories or grades are negotiated by representatives drawn from employees or by representatives of a trade union. In many medium-sized and large organisations the usual process of consultation and negotiation is between management and unions.

The development of unions has meant that conflict over pay and conditions can be guided into agreed channels with a process of discussion, consultation and negotiation. Basic pay and working conditions may be negotiated at a national level, while the details are negotiated at a local level. While the system may be a familiar process for both unions and management, the expectations of the two 'sides' may differ considerably. Management will have priorities in relation to minimising costs and maintaining competitiveness or keeping within spending limits. Unions will be attempting to obtain the best pay and working conditions for their members. What is involved in the process of negotiation and the eventual arrival at an acceptable compromise is the 'structuring' or 'conditioning' of such contrasting expectations to meet on common ground (*see* Fig 9.9).

In this negotiating process, both management and unions will start with an initial position which may be more extreme than they expect the other side to accept. At the same time, each side has a fall-back position which is the absolute limit to which it would consider being pushed by the other side. In between these two position it is necessary to establish common ground. This is an area within which each side will receive something of what it wants, and will be prepared to make concessions in order to achieve it. Somewhere in this common ground there is a realistic position where agreement can be reached. Where agreements are not reached, strikes and lock-outs may occur, but in the end, if the organisation is to continue to operate, agreement has to be reached.

In this process managers need negotiating skills, patience and a clear view of their objectives. The goal of negotiation is to arrive at a position where both sides feel that they have won something, a 'win–win' situation. If one side feels it has lost heavily (a 'win–lose' outcome), the resulting agreement may be difficult to manage in the future because one side will be attempting to make up for its 'loss' and disagreements may become frequent. Negotiating skills involve:

- testing and summarising what is being agreed to make sure that everybody interprets the substance of the agreement in the same way – an agreement has to work and ignoring even small points of dispute will make this very difficult;

- understanding the other side's need in order to discover and explore the common ground;

- communicating the reasons for a particular suggestion or action so that the other side knows what the motives are for a particular policy;

- assessing the process of negotiation to see if it could be improved.

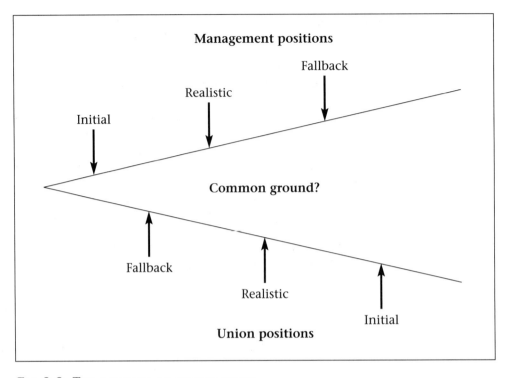

FIG 9.9 THE PROCESS OF NEGOTIATION

Organisational culture will have a marked effect on the context in which these negotiations will take place. Open communication with an organisation can reduce the possibility of conflict arising and can develop trust and confidence between all employees. Where changes are being proposed, they need to be discussed in detail with all employees, explaining the need for them and consulting on alternative methods of implementation. Managers need to show that they understand the employees' concerns and to involve them in the process of change.

The history of industrial relations has seen rises and falls in the relative power of unions, reflected in their membership. In the UK, unions were strong in the 1960s and 1970s. In the 1990s the membership of many unions in the UK has declined as a result of high unemployment, reductions in the labour force of many organisations and legislation controlling union activities. At the same time investment in the UK by overseas companies, such as Japanese-owned corporations, has been based on 'no-strike' deals, with firm structures and systems for agreeing pay and conditions. The process for 'delayering' and 'restructuring' in many companies has often been accompanied by the development of self-managed teams at various levels, with the objective of placing more decision making in the hands of employees. In some organisations, particularly in Germany, employee and/or union representatives are members of the highest decision-making bodies.

The way that managers consult and negotiate in an organisation provides a clear indication of its culture. If senior management believes in and supports a process of open consultation with all employees, and promotes a situation where self-managed teams can make decisions about matters important to them, then the possibility of conflict within the organisation can be reduced. Where there is a co-operative approach, the role of unions and negotiation can be viewed by managers as essential for the future success of the organisation.

MANAGERS AND CULTURAL CHANGE

Few would dispute the assertion that effective leadership is vital to the success of all large-scale change programmes. Research studies have repeatedly demonstrated that the absence of top leadership support for a project is often a key factor in that project's ultimate failure. The successful management of culture also requires the backing of top managers, especially the most senior executive in any organisation. The leader of an organisation obviously has a crucial role to play in setting the vision that the organisation is going to move towards. The leader also has responsibility for allocating tasks and duties, structuring the organisation, and distributing material and financial resources. If human resource policies, programmes and systems are to be used as cultural levers, then organisational leaders must be centrally involved in their redesign, for it is only they who have the authority to sanction such a strategy.

According to Peters (1978) symbols are the means by which managers achieve their work goals. His argument is that executives:

> *'do not synthesize chemicals or operate lift trucks; they deal in symbols. And their overt verbal communications are only part of the story. Consciously or unconsciously, the senior executive is constantly acting out the vision and goals he is trying to realize in an organisation that is typically far too vast and complex for him to control directly.'* (Peters, 1978, p 10)

Peters identifies a number of different symbolic means by which executives may impose on the culture of their organisation. Among the most interesting of these are: how top executives spend their time, their use of language, their use of meetings, agendas and minutes, and their use of settings.

A chief executive can communicate important messages to employees through his or her actions. Most senior and middle managers in organisations are acutely sensitive to what the leader is doing, and spend considerable time working out the implications of what they see and hear for their careers.

In attempting to manage organisational culture a leader is seeking to manage *meaning*, that is, how employees think and feel about their colleagues, work activities, the marketplace, and all other elements of organisational life. If a chief executive makes a public announcement that R&D (Research & Development) is important, or that quality is the organisation's most pressing concern, then employees will listen. If the chief executive makes the point on a continual basis, and especially if the argument is made forcibly and memorably, perhaps by using anecdotes and stories, then over time people may begin to adjust the way they think about the organisation. Leaders occupy privileged positions which allow them to communicate with all their employees.

Organisational leaders have the power to call and postpone meetings, shape agendas and determine the way in which minutes are written up. They thus possess considerable influence to define those issues which are important to an organisation, and the organisation's official view on key matters. These subtle tools also have a role to play in shaping employees' understandings of what is expected of them, what views are considered *appropriate* for them to hold, and how they are expected to conduct their work activities. When these means are used skilfully and backed up by the use of questions which indicate the direction in which the chief executive wants to push the organisation ('What about quality?', 'What's happening with customers?', 'What's new in R&D?'), then they can be particularly effective. For example, if the chief executive puts discussion of the latest customer satisfaction report top of the agenda and insists on questioning his senior executives on its implications for some hours at every board meeting for the next six months, then this is likely to have a marked impact on how the organisation operates, at least in the short term. If the same customer satisfaction survey is repeated on an annual basis and the chief executive pursues its findings with consistent enthusiasm, then over time this may well have an impact on the underlying beliefs, values and behaviours of employees throughout the organisation.

Leaders exercise their power in various physical settings, some of which reinforce and some of which may attenuate the impact of their messages. Merely by turning up to a meeting or turning down an invitation to attend a meeting a leader can communicate much about the relative importance of teams, functions and issues. If the chief executive always attends top level R&D meetings but rarely bothers with meetings of senior marketing executives, then the importance of R&D over marketing to the organisation will be widely noted. The location in which meetings are held can also be symbolically significant. For example, moving a senior management board meeting from an isolated headquarters to the centre of operations might be employed to signal a genuine attempt by executives to really understand field problems. How leaders choose to use their personal office space and the nature of the buildings in which they choose to house their organisations can also be of symbolic importance.

It should be borne in mind that it is an organisation's leader (especially if the leader is also the founder) that is often most resistant to change. Founders have generally made a success of themselves and their organisation for a number of years, and believe that they have a winning formula.

Even extremely competent symbolic leaders may not always be good transformational leaders, that is, able and willing to create a culture that can cope with change.

An organisation's culture may well exert an influence over the strategies it pursues (Beach, 1993). Strategic analyses are never value free. Moreover people are often locked into traditional or habitual ways of doing and seeing things, and this undoubtedly affects their ability to contemplate new options and new solutions. For example, organisations typically exist in highly complex and dynamic environments in which trends (in competitive forces, technology, the labour market and so forth) are difficult to discern. Under these conditions selective perception can mean that organisations in the same market but with different cultural assumptions can interpret their environment significantly differently, giving rise to radically opposed strategies. Of two large clearing banks one might interpret the competitive environment as favourable to an expansion of its international division, while the other might decide on retrenchment. The decision regarding which strategy to follow will depend in part on what information has been selectively focused on, how this information has been interpreted, the values and assumptions of the organisation, and the power relationships between sub-cultures.

It can be argued that organisational culture is the key to understanding why some firms succeed in implementing their strategies while others fail. According to this perspective, an understanding of how to evaluate culture would make it possible to manage organisations through periods of strategic change. Culture, then, is both the means to effective organisational performance through the medium of strategy, and a potential barrier inhibiting required strategic realignment which can adversely affect strategy implementation.

While culture exerts an influence over both strategy formulation and strategy implementation, there is nevertheless scope for organisations to develop strategies which are incompatible with their cultures. In fact, a certain degree of cultural risk is associated with any organisational strategy, and the implementation plans involved in pursuing it.

There are a number of ways of dealing with this. On the one hand, attempts should be made to make implementation plans compatible with the culture, and on the other, advantage should be taken of any scope for reducing the strategic significance of the new behaviours. Depending on a variety of contextual variables some options available to the strategist include:

- **Ignoring the culture:** this is not usually a viable alternative, except where the organisation is relatively young and has not yet developed a strong sense of identity or has suffered a major haemorrhage of employees.

- **Managing around the culture by changing the implementation plans:** if the strategy is vital to the success of an organisation but its culture cannot accommodate the implementation plans designed to realise it, then there is a good case for managing around the culture.

  For example, consider an organisation that needs to focus its marketing on the most profitable market segments. While the most obvious means of pursuing the strategy involves developing a reward system which encourages such behaviour and adjustment of the management information systems, cultural barriers in the form of diffused power, highly individualised operations and a relationship-oriented ethos preclude these measures. However, by dedicating full-time personnel to each key market the organisation can bypass cultural constraints and maintain its strategic intent.

- **Modifying the culture to fit the strategy:** this is an extremely difficult, time-consuming, expensive and uncertain option.

- **Adapting the strategy to fit the culture:** this needs to occur in certain situations, notably after a merger, when particularly complex and involved cultural situations are likely to emerge. A strategy suffering greatly from cultural blocks and pressures may require that other action be taken, including managing around the culture in order to make cultural risk manageable.

Executives managing large corporations will need to assess cultural risk throughout a portfolio of businesses, each with its own strategy, culture and implementation plans. Such executives require answers to questions such as:

- How much cultural risk is there in the corporation as a whole, including all the subsidiaries?

- How is this risk spread across the businesses?

- What are the specific sources of cultural risk? Are there any detectable patterns of risk in the business portfolio?

- Given the level of risk identified, is the total corporate strategy in danger?

In order to answer these (and related) questions managers have to consider the environment in which they operate, their corporate objectives and the systems they have in place.

STRATEGY AND CULTURAL CHANGE

In order to be effective, organisation strategies require the participation not just of the senior executive team, but of the organisation as a whole. For example, Xerox's pursuit of total quality necessitates that all organisational members adopt standardised procedures and a *quality mentality*. Without this organisation-wide embracing of a quality orientation the pursuit of a quality-led strategy in which things are done right first time would be impossible. The same is true at CSL (*see* the Case Study on pp 262–4). The realisation of such a strategy will be more likely where the cultural inclinations of the organisation support it. As a matter of fact most organisational attempts to emphasise quality are normally represented as a form of culture change, blurring the distinction between strategic intent and culture. The important point being made here should, however, be clear: an organisation's culture can be a useful source of high reliability in the pursuit and realisation of strategy.

Where two organisations with very different cultures seek to merge there can be extreme problems of integration, co-ordination and control which in turn often lead to a lower level of post-merger performance. This failure adequately to take culture into account can mean that 'synergy' is a strictly pre-merger concept. One company that has made a large number of successful acquisitions, and which attributes this in part to its careful consideration of cultural fit, is the Dana Corporation, based in Toledo, Ohio. According to Dana's philosophy, firms should not only be prepared to walk away from potential acquisitions which do not fit their culture, but having acquired a company should honour its traditions and heritage.

Strategy can in fact be thought of as a cultural artifact, and within an organisation any given strategy is likely to have symbolic associations for employees. Some of the many functions that strategy plays in its role as artifact and symbol include the following.

- **A focus for organisational and individual self-understanding:** it allows individuals to formulate answers to questions such as 'where is the organisation going?', 'How is it going to get there?' and 'What is my role in the life of the organisation?'

- **A focus for identification, loyalty and motivation:** it provides individuals with goals and longer-term objectives with which they are able to identify and value, and in the pursuit of which they are prepared to exchange energy and enthusiasm for material gains.

- **A means for comprehending social phenomena:** an organisation's strategy is often encoded in various written statements and reports and plays a key role in general conversation between employees. From these sources individuals gain the information they require to understand and classify people, businesses, markets and events. It provides a context and a vocabulary for understanding the past and making guesses about the future state of the organisation and its markets.

Organisational strategy is not just a reflection of organisational culture. The formulation and implementation of strategy is generally influenced by a wide variety of non-cultural environmental factors such as the activities of competitors, customers and suppliers. Certainly the resulting trends, activities and events will be interpreted through the perception filter of culture, but this fact does not make a new technological breakthrough or a reduction in the number of supplier companies any less real. This means that it is impossible accurately to predict an organisation's strategy from knowledge of its culture alone. It also means that when an organisation is observed it is possible for its strategy to appear not to match its culture because of the influence of external exigencies. For example, Hewlett Packard was effectively forced to follow the IBM standard when manufacturing personal computers, even though its natural cultural inclination was to create its own specification: to have done anything else was to have risked disaster.

STRONG ORGANISATIONAL CULTURES

One of the most widely cited hypotheses is that a *strong* culture enables an organisation to achieve excellent performance. Deal and Kennedy (1982), for example, have argued that: 'The impact of a strong culture on productivity is amazing. In the extreme, we estimate that a company can gain as much as one or two hours of productive work per employee per day.' 'Strong' is usually used as a synonym for consistency. Thus the phrase 'strong culture' is frequently employed to refer to companies in which beliefs and values are shared relatively consistently throughout an organisation.

Advantages of a strong culture

- A strong organisational culture facilitates goal alignment. The idea is that because all employees share the same basic assumptions they can agree not just on what goals to pursue but also on the means by which they should be achieved. As a result employee initiative, energy and enthusiasm is all channelled in the same direction. In these organisations there are few problems of co-ordination and control, communication is quick and effective, and resources are not wasted in internal conflicts. This all means that organisational performance is likely to be healthy.

- A strong culture leads to high levels of employee motivation. There are two main arguments here. First, it has been suggested that there is something intrinsically appealing about strong cultures that encourage people to identify with them. In short, employees like to be part of an organisation with a distinctive style and ethos with its own peculiarities and idiosyncrasies, and with others who share their view on how an organisation should work. Second, it is sometimes thought that strong culture organisations incorporate practices which make working for them rewarding. These practices tend to include employee participation in decision making and various recognition schemes. High levels of motivation among employees, so the argument states, translates into high organisational performance.

- A strong culture is better able to learn from its past. The idea is that strong cultures characteristically possess agreed norms of behaviour, integrative rituals and ceremonies, and well-known stories. These reinforce consensus on the interpretation of issues and events based on past experience, provide precedents from the organisation's history which help decide how to meet new challenges and promote self-understanding and social cohesion through shared knowledge of the past. The suggestion here is that an organisation which is able to reflect on its development and which is able to draw on a stock of knowledge encoded in stories, rules of thumb and general heuristics is likely to perform better than competitors unable to learn from their past successes and failures. However, serious questions can be raised concerning the validity of the argument.

Problems of a strong culture

- A strong culture may facilitate goal alignment, but the goals set by a culture may not always be positive in two senses: they may not be ethical, and they might not encourage good economic performance. In the first case we can imagine an organisation such as a political or religious sect that brainwashes its members into pursuing violent ends, or an economic organisation that pursues environmentally catastrophic objectives. An example of the second case would be an organisation with a culture which dictated that care for employees was of greater value than profitability or market share, with the result that economic objectives were made subservient to human resource objectives.

- It cannot be assumed that all strong cultures are associated with high levels of employee motivation. Many UK public services have well-developed and strong cultures, but it is at least questionable whether all these organisations are populated by highly motivated individuals. The point is that strong cultures may encourage many different attitudes toward the organisation and to work other than the purely positive. As regards motivation, therefore, strong cultures can work both ways.

- It is probably true that an organisation which appreciates its past and which encodes information about past decisions in stories and anecdotes is advantaged compared with similarly placed organisations which do not. However, it is also true that organisations can become too wrapped up in the past and fail to focus on the present and in the future. It is also possible for organisations to reapply lessons learned in the past to current situations where the old rules no longer apply, perhaps because of technological innovation or increased competition. In other words, there is a thin dividing line between being able to learn from the past and being a prisoner of the past.

- There are in fact quite a few well-known examples of organisations with both strong cultures and strong economic performances. Yet even these companies do not necessarily lend credence to the strong culture argument. The reason for this is the problem of determining causality. After all, it may be that good economic performance is the cause of a strong culture rather than a strong culture being responsible for high performance. It therefore seems more than reasonable to suggest that economic success can strengthen a culture.

- The strong culture argument fails to take account of the fact that few organisations have a single, unitary culture. Most scholarly commentators suggest that not only do organisations tend to have multiple sub-cultures, but that there are often highly complex operational and power relationships between them. Certainly some or even all of these sub-cultures may be strong in the sense of being cohesive, but this may mean that they function to undermine the initiatives of other sub-cultures rather than to support them. Figure 9.10 illustrates that an organisational culture develops under the influence of its wider environmental context and in response to the unique factors that have characterised its evolution. The result is an intricate web of rites, symbols and cognitions that can be described as an organisational culture, and which find expression as a complex of cultural dynamics.

CULTURE FIT

In order for an organisation to have long-term success it must have more than just a strong and appropriate culture, it must be able to continuously adapt to its environment. An adaptive culture is generally characterised as one in which people will take risks, trust each other, have a proactive approach to organisational life, will work together to identify problems, share considerable confidence in their own abilities and those of their colleagues, and have enthusiasm for their jobs. While the specific qualities associated with adaptive cultures vary from author to author the organisations most frequently cited as possessing exemplary adaptive cultures are corporations like Digital Equipment Corporation, Honda and 3M. The third of Denison's (1990) hypotheses (adaptability) concerns these issues. The adaptability hypothesis states that a culture which allows an organisation to adapt to changing demands and circumstances will promote effectiveness. Adaptability aids organisational effectiveness in

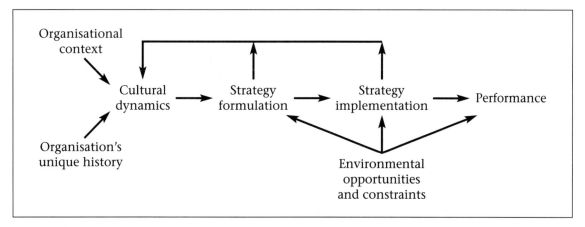

FIG 9.10 UNDERSTANDING CULTURE, STRATEGY AND PERFORMANCE

three ways. First, it allows an organisation to recognise and respond to its external environment. Second, it means an ability to respond to internal constituences, such that different functions, departments, and divisions interact positively with each other. Third, in response to either internal or external prompting it requires the capacity too restructure and reinstitutionalise behaviours and processes as appropriate.

In its most general form the 'adaptive culture equals high performance' equation is open to criticism. Not only can it not account for those organisations which are not obviously adaptive but which are successful because they fit the relative stability of their organisation's environment, but it is unconvincing in important respects. For example, risk-taking cultures may well go out of business if they take too many bad risks, and not all innovations are always good for the organisation. In fact, too much change can lead to instability and loss of sense of direction. Refinement of the perspective is, therefore required.

First, the culture must be one which values and supports all the large stakeholders in the organisation. In the case of commercial organisations these will be customers, stockholders and employees, and in the case of public organisations may well include the government, regulatory agencies and the general public. Second, the culture must also value excellent leadership from its managers at all levels.

An organisational culture, or rather the dynamics it generates, thus directly affects strategy formulation in at least five different ways: culture acts as a perception filter, affects the interpretation of information, sets moral and ethical standards, provides rules, norms and heuristics for action, and influences how power and authority are wielded in reaching decisions regarding what course of action to pursue. The formulated strategy is a cultural artifact which helps employees understand their role in the organisation, is a focus for identification and loyalty, encourages motivation, and provides a framework of ideas that enables individuals to comprehend their environment and the place of their organisation within it.

An organisation's culture, then, influences how its strategy is implemented. It is suggested that the more consonant a strategy is with the prevailing culture the more effectively that strategy will be put into practice. It is further anticipated that the stronger and richer the culture (in the sense that there is agreement on beliefs, values and assumptions, and many relevant strategy-supportive stories) the more likely it is that the strategy will be successfully implemented. The idea that the process of strategy formulation and the dynamics of strategy implementation will also have an impact on culture is worthy of note. It should also be observed that environmental opportunities and constraints are significant here, influencing both strategy formulation and implementation. In fact, the resulting level of performance will depend as much on environmental factors as it will on culture.

It can be argued that certain cultural features are more likely to be associated with high levels of economic performance than others. It is at least arguable that the most effective cultures are those which are not only strong (in the sense of being consistent), but actively involve large numbers of individuals in consultative and decision-making bodies. In addition, it seems reasonable to suggest that some cultures allow an organisation to exploit a given environment more effectively than others, and are thus more 'strategically appropriate'. If a culture is able to adapt to changing circumstances in order to maintain its strategic appropriateness over time, then this too may well be advantageous. There is also evidence that cultures which value large stakeholders and leadership at all levels are associated with superior economic performance.

SUMMARY

■ Organisational cultures are neither static nor permanent. Rather, they evolve over time in response to changes in the external environment, new technologies and products, and various macro-social and political trends. Indeed, small-scale incremental changes occur on a daily basis as some individuals leave and others join, new systems and procedures are introduced and some are modified to reflect changing personalities, the latest fads and fashions, and the recommendations of the most recent training courses. Thus culture change (where 'culture' is understood in its broadest sense) is a feature of organisational life. The real point at issue is how much control managers can exert over the dynamics of culture change processes. While most of this chapter has been taken up with reviewing the sorts of measures that might be employed to engineer change towards a desired state culture, their effectiveness is largely yet to be proven.

■ Culture change is difficult to realise because most employees in an organisation have a high emotional stake in the current culture. People who have been steeped in the traditions and values of an organisation and whose philosophy of life may well be caught up in the organisation's cultural assumptions will experience considerable uncertainty, anxiety and pain in the process of change. For many middle and senior managers change may also seem to threaten a loss in status, loss of power over resources and less security. Even if there are personal gains to be made from altering the habits of a lifetime these are likely to be seen as potential or theoretical only, as against the certainty of the losses. These multiple sources of perceived risk will usually result in *resistance* to change, resistance which is often culturally based. Depending on the organisation this resistance may be more or less organised and more or less overt, the form it takes being of far less significance than the possible consequence, namely the gradual failure of the culture change strategy.

■ Using human resource programmes, policies and procedures to manage a culture seems an intuitively plausible plan, but is only likely to have much impact in the long term. This may mean that a given culture management strategy has to be pursued with persistence and enthusiasm for years to have any noticeable effect.

■ Organisational strategies and structures and their implementation are shaped by the assumptions, beliefs and values which can be defined as culture. Furthermore, it has been suggested that this culture both constrains and presents opportunities for what an organisation is able to accomplish. Thus organisational effectiveness must, in large part, be interpreted as a cultural phenomenon, albeit mediated by various management systems, strategies and procedures. This does not mean that it is easy to argue that culture causes good and poor performance, because culture is itself massively affected by, for instance, changes in strategy and in organisational structures. The complexity of the intercausal relationship between strategy, culture and performance makes hard and fast generalisations difficult to make.

REVIEW AND DISCUSSION QUESTIONS

1   Why have some theorists suggested that organisational culture cannot be managed? Are they right?

2   What factors affect the relative ease (or difficulty) of managing organisational culture?

3   Which individual human resource programme, policy or system is most important for leaders attempting to manage their organisation's culture?

4   What are the most effective symbolic means that leaders can use to manage their organisation's culture? What are the least effective symbols that leaders may choose to employ?

5   In what ways can organisational culture affect strategy formulation?

6   How can an organisation's culture promote internal consistency and reliability? Why are these characteristics desirable? What are the potential disadvantages associated with consistent and reliable cultures?

7   Can strategy influence the development of a culture and if so how?

CASE STUDY: QUALITY AT CSL

Communication Systems Limited (CSL) is a wholly owned subsidiary of Siemens and GEC, both of which have a 50 per cent stake in the company's equity. CSL is primarily concerned with selling, installing and maintaining business telephone communication solutions in the UK, and in order to maintain its customer base effectively employs approximately 1500 people on 11 sites. From 1987 onwards CSL became interested in the idea of quality as a means of competing in an increasingly hostile global market. A focus on overall quality was recognised by CSL management as a potential solution to the problem the organisation faced of distinguishing themselves from competitors selling essentially similar products.[1] As the senior executives at CSL saw it, differentiating on the basis of quality was a means to an end: better-quality products and services meant more satisfied customers, and happier customers meant an increase in market share and profitability.

The first step towards creating a quality-oriented culture was, from July 1992, to embark on the process of becoming BS 5750 accredited. While still not widely recognised in other parts of the world, BS 5750 is a well-known and highly regarded UK quality specification that encourages organisations to formally define procedures, create job descriptions and invent formal systems for dealing with work activities in a rational and coherent manner. In order to facilitate the acceptance of the new quality standards the quality programme director at CSL customised them to suit the organisation's culture and work patterns. As the quality director said, 'we put it into more friendly terms, made it more meaningful for our people'. Such was the success of the programme of change that 15 months later the firm attained accreditation to BS 5750, and so became only the twelfth company to gain the standard across the whole organisation.

Crucial to the success of the enterprise was the support of the managing director, who not only had a good knowledge of the quality programme but visibly demonstrated his commitment to it by visiting customers on a regular basis and chairing a monthly 'quality council' meeting in which he probed senior managers for detailed information regarding issues of quality and customer satisfaction. The quality programme director himself was another key player, who was expected not just to regularly update other members of the organisation concerning progress towards agreed quality and service targets, but also to visit customers and suppliers and to foster long-term partnerships with CSL. In this way it was hoped to mirror the success some Japanese corporations have had in forming close alliances with main suppliers and important customers, and involve them in the process of quality improvement and service enhancement. A visible demonstration of CSL's commitment to the ideal is its decision to base engineers on the sites of some big clients, such as IBM and BP: now, if there is a problem, CSL can offer these corporations an immediate solution.

The attempt to create a quality culture did not always run smoothly. There was some initial resistance to the burden of documenting systems and formalising procedures needed to achieve BS 5750, and building the internal partnership relations within CSL that are required to make it work. Such were the advantages which emerged, however, and the determination of the managing director and quality programme director that resistance to the programme quickly withered. The change in the relations between marketing and sales amply demonstrates the kind of practical benefit which emerged from this process. Before BS 5750, marketing had always considered itself exploited and made a scapegoat by other departments, especially sales, which landed all sorts of product-related problems at the marketing door. Sales, on the other hand, thought that marketing did very little and was poor value for money. But with the introduction of the quality specifications both sides had to come together to agree what they wanted from each other, allocate duties and responsibilities, and define these in written documents. With the sorting out of all the old grey areas around which disputes used to emerge a more professional working relationship has evolved in which marketing receives adequate information from sales and knows what is expected of them, while sales can now see clear deliverables emanating from marketing. Thus greater formalisation has resulted in a general reduction in interpersonal and interdepartmental

conflict and a greater willingness to work collaboratively to solve mutual problems.

The pursuit of quality and the alteration of employees' beliefs, values and assumptions in order to support this strategic pattern is, of course, an ongoing process. Moreover the quality system needs to be kept under regular review to ensure that it continues to be appropriate and to be followed. There are, therefore, continual reviews of procedures and periodic assessments of what is being achieved. These internal assessments are engaged in at two levels. First, each department conducts a self-appraisal on an annual basis using a checklist of questions covering all aspects of quality and work activities. Second, there is regular peer appraisal, in which managers (and more junior employees) from other departments audit the quality of a department other than their own. The quality consequences have been dramatic: for example, customer complaints are now answered within a matter of a few hours and have shown a hefty reduction in volume. Certainly there are still problems. For instance, no one has yet figured out how adequately to predict lightning strikes, one of the main causes of maintenance backlogs. Terrorist attacks on London's financial centre also initially caused a few headaches, as finance organisations often need a lot of telecommunications equipment (and they need it immediately) once their offices are destroyed. CSL overcame the problem of the huge costs of storing spare equipment by developing a Disaster Recovery contract (a form of insurance for financial organisations under threat), thus tackling a thorny problem with an imaginative customer-focused solution.

With the reduction in conflict, mutual blame and finger-pointing has come the opportunity to enhance quality still further. Despite obvious advantages BS 5750 is not a perfect measure of quality, being far more concerned with formal systems than intangibles like leadership, human resources and culture. Significant improvements in quality, then, were going to require the pursuit of a more subtle strategy. To ensure that the company was 'doing the right things' as judged by the customer as well as 'doing things right', an additional strategy was required. A little over

▶

a year ago CSL management adopted the 'Baldrige Award' criteria.[2] With IBM, one of CSL's biggest customers, also pursuing this quality award, it is little wonder that CSL are in the vanguard of GEC/Siemen's quality accreditation efforts. Under the generic name of *Market Driven Quality* a new phase in the quality journey has been announced, with Areas For Improvement (AFIs) now routinely identified and neutralised by senior management on a six-monthly cycle. This is currently being cascaded downwards to involve the whole organisation. While full accreditation to Baldrige is recognised to be some years away, there is now a confidence about CSL that the cultural shift required will ultimately be achieved. ■

Notes

1 In fact, CSL was formed in 1991, and it was the antecedents of CSL that first flirted with quality in the late 1980s.
2 The Baldrige Award is an American quality award.

Source: Compiled from information supplied by Ralph Morris, Quality programme Director, CSL. Quoted in Brown (1995).

REFERENCES FOR FURTHER READING

Anthony, P (1994) *Managing Culture*, Buckingham: Open University Press.

Beach, L R (1993) *Making the Right Decision: Organizational Culture, Vision and Planning*, Englewood Cliffs, NJ: Prentice-Hall.

Brown, A (1998) *Organisational Culture*, 2nd edn, London: Financial Times Pitman Publishing.

Deal, T and Kennedy, A D (1982) *Corporate Cultures: The Rites and Rituals of Corporate Life*, Reading, Mass: Addison-Wesley.

Denison, D (1990) *Corporate Culture and Organizational Effectiveness*, New York: John Wiley.

Hampden-Turner, C and Trompenaars, F (1994) *The Seven Cultures of Capitalism*, Judy Piatkus.

Handy, C B (1978) *The Gods of Management*, London: Souvenir Press.

Handy C B (1985) *Understanding Organizations*, Ch 7, London: Penguin.

Harrison, R (1972) 'How to Describe Your Organisation', *Harvard Business Review*, September–October.

Hassard, J and Sharifi, S (1989) 'Corporate Culture and Strategic Change', *Journal of General Management*, 15(2), 4–19.

Hofstede, G (1980) *Culture's Consequences: International Differences in Work-Related Values*, London: Sage.

Hofstede, G (1983) 'National Cultures in Four Dimensions', *International Studies of Management and Organisations*, 13.

Hofstede, G (1991) *Cultures and Organizations*, New York: McGraw-Hill.

Hofstede, G, Nenijen, B, Ohayv, D D and Sanders, G (1990) 'Measuring Organizational Cultures: a Qualitative and Quantitative Study across Twenty Cases', *Administrative Science Quarterly*, June, 35(2), p 291.

Kerr, J and Slocum, J W (1987) *Managing Corporate Culture through Reward Systems*, Academy of Management Executive, 1.

Kotter, J P and Heskett, J L (1992) *Corporate Culture and Performance*, New York: Free Press.

Lessem, R (1990) *Managing Corporate Culture*, Gower.

Morgan, G (1986) *Images of Organisation*, London: Sage.

Peters, T and Waterman, R (1982) *In Search of Excellence*, New York: Harper & Row.

Peterson, R B (ed) (1993) *Managers and National Culture: A Global Perspective*, Quorum Books.

Pheysey, D (1993) *Organisational Cultures*, Routledge.

Quinn, R E and McGrath, M R (1985) 'The Transformation of Organisational Cultures: A Competing Values Perspective', in P J Frost *et al.* (ed) *Organizational Culture*, Sage.

Randlesome, C (1990) *Business Cultures in Europe*, Heinemann.

Robbins, S (1990) *Organization Theory*, 3rd edn, Englewood Cliffs, NJ: Prentice-Hall.

Schein, E (1985) *Organization Culture and Leadership*, San Francisco: Jossey-Bass.

Schneider, S (1989) 'Strategy Formulation: The Impact of National Culture', *Organization Studies*, 10/2, 149–68.

Schneider, S and De Meyer, D (1991) 'Interpreting and Responding to Strategic Issues – The Impact of National Culture', *Strategic Management Journal*, 12, 307–20.

Scholz, C (1987) 'Corporate Culture and Strategy – the Problem of Strategic Fit', *Long Range Planning*, Vol 20, 4.

Smith, P (1992) 'Organizational Behaviour and National Cultures', *British Journal of Management*, Vol 3, 39–51.

Whitley, R (1992) *Business Systems in East Asia: Firms, Markets and Societies*, Sage.

ORGANISATIONAL COMMUNICATION

Len Holden

OBJECTIVES

The purpose of this chapter is to cover the following topics:

◆ definitions of organisational communication

◆ communication media

◆ downward, upward and horizontal types of communication

◆ models of communication

◆ the Krone, Jablin and Putnam definitions of communication

◆ Clampitt's models of communication

◆ international aspects of communication

◆ communications and the future

ORGANISATIONAL COMMUNICATION: DEFINITIONS

Communication must exist in all organisations to enable them to function. The concerns in management literature over the past twenty years have been to recognise the importance of communication to the efficiency of the organisation and to seek ways to improve the channels and processes of communication.

Communication is pervasive, continually in operation and covers an enormous range of activities. For example, some of the more obvious modes of communication with which most people would readily identify are:

- sending a memo to an employee as a reminder to do a task;

- telephoning an order for new stock;

- posting a notice of a forthcoming meeting on the noticeboard;

- sending an E-mail message or a fax to an overseas subsidiary;

- writing a letter to placate an angry customer.

From these examples the Advisory, Conciliation and Arbitration Service (ACAS) definition would suffice in describing organisational communications as:

> *'the provision and passing of information and instructions which enable a company or any employing organisation to function efficiently and employees to be properly informed about developments. It covers information of all kinds which can be provided; the channels along which it passes; and the means of passing it.'* (ACAS, 1982, p 2)

However, communication is also a very complex series of processes operating at all levels within organisations, ranging from the 'grapevine' heavily laden with rumour, to formalised systems such as joint consultative committees (JCCs) or works councils. They can operate at the localised level of the shop floor or office between supervisor and staff and the staff themselves, or at a distance by means of representatives such as union officials or messages from the boardroom or the chief executive to various branches or subsidiaries of large and complex organisations. They can be one-way or two-way, top-down or down-up as well as across the organisation.

Communication can operate at a personal level and informal level as well as through formal channels such as those cited above. Thus the following examples can equally be categorised as organisational communications and can contribute as much to the efficiency or inefficiency of the organisation.

- An unsympathetic supervisor ignoring the explanations of lateness by an employee.

- An angry discussion in the canteen between employees about a low pay-rise.

- An employee sitting with crossed arms and legs while a line manager attempts to broach a delicate subject about lack of commitment to work.

- A rumour that large-scale redundancies will be made by the company shortly.

These examples embrace informal channels of communication, such as gossip or the grapevine, body language and interpersonal behaviour. They are based in organic or human interactive processes and can be as important as mechanistic and formal channels of communication in conveying positive or negative messages. It is only relatively recently that these informal processes have come to be recognised as being as important as the formal processes.

What can also be added to the ACAS definition is that communication is a two-way process. What is being increasingly recognised is that messages to and, equally important, from the workforce have considerable significance. Thus communication is important for conveying the organisation's mission, business aims and objectives, and its general ethos or culture. It is also needed to enable the thoughts and feelings of the workforce to be expressed and, of equal significance, heeded and acted upon. Such policies are being heavily influenced and underscored by human resource management practices.

Communication systems also carry implicit messages about the mediation of power within organisations. Employee-involvement communication systems (which are examined more closely below) are processes which enable the workforce to have a greater say in decision making to varying degrees, with the concomitant loss of managerial prerogatives; an issue which can create, as well as attempting to allay, conflict. Communication systems are also influenced by political, social and economic trends within society which change and evolve over time and in turn influence the perceptions of those engaged in the employment relationship. In addition, the nature of the communication channel can affect the message as does the culture(s) existing within and outside the organisation (Clampitt, 1991; Jablin *et al.*, 1987).

Thus even the simplest message can be misunderstood or misconstrued because of the complex influences which act on the communication process. Equally important and potentially disastrous is that communication channels can send conflicting messages. An oft-cited case is the company which encouraged employees to take up share options entitling them to attend the annual shareholders meeting, where they were told how successfully the company had performed over the previous year. Many of these same employees were also in the trade union to which management communicated later that, because of the poor performance of the company over the previous year, the pay increases requested could not be met!

COMMUNICATION MEDIA

The number and types of channels of communication have increased at a phenomenal rate since 1945 and with even greater acceleration and facilitation since the 1980s, transforming organisations and the way they operate. Within a 50-year timeframe most organisations have moved from pencil and typewriter-dominated environments, with the telephone as the main medium of distant communication, to computer-terminal oriented environments with the increasing predominance of voice mail, fax, E-mail, modem systems and the Internet. In addition, we have moved towards teleconferencing as well as computer conferencing. Indeed in the world of the telecommuter in his or her telecottage, he or she may do a job but never leave home. This is the world of work made possible by increasingly advanced channels of communication.

Despite these developments, face-to-face communication is probably what most people prefer and what still predominates in most organisations. It enables instant feedback, allows re-explanation and there is no substitute, as yet anyway, to meeting someone in the flesh. Recent studies of why telecommuting has not been as popular as predicted is that 'loneliness' is an important factor in its unpopularity. Meeting people and hearing the office gossip is part of the social communication process which people enjoy about work.

Figure 10.1 attempts to categorise multifarious communication mechanisms in accordance with their feedback potential and how quickly (immediacy) the feedback can operate in organisations.

TYPE	CHANNEL	FEEDBACK POTENTIAL	FEEDBACK IMMEDIACY
Written/printed	Memos	low	low
	Post – internal/external	low	low
	Company newspaper/journal	low	low
	Newsletters	low	low
	Company reports	low	low
	Bulletins	low	low
	Noticeboard	low	low
	Suggestion scheme	med/high	low
	Attitude survey	high	low
Speech	Formal presentations	low	low
	Mass meetings	low	low
	Departmental meetings	medium	high
	Team briefing groups	medium	high
	Quality circles	high	high
	Grapevine	high	high
	Face-to-face/one-to-one	high	high
	Appraisal	high	high
Non-verbal	Body language	high	high
Mechanical	Audio tape	low	low
	Video tape	low	low
	Television	low	low
	Voice mail	low	low
	Fax	medium	medium
	E-mail	medium	medium
	Telephone	high	high
	Teleconferencing	high	high
	Internet	high	high

(Please note this is not an exhaustive list)

FIG 10.1 COMMUNICATION CHANNELS AND FEEDBACK

DOWNWARD, UPWARD AND HORIZONTAL TYPES OF COMMUNICATION

Another way of categorising communications is by their route through organisations, the most common being downward and upward. More recently emphasis has been on the horizontal channels in organisations, particularly in quality, customer service (internal and external) and similar schemes. Delayering, downsizing, empowerment and devolvement have led to flatter organisational structures in which the team unit has become the operational pivot. Thus communications within the team and with other teams (departments or internal customers) is seen to have considerable significance.

- **Downwards communication (top-down)**, e.g. from managers to other employees. This includes channels such as house journals, company newspapers, employee reports and regular briefing sessions, often with videos.

- **Upwards communication** is designed to tap into employees' knowledge and opinions, either at an individual level or through the mechanism of small groups; this includes practices such as suggestion schemes and attitude surveys.

- **Horizontal communication** takes place between individuals and teams, and within and between departments or work groups, such as operate in quality circles, total quality management and customer care programmes.

In many organisations a combination of these forms of communication will exist, hopefully supporting and complementing each other.

In a book of this nature it would be impossible to examine all of these approaches in detail, but a closer study of some of the more popular and recent schemes in each category may serve to illustrate current trends.

Downward communication

THE COMPANY MAGAZINE OR NEWSPAPER

One of the most common methods of downward communication which has witnessed a considerable increase since the mid-1970s is the proliferation of company newspapers or magazines (CBI, 1989). Reviewing methods of communications in six surveys of organisations conducted between 1975 and 1983, Townley (1989) indicated that most put the company newspaper or house journal either as the most popular or second most popular form of communication. The problem is that they can vary in quality from amateur desktop-published affairs produced by employees in their 'spare' time, to lavish glossy productions, which have been part of the communications systems of many large companies for a number of years.

There is also the question of editorial control which may restrict the messages that are conveyed to the workforce. Continual, glowing reports of the company successes or anodyne and meaningless information may have negative results in the long run. Genuine expressions of employee feelings via letters pages or forthright quotes from employee representatives, even of a negative nature, may show the desire of management to achieve fairness. Of course, the judgement of the editor will come into play in deciding the content of the newspaper or journal, which in turn will be affected by the organisational culture and management views.

For example, a militant shop steward during a dispute called the managing director a 'fascist' which the personnel director urged the editor to expunge as being insulting. The editor defended the decision to retain the quote on the grounds that he had sought one from the shop steward and not to print it would look like corporate censorship. In addition, such a quote was so patently absurd that it would have a negative effect. In the event the quote was left to stand and the prediction of the editor proved true when the shop steward was spurned by his fellow employees and the union felt moved to publicly apologise for the comment (Wilkinson, 1989).

TEAM BRIEFINGS

Team briefings have witnessed a considerable increase in the past five years, although they have been in existence in some organisations for longer (Marchington *et al.*, 1992). They are often used to cascade information or managerial messages throughout the organisation. The teams are usually based round a common production or service area, rather than an occupation, and usually comprise of between four and fifteen people. The leader of the team is usually the manager or supervisor of the section, and should be trained in the principles and skills of how to brief. The meetings last for no more than 30 minutes, and time should be left for questions from employees. Meetings should be held at least monthly or on a regular prearranged basis.

Surveys often reveal considerable satisfaction with team briefings by both employers and management (e.g. CBI, 1989) as they are effective in reinforcing company aims and objectives at the personal face-to-face level. Ramsay (1992a, p 223), however, urges caution in accepting this rosy picture because success depends on context 'to a significant extent'. For example, they might be postponed or cancelled in times when business is brisk, which may undermine commitment to holding them at all in the long run. If the intention is to undermine union messages, the success will very much depend on the strength of the union and the conviction of management. A sceptical and undertrained management and supervisory force can do much to undermine the effectiveness of team briefings.

Upward communication

These schemes can also be described as two-way communication and are most associated with 'new' managerial concepts such as human resource management (HRM). They are clearly aimed at increasing employee motivation and 'influence' within the organisation. They also aim to improve employee morale, loyalty and commitment, with a view to improving service and efficiency. Another facet of these types of scheme is to facilitate acceptance of changes in work practices, functional flexibility and new technology, as well as engender an atmosphere conducive to co-operation and team building (Ramsay, 1992a).

ATTITUDE SURVEYS

Although not a new concept, attitude surveys have witnessed a considerable increase in vogue in recent years. They are often conducted by personnel or HR departments and sometimes consultants are hired to carry them out. They most often take the form of questionnaires, but can also involve face-to-face or telephone interviews. Employee responses are often marked with the intention of eliciting the feelings of numbers of employees on a range of issues, for example feelings of involvement in various organisational issues and procedures, and what employees think of various schemes. This not only is seen as useful in that employees have a chance to air their views, but it also helps to monitor the success or failure of initiatives, enabling management to decide whether to retain, remove or improve them.

Employees can come to view them with an air of cynicism as time-wasting exercises if there is little or no feedback. It is important to communicate to employees how surveys have been used and how they have affected the organisation and its policies. Publication of the results can be made in the company newspaper, journal or news sheet.

SUGGESTION SCHEMES

Suggestion schemes have had a long history and many organisations still retain them, although many have abandoned them in favour of feedback and new ideas emanating from problem-solving sessions such as quality circles. Suggestion schemes have come into and gone out of fashion many times over the years, and the suggestion box limply hanging off the wall with a solitary yellowing note upon which is written an anonymous rude message to the managing director is a familiar joke. When operated seriously, these schemes can be very effective. Suggestions on how to improve work and improve the working environment have saved companies enormous amounts of money, and in the best schemes the originator of the idea is justly rewarded with a cash bonus or other perquisites, and often with a picture and story in the company newspaper. Publicising the event is important because it shows that the scheme is working, that employees are listened to and their ideas are valued, and it will encourage others to do the same. These days the suggestion box itself is no longer necessary as suggestions can be channelled through the company newspaper or magazine, or some other point of collection, such as through team briefing.

Horizontal communication

These schemes are often associated with attempts at culture change and restructuring within organisations, and emphasise employee ownership and empowerment, in the hope of increasing employee commitment, and consequently giving greater productivity and better service.

QUALITY CIRCLES

One of the first methods identified with the 'new', involved approach to management was the quality circle (QC) (*see also* Chapter 7). It first arrived in the UK via the USA from Japan and, as has been noted in Chapter 7, although QCs were implanted in Japan in the post-war years by two American consultants, W Edwards Deming and J M Duran (Clutterbuck and Grainer, 1990).

QCs are made up of six to ten employees holding regular meetings weekly or fortnightly during working time. The principal aim is to:

'identify problems from their own area and, using data collection methods and statistical techniques acquired during circle training, analyse these problems and devise possible solutions; the proposed solutions are then presented formally to the manager of the section who may decide to implement the circle's proposal.' (Brennan, 1991)

There was tremendous interest shown in QCs by British managers in the early 1980s, but within a few years they began to decline in popularity. A number of reasons have been identified for this decline but principal among them was the attitude of middle managers. For example, it is crucial that a manager or supervisor with the requisite qualities and training leads the circle. Technical competence alone is not enough to guide the circle and studies began to highlight the necessity for interpersonal skills. Some managers also felt that their power and authority was undermined by the QC, and others just lacked commitment in the initial stages, which had the effect of making QCs difficult to develop effectively. There were also difficulties from the over-enthusiastic facilitator who deliberately gave an overtly positive but false impression of the circle's operation, possibly for career progression reasons. This makes it difficult to identify problems within the circle to improve its effectiveness (Brennan, 1991).

Suspicion of circles could be engendered if they were seen as a way of undermining trade union functions. Non-consultation with the union, particularly when setting up QCs, often bred suspicions that this was another anti-union management ploy, and the QC was, therefore, effectively undermined by non-co-operative attitudes.

Other circles failed because suggestions by the workforce were not actually applied or even considered, thus rendering them a waste of time in the minds of the participants.

Finally, many circles simply 'ran out of steam' after the initial burst of enthusiasm. The need for continual reinforcement of their function and purpose was evident (Collard and Dale, 1989; Ramsay, 1992a).

TEAMWORKING

Teamworking is an initiative in employee involvement (EI) and like QCs originated in Japan. It emphasises problem solving in a teamworking situation and in order to function effectively it must be bound up with policies of task flexibility and job rotation (Price, 1989). Teams vary in size from seven to ten people or even more, and large elements of training are necessary to ensure that workers, team leaders, supervisors and managers have the requisite skills to enable the team to function efficiently. A large part of such training is of a managerial or interpersonal skill and communicational nature, as well as of a technical nature.

TOTAL QUALITY MANAGEMENT

Whether employee involvement works or not depends on the aims and objectives of the EI scheme. In addition, there are times when certain schemes will work successfully and times when they will be unsuccessful, and this is why EI, like many other HRM policies, goes through changes in fashion. The economic, political and social context influences the type and success of the scheme which organisations adopt (Ramsay, 1992a). A further factor is the type, size and sector of the organisation. What may work in a small firm, for example, may not work so well in a large bureaucratic organisation. What may work in a democratic organisational culture will probably be unsuccessful in a more authoritarian one (Wilkinson, 1989).

Even schemes, such as TQM, which begin life for the most positive reasons, such as the enhancement of employee commitment, motivation and empowerment, may become distorted. Factors, both internal and external, may turn them into something unworkable and, from the employee point of view, they may be seen as a sinister attempt to gain more commitment, work and productivity, without the concomitant reward, control or empowerment.

TQM IN PRACTICE

Total quality management has witnessed a rise in popularity in many organisations in recent years and is often bound up with culture changes and other HRM and managerial initiatives, such as customer service programmes (*see also* Chapter 7).

TQM operates at both a local and establishment-wide level and is pervasive throughout the whole organisation. It is concerned with concepts such as culture change, which in turn engender attitudinal changes in the workforce. At workplace level emphasis can be placed purely on improving the quality of product or service. Like customer service schemes, this can also be the implementation of more efficiency between internal departments (which can be seen as internal customers) and external customers themselves. Like quality circles, the idea stems from the writings of Deming, Juran and, more recently, Crosby (1979, 1984). They have also been linked to British Standard BS 5750 and ISO 9000 approaches, although many claim that this is more suitable for production-oriented rather than service sector work.

Wilkinson *et al.* (1992) point out clearly the differences (and therefore the implications) between QCs and TQM (*see* Fig 10.2).

The compulsory nature of TQM with its top-down overtones suggests a system whereby worker empowerment is restricted very much within the boundaries set by management. In its operation in production companies, Sewell and Wilkinson (1992) also propose that it has an air of surveillance, whereby the performance of individual workers is monitored by electronic devices which control his or her work to conform to the group norm – a norm set by management. They describe how in an electronic components factory the teams – especially the team leader – which

	QUALITY CIRCLES	TQM
Choice	voluntary	compulsory
Structure	bolt-on	integrated quality system
Direction	bottom-up	top-down
Scope	within departments or units	company-wide
Aims	employee relations' improvements	quality improvements

FIG 10.2 IDEAL TYPES

make the components 'have a great deal of discretion in the way labour resources are deployed across the cell (the unit of manufacture)' (Sewell and Wilkinson, 1992). Multi-skilling is encouraged and work rotation allocated by the team and team leader. Within the team individuals are encouraged to improve personal performance and innovations should be made to improve productivity and product quality. Team meetings provide the forum where such issues are debated and information shared.

Quality is controlled by a visual inspection and electronic tests, which also trace the individual responsible for the fault. This information, together with data on absenteeism, conformity to standard times and production planning targets, is prominently displayed for all the team to see. Naturally, the information forms the basis of much discussion between team members. In turn this creates a situation where the team will 'discipline' those that they feel are not conforming to the norms. This is a form of what Friedman (1977, quoted in Sewell and Wilkinson, 1992) called 'responsible autonomy', a situation where the group acts as the controller of the individual and therefore the team. Thus managers can clearly claim that the workforce is being 'empowered'. This delegation of power, however, has a dual nature which according to Muetzfeldt (quoted in Sewell and Wilkinson, 1992) 'can actually increase the power of the delegating agency, so long as it can legitimate and retain its authority, and undermine it if the obedience of the delegated agents cannot be assured'.

Sewell and Wilkinson see this system of TQM as an analogy of the work of Foucault, who stressed the importance of tracing the loci of power in organisations in order to understand its importance and how it is used.

Wilkinson *et al.* (1992) in their research into EI for the Department of Employment (*see* Marchington *et al.*, 1992) visited 25 organisations, of which the majority had TQM programmes in operation. In examining these practices it was evident that TQM operated in a wide variety of forms and, like HRM, was open to a variety of definitions and interpretations. In a close examination of TQM in three typical UK companies in engineering, finance and marketing, they discovered several problems in its implementation and operation. All of the schemes were difficult to sustain for four basic reasons:

1   The schemes were narrow in conception and 'bolted-on to, rather than integrated into, key management policies' (Wilkinson *et al.*, 1992). As a result, some schemes looked very similar to quality circles and thus had many of their faults. Companies tended to look for immediate gains rather than look to long-term cultural changes. 'If these are not forthcoming TQM is short-lived' (Wilkinson *et al.*, 1992). In turn this created an obsession with 'the cost of quality and immediacy of return, concepts which are totally different from Japanese thinking' (Wilkinson *et al.*, 1992).

2   The role of middle managers became unclear and confused, and was looked upon as one group of managers imposing itself on another. This had the effect of creating conflicts. Because TQM was carried out in a highly centralised framework in most organisations, teams were reliant on the services of other departments, with which they were competing for resources, and each department was often in ignorance of how they were affected by each other. The competition thus militated against mutually co-operative solutions.

3 Industrial relations, while impacting on TQM programmes, are rarely considered by employers. Thus there was usually neglect in obtaining union agreement or establishing a positive working climate before implementing TQM schemes, a situation almost guaranteed to create suspicions either in the unions or the workforce. TQM affects strongly such issues as job control, working practices and reward, all of which can, if not handled sensitively, create problems, as unions and workers may place obstacles in the way of the system's operation.

4 Aspects of employee involvement in TQM schemes can have contradictory elements. Similarly to the findings of Sewell and Wilkinson (1992), it was discovered that there was a contradiction in the language of employee involvement (empowerment of the workforce, etc.) and the actuality of the work situation in which power very much rested in the hands of management.

These studies point to a number of problems in the implementation of TQM. Ramsay (1992a) has noted, with some laconic interest, the rise and fall of fads and fashions in employee involvement and speculates what might be next on the agenda if TQM does not succeed! What is certain is that easy solutions do not exist and the implementation of new systems has to be viewed in a long-term framework and reviewed constantly with the full consent and approval of the workforce.

MODELS OF COMMUNICATION

It would be apposite at this point to examine some models of communication before proposing more sophisticated definitions of organisational communication and examining other forms of communication.

The first model of communication to emerge was conceived by Shannon and Weaver (1949) and initially had a mathematical basis (*see* Fig 10.3). It was devised to help Bell Telephone Company engineers understand how to transmit electrical impulses most efficiently from one place to another. Although created for mechanistic reasons, it is applicable to organisational and other communication processes.

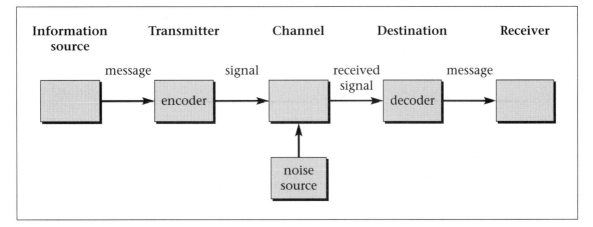

FIG 10.3 THE SHANNON AND WEAVER MODEL OF COMMUNICATION

Source: C Shannon and W Weaver, *The Mathematical Theory of Communication*. Copyright 1949 by the Board of Trustees of the University of Illinois. Used with permission of the author and the University of Illinois Press.

The message is encoded, i.e. turned from an idea into a verbal or written message; the message is then sent from the information source to the receiver, travelling via a channel, and is then decoded by the receiver, either by hearing or reading the message. The problem is that the message can get distorted by noise sources or interference. In the mechanistic version of the telephone this might be interference on the telephone line, thus making the communication difficult and unclear. In the case of a manager speaking to an employee, it could be more subtle. The noise source which distorts the message could be personal. For example, the employee may dislike the manager, or be unhappy with the situation in which he or she works, or have a headache or personal problems at home.

One criticism of the Shannon and Weaver model is that communication is seen as only a one-way process. Observers in the field of human behaviour have stated that this is not so, even in communications between the most seemingly compliant employee and manager. The employee may communicate dissatisfaction through body language or through another source, such as his or her work group. Later communication model builders therefore added the element of 'feedback' to the communication model (Schramm, 1954; DeFleur, 1966).

Thus while the Shannon and Weaver model concentrates on the channels between sender and receiver, the Schramm model devotes its discussion to the main actors in the communication process, allowing both to send and receive messages (*see* Fig 10.4).

While these communication models have been refined and elaborated (McQuail and Windahl, 1981), they nevertheless contain the essence of the communication process as represented in most organisations.

The medium is the message

The communication models clearly show that messages, whether one-way or two-way, can be influenced by a variety of distorting influences (noise), which may be part of a contextual influence of the communication medium. Indeed McLuhan (1964) has gone so far as to suggest that 'the medium is the message', that the message is influ-

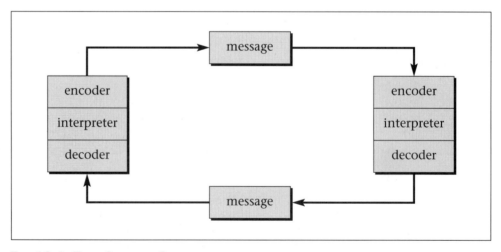

FIG 10.4 THE OSGOOD SCHRAMM MODEL OF COMMUNICATION

Source: W Schramm, 'How Communication Works' from *The Process and Effects of Mass Communication*. Copyright 1954 by the Board of Trustees of the University of Illinois. Used with permission of the author and the University of Illinois Press.

enced by the kind and type of channel or medium used. A well-known example was the live US presidential debate between Kennedy and Nixon in 1960. Listeners on the radio thought Nixon won the debate with a convincing set of arguments, whereas viewers of the television broadcast gave the debate to Kennedy. Analysts later pointed to the visual power of the television medium which showed a young, handsome Kennedy opposing a seedy-looking Nixon who was sweating, had 'five-o'clock shadow' and was wearing a suit which did not allow him to stand out from his background. The visual imagery acted as a powerful influence on the message.

The Krone, Jablin and Putnam definition

With these diverse influences on communication in mind, Krone, Jablin and Putnam in 1987 posed a more complex series of definitions. While they acknowledged that empirical research exploring organisational communication processes had burgeoned over the last two decades, they also recognised the necessity of developing a theoretical base, the starting point from which attempts should be made at a more rigorous definition of organisational communication.

They focused on four 'fairly comprehensive yet parsimonious' perspectives: mechanistic, psychological, interpretive-symbolic and systems-interaction (Jablin *et al.*, 1987).

The mechanistic perspective

This concentrates on the channel of communication and the transmission of the message. It follows very much the model posed by Shannon and Weaver. Thus the mechanistic perspective views communication as a linear connection between communicators in which A causes B. The clarity of the message is thus affected by the degree of interference or 'noise' in transmission. An example of this type of organisational communication exists very strongly in military structures where officers pass orders down through various communication channels which are understood by the recipients and acted upon. As we are all aware, this image of communicational efficiency is not always lived up to in the heat of battle, as Tolstoy (in *War and Peace*) and many other writers have attested.

The psychological perspective

The psychological perspective focuses specifically on how characteristics of individuals (personality, mood, ideology, etc) impact on the reception and interpretation of communications. As a result: 'the conceptual filters of individuals become the locus of communication. These filters consist of the communicators' attitudes, cognitions and perceptions' (Krone *et al.*, 1987). These filters thus become vital in the encoding and decoding process. From this perspective organisational communication is seen very much as an interpersonal activity, and individuals as information processors influenced by conceptual filters – for example, how individuals view themselves, perceptions of power and control in the organisation, work expectations and other factors.

One psychological barrier to communication pointed to by many surveys is the gulf between hierarchical levels in the organisation. Consistent studies in the

United States and the UK since the 1950s have shown that superiors think they adequately communicate with their subordinates, whereas subordinates think the opposite – that they send more messages upwards but receive less feedback from their bosses. Psychological explanations of this phenomenon regard the prime cause as perceptual differences of the same processes, and how each relates to those processes and the people who carry them out.

Vicki Smith, in studying a Californian bank, clearly shows how the strategy conceived at boardroom level becomes increasingly distorted as it travels down the line to workplace level. Each level in the hierarchy perceives the strategy slightly differently, and sometimes very differently. The implementers of strategy have their own personal and psychological agendas. For example, if the implementation of strategy means taking painful decisions which would upset subordinates, line managers would distort the messages to fit in with their perceptions of creating less distress but conforming to what they perceive to be the received strategy (Smith, 1990).

The interpretive-symbolic perspective

This perspective extends the psychological perspective into the realms of socially-shared meanings of what constitutes the organisation.

> *'Thus, rather than passively submitting to some organisationally determined view of the workplace, the interpretive symbolic perspective posits that by virtue of their ability to communicate, individuals are capable of creating and shaping their own social reality.'*
>
> (Krone, Jablin and Putnam; *see* Jablin *et al.*, 1987)

Within this perspective *shared meanings* of common events and actions become important.

> *'Thus behaviour is not simply the response of conceptual filters to information stimuli; rather, it develops through social interaction and it changes as the social context changes.'*
>
> (Krone, Jablin and Putnam; *see* Jablin *et al.*, 1987)

In essence the interpretive-symbolic perspective emphasises how culture has an impact on the interpretive processes, and how interpretive processes through shared meanings impact on and create organisational culture.

In illustrating this, most people entering a new organisational environment quickly become aware of the 'ways of doing things' and how the organisation is constituted, constructed and perceived by their fellow workers. If a newcomer, for example, proposes a different way of carrying out a work function, this can be received in a hostile manner if it is perceived that this does not fit into or threatens the previous ways of doing things or the perceptions of the existing work culture.

THE CHALLENGER SPACE SHUTTLE DISASTER

Perhaps the most startling example of this operating in a dysfunctional way was the Challenger space shuttle disaster in the 1980s in which all the members of the crew were killed. Concerns about the shuttle's safety had not been adequately relayed back from the engineers at the launch base to top management at control. This was not a simple breakdown in communication but the subconscious misreading of messages, influenced heavily by organisational culture. The overriding shared cultural meaning of the event was that the shuttle launch had to be a success in every way as the future programme budgets from Congress hinged upon it. The launch thus had to be publicly seen as successful in all respects, including a punctual lift-off for the waiting world media. These concerns overrode the safety messages and the resulting disaster ironically put an effective end to those original objectives of the programme.

Pace and Boren (1973) sum up this situation well by stating that 'messages in serial production, like water in a great river, change through losses, gains, absorptions and combinations along the route from the headwaters to their final destinations'. A well-known example is the famous First World War communication in which an officer in a trench asks the soldier next to him to pass on down the line of soldiers the following message for headquarters:

'We're going to advance. Send reinforcements.'

By the time the message has passed along the line it has become distorted to:

'We're going to a dance. Send three and fourpence!'

The systems-interactive perspective

The systems-interactive perspective has similarities with the mechanistic approach, in concentrating on external behaviours of groups and individuals, and examining how and with what frequency communication systems are used. The emphasis is thus on *patterned sequential behaviour* which examines the categories, forms and sequential patterns of message behaviour. However, this systems-interactive perspective is different from the mechanistic perspective in the sense that an individual does not 'do' communication, but becomes 'part' of communication.

This approach has been used to look at superior–subordinate communication and conflictual relations in industrial relations by examining responses to communication acts and tracing their processes. For example, Fairhurst, Rogers and Saar (1987) examined dominance patterns of manager–subordinate interactions. Their findings indicated that managers who displayed a high number of dominant attitudes in their communications perceived that their subordinates had less interest in decision involvement and rated them as being lower in performance than managers who used fewer controlling patterns. Putnam and Jones (1982) in examining labour–management communication found that labour (trade unions) specialised in using offensive manoeuvres such as attacking arguments and threats, while management relied on defensive tactics such as commitments and self-supporting arguments. Thus, reversing this pattern, with the unions providing information to an enquiring management seems to have the tendency to prevent or lower conflict. If each side tries to match each other in a one-upmanship pattern, it tends to lead to higher conflict and a bargaining impasse.

These four communication perspectives are summarised in Fig 10.5.

PERSPECTIVE	LOCUS OF COMMUNICATION	CHARACTERISTICS/ IMPLICATIONS
Mechanistic	Channel and message transmission	Focus on conveying of information and accuracy of message reception
		Message sending/receiving considered as linear process
		Somewhat dehumanising; little attention to receiver and role of meaning in communication
		Tendency to oversimplify and reidentify the communication process
Psychological	Conceptual filters	Receiver as active message interpreter
		Emphasises intentions and human aspects of communications
Interpretive-symbolic	Role taking	Considers role of self and group – cultural context of communication
		Emphasis on symbols and 'shared' meaning
Systems-interaction	Sequences of communication behaviour	Feedback patterns; conflict management, work group development
		Treats communication as an evolving system
		Focuses on types of message sequence functions and behaviours

FIG 10.5 ALTERNATIVE PERSPECTIVES TO ORGANISATIONAL COMMUNICATION

Source: Adapted from Krone, Jablin and Putnam (1987), p 33, in F Jablin, L Putnam, K Roberts and L Porter (eds) (1987) *Handbook of Organisational Communication: An Interdisciplinary Perspective*. Copyright © by Sage Publications, Inc. Reprinted by permission of Sage Publications, Inc.

CLAMPITT'S MODELS OF COMMUNICATION

Other writers, most notably Clampitt (1991), have also developed models of communication. He identifies three main approaches to communication: the arrow, the circuit and the dance.

The arrow approach

The 'arrow' is closely identified with the mechanistic view and the Shannon and Weaver communication model and is concerned with the conveyance of clear messages unhindered by 'noise'. For example, when a manager gives instructions to an employee, the manager 'A' conceives instructions which are sent by a medium (face-to-face, telephone, memo, etc) to 'B', an employee. The arrow metaphor is the direction of the communication from A to B. Clampitt believes that within each form of communication a number of assumptions are made. The arrow manager's assumptions are illustrated in Fig 10.6.

As can be imagined, there could be enormous differences between the perceived communication effectiveness and the underlying assumptions, and the actual communication reception by the receiver, i.e. the employee. For example, it is possible that the employee may not share the assumptions of the manager either consciously or subconsciously, thus causing a communication breakdown.

Managers who hold dear to this view of the communication process are liable to blame the employee:

'Why didn't they just follow my instructions?'
or
'Why can't they get it right? If I've told them once, I've told them a thousand times.'

COMMUNICATION EFFECTIVENESS	UNDERLYING ASSUMPTIONS
Being able clearly and precisely to put my thoughts into words.	What is clear and precise to one person is clear and precise to another.
Speaking with credibility and authority.	Credibility is something the speaker possesses and not something given to the speaker by the audience.
Getting the results I want by talking to my people.	Communication is primarily a one-way activity.

FIG 10.6 EVALUATION OF ARROW MANAGERS' ASSUMPTIONS

Source: P Clampitt (1991) *Communicating for Managerial Effectiveness*, p 3. Copyright © 1991 by Sage Publications, Inc. Reprinted by permission of Sage Publications, Inc.

The circuit approach

> *'The circuit approach represents an evolution from the arrow to the circle. Circuit managers stress feedback over response, relationship over content, connotation over denotations, understanding over compliance. Communication is seen as a two-way process involving the dynamic interplay of an active sender and receiver.'*

(Clampitt, 1991)

This approach conforms much more to the Osgood Schramm Model (*see* Fig 10.4), which emphasises that communication is a two-way process. This is also congruent with recent trends towards employee participation styles of management as embodied in total quality management (TQM), business process re-engineering, and customer service schemes. As with the arrow manager, the circuit manager holds a set of assumptions, as shown in Fig 10.7.

The circuit manager recognises that there will be communication breakdowns and the oft-cited reasons are as follows:

- People just 'don't connect' in the sense that their values, emotions and ideas are too dissimilar.

- Poor listening skills often mar and distort the communication.

- There may be 'hidden agendas' or unarticulated goals which may cause friction when revealed at a later time or in another context.

- Communicational relationships can only operate under certain conditions. For example, if a proper climate for the exchange of information and ideas does not exist, then this will hamper attempts at communication.

COMMUNICATION EFFECTIVENESS	UNDERLYING ASSUMPTIONS
Listening to employees, in order to make them happy.	Job satisfaction is the goal of organisational communication.
Being sensitive to employees in order to adapt messages to each individual.	Messages are exclusively interpreted in the context of interpersonal relationships.
Being open and understanding.	Openness is useful in all circumstances. Understanding is always more acceptable than ambiguity.

FIG 10.7 EVALUATION OF CIRCUIT MANAGERS' ASSUMPTIONS

Source: P Clampitt (1991), *Communication for Managerial Effectiveness*, p 3. Copyright © 1991 by Sage Publications, Inc. Reprinted by permission of Sage Publications, Inc.

Despite these potential weaknesses the circuit approach to communication is much more empathetic and more likely to succeed in work environments of high trust. Problems arise when these approaches are inadvertently applied to environments of low trust in the belief that they can act as an agent for change.

The dance approach

Clampitt finally describes what he sees as a superior approach to communication by using the metaphor of dance. Comparing communication to dance may seem odd but Clampitt justifies it by suggesting that:

> *'Dance involves patterns, movements and creativity. It can be enjoyed by participants as well as observers. There are as many styles as people. Tastes vary. Standards differ. Styles change. Trends come and go. But dance has been and always will be part of the human community. Once a dance is performed it can never be recaptured in the same way again . . . It may be one of the highest and unique forms of human expression. So, too, is communication.'*
>
> (Clampitt, 1991)

The dance metaphor is used by Clampitt to illustrate the complexity and diversity of communication and the communication process, and that simple explanations can be misleading. For example, the purpose of communication is not always clear, and communicators may have multiple goals for a single message.

> *'Effectiveness can only be determined in the light of the communicators' goals – whatever they may be – including obfuscation, confusion, or deception . . . hence, there is no single measure of communication effectiveness.'*
> (Clampitt, 1991)

For example, politicians can be very effective communicators in hard-hitting election campaigns, using slogans, simplifying complex ideas and relating party policy to the average voter; but in times of adversity they can use those same skills to obfuscate, fudge and mislead their audiences. Similarly, hidden agendas and multiplicity of purpose can pervade the communication process in organisations, be it the managing director making reassuring noises to shareholders about profits or to the workforce about redundancy at a time when market share and sales are falling. This means recognising that communication is used for multiple purposes and, importantly, requires the co-ordination of meanings – so that the diversity of meanings are implicitly and explicitly guided towards the same objectives within the organisational culture.

Communication, like dance, tends to be rule-governed. Thus, just as in dance certain steps and movements are acceptable, so too in communication there are implicit and explicit rules. For example, effective listeners may use the following rules (Clampitt, 1991):

- **Initiate conversations with questions about unrisky topics.**

- **If a person's comments are unclear, then ask for clarification.**

- **If a person appears defensive, nod head.**

- **Terminate conversations by summarising the conversation.**

Communicators develop a repertoire of skills. Just as the dancer no longer thinks about the execution of certain steps and movements, so too does the communication process become a subconscious and automatic process to the experienced communicator.

Communication can also be viewed as a pattern activity in which certain exchanges can become inured into positive and, more worryingly, negative patterns of communication, just as dancers can develop 'bad' habits in the execution of movements. For example, Clampitt uses the following conversation to explain these communicational difficulties caused by negative patterns of reinforcement.

A manager may jokingly insult an employee:

'Hey, Pat! Has your golf game improved yet?'

The manager interprets this as a greeting; the employee as an insult. The employee replies, however, with what she sees as a placatory response – a factual reply to the question:

'I haven't been golfing lately.'

The manager interprets this as meaning that the employee is ignoring him, and tries to re-establish the conversation with another 'playful' question:

'Well how's that old banger of a car going?'

The employee regards this as another insult and mentally asks 'What kind of a game is he playing?' She again responds to the 'insult' with a placatory and factual answer:

'I sold it.'

The manager thinks, 'She's catching on, but still takes the conversation too seriously.' He continues the conversation with another 'jokey' insult:

'I hope you didn't buy another heap of rubbish.'

The employee sees this as another insult and that he is now questioning her decision-making ability. This time she is not placatory:

'Why don't you just get off my back and mind your own business!'

The manager interprets this: 'Why is she so upset? I'm just trying to build some rapport. The employee has no sense of humour.'

The employee interprets this: 'If placating doesn't work then stand up for yourself. My only alternative is to be assertive. He's insensitive and unprofessional.'

Neither the manager nor the employee see the overall pattern resulting from their personal rules of interaction. In a group situation the margin for error multiplies considerably. Recognising these negative patterns and changing them therefore becomes an important aspect of communication.

Organisations where communications flow in a positive way are those where the rules and patterns, together with the subconscious understandings, create a culture of commitment and congruence, as Clampitt would suggest, like the most beautiful and creative dance partners performing a work of magnificence with elegant ease.

Criticism can be levelled at these perspectives in that they do not fully consider external influences on the organisation such as social, economic and political trends. Investigators into employee involvement (EI) operations have attempted to take these factors into consideration, most notable Poole (1986) and Ramsay (1977).

INTERNATIONAL ASPECTS OF COMMUNICATION

In many countries in Europe and the rest of the world, trade unions still act as one of the most important communication channels, despite the fact that indications are that there has been a decline in membership worldwide since 1983 (ILO, 1993). Their importance is still central in Scandinavian countries, especially Sweden, and they still carry considerable weight in Germany and the UK, although the rise in long-term unemployment and the decline in the old staple industries like shipbuilding, coal, iron and steel, and engineering, where unionism had a strong traditional base, has tended to erode their power (*see* Chapter 9).

The Price Waterhouse Cranfield Survey into International Strategic HRM investigated trends in employee communications in five countries (the UK, Sweden, West Germany, Spain and France) in 1990, and ten countries in 1991 (the original five plus the Netherlands, Norway, Denmark, Italy and Switzerland). Both survey years revealed a marked increase in attempts at communicating with the workforce, both via staff representative bodies, such as trade unions, and by more direct methods associated with HRM initiatives (Holden, 1990; Price Waterhouse Cranfield Survey Reports, 1990 and 1991). Only in UK organisations did personnel managers report the greatest decrease in trade union influence, at 49 per cent, and the greatest decrease in communication through staff representative bodies, as shown in Fig 10.8.

This survey and the ten-country survey in the following year were both conducted before the recession of the early 1990s began to bite in the UK, and the decrease in communication via staff representative bodies obviously echoes the declining influence in trade union power in the UK. Despite this decline, it would be a mistake to underestimate the still relatively strong role which trade unions

	UK	France	Spain	Sweden	Germany
Increased	18	22	53	38	23
Decreased	20	12	3	7	3
Same	49	58	44	55	64

FIG 10.8 COMMUNICATION THROUGH STAFF REPRESENTATIVE BODIES, 1990 – AS PERCEIVED BY PERSONNEL MANAGERS (PERCENTAGES)

Source: Holden, (1990).

285

play in communication. This is demonstrated by Spain, which showed an enormous increase of 53 per cent and clearly reflects the comparatively strong growth in trade unionism (albeit from a low base, and now around 10 per cent density) in the 1980s, backed by legislation requiring works committees in organisations employing more than 50 people (Filella and Soler, 1992).

The aims and objectives of an increase in the number and intensity of communication channels may have specific 'political' reasons. For example, in times of dispute with the union, the management may feel they need to put their side of the case more effectively to the workforce. In the past many companies found themselves at a comparative disadvantage in disputes as the unions virtually had a monopoly of the informational channels to the workforce. This was no fault of the unions but more a reflection of the incompetence of management. Management appeared incapable of creating effective communication channels but this was because they suspected these could be used at other times for what might be perceived as more negative purposes (Monks, 1989). In other words, management can themselves suffer from their own ideology of operating 'mushroom systems' (keeping the workforce in the dark, and piling 'manure' on them) which maintains a climate of distrust and attitudes of 'us and them'. Fortunately, other surveys supporting the findings from the Price Waterhouse Cranfield survey indicate that in many organisations such ideas are becoming less popular (CBI, 1989; Marchington *et al.*, 1992).

Parallel to overall increases via staff representative bodies in four of the five countries surveyed were even larger increases in verbal and written communication in all five countries (*see* Fig 10.9). The ten-country survey revealed similar trends (Price Waterhouse Cranfield Survey Report, 1991).

These increases shown in Fig 10.9 obviously indicate a greater desire by employers to increase communication, probably inspired by HRM trends which spread in the 1980s. France and the UK show particularly large increases in both verbal and written communications which parallel the rise in team briefing and other teamwork methods, as well as increases in the more traditional written forms of

	UK	France	Spain	Sweden	Germany
Verbal					
Increased	67	68	45	64	34
Decreased	1	2	8	1	3
Same	31	28	47	34	54
Written					
Increased	63	64	49	47	26
Decreased	1	4	3	3	3
Same	34	29	48	47	58

FIG 10.9 CHANGES IN VERBAL AND WRITTEN COMMUNICATION – AS PERCEIVED BY PERSONNEL MANAGERS (PERCENTAGES)

Source: Holden, (1990).

communication. The survey in the following year, however, added questions to establish the major ways by which employees communicated their views to management, and trade unions and/or works councils still predominated in all ten countries (Price Waterhouse Cranfield Survey Report, 1991).

It would seem that communication with and from the workforce is increasing at workplace level but the more established forms of communication and forms of EI such as unions, works councils and JCCs are still important in those organisations where they are established. The survey conducted by Marchington *et al.* (1992) in UK organisations would seem to confirm this.

Nevertheless, these surveys do not indicate the degree of participation by employees in organisations. Research by Fröhlich and Krieger (1990), Cressey and Williams (1990), Boreham (1992) and Gill (1993) have tried to address this issue in comparative contexts.

Fröhlich and Krieger examined the extent of employee participation in technological change in five of the then EC countries – the UK, France, Germany, Italy and Denmark. They discovered that in the four phases of introducing new technology (planning, selection, implementation and subsequent evaluation) workers were more likely to be involved in the latter stages and that full participation, particularly in decision making, remained relatively low for all countries and for all stages. Cressey and Williams in a similar survey, but covering all of the 12 countries in the then EC, found comparable results and posed a 'paradox of participation'. As the scope for influence by employees over the processes of technological change decreased, so the intensity of participation increased. In other words there was more scope for participation in the implementation stage (the latter stage) when participative influence concerning fundamental decisions was reduced, and less participation in the crucial earlier planning stages in the introduction of new technology.

Gill (1993), using the same 12-country EC data analysed by Cressey and Williams (1990), perceives differences in attitudes between Northern European and Mediterranean countries which result in a wide diversity in levels of participation. Denmark, Germany, the Netherlands and Belgium have much greater employee participation than Portugal, Spain, Italy, Greece, France, Luxembourg and the UK. In France and the UK, however, he argues, 'there is a dependence by management on the skills and problem solving abilities of the labour force' (Gill, 1993). Nevertheless, he claims that 'in the United Kingdom there has been a shift away from negotiation towards more consultation during the last decade and management has become increasingly paternalistic in their style' (Gill, 1993). These differences are caused, he argues, by the diverse industrial relations practices in each country shaped by historical and cultural factors.

In all three studies managers were of the view that increased participation was effective for the efficient implementation of new technology, but this may have the effect of compromising their prerogatives.

Boreham (1992) investigated the degree of employee control over labour processes in seven countries (Australia, Britain, Canada, Germany, Japan, Sweden and the USA). He was particularly interested to know whether employee control was enhanced by the introduction of new practices associated with post-Fordist systems such as flexible working linked to quality improvement and greater response to market conditions. The assumption here was that efficiency was improved by decentralisation and democratised decision-making practices. The findings clearly indicated that 'the nearer one approaches the core of status and power in the enterprise the more likely it is that one be allowed discretion over one's work arrangements' (Boreham, 1992). He also found that there was little evidence 'to support the view that management will cede its decision-making prerogatives in the interests of more rational production methods' (Boreham, 1992). This pattern was generally true of Japanese and Swedish organisations which are associated with employee involvement styles of management.

These surveys clearly indicate a contradiction in managers' perceptions that employee involvement is an effective way of increasing work efficiency but such involvement is outweighed by the challenge to managers' prerogatives over decision making. Thus employee involvement is very limited and is more likely to take the form of managements' information dissemination to, and consultation with, the workforce, which is not the same as the 'empowerment' to which many HRM textbooks allude.

Boreham (1992) also stresses the significance of flexible employment patterns and involvement. In a world where increases in part-time, fixed contract and short-term working is becoming more pronounced, he shows that these employees have even less involvement in workplace decisions, and that core groups, particularly in management categories, still hold far greater sway over the organisation and control of work. Such evidence casts huge question marks over involvement schemes aimed at motivating workers.

Employee involvement and the European Union

One of the most controversial issues surrounding the European social dimension has been the issue of employee involvement. The refusal to adopt the Social Charter and the Works Council Directive of 1991 by the UK government is also reflective of some employer attitudes throughout Europe in which legislation is viewed as a threat to managerial prerogatives. Nevertheless, many European countries have in place laws supporting works councils and other employee rights to consultation.

- **The Fifth Directive 1972** embodied the first separate EU legal proposals on communication and participation. This aimed to establish formal participation structures in the then EC. The aim was to achieve harmonisation of company law.

- **The Vredeling Directive 1980** aimed to introduce formal employee information and consultation procedures into companies and groups with more than 1000 employees. The proposal would require them to disclose to employee representatives a considerable amount of information concerning their activities, e.g. company structures, financial position, employment situation and probable trends concerning production, sales and future developments. The directive would also require parent companies to establish formal consultative procedures to take place on any decision 'liable to have serious consequences for the interests of employees of its subsidiaries in the community'.

- **The Val Duchesse Meetings in 1985** between UNICE (Union of European Community Industries), the main community employers organisation, ETUC (European Trade Union Confederation) and CEEP (the European Centre of Public Enterprises) agreed that information was to be furnished and consultation was to be carried out in the implementation of new technologies.

Most of these provisions were adopted into the Social Charter, particularly for the following cases:

- When technological changes which, from the point of view of working conditions and work organisation, have major implications for the workforce are introduced into undertakings.

- In connection with restructuring operations in undertakings or in cases of mergers having an impact on the employment of workers.

- In cases of collective redundancy procedures.

- When transfrontier workers in particular are affected by the employment policies pursued by the undertaking where they are employed.

After considerable pressure from the UK government and UNICE, the adoption of the 1989 version of the Social Charter allowed the process of 'subsidiarity' to replace enforcement and obligation on these issues, much to the disappointment of its advocates. Subsidiarity in effect means that each member state shall interpret these rulings in its own way.

This will inevitably mean that workers' participation rights will be more substantive in countries with supportive legislation such as Germany, Belgium and the Netherlands. EU initiatives are controversial and will be a long time in being implemented. Even in those countries which have employee involvement legislation in place, 'the shift from management to workers, in terms of control has been slight' (Lane, 1989).

However, employee involvement rooted in industrial democratic processes has witnessed a surer growth over the past twenty years in legislatively supported systems such as co-determination in Germany and Sweden. The operation of these two contrasting styles of industrial democracy is also reflected by the relative union strength in each country – 85 per cent in Sweden and 35 per cent in Germany in 1988 (OECD, 1991).

THE UNITED KINGDOM AND THE WORKS COUNCIL ISSUE

As already mentioned, the UK government was opposed to the Works Council Directive 1991 and the directives on participation embodied in the Social Charter. However, the adoption of the Maastricht Treaty and with it the Social Chapter could possibly mean that works councils could be instituted in the UK through foreign-owned subsidiaries (Gold and Hall, 1992). Considerable debate has been engendered by the fact that even if the UK does not sign the Maastricht Protocol (the part of the Maastricht Treaty which embodies the Social Chapter), large British-owned subsidiaries operating in two or more other EU countries will have to conform to the Works Council Directive. Once such bodies exist it would be difficult politically to exclude British workers. Hall (1992) states that 'companies covered by the Directive [on Works Councils], whether based in the UK or elsewhere, could well decide voluntarily to bring their UK employees within the ambit of their European works councils; they would certainly come under pressure from UK unions to do so'.

The current Directive makes it obligatory for any company with over 1000 employees in the EU and more than 100 employees in two different countries to set up a council comprised of worker representatives.

The ex-President of the Commission, Jacques Delors, a strong believer in works councils, believes that the bad feeling engendered by the Hoover dispute – in which the white goods company transferred its plant from France to Scotland as workers would accept lower pay there – could have been avoided by directing the argument via a works council in each country (Wolf, 1993).

While the government has claimed that employee involvement is adequate at present in Britain and should be left to the discretion of each employer, a recent comparison of British and Dutch employee participation practices shows that this voluntary approach does not do well when compared to countries like the Netherlands, which has legislation compelling organisations to set up EI mechanisms like works councils. Wenlock and Purcell (1991) state that:

> *'Existing British practice does not go far enough in its provision of employees' rights to information, consultation and participation in the management of transfer of undertakings, whereas the Dutch jurification model exceeds even the EU legislation in its provision of employees' rights to participate in strategic management decision making.'*

A survey has shown that most of Britain's top 100 companies have had to set up Europe-wide workforce consultation committees by 1996. Under the re-drafted directive rules an EU company 'with more than 1000 employees in the other 11 member states and more than 100 workers in at least two of those states would have to negotiate Europe-wide employee consultation machinery if there is a request for it. Although British workforces do not have to be included by law, many firms admit privately that it would be impossible in practice to exclude them' (Milne, 1994).

With the election of a Labour government in 1997 it seems certain that the UK will officially adopt the directive.

Japanese employee involvement

Japan is often cited as an exemplar of excellent organisational communication, particularly through employee participatory practices, most notably in giant corporations such as Komatsu, Hitachi, Nissan, Honda, Mitsubishi and Toyota. The most commonly emulated participatory technique has been quality circles, implanted in Japanese organisations in the 1950s. Since then employee involvement techniques such as QCs and teamworking have been part and parcel of the working practices of Japanese subsidiaries such as Nissan in Sunderland and Toyota in Derby. Many studies have been made of Japanese organisations in order to discover the secrets of their economic success, and teamworking techniques have received much attention as a perceived key to efficient work practices.

Pascale and Athos (1982) emphasise that the work group is the basic building block of Japanese organisations.

> *'Owing to the central importance of group efforts in their thinking, the Japanese are extremely sensitive to and concerned about group interactions and relationships.'*

They liken the Japanese worker's view of the group to that of a marriage which rests on commitment, trust, sharing and loyalty and, while power ultimately rests with management, the group leader handles the interaction within the group carefully.

This 'participation assumption' is also related to a lifetime employment assumption, which ensures the worker has a strong stake in the firm and its success. Finally, and perhaps most importantly, participation is backed up by training of both group leaders and workers in the skills of group participation (Dore and Sako, 1989). Employee involvement, like training, is thus embedded in Japanese organisations.

A number of observers have pointed out that employee involvement should not be confused with decision making, particularly at the higher levels within the organisation.

> *'The reality is that not all employees wield real power . . . [and] when it comes to making the decision, workers feel under great pressure to agree with supervisors and unpopular decisions are simply ignored.'*
>
> (Klaus and Bass, 1974; Naoi and Schooler, 1985, quoted in Briggs, 1991)

Briggs sees this paradox of employee involvement and emasculation of power as being explained by the split between opinion and behaviour. In a number of surveys Japanese workers have rated themselves low on job satisfaction and yet they work far more hours for less reward than their American and British counterparts. This cannot be explained by coercive methods alone, and Briggs points to the extent of unionisation, albeit organised around large corporations, and finds this view untenable. Her explanation is based on cultural factors in that the Japanese have 'a deep felt desire to keep the realm of duty separate from the realm of personal feeling . . . duty must come first and must exist totally separate from the domain of personal feelings' (Briggs, 1991).

If this is the case, then this has ramifications for the export of such EI practices to other countries, most notably Britain, which has received enormous amounts of Japanese investment. Wickens (1987) in his exposition of how Nissan implanted Japanese practices into its Sunderland factory, strongly believes that people are capable of change and the institution of Japanese-style working practices was partly effected by a watering-down process to meet British attitudes, combined with a process of education and training to enable newly hired (often novice) workers in car manufacturing to be imbued with Japanese-style practices. This was reinforced by a 'greenfield' culture, with workers who had predominantly been recruited from regions where high unemployment meant an eagerness to gain and retain employment.

A number of observers have pointed out that control and the mechanisms of employee involvement in Japanese-owned British organisations still resides firmly in the hands of management. Lewis (1989) in his study of employee participation in a Japanese-owned electronics factory found that, while a board was set up (a kind of JCC) to represent employee interests, employees were not quite sure what was meant by involvement. Most of the issues raised were not about the overall running of the operation but more parochial shopfloor concerns, and the real aim in setting up the board was to introduce unitarist principles in the company, such as single-status terms and conditions, no-strike arrangements and flexible working practices. All were reinforced with powerful symbols of unitarism, such as brightly coloured jackets which everyone wore, replete with the owner's forename. This sent messages of egalitarianism and that the organisation was one happy family. The single-status restaurants and toilets were also part of this symbolic reinforcement of unitarism. Oliver and Lowe (1991) endorse this unitarist view of Japanese-style management. In comparing styles of HRM in Japanese, American and British computer companies based in the UK, they found the Japanese emphasised consensus and collectivism with 'a thin dividing line between the public and the private and a strong sense of mutual support and awareness'.

In essence the implementation of EI, even in Japanese organisations which have strong commitments to such systems, are not in existence as decision-making instruments *per se* or even conduits of employee criticism, but as mechanisms which reinforce common aims and goals within the unitarist organisational context.

Ramsay (1992b) has also pointed out that few non-Japanese owned British organisations have adopted Japanese EI measures in the long term. Quality circles, after an initial flurry of interest, dropped from 63 per cent in 1980 to 10 per cent in 1989 in British organisations, and by the late 1980s only a few companies were still experimenting with teamworking. He concludes: 'no matter what the degree of genuine autonomy or control in Swedish or Japanese work group experiments, the greater constraints on the prospect for worker influence came from the institutional settings and – even more critically – the broader social and cultural contexts' (Ramsay, 1992b).

COMMUNICATIONS AND THE FUTURE

The 'communications revolution', as some people have dubbed recent developments in new technology, will have a profound effect on the way companies and workplaces are organised. However, the process of radical restructuring of communicational modes and channels had already begun to get under way in the late 1980s with the introduction of managerial policies such as 'delayering' – which were partly devised to shorten communicational lines in the vertical organisational structure. In the 1990s these are increasingly being combined with management-driven policies which embody ideas of 'empowerment' and 'employee influence' at workplace level and are justified as ultimately increasing the efficiency of the organisation. In these delayered and downsized organisations the core workforce will increasingly be composed of highly educated personnel, empowered and willing to take decisions. The teams of which they will be part will be democratic units. These future workers will expect consultation, information and involvement.

Studies have already indicated that the transition to such 'ideal' workplaces will not be smooth. Management will be posed with the dilemma of how much power to extend to the workforce while harnessing their creative energies, while at the same time not undermining managerial prerogatives. However, a number of suggestions can be made which may well enable these new EI and communicational mechanisms to function more efficiently. There must be:

- a willingness by management to concede some of their prerogatives;
- recognition of the necessity to train managers in EI initiatives such as teamworking;
- a clear policy regarding the role and prerogatives of line managers in relation to senior management and the workforce under their supervision;
- recognition of the necessity to train workers in group working skills such as presentation, leadership, assertiveness, problem solving, etc;

- recognition of the necessity of providing proper feedback mechanisms which clearly indicate the workforce is being listened to and not purely in a 'lip-service fashion';

- action taken to implement group decisions, to reinforce the view among the workforce that their contributions are well received;

- the recognition that conflicting views have a place in developing initiatives.

Futurologists are already predicting that even this view will eventually diminish and even vanish as new technology increasingly impacts on communications in organisations. As Nick Land, a philosopher and researcher in the field of new technology, states:

> *'There is a similar pattern that you find in the structure of societies, in the structure of companies and in the structure of computers, and all three are moving in the same direction. That is, away from a top-down structure of a central command system giving the system instructions about how to behave, towards a system that is flat, which is a web, in which change moves from the bottom up. And this is going to happen across all institutions and technical devices. It's the way they work.'* (Quoted in Harrison, 1995)

In physical terms office blocks, defined as the corporate ego trip of the 1980s, will be the social and economic dinosaurs of the next century. 'Businesses will concentrate on fewer, more efficient buildings, with all but management and key workers operating from home or satellite offices in the suburbs' (Brown, 1994). This vision of a cyberspace heaven in which the Internet and other technological developments will create a work–home environment, has been contrasted with a societal hell in which those dispossessed of the new technology will languish in crumbling ghettos in the giant hulks of decaying cities (Handy, 1994; Harrison, 1995). Whatever the future holds, communication will still continue to be important, as will the skills needed to do it effectively.

SUMMARY

- In this chapter an outline of communication models was undertaken, examining the mechanistic concepts of the Shannon and Weaver model and the feedback concept indicated in the Schramm model. Definitions of organisational communication were considered, including those of Krone, Jablin and Putnam, who view the communication process as being influenced by mechanistic, psychological, interpretive-symbolic and systems-interactive perspectives.

- Clampitt identified three approaches to communication which he calls the arrow, circuit and dance models. The first two follow respectively the Shannon and Weaver mechanistic model, and the Schramm feedback model. The dance model he believes to be superior as it incorporates elements of organisational culture and other organic or human influences.

■ A review of various media channels was undertaken in the light of their classification into downward, upward and horizontal forms of organisational communication.

■ Trends in international communication were highlighted through the findings of a number of surveys, and a more detailed examination of Japanese communication and employee involvement practices was undertaken. Communications in an employee involvement context within the European Union were considered with special attention given to the issue of the influence of the Works Council Directive on the UK.

■ The chapter ended with some speculations and prognostications about the influence and direction of organisational communications in the future.

REVIEW AND DISCUSSION QUESTIONS

1 Why did quality circles enjoy increased popularity in the 1980s, but witness a decline in their use in the UK in the early 1990s?

2 What lessons can be learned from Japanese communication and employee involvement practices?

3 What editorial policies would you decide to adopt in creating a company newspaper? What difficulties could you foresee in their implementation?

4 Make a network analysis of a workplace or department, with an individual at the centre. By means of flow lines and arrows show with whom this person communicates (a) within the department and (b) outside the department. Do not forget to put in feedback arrows. State what methods of communication are used, e.g. telephone, memo, face-to-face. From this exercise it should be possible to see what improvements can be made in communication flows for the individual and the department.

5 Outline the processes for conducting an employee attitude survey. To what uses could the survey be put?

CASE STUDY: NO NEWS IS BAD NEWS

Future Fashion is a string of high street retail outlets selling fashion clothes and accessories. Although hit badly by the recession from 1991, by means of price cutting and shrewd marketing the company has managed to remain solvent and make a small profit. However, by 1995 the crunch had come and the Managing Director, Paul Brown, is holding a board meeting to review the situation.

The Financial Director, John Green, states the facts baldly.

'We are now just losing too much money to stay in the position we are in. We will have to make some savings or the business will disappear.'

Paul addresses the meeting generally.

'Well are there any suggestions as to how we can make savings?'

Steve White, Director of Operations, speaks candidly:

'There are few alternatives left open to us. We've got to cut staff, and introduce a tighter contract based on zero hours working. If we don't, we all lose our jobs!'

Jane Black, the Human Resource Director, agrees that staff costs have to be cut but suggests that a redundancy and outplacement programme be implemented. This is rejected forcefully by Steve as a waste of time and money and John agrees.

'As long as we stick to the letter of the law we're OK. We don't have to go beyond that.'

Jane argues:

'We should be preparing the workforce for the bad news. They need time to absorb it and make other plans for their working lives. If we don't, we will end up having bad publicity which won't help the business, and more importantly we will have a lot of disgruntled workers on our hands as well as the union on our backs.' ■

REFERENCES AND FURTHER READING*

Advisory Conciliation and Arbitration Service (ACAS) (1982) *Workplace Communications*, Advisory Booklet No 8, London: ACAS.

Boreham, P (1992) 'The Myth of Post-Fordist Management: Work Organisation and Employee Discretion in Seven Countries', *Employee Relations*, Vol 14, No 2, 13–24.

Brennan, B (1991) 'Mismanagement and Quality Circles: How Middle Managers Influence Direct Participation', *Employee Relations*, Vol 13, No 5.

Briggs, P (1991) 'Organisational Commitment: The Key to Japanese Success?', in C Brewster and S Tyson (eds) *International Comparisons in Human Resource Management*, London: Pitman Publishing.

Brown, P (1994) 'Dinosaur offices heading for extinction', *Guardian*, 14 November.

CBI, *see* Confederation of British Industry.

*Clampitt, P (1991) *Communicating for Managerial Effectiveness*, Newbury Park: Sage.

Clutterbuck, D and Grainer, S (1990) *Makers of Management: Men and Women who Changed the Business World*, London: Macmillan.

*Collard, R and Dale, B (1989) 'Quality Circles', in K Sisson (ed) *Personnel Management in Britain*, Oxford: Blackwell.

Confederation of British Industry (1989) *Employee Involvement: Shaping the Future Business*, London: CBI.

Cressey, P and Williams, R (1990) *Participation in Change: New Technology and the Role of Employee Involvement*, Dublin: European Foundation for the Improvement of Living and Working Conditions.

*Crosby, P (1979) *Quality is Free*, New York: McGraw-Hill.

Crosby, P (1984) *Quality Without Tears*, New York: McGraw-Hill.

DeFleur, M (1966) *Theories of Mass Communication*, New York: David Mckay.

Dore, R and Sako, M (1989) *How the Japanese Learn to Work*, London: Routledge.

Fairhurst, G, Rogers, L and Saar, R (1987) 'Manager–subordinate control patterns and judgement about relationship', in M McLaughlin (ed) *Communication Yearbook* 10, 395–415, Newbury Park, Ca: Sage.

Filella, J and Soler, C (1992) 'Spain', in C Brewster, A Hegewisch, L Holden and T Lockhart (eds) *The European Human Resource Management Guide*, London: Academic Press.

Fröhlich, D and Krieger, H (1990) 'Technological Change and Worker Participation in Europe', *New Technology, Work and Employment*, Vol 5, No 2, Autumn.

Gill, C (1993) 'Technological Change and Participation in Work Organisation: Recent Results from a European Survey', *The International Journal of Human Resource Management*, Vol 4, No 2, May.

Gold, M and Hall, M (1992) *Report on European-level Information and Consultation in Multinational Companies – Evaluation and Practice*, Dublin: European Foundation for the Improvement of Living and Working Conditions.

Hall, M (1992) 'Behind the European Works Council Directives: The European Commission's Legislative Strategy', *British Journal of Industrial Relations*, Vol 30, No 4, December.

Handy, C (1994) *The Empty Raincoat: Making Sense of the Future*, London: Hutchinson.

Harrison, M (1995) *Visions of Heaven and Hell*, London: Channel 4 Television.

Holden, L (1990) 'Employee Communications in Europe on the Increase', *Involvement and Participation*, November.

ILO (1993) *World Labour Report*, Geneva: International Labour Organisation.

*Jablin, F, Putnam, L, Roberts, K and Porter, L (eds) (1987) *Handbook of Organisational Communication: An Interdisciplinary Perspective*, Newbury Park: Sage.

Klauss, R and Bass, B (1974) 'Group Influence on Individual Behaviour across Cultures', *Journal of Cross-cultural Psychology*, Vol 5, 236–46.

Lane, C (1989) *Management and Labour in Europe*, Aldershot: Edward Elgar.

Lawler, E (1986) *High-Involvement Management*, San Francisco: Jossey-Bass.

McLuhan, M (1964) *Understanding Media*, London: Routledge & Kegan Paul.

McQuail, D and Windahl, S (1981) *Communication Models*, Harlow: Addison-Wesley Longman.

Marchington, M (1992) *Managing the Team: A Guide to Successful Employee Involvement*, Oxford: Blackwell.

*Marchington, M, Goodman, J, Wilkinson, A. and Ackers, P (1992) *New Developments in Employee Involvement*, Manchester School of Management, Employment Department Research Series No 2.

Milne, S (1994) 'Works councils net snares majority of top firms', *Guardian*, 7 June, p 17.

Monks, J (1989) 'Trade Union Role in Communications', in T Wilkinson (ed), *The Communications Challenge*, London: IPD.

Naoi, A and Schooler, C (1985) 'Occupational Conditions and Psychological Functioning in Japan', *American Journal of Sociology*, Vol 9, No 4, 729–52 (quoted in Briggs, 1991).

OECD (1991) *OECD in Figures: Statistics on the Member Countries*, Paris: Organisation for Economic Cooperation and Development.

Oliver, N and Lowe, J (1991) 'UK Computer Industry: American, British and Japanese Contrasts in Human Resource Management', *Personnel Review*, Vol 20, No 2.

Pace, W and Boren, R (1973) *The Human Transaction*, Glenview, Il: Scott Foreman.

Pascale, R and Athos, A (1982) *The Art of Japanese Management*, London: Allen Lane.

*Pease, A (1984) *Body Language*, London: Sheldon Press.

*Poole, M (1986) *Towards A New Industrial Democracy: Workers' Participation in Industry*, London: Routledge & Kegan Paul.

Price, R (1989) 'The Decline and Fall of the Status Divide?', in K Sisson (ed) *Personnel Management in Britain*, Oxford: Blackwell.

Price Waterhouse Cranfield Project on International Strategic Human Resource Management (1990) *Report*, London: Price Waterhouse.

Price Waterhouse Cranfield Project on International Strategic Human Resource Management (1991) *Report*, Cranfield: Cranfield School of Management.

Putnam, L and Jones, T (1982) 'Reciprocity in negotiations: An analysis of bargaining inerreaction', *Communication Monographs*, 49, 171–91.

Ramsay, H (1977) 'Cycles of Control', *Sociology*, 11, 481–506.

*Ramsay, H (1991) 'Reinventing the Wheel? A Review of the Development and Performance of Employee Involvement', *Human Resource Management Journal*, Vol 1, No 1, Summer.

Ramsay, H (1992*a*) 'Commitment and Involvement', in B Towers (ed) *The Handbook of Human Resource Management*, Oxford: Blackwell.

Ramsay, H (1992*b*) 'Swedish and Japanese Work Methods – Comparisons and Contrasts', *P+ European Participation Monitor*, Issue No 3, No 1.

Schramm, W (1954) 'How Communication Works', in W Schramm (ed) *The Process and Effects of Mass Communication*, Urbana: University of Illinois Press.

Sewell, G and Wilkinson, B. (1992) 'Empowerment or Emasculation? Shopfloor Surveillance in a Total Quality Organisation', in P Blyton and P Turnbull (eds) *Reassessing Human Resource Management*, London: Sage.

Shannon, C and Weaver, W (1949) *The Mathematical Theory of Communication*, Urbana: University of Illinois Press.

Smith, V (1990) *Managing in the Corporate Interest: Control and Resistance in an American Bank*, Oxford, England: University of California Press.

Townley, B (1989) 'Employee Communication Programmes', in K Sisson (ed) *Personnel Management in Britain*, Oxford: Blackwell.

Wenlock, H and Purcell, J (1991) 'The Management Transfer of Undertakings: A Comparison of Employee Participation Practices in the United Kingdom and the Netherlands', *Human Resource Management Journal*, Vol 1, No 2, Winter.

Wickens, P (1987) *The Road to Nissan: Flexibility, Quality and Teamwork,* Basingstoke: Macmillan.

Wilkinson, A, Marchington, M, Ackers, P and Goodman, J (1992) 'Total Quality Management and Employee Involvement', *Human Resource Management Journal,* Vol 2, No 4, Summer.

*Wilkinson, T (1989) (ed) *The Communications Challenge: Personnel and PR Perspectives,* London: IPD.

Wolf, J (1993) 'Britain fights works councils plan', *Guardian,* 7 April.

HUMAN RESOURCES MANAGEMENT

Roger Bennett

OBJECTIVES

This chapter surveys the approaches and methods that an organisation can apply to the management of its human resources. The objectives of the chapter are to help the reader to:

◆ understand and explain the difference between personnel management and human resources management

◆ recognise good practice in the fields of recruitment, selection and appraisal

◆ appreciate the importance of human resources planning for the efficient management of enterprises

◆ identify key legal requirements in relation to equal opportunities

◆ assess the training needs of a business or large department

◆ analyse the significance of current trends in the techniques for managing human resources

NATURE OF HUMAN RESOURCES MANAGEMENT

Human resources management concerns the human side of enterprises and the factors that determine workers' relationships with their employing organisations. It is a wide-ranging subject that covers, among other things: management/worker communications; elements of work psychology; employee relations, training and motivation; organisation of the physical and social conditions of work; and (of course) personnel management.

Everyone who has control over others shares in human resources management. Accordingly, HRM is not a function that the individual manager can leave to specialists, although HRM professionals do play a vital role.

Human resources management and personnel management

In contrast with 'personnel management' which deals with the practical aspects of recruitment, staff appraisal, training, job evaluation, etc, HRM has a *strategic* dimension and involves the total deployment of all the human resources available to the firm (Guest, 1987; Legge, 1989; Ferris and Buckley, 1996). Personnel management is practical, utilitarian and instrumental, and mostly concerned with administration and the *implementation* of policies. Human resources management, in contrast, encompasses such broader matters as:

- **The aggregate size of the organisation's labour force** in the context of an overall corporate plan (how many divisions and subsidiaries the company is to have, design of the organisation, etc).

- **How much to spend on training the workforce**, given strategic decisions on target quality levels, product prices, volume of production and so on.

- **The desirability of establishing relations with trade unions** from the viewpoint of the effective management control of the entire organisation.

- **Human asset accounting**, i.e. the systematic measurement and analysis of the costs and *financial* benefits of alterative personnel policies (e.g. the monetary consequences of staff development exercises, the effects of various salary structures, etc) and the valuation of the human worth of the enterprise's employees.

The strategic approach to HRM involves the integration of personnel and other HRM considerations into the firm's overall corporate planning and strategy formulation procedures (Stroh *et al.*, 1998). It is proactive, seeking constantly to discover new ways of utilising the labour force in a more productive manner, thus giving the business a competitive edge. Practical manifestations of the adoption of a strategic approach to HRM might include:

- incorporation of a brief summary of the firm's basic HRM policy into its mission statement;

- explicit consideration of the consequences for employees of each of the firm's strategies and major new projects;

- designing organisation structures to suit the needs of employees rather than conditioning the latter to fit in with the existing form of organisation;

- having the head of HRM on the firm's board of directors.

More than ever before, human resource managers are expected to contribute to productivity and quality improvement, the stimulation of creative thinking, leadership and the development of corporate skills.

Further differences between personnel management and HRM are as follows:

1 HRM is concerned with the wider implications of the management of change and not just with the effects of change on working practices. It seeks proactively to encourage flexible attitudes and the acceptance of new methods.

2 Aspects of HRM constitute major inputs into organisational development exercises.

3 Personnel management is (necessarily) reactive and diagnostic. It *responds* to changes in employment law, labour market conditions, trade union actions, government codes of practice and other environmental influences. HRM, conversely, is *prescriptive* and concerned with strategies, the initiation of new activities and the development of fresh ideas.

4 HRM determines general policies for employment relationships within the enterprise. Thus, it needs to establish within the organisation a *culture* that is conducive to employee commitment and co-operation. Personnel management, on the other hand, has been criticised for being primarily concerned with imposing *compliance* with company rules and procedures among employees, rather than with loyalty and commitment to the firm.

5 Personnel management has short-term perspectives; HRM has long-term perspectives, seeking to *integrate* all the human aspects of the organisation into a coherent whole and to establish high-level employee goals.

6 The HRM approach emphasises the need:

  — for direct communication with employees rather than their collective representation;

  — to develop an organisational culture conducive to the adoption of flexible working methods;

  — for group working and employee participation in group decisions;

  — to enhance employees' long-term capabilities, not just their competence at current duties.

Human resources management and competitive advantage

There are a number of reasons why the effective management of human resources can give a business a competitive edge over rival firms, as follows.

- Contented and hard-working employees are more likely to produce excellent work that genuinely adds value to the enterprise.

- The stability of a company that possesses sound employee relations will encourage outside investors to buy shares in the business, so that it becomes easier for the company to raise funds.

- The existence of common values upheld throughout the organisation facilitates the development of long-term strategies and plans.

- Company resources should be used in the most efficient ways (via the recruitment of the best people, use of high-level skills developed through top class training programmes, etc).

- An organisational culture conducive to quality performance is likely to prevail.

- Change can be implemented with less disruption.

- The organisation's core competencies are strengthened and enhanced.

HUMAN RESOURCES PLANNING

Definition of human resources planning

Human resources planning (HRP) is the comparison of an organisation's existing labour resources with forecast labour demand, and hence the scheduling of activities for acquiring, training, redeploying and possibly discarding labour. It seeks to ensure that an adequate supply of labour is available precisely when required. Specific human resource planning duties include:

- estimation of labour turnover for each grade of employee and the examination of the effects of high or low turnover rates on the organisation's performance;

- analysis of the consequences of changes in working practices and hours;

- predicting future labour shortages;

- devising schemes for handling the human problems arising from labour deficits or surpluses;

- introduction of early retirement and other natural wastage procedures;

- analysis of the skills, educational backgrounds, experience, capacities and potentials of employees.

Effective HRP should result in the right people doing the right things in the right place at precisely the right time. The process of human resources planning is illustrated in Fig 11.1.

301

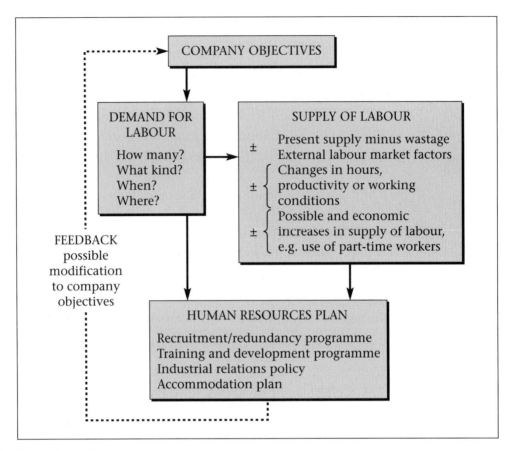

FIG 11.1 THE HUMAN RESOURCES PLANNING PROCESS

HRP should help management in making decisions concerning recruitment, the avoidance of redundancies, training and staff development, and the estimation of the costs of employing labour. Sometimes redundancies can be avoided through the preparation of 'skills inventories' (i.e. detailed listings of all the competencies, work experiences and qualifications of current employees – even those characteristics not relevant to present occupations). The purpose of a skills inventory is to inform management of all the jobs that existing employees might be capable of undertaking.

Benefits of human resources planning

In preparing a human resources plan, management can co-ordinate and integrate all the organisation's HRM activities, avoiding duplication of effort and eliminating unnecessary waste (Schuler and Walker, 1990). Specific advantages to HRP include the following:

1 The organisation will be ready to adapt future HRM activities to meet changing circumstances.

2 Careful consideration of likely future events might lead to the discovery of better means for managing human resources. Foreseeable pitfalls might be avoided.

3 Measures to influence future events can be initiated by the organisation itself.

4 Decisions concerning future HRM activities can be taken in advance, unhurriedly, using all the data available and considering all available options. This avoids decision making in crisis situations with management unable to study all relevant issues judiciously and at length.

5 Planning forces the organisation to assess critically the feasibility of its HRM objectives.

6 Labour shortfalls and surpluses may be able to be avoided.

7 It helps the firm create and develop employee training and management succession programmes.

8 Some of the problems of managing change may be foreseen and their consequences mitigated. Consultations with affected groups and individuals can occur at an early stage in the change process.

9 Management is compelled to assess critically the strengths and weaknesses of its labour force and personnel policies.

10 Duplication of effort among employees can be avoided; co-ordination and integration of workers' efforts is improved.

Planning procedures

Principles of effective human resources planning (HRP)

Certain fundamental principles should always be applied when preparing a human resources plan, as follows:

- The plan should be as detailed as expenditure constraints allow.

- Plans should not extend too far into the future – accurate prediction of the distant future is simply impossible.

- *All* alternative courses of action should be considered.

- Side effects and implications of the actions envisaged should be examined.

- Instructions to individuals and departments must be incorporated into the plan.

- Plans should be concise and easy to understand.

As the plan is executed its effectiveness in achieving stated objectives should be monitored. Differences between actual and desired positions must be quickly identified and remedial measures introduced.

Labour turnover analysis

Employees may be categorised according to age, length of service, occupation, educational background, job experience and promotion potential. *Labour turnover* is commonly measured by the ratio of the number of workers who left the firm during a certain period (normally six months or a year) to the average number of workers employed during the same period. If this is relatively constant over time, the organisation can predict the recruitment needed to keep all existing posts occupied. The problem is that if just one or two posts are filled and vacated many times during a particular period, the index becomes artificially high. For instance, if a single job is filled ten times in a year, the effect on the index is identical to that of ten people leaving different jobs during that year. To overcome (partially) this problem the 'labour stability index' can be used to show the extent to which employees with longer service are leaving the organisation:

$$\frac{\text{Number of employees with more than one year's service}}{\text{Total number of people employed one year ago}}$$

Note that this index does not reveal the average length of service of employees, which should be computed separately for each category of staff.

Another useful exercise is to compute the percentages of a group of employees – all of whom are hired on the same date – who are still with the firm after certain periods. Thus for example, 10 per cent might have left by the end of one year, 25 per cent after two years, 70 per cent after five, and so on. The firm can then predict how long, on average, it takes for (say) half of all workers recruited on a particular date to leave the firm. The exercise can be repeated for various occupational groups.

High labour turnover may be due to low pay, inadequate holiday entitlement, long working hours or other conditions of employment regarded by workers as unsatisfactory. Other causes include:

- **excessively monotonous work;**
- **absence of promotion prospects;**
- **bad recruitment and staff induction procedures;**
- **ineffective grievance procedures;**
- **poor communications within the organisation.**

High labour turnover is undesirable for several reasons. Recruitment and training costs increase, new entrants are relatively unproductive during the early stages of their service, and additional demands are placed on the remaining staff. Morale is typically lower in organisations with high labour turnover. Note, however, that certain categories of employee exhibit, on average, exceptionally high labour turnover rates – notably young workers and those engaged in boring and repetitive duties. Also, workers are more likely to quit their jobs in rapidly expanding industries.

Steps in the HRP process

In drafting a human resources plan the organisation must consider the demand for labour, its potential supply (with corrections for its present misuse, over-use or under-use) and the external environment. By studying the interaction of all these factors, it can then produce a plan showing how many and what kind of employees are expected to be required in the future. The main points to be considered are as follows:

1 **The creation of an HRP group**, including the managers in charge of the main functions within the organisation.

2 **The statement of human resources objectives** in the light of the organisation's objectives by considering:
- capital equipment plans;
- reorganisation, e.g. centralisation or decentralisation;
- changes in products or in output;
- marketing plans;
- financial limitations.

3 **The present utilisation of human resources,** in particular:
- numbers of employees in various categories;
- estimation of labour turnover for each grade of employee and the analysis of the effects of high or low turnover rates on the organisation's performance;
- amount of overtime worked;
- amount of short time;
- appraisal of performance and potential of present employees;
- general level of payment compared with that in other organisations.

Note that, for all the above, accurate and complete personnel records are essential.

4 **The external environment of the organisation:**
- recruitment position;
- population trends;
- local housing and transport plans;
- national agreements dealing with conditions of work;
- government policies on education, retirement, regional subsidies, etc.

5 **The potential supply of labour,** in particular:
- effects of local emigration and immigration;
- effects of recruitment or redundancy by local firms;
- possibility of employing categories not now employed, e.g. part-time workers;
- changes in productivity, working hours and/or practices.

FORECASTING AND THE HUMAN RESOURCES AUDIT

Human resources plans are predetermined responses to anticipated future events (Greenberg and Baron, 1997). It is axiomatic that possible future events must be predicted, so mechanisms for forecasting the future need to be devised. The demand for labour is a 'derived demand', depending as it does on the number and types of people needed to produce and distribute goods. Factors influencing the demand for a particular company's products include the rate of growth of total consumer spending, the intensity of competition including competition from imported goods), changes in tastes and fashion, and possibly seasonal variations in levels of purchases. All these factors affect the volumes and characteristics of a firm's production and hence the labour it needs to employ. Unfortunately, accurate forecasting of such variables is notoriously difficult, for several reasons, as outlined below:

- Many variables (tax levels, business laws, interest rates, consumer incomes, etc) are determined by government and are thus beyond the organisation's control.

- Consumer tastes can change quickly and unpredictably.

- New technical inventions may occur.

- Competitors might alter their behaviour; fresh competition could emerge.

- Past events upon which forecasts are based might not occur in the future.

- Existing suppliers, distribution options, harmonious industrial relations, etc, could suddenly disappear.

- Technical difficulties (unreliable data, incorrect choice of statistical forecasting technique, etc) might arise.

The longer the period of the forecast, the greater the likelihood of serious error. It is wise, therefore, to generate several different forecasts, with a greater amount of detail the shorter the timespan involved, and each forecast assuming a different scenario of events. The accuracy of predictions should be monitored by comparing them with events as they occur, and sources of error (inadequate or incorrect data, faulty forecasting techniques, poor judgements by forecasters, etc) should be identified. It is useful to know whether forecasts are on average persistently overestimating or underestimating actual performance.

The human resources audit and the final HR plan

Alongside its forecasts of the demands for various categories of labour, management needs to set out all its available information on the organisation's existing personnel, taken perhaps from a skills inventory (*see* p 302 above) plus appraisal reports on the quality of employees' work. Analysis of this information might be set out in a separate document, the 'human resources audit' that lists the abilities, performance records and apparent potential of each of the organisation's departments and its employees. The aim of the exercise is to match the organisation's present and future human resources against current and forecast requirements, thus enabling it to produce the final human resources plan showing in detail, by function, occupation and locations, how many employees it is *practicable* to employ at various stages in the future (Graham and Bennett, 1998). The following should appear in it:

- jobs which will appear, disappear or change;

- to what extent redeployment or retraining is possible;

- necessary changes at supervisory and management levels;

- training needs;

- recruitment, redundancy or retirement programmes;

- industrial relations implications;

- arrangements for feedback in case modifications in the plan or company objectives are necessary;

- details of arrangements for handling any human problems arising from labour deficits or surpluses (e.g. early retirement or other natural wastage procedures).

Short-term plans

Many organisations do not have the financial or managerial resources to forecast long-term HRP variables, or they feel that the nature of their business makes it impossible to look ahead for more than one year. Hence they might prepare short-term plans covering just the next 12 months. A short-term human resources plan is comparatively easy to put together because an organisation will usually make a production or marketing plan for a year ahead involving budgets, orders for new materials and components, and sales quotas. From this can be derived the amount of *direct labour* in terms of labour-hours required in future, and then, by dividing into this figure the number of available working hours, the number of workers can be obtained. Overtime and the average level of sickness absence and machine breakdowns must be taken into account when available working hours are calculated.

The amount of *indirect labour* may be estimated partly by fixed commitments and partly as a rule of thumb percentage of indirect to direct labour. From the total labour requirements a recruitment or redundancy plan can be derived, but the period is usually too short for any worthwhile training plan to be made.

An advantage of the short-term plan is the ease with which the forecast can be compared with the labour that was actually required, and any discrepancies analysed.

RECRUITMENT

Recruitment is the first stage in the process of filling a vacancy. It involves the examination of the requirements for filling the vacancy (particularly in relation to job and person specifications); consideration of the sources of suitable candidates; drafting job advertisements and selecting media suitable to carry them; assessing appropriate salary levels for new employees; and arranging interviews and other aspects of 'selection', the second stage in the staffing process (Chessington, 1995). Selection requires the assessment of candidates by various means and the choice of successful candidate. It is considered further in the section on selection and recruitment below.

The recruitment process

The department in which the recruit will work must draft or revise a comprehensive job specification for the vacant position, outlining its major and minor responsibilities; the skills, experience and qualifications needed; grade and level of pay; starting date; whether temporary or permanent; and particulars of any special conditions (shift-work, for example) attached to the job. Then the vacancy is advertised in suitable media and/or recruitment agencies are approached.

External recruitment is expensive. It involves advertising, agency fees, distribution of application forms, preparation of shortlists, writing for references, interviewing, payment of travelling expenses, etc. If the candidate appointed is unsuitable or leaves within a short period then the entire procedure has to be repeated. The advantages of filling the vacancy internally rather than externally are:

- better motivation of employees because their capabilities are considered and opportunities offered for promotion;
- better utilisation of employees, because the organisation can often make better use of their abilities in a different job;
- greater reliability as compared with an external recruitment because a present employee is known more thoroughly than an external candidate;
- that a present employee is more likely to stay with the organisation than an external candidate.

Job advertisements

It has been estimated that about 10 per cent of all press advertising expenditure is devoted to situations vacant advertising. There is no doubt that much of this huge sum is wasted, chiefly because so little research has been carried out, compared with research in the field of product advertising. Many employers have been able to reduce their job advertising costs with no adverse effect on the quality or quantity of candidate response by experimenting with styles of advertisements, media and wording, and keeping careful records of the number of replies received to each advertisement and the candidate who was eventually selected. The only reliable guidance about advertising comes from the person who receives and analyses the replies, i.e. the employer. Newspapers and advertising agencies, which often claim to advise on the style and size of advertisements, are not usually in a position to know and evaluate the response.

Job advertisements should aim at procuring a small number of well-qualified candidates quickly and as cheaply as possible. Note the high cost of placing job advertisements in newspapers. A single advertisement covering 140 mm × 2 columns (approximately one-eighth of a page) in one issue of a quality daily news-paper will cost between £4000 or more depending on the newspaper's circulation and the page position of the advertisement. Even a small advertisement in a regional newspaper can cost £700 or more. An advertisement which produces hundreds of replies is a disadvantage to the organisation because the employer will then be faced with the lengthy and expensive task of sorting out a few candidates for interview.

The advertisement can become the first stage in selection by describing the job and qualifications required so comprehensively that borderline candidates will be deterred from applying and good candidates encouraged.

Headhunting

Very senior managers are sometimes recruited by a process known as 'executive search' or 'headhunting'. Its advocates believe that the best candidates are not those who reply to advertisements or look for new jobs in other ways, but those who are successful in their present jobs and are not thinking of moving elsewhere.

On receipt of a commission from a client the headhunter will search for potential candidates

- in competing businesses (possibly obtaining their names from company reports, brochures, etc);

- in the membership lists of professional bodies, trade association yearbooks, newspaper and magazine reports that mention successful managers in the relevant industry; and

- through confidential headhunting networks. Selected individuals are then approached discreetly and, following a discussion regarding the job and its remuneration, one or two of them are introduced to the client firm.

Advantages of headhunting are as follows:

- Headhunters should possess expert knowledge of the salary levels and fringe benefits necessary to attract good calibre candidates. Also, they will analyse the vacancy and offer an opinion about the type of person required, will conduct initial screening, administer psychometric tests, etc. This saves the client many administrative costs and advertising expenses.

- Possibly, top managers already in employment will not bother to read job advertisements, newspapers and other conventional media and hence cannot be reached by these means.

- Senior managers prepared to consider a move sometimes make this known to leading headhunters, even though they would not openly apply to competing companies.

- If a targeted candidate does not want the job, he or she may suggest someone else who is equally suitable and who may in fact be interested.

- Recruiting firms are assured that candidates presented to them will almost certainly be well equipped for the vacant position.

- The anonymity of the recruiting organisation is preserved until the final stages in the procedure.

Criticisms of executive search include the following.

- Headhunting is highly disruptive to successful businesses, which stand to lose expensively trained senior managers.

- It can be used to avoid equal opportunities laws on recruitment and selection.

- A headhunted individual might subsequently be enticed by other headhunters to leave his or her new firm after a short period. To avoid this some companies attach 'golden handcuffs' to senior management positions, i.e. they pay large cash bonuses which are only available to executives who stay with the firm a certain number of years.

- Arguably, headhunters rely too heavily on existing networks and trade contacts, creating thereby a glorified 'old boy system' which ignores good people from other sources.

- Headhunters' fees are far higher than for conventional employment agencies (up to 50 per cent of the recruited individual's initial salary in some instances).

- An unsuitable candidate might bribe the headhunter to recommend that person for the vacant job.

- The headhunter might acquire confidential information about the client company which could then be passed on to competing firms.

- Headhunters are not subject to the same long-term accountability as personnel managers employed within the business. Also they lack detailed knowledge of the client organisation's culture and operations.

- A headhunter might misleadingly suggest to potential candidates that a job carries a high level of salary when this is not actually the case. The salary quoted may in fact depend on meeting unrealistic targets. Equally, a recruiting firm might expect a headhunter to find a candidate capable of solving all its difficulties, when in reality the business is so weak it is bound to fail.

EQUAL OPPORTUNITIES

The Sex Discrimination Act 1975 sought to ensure that men and women and married persons be treated equally in employment situations. Thus, employers are not allowed to discriminate against women in:

- **selection procedures;**

- **terms on which employment is offered;**

- **access to opportunities for training or promotion;**

- **fringe benefits;**

- **deciding which workers shall be made redundant.**

Sex discrimination can be direct or indirect. The former means treating people unfavourably simply because of their sex, for example segregating women employees into separate departments and paying them lower wages. Indirect discrimination occurs when an employer applies a test or condition that puts one of the sexes at an unfair advantage. An example here would be a condition that all job applicants be over six feet three inches tall for work where the employee's height is not important. There are, however, exemptions available under the Act. These relate to:

- **employment manually outside the United Kingdom;**

- **employment in religious organisations that operate a sex bar;**

- **employment in the armed services.**

Also, jobs where sex is a 'genuine occupational qualification' are exempt. Examples would be actors playing male or female roles, jobs in single-sex schools, hospitals or other institutions; and jobs where decency or privacy require employment of a particular sex.

The Race Relations Act 1976 offers similar rights to ethnic minorities. As with the Sex Discrimination Act there are exemptions, including work where membership of a particular race is a genuine occupational qualification. Complaints against discrimination are heard by industrial tribunals.

Sexual harassment

Sexual harassment in the workplace can involve unwelcome sexual advances, requests for sexual favours, improper physical contact or other conduct of a sexual nature (sexist comments, jokes and so on) where such conduct unreasonably interferes with an individual's performance at work and/or creates an intimidating, hostile or offensive working environment. It is especially serious when someone's conditions of employment or benefits (promotions, pay rises, etc) depend on submission to this form of behaviour. Psychological distress within the victim and his or her eventual resignation from a job is likely to result from the practice. Sexual harassment is an infringement of personal freedom because it restricts an individual's ability to act as he or she wishes. It represents a loss of *control* over one's personal affairs.

Responses to sexual harassment can be confrontational or acquiescent. The latter involves feelings of helplessness about the situation and/or nervousness at the prospect of having to complain. Confrontational reactions (shouting, assertive complaints to supervisors, etc) carry the risk of long-term embarrassment if management simply ignores the victim's plight.

Companies can deal with sexual harassment via the establishment and publication of complaints procedures for use by victims, by informing all members of a firm that sexual harassment will not be tolerated, and through the development of appropriate policies and codes of practice. Problems with sexual harassment policies are that:

- **sexual harassment in practice is extremely difficult to prove;**

- **targets of sexual harassment are frequently reluctant to report the problem,** fearing adverse consequences if a complaint is not upheld;

- **most accusations of harassment are made against men.** It may be that males who engage in sexually harassing behaviour are most likely to be accused of impropriety than are women who act in exactly the same way! Consequently, sexual harassment might come to be regarded as an exclusively male-initiated activity, hence discouraging men from complaining about being harassed;

- **policies are useless if the people guilty of harassment are themselves top managers within the firm;**

- **it can be difficult to distinguish between sexual harassment and 'normal' male/female flirting behaviour.**

Equal pay

The Equal Pay Act 1970 requires that men and women receive equal pay for work of equal value. All the terms and conditions of a woman's (or a man's) contract of employment must not be less favourable than that which would be issued to a member of the opposite sex. It is illegal to lay down separate rates of pay for men and women.

In 1996 the Equal Opportunities Commission published a code of practice on equal pay containing practical guidance to businesses concerning the elimination of pay discrimination between men and women. The code has sections covering, inter alia, the meaning of pay, implications of the law for employers, pay systems, the identification of discrimination, and job evaluation and grading, plus a model equal pay policy. The code is admissible in evidence before an industrial tribunal in any proceedings under the Sex Discrimination Act 1975 and the Equal Pay Act 1970.

Since 1 January 1984, any person has been able to claim equal pay relative to a member of the opposite sex employed by the same firm who does work of *equal value*, as determined by a job evaluation study. Hence, a woman (say) need not identify a man who is doing identical work for the firm on higher wages; she merely has to demonstrate that her job is *worth* the same in terms of its 'demands'. Such demands might relate to the effort, skill, responsibility assumed, working conditions or decision-taking capacities required for effective performance.

Disabled workers

Attitudes towards the disabled in the workplace can be extremely negative, with disability being perceived as the source of poor performance, low levels of skill, absence of work ethic, accident-proneness and taking long periods off work. None of these beliefs stand up to proper scientific scrutiny, yet they continue to distort non-disabled observers' perceptions of the person concerned.

The Disabled Persons (Employment) Acts 1944 and **1958** provide for the following.

- A register of disabled persons, open to all who are substantially handicapped in getting or keeping suitable employment.

- A requirement that every employer with 20 or more workers should employ at least 3 per cent registered disabled workers.

- An employer may not dismiss a registered disabled person without reasonable cause if the firm is below its quota or if the dismissal would bring its numbers below it.

- The designation of two jobs, passenger lift attendant and car park attendant, which may only be filled by registered disabled persons.

The Acts have helped many disabled persons to find work, but in some areas employers find the quota difficult to fulfil, although they employ a reasonable number of disabled people. The reason for the difficulty is that, although there is a legal requirement for employers to maintain a 3 per cent quota, there is no legal requirement for disabled persons to register. Indeed, many disabled people maintain that being registered may be a drawback in their careers and that they prefer not to indicate that they regard themselves as in a different category from other people.

THE DISABILITY DISCRIMINATION ACT 1995

This legislation introduced new rights for disabled people in the areas of employment, education, public transport and access to goods, facilities and services. A 'National Disability Council' was established to advise the government on eliminating discrimination against disabled people, and a code of practice was published containing a wide range of examples to illustrate how employers and others can comply with the Act. The code is not legally binding of *itself*, but is admissible as evidence in courts and industrial tribunals in order to establish whether discrimination has occurred. 'Disability' is defined as 'a physical or mental impairment which has a substantial and long-term adverse effect on a person's ability to carry out normal day-to-day activities'. Hence a severe disfigurement represents a 'disability' (though not if it results from tatooing or body piercing), as does anything likely to restrict an individual's mobility, manual dexterity, physical co-ordination, speech, hearing or eyesight, or perception of danger, or his or her capacities to learn or understand or to lift or carry everyday objects. However, addictions and anti-social behaviour do not entitle people to protection under the Act. Hay fever is also excluded (unless it aggravates another condition), together with behavioural tendencies towards theft, setting fires or exhibitionism. Specific provisions of the legislation are as follows.

- **It is unlawful for an employer with 20 or more workers to treat disabled people less favourably than others unless there are justifiable reasons.** Employers have to make 'reasonable adjustments' to working arrangements or environments where that would overcome the practical problems created by an individual's disability.

- **No service-providing firm of any size may discriminate against the disabled, who have a legal *right* to be served.** Thus, for example, a hotelier who pretends that all rooms are fully booked in order to refuse a booking from a mentally ill person is breaking the law.

- **People letting or selling land or property must not discriminate against disabled persons.**

- **Colleges of further education are required to publish 'Disability Statements' to inform students about the arrangements they have made to help them to gain access to college facilities.**

- **A disabled person who feels that he or she has been unfairly discriminated against in employment or when applying for a job has a right of redress through an industrial tribunal.**

- **New buses, taxis, trains and trams must satisfy minimum standards for access by disabled people.**

Job applicants with criminal records

A person with a criminal conviction is not necessarily obliged to disclose this to a recruiting company, provided the conviction has been 'spent', i.e. a certain period has elapsed since the time of the offence.

313

The Rehabilitation of Offenders Act 1974 contains a table of the time intervals that must pass by before a conviction becomes spent. For example, sentences of imprisonment are spent after seven years if the sentence was for less than six months, or ten years for sentences of between six and 30 months. Fines become spent after various periods according to the level of fine imposed. A probation order is spent after 12 months. The periods are halved if the person involved was under 17 years of age when he or she was convicted.

However, some sentences can never be spent, notably life imprisonment (which in practice can mean that only a short period is actually spent in jail) and other periods of imprisonment for more than 30 months. Also, there are exceptions to the Act whereby candidates for certain jobs do have to reveal past convictions, namely: any form of work with young people under the age of 18; lawyers; chartered accountants; nurses; vets; dentists; medical practitioners; social and health workers; firearms dealers; and prison officers.

Under the Act it is unlawful for an employer to deny someone a job solely on the grounds that the applicant has a spent conviction and, if the person is asked to declare on an application form whether he or she has a criminal record or is questioned about this during an interview, the applicant is legally entitled to 'forget' about ever having been convicted. If an employee is dismissed in consequence of a spent conviction being discovered, the dismissal is regarded in law as being unfair. Indeed, the employer may not reveal that the employee possesses a spent conviction to third parties (when writing references for example). The justification for the Act is twofold:

- that in the absence of legislation the possession of a criminal record would effectively debar the vast majority of petty criminals from obtaining employment, hence encouraging them to commit further offences;

- that criminal records are held only by people who have *already* been punished for their crimes, so that it is improper for such individuals to be punished again through not being able to get a job.

Age discrimination

At present there is no UK law forbidding ageism, which is frequently criticised as unfair on the grounds that older employees may in fact make extremely good workers. Older employees have lower-than-average absenteeism, lateness and labour turnover, and it has been demonstrated that older employees tend to be more satisfied with their jobs (possibly because their expectations are lower and because they are better adjusted to work routines than younger workers). Age-related decreases in individual productivity are likely to be very marginal and outweighed by the benefits of experience (Johnson and Neumark, 1997). Training difficulties might be due more to older people being out of practice than to lack of ability, and training programmes can be adapted to take this into account.

Specific problems confronted by older workers include:

- early loss of employment because of age;

- difficulties in finding fresh employment;

- targeting of older people in company downsizing exercises;

- what are in effect compulsory early retirement schemes;

- exclusion from government retraining programmes and, where such programmes exist, the training materials used to reskill older workers being based (unsuitably) on those applied to the training of very young people;

- loss of statutory protection against unfair dismissal once an employee has reached a certain age.

Note that companies which recruit large numbers of older employees might become unattractive to young people because of the consequential loss of immediate short-term promotion prospects for young workers. Also, since older employees are likely to quit their jobs, reduction of the size of a firm's labour force through natural wastage can become extremely difficult. This is because a freeze on recruitment means that younger people (who tend to leave their employers more frequently) are not replaced, thus increasing the average age of remaining workers. Consequently staffing crises arise when older cohorts simultaneously retire.

Equal opportunities policies

Today, many organisations have 'equal opportunities policies' in which they formally state their commitment to equal opportunity ideals. The advantages to having such a policy are that:

- top management is seen to endorse equal opportunity measures, creating an example to be followed at lower levels;

- as part of its policy the organisation might critically examine the sex and ethnic compositions of all its departments, divisions, occupational categories and levels of worker, exposing any unfair employment practices currently operating;

- the best candidates for jobs will (or should) be recruited or promoted regardless of their sex or ethnic origin;

- discontent among existing minority-group employees may be avoided.

Problems attached to equal opportunity policies are as follows:

- Organisations sometimes publish extensive equal opportunity policy documents in order to placate existing minority group workers and/or external bodies (local authorities, government purchasing agencies, the Equal Opportunities Commission (EOC) or Commission for Racial Equality (CRE), etc) but in fact have no commitment to equal opportunities whatsoever. They have no procedures for *implementing* their equal opportunity policy documents. This creates disillusion and cynicism among all concerned.

- Recruitment costs increase substantially. Job advertisements have to be placed (expensively) in magazines and newspapers read by each of the sexes and by various ethnic minorities. All applications have to be examined carefully from an equal-opportunities viewpoint, interview panels need to be larger, more candidates must be interviewed and more time has to be spent in interviewing.

- An organisation might apply an equal opportunities policy to operatives and low-grade managers, but not to middle managers or senior executives. Hence the representation of minority groups collapses at higher levels, so that corporate strategy cannot be influenced by individuals from minority groups.

Both the EOC and CRE publish codes of practice setting out the steps to be taken to eliminate unfair discrimination in recruitment and other employment matters. The codes offer practical guidance on how personnel policies and procedures should be constructed in order to avoid discrimination, and how existing employees must be instructed about preventing contravention of the Act when interviewing, dealing with subordinates, selecting staff for promotion, etc.

SELECTION AND INDUCTION

Selection is the assessment of candidates for vacant jobs and the choice of the most suitable people. It involves matching the requirements of a job with the attributes of candidates (Boerlijst and Meijboom, 1989). This is facilitated by drafting a 'person specification' defining the background, education, training, personality and other characteristics of the ideal candidate. The person described may not exist, but the process of drafting a person specification creates a standard against which candidates can be compared.

Schemes for categorising the various attributes required to perform certain types of work have existed for many years (Rodger, 1952; Fraser, 1954), usually presented in the form of a checklist describing the demands of the vacant job, as in the following example:

1 **Physical aspects of the work.** Does the job require someone with exceptional strength or fitness (heavy lifting work for instance), or a specific physical appearance, dress, speech or manner (e.g. for a position as a salesperson or receptionist)?

2 **Need to communicate.** Some work involves regular contact with others. Workplace supervisors, salespeople, receptionists, training instructors, etc, need an external appearance, manners and communication skills that are not so important for socially isolated jobs (long-distance lorry driving, for instance). Jobs with social interaction require agreeable people who mix easily. Such jobs are unsuitable for hostile, aggressive individuals.

3 **Formal qualifications.** What is the minimum level of education and professional qualifications necessary for the job? It is important not to recruit people who are massively overqualified for the vacancy as they might quickly become bored and underperform, or leave the company.

4 **Experience needed.** Should the person selected have personal experience of specific tasks, and if so for what periods and at what levels?

5 **Specific competences.** Does the work require a person with particular abilities, such as mathematical competence, manual dexterity, or the capacities to think

quickly, assimilate large quantities of information, exercise mental agility and interpret complicated issues? Employees who cannot easily withstand stress should not attempt harrowing or emotionally arduous duties.

6 **Personal ambition.** Repetitive production-line work is not intellectually stimulating; financial reward is probably the major motivating factor here. Other jobs present opportunities for creativity and self-development, and thus would be appropriate for people with drive, enthusiasm, self-direction and personal ambition.

Interviewing

The purpose of a job interview is to obtain information. Therefore, applicants should be put at ease as quickly as possible and hence into a frame of mind in which they will disclose the maximum amount of information about themselves. Uncomfortable, ill-at-ease candidates will not be as frank as those who are relaxed, confident and in full control of their responses. Accordingly, candidates should be interviewed promptly at the appointed time or, if delay is inevitable, apologies should be offered. Interruptions from telephone calls, secretaries, etc, disturb concentration and should be avoided.

The following rules should be followed when conducting interviews.

1 Opening remarks should be supportive and uncontroversial.

2 Questions which simply ask for repetition of information already provided on application forms should be avoided. Rather, the interviewer should seek supplementary information to probe in depth the candidate's potential.

3 Detailed notetaking by interviewers is inadvisable because of its disturbing effects on the interviewee. Candidates should be assessed immediately after their interviews. Otherwise, important points in earlier interviews will be forgotten in the final end-of-session appraisal.

4 Open-ended questions such as 'what made you decide to do that?' or 'why did you enjoy that type of work?' are usually more productive in obtaining information than direct queries. Generally-worded questions invite the candidate to discuss feelings, opinions and perceptions of events. Simple yes/no questions will not draw out the candidate's opinions. Interviewers should not make critical or insensitive remarks during the interview.

5 Interviewers should not compare candidates with themselves.

6 Only job-relevant questions should be asked.

7 The 'halo effect', i.e. assuming that because a candidate possesses one desirable characteristic (smart appearance or a good speaking voice, for example), then he or she must be equally good in all other areas, must not be allowed to influence the selection.

8 'Revealing' questions should not be asked. A revealing question discloses attitudes and beliefs held by the questioner. An example would be 'I like watching football, don't you?'

9 Inappropriate criteria must not be applied. This could involve, for example, males who interview females associating attractive physical appearance with work ability, or appointing people the interviewer knows socially.

10 Interviewers should not behave in a pompous manner. This wastes time and contributes nothing to the quality of the interview.

11 Interview panels should be as small as possible. Overlarge panels create unhelpful dramatic atmospheres, and panel members might ask irrelevant and disconnected questions.

Testing

At best, selection tests are a useful complement to interviews. At worst, they are confusing and irrelevant appendages to the selection process. The purpose of an interview is to obtain information. Thus, tests can be justified only to the extent that more and better information about a candidate is actually generated.

There are many serious problems involved in setting tests and correctly interpreting the results. Tests are particularly useful where interviews are not possible, as for example when large numbers of employees are to be engaged within a very short period, and for situations where candidates have no formal qualifications or experience of work, as in the case for instance of recruiting school leavers who have no academic certificates. Advocates of selection testing claim that tests remove subjectivity in selection procedures. In principle, a good test should measure objectively the subject's abilities and characteristics. An effective test moreover will:

- **be cheap to administer** (note that a single test can be given to a roomful of perhaps forty or fifty people at each sitting, and only a couple of people will be needed to organise and invigilate the test);

- **measure precisely what it is intended to measure.** An intelligence test should assess intelligence, not learned responses; aptitude tests should indicate candidates' true potentials for undertaking the jobs for which they are being considered, not other occupations;

- **give consistent results when repeated.** Only then can the results obtained from a single sitting be accepted as sufficiently reliable for appointment decisions;

- **discriminate between candidates.** Good quality applicants should, if the test is working properly, obtain high marks and poor candidates should consistently fail. If candidates pass the test but then turn out to be incompetent, the test has not achieved its purpose;

- **rank the candidates.** The best candidate should obtain the top mark, the next best should get the second highest mark and so on.

- **be relevant to the job.** The characteristics exposed by performance in the test should relate directly to the job specification for the vacant post.

Induction

Once an offer of appointment is accepted, a contract of employment exists. The letter of appointment must include details of terms and conditions attached to the work: wages, working hours, holidays, sick pay, pension schemes, company rules, safety regulations, etc. Having considered all the terms and conditions, the recruit now signs a document saying he or she understands and will abide by them. Subsequent breach of the contract will offer grounds for fair dismissal.

Induction is the process of introducing recruits to an organisation and explaining their role within it and usually begins with a guided tour of the building. Induction is important because impressions gained by new employees during this period can influence their perceptions of the organisation for many years to come. Good induction procedures also help employees to fit into strange and initially uncomfortable environments quickly and without fuss. Recruits should be welcomed personally by senior members of staff and then introduced to colleagues, supervisors and subordinates. Recruits might be given copies of the firm's organisation chart, and an explanation of individual positions within it. Particular aspects of specific jobs can be discussed and, if appropriate, training arrangements made. Efficiency standards, expected output quality, security arrangements and so on will be detailed.

A crucially important aspect of the induction process is that of informing recruits where to go for help if they experience problems. Entrants should know whom to approach, and the correct procedures to follow. Appropriate contacts might be supervisors, personnel officers, higher managers or trade union representatives. In any event the recruit should know what to do if he or she:

- has a problem with money or understanding the wage system;
- has a medical problem;
- feels that working conditions are unsafe;
- does not get on with other people in the department;
- has difficulty with the work;
- is bullied or harassed;
- has a complaint;
- does not receive adequate training.

TRAINING AND DEVELOPMENT

The purpose of training is to improve employees' performances in their current jobs and/or equip them for more demanding roles. It is expensive: special instructors may have to be employed; external courses must be financed; internal courses require resourcing with materials, personnel and physical facilities. Moreover, there is no guarantee that trainees will actually benefit from participating in programmes. Employees are usually unproductive while undergoing training, and there are many incidental expenses (hotel accommodation, travel, meal allowances, etc).

Putting aside questions of staff morale, it might not make economic sense to spend enormous sums on training existing employees for higher-level work if competent people can be recruited cheaply from outside. Equally pointless is the (not uncommon) practice of training far more employees in a certain type of work than there are vacancies in that area. This policy, while ensuring a ready supply of qualified internal applicants whenever needs for a particular skill arise, causes high labour turnover as workers become increasingly frustrated at not being able to perform the work for which they were trained. Indeed, 'overtraining' policies can backfire, resulting in shortages of trained internal applicants for higher-level jobs (Schuler, 1992).

Training seeks to improve and develop the knowledge, skills and/or attitudes of employees. Apart from the benefits accruing to the individual worker (greater versatility, extra skills, etc), many advantages accrue to the organisation. Employees become more flexible, the productivity and quality of work should improve, job satisfaction might increase (with consequent reductions in absenteeism and staff turnover rates) and the organisation need not fear the consequences of new technology.

Assessing training needs

Needs for employee training may arise from the introduction of new technologies, or the organisation's diversification into different fields (Bernardin and Russel, 1993). Other causes of the need for training might be poor-quality output, high accident rates, high absenteeism or staff turnover, or unfavourable performance appraisal reports submitted by managers on their subordinates. Note, however, that any one of these might be caused by factors other than inadequate training.

Like any other business process, training can be very wasteful if it is not carefully planned and supervised. Without a logical, systematic approach, some training may be given which is not necessary, and vice versa, or the extent of the training may be too small or too great. When the training is complete, *validation* will show whether it has been successful in achieving its aims and *evaluation* will attempt to measure its cost-benefit.

The systematic approach to training follows this programme.

1 The job is analysed and defined.

2 Reasonable standards of performance are established, perhaps by reference to experienced employees.

3 The employees being considered for training are studied to see if the required performance standards are being attained.

4 The difference (if any) between 2 and 3 is considered. It is often called the 'training gap', though it may be partly due to faults in the organisation, poor materials or defective equipment.

5 Training programmes are devised to meet the training needs revealed in 4.

6 Training is given and appropriate records kept.

7 The performance achieved after training is measured; if the training programme has been successful, the performance standards set in 2 should now be achieved (validation).

8 An attempt is made to calculate the cost of the training and compare it with the financial benefit gained by the improved performance of the employees. The training programme may be revised if a method can be seen of achieving the same result at lower cost (evaluation).

Evaluation of training

For manual workers the success of a training programme might be quantified in terms of better productivity, higher quality of output, less absenteeism, lower staff turnover, greater adaptability, fewer accidents and less need for close supervision. Unfortunately, improved performance in many jobs is difficult to express quantitatively in the short term. And some skills acquired on courses undertaken today might not be used until the future.

Training can improve workers' morale, create better interpersonal relationships, instil in employees a sense of loyalty to the organisation, and provide other intangible benefits (Beer *et al.*, 1985). Note, however, that it is not sufficient merely to ask workers whether they feel more efficient as a consequence of attending a course; hard, objective evidence is also required. Courses which participants have particularly enjoyed (especially residential courses) may be popular not because of their intrinsic educational value but because of their 'holiday camp' atmosphere, recreational facilities, friendships established among course members, and so on.

The following procedure should be adopted when evaluating the effectiveness of training.

- Ask the question, 'What difference would it make if the training did not take place?' If the answer is 'not very much' then critically reassess the value of the training.

- Relate the outcomes of the training to the organisation's initial training objectives. Isolate divergences and explain why they occurred.

- Interview people on completion of a course and ask them whether it was relevant to their work, whether it taught them things they did not previously know, whether is was too easy or too difficult, how well supported the programme was in terms of course materials, instructors, facilities, etc, and how they think the knowledge gained will help their future careers. Keep a written record of the answers, and repeat the interview after at least six months have elapsed since finishing the course.

Staff development

Staff development seeks to improve a person's overall career prospects rather than train him or her to perform duties necessary for the present job. Hence it normally comprises a series of planned training activities and work experiences designed to improve a manager's performance and equip him or her for higher-level work. Activities might include attendance at courses, job rotation, understudying (i.e. spending a short period as a personal assistant to a more senior manager), attachments to project committees and special working parties, and the completion of longer-term academic qualifications in the management field. Programmes may cover:

- background knowledge of the organisation, its trading environment, products, production methods, markets and personnel;

- administrative procedures, the legal environment, specialist techniques;

- management methods, analytical skills, organisation, delegation and control, time management;

- interpersonal skills, communication, leadership and co-ordination;

- creative abilities, decision making and problem solving.

Note that some organisations insist that managerial ability cannot be taught, and that management training courses are therefore a waste of time. They argue that few courses contain material that is directly relevant and immediately applicable to real-life management situations, and that normal competition between managerial staff should ensure the 'survival of the fittest'.

In organisations which do train managerial staff, new approaches to training are increasingly common – they want to develop the initiative, self-reliance, leadership and interpersonal communication skills of managers as well as their technical abilities. An interesting recent development in the training field has been the increasing use of outdoor management training, which assumes the existence of direct parallels between the personal qualities necessary for successful management and those cultivated through participation in outdoor pursuits such as rock-climbing, canoeing, sailing or orienteering. The essential demands of these activities – planning, organising, team-building, dealing with uncertainty, direction and control – are the same, advocates argue, as those needed for management.

PERFORMANCE MANAGEMENT AND APPRAISAL

Performance management is the integration of employee development with results-based assessment (*see* Chapters 6–9). It encompasses performance appraisal, objective-setting for individuals and departments, appropriate training programmes and performance-related pay. Appraisal of managers by their subordinates, peers and people in other departments (perhaps even customers) might also be included in the scheme (Philpott and Sheppard, 1992).

Target setting

An employee's targets could be stated in terms of achieving a certain standard (i.e. an ongoing performance criterion, such as a specified departmental staff attendance rate or the attainment of minimum quality levels) that is to be maintained indefinitely, or as an *ad hoc* goal (Fletcher and Williams, 1992). The advantages of bosses and employees jointly setting personal objectives are as follows:

- it forces everyone in the department to think carefully about his or her role and duties, about why tasks are necessary, and how best to get things done;

- targets are clarified and mechanisms created for monitoring performance;

- crucial elements are identified in each job. This information is useful for determining training and recruitment needs;

- personal achievements of employees are recognised and rewarded;

- bosses and their colleagues are obliged to communicate – in consequence, bosses can quickly identify which employees are ready for promotion and the help they will need in preparing themselves for this;

- performance is appraised against quantified targets, not subjective criteria;

- there is forced co-ordination of activities – between departments, between junior and senior management, and between short-term and long-term goals.

The targets set should adhere to the following guidelines:

- Targets should be precise, unambiguous and (if possible) expressed numerically. Generic objectives such as 'increase profits' or 'cut costs' are not acceptable.

- Targets should relate to the crucial and primary elements of employees' jobs and not to trivial matters.

- Targets should be consistent.

- Each target should be accompanied by a statement of how it is to be achieved, by when, the resources necessary and how and where these will be acquired.

A good way to assess the usefulness of objectives is to ask whether they pass the SMART test, i.e. targets need to be:

> **S**pecific
> **M**easurable
> **A**greed between boss and worker
> **R**ealistic
> **T**ime related

Both parties should share a common perspective on the situation intended to exist after the achievement of objectives and on how soon results may reasonably be expected.

Appraisal

Managers frequently make *ad hoc* judgements about employees, but are loath to discuss the grounds on which the opinions are based. Performance appraisal replaces casual assessment with formal, systematic procedures. Employees know they are being evaluated and are told the criteria that will be used in the course of the appraisal. (Indeed, knowledge that an appraisal is soon to occur could motivate an employee into increased effort aimed at enhancing the outcomes of the assessment.) Specifically, appraisal is the analysis of employees' past successes and failures, and the assessment of their suitability for promotion or further training. Its advantages include the following:

- Boss and employee are compelled to meet and discuss common work-related problems. Appraisees become aware of what exactly is expected of them and of their status in the eyes of their line managers.

- Appraisal monitors the feasibility of targets set by higher management, who receive valuable feedback on problems encountered when implementing policies. Thus, it creates a cheap and effective early warning system within the organisation's management information structure.

- It enables bosses to learn about employees and the true nature of their duties. Conducting appraisals helps a manager to remain in touch with the staff in his or her department. Unknown skills and competences might be uncovered. This data can be incorporated into the firm's human resource plan and hence assist in avoiding compulsory redundancies, in career and management succession planning, and in identifying needs for employee training (Kinnie and Lowe, 1990).

A successful appraisal is one that results in:

- reasonable targets which are mutually agreed, not arbitrarily determined;

- recognition of the employees' achievements;

- clear identification of obstacles to improved performance (organisational problems as well as individual difficulties);

- enthusiastic pursuit of measurable objectives;

- two-way communication between boss and worker.

It is important for appraisal to be seen as a staff development exercise, intended to be helpful to everyone concerned, and not as a form of restrictive control or disciplinary measure. The purpose therefore must be to assist both individuals and the organisation in improving their performances. Appraisal reviews are usually categorised into three types.

1 **Performance reviews**, which analyse employees' past successes and failures with a view to improving future performance.

2 **Potential reviews**, which assess subordinates' suitability for promotion and/or further training.

3 **Reward reviews**, for determining pay rises. It is a well-established principle that salary assessments should occur well after performance and potential reviews have been completed, for two reasons:

  - performance reviews examine personal strengths and weaknesses in order to improve efficiency. If salary matters are discussed during these meetings, they might dominate the conversation;

  - ultimately, salary levels are determined by market forces of supply and demand for labour. Staff shortages could cause the firm to pay high wages quite independent of the objective worth of particular workers.

Self-appraisal and peer group appraisal

Appraisal might be more useful to the appraisee, and lead in the longer term to greater efficiency, if it is conducted either by the employee or by a colleague of equal occupational status. Such appraisals may analyse issues more critically than when people fear the career consequences of admitting mistakes. Appraisees state – using any of the methods previously discussed – how they regard their performance, the adequacy of the training they have received, effects of alterations in job content, perceptions of key objectives and future aspirations. They identify their own strengths and account for their failures and weaknesses, suggesting ways in which the firm might better use their talents, skills and recently acquired experiences.

There are, of course, problems with self-appraisal, including the following:

- Many people are quite incapable of analysing themselves. It is unusual for individuals to assess their own competence in other walks of life. At school, college and during the early stages of a career the individual becomes accustomed to being directed and evaluated by others. The transition of appraisee to self-assessor might require skilled and detailed guidance by someone already competent in appraisal techniques. Most appraisees in lower-level positions will have received no training in self-analysis or appraisal.

- To the extent that appraisals form a basis for future career development, appraisees might overstate their successes while ignoring their failings.

On the other hand, employees are compelled to think carefully about the adequacy of their contribution, about barriers preventing improved performance, about their future and about the quality of their relationships with others.

Problems with performance appraisal

There are a number of problems with performance appraisal, including the following:

- dangers of favouritism, bias and stereotyping by managers who conduct appraisals;

- possibilities that inconsistent criteria will be applied by different managers when assessing the calibre of subordinates (Schneier *et al.*, 1991);

- all the information relevant to a particular case might not be available;

- information might not be interpreted objectively;

- assessors might seek to evaluate every subordinate as 'fair' for all performance categories;

- assessors might focus on specific cases of outstandingly good and bad performance while ignoring the employee's average overall ability;

- appraisal systems require appraising managers to undertake extra work, which they might be reluctant to accept. Hence the process becomes a ritualistic chore to be completed as quickly as possible in a manner that causes the least comment from those affected by the scheme.

Douglas McGregor noted the great reluctance with which many managers under-take assessment responsibilities; preferring to treat subordinates as professional colleagues rather than as inferiors upon whom they are entitled to pass judgement (McGregor, 1957). Senior managers, McGregor asserted, dislike 'playing God'. Usually they are fully cognisant of their own biases and thus rightly seek to avoid situations where prejudice could arise. Also, subordinates may bitterly resent their personal qualities being commented upon, seeing the appraisal as a patronising exercise designed to humiliate or to punish past inadequacies in their work.

Appraisal requires concentration, diligence and competence in the manager con-ducting the appraisal. Training in appraisal techniques is required, followed by substantial guided experience in their practical application. McGregor pointed out the facts that:

- few managers receive any instruction in appraisal methods;

- even managers who are properly trained might not possess all the informa-tion needed to undertake fair appraisals. They may be out of touch with current working practices or unfamiliar with environmental problems affect-ing subordinates' work.

Promotion, transfer, demotion and dismissal

Promotion and demotion

Apart from improvements in pay and conditions of work, the most immediate incentives available to employees are opportunities for promotion. If the organisa-tion has trained its staff adequately and ensured that employees' work experiences are sufficiently wide, internal promotion should be feasible. Thus, external recruit-ment will be necessary only for specialist positions or when no one within the organisation possesses appropriate qualifications for a post. Prospects of promotion often represent significant motivators (van Ham *et al.*, 1986). Promotion methods are worthy, therefore, of serious discussion.

The criteria used in selecting individuals for promotion may be based on ability or seniority. Ability-related systems accelerate the careers of staff who are excep-tionally competent, whereas seniority-based procedures have the advantage of ensuring steady progression for all employees; and knowledge that promotion is reasonably assured can improve morale throughout the organisation. Promotion follows logically from training, performance appraisal, management development and management by objectives programmes.

People can be selected for promotion directly – management simply appointing chosen employees to higher posts – or vacancies can be advertised within the firm. Direct selection is quick, inexpensive and suitable where management knows the abilities of all its subordinates. Internal advertisement is appropriate in large organi-sations where several candidates of about the same level of ability might apply.

Unfair discrimination in promotion will upset and demotivate staff: it should be avoided at all costs – promotion should never be denied on grounds of race, sex, colour or creed. Organisations that operate in sensitive multicultural or multiethnic environments sometimes monitor the consequences of their promotion policies by checking whether certain groups are over-represented among those who do not achieve promotion. Hence, if it is found that females, ethnic minorities or certain religious groups are prominent in the non-promoted category, reasons for this can be identified and remedial measures applied. Specifically, the following questions can be asked of any promotion system.

1 What are the characteristics of non-promoted groups, and are there valid reasons explaining why individuals in these groups are not promoted?

2 What contributions have non-promoted groups made to the work of the organisation? Have they been adequately rewarded for their contributions?

3 Why do non-promoted individuals remain with the organisation?

4 What help can be given to non-promoted groups in order to help them qualify for promotion? What are the obstacles confronting non-promoted categories, and how can they be removed?

5 What can management itself do to improve its knowledge of the backgrounds and difficulties experienced by non-promoted groups? How does management feel about these people?

A non-discriminatory promotion policy has numerous benefits. Internal personal relationships between managers and subordinates are improved; labour turnover will fall, since able staff do not need to leave the organisation to do higher-level work. Efficiency should increase through utilisation in senior positions of the accumulated experience of long-serving employees. Additionally, there is little risk of the individuals promoted possessing unknown deficiencies, as can occur with externally recruited senior staff. On the other hand, outsiders can inject fresh ideas and apply new perspectives to existing problems: external recruits might be of much higher calibre than internal candidates.

Demotion is a move to a job within the company which is lower in importance. It is usually, though not always, accompanied by a reduction in pay. An employee may be demoted for the following reasons.

- His or her job may disappear or become less important through a departmental or company reorganisation.

- The worker may no longer be thought capable of carrying out his or her present responsibilities efficiently.

Unless the employee has requested it, demotion will probably have adverse effects.

- There will be less satisfaction of esteem and self-actualisation needs. The employee may show negative reactions to frustration.

- The employee may become a centre of discontent in the organisation.

- Other employees may lose confidence in the organisation.

An employee who resigns in consequence of a demotion may complain of unfair dismissal under a special category known as 'constructive dismissal' (*see* below).

327

Transfers

A transfer is a move to a job within the company which has approximately equal importance, status and pay. To manage human resources in a constructive way, it is sometimes necessary to transfer employees to other jobs, sometimes because of changed work requirements and sometimes because an employee is unhappy or dissatisfied in his or her present job.

In some organisations it is the custom for the least satisfactory employees to be transferred from one department to another, with the result that a transfer is regarded as discreditable, particularly if it occurs at short notice and without explanation. An unhappy employee may therefore prefer to leave rather than seek a transfer.

In other organisations transfers are used as a means of developing promising employees by giving them experience in several departments. A few organisations advertise all vacancies internally and consider applicants for whom the new job would be a transfer rather than a promotion.

Transfers can increase job satisfaction and improve utilisation under the following circumstances.

- A transfer is regarded as a re-selection.

- The need for a transfer is explained.

- Unsatisfactory employees are not dealt with by transferring them to other departments.

- Requests by employees for transfers are fully investigated.

- No employee is transferred to another district against his or her will.

- An employee transferred to another district is given financial assistance from the organisation to cover removal costs, legal fees, refurnishing, etc.

Dismissal

Dismissal means the termination of employment by:

- the employer, with or without notice; or

- the failure of the employer to renew a fixed-term contract; or

- the employee's resignation, with or without notice, when the employer behaves in a manner that demonstrates refusal to be bound by the contract of employment.

The latter is termed *constructive dismissal*. It means the employer is behaving so unreasonably that the worker has no alternative but to quit.

Normally, an employer must give the employee notice of dismissal as stated in the worker's contract of employment. Occasionally, however, dismissal without notice is permissible. This is known as *summary dismissal* and could occur when an employee's behaviour makes impossible the fulfilment of a contract of employment. Examples are theft, persistent drunkenness, violence, abusiveness to colleagues or customers, wilful disobedience, or incompetence that immediately causes damage to the employer's business.

Many countries have statutes that govern how employees may be fairly dismissed. Under the Employment Rights Act 1996, employees covered by the Act (i.e. those with at least two years' continuous service) may only be fairly dismissed for genuine redundancy or for:

1 **gross misconduct**, e.g. refusal to obey reasonable instructions, dishonesty, persistent absenteeism, neglect of duties, etc;

2 **incapacity** to do the job, caused by such things as incompetence, illness (once the workers' contractual sick pay entitlement has expired), or the person not having the skills or aptitude for the work;

3 **some other substantial reason**, e.g. going on strike, disruption of staff relations, or a temporary job coming to an end, provided the impermanent nature of the work was fully explained to the worker when the employment started.

'Redundancy' means that the organisation's need for employees to do work of a particular kind has ceased or diminished, so that someone has to lose their job. The criteria used to select individuals for redundancy must by law be fair and reasonable. Workers declared redundant are entitled to redundancy payments. The redundancy process is illustrated in Fig 11.2.

'Wrongful', as opposed to 'unfair', dismissal occurs when insufficient notice is given. It gives rise to a civil action for damages equivalent to the actual loss incurred. Wrongful dismissal may be claimed by any dismissed worker, regardless of length of service – a worker who has been with the organisation for only a few days may be 'wrongfully' sacked.

Allegations of wrongful dismissal are heard by normal county courts; cases concerning unfair dismissal are heard in industrial tribunals. Note that whereas costs in the latter are intended to be minimal (and in normal circumstances are never awarded to the other side), costs in the county court can be huge.

The ACAS Code on dismissal

Disciplinary procedures should be in writing, easy to understand and made known to employees and their representatives. The UK Advisory, Conciliation and Arbitration Service (ACAS) has issued an important code of practice on these matters. This code recognises that the maintenance of discipline is a management responsibility, but emphasises the desirability of involving workers' representatives when drafting procedures. In addition to the points outlined above, the main recommendations of the ACAS Code are as follows.

1 Employers should indicate the forms of conduct that are considered unacceptable, and in what circumstances. Rules should be particular rather than universal and justified in terms of the objective requirements of a job.

2 All workers should be given a copy of the organisation's rules and have them explained orally as part of an induction programme. Employees should be informed of the consequences of breaking rules, particularly those rules which if broken may result in summary dismissal.

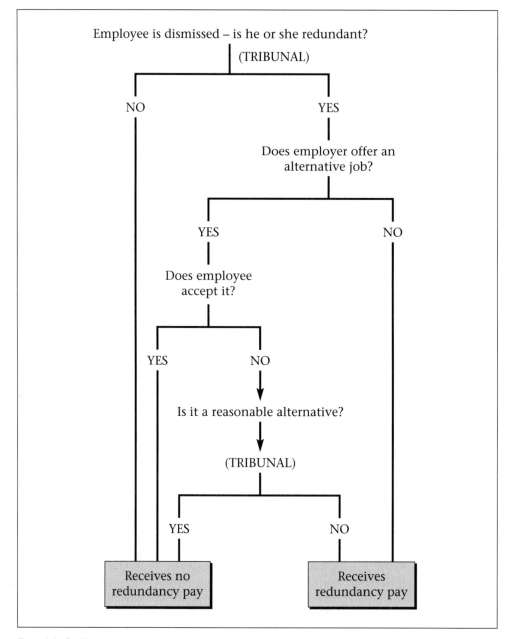

FIG 11.2 THE REDUNDANCY PROCESS

3 Only senior management should have the power to dismiss.

4 The accused person should have the right to be accompanied at disciplinary hearings by a trade union representative or by a fellow employee of his or her own choice.

5 Employees should not be dismissed for a first offence (except for gross misconduct). The code distinguishes between informal oral warnings for minor infringements of rules, and formal written warnings issued following serious offences. Formal warnings should set out the nature of the breach of discipline, the likely consequences of further offences, and should state that the warning constitutes stage one of the formal procedure. If misconduct is repeated, a second and final written warning should be issued containing an unambiguous statement that a further recurrence of the offence will lead to whatever action (suspension, dismissal or some other sanction) has been determined. Assuming the errant worker's behaviour does not improve, the next step is suspension or dismissal, accompanied by a written statement of reasons for the action taken and details of the right of appeal.

6 The employer should take into account the employee's age, position, length of service and general performance, and whether domestic problems etc make it appropriate to reduce the severity of the disciplinary action taken.

Appeals should be considered quickly and be heard by a higher level of authority than took the original disciplinary action. Wherever possible the appeal should be considered by independent people who are not the immediate superiors of the manager who decided to dismiss the worker. The procedure should spell out the actions that may be taken by those hearing the appeal, and enable any new evidence to be made known to the employee.

Employees who believe they have been unfairly dismissed may take their case to an industrial tribunal, i.e. a three-person court, with a qualified solicitor or barrister in the chair plus two lay members, that hears cases relating to alleged unfair dismissal, health and safety at work, equal opportunities and certain other employment matters. Each of the lay members represents one of the two sides of industry (unions and employers' associations, which supply the UK legal authorities with lists of persons they wish to sit on tribunals).

THE FOUR CS MODEL OF HUMAN RESOURCES MANAGEMENT

The four Cs model was developed by researchers at the Harvard Business School as a means of investigating HRM issues in a wider environmental context than the mundane and instrumental tasks of recruitment and selection, training, appraisal, maintenance of employee records and so on (Beer *et al.*, 1985). According to the Harvard model, HRM policies need to derive from a critical analysis of:

- the demands of the various stakeholders in a business; and

- a number of 'situational factors'.

Stakeholder theory

This asserts that since organisations are owned and operated by differing interest groups (stakeholders), management's main task is to balance the returns to various group interests. Examples of stakeholders are shareholders, different categories of employee, customers/users of the product, creditors (including banks), unions and (possibly) local or national government. Managers, therefore, need to be politicians and diplomats. They must establish good relations with each group, develop persuasive skills, create alliances, represent one faction to others, etc.

Stakeholder theory implies the recognition that each interest group possesses certain basic rights. Thus, for example, management should consider workers' interests as well as those of shareholders when taking important decisions.

Stakeholders may or may not hold formal authority, although each will have invested something in the organisation, whether this be work, finance or other resources. Accordingly, every stakeholder will expect a reward from the enterprise and normally will wish to influence how this is determined. Management must:

- identify the stakeholders in the organisation;

- determine the minimum return each stakeholder is willing to accept;

- seek to influence stakeholders' perceptions of the organisation (e.g. by persuading shareholders that a high dividend is not in a company's best long-term interest or convincing workers that a high wage settlement is not possible during the current year);

- identify key individuals in specific stakeholder groups and establish good relations with these people.

Situational factors

These include the state of the labour market, the calibres and motivation of employees, management style (which itself depends in part on the culture of the local community), the technologies used in production and the nature of working methods (e.g. whether specialisation and the division of labour are required). Labour market situations are crucial to the analysis. The labour market comprises all the people seeking work and all the companies, government bodies and other organisations that require employees. Labour markets operate at regional, industry sector, national and (increasingly) international levels. There are sub-markets for various categories of occupation, skill, educational background and other employee characteristics and for different types of task.

Further situational factors that might be relevant are:

- form of ownership of the organisation (and hence to whom management is accountable);

- influence of trade unions and employers' associations;

- laws and business practices of the society in which the organisation operates;

- the competitive environment;

- senior management's ability to co-ordinate and control.

Stakeholder expectations and situational factors need to be taken into account when formulating human resources strategies, and will affect HRM policies concerning such matters as remuneration systems, degree of supervision of workers, use of labour-intensive rather than capital-intensive methods, etc. An increase in the intensity of business competition may cause a firm to improve labour productivity, discard employees, restructure administrative systems, and so on. A change in the age structure of the population could lead an organisation to hire more women. Rising educational standards might make it appropriate to redesign jobs in order to give workers more autonomy.

Outcomes to human resources management

According to the Harvard researchers, the effectiveness of the outcomes to human resources management should be evaluated under four headings: commitment, competence, congruence and cost-effectiveness.

1 **Commitment** concerns employees' loyalty to the organisation, personal motivation and liking for their work. The degree of employee commitment might be assessed via attitude surveys, labour turnover and absenteeism statistics, and through interviews with workers who quit their jobs.

2 **Competence** relates to employees' skills and abilities, training requirements and potential for higher-level work. These may be estimated through employee appraisal systems and the preparation of skills inventories (*see* p 302 above). HRM policies should be designed to attract, retain and motivate competent workers.

3 **Congruence** means that management and workers share the same vision of the organisation's goals and work together to attain them. In a well-managed organisation, employees at all levels of authority will share common perspectives about the factors that determine its prosperity and future prospects. Such perspectives concern the guiding principles that govern the organisation's work: how things should be done, when, by whom, and how enthusiastically.

   To some extent these perceptions may be created by management via its internal communications, style of leadership, organisation system and working methods, but they can only be sustained and brought to bear on day-to-day operations by the organisation's workers. Staff should *feel* they possess a common objective. They need to experience a sense of affinity with the organisation and *want* to pursue a common cause. Congruence is evident in the absence of grievances and conflicts within the organisation, and in harmonious industrial relations.

4 **Cost-effectiveness** concerns operational efficiency. Human resources should be used to the best advantage and in the most productive ways. Outputs must be maximised at the lowest input cost, and the organisation must be quick to respond to market opportunities and environmental change.

Problems with the four Cs approach

The Harvard model suggests that human resources policies should seek to increase the level of each of the four Cs. For example, commitment might be enhanced through improving the flow of management/worker communication, while competence could be increased through extra training. Problems with the four Cs approach are:

- how *exactly* to measure these variables;

- possible conflicts between cost-effectiveness and congruence (especially if the drive for the former generates low wages);

- the huge variety of variables potentially relevant to any given HRM situation. Often it is impossible to distinguish the key factors defining the true character of a particular state of affairs;

- the fact that sometimes a technology or set of working conditions make it virtually impossible to increase the levels of some of the Cs. Certain jobs are inevitably dirty, boring and repetitive, yet they still have to be done.

THE MANAGEMENT OF HUMAN RESOURCES

The modern approach to the management of human resources is to emphasise co-operation rather than conflict and to integrate HRM policies into the overall corporate strategies of the organisation. This requires senior management to:

- recognise the critical importance of harmonious relations with the workforce; and

- relate HRM to the attainment of increased competitiveness, improved product quality and better customer care.

Well-constructed human resources policies are essential for the well-being of the firm, and all efforts must be made to minimise the potential for conflicts between management and workers.

Role of the personnel department

In most (but not all) organisations human resources management is the responsibility of the personnel department. The personnel officer is necessarily a generalist, since the variety of issues typically dealt with in a personnel department is so diverse that no one person could master all aspects of the job. Thus, a personnel manager requires a working rather than a detailed knowledge of:

- the organisation, its products and the industry or sector in which it operates;

- production methods and organisational structure;

- pension schemes, wage and bonus arrangements;

- law relating to employment;

- the fundamentals of management theory and practice.

Consequently, the personnel manager requires wide-ranging knowledge and skills, in contrast to the highly specialised qualifications and experience of many of the line managers whom the personnel manager will advise.

The mundane tasks of writing copy for job advertisements, organising training courses, keeping personnel records, operating wages systems, looking after health and safety at work arrangements, etc, are known collectively as the *service* function of the personnel role. Other major personnel management functions are as follows.

The control function, comprising:
- analysis of key operational indices in the personnel field: labour turnover, wage costs, absenteeism and so on;
- monitoring labour performance (staff appraisal, for example);
- recommending appropriate remedial action to line managers.

The advisory function, whereby the personnel department offers expert advice on personnel policies and procedures, for example:
- which employees are ready for promotion;
- who should attend a certain training course;
- how a grievance procedure should be operated;
- interpretation of contracts of employment, health and safety regulations, etc.

Evaluating the effectiveness of a personnel department

Effective personnel management should feed through into improved organisational performance, higher productivity among employees, better customer service and hence increased long-term sales (Burn, 1996). Measuring the value of the short-run activities of a personnel department, however, can be problematic. Specific difficulties attached to the evaluation of the personnel function are that:

- since organisations operate in widely disparate commercial environments, wide differences in labour turnover, absenteeism, etc are to be expected among firms engaged in similar lines of work;

- personnel management is such a wide-ranging activity that it might not be appropriate to select just a handful of variables for appraisal.

Quantitative indices of a personnel department's work may be available in relation to:

- unit labour costs compared to those in competing companies;

- staff turnover;

- absenteeism rates;

- incidence of invocation of grievance procedures;

- the proportion of the personnel department's staff that obtain professional qualifications;

- number of days lost through strikes;

- how long it takes to recruit a new employee;

- successes achieved in the implementation of equal opportunities policies.

Subjective criteria include employee motivation, team spirit and willingness to accept change; the extent to which proposals emerging from the personnel department are accepted by senior management; quality of relationships with trade unions; calibre of job applicants responding to job advertisements; usefulness of documents drafted by the department (job descriptions and person specifications, for example), and so on. Staff from other parts of the firm may be questioned in order to ascertain how they rate the personnel department in terms of such matters as:

- how promptly it responds to requests for information or advice;

- the quality of advice given by personnel department staff;

- politeness and approachability of the department's members;

- individual knowledge of technical personnel matters;

- the department's overall contributions to the work of other sections.

Senior management may evaluate a personnel department's contributions on the basis of its ability to handle satisfactorily sensitive human relations problems arising from downsizing, organisational restructuring and the implementation of change. Also the personnel/human resources officer will be expected to make meaningful contributions to top management team decisions and to assist with strategic issues such as the formulation of mission statments, determination of corporate culture, facilitation of technological change, and so on.

Decentralisation and devolution

Many personnel and HRM functions can be undertaken by managers in local units rather than through a central personnel department. Note that the individuals completing such duties in subsidiaries, divisions, etc, might *themselves* be personnel specialists rather than general line managers, although in practice this is rare because of the duplication of effort involved. The main problem with devolution of personnel and/or HRM work to non-specialist line managers is that they may be neither competent nor interested in personnel or HRM issues, and might not be motivated to complete HRM duties properly, so that critically important personnel tasks are neglected. Bad HRM decisions lead to a poor corporate image, higher long-run costs and loss of output due to industrial conflict. Also line managers might focus all their attention on immediately pressing personnel problems at the expense of long-term HRM planning, and it could result in HRM considerations not influencing strategic management decisions.

Effective devolution requires:

- the provision of back-up services in relation to technical problems arising from contracts of employment, legal aspects of redundancy and dismissal, union recognition, etc. An outside consultancy might assume this role;

- acceptance by everyone that line managers' workloads will have to increase following their assumption of personnel responsibilities;

- training of line managers in HRM techniques and concepts.

EUROPEAN UNION INFLUENCES

Following the UK general election of 1997 the incoming government announced its policy of positive engagement with the European Union and, in particular, that the UK would accept the European Social Charter. The latter originated during the 1987 Belgian Presidency of the EU's Council of Ministers. It was put forward as a suggested device for ensuring that basic employment rights would not be eroded following the intense business competition expected to occur in consequence of the completion of the single internal market. Further objectives were to encourage EU governments to harmonise national employment laws and practices and to confirm the EU's commitment to an active social policy. The Social Charter was intended as a grand gesture towards the EU's labour force, representing an unequivocal statement that *people* matter as well as business competition and that the interests of employees are just as important as those of firms.

The first draft of the Charter was published by the European Commission in May 1989 with the intention that each member state would implement its requirements at the national (rather than EU) level. Action would not be taken by the EU (via Directives, Regulations, etc), provided the Charter's basic objectives could be effectively attained by member states or bodies within them.

Contents of the Social Charter

The basic rights to be established by the Charter were as follows:

- **Fair remuneration.** This would involve the specification of rules for establishing a fair wage.

- **Health, protection and safety at the workplace.**

- **Access to vocational training throughout a person's working life, including the right to retraining.**

- **Freedom of association and collective bargaining**, i.e. to belong or not belong to a trade union and for unions to have the right to bargain with employing firms.

- **Integration into working life of disabled people** – the provision of training for the disabled, accessibility to work premises, availability of special transport and explicit consideration of disabled people during the ergonomic design of equipment.

- **Information, consultation and worker participation in company decision making,** especially in enterprises that operate in more than one EU country.

- **Freedom of occupation, residence and movement of workers,** including equal treatment as regards local taxes and social security entitlements.

- **Improvement in living and working conditions.** This embraces equality of treatment for part-time and temporary workers, controls on night working, and requirements for weekly rest periods and paid holidays.

- **Social protection**, including adequate unemployment and other social security benefits.

- **Equal treatment of men and women.**

- **Protection of young people**, with a minimum working age of 15 years (16 for full-time employment) and a ban on night work for those under 18.

- **Reasonable living standards for senior citizens**, with a specified minimum income underwritten by the state.

To date only two EC Directives have emerged from the Charter: a Directive giving parents of either sex the right to take three months' unpaid leave following the birth of a child and the Works Council Directive.

The Works Council Directive

Works councils are bodies comprising representatives of management and employees who meet regularly to discuss matters of mutual interest (Cressey, 1998). In 1994 the 14 EU countries other than the UK implemented the Works Council Directive under which EU-wide companies with more than 1000 European employees and at least two establishments in EU states had to establish cross-border group or company-wide works councils. Managements became legally obliged to inform and consult these councils on matters relating to job reductions, the introduction of new technology and changes in working patterns. The UK accepted the Directive in 1997.

Under the Directive a cross-frontier group or company-wide works council must have up to 30 members and the right to at least one meeting with management each year. A second meeting can be called in exceptional circumstances. A group or company is not compelled to form such a works council if its employees do not want one, but if the workers express a wish to have a cross-border works council and management fails to respond to a written request for a council to be implemented then legal processes can be invoked to force management to comply with the demand.

The Directive applies to:

- **EU scale undertakings**, i.e. those with at least 1000 employees within the EU and at least 150 employees in at least two member states; and

- **EU scale groups of companies**, i.e. groups controlled by a single parent and with at least 1000 employees within the EU and possessing at least two undertakings in separate EU states each with at least 150 employees.

The nature, composition and *modus operandi* of a European works council must be set out in a written agreement between management and a 'special negotiating body' (SNB) elected by employee representatives and containing at least one worker representative from each EU state in which the company operates. Negotiations must begin within six months following a request from the SNB, and the council must be established within the next three years. The process of forming a works council is activated when the central management receives a written request from at least 100 employees or their representatives in at least two EU states (or Norway and/or Iceland).

The written agreement itself needs to cover the scope and powers of the council, number of members and their durations of office, election procedures, consultation mechanisms, and the resources and assistance to be given to the council by central management (such assistance is required by law to be of 'appropriate' dimensions). Council members are entitled to paid time off work to attend meetings. Consultations must be 'timely' and conducted on the basis of a report prepared by the central management. However, confidential information that if disclosed would 'substantially damage' the business may be withheld from the council. Whether a specific item of information might cause substantial damage is open to legal challenge. All council members are obliged not to disclose confidential information to third parties. The council is entitled to have professional help of its own choosing, paid for by the management. Even if a workforce decides not to have a works council, its representatives must still be informed of any management proposal likely to have serious consequences for employees in more than one EU state, notably in relation to mergers, relocations, planned redundancies and intended closures of establishments, organisation changes and/or the introduction of substantially new technologies or working methods.

SUMMARY

■ Human resources are an organisation's most important asset and the effective management of human resources is a key determinant of an organisation's success. All managers who control others are necessarily involved in human resources management and thus require at least a rudimentary understanding of what the subject is about; its problems, possibilities and prospects; and how it relates to the organisation's strategy and management overall.

■ Human resources are much more difficult to manage than material resources, partly because conflict often occurs between the employer's and employees' wishes and partly because, to an increasing extent, employees try to share in making decisions about their working environment. Management must recognise workers' aspirations, and harness and develop their innate abilities for the good of the organisation. Employees will not submit passively to manipulation or dictatorial control by management but more and more expect and demand some influence in the way they are employed. Research in the behavioural sciences shows that an appropriate response by management will benefit the organisation.

■ HRM is much more than the application within an organisation of a set of management techniques. It is concerned with the wider implications of the management of change and not just with the effects of change on working practices. It seeks proactively to encourage flexible attitudes and the acceptance of new methods.

REVIEW AND DISCUSSION QUESTIONS

1   What is the definition of 'human resources management'? Explain the relationships between human resources management and personnel management.

2   Examine the training policies of an organisation. How effective are these policies and how could they be improved?

CASE STUDY: BULLIES IN THE BOARDROOM

After years of downsizing, de-layering and re-engineering, a punch-drunk British workforce hardly looks ready for a return to confrontational industrial relations. Yet the strike at British Airways, complete with management pressure and inter-union rivalry, raises questions. Is this the first sign of a shift in power back to the workers as labour market conditions tighten? And have managers become complacent in their attitudes to the workforce?

The British Airways saga admittedly looks more of a throwback than a forward indicator. Most occupants of British boardrooms would reject charges of complacency or macho management. Yet there is evidence that business leaders are failing to carry employees with them as they continue to restructure. The standard rhetoric about 'empowered' employees being vital corporate assets rings increasingly hollow.

Consider recent data from International Survey Research (ISR), a consultant whose employee opinion surveys cover 450 companies in 18 countries. Some findings in its latest survey, such as the free-fall in feelings of employment security throughout Europe, are predictable enough. Nor is it surprising that stakeholder-type economies such as Switzerland, Norway and the Netherlands tend to have the most contented workforces. The UK's ignominious position – second only to Hungary at the bottom of the league for employee satisfaction – will no doubt be dismissed as British workers enjoying a moan. And the fact that UK management is judged less favourably by employees than managers elsewhere will prompt a similar response.

Yet when ISR's work is looked at over a period of years, it is less easily brushed aside. Take the progressive collapse in the morale of the UK workforce since 1990. The trend is odd because it defies the logic of the economic cycle. Recovery has brought deterioration, not improvement. Also odd is the workforce's view of management. At the depths of the recession earlier in the decade, UK employees, though dissatisfied, were still taking a favourable view of their managers compared with the rest of Europe. Today, in spite of a marked increase in the rate of UK earnings growth, disillusionment appears total.

The clue comes with the ISR survey published at the end of 1995. This revealed that UK worker attitudes had suffered 'the most precipitate decline' of any European country over the previous 10 years. Motivation and commitment to the company were lower even than in the strife-torn days of the mid-1970s. The timing is significant because this was the first survey after the notorious British Gas annual general meeting at which the investment institutions sanctioned a much-increased pay package for the company's chief executive, Mr Cedric Brown – this when profits were down, customer service was deteriorating and employees were being shed in large numbers. The message is clear enough. Far from being a little local difficulty in the privatised utilities, the 'fat cat' pay saga had a much wider demoralising impact which is still being felt.

It does not follow that British workers are about to take to the picket lines en masse. As long as insecurity is endemic, and the main legislative reforms of the past 18 years remain intact, the unions will not resume their former mantle. Nor does the government of Mr Tony Blair, a friend of BA chief executive Mr Bob Ayling, appear keen to take an active role in the dispute at the airline. The more practical conclusion is that business does have a problem of legitimacy. There is much talk about a new psychological contract, whereby companies tell employees they can no longer offer security but will offer training in lieu to enhance employability.

There is also a view that employee satisfaction is a key performance indicator. Yet surveys show that workers feel diminishing loyalty. In effect, a contract which views the employee as both an asset and a cost has an innate tension. If it operates against the background of ever-widening pay differentials between shopfloor and board, or runs into the BA style of management, it may become untenable. There is a growing recognition among economists that trust is a valuable commodity. At national level – as in the stakeholder economies mentioned earlier – it can enhance growth. When it exists between the various stakeholders in a business it reduces costs and enhances competitive advantages. If British business wants to achieve the highest standards on a sustainable basis, it badly needs to absorb this lesson. ■

Source: *Financial Times*, 15 July 1997. Reprinted with permission.

REFERENCES FOR FURTHER READING

Beer, M, Spector, B A, Lawrence, P R and Walton, R E (1985) *Human Resource Management*, The Free Press.

Bernardin, H J and Russel, J (1993) *Human Resource Management: an Experimental Approach*, McGraw-Hill.

Boerlijst, G and Meijboom, G (1989) 'Matching the Individual and the Organisation', in P. Herriot (ed), *Assessment and Selection in Organisations: Methods and Practice for Recruitment and Appraisal*, Chichester: Wiley.

Burn, D (1996) *Benchmarking the Human Resources Function*, Hutchin Technical Communication.

Cherrington, D J (1995) *The Management of Human Resources*, 4th Edition, Prentice-Hall International.

Cressey, P (1998) 'European Works Councils in Practice', *Human Resource Management Journal*, 8(1), 67–79.

Fletcher, C and Williams, R (1992) 'The Route to Performance Management', *Personnel Review*, 24(10), 42–7.

Ferris, G R and Buckley, R M (1996) *Human Resources Management: Context, Functions and Outcomes*, Prentice-Hall.

Fraser, J M (1954) *A Handbook of Employment Interviewing*, Macdonald & Evans.

Graham, H T and Bennett, R (1998) *Human Resources Management*, 9th edn, Financial Times Pitman Publishing.

Greenberg, J and Baron, R A (1997) *Behaviour in Organisations: Understanding and Managing the Human Side of Work*, Prentice-Hall International.

Guest, D (1987) 'Human Resource Management and Industrial Relations', *Journal of Management Studies*, 24(5), 503–21.

Ham, J van, Paauwe, J and Williams, R (1986) 'Personnel Management is a Changed Environment', *Personnel Review*, 15(3), 3–17.

Johnson, R W and Neumark, D (1997) 'Age discrimination, job separations, and employment status of older workers', *Journal of Human Resources*, 32(4), 779–811.

Kinnie, N and Lowe, D. (1990) 'Performance Related Pay on the Shop Floor', *Personnel Management*, 21(11), 45–9.

Legge, K (1989) 'Human Resource Management: A Critical Analysis', in J. Storey (ed), *New Perspectives on Human Resource Management*, Routledge.

McGregor, D (1957) 'An Uneasy Look at Performance Appraisal', *Harvard Business Review*, 35(3).

Philpott, L and Sheppard, L (1992) 'Managing for Improved Performance', in M. Armstrong (ed), *Strategies for Human Resource Management*, Kogan Page.

Plender, J (1997) 'Bullies in the boardroom', *Financial Times*, 15 July.

Rodger, A (1952) *The Seven Point Plan*, London: NIIP.

Schneier, C E, Shaw, D G and Beatty, R W (1991) 'Performance Measurement and Management: A Tool for Strategy Execution', *Human Resource Management*, 30(4), 279–303.

Schuler, R S (1992) 'Linking People with the Strategic Needs of Business', *Organisational Dynamics*, Summer 18–32.

Schuler, R S and Walker, J W (1990) 'Human Resources Strategy: Focusing on Issues and Actions', *Organisational Dynamics*, Summer 5–19.

Stroh, C K and Caliguiri, P M (1998) 'Strategic human resources: a new source of competitive advantage in the global arena', *International Journal of Human Resouce Management*, 9(1), 1–17.

WORK MOTIVATION: PERSONAL AND SITUATIONAL INFLUENCES ON BEHAVIOUR

Dominic Cooper

OBJECTIVES

The objectives of this chapter are to:

◆ explain what motivation is

◆ outline the psychological and situational features that affect people's motivation

◆ describe the main theoretical approaches to motivation

◆ highlight the motivating characteristics common to all the theories

INTRODUCTION

Work motivation is a psychological concept that is primarily concerned with increasing the *strength* and *direction* of people's work-related behaviours to influence the quality and quantity of people's performance output. Work motivation has been the subject of much debate since the early 1940s. This has led to the development of various motivational theories, which chronologically have broadly focused upon:

- **genetic and hereditory factors** (e.g. Maslow's hierarchy of relative prepotency);

- **people's needs, personality and interests** (e.g. McClelland's managerial needs theory);

- **organisational justice and fairness** (e.g. Adams' equity theory);

- **incentives and rewards** (e.g. Vroom's expectancy theory);

- **behavioural change** (e.g. Luthans and Kreitner's organisational behaviour modification);

- **the design of people's jobs** (e.g. Hackman and Oldham's job characteristics model);

- **setting targets** (e.g. Locke and Latham's goal-setting theory);

- **role modelling and self-efficacy** (e.g. Bandura's social learning theory).

Early work on work motivation attempted to address the question 'Can work motivation make a difference to work performance?' By the mid-1980s development work had shifted the emphasis to a more practical viewpoint by attempting to discover 'How' the various factors of the different motivation theories affect people's motivation and subsequent task-performance. This focus on the more practical aspects led to the effectiveness of the different motivational theories being assessed on the basis of their usefulness to managers, practitioners and research psychologists. These evaluations consistently rated behaviour modification and goal-setting theory as the two most valid and effective work motivation theories, closely followed by expectancy theory, social learning theory and equity theory, suggesting that positive reinforcements, goals, expectancies, social learning, participation and enriched jobs are the main factors that *actually* motivate people to perform well (Pinder, 1984). Importantly, despite the prominence given to Maslow's hierarchy of prepotency in the majority of management texts and student courses since its inception, evaluations reveal that the theory has little practical utility or predictive validity. Indeed this is beginning to be recognised by many human resource managers, as they analyse the results of the organisational downsizing exercises conducted over the last two decades (Bower, 1996; Wooldridge, 1995).

Because every employee is motivated to some end or other, it is nonsense to talk about an unmotivated person. In reality, it is often the case that employees are simply directing their energies to achieve different aims. This type of behaviour tends to puzzle managers who often ask why it is that some employees do not invest their energies in the way that is desired. More often than not, the reason is

343

because the organisation's or manager's goals are not very clear, which tends to give employees the leeway to interpret the effectiveness of their performance against a multitude of indicators. Alternatively, employees may be less enthusiastic about achieving management's goals because they either do not coincide with the person's long-term career goals, or management's goals are thought to be focused in the wrong direction to achieve the required levels of performance.

It must be stressed at the outset that there are no easy solutions or magic managerial formulae that can be applied to motivate people to produce better performance. Nonetheless, insights into the various factors that affect people's behaviour can go a long way toward helping a manager understand why some people behave in the way they do, and the reasons that lie behind their choice of behaviours. Armed with this knowledge, managers may be better placed to direct employee behaviour for the good of the organisation.

Among many other outcomes, the strength and direction of a person's motivation will determine both the quality and quantity of a person's performance output. In turn, a person's motivation is affected by organisational, job and personal factors. Thus, motivation is dynamic: it needs constant nurturing as it can be positively or negatively affected by so many day-to-day features of organisational life. Some of the factors proven to influence people's motivation are their:

- **commitment to the organisation;**

- **involvement at work;**

- **job satisfaction;**

- **mental health.**

Each of these factors have been linked with specific work behaviours such as performance, absenteeism, tenure, turnover and organisational citizenship. Consequently, these factors must be taken into account when managers attempt to address these issues via motivational strategies. In practice, they are often overlooked because managers are primarily interested in observable and measurable work-related behaviours or other key performance indicators that focus on the outcomes of various behaviours. Although laudable, as behaviour is *the* common denominator to every key performance indicator, this can create many difficulties if other factors known to impact on people's motivation are ignored or overlooked.

Influencing factors

It is well known that psychological qualities, such as disposition, temperament, intelligence, abilities and skill, exert large influences on people's behaviour. Nonetheless, people's behaviour is not entirely determined by the kind of person they are, as the strength of a particular situation will also interact with the person's personal qualities to influence their subsequent behaviour. This can be illustrated by a confident, dominant person's behaviour during a selection process at an assessment centre. During leaderless group-discussion exercises, where each candidate was being assessed on their leadership potential, interpersonal skills, problem solving and business awareness, the person was extremely forceful to the extent that he completely dominated the proceedings. Conversely, during the selection interview the person was quiet and deferential as he deferred to the interviewer's persistent questioning. Thus, the two different situations faced by the candidate altered the way the person behaved: in the leaderless group discussion the person's disposition to dominate was allowed free rein, whereas the power relationships between the selector and candidate completely restrained the candidate's dominating behaviour. Importantly, a person's behaviour can also alter a situation. An extreme example might be that of the 1996/1997 collapse of Barings, the British merchant bank, brought about by Nick Leeson's behaviour in the Tokyo stock markets.

In the workplace, the type of work a person does, the size of the organisation they work in, the working environment (e.g. office or factory), the presence and quality of the management control systems, the effectiveness of organisational communication systems, reward systems, organisational norms and the other people they work with are all situational factors that will exert an influence on people's behaviour. In normal circumstances, the most important situational features at work tend to be other people. This was aptly illustrated in the famous 'Hawthorne' studies conducted in the Hawthorne plant of the Western Electric Company in Chicago (Roethlisberger and Dickson, 1939). In the Bank Wiring Observation Room the work groups had established an output 'norm' averaging 6000 units per day. This 'unofficial' production norm was enforced by various methods. Workers would give each other verbal warnings or resort to physical violence to prevent 'rate-busting' (producing too much) or chiselling (producing too little). Another behavioural 'norm' was that inspectors should not be officious or pull rank on the workers. One inspector who violated this 'norm' was ostracised by all the workers and subjected to vindictive pranks until he requested a transfer to a different department. This example makes the point that the situations people find themselves in, their personal psychological qualities and their ongoing behaviour all interact to reciprocally determine the way that work is done. These reciprocal relationships are illustrated by the framework in Fig 12.1, which is derived from social learning theory (Bandura, 1986).

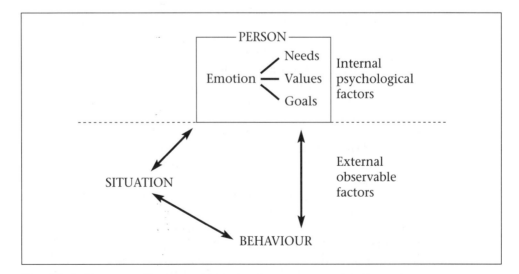

FIG 12.1 BANDURA'S MODEL OF RECIPROCAL DETERMINISM

Source: Bandura, Albert, *Social Foundations of Thought and Action: A Social Cognitive Theory* © 1986, pp 22–25. Adapted by permission of Prentice Hall, Upper Saddle River, New Jersey.

345

In this framework, behaviour is a function of both person and situational variables. Conversely, behaviour will exert a reciprocal influence on both situational and personal factors. Importantly, this framework also recognises that a change in any one element of the framework may take time to exert its reciprocal influence on the other two elements. For example, the impact of changing the design of a job (situation) may not have an immediate influence on people's work-related behaviour or attitudes. It may take six months or more. This framework is supported by a great deal of research evidence showing that specific dispositional factors have an impact on behaviour; that specific situational or environmental features also impact on behaviour; and that behaviour can impact on a person's disposition and the situation. When applied to motivation, it is clear that a manager must take all three elements of this framework into account.

Person factors

The extent to which person or dispositional variables help to reciprocally determine behaviour in organisations can best be illustrated with the psychological concept of job satisfaction. Job satisfaction is an all embracing concept that refers to job-related attitudes about various job-related characteristics, such as an organisation's structure, pay and reward policies, leadership behaviours, management styles, co-workers, etc. Much of the research on job satisfaction has been concerned with showing the influence of situational and dispositional factors (*see* Arvey *et al.*, 1991). The work of Staw and Ross (1985) provides a good example of this. They examined longitudinal data collected from a sample of 5000 45- to 59-year-old men at three points in time, over a period of five years. A number of these people had changed their occupation or employers during this period. Despite the job changes, these people's levels of job satisfaction remained relatively stable over the five-year period. Of particular interest to motivation, Staw and Ross also found that a person's previous attitudes were stronger predictors of job satisfaction than either changes in pay or the redesign of jobs. Importantly, this research demonstrates that job satisfaction is not entirely determined by the kind of job a person does or the type of organisation they work in, but is also linked to dispositional or personality factors. Follow-up research by Gerhart (1987) with a cohort of younger men confirmed Staw and Ross's findings that job satisfaction was stable across time and was influenced by a person's previously held attitudes. However, it was also found that changes in the complexity of people's jobs were more predictive of job satisfaction for the younger workers than was the case for older workers. Thus, Gerhart illustrated the influence of both situational and dispositional or person factors on job satisfaction. The case study outlined in Fig 12.2 further demonstrates how dispositional and situational factors might interact to affect performance.

Other evidence to support the stability of personal qualities and their origins was provided by Arvey *et al.* (1989), who were also interested in job satisfaction. This study involved the use of 34 pairs of twins who were reared apart from an early age. The results indicated that there is a significant genetic component to job satisfaction, in so far as people inherit a tendency to view the world in an emotionally negative or positive way. Those who view the world in an emotionally negative way are less likely to be satisfied in their jobs than those who interpret events in a more positive way. This spills over into the way we view our working environment and affects our attitudes and motivation towards our job or work, and may even influence the type of work an individual seeks and finds. Evidence provided by

Barrick and Mount (1993) investigated the moderating effects of strong and weak situations on the relationship between people's disposition and their job performance in the workplace.

In the first instance, using the Personal Characteristics Inventory (PCI), they measured the personality of 146 first-line supervisors and middle-level managers. The PCI utilises the 'big-five' factor model of personality and measures the constructs of:

- **conscientiousness** (e.g. responsible, dependable, persistent and achievement-orientated);
- **extraversion** (e.g. sociable, talkative and assertive);
- **emotional stability** (e.g. calm, secure and relaxed);
- **openness to experience** (e.g. imaginative, artistically sensitive and intellectual);
- **agreeableness** (e.g. good-natured, cooperative and trusting).

The job performance of these 146 people was subsequently rated by their own managers, based on a standardised performance appraisal form that measured eight distinct facets of effective managerial performance.

The initial results indicated that the conscientiousness and extraversion personality constructs positively correlated with the job performance ratings. Subsequently, to assess the effects of the situation on personality and job performance, the degree of autonomy enjoyed by the 146 managers was measured. Low autonomy situations are those that demand high levels of conformity where an individual's personality is suppressed (e.g. closely-supervised machine-paced assembly work). High autonomy situations are those which allow an individual a high degree of discretion to choose their own work behaviour (e.g. a company salesperson).

The results indicated that managers with higher scores on the personality constructs of conscientiousness and extraversion performed much better in jobs with a high degree of autonomy. Conversely, managers who scored highly on the agreeableness construct performed much better in low autonomy jobs. These results indicate that the situation (degree of autonomy) interacts with a manager's disposition (personality) reciprocally to determine job performance. In practical terms, this means that those high in conscientiousness will exhibit better performance if allowed to set their own performance goals. rather than being assigned performance goals.

FIG 12.2 INTERACTING EFFECTS OF DISPOSITIONAL AND SITUATION FACTORS

Source: Barrick and Mount. Copyright © 1993 by the American Psychological Association. Reprinted with permission.

Levin and Stokes (1989) confirms these relationships. They conducted a laboratory study with 140 subjects and a field study with 315 staff from a professional services company. In both studies, the results showed a small but significant link between negative emotions and job satisfaction. However, the presence of certain job characteristics was shown to exert the largest effects on job satisfaction, suggesting that a motivating environment will exert much larger effects on performance than dispositional factors. This proposition was supported in recent work conducted by Orpen (1994) with 135 employees from three financial services companies. Orpen found that the degree of autonomy within a person's job moderated the effects of motivation on both job satisfaction and performance, in that highly motivated people's job satisfaction and performance was adversely affected by a lack of autonomy.

Situational factors

The extent to which situational or environmental factors exert an influence on behaviour and job-related attitudes was recently demonstrated by Clegg and Wall (1990). Undertaking research in a British electronics factory, they showed that people's mental health was associated quite directly with the complexity of people's jobs: simple jobs were associated with poor mental health, and high complexity jobs were associated with better mental health. Initial results suggested small differences between the two levels of mental health. The differences became much larger when person variables were also considered. People with low levels of perceived skill use, who also engaged in frequent daydreaming, and did a simple job, consistently exhibited poorer levels of mental health. In contrast, those individuals who did complex jobs, perceived that they used a whole range of skills and experienced few failures had much better levels of mental health. This and other studies such as that of Kohn and Schooler demonstrates the complexity of the interactions between person and situational factors. Kohn and Schooler (1982) conducted a longitudinal study with a cohort of men, and showed that a person's disposition affected their choice of occupation. People who could view problems from many perspectives were attracted to jobs where they could use their intellectual skills. In turn, over a period of time, their intellectual skills improved because of the kind of work they were doing. The more these skills improved, the more they tended to seek out even more intellectually demanding jobs. In other words, these people's disposition affected their initial choice of job, and the demands of their jobs reciprocally affected their disposition, leading them to seek out further intellectual challenges. This work and others (e.g. Mortimer *et al.*, 1986) confirms the bi-directional and reciprocal nature of work and people's personal development.

The above body of evidence demonstrates how person and situational variables interact to affect motivation, performance and other work-related behaviour. It makes sense, therefore, to match job demands with people's skills and abilities. The results of seven case studies (shown in Fig 12.3) conducted by Caldwell and O'Reilly (1990) in a variety of organisations showed that where the person and the situation were well matched in terms of skills, abilities and job demands, etc, motivation, performance and job satisfaction was also high. Conversely, work by Stadler (1994) and Baillod and Semmer (1994) in a two-year study of turnover among computer specialists showed that where person–job fit was low, organisational commitment and job satisfaction were also low. In all instances, leaving was preceded by low job satisfaction. Only when changes in job design led to an improvement in job satisfaction did people stay with the organisation.

Organisation	Job	Correlations of person–job fit with job performance (job satisfaction)
Consumer products	Production supervisors	0.98
Insurance company	Claims adjustment supervisors	0.60
Utility company	Senior finance managers	0.53
	Senior engineering managers	0.65
Computer manufacturers	Production supervisors	0.85
Computer distributor	Sales representatives	0.35
University	Departmental secretaries	0.53

FIG 12.3 THE EFFECTS OF MATCHING PEOPLE TO JOBS
Source: Caldwell and O'Reilly. Copyright © 1990 by the American Psychological Association. Reprinted with permission.

MOTIVATIONAL THEORIES

In line with the above framework, the following discussion addresses the major work-based motivational theories from two perspectives:

- from the viewpoint of the personal psychological factors involved; *or*

- by exploring the impact of situational or environmental factors on workplace motivation, behaviour and performance.

Broadly speaking, motivational theories focused on psychological factors are divided into either content or process theories. Content theories concentrate on what motivates people by attempting to develop an understanding of fundamental human needs. On the other hand, process theories are more concerned with how motivation is aroused and maintained.

Content theories

MASLOW'S 'HIERARCHY OF RELATIVE PREPOTENCY'

The first comprehensive attempt to classify human needs (motives) and develop a universal motivational theory was that of Abraham Maslow (1942), an American organisational psychologist. As shown in Fig 12.4 Maslow proposed that human needs can be classified into motivating factors that influence people's behaviour, which he described as 'a hierarchy of relative prepotency'. In essence, Maslow's theory consists of two parts. The first concerns the classification of needs or

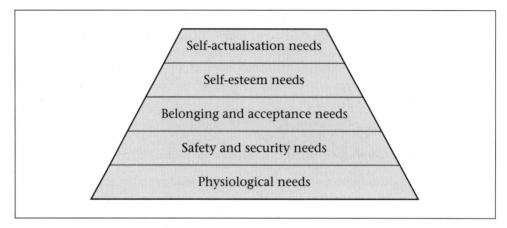

FIG 12.4 MASLOW'S HIERARCHY OF RELATIVE PREPOTENCY
Source: Maslow, 1942.

motivating factors, while the second is concerned with how these needs or motivators relate to each other. In other words, he postulated that people have several areas of need, each of which needs to be satisfied before other needs become predominant. Once satisfied, a previous need is no longer a motivator.

The plausibility of the 'hierarchy of prepotency' is immediately apparent. The most basic physiological needs such as hunger, thirst and sex must be satisfied first. Once satisfied, people turn their attentions to their safety and security needs such as providing shelter to protect themselves from the elements or other dangers. The next level relates to satisfying social needs, for example by belonging to and being accepted by a social or work group. Once these needs are met, they are replaced with a need for self-esteem, such as the desire for high status within a peer group. The ultimate need resides at the top of the hierarchy: the need for self-actualisation, which refers to the need for a person to fulfil their potential. Thus, Maslow asserts that the five levels of need are activated one after the other, beginning with the physiological needs. The basic needs must be satisfied before the next level of needs becomes important. For example, social needs become important only after perceived safety needs have been met. When a person's level of need is adequately satisfied, it ceases to dominate and influence behaviour. The next level of need then becomes the important motivating factor.

Although Maslow's hierarchy is a useful way of describing various types of motivators it is extremely weak in several respects:

- Although all five needs are claimed to exist within everyone, they are not uniformly motivating. At any given moment, different people are likely to be striving to fulfil different need levels of the hierarchy. For example, an individual whose belonging needs are dominant (level 3), is likely to behave differently to someone attempting to satisfy safety and security needs (level 2). This presents a problem for managers, in that, 'If each worker has a different hierarchy of needs, how does a manager provide motivators for all his or her staff?'

- The simplicity of the hierarchy does not reflect the reality that behaviour in the real world is shaped by situational pressures and controls that are often beyond a person's individual control. As such it does not recognise that people's behaviour can only be fully understood by examining the reciprocal relationship between person, and behavioural and situational characteristics.

- The model assumes that one motive should predominate at any one moment in time. However, humans are more complex than this. For example, people work to simultaneously attain pay and rewards (security), social contact (belonging), status (self-esteem), etc.

- A major problem occurs from trying to infer the timescale elapsing between lower-order need satisfaction and the emergence of higher-order needs. It could be almost immediately or over a period of several years, when an individual turns directly from a satisfied lower-order need to an unsatisfied higher need. This fits with Maslow's stated position that the hierarchy was supposed to represent a life-time developmental model of motivation.

- The hierarchy is difficult to relate to work processes, because people do not necessarily satisfy their higher-order needs through their jobs or occupations. Many people prefer to satisfy their needs outside the workplace, for example through leisure activities.

- The five needs are not defined with sufficient precision, making it difficult to define the various needs in operational terms. For example, it would be difficult, if not impossible, for a personnel manager to make use of the hierarchy to address problems of mass absenteeism every Monday morning.

Much research has attempted to test the hierarchical structure of Maslow's hierarchy, but overall, only modest support has been obtained. Typical results suggest that:

- There is greater support for three levels of need, rather than five (*see* Fig 12.5).

- There is little consistent support for the notion that needs are hierarchically organised.

- Those who find it difficult to satisfy a higher-order need revert to satisfying lower-order needs, even though they have been satisfied previously.

- A satisfied lower-order need is not a motivator. Conversely, the motivational value of higher-order needs grows in strength the more they are satisfied.

These types of result are in complete contrast to those postulated by Maslow. Therefore, despite the considerable influence that Maslow's theory has exerted in the workplace, it actually rests on very little empirical evidence.

Content theories such as Maslow's need hierarchy are flawed because they propose that everyone's needs are organised in the same hierarchical order, and to a large extent that everybody strives for the same fundamental goals such as self-actualisation. However, everyday experience suggests that people are more varied and complex than this, and are not all alike. In any organisation, different employees will operate at many different motivational levels in these types of hierarchy. This pre-

Hall and Nougaim (1968) conducted a longitudinal study in the American Telephone and Telegraph (AT&T) company over five years with 49 managers. They tested the hypotheses that as lower-order needs are satisfied, higher-level needs emerge. This aspect of Maslow's model was not supported, but moderate support was found for the hypotheses that lower needs decline in strength when satisfied, while higher-order needs grow in strength. The authors concluded that the study results could be better explained in terms of a person's sequential career progression, rather than by progressing through Maslow's hierarchy of needs.

Alderfer (1969) ERG Model

A variation on Maslow's model was proposed by Alderfer (1969) who combined Maslow's physiological and safety needs into one level of existence needs, retained his social need level, and combined the self-esteem and self-actualisation needs into one level of growth need. Alderfer compared the predictive power of this variant model with Maslow's 'hierarchy of prepotency'. Questionnaires were distributed to 110 bank employees from various levels in the organisation. The results indicated that the less a higher-order need was satisfied, the more likely it was that an individual would revert to satisfying the next level of need below, even though it had previously been satisfied. Thus Alderfer found that the satisfaction of a level of need appears to be associated with its own importance, rather than the importance of the next higher-level need. From these results he concluded needs are not necessarily hierarchically organised.

Wahba and Bridwell (1979)

In a review of the literature, Wahba and Bridwell (1979) tested Maslow's notion that there are five needs. No support was found for five needs, although it was found that, in general, there was a main trend towards three needs. Similarly, no consistent support was found for the notion that needs are organised hierarchically.

FIG 12.5 TESTS OF MASLOW'S HIERARCHY OF RELATIVE PREPOTENCY

sents many problems for employers as it is very difficult to satisfy all employees' needs simultaneously. Other problems reside in the fact that need hierarchies do not recognise that situational and environment factors such as managerial policies and practices, an organisation's structure, the type of technology used and the external environment all influence our needs. Any motivational theory that proposes strong similarities between people can only lead to the conclusion that there is 'one best way' to manage and motivate others, which is simply not true.

Individual differences in motivational needs

In general, many early need theories of human motivation were flawed because they failed to take account of people's individual differences. One need theory that explicitly recognises individual differences in motivation is McClelland's (1961) 'managerial needs' theory. McClelland conducted research with over 500 managers from 25 different US corporations to determine just what motivates a good manager. Upon the basis of this research he argues that managers possess three basic motivational needs: achievement, affiliation and power. Importantly, each of these three levels of needs has been demonstrably linked to both job satisfaction and competence in a number of occupations, particularly management (Medcof and Hausdorf, 1995).

NEED FOR ACHIEVEMENT

According to McClelland, the need for achievement (nAch), or the desire to do something better or more efficiently than it has been done before, is one of the keys to economic growth. Those who are high in nAch are people who prefer personal responsibility, positively enjoy competition, like to set, strive for and reach difficult goals, like to take calculated risks, like immediate short-term feedback on their performance and work hard until they attain excellence. Not surprisingly, in the workplace, those scoring highly on nAch will be attracted to an entrepreneurial role. McClelland suggests that people high on this motive are likely to have grown up in environments which expected competence of them, gave them independence at an early age and evaluated them highly. A great deal of work has been conducted on the achievement motivation of managers. In essence, the results show that companies whose executives have high achievement motivation produce better results. This is particularly true in an entrepreneurial rather than a bureaucratic organisation. For example, McClelland examined the motives of 51 technical entrepreneurs and calculated the growth rate of their companies in terms of the value of their sales. The growth rate of those companies led by entrepreneurs with high nAch was almost 250 per cent higher than companies led by entrepreneurs with moderate needs for achievement.

NEED FOR AFFILIATION

During the course of his work, McClelland found that some major figures in industry did not score highly on nAch as he had expected. He reasoned that as a large part of working life in organisations was concerned with co-ordinating the activities of others, the ability to relate to others was an important component of being a manager. He proposed that those who have this ability, are high on need for affiliation (nAff), and that these people strive for approval from both their subordinates and superiors. Consequently, those high on nAff are sensitive to the needs of others. It has been suggested that there are two forms of nAff, one more managerially effective than the other.

1 The first, **affiliative assurance**, is best described as a striving for close relationships, due to the perceived security that they provide. Such a person tends to look for continual approval, and is anxious about possible rejection. In other words, these managers want to be liked. These managers will expend a lot of energy on maintaining relationships, at the expense of getting the job done.

Generally speaking, those high on affiliative assurance would rather hang on to team members, than see them promoted.

2 The second, **affiliative interest**, is best described as a care and concern for the feelings of others, but not at the expense of getting the job done. It is a concern for the legitimate needs and feelings of others, which is the type of affiliation that will lead to greater organisational effectiveness.

NEED FOR POWER

McClelland also discovered that a good manager was high in interpersonal skills. This was combined with a need to influence people for the good of the organisation by being in control of events, forcefully expressing opinions and being the leader. In other words these people had a greater need for power (nPow) than the need to achieve or need to be liked. A need for power, however, has both positive and negative aspects. The positive side shows itself as an interest in persuasion and interpersonal influence. The negative side shows itself as an unsocialised concern for personal dominance at the expense of others. The aspect that dominates is determined by the degree of self-control or activity inhibition a manager possesses. Managers with a high degree of self-control will satisfy their need for power in socially acceptable ways via interpersonal influencing skills. These managers tend to be committed to organisational goals, want to serve others and rather than dominate employees they try to make them feel that they too have power. In contrast, managers who are more concerned with personal power show little signs of self-control and tend to exercise their power impulsively and in a haphazard manner. This inconsistency creates many difficulties for the manager's subordinates and can lead to major productivity problems.

Another important line of research arose from the work of McClelland: the leadership motive pattern. Achievement motivation is usually measured alongside the motives for power and for affiliation. McClelland noted that a certain pattern enabled people to be effective managers at the highest levels in an organisation. For senior managers, success tended to be associated with a low level of affiliation motive and a moderate to high need for power together with an ability to inhibit spontaneous impulses (i.e. good self-control). However, with lower level managers, success was related to a combination of a high need for both power and achievement. These findings have been supported by other researchers (*see* Fig 12.6), who have found that those scoring high on both nPow and nAch exhibited better managerial performance and had a higher promotion rate than others. The opposite was true for those who scored low on these needs. Taken as a whole these findings suggest that a manager's motivating potential appears to be predictive of effective managerial behaviour, which has obvious implications for personnel selection and placement practices (*see* Cooper and Robertson, 1995).

McClelland's work is important in the sense that it recognises that people have different needs. Although his findings are extremely useful for selection purposes, in line with other need theories, McClelland does not specify the motivational links between a manager's individual needs and actual performance. Indeed, attempts to link nAch with performance have generally been unsuccessful. Matsui *et al.* (1982), for example, found that although nAch positively correlated with people's tendency to set goals, nAch did not actually correlate with performance.

Much of the early research on managerial motivation was conducted with the Thematic Apperception Test (TAT) which involves people writing stories about a series of pictures. Unfortunately, the TAT was later found to be both unreliable and invalid. Because of these problems, Stahl (1983) used the Job Choice Exercise (JCE) to re-examine McClelland's concepts of managerial motivation. The JCE requires respondents to make 24 decisions about the attractiveness of jobs in motivational terms (i.e. nPow, nAch, nAff). In seven separate distributions, the JCE was administered to a total of 1741 respondents that included managers and shopfloor workers from a variety of industries, as well as students and Air Force cadets.

Examining the data in a number of different ways, Stahl showed that respondents who scored above 3.14 on nPow and 4.64 on nAch exhibited better levels of job performance, had a higher promotion rate than others and were more likely to be managers than shopfloor workers. The opposite was found for those with lower scores for nPow and nAch.

These findings supported the work of McClelland, who had asserted that 'power is the great motivator' for senior executives. Stahl, however, found that this also held for middle and junior managers. Thus, McClelland's model of managerial needs appears to apply to all managerial levels.

FIG 12.6 A TEST OF MCCLELLAND'S MANAGERIAL NEEDS MODEL

Not surprisingly, it was found that the goals themselves were related to performance. Thus, nAch appears to be indirectly related to performance, in so far as those high in nAch are likely to set goals. In turn, it is the actual goals that affect performance (*see* the section on goal-setting later in the chapter).

Process theories

An alternative and complementary approach to understanding motivation lies in examining the psychological processes that are involved in motivation. Process theories recognise that people have different competing needs; that behaviour is a function of both the person and the situation; that people are decision-making organisms; and that any decisions made are based on the link between behaviour and outcomes. Thus, as Fig 12.7 makes clear, process approaches recognise that there is a direct link between effort, performance and outcomes.

In essence, the process approach to motivation proposes that people will direct their efforts towards goals that they value. However, while the existence of a valued goal is a necessary condition for action, on its own it is not a sufficient condition: people will only act, if they have a reasonable expectation that their actions will lead to the desired goals and the benefits that flow from reaching the goals are of significant value.

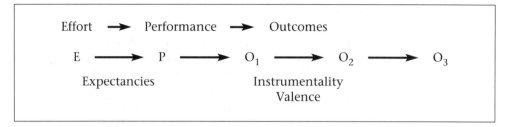

FIG 12.7 EXPECTANCY THEORY RELATIONSHIPS

Expectancy theory

The important role of these characteristics for motivating human behaviour was explicitly recognised by Vroom (1964) in his expectancy model of motivation. The model states that motivation (M) is a function of the expectancy (E) of reaching a certain outcome, multiplied by the value (V) of the outcome for that person:

Motivation = Expectancy × Value

Vroom's theory predicts that outcomes which have a high expectancy of being reached (e.g. greater efficiency) and the rewards of which are highly valued (e.g. increased profits) will direct people to exert much greater effort in their task. Conversely, outcomes with high expectations (e.g. promotion) and neutral or even disliked values (e.g. working away from home) will reduce the amount of effort the person is prepared to invest. Similarly, outcomes with relatively low expectancies of being reached (e.g. zero accidents in a manufacturing organisation) and neutral valuations (e.g. no perceived personal benefits) will not have an influence on a person's level of motivation. In a sense, therefore, Vroom's expectancy theory is hedonistic. People will only decide how much effort they are going to put into their work according to what they perceive they are going to get out of it and according to how much they value the potential outcomes.

More recent refinements (*see* Heckhausen *et al.*, 1985, for an excellent review) have extended Vroom's original theory to include an instrumentality component, based on a division of expectancy into two separate parts:

- **the perceived probability of achieving the expected outcome;** *and*

- **the perceived probability of actually being rewarded for achieving the expected outcome.**

Instrumentality is concerned with the latter. The heart of the issue here is the extent to which good performance is actually rewarded, and whether the rewards on offer adequately offset the costs and risks borne by an employee. For example, many MBA graduates are offered positions that attract a low salary but with greater opportunities for more rapid advancement to the higher echelons of management. Similarly, many are offered positions with very attractive salaries, but little opportunity for advancement. A graduate fortunate to be offered both is likely to choose between the two on the basis of his or her perceptions that the likelihood of rapid advancement is a reality. These refined versions are referred to as VIE models, where:

1 **Expectancy (E)** concerns the perceived relationship between the amount of effort people put into their work and the levels of performance achieved. In other words: 'Do they expect greater effort to lead to better performance?' Of extreme importance here is not the actual relationship between effort and performance, but what the person believes the relationship to be. Thus the precise behaviours that constitute good levels of performance must be specified. Employees must believe they can control the quality of their job performance: if they do not, they will see no point in trying harder.

2 **Instrumentality (I)** refers to the perceived relationship between an employee's performance and outcomes in terms of rewards and punishments. The probability of increased effort leading to increased reward (e.g. pay), will affect the amount of effort people think it worthwhile to expend in the first place, and therefore constitutes an important feedback loop. Even if the person concludes that greater effort on their part leads to better performance, this effort is unlikely to be enacted and sustained if it does not lead to some tangible reward.

3 **Valence (V)** concerns the attractiveness of the rewards on offer. This aspect of the theory explicitly recognises that there are significant differences between people in terms of the outcomes that they find attractive. An employee may believe that increased effort leads to better performance, and that better performance leads to increased rewards. However, if the rewards on offer are not highly valued, the person may say, 'Why should I bother?' The motivating potential of a reward, therefore, depends solely on the value the person places on it. If the reward (e.g. promotion) is highly valued, motivation is likely to be high. Conversely, if promotion is not valued, motivation is likely to be low. The notion of fairness may also enter employees' minds, to the extent that they will have a view of the level and kind of rewards which ought to be available to the person for performing a particular type of work. The issue of equity also enters into the way rewards are distributed in relation to performance and to any deprivations people may suffer in carrying out their work, such as working on a night shift. The important point here is that employees are unlikely to be satisfied with the rewards they receive if they are perceived as inequitable. Dissatisfaction will weaken the motivating power of any potential rewards.

Contemporary elaborations of expectancy theory are expressed as:

$$\textbf{Motivation} = \textbf{E} \sum_{i=1}^{n} \textbf{IV}$$

This formula clearly shows that motivation and performance are influenced by a person's beliefs about the links between effort and performance (E), the perceptions about the links between performance and rewards (I), and the perceived value (V) placed on the rewards. The numerical values for each component can range from plus one to minus one (+1 to –1) with a mean of zero. Thus, an expectation with a guaranteed certainty of success can be expressed as (+1), absolutely no guarantee of success as (–1), and indifference as (0). The same would apply to both instrumentality and valence. In reality, a particular course of action can lead to many simultaneous outcomes. Therefore, the theory proposes that instrumentality and valence be summed (Σ IV) across the total number (n) of possible outcomes. The degree to which a person is motivated is the sum of the perceived value of all possible rewards multiplied by the strength of the expectancies. Importantly, it will prove difficult to motivate a person who places little credence on any one of the three components.

The formula therefore represents:

Motivation = Expectation × rewards (i.e. the sum of Instrumentality and Valence) across the total number of outcomes

Each of these must be given a value between +1 and –1, dependent upon how successful they are likely to be.

Although quite complicated, expectancy theory does recognise that situational and person factors appear to account for the variability in people's performance. Primarily, however, expectancy theory is a means to identify what rewards are valued by employees for particular courses of action, rather than a means with which to translate motivation into performance. As such, it shows that a person's level of performance varies directly in proportion to a person's need for achievement and anticipated satisfaction with any rewards offered.

Although this sounds little more than common sense, it does draw attention to certain requirements for directing motivation that are frequently neglected in practice. For example, managers should try and ensure that an employee's personal goals match those of the organisation. This might best be achieved by closer matching of the person to the job via effective personnel selection practices (*see* Cooper and Robertson, 1995). Similarly, managers must provide feedback in one form or another (e.g. praise) to employees so that their efforts can actually be seen to be rewarded. Other, important implications for managers and organisations are listed in Fig 12.8.

Goal-setting theory

Expectancy theories have proved popular and have influenced much subsequent research into motivation in the workplace. One approach that has successfully incorporated the notions of expectancy theory and many others besides is goal-setting theory. This is perhaps because any and all attempts to motivate performance in the workplace inevitably include targets or goals in some form or other (e.g. vision statements, deadlines, etc). First proposed by Ed Locke, an American psychologist, in 1968, at present goal-setting is one of the most influential theories of work motivation applicable to all cultures. Over 400 empirical studies, conducted on over 88 different types of tasks, have investigated the influence of goal-setting on task performance. This body of evidence has repeatedly shown that provided a goal is related to specific task requirements and is accepted by employees, virtually any type of action that is able to be measured and controlled can be improved (*see* Locke and Latham, 1990, for a comprehensive review of goal-setting theory). Indeed, it has been stated that 'Goal-setting theory has demonstrated more scientific validity to date than any other theory or approach to motivation ...' (Pinder, 1984, p 169).

Implications for managers

- Find out what rewards employees value.
- Specify the exact behaviours that reflect good levels of performance.
- Ensure the desired levels of performance are within employees' capabilities.
- Ensure that the links between effort–performance–outcomes are clear to all employees.
- Ensure that the rewards on offer do not conflict with other rewards from different organisational sources.
- Ensure that the rewards are not seen as trivial.
- Ensure that the level of rewards actually matches levels of performance.
- Ensure the reward system is fair and equitable.

Implications for organisations

- Design pay and reward systems so that performance is rewarded, not other factors such as length of service.
- Design jobs in such a way as to provide opportunities for people to satisfy their own needs through their work.
- Allow employees to be involved in decisions affecting the type of rewards on offer.

FIG 12.8 MANAGERIAL IMPLICATIONS OF EXPECTANCY THEORY

Source: Nadler and Lawler, 1979

CORE FINDINGS

Derived from both management and academic theories, goal-setting is primarily based on the central notion that specific, difficult goals are the immediate, though not only, precursors of human action. Reviews (e.g. Locke *et al.*, 1981) have revealed that approximately 90 per cent of all goal-setting studies have shown a beneficial effect of goal-setting on performance. The core findings of this vast body of research have shown that:

- difficult goals lead to higher performance than moderate or easy goals;

- specific, difficult goals lead to higher performance than vague, broad goals or 'do your best' goals;

- feedback about goal-directed behaviour is necessary for goal-setting to work;

- people need to be committed to achieving the goals.

These core findings make clear that the main aim of any goal is to place sufficient demands upon people to motivate them to achieve higher levels of performance. However, a goal on its own is insufficient to motivate people. Any goals that are set must be both specific and difficult. In addition, people must be committed to the process and they must also be able to track their progress. By their very nature, specific, difficult goals affect performance by:

- presenting challenges that cause people to focus their attention and actions on the task requirements;

- mobilising people's effort;

- boosting people's commitment to try harder and persevere until the goals are achieved;

- motivating people to search for the optimum performance strategy.

SPECIFIC GOALS

Specific goals remove any doubt about what is expected, enabling people to focus their attentions solely on the activities specified. A recent goal-setting study conducted in a British manufacturing organisation demonstrated this effect (Cooper *et al.*, 1994). In an attempt to reduce accident rates, goals were set for specific unsafe behaviours in each of 14 departments. The results, illustrated in Fig 12.9, showed considerable reductions in accidents related to unsafe behaviours for which goals had been set. Conversely, accidents related to other safety behaviours, for which no goals had been set, either continued at their previous rate or increased. Similar results were found in the UK construction industry (Duff *et al.*, 1993). Improvements in safety performance were found for scaffolding, access to heights and housekeeping categories for which goals had been set, whereas no appreciable improvement was found in a personal protective equipment category for which no goals were set.

In practice, managers often set goals that are too broad (e.g. an accounts manager may set a productivity improvement goal of 10 per cent for the processing of orders and invoices). Unfortunately, broad goals allow people to interpret the effectiveness of their performance against a variety of performance indicators. Greater productivity improvements would be found for goals that specified exactly the

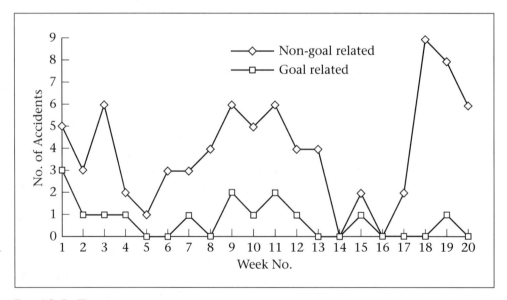

FIG 12.9 THE EFFECTS OF SPECIFIC GOALS ON ACCIDENT RATES
Source: Cooper *et al.*, 1994.

performance to be improved. For example, reducing invoice 'receipt to payment' processing time from 45 days to 28 days is a much more specific productivity goal. As such, clerks can only compare their performance to the amount of time taken. Interestingly, most people are reassured by, and more satisfied, from having a clear appreciation of what is expected of them, rather than a vague approximation.

DIFFICULT GOALS

The amount of effort and energy directed towards goal-achievement depends upon how challenging the goal is believed to be. In general, assuming the goals are accepted, the more of a challenge the goal represents, the more effort people will be prepared to employ. When people rise to a challenge, they tend to be much more determined and try harder, by drawing upon more of their skills, abilities and experiences until the goal is reached. In turn this boosts people's confidence in their abilities, causing them to set even higher goals, reflecting the old adage that 'success breeds success'.

Nonetheless, it should be recognised that people will be reluctant to try and reach a goal that they think is unrealistic or impossible to achieve (e.g. zero accidents in the workplace). Impossibly difficult goals are demotivating. They lower people's goal-commitment to such an extent that the goals are rejected out of hand, and people will not even try to reach them. This raises the question of when is a goal sufficiently challenging, but not beyond the capabilities of those concerned? The answer to this question depends on whether or not the goals are related to individual or group performance. If the goal is related to individual performance, goal-difficulty is usually determined by comparing the output (e.g. productivity) of a few high-performing people with that achieved by the majority. The average output of the high performers is then used as the difficulty level of the goal, as it is challenging to the majority but still achievable. If a goal is to be set for a workgroup, it will be necessary to establish the average levels of current output for the group as a whole over a relatively small period of time, to provide an average baseline figure. This baseline figure is then used as the basis for discussions about the degree to which performance improvements are possible, while also providing a benchmark with which to compare future performance.

CONTINGENT FACTORS

Although a goal should be challenging, realistic and expressed in very specific terms, being confronted with a challenge does not always guarantee high performance. Locke and Latham (1990) have identified various characteristics that are known to affect goal-directed performance and include:

- **People's skills, abilities and knowledge**. An individual's or work group's ability to perform a task will obviously limit the extent to which a task goal will be reached. Ability is normally judged by how well someone has done on the same or similar tasks in the past. In general, people with high levels of ability tend to achieve difficult goals, whereas those with less ability tend to struggle, although this will be related to the complexity of the task.

- **Self-confidence**. People's confidence in their own abilities to perform a task will influence their choice of how difficult a goal should be, and the amount of effort they will spend in trying to reach a goal. Someone who is very sure, and has every confidence in their own task abilities is more likely to set a challenging goal, and be more committed to reaching it, than someone who is uncertain.

- **Task complexity**. Research findings indicate that specific, challenging goals produce better performance improvements on simple rather than complex tasks, although improvements can be expected for both types of task (Wood, Mento and Locke, 1987). This is because when people work on simple tasks, their efforts lead directly to improved task performance. Conversely, complex tasks involve decisions about when, where and how to allocate effort for maximum effect. This means that any effort used has indirect effects upon performance. Managerial and supervisory functions are deemed to be complex tasks because they include multiple demands upon the individual from various organisational sources. Therefore, the complexity of the managerial function also inevitably incorporates competing goals, of which one will be reached at the expense of the others at a particular moment in time.

- **Goal-choice**. The choice of how difficult a goal should be will be influenced by what the individual or work group would ideally like to achieve, what they expect to achieve and what is believed to be the minimum that should be achieved. A goal determined by ideals is more than likely to be based upon wishful thinking more than reality and represents what could happen if everything went right. This type of goal is typically reflected through mission or vision statements issued by boardroom executives (e.g. that safety is a top priority; that the company has set a goal of zero accidents and that all employees should behave safely and follow company safety policies). A goal based on expectations is typically based on a realistic assessment of what can be accomplished in the light of past experience. Success or failure in attaining previous goals, the likelihood of adequate resources, the expected amount of managerial support and the importance of the goal are all primary factors likely to influence assessments when choosing the difficulty level of a goal. A goal based on the minimum that should be achieved reflects the minimum levels of performance that people will be satisfied with. Assessments of goal-difficulty levels based on minimum requirements perhaps reflect the fact that organisations typically have multiple goals. Very often, however, these organisational goals are in conflict with one another, the case of productivity vs safety being a familiar one. Organisations faced with conflicting goals, typically, trade off goals, so that one goal will be reached at the expense of another. Choosing the goal-difficulty level based on minimum requirements is often seen to be a compromise that leads to the satisfaction of several conflicting goals. Indeed, a goal based upon the minimum required is the typical choice, rather than the expected or ideal goal.

- **Goal-commitment**. Challenging goals only lead to higher performance when people are committed to them. Commitment refers to the degree to which the person is attached to the goal, considers it significant or important, and is determined to reach it, even in the face of setbacks and obstacles. Acceptance of and commitment to goals is a crucial factor in performance, in that as commitment declines, performance also declines (Erez and Zidon, 1984). Factors which have been found to enhance commitment fall into two broad categories: those which convince people that achieving the goal is possible, and those which convince people that achieving the goal is important. Managers can play an important role in facilitating commitment to goals by persuading employees that the desired goals are both achievable and important. In addition they should provide visible ongoing support. If they don't, the importance of the goal could be undermined, resulting in goal-rejection. Commitment to a challenging goal could also be considerably improved by allowing employees to participate in the goal-setting process.

For many people, a goal set and delegated by others serves as a disincentive, which may lead to people rejecting it. However, in the USA, Locke and colleagues have consistently argued that provided a goal is sufficiently difficult, delegated goals are as effective as participatively set goals for inducing high commitment and high performance. In contrast, Erez and her colleagues (e.g. Erez *et al.*, 1985) consistently reported that participative goals were better in studies conducted in the USA and Israel. Disputes between the two schools of thought led to a joint laboratory study in an attempt to settle the issue, a very unique scientific venture (Latham *et al.*, 1988). The results indicated that the main differences between the two camps could be attributed to various methodological differences in the way goals were set. In essence, Erez and colleagues used a 'tell' approach, whereas Latham and colleagues used a 'tell and sell' approach.

These same issues were examined in the UK construction industry, by Cooper *et al.* (1992). Controlling for all the methodological problems noted in Latham *et al.* (1988), on those sites where operatives participated in the goal-setting process there was much greater improvements in safety performance than on those sites where goals were delegated (assigned) to operatives. Similarly, a meta-analysis of the extant goal-setting literature revealed the potency of participative goals, rather than delegated goals, for improving a variety of task performances (Cooper, 1992).

- **Information feedback.** Feedback is usually defined as 'information about the effectiveness of particular work behaviours' and is thought to fulfil several functions. For example, it is directive, by clarifying specific behaviours that ought to be performed; it is motivational, as it stimulates greater effort; and, it is error correcting, as it provides information about the extent of errors being made. Research has shown that feedback by itself, can lead to higher levels of performance (e.g. Pritchard *et al.*, 1988). However, in combination, goals and feedback are far more powerful than either one alone (Balcazar *et al.*, 1986). Goals inspire individuals to achieve particular levels of performance, while feedback allows the person to track how well he or she is doing in relation to the goal, so that if necessary, adjustments in effort can be made.

Thus the message from goal-setting theory is simple. A specific, challenging goal has maximum effect when an individual has confidence in his/her ability to perform the task, is committed to the goal, the task is simple, and accurate feedback is made available so that the person can track their progress in relation to the goal. As these kinds of contingent factors make clear, goal-setting theory explicitly recognises the influence of person and situational variables. The reciprocal relationships between important goal-setting characteristics are illustrated in Fig 12.10 which indicates how each characteristic might interact with and affect other goal characteristics. For example, productivity goals will be affected by the person's commitment to improving productivity, whether or not the productivity goals conflict with other organisational goals (e.g. productivity vs safety), and whether or not management is committed enough to provide the necessary support and resources for people to reach the goals.

More recent applications of goal-setting have incorporated the notions of self-efficacy, self-regulation and self-management training derived from social learning theory (Bandura, 1986) and expectancy theory (*see* Heckhausen and Kuhl, 1985). For a recent review of goal-setting and other motivational theories *see* Kanfer (1992) and Kleinbeck *et al.* (1990).

SITUATIONAL MOTIVATION THEORIES

Extreme examples of the effects of situational influences can be found in the work of behavioural psychologists, who essentially take the view that situations condition people's behaviour. This approach proposes that because behaviour is a

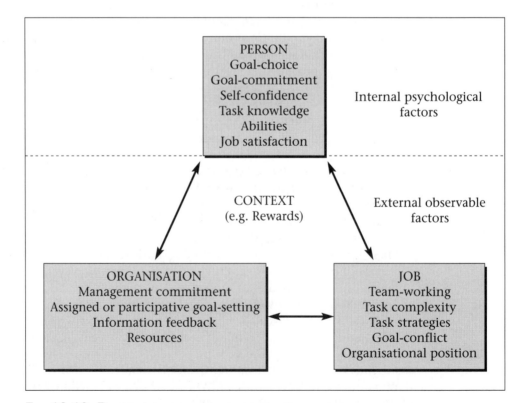

FIG 12.10 RECIPROCALLY DETERMINED MODEL OF GOAL-SETTING

function of its consequences, behaviour that is reinforced in some way will strengthen and continue. On the other hand, behaviour that is punished or behaviour that produces unimportant outcomes for the person will be less likely to occur. Thus, behaviourist approaches emphasise that people's behaviour is learnt through a trial and error process that is shaped by the type of punishment or reward the person receives.

The different types of reinforcers and their controlling effects on behaviour shown in Fig 12.11 indicate that a positive reward strengthens and increases the probability of a person behaving in a particular way. In the workplace, for example, an employee praised by a manager for completing a difficult job within a certain deadline will be more likely to repeat that type of performance in the future. Conversely, if the employee received no acknowledgement of any kind, continuation of this type of good performance would be extinguished because their performance was ignored. Similarly, a negative reward can also strengthen the way people behave. For example, removing an aspect of a job that an employee dislikes (e.g. making the tea) due to that person's good job performance would also reinforce the employee's behaviour by rewarding their performance. Punishment, on the other hand, is purported to stop or decrease certain behaviours. For example, issuing a written warning to an employee for persistent lateness is a punisher that is meant to stop this type of behaviour. However, the influence of punishment and rewards on behaviour differs considerably. To be effective, a punisher has to fulfil two conditions: it must be given immediately, and every single time the unwanted behaviour(s) occurs. In most workplace situations this is not always possible. Rewards, on the other hand, need be given only every so often. Initially, rewards should be given as soon as possible after the desired behaviour. To ensure that employees are clear about the linkages between the desired behaviour(s) and the rewards, they should be given only when the desired behaviour has actually occurred. Once the desired behaviour starts to become established in the employee's repertoire, the frequency of reward (e.g. praise) can be reduced over a period of time.

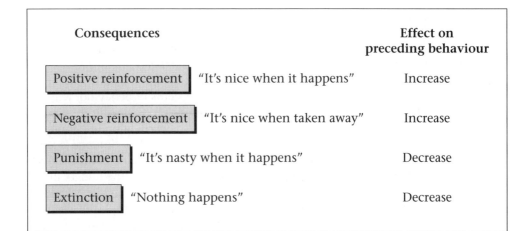

Consequences		Effect on preceding behaviour
Positive reinforcement	"It's nice when it happens"	Increase
Negative reinforcement	"It's nice when taken away"	Increase
Punishment	"It's nasty when it happens"	Decrease
Extinction	"Nothing happens"	Decrease

FIG 12.11 DIFFERENT REINFORCERS AND THEIR CONTROLLING EFFECTS ON BEHAVIOUR

Organisational behaviour modification

Focusing solely on behaviour, this approach does not make use of any underlying psychological processes such as motivation or personality. Nonetheless, it has been successfully used to influence behaviour in a variety of work settings. When used in a strategic planned way to motivate organisational behaviour, the behavioural approach outlined in the previous section is referred to as organisational behaviour modification (OBM). OBM has been used to successfully improve a variety of work-related performances that includes absenteeism, productivity and quality in a variety of settings (Andrasik *et al.*, 1981; Luthans and Martinko, 1987). Several key features of OBM, that significantly add to its success as a motivational technique, include:

- its focus on current rather than past determinants of behaviour;
- its emphasis on overt behaviour change as the major criterion in evaluating its motivational effects;
- its careful choice of the specific behaviours to be targeted;
- its use of structured observational checklists for measuring performance;
- its use of reinforcers.

At the theoretical level, behaviourist terminology describes the flow of these procedures as antecedents–behaviour–consequents (ABC model). Antecedents are described as 'controlling stimuli' that trigger or elicit observable behaviours. Consequents are any events that follow as a direct result of the behaviour, and as such are described as reinforcers. For example, a ringing phone would be described as an antecedent when someone picks it up (behaviour) to speak (consequent) with the caller. Speaking to the caller reinforces the behaviour of answering the phone. Although some might think that the antecedent is the most important aspect of determining behaviour, it is the consequent that has the most powerful influence. For example, if the phone rang repeatedly and there was no caller each time it was answered, it would not take long before the ringing phone was ignored. Thus, antecedents trigger certain behaviours because they signal consequences. Using the ABC model, organisational behaviourists try to discover which consequents are controlling which behaviours. When identified, the consequents are changed, so that the target behaviours also change to what is desired (*see* Fig 12.12).

Managerial attempts to change employee behaviour often fail in practice because they focus almost exclusively on the antecedents of behaviour (e.g. rules, procedures, etc) instead of the consequents (e.g. time saved, extra production). In some cases, organisations even reward the behaviours they are trying to eliminate. Attempting to save money by reclaiming surpluses from annual departmental budgets and reducing the following year's budget allocation is a classic example. In these circumstances the organisation is rewarding managers who spend up to the budget limit, while simultaneously punishing thrifty managers! Allowing departmental managers to keep a certain percentage of budget savings for other work-related uses (e.g. updating computer equipment) is more likely to result in across-the-board savings. Nonetheless, it is important to recognise that a behaviour may have more than one consequent, some of which will exert stronger reinforcing effects than others. Three features are known to determine the strength of a consequent (reinforcer):

A student working in a drugstore to pay her way through an American college tried to identify the rewards for different types of work-related behaviour. She observed the average length of time taken to complete certain tasks. She related the timings to two factors that she thought were acting as reinforcers (consequents). The average timings for the different types of tasks were as follows:

Task	Average timings in minutes	
	Situation A	*Situation B*
Restock sweet shelves	20	35
Restock cigarette shelves	5	15
Vacuum floor	5	15
Dump rubbish	5	10
Clean store	45	90
Check in deliveries	30	60
Help pharmacist	50	60
Deliver orders	50	60
Totals	210	345

The average timings for each factor were found to be very different. What she had noticed was that people worked faster when a nice job was to follow what was seen as a nasty job, and took much longer when a nice job was followed by a nasty job. This effect is termed the 'Premack Principle', after a researcher who had observed the same phenomena in animals. Utilising this principle, it is possible for managers to identify tasks that employees see as nice or nasty, and change the situation by rescheduling work so that a nice job always follows a nasty job. In this way, a manager can easily rearrange the consequents of employees' behaviour without the use of incentives or other inducements.

FIG 12.12 REARRANGING CONSEQUENTS
Source: O'Brien *et al.*, 1982.

- **timing** – the sooner a consequent follows a behaviour, the more powerful it will be;

- **consistency** – the more certain it is that a consequent will follow a behaviour, the more powerful it will be in controlling subsequent behaviour;

- **significance** – positively valued consequents exert greater effects than negative (i.e. punishing) consequents.

This means that the more a manager can ensure that the consequents of a behaviour are soon, certain and positive the more likely that behaviour will be repeated. Consequents that are late, uncertain and negative will have little, if any, effects on behaviour. For example, an employee may never follow certain safety procedures (antecedent) because he or she is consistently (certain) rewarded by an immediate (soon) time saving and extra production (positive). To ensure employees follow the correct procedures a manager must ensure that the consequents of following the correct procedures outweigh the consequents of behaving unsafely (*see* Cooper, 1998). Because social rewards are one of the most powerful consequents known to man, a manager might try to address this problem by harnessing peer pressure and give immediate positive feedback (e.g. praise) to those who behave safely. In addition, senior management would also need to accept that productivity might not be as high. Many managers have great difficulty with this idea, even though just one accident could cost the company far more money than that gained from any extra productivity. For example, the HSE (1993) estimated that only £1 out of every £11 of accident costs were recoverable from insurance. Figure 12.13 outlines how an intervention utilising OBM techniques increased the safety performance of employees in an American farm machinery manufacturers.

A farm machinery manufacturing plant had been experiencing three times as many accidents as its competitors. The company management sought a motivational programme to rectify the situation, that did not involve the use of monetary bonuses, safety prizes or disciplinary actions. They contacted licensed psychologists at their local university, who analysed the company's accident records for the previous five years. This revealed that 95 per cent of all accidents had occurred in 11 shopfloor departments. Based on recently-developed company safety manuals, the psychologists devised behavioural observation checklists for each of the 11 departments.

Employees were observed at their place of work for 15–20 seconds by the psychologists three or four times a week to establish the current baseline level of safe behaviour. This continued for 14 weeks. After the baseline had been established, employees were provided with safety training. Their behaviour was monitored for a further 10 weeks, during which their safety behaviour improved from an average of 62 per cent to 71 per cent. Subsequently, further training sessions were held, whereby employees were given specific safety performance goals. After a further 16 weeks, safety behaviour improved from an average of 71 per cent to 78 per cent. Employees attended further training sessions where the goals were restated, and employees were informed that the results of the weekly observations would be posted on departmental feedback charts.

After 12 weeks dramatic improvements were demonstrated. Safety performance had leapt from 78 per cent to 95 per cent, due to the provision of regular performance feedback (consequent) during this period. The lost time accident rate also decreased from 21.2 to 9.88 during the study period. Thus, OBM techniques were proven to be successful for motivating safety behaviour improvements in the USA. Applications of OBM-type techniques in the UK have produced similar results (Cooper *et al.*, 1994; Duff *et al.*, 1993).

FIG 12.13 IMPROVING SAFETY BEHAVIOUR WITH OBM TECHNIQUES

Source: Reprinted by permission of *Academy of Management*. From 'The effects of training, goal-setting and knowledge of results on safe behaviour: a component analysis' by R A Reber and J A Wallin (27, pp 544–60, 1984).

Recent innovations

Primarily due to the work of Bandura (1977), more recent OBM applications have begun to incorporate the notion of social learning theory (SLT), whereby person, situational and behavioural variables interact to reciprocally determine people's behaviour. SLT incorporates many key notions, such as role modelling and self-efficacy, each of which may interact with each other. For example, a security guard does not need to directly experience an armed robbery to know that he or she should take certain precautions. People watch and learn from the experiences of others. In turn they develop expectations about what may happen from pursuing various courses of action, and how certain events can be avoided or achieved.

- **Role modelling** is a powerful motivational technique for influencing behaviour. In essence, role modelling research (e.g. Rakestraw and Weiss, 1981) has shown that people who watch a high-performing role model (e.g. a trainee salesperson watching a company's top salesperson) will imitate the role model's behaviour until it is thoroughly learnt. Thereafter, as the person gains experience, he or she becomes more confident and more motivated to perform at a much higher level. Ultimately, the trainee's performance will be better than the original role model (the old adage that the pupil becomes the teacher of the master illustrates the principle here). Simon and Werner (1996) demonstrated the superiority of behaviour modelling over self-paced and instructional learning with 160 novice computer users. Compared to the other training methods, trainees in the behaviour modelling condition learned significantly more than other trainees and did best when demonstrating the skills taught in a hands-on test.

- **Self-efficacy** is very close in meaning to the expectancy concept in expectancy theory, and is defined as 'how well one can execute courses of action required to deal with prospective situations' (Bandura, 1982). However, self-efficacy is broader in meaning as it encompasses the individual's estimates of their total capacity to perform in a given situation, and therefore reflects a person's degree of self-confidence. Much research has demonstrated very strong links between self-efficacy and a wide variety of work-related performance (Sadri and Robertson, 1993; Robertson and Sadri, 1993). This has shown that the more confident a person is in their abilities, the more likely they are to set high goals and be committed to them. In turn this results in high levels of performance (e.g. Locke et al., 1984).

Although recent innovations have included person factors, OBM basically represents the systematic and applied use of the idea that situations can determine the strength and direction of behaviour (motivation). Changes in the situation will bring about changes in behaviour. For many people, however, the most important aspect of the situation is the nature of the job they are required to do. For example, many manufacturing jobs involve closely supervised, machine-paced, repetitive tasks. Other jobs involve a great degree of autonomy and variety of work (e.g. university lecturers). The way that these type of job characteristics influence people's work-related behaviour and motivation is important. However, these issues are unlikely to be successfully addressed purely from an OBM perspective. It may also require job design changes.

Job characteristics

A large stream of research has shown that the design of jobs can have an enormous impact on motivation, behaviour, productivity and job satisfaction (*see* Wall and Martin, 1987). Two main steps have been taken in moves toward optimising the redesign of jobs. The first step has been concerned with broadening the scope of people's work to introduce greater task variety. This has generally taken the form of job enlargement or job rotation. Job enlargement strategies have generally combined two or more specialised jobs so that the worker is able to use a wider range of skills. Job rotation is thought to increase task variety by moving at regular intervals between different jobs. However, research has shown that these types of job redesign are inadequate. This is partly because these aspects have only been attempted horizontally at the same organisational levels, and partly because simply adding two boring repetitive mundane type jobs, or rotating people between them, is neither satisfying or motivating. As succinctly pointed out by Herzberg *et al.* (1959): 'Adding one Mickey Mouse job to another Mickey Mouse job, adds up to an enlarged Mickey Mouse job.' Recognition of these types of problems led to job enrichment schemes in attempts to make jobs more challenging rather than just more of the same. Job enrichment schemes add discretion and responsibility by vertically expanding the scope of a job while also providing some degree of autonomy.

One of the most widely known and influential attempts to link the situational characteristics of a job with motivation is Hackman and Oldham's (1975, 1976, 1980) job characteristics model (JCM). As illustrated in Fig 12.14, the JCM suggests that five job characteristics are important as they determine various aspects of employees' attitudes and behaviour.

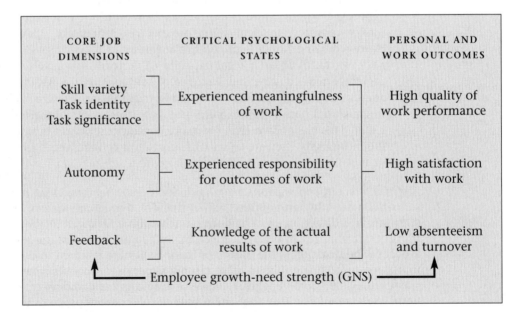

FIG 12.14 JOB CHARACTERISTICS MODEL

Source: Adapted from Hackman and Oldham. Copyright © 1975 by the American Psychological Association. Reprinted with permission.

According to the model, a highly motivating job will be designed to incorporate a high degree of each of the following job characteristics:

- **Skill variety** – the degree to which a job provides for the use of a number of different activities and skills.

- **Task identity** – the degree to which people complete a whole piece of work, rather than part of it.

- **Task significance** – the extent to which a job exerts a substantial influence on the lives or work of others.

- **Autonomy** – the extent of freedom and independence a job holder has to make his or her own decisions.

- **Feedback** – the extent to which the job itself provides feedback about the job holder's ongoing performance.

The theory proposes that skill variety, task identity and significance collectively influence the *experienced meaningfulness* (EM) of the work. Somebody low in EM is not likely to care much about the job, and will therefore be less likely to produce quality products or services. Similarly, autonomy is thought to affect an employee's *experienced responsibility* (ER), i.e. the extent to which the job holder feels personal responsibility for the outcomes. For example, a finance director with high ER will be concerned to deliver a quality service to suppliers by personally ensuring that his or her staff promptly process and pay invoices by the due date. Feedback is based on the notion of personal reward or reinforcement, because it provides ongoing personal knowledge of how the person is performing. As a whole, these characteristics are thought to be motivating if a person feels that they have been personally responsible for producing something worthwhile that he or she cares about. In essence, the JCM posits the notion that jobs which are more satisfying or motivating are those which are generally more productive. However, research has shown that the model best applies to individuals who have a strong need to grow and develop through the kind of work they do. For these kinds of people, improvements in the five core job characteristics will likely lead to greater productivity. However, people low in *growth need strength* (GNS) are much less likely to respond to such changes, perhaps because they do not feel that they can cope with more complex demands.

Figure 12.15 shows how the JCM can be used to adopt certain kinds of change principles to design jobs so as to influence each of the five core job dimensions.

Building on earlier models of job design, Hackman and Oldham (1975) suggest that tasks can be combined to enhance both skill variety and task identity. Task identity could also be further enhanced by forming natural work groups. Modern examples of this can be found in organisations that have introduced quality circles, or interdepartmental project teams within a matrix type organisational design (*see* Robertson *et al.*, 1992). Establishing client relations addresses people's social needs and is thought to enhance skill variety and the degree of autonomy, and to provide opportunities for feedback about their performance. TQM organisations embracing the notion of internal markets provide many opportunities to establish client relations for jobs where this has previously been very difficult. Vertical loading, similar

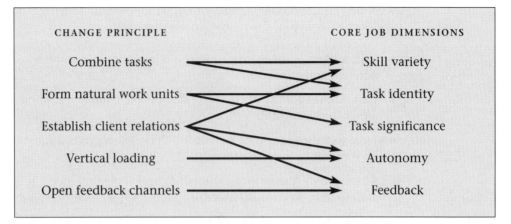

FIG 12.15 IDEAS FOR JOB ENRICHMENT

Source: Hackman and Oldham. Copyright © 1975 by the American Psychological Association. Reprinted with permission.

to job enrichment schemes, enhances people's autonomy as responsibility is pushed down the organisation, enabling people to make their own decisions. Indeed, this is one of the central features of TQM systems, which advocate that people should be given the responsibility and authority for identifying and solving quality problems. Multiple feedback and/or communication channels assist people to monitor their performance so that they can assess how well they are doing. As such, feedback fulfils many functions, not least of which is its motivational function. An example of an application of the JCM in a British food manufacturing company is presented in Fig 12.16.

The JCM model also provides a basis for measuring the motivational potential of individual jobs. Based on the major components of the JCM, Hackman and Oldham developed the job diagnostic survey (JDS) with which to assess the motivating potential of a job (*see* Fig 12.17).

The JDS is intended to be used to:

- **diagnose existing jobs to assist in job-redesign;**

- **evaluate the effects of job-redesign activities;**

- **evaluate the effects of job-redesign on people's motivation and job satisfaction.**

Scores for each job dimension range from one to seven, making a total score of 343 possible, although research suggests that the average score for most jobs is in the region of 150. Although Fig 12.17 shows that certain elements should be multiplied, Fried and Ferris (1987) have shown that simply adding the components together is just as good at identifying the motivational potential of people's jobs. Other approaches to the measurement of motivation at work and their uses are outlined in Robertson *et al* (1992).

Kemp *et al.* (1983) redesigned jobs to introduce more variety and autonomy in a UK food manufacturing company. Employees in the existing jobs had little control over their work, and had little input to the decision-making process, as most decisions were made by the supervisors. The jobs were re-designed into semi-autonomous work groups consisting of 8–12 employees. Each group was allocated and collectively responsible for eight different tasks within the production process. These tasks involved employees:

- allocating jobs among themselves;
- reaching performance targets and quality standards;
- recording production data;
- solving local production problems;
- ordering and collecting raw materials;
- delivering the finished product to the stores;
- selecting and training new recruits;
- managing their day-to-day activities.

Because the redesign process abolished the supervisory function, each of the teams reported directly to first-line managers.

Changes in the attitudes and behaviours of members of the redesigned jobs over a six-month period were compared to three control groups. Experimental groups reported an enhanced degree of autonomy and greater job satisfaction. Productivity also improved. A follow-up study two years later (Wall *et al.*, 1986) confirmed these findings.

FIG 12.16 THE EFFECTS OF JOB REDESIGN
Source: Kemp *et al.*, 1983.

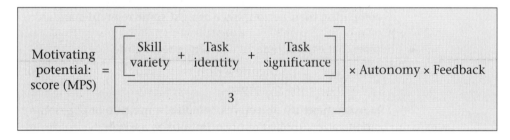

$$\text{Motivating potential score (MPS)} = \left[\frac{\text{Skill variety} + \text{Task identity} + \text{Task significance}}{3} \right] \times \text{Autonomy} \times \text{Feedback}$$

FIG 12.17 MOTIVATING: POTENTIAL FORMULA FOR THE JOB DIAGNOSTIC SURVEY
Source: Hackman and Oldham. Copyright © 1975 by the American Psychological Association. Reprinted with permission.

SUMMARY

■ The key to effective work performance lies in an understanding of human motivation. This chapter has covered motivational theories concerned with the internal person factors that motivate people, in terms of satisfying various needs. As such these have focused on what motivates people. Other theories have been outlined that concentrate on how people can be motivated, by clarifying the behavioural links between effort, performance and outcomes. In addition, motivational theories concerned with the impact of situational factors on motivation have been discussed. As this chapter has tried to make clear there is no one best way to motivate others. Managers must take account of the reciprocally determined relationships between situations, psychological variables and people's behaviour. In practice, therefore, managers are well-advised to use a combination of approaches that best suit the circumstances.

■ Nonetheless, three elements appear to be common to all of the motivational approaches previously discussed: setting targets, monitoring performance and providing feedback. These elements are implicit in some of the motivational theories and explicit in others. Theories that implicitly recognise target setting as the motivator for action include:

  – **Maslow's hierarchical model** – whereby the satisfaction of a particular level of need is the target, prior to the next need level in the hierarchy becoming dominant.

  – **McClelland's 'managerial needs model'** – the concept of need for achievement is concerned with the frequency of behaviour in setting and attaining targets, albeit moderated by the person's need for power or affiliation.

  – **Organisational behaviour modification** – this model focuses on the notion of reinforcers to motivate people to attain certain performance standards, in other words 'targets'.

  – **Job characteristics model** – job design and job enrichment schemes are concerned with increasing people's sense of achievement and providing employee's with a sense of personal responsibility for their work. In order for people to know whether or not they have achieved something, they must be comparing their performance against some referent standard (i.e. targets).

■ Theories that explicitly recognise target setting include:

  – **Expectancy type theories**, with their emphasis upon the link between effort, performance and outcomes.

  – **Management by objectives**, which is a mixture of goal-setting and behaviour modification applied to organisations as a whole.

  – **Goal-setting theory**.

■ Knowledge about the achievement of performance standards (targets) requires the monitoring and tracking of performance to provide feedback. Performance feedback is vital if the people concerned are to know where they are in relation to the targets. Most of the theories of motivation that have been discussed explicitly recognise the importance of feedback. They include behaviour modification, goal-setting theory, job design theory and job enrichment programmes. Feedback is also implicitly recognised as important in both need and expectancy theories. If targets are set then it follows that some mechanism must be available to let people know if the targets have been attained. However, managers implementing these motivational strategies need to recognise that the effectiveness of these three basic principles can be moderated by other factors such as:

1 Individual differences in the strength of various needs.

2 The degree of employee involvement in decision making.

3 Organisational variables such as the structure of the organisation in hierarchical terms, the types of control systems and technology used, and the views of human behaviour held by those who manage the organisation.

■ The importance of these moderating factors cannot be underestimated, and may be addressed by ensuring that the characteristics of a motivating environment are in place. The following characteristics are derived from the main motivational elements common to all the theories discussed in this chapter and include ensuring that:

1 Employees have a realistic understanding of the links between effort and performance.

2 Performance requirements are expressed in terms of specific, hard, but attainable targets.

3 Employees participate in the process of setting targets.

4 Feedback to employees is regular, informative and easy to interpret.

5 Rewards (including pay) are seen as equitable and are tailored to individual requirements and preferences.

6 Jobs are designed, where possible, to maximise skill variety, task identity and significance, autonomy and feedback, and to provide opportunities for learning and growth.

■ The motivation of employees is a major concern for all managers. However, it is no easy responsibility and there are no easy answers. Individuals are motivated by different things, depending on the situation they find themselves in. This can considerably complicate matters. Nonetheless, the presence of the above motivating characteristics will allow managers to make a great deal of progress in motivating employees for the good of the organisation.

REVIEW AND DISCUSSION QUESTIONS

1 What motivates people at work?

2 What factors affect people's motivation?

3 Describe the controlling factors that cause people to behave in the ways they do.

4 What factors are important for goal-setting to work?

5 How do expectancies influence performance outcomes?

6 In what ways could you measure a person's motivation?

7 What are the practical implications of need theories?

8 In what way are behaviourist and expectancy theories linked?

9 What are the common factors that link self-efficacy, expectancy and need for achievement?

10 How is people's motivation affected by the type of job they do?

CASE STUDY: JAPANESE BANKS' LOCAL FEEL   **FT**

Japanese banks have been used to running their foreign operations from Tokyo and have been slower than their counterparts in manufacturing to cede control to local staff. Now they are under pressure to undertake more local recruitment. The motivation for many is to cut costs, rather than to improve international perspective: expensive expatriates are being replaced with non-Japanese staff and managers. The strategy is creating tensions within some organisations. As many decisions are still made in Tokyo, the language and cultural barriers have been hard to break for non-Japanese.

Japanese institutions still emphasise consensus. Nemawashi, the behind-the-scenes sounding out of issues, and ringi, the official consensus-building process usually accomplished through internal memos in Japanese, are still important. Managers who do not speak Japanese have little means of communicating with counterparts in Tokyo and have been left out of the decision-making process. While this is frustrating for non-Japanese managers, Japanese staff have also found the situation stressful. 'We end up taking on those deals and work which belong to other managers,' says one middle manager at a bank in the City of London.

The Japanese are feeling squeezed between Tokyo and the non-Japanese staff. Some Japanese banks in the City are now circulating ringi memos in English. Yutaka Kitamura at Sanwa Bank's London branch says the proportion of paperwork in English has increased greatly. A few banks are trying to take the process forward. 'We want to compete against other European banks and for that we need local specialists,' says Shunichi Okuyama, managing director of Sumitomo Bank in London. The bank's financial products and loan divisions are staffed by non-Japanese officials.

The bank also surprised other Japanese institutions by transferring a team of UK managers to Hong Kong three years ago: it was the first time a Japanese institution had moved a non-Asian manager into the region. For local empowerment really to take effect, however, regional decision-making bodies need to be set up outside Tokyo. Divisions overseeing loans, budgets, strategy and auditing that can be shifted out of head office should be, says Okuyama. In the US Sumitomo has an American head office making business decisions in the region.

Fuji Bank too is trying to accelerate local control. The bank is working on an international personnel system with a full benefit and pensions scheme for non-Japanese staff. With Japanese clients now accounting for just a fifth of all business, Fuji must become a truly European bank, says Akio Takeuchi, general manager of

Fuji in London. To do so, it must keep qualified specialists who demand high salaries and are wooed from other institutions: 'For us localisation is no longer a cheap alternative.'

In spite of all their efforts, Japanese banks are a long way behind their US and European counterparts, say Japanese banking executives in the City. As one London-based Japanese banker comments: 'We see European banks which have their eyes set on the world bringing in international executives as board members and changing their internal official language to English. This is something the bank executives in Tokyo do not seem to realise.' ∎

Source: *Financial Times*, 29 January 1997. Reprinted with permission.

Note: This chapter was originally based on a paper presented by Robertson, I T & Cooper, M D (1992) *Motivation: Evolution or Revolution*. IPM National Conference, 'Investing in People': Harrogate, UK, 28 October.

REFERENCES AND FURTHER READING

Adams, J S (1965) 'Inequity in social exchange', in L Berkowitz (ed), *Advances in Experimental Social Psychology*, Vol 2, New York: Academic Press, pp 267–99.

Alderfer, C P (1969) 'An empirical test of a new theory of human needs', *Organisational Behaviour and Human Performance*, 4, 142–75.

Andrasik, F, Heimberg, J S and McNamara, J R (1981) *Behaviour Modification of Work and Work-Related Problems*, New York: Academic Press.

Arvey, R D, Bouchard, T J, Segal, N L and Abraham, L N (1989) 'Job satisfaction: environmental and genetic components', *Journal of Applied Psychology*, 74, 187–92.

Arvey, R D, Carter, G W and Buerkley, D K (1991) 'Job satisfaction: dispositional and situational influences', in C L Cooper and I T Robertson (eds) *International Review of Industrial and Organisational Psychology*, Vol 6, Wiley: Chichester.

Balcazar, F, Hopkins, B L and Suarez, Y (1986) 'A critical objective review of performance feedback', *Journal of Organisational Behaviour Management*, 7, 65–89.

Balliod, J and Semmer, N (1994) 'Turnover and patterns of job change among computer specialists', *Zeitschrift fur Arbeits und Organisations Psychologie*, 38, 152–63 (in German).

Bandura, A (1977) *Social Learning Theory*, Engelwood Cliffs, NJ: Prentice-Hall.

Bandura, A (1982) 'Self-efficacy mechanism in human agency', *American Psychologist*, 37, 122–47.

Bandura, A (1986) *Social Foundations of Thought and Action: A Social-Cognitive Theory*, Upper Saddle River, NJ: Prentice-Hall.

Barrick, M R and Mount, M K (1993) 'Autonomy as a moderator of the relationships between the big five personality dimensions and job performance', *Journal of Applied Psychology*, 78, 111–18.

Bower, D (1996) 'Higher aspirations only grow from strong roots', *People Management*, 8 August.

Caldwell, D F and O'Reilly, C A (1990) 'Measuring person–job fit with a profile-comparison process', *Journal of Applied Psychology*, 75, 648–57.

Clegg, C W and Wall, T D (1990) 'The relationship between simplified jobs and mental health: a replication study', *Journal of Occupational Psychology*, 63, 289–96.

Cooper, M D (1992) *An examination of assigned and participative goal-setting in relation to the improvement of safety in the construction industry*. Unpublished PhD thesis, School of Management, UMIST.

Cooper, M D (1998) *Improving Safety Culture: A Practical Guide*, J Wiley & Sons: Chichester.

Cooper, M D and Robertson, I T (1995) *The Psychology of Personnel Selection: A Quality Approach*, The Essential Business Psychology Series (C Fletcher, ed), London: Routledge.

Cooper, M D, Phillips, R A, Sutherland, V J and Makin, P J (1994) 'Reducing accidents using goal-setting and feedback: a field study', *Journal of Occupational and Organisational Psychology*, 67, 219–40.

Cooper, M D, Robertson, I T, Duff, A R and Phillips, R A (1992) *Assigned or Participative Goals: Do They Make a Difference?* British Psychological Society, Annual Occupational Psychology Conference, Liverpool, 3–5 January.

Duff, A R, Robertson, I T, Cooper, M D and Phillips, R A (1993) *Improving Safety on Construction Sites by Changing Personnel Behaviour*, HMSO Report Series CRR51/93, London: HMSO.

Erez, M and Zidon, I (1984) 'Effect of goal-acceptance on the relationship of goal-difficulty to performance', *Journal of Applied Psychology*, 69, 69–78.

Erez, M, Earley P C and Hulin, C L (1985) 'The impact of participation on goal-acceptance and performance: a two-step model', *Academy of Management Journal*, 28, 50–66.

Fried, Y and Ferris, G R (1987) 'The validity of the job characteristics model: a review and meta-analysis', *Personnel Psychology*, 40, 287–322.

Gerhart, B (1987) 'How important are dispositional factors as determinants of job satisfaction? Implications for job design and other personnel programs', *Journal of Applied Psychology*, 72, 366–73.

Hackman, J R and Oldham, G R (1975) 'Development of the job diagnostic survey', *Journal of Applied Psychology*, 60, 159–70.

Hackman, J R and Oldham, G R (1976) 'Motivation through the design of work: test of a theory', *Organisational Behaviour and Human Performance*, 16, 250–79.

Hackman, J R and Oldham, G R (1980) *Work Redesign*, New York: Addison-Wesley.

Hall, D T and Nougaim, K E (1968) 'An examination of Maslow's need hierarchy in an organisational setting', *Organisational Behaviour and Human Performance*, 3, 12–35.

Health and Safety Executive (1993) *The Costs of Accidents at Work*, London: HMSO.

Heckhausen, H and Kuhl, J (1985) 'From wishes to action: the dead ends and short cuts on the long way to action', in M Frese and J Sabini (eds) *Goal-Directed Behaviour: The Concept of Action in Psychology*, Hillsdale, NJ: Lawrence Erlbaum Associates.

Heckhausen, H, Schmalt, H D and Schneider, K (1985) *Achievement Motivation in Perspective*, New York: Academic Press.

Herzberg, F, Mausner, B and Syndorman, B B (1959) *The Motivation to Work*, New York: Wiley.

Kanfer, R (1992) 'Work motivation: new directions in theory and research', in C L Cooper and I T Robertson (eds) *International Review of Industrial and Organisational Psychology*, Vol 7, Wiley: Chichester.

Kemp, N J, Wall, T D, Clegg, C W and Cordery, J L (1983) 'Autonomous work groups in a greenfield site: a comparative study', *Journal of Occupational Psychology*, 56, 271–88.

Kleinbeck, V W E, Quast, H H, Thierry, H and Hackor, H (eds) (1990) *Work Motivation*, Hillside, NJ: Lawrence Erlbaum Associates.

Kohn, M L and Schooler, C (1982) 'Job conditions and personality: a longitudinal assessment of their reciprocal effects', *American Journal of Sociology*, 87, 1257–86.

Latham, G P, Erez, M and Locke, E A (1988) 'Resolving scientific disputes by the joint design of crucial experiments by the antagonists: application of the dispute regarding participation in goal-setting', *Journal of Applied Psychology*, 73, 753–72.

Levin, I and Stokes, J P (1989) 'Dispositional approach to job satisfaction: role of negative affectivity', *Journal of Applied Psychology*, 74, 752–8.

Locke, E A and Latham, G P (1990) *A Theory of Goal-setting and Task Performance*, Prentice-Hall.

Locke, E A, Frederick, E, Buckner, E and Bobko, P (1984) 'Effect of self-efficacy, goals, and task strategies on task performance', *Journal of Applied Psychology*, 69, 241–51.

Locke, E A, Shaw, K M, Saari, L M and Latham, G P (1981) 'Goal-setting and task performance: 1969–1980', *Psychological Bulletin*, 90, 125–52.

Luthans, F and Krietner, R (1975) *Organisational Behaviour Modification*, Glenview, IL: Scott, Foresman.

Luthans, F and Martinko, M (1987) 'Behavioural approaches to organisations', in C L Cooper and I T Robertson (eds) *International Review of Industrial and Organisational Psychology*, Vol 2, Wiley: Chichester.

McClelland, D C (1961) *The Achieving Society*, Princeton, NJ: Van Nostrand.

Maslow, A H (1942) 'A theory of human motivation', *Psychological Review*, 50, 370–96.

Matsui, T, Okada, A and Kakuyama, T (1982) 'Influence of achievement need on goal-setting, performance and feedback effectiveness', *Journal of Applied Psychology*, 67, 645–8.

Medcof, J W and Hausdorf, P A (1995) 'Instruments to measure opportunities to satisfy needs, and degree of satisfaction of needs, in the workplace', *Journal of Occupational and Organisational Psychology*, 68, 193–208.

Mortimer, J T, Lorence, J P and Kumka, D S (1986) *Work, Family and Personality: Transition to adulthood*. Hove, UK: LEA ltd.

Nadler, D A and Lawler, E E (1979) 'Motivation: a dianostic approach', in R M Steers and L W Porter (eds) *Motivation and Work Behaviour*, 2nd edn, New York: McGraw-Hill.

O'Brien, R M, Dickson, A M and Rosow, M P (eds) (1982) *Industrial Behaviour Modification: A Learning-based Approach to Industrial Organisational Problems*, New York: Pergamon Press.

Orpen, C (1994) 'Interactive effects of work motivation and personal control on employee job performance and satisfaction', *Journal of Social Psychology*, 134(6), 855–6.

Pritchard, R D, Jones, S D, Roth, P L, Stuebing, K K and Ekeberg, S E (1988) 'Effects of group feedback, goal-setting, and incentives on organisational productivity', *Journal of Applied Psychology*, 73, 337–58.

Pinder, C C (1984) *Work Motivation*, Glenview, IL: Scott, Foresman.

Rakestraw, T L and Weiss, H M (1981) 'The interaction of social influences and task experience on goals, performance, and performance satisfaction', *Organisational Behaviour and Human Performance*, 27, 326–44.

Reber, R A and Wallin, J A (1984) 'The effects of training, goal-setting and knowledge of results on safe behaviour: a component analysis', *Academy of Management Journal*, 27, 544–60.

Robertson, I T and Sadri, G (1993) 'Managerial self-efficacy and managerial performance', *British Journal of Management*, 4, 37–45.

Robertson, I T, Smith, J M and Cooper, M D (1992) *Motivation: Strategies, Theory and Practice*, London: IPM.

Roethlisberger, F J and Dickson, W J (1939) *Management and the Worker*, Cambridge, MA: Harvard University Press.

Sadri, G and Robertson, I T (1993) 'Self-efficacy and work-related behaviour: a review and meta-analyses', *Applied Psychology: An International Review*, 42, 139–52.

Simon, S J and Werner, J M (1996) 'Computer training through behaviour modelling, self-paced, and instructional approaches: a field experiment', *Journal of Applied Psychology*, 81(6), 648–59.

Stadler, R (1994) *Berufliche Veranderungen bei Computerfachleuten (Job Changes among Computer Specialists)*, unpublished masters thesis, University of Bern, Dept of Psychology.

Stahl, M J (1983) 'Achievement, power and managerial motivation: selecting managerial talent with the job choice exercise', *Personnel Psychology*, 36, 775–89.

Staw, B M and Ross, J (1985) 'Stability in the midst of change: a dispositional approach to job attitudes', *Journal of Applied Psychology*, 70, 469–80.

Vroom, V H (1964) *Work and Motivation*, New York: J Wiley.

Wahba, M A and Bridwell, L G (1979) 'Maslow reconsidered: a review of research on the need hierarchy theory', in R M Steers and L W Porter (eds) *Motivation and Work Behaviour*, 2nd edn, New York: McGraw-Hill.

Wall, T D and Martin, R (1987) 'Job and work design', in C L Cooper and I T Robertson (eds) *International Review of Industrial and Organisational Psychology*, Vol 2, Chichester: Wiley.

Wall, T D, Kemp, N J, Jackson, P R and Clegg, C W (1986) 'An outcome evaluation of autonomous working groups: a long-term field experiment', *Academy of Management Journal*, 29, 280–304.

Wood, R E, Mento, A J and Locke, E A (1987) 'Task complexity as a moderator of goal-effects: a meta-analysis', *Journal of Applied Psychology*, 72, 416–25.

Wooldridge, E (1995) 'Time to stand Maslow's hierarchy on its head?', *People Management*, 21 December.

CONTROLLING

MANAGEMENT DECISION MAKING

Mik Wisniewski

OBJECTIVES

The objectives of this chapter are to create an understanding of:

◆ the different types of management decision

◆ the key elements of the decision-making process

◆ what is meant by a model in business

◆ some of the more common models useful to the business decision maker

INTRODUCTION

Today's environment for an effective manager in any organisation is increasingly difficult. No matter whether the manager is involved in a private sector company, a public sector organisation or a non-profit organisation, his or her job has become increasingly difficult and complex. There are many contributory causes to this, of which Fig 13.1 illustrates some of the more obvious. All organisations must respond to a variety of pressures. Some of these may be internal to the organisation: the constant search for improved efficiency, for increased effectiveness and for the creation and strengthening of competitive advantage. Other factors may be largely external but generate pressure for change and decision making in their own right. These may include the following.

Increasing competition

In the private sector competition is becoming increasingly severe. Markets that were thought secure now look vulnerable to competition from other domestic companies, from the Pacific rim economies, from the emerging market economies of what was Eastern Europe. Managers must decide how best to respond to this competition: which markets to compete in (and which not to) and on what basis to

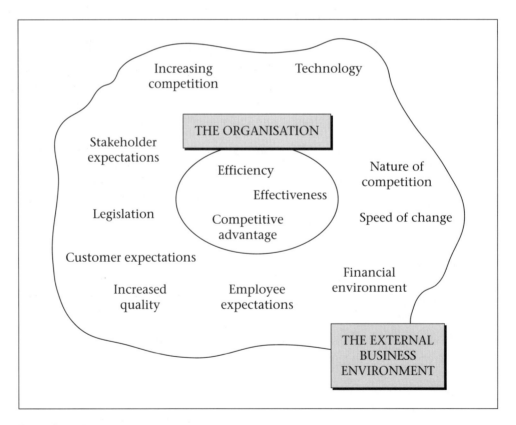

FIG 13.1 PRESSURES FOR CHANGE

compete – price, quality, customer service, availability. In the public sector competition is also increasingly becoming the norm. In local authorities more and more internal services must engage in competitive tendering with the private sector to win contracts. In the National Health Service providers must 'win' work from healthcare purchasers. Managers in these public sector organisations must take critical decisions on how to compete and in which areas.

Changing nature of competition

The way in which businesses compete is also rapidly changing. Organisations must constantly strive to offer 'better' products and services than their competitors. The problem, of course, is deciding what changes to the product or service will be most valued by customers. Should a company reduce its price in order to compete? Should it keep the price the same but offer extended features to the product or service? Similar problems face managers in the public sector.

Increasing focus on quality and customer satisfaction

Customers in both public and private sectors have increasingly higher expectations in terms of product and service quality. With increasing choice, customers are able to favour organisations which deliver 'quality' products and services. Managers must decide how best to respond to this pressure and how to overcome the many problems that prevent quality products and services from being delivered.

Financial environment

Financial markets today are global, with sources of investment funding and opportunities for savings and investment no longer limited to domestic financial organisations. Couple this with the fact that many capital investments for business will cost billions of pounds, and strategic alliances between different businesses – often competitors – become the norm. Consortia of organisations collaborate on ventures such as the Channel Tunnel and the development of new aerospace technology, and multi-agency initiatives are commonplace in the public sector where no one organisation has the resources to develop an initiative single-handed. Decisions are required on who to form such alliances with and the detailed nature of such co-operative ventures.

Technology

Rapid technological change creates both opportunities and problems for managers. Technology can offer the potential for improved efficiency and related cost savings and the creation of real competitive advantage. However, an organisation needs to ensure that it invests in the 'right' technology. A few years – or in some cases, months – later and the business might find its technological investment outdated and inappropriate.

Rate of change

As if these pressures were not problem enough for a manager, the speed at which change is taking place is actually increasing (*see* Chapter 1). Changes in technology, working practices, legislation, the competitive environment and so on take place with alarming frequency. Technological products such as computers, personal CD players and mobile phones have a life span measured in months, not years, before they are overtaken by more technologically advanced products.

A simple business scenario will be used to illustrate some of the points in this chapter and the increasingly difficult task of management decision making. A company operates a number of medium-sized hotels throughout Scotland: in Glasgow, Edinburgh, Aviemore and a number of other key towns and cities. The structure of the company is typical of many. Each hotel in the group acts as a profit centre and has a manager who is responsible for the day-to-day running of that hotel, although many of the routine decisions may be delegated to other staff. The managing director (MD) of the company has the responsibility for longer-term decisions relating to the future of the business. Consider many of the factors that will influence the business environment in which the group operates. Some hotels in the group may well face increased competition for customers from other hotels, both in Edinburgh and perhaps other parts of Scotland, for the tourist part of the market. Customers are becoming more articulate and demanding in terms of the levels of customer service which hotels provide and the overall quality levels. Changing patterns of business and leisure both offer opportunities and create problems for the business. An increasing number of tourists visiting Scotland offer the potential for increased business, as does the increasing foreign trade in which Scottish industry is becoming involved.

Because of the extent and rate of the change pressures discussed earlier, managers in many organisations find they have to take an increasing number of decisions: some of these are relatively minor and deal with day-to-day problems that arise. The hotel manager, for example, has to take routine decisions about the quantity of fresh food to order each day. Too much and the hotel's costs will escalate. Too little and there are obvious problems in terms of serving meals to customers. Others are more complex and may well affect the long-term future and success of the organisation. The MD may feel that, with an increasing number of foreign tourists visiting Scotland, the company should undertake an advertising campaign in selected foreign newspapers to attract customers. However, if the wrong newspapers are used, in terms of market penetration, or the wrong countries are targeted, then the consequences could well be both adverse financial costs and lost business.

In a comparable development the consequences of these decisions take on increasing importance in terms of the future success of the organisation. Yet, at the same time as managers find themselves in a position of having to take more decisions, they also find that they have less and less time available in which to make a decision. That is, the timescale between recognising that a decision needs to be taken and having to make a decision to resolve a problem or capitalise on an opportunity is becoming ever shorter. This is illustrated in Fig 13.2. Managers are faced with taking decisions in situations of increasing complexity: there may be many different aspects to the situation that need to be carefully considered, decisions taken in one area may well have consequences for other areas of activity, there may be legal implications for certain decisions, there will certainly be financial implications, and so on. Additionally, with technological change the quantity of information available to managers steadily increases, making the task of deciding what is relevant and irrelevant more difficult. In the hotel group scenario a decision as to which countries in Europe to target as part of a promotional campaign might sound relatively

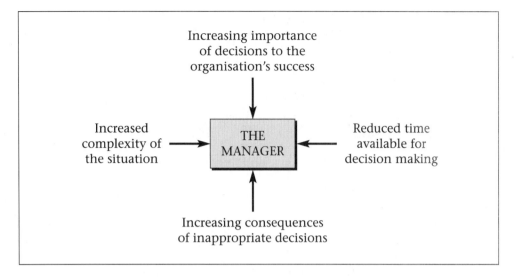

FIG 13.2 DECISION-MAKING PRESSURES

straightforward. However, such a decision has to be put into the context of evaluating information about population trends, income and spending patterns, leisure habits, travel patterns and the like in a number of different countries.

Decisions are also becoming increasingly important to organisational success. There are no such things as 'trivial' decisions in business any longer. Even apparently routine, day-to-day decisions may have longer-term consequences. Equally, the consequences of taking decisions which later turn out to be wrong or inappropriate became more significant. With many decisions having major financial consequences for an organisation, 'getting it wrong' might well send a company out of business. To compound these problems for the decision maker, the time available to evaluate alternatives, to research the problem and to ponder what decision should be taken is decreasing. Decisions typically must be taken in a much shorter timescale. One illustration of this relates to decisions of financial institutions in terms of buying and selling foreign currency via the financial markets. Exchange rates are particularly volatile and hesitation on the part of a key decision maker as to whether to buy or sell a particular currency and which currencies to deal in need to be taken in minutes.

It is hardly surprising that considerable attention has been given both to examining the nature and methods of management decision making and to tools and techniques which can assist the manager in the decision-making process. In the rest of this chapter we shall examine some of these in more detail.

TYPES OF DECISION

It will be worthwhile at this stage considering the different types of decision that managers face. There are many different ways in which we can categorise the types of decisions that managers take, and one of the more useful of these is shown in Fig 13.3. Although any such categorisation is to some extent artificial, it is possible to envisage three generic types of decision: at the operational, administrative and

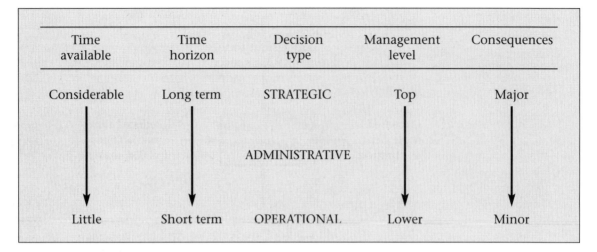

Time available	Time horizon	Decision type	Management level	Consequences
Considerable	Long term	STRATEGIC	Top	Major
		ADMINISTRATIVE		
Little	Short term	OPERATIONAL	Lower	Minor

FIG 13.3 DECISION TYPES

strategic levels. Naturally, the distinction between these types can be somewhat blurred at the edges – a series of apparently operational decisions, for example, could build into a strategic one. However, each type of decision is typically characterised by a number of features.

Operational decisions are typically routine, day-to-day decisions that will have little direct and immediate impact on the business as a whole and may well be repetitive, in the sense that such decisions have to be taken repeatedly, perhaps several times a year. Examples might be deciding how to deal with an individual customer's complaint, when to reorder office supplies and so on. Typically such decisions are governed primarily by predetermined 'rules' established by the organisation and will involve routine systems and procedures designed to help decision making. Thus there may be a formal procedure to follow in the case of a customer complaint or there may be preset guidelines as to when to reorder basic office supplies. Such decisions are typically taken by managers at the lower levels of the organisational hierarchy. Similarly on an individual basis the consequences of wrong or poor decisions will be minor (although a series of wrong decisions can build into major consequences). Managers typically have little time available in which to reach such a decision (and this is one of the reasons why predetermined procedures are in place) and are operating in a short-term time horizon.

At the other end of the spectrum there are what can be termed *strategic* decisions, which are more concerned with the achievement of corporate aims and objectives and long-term corporate plans. Strategic decisions may well involve determining which products/services to offer in the future and which to discontinue; which markets the organisation will compete in; on what basis the organisation will compete, and so on. Understandably such decisions tend to be taken by the top layer of management in an organisation and will benefit from lengthy consideration, simply because they have major consequences for the future success of the organisation. Unlike operational decisions strategic decisions cannot be taken by following a set procedure or a pre-established set of rules. Typically such decisions relate to situations that are more or less unique, or one-off, or where each situation needs to be considered on an individual basis.

In between these two types of decision we have what can be termed *administrative* decisions. Such decisions are typically concerned with establishing systems for control and organisation within the business, and may well relate to the administrative decisions that follow from key strategic decisions which will help establish systems and procedures to support the operational decision-making process.

To return to the hotel scenario. Strategic decisions may relate to the expansion of the chain of hotels the company owns. Clearly such a decision will be taken by senior managers in the organisation, it will have major consequences for the entire organisation (opening hotels in the wrong locations may lead to the company going out of business), and senior managers will take some considerable time (and analysis) before reaching such a decision. Such decisions will also typically be required relatively infrequently. Administrative decisions might then relate to the establishment of appropriate systems to ensure that the new hotel functions properly. Payroll and financial systems will need to be set up; supplies and logistics systems will be required, as will human resource systems and so on. Such administrative decisions are likely to be taken by middle managers in the organisation and, although they are critical to the successful running of the business, taking the wrong decision – about a particular supplier for example – is unlikely to send the company out of business. Operational decisions will then be required by front-line managers responsible for the smooth running of the hotel on a day-to-day basis. The relevant manager – or perhaps an individual employee if operational decisions have been delegated – will have to take decisions about ensuring the hotel bar is adequately stocked. Such decisions will be taken frequently (perhaps daily) and clearly will need to be taken quickly. Such operational decisions may well be based on earlier administrative decisions. An automated stock control system, for example, may be in place to assist in such operational decisions, perhaps by producing a daily report on yesterday's sales and today's stock levels.

Clearly not all decisions fit neatly into this – or any other – classification structure. Consider, for example, an organisation which is seeking to introduce an effective equal opportunities policy. Such a decision will have to be taken by top management and will have major consequences for the organisation. However, it cannot really be called a strategic decision in the business sense of the word. It is also evident that it is not a decision for which procedures or systems can be applied. While such a classification system does not do justice to the complexity and variety of many managerial decisions, it does provide a useful framework for the different types of decision, their implications and for the roles of the different types of manager in an organisation.

THE DECISION-MAKING PROCESS

It will also be helpful at this stage to develop an overview of what can be described as the decision-making process. Consider the hotel scenario described earlier. The manager of one of the hotels in the group has received a complaint from a guest that the morning newspaper requested has not been delivered. The manager has to decide what to do. While this may seem a relatively trivial decision problem – and one which is clearly operational in terms of our earlier framework – it will serve to illustrate the various stages of the decision-making process. One immediate decision that the manager should make is to apologise to the guest and try to rectify the immediate problem. This might solve the immediate – and obvious – problem, but it is not clear what has caused

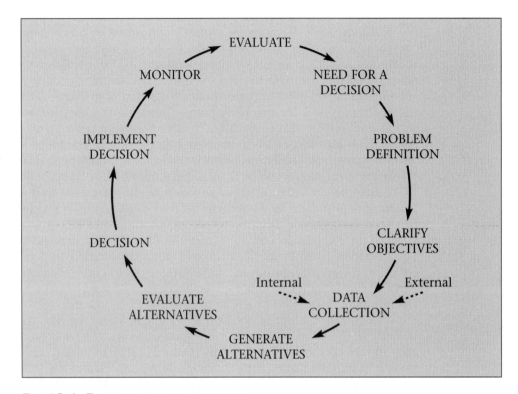

FIG 13.4 DECISION-MAKING PROCESS

the problem in the first place, nor whether the problem is likely to occur again in the future. There are various ways in which we can describe the process involved in decision making for this and any other decision situation. One of these is illustrated in Fig 13.4. (*see also* Chapter 4).

Need for a decision

It is possible to begin at the stage described as 'need for a decision'. At some stage it will become evident to a manager that a decision is required relating to a particular situation. Such a decision might relate to a problem or crisis at the operational level as in this case, or to dealing with a key strategic threat (a competitor lowering the price of their product, for example). It might also relate at a more strategic level to the realisation that an opportunity exists (for expansion, increased market share, enhanced competitive advantage). This stage seems a very obvious one, but implies that both the organisation and manager have formal and informal monitoring systems to assess performance and standards and scan for opportunities. In the hotel scenario the manager becomes aware of the need for a decision at a relatively late stage – when the customer complains. This by itself indicates that the organisation does not appear to have appropriate information systems in place to resolve such potential difficulties as they are happening or preferably before they can happen.

Problem definition

Once the decision recognition phase has occurred, then the problem definition phase is reached. The manager needs to ensure that a clear definition of the problem (or opportunity) is provided. Again, in the hotel context the problem appears to be that a customer did not receive their morning newspaper. But the manager needs to ensure a clear, concise and accurate definition of the situation is produced. Did the newspaper not arrive at all or did it arrive late? Was the wrong newspaper delivered rather than the one the customer requested? Have other customers complained of the same problem? Did this happen just today or has it happened in the past? The manager must develop an appropriate understanding of what exactly the problem is, its extent and scope.

Clarify objectives

With such a definition the manager can then develop appropriate decision objectives: what the decision (still to be taken) is intended to achieve. Clearly this in part will depend on the definition phase. A situation which has occurred only today with one customer will have very different decision objectives from one which has occurred repeatedly over the last month with a number of customers. The objectives phase is a particularly important one, however. The manager must be clear about what a particular decision, or set of related decisions, is to achieve. Without this clarification the manager will not be in a position in the future to determine whether a particular decision that was taken was effective or not.

Data collection

When the objectives have been clarified data must be collected about the problem. Again, this will depend on the scale of the decision situation. Such data may be collected from within the organisation or from external sources. For the hotel scenario management may collect data on the number of times this situation has arisen over the past month; whether the situation appears to occur at weekends or during the week; at times when the hotel is busy or when it is quiet; discussions might take place with both customers and staff to gain their perception of the scale and extent of the situation. Externally management may contact other hotels in the group to see if they experience a similar problem. Contact may also be made with the newsagent who supplies newspapers to the hotel to see what their records indicate in terms of the number of copies of different newspapers ordered and supplied. Equally the data collected may be 'hard' data – factual or numerical – or it may be 'soft' – opinions of customers and staff.

Generate alternatives

The manager must now try to generate alternative decisions in the context of the problem or options which could be designed to resolve a particular problem. Clearly much will depend on the situation itself. The generation of such alternatives or options may take place through formal problem analysis using a number of techniques and decision tools (some of which are introduced later in this chapter). Other situations may call for a more 'creative' approach, particularly when the situation is unstructured.

Evaluate alternatives

Once a number of alternatives or options have been generated, then the decision maker must evaluate these. Clearly this must be done in the context of the 'clarify objectives' phase, with alternatives evaluated in the context of how far they contribute to the achievement of the declared decision objectives. Other criteria will also be used: the financial implications of each alternative, the wider organisational implications, and so on.

Decision

The critical part of this process is then reached where a decision must now be made. Of the alternatives which have been generated and then evaluated, a choice must be made as to which is most preferable and feasible.

Implement and monitor

However, decision making is about more than simply making a decision. The decision once made must be implemented and change effected in the organisation. It is tempting to conclude that the decision-making process ends here. However, the circle of the process in Fig 13.4 has yet to be closed. Some sort of monitoring system – either formal or informal – must be established to monitor the impact of the decision taken on the situation. This assists in an evaluation of the decision taken at some later date. Not only does this assist the organisation in assessing whether decisions taken to resolve particular problems have been effective, but it also helps the manager learn through experience in terms of which decisions proved effective and which did not and the reasons for this effectiveness or lack of it.

MODELS IN THE DECISION PROCESS

While a manager may encounter difficulty at any of the stages in the decision-making process, two in particular are likely to be problematic: the generation of alternatives and the evaluation of those alternatives. In either of these stages a manager may wish to apply appropriate quantitative models or techniques. A model can best be understood as a representation, or simulation, of reality. Perhaps the most familiar use of models is in the fields of science and engineering. Architects often construct a model of a new building or construction project to help visualise what it will look like and to facilitate analysis of the construction process. An engineer may build a physical model of a new piece of engineering equipment – a new aircraft type, for example, or a new model of car. Such models help in the process of trying out new ideas and assessing the impact they will have on the building or piece of equipment, without the expense and risk involved in instituting such changes on the real building or piece of equipment. Models have an equally important role to play in business. Naturally in business such models are not physical, as they are for the engineer or architect, but typically mathematical or statistical. A number of common business models will be introduced in the rest of this chapter and their potential role in the decision-making process illustrated. Similarly, we shall introduce a small number of techniques used in decision making. Naturally, we can only illustrate how models and techniques can contribute to the decision-making process. The number of models and techniques available to the manager is considerable and we are able only to introduce a few of the more basic. The Further Reading section provides details of others (*see also* Chapter 6).

THE BREAKEVEN MODEL

One of the simplest models is the breakeven model. Consider the following scenario. One of the hotels in the group has realised that an increasing part of its business consists of being the venue for meetings and small conferences. Typically, an outside organisation will hire a number of the larger rooms in the hotel for a meeting, seminar or training and development programme. The hotel has had an increasing number of requests from the organisers of such events to provide sophisticated on-site photocopying facilities. Naturally, the event organisers expect to have to pay for such additional facilities, but as hotel manager you are trying to decide what to do. Clearly the option of providing such facilities is an attractive one, since it will satisfy a customer request and help contribute towards customer satisfaction and repeat business. However, there will clearly be financial consequences, and one of the key decisions would relate to how much to charge event organisers for the use of such facilities. The hotel manager has investigated the situation and collected some relevant data, and found that a local company will rent a suitable photocopier to the hotel on an annual basis for £600. This company is also willing to take responsibility for the running costs of the machine (consisting of the cost of paper and toner together with routine maintenance) for £40 per 1000 copies. To assist the manager the total cost to the hotel can be broken into two elements. One is fixed or constant, the £600 rental fee, while the other varies with the number of copies produced by the machine. Referring to these as fixed cost and variable cost respectively this gives:

Total cost = Fixed cost + Variable cost

TC = FC + VC

using FC to represent fixed cost and VC variable cost. Further, the two costs are readily quantified. FC is clearly £600, while VC will be 4p per copy (£40/1000). If the variable X is used to denote the number of copies made, then this gives:

$$TC = 600 + 0.04X$$

This equation allows the manager to determine the total cost incurred for any number of copies, X, produced by substituting a given numerical value for X in the equation and calculating the corresponding value for TC. It is often advantageous to show mathematical information graphically wherever possible (since a diagram usually conveys a much more immediate picture to a manager than does an equation). The graph corresponding to the TC equation is shown in Fig 13.5. The FC line is constant and parallel to the X axis on the graph, indicating that this cost element does not vary with the number of copies. The VC line starts from the origin (since variable costs will be zero when zero copies are produced) with a slope of 0.04 and reaches £800 when X is 20 000. The TC line, which is the combination of

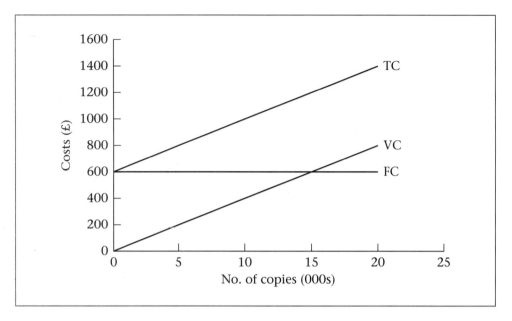

FIG 13.5 COSTS

FC and VC, starts from 600 and has the same slope as the VC line, reaching £1400 when X is 20 000.

However, this is only one side of the situation. Clearly the hotel expects to generate revenue from the use of the equipment. Assume that the manager believes a price of 10p per copy would be acceptable to event organisers. The manager is trying to assess how this would affect the financial implications of the decision under consideration. Denoting R as revenue from copies made, the revenue equation is then:

$$R = 0.10X$$

How does this help the manager decide what the financial effects of installing the photocopier will be? Examine Fig 13.6 which shows the TC equation together with the R equation. Both the total costs and revenue implications of the decision are clearly seen, based on the information given. If the photocopier is used to produce less than 10 000 copies a year then TC exceeds R, that is the total cost of providing this service exceeds the revenue that it generates. However, if the level of use exceeds 10 000 copies the revenue exceeds costs. The figure of 10 000 copies is referred to as the breakeven point, since it indicates the level of use which generates neither a profit nor a loss and shows where costs and revenue are equal.

Clearly, this model does not indicate to the manager what the appropriate decision should be. However, it does serve its purpose in generating information about options and alternatives to be used in the decision process. The manager must now decide, based on other information, whether it is likely that usage levels will be above the breakeven figure. If the view is that they will not, then the manager has to assess whether to provide the service anyway, add to the hotel's competitive advantage and accept the extra financial consequences of this decision. One of the benefits of the model is that the manager can readily quantify what the exact financial consequences of a particular decision would be.

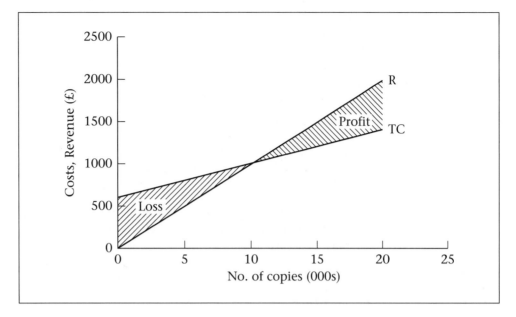

FIG 13.6 TOTAL COSTS AND REVENUE

Such models can play a potentially important role in the decision-making process. This is further illustrated if the model is developed further. The graph has been used so far to determine the breakeven point. With some simple algebra this value can be determined mathematically.

$$TC = 600 + 0.04X$$

$$R = 0.1X$$

By definition the breakeven point occurs where TC = R:

$$TC = 600 + 0.04X = 0.1X = R$$

or where $600 + 0.04X = 0.1X$

Rearranging gives:

$$600 = 0.1X - 0.04X \text{ or } 600 = 0.06X$$

and then:

$$X = 600/0.06 = 10\,000$$

However, this applies only to the specific values we have for FC, VC and price charged per copy. In general:

$$TC = a + bX$$
$$R = cX$$

where a, b, c would take the appropriate numerical values. The breakeven point will then be given by:

$$X = a/(c - b)$$

This provides a general solution to the breakeven problem and the manager can generate 'what if' analysis relating to the decision situation. What if the fixed cost rises to £750? What if price charged rises to 12p per copy? What if customers are only willing to pay 8p a copy? Such analysis allows a manager to investigate other possible options in the context of the decision situation. In the first instance, for example, the new breakeven position is readily calculated as:

$$X = 750/(0.1 - 0.04) = 750/0.06 = 12\,500$$

That is, a rise in the fixed cost element would have the effect of pushing the breakeven point up by 2500 copies a year. As with all such quantitative models, the results of the analysis do not provide the manager with a decision. What they do provide is additional information about the decision situation and the various alternatives that may be under consideration. They also provide an analytical framework for the manager to evaluate such alternatives. This is illustrated further with the second model we shall examine: the payoff table.

PAYOFF TABLES

It will be evident that one of the key characteristics of business decision making is that it takes place under considerable uncertainty. A manager must take a decision typically with incomplete knowledge about the situation or knowing that the future outcomes of decisions taken now are uncertain. There are ways of examining these decision problems that can help clarify how decisions can be made.

This will be illustrated with a second scenario. The hotel group is considering its future direction and strategy. It has decided that there is the potential for increasing the number of business people from abroad who use the group's hotel facilities in Scotland. In particular, it feels that concentrated advertising in selected markets in Europe would increase this type of business. What the group's managing director has in mind is an advertising campaign aimed at businesses which wish to develop commercial and industrial links with companies in Scotland. What the hotel will offer to these businesses is a special 'package' deal. It will arrange air travel for the foreign business person, a chauffeured executive car to collect them from the airport and take them to one of the group's hotels, and translation and interpretation facilities while they are in Scotland.

Three potential markets are currently under investigation; Scandinavia, Germany and Eastern Europe. The group has estimated that a suitable advertising campaign in each country (through TV, radio, the business press) would cost respectively:

Scandinavia	£150 000
Germany	£200 000
Eastern Europe	£300 000

The financial director has indicated that the group only has financial resources to fund one of these campaigns, and the critical decision is: which one? Naturally, the group expects a return for this expenditure through the increased business it attracts to its hotels. However, the situation is made difficult by the fact that the additional revenue generated will, in part, depend on the effectiveness of the campaign in each area. The group's marketing function has concluded that the overall

AREA	OUTCOME		
	Low	Medium	High
Scandinavia	175	225	250
Germany	150	300	350
Eastern Europe	100	250	600

FIG 13.7 FINANCIAL RETURNS FROM THE CAMPAIGN (£000s)

effect of the campaign in each of the three areas could be classed as: low, medium, high. For each possibility they have quantified the financial return the group could anticipate from each area in terms of increased business. This is summarised in Fig 13.7.

So, for example, if the group decides to campaign in Germany and the campaign has a low impact, then it is expected the campaign will generate an additional £150 000 of business for the group. On the other hand, if the campaign is focused on Scandinavia and the outcome is high, then £250 000 of additional business is expected.

This scenario is typical of many situations that organisations have to face. The group is faced with a range of decision alternatives over which it has control (it can choose between them), but it also faces uncertainty in terms of the impact of each of these alternatives. These future outcomes are referred to as 'states of nature': they are outside the direct control of the group. However, they do include all possible outcomes and only one of them can actually occur. How does the group decide what to do *now* given that it does not know the outcome from the campaign that will be achieved in the *future*? Figure 13.7 shows only one side of the situation. The cost of the campaign must also be taken into account. This can be achieved by constructing what is known as a payoff table, which shows the net effect of each possible decision and each outcome. Figure 13.8 shows the results where the campaign costs for each area have been subtracted from the expected returns shown in Fig 13.7.

AREA	OUTCOME		
	Low	Medium	High
Scandinavia	25	75	100
Germany	–50	100	150
Eastern Europe	–200	–50	300

FIG 13.8 CAMPAIGN PAYOFFS (£000s)

The payoff table can now be used to consider the attractiveness of alternative decisions. Clearly the decision taken will be influenced by a number of factors other than the payoff table: how reliable the information is about the alternative decisions, how risky the various options are, how critical the decision is to the company's future, and so on. One of the key factors, however, will depend on the organisation's attitude to these future states of nature. In the absence of any other information on the likelihood of each state of nature, we can consider a number of options.

The maximax criterion

Assume that the hotel group's senior managers take an optimistic view of the future outcome. If this were the case then they would choose the decision which generated the highest possible payoff, since they feel that the 'best' state of nature will occur. Such an approach is known as the maximax criterion since we are searching for the *max*imum of the *max*imum payoffs. In this problem the maximax decision would be to launch the campaign in Eastern Europe since this – potentially – generates the highest payoff at £300 000, compared with the best possible payoff of £150 000 for the German campaign and £100 000 for the Scandinavian. In general for this approach the maximum payoff for each decision is found and then the largest of these chosen. This approach has the advantage of focusing on the best possible outcome from the alternative decisions under consideration.

The maximin criterion

The maximax decision is based on an optimistic view of the future in terms of the states of nature that could occur. However, the group may take a different attitude and consider the worst-case scenario – a pessimistic view about future outcomes. In such a situation the maximin criterion can be applied: the *max*imum of the *min*imum payoffs. The basic logic is to find the best decision given the assumption that the worst possible future outcome will occur. For each alternative decision the minimum (worst) payoff is found and then the largest of these chosen to find the most desirable decision. In this case this would lead to a decision to launch the campaign in Scandinavia since this is the largest of the minimum payoffs at £25 000 (the minimum payoffs being 25 000, –50 000 and –200 000 respectively). Such an approach ensures that management has taken the best decision if the worst outcome happens. However, it is also evident that the approach ignores the potentially larger payoffs from other decisions.

The minimax regret criterion

A third approach uses the concept of opportunity loss or regret. Assume the decision is taken to launch the campaign in Scandinavia. Having committed itself to this course of action, management later observes that the impact of the campaign was high. With hindsight management realises that the decision taken was not the best given the state of nature that actually occurred (even though when it took the decision it had no way of knowing which state of nature would prevail). The optimal decision for this state of nature would have been to campaign in Eastern Europe since this has a higher payoff given this state of nature. Effectively the group has 'lost' £200 000 by taking the decision to launch in Scandinavia. This figure is referred to as the opportunity cost – or regret – of the decision for that state of nature. The opportunity loss, or regret, associated with each possible decision and the various states of nature can be calculated using the same logic. This is summarised in Fig 13.9.

Each column (state of nature) in the payoff table is considered in turn and it is determined, for that state of nature, what the optimum decision would be. So, if the campaign impact was low the optimum decision would be to campaign in Scandinavia. If this decision had actually been taken the 'regret' in financial terms would be zero, since it was the best decision given this state of nature. On the other hand, if it had been decided to campaign in Germany the regret would be £75 000, since a payoff of £25 000 could have been achieved whereas the decision actually incurred a loss of £50 000. Similarly, if the decision had been to campaign in Eastern Europe the regret would be £225 000. These calculations can be performed for the other two states of nature columns. This process can be repeated for each outcome in turn, producing the data in Fig 13.9.

	OUTCOME		
AREA	Low	Medium	High
Scandinavia	0	25	200
Germany	75	0	150
Eastern Europe	225	150	0

FIG 13.9 REGRET (£000s)

For each of the decision options the maximum of these regret values is then obtained: £200 000 for Scandinavia, £150 000 for Germany, £225 000 for Eastern Europe. Each decision is considered in turn and the maximum regret value shows the maximum opportunity cost associated with this decision on the assumption that the worst state of nature happens. Management would then wish to take the decision where this maximum regret was minimised. This would be the decision to campaign in Germany, since this has the lowest maximum regret at £150 000. The basic logic of the approach is to say: how much does the group stand to 'lose' from each decision if that decision turns out to be the wrong one? Management then chooses the decision where this potential 'loss' is minimised.

It is worth noting that in this scenario the three different approaches have led to three different decisions, with the decision taken depending on the decision maker's view of the future. One of the benefits of this approach is that it requires the decision maker to consider and justify explicitly their view of future states of nature. One of its main drawbacks is that the three states of nature have been treated as being equally likely. Management needs to be able to incorporate such likelihood information into the decision-making process, which can be achieved by introducing the concept of expected value.

EXPECTED VALUE

It is clear that management is currently assuming that the three outcomes from the campaign are equally likely. This will not necessarily be a realistic assumption. Based on further analysis, market research or simply personal intuition and experience, management might feel that some of the outcomes are more likely than others. If this is the case, and such likelihoods can be quantified, then management will clearly want to take this extra factor into account when trying to reach an appropriate decision. Assume that the group has been able to quantify such likelihoods, referred to as probabilities, as shown in Fig 13.10.

It can be seen that the probabilities of each outcome for Scandinavia and Germany are the same, but different from those for Eastern Europe. By convention a probability is shown as a value between 0 and 1, with 0 indicating something which can never happen and 1 indicating that it is certain to happen. For example, the Low outcome has a probability of 0.2 for Scandinavia and for Germany: there is a 20 per cent chance that this is the outcome that will occur, compared with 40 per cent for Medium and 40 per cent for High. For Eastern Europe, however, the probability of Low is higher (that is, this outcome is more likely to occur) at 50 per cent. Note that the total of the probabilities for each area individually total to 1: one of the three outcomes must occur.

Clearly management now needs to be able to use this additional information to help it reach a decision. The approach taken is to calculate the *expected value* for each of the alternative decisions. Consider the decision to campaign in Scandinavia. For this decision there are three possible states of nature, each with a payoff, and for each state of nature there is now a probability. It seems reasonable to use these probabilities to calculate a weighted average outcome for this decision. That is:

$$(£25\ 000 \times 0.2) + (£75\ 000 \times 0.4) + (£100\ 000 \times 0.4)$$

That is, if we campaign in Scandinavia there is a 20 per cent chance of a £25 000 payoff, a 40 per cent chance of a £75 000 payoff and a 40 per cent chance of a £100 000 payoff. The calculation gives a figure of £75 000 as the expected value (EV) of this decision: the alternative payoffs weighted by the respective

AREA	OUTCOME		
	Low	Medium	High
Scandinavia	0.2	0.4	0.4
Germany	0.2	0.4	0.4
Eastern Europe	0.5	0.2	0.3

FIG 13.10 PROBABILITY OF OUTCOMES

probabilities. Care needs to be taken in terms of what the EV represents. It is not a guaranteed payoff from this decision. Rather it is a measure taking into account both the payoffs and their likelihood. The purpose of such EVs is to facilitate comparison between alternative decisions under such conditions of uncertainty. The EVs for the three alternative decisions are:

Scandinavia	£75 000
Germany	£90 000
Eastern Europe	–£40 000

Based on this information it would be logical to recommend that the campaign is launched in Germany since it has a higher EV. Note that the option for Eastern Europe actually has a negative EV: its weighted payoff indicates a loss rather than a profit. Once again it must be stressed that taking a decision on such a basis does not guarantee a positive payoff to the group. The state of nature that actually occurs in Germany could generate a payoff of –£50 000, £100 000 or £150 000. Overall, however, the German option is to be favoured since the weighted combination of payoffs and probabilities is higher than that for the other two options.

DECISION TREES

It is also possible to examine this type of decision situation by constructing a decision tree which shows the relationship over time between decisions, outcomes, payoffs and probabilities (*see also* Chapter 2). The tree diagram for this problem is shown in Fig 13.11. The tree starts on the left. The box symbol (known as a decision node) is used to denote that at this point a decision must be taken and the alternative decisions faced branch out from this node: to campaign in Scandinavia (S), Germany (G) or Eastern Europe (E). Each of these branches leads to an outcome node (represented by a circle) showing the states of nature: future outcomes from the decisions over which the decision maker has no control. In this example the node along each decision branch is the same: the campaign impact could turn out to be low (L), medium (M) or high (H). At the end of each branch there is a payoff: a total of nine possible payoffs of this problem. Information is then added on the payoffs, the probability of each outcome and the EVs of each decision branch. The decision maker now sees clearly the potential payoffs from each decision and state of nature combination. Also the EVs for each decision can be identified and used to assist in the decision-making process, as we have discussed.

Decision trees are useful ways of showing the outcomes and potential consequences of alternative decisions. They are also particularly useful in situations where a series of decisions may need to be taken over time and where subsequent decision options may depend on future outcomes. Consider an expansion of the existing scenario. One of the members of the group's board is still not convinced that the Eastern Europe option should be ruled out at this stage, particularly given that potentially it offers the largest payoff of the three (at £300 000). The director believes that if the company chooses this option for its promotion campaign and if the impact of that campaign is either low or medium in the future (leading to a negative payoff), then there is the possibility of a supplementary advertising campaign to try to boost business further. Some additional research has been conducted into this. If, six months after the initial campaign in Eastern Europe, the

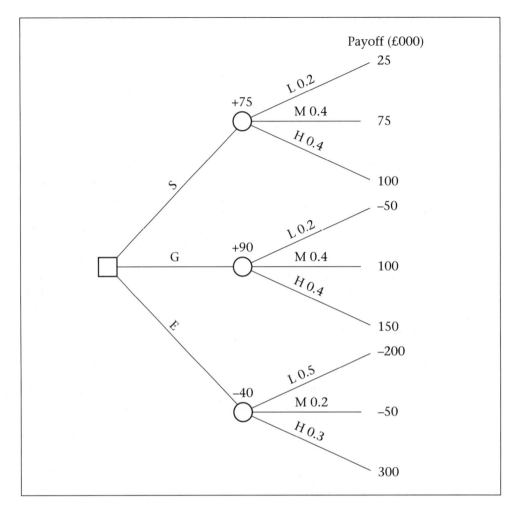

Payoff (£000)

FIG 13.11 DECISION TREE

impact turns out to be low or medium, then a supplementary campaign can be conducted at an additional cost of £100 000. If the initial impact is Low then it is felt that this additional campaign has a probability of 0.3 of increasing the payoff by £300 000. However, there is a 0.7 probability that the additional campaign will have no further impact on payoff at all. If the initial outcome is Medium then the supplementary campaign has a 0.4 probability of having a zero effect and a 0.6 probability of increasing payoff by £300 000.

Clearly the group needs to evaluate the effect of this additional option on the original decision. However, there is an additional difficulty. The finance department has indicated that it needs to know now – and not in six months' time – whether the additional £100 000 will be needed for the campaign in order to ensure that the group's cash flow is not adversely affected. In other words, the group cannot wait until it knows the outcome of the initial campaign before making a further decision. It needs to decide now what this second decision will be. It will be helpful if the additional information is summarised. For the Eastern European option:

Initial outcome Low			*Initial outcome Medium*		
Initial payoff	–£200 000		Initial payoff	–£50 000	
Supplementary costs	£100 000		Supplementary costs	£100 000	
Supplementary payoff:			Supplementary payoff:		
£0	(probability 0.7)		£0	(probability 0.4)	
£300 000	(probability 0.3)		£300 000	(probability 0.6)	

The part of the original decision tree relating to Eastern Europe has been updated to help decide what to do. Figure 13.12 shows the amended tree. The decision options relating to Scandinavia and Germany have been simplified to show only their respective EVs. If the Eastern Europe option is examined in detail it can be seen how the additional information is incorporated. The initial decision is one of three: S, G, E. For the Eastern Europe decision there are the three original initial outcomes, Low, Medium, High. For the High outcome nothing alters in terms of probability or payoff. For Low and Medium, however, a second decision node is needed to help determine whether or not to launch a supplementary campaign. These decisions are shown as Supp (supplementary campaign is launched) and No supp. For the No supp decision in both cases the payoffs remain as they were in the original problem. For the Supp decision option, however, there is a change. If the

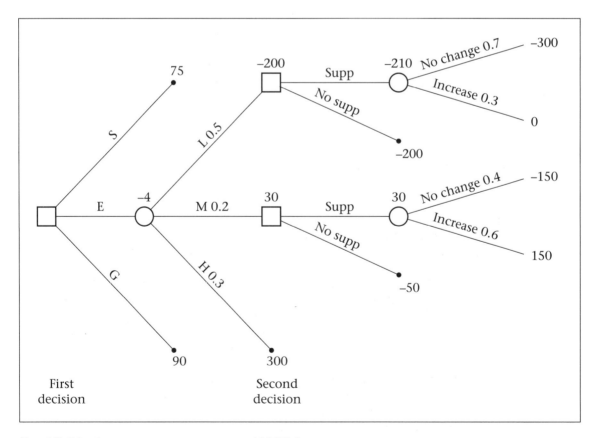

FIG 13.12 AMENDED DECISION TREE (£000s)

initial impact is Low and the supplementary campaign is launched, there are two secondary outcomes: the supplementary campaign could lead to a change in payoff or could leave the payoff unchanged. The respective probabilities and net payoffs are shown. It can then be seen that the EV of launching the supplementary campaign *if* the initial impact is Low would be –£210 000. This is actually a lower EV than the alternative decision of No supp. This implies that if management decides to target Eastern Europe (the initial decision) and if the campaign impact is Low, they know *now* that a supplementary campaign is not worthwhile. In other words, management can predict now what a future decision would be relating to a particular set of outcomes based on the information given. For the initial impact of Medium a similar process takes place. It can be seen that the EV of launching the supplementary campaign is £30 000 compared with the EV of not launching this campaign of –£50 000. Again, management can predict a future decision. If it decides to campaign in Eastern Europe and if the initial impact is Medium, then a supplementary campaign should be launched.

However, does this affect management's initial decision to campaign in Germany and not Eastern Europe? This can be answered by working backwards through the amended diagram. The payoffs for each of the three initial outcomes are then –£200 000 (since if the initial outcome is Low the group would do nothing further), £30 000 (which has changed from the original –£50 000 since the group would now launch the supplementary campaign) and £300 000 (which is also unchanged). Using the original probabilities the EV for the Eastern Europe option is now –£4000. This is still negative and would not affect the original decision to target Germany. It can also illustrate how such an approach can be used to assess in the present decisions that may have to be taken at some time in the future. Management does not have to wait for an outcome to occur before considering and choosing between alternative decisions; with the right information management can make that decision now and be ready to implement it should that particular outcome occur.

ISHIKAWA DIAGRAMS

The next management technique is descriptive rather than quantitative. This is the Ishikawa diagram – alternatively known as the cause–effect diagram or the fishbone diagram (*see also* Chapter 7). Originally developed for use in the area of quality management, organisations have found it equally useful in terms of wider problem solving and decision making. Consider the problem scenario we developed earlier, relating to customer complaints in the hotel about non-delivery of morning newspapers. An initial investigation has revealed that the problem is not a one-off: it has been happening for some time and a number of customers have experienced the problem. One of the difficulties the decision maker has in such a context is trying to determine the fundamental causes of the problem, the relative importance of each cause and possible relationships between causes. An Ishikawa diagram can help the decision maker by providing a framework to identify such causes and their relationships. The general format of the diagram is shown in Fig 13.13, although the approach is readily adapted to the exact situation under examination.

The diagram starts at the right-hand side with the observed effect. This is the issue, situation or problem that management is focusing on. The major causes, or contributory factors, relating to this effect are then identified and used to label the

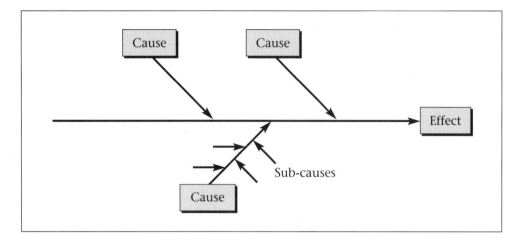

FIG 13.13 ISHIKAWA DIAGRAM: EFFECT, CAUSES AND SUB-CAUSES

ends of each major branch as shown. One common approach is to consider five major factors: manpower (shortage of staff perhaps, inadequate training, poor communication between staff); materials (resources, quality of resources); machines; methods (work practices, data capture systems) and measurements. Factors which contribute to each of these major causes can then be determined and used to label sub-branches coming from each main cause branch, as in Fig 13.14.

The Ishikawa diagram is a method of focusing on the major factors causing a particular effect. It seems very simple and straightforward, but is deceptively powerful when used in the right way. A team approach to identify causes is likely to be needed since most activities will involve a group of people rather than one individual. Figure 13.15 shows a completed diagram that might have been produced by the hotel manager after consultation with key members of staff.

On the manpower side, factors have been identified as: understaffing in the hotel, key staff away ill, staff having an unclear idea as to who was responsible for providing this service, new staff who had not been told it was part of their duties. On the materials side management has identified that on occasion the wrong newspapers are delivered to the hotel and sometimes not enough newspapers are

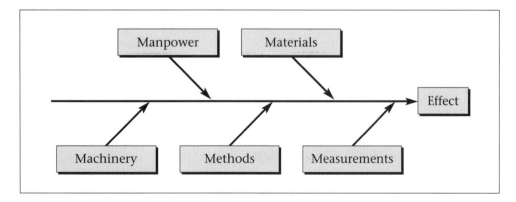

FIG 13.14 ISHIKAWA DIAGRAM: THE FIVE MS

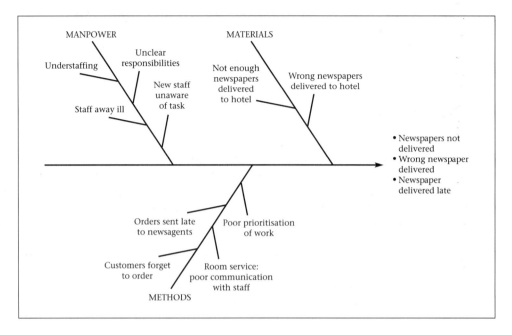

FIG 13.15 ISHIKAWA DIAGRAM FOR HOTEL PROBLEM

delivered. On the methods side it can be seen that orders are often sent late to the supplying newsagent (possibly linked to some of the materials causes), the room service staff (who take orders for morning papers from customers) do not communicate adequately with the staff who have to deliver the papers, occasionally the effect can be caused by customers in the hotel simply forgetting to place an order for a specific newspaper, and there can be a problem with staff prioritisation of this task with others that are expected of them (linked to one of the manpower causes). Note that the manager has decided to drop the machinery and measurement branches as redundant to this problem analysis.

What the diagram provides is a focused analysis of key factors contributing to the problem. The manager now has a clear perspective on contributing factors and can begin the process of prioritising between them and seeking solutions to them. In some cases there may be no direct solution. Understaffing, for example, may be a perennial problem if the group is exercising central control over staff numbers. However, it is evident that improved training is needed for new staff to ensure they are aware of all their duties and it is also evident that communication needs to be improved between management, room service and staff, and also between the hotel and the supplying newsagent. Perhaps an agreement for the hotel to fax its order last thing in the evening might help resolve some of these causes. Similarly, a new system is needed to ensure that customers are aware of their need to order before a specific time.

The diagram demonstrates the potential in terms of assisting the decision maker. Whatever the possible solutions, the diagram allows management to assess the impact each solution could be expected to have on the effect. This by itself can be a valuable conclusion to reach. Improving staff training, for example, will not solve the entire problem given that there are other factors contributing to the problem that will not be solved by this initiative. Similarly, although the diagram is readily applied to effects in the guise of problems, it can also be applied to effects which indicate 'success'. If one feature of a product or service is seen as particularly successful, this method can be a useful mechanism for identifying the key factors that have contributed to this success with a view to replicating these factors for other products/services.

FORCEFIELD ANALYSIS

The techniques and models introduced so far are focused on the stages of the decision-making process which relate to the generation of alternatives and the evaluation of those alternatives. As has already been discussed, part of the management decision-making process involves the successful implementation of the decision taken: making it work, in other words. No matter how well designed the decision, a manager may well find in practice that once implemented the decision does not have the desired or expected effect.

Naturally there may be many reasons for this, but forcefield analysis considers one aspect of such a situation (*see also* Chapters 1 and 5). A decision situation – where some change is seen as necessary – can be visualised as comprising two mutually opposed forces: what can be described as restraining forces which resist the change implied in some decision, and driving forces which support or encourage change. The purpose of forcefield analysis is to help the manager identify in advance of decision implementation what these critical forces are likely to be, and consider how best the restraining forces can be removed or minimised and how the driving forces can be strengthened. The approach in forcefield analysis is straightforward. Consider the decision situation shown in Fig 13.16.

The current situation is shown as the solid line and the desired situation – after successful implementation of some decision – is shown as a dotted line. The gap between the two implies change. In the move to push towards the desired situation it is likely that a number of restraining forces will be encountered. These need to be individually identified and used to label each arrow line. A number of key driving forces can be identified in the same way. The next stage is to assess the relative strengths of each force: some will be stronger than others in either driving or restraining the change. The forcefield – and the current situation – can now be regarded as representing an

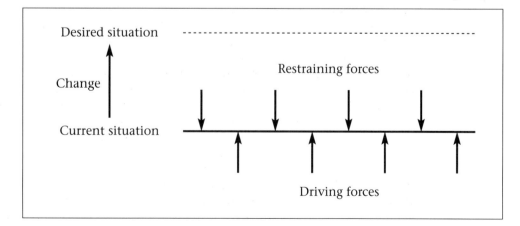

FIG 13.16 FORCEFIELD ANALYSIS

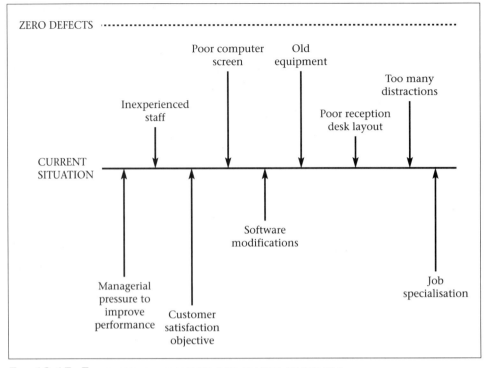

FIG 13.17 FORCEFIELD ANALYSIS FOR HOTEL PROBLEM

equilibrium position: a position of balance. In order to push towards the desired situation management must either strengthen the driving forces to push the situation forward or weaken the restraining forces (or, of course, do both).

Consider another hotel scenario. In one hotel in the group the main reception desk is responsible for taking telephone bookings for accommodation from customers. Typically, a customer will telephone the reception desk to make a booking, various details will then be entered into the computerised booking system and, at a later date, written confirmation sent to the customer. However, the hotel manager has recently become aware that an unacceptable number of errors occur in the input of customer details into the computerised booking system. In some cases this causes relatively minor problems – the customer is greeted by the wrong name when they check into the hotel – in other cases it is more serious, with the bill sent to the wrong customer address. The manager has decided that a zero defect target will be established: that no errors of this kind will be tolerated.

Figure 13.17 shows the results of a forcefield analysis on the situation. A number of restraining forces have been identified and the relative importance of each shown in relation to the size of the arrowed line (with longer lines implying more importance). It can be seen that the effective implementation of the zero defect decision will be restrained by inexperienced staff, inadequate equipment (with both poor screen layouts and antiquated equipment), physical difficulties caused by the layout of the reception area, and too many distractions when staff are on the phone and keying in details. Similarly a number of driving forces have also been identified, including managerial pressure, the corporate objective of achieving customer satisfaction, planned modification to computer software and an initiative to allow reception staff some degree of job specialisation.

The decision maker can now use the analysis to evaluate how the restraining factors can be removed or reduced (and indeed whether this will happen with some of the initiatives under way) and how to reinforce the driving forces. For example, the manager might decide to improve communications with reception staff so that they are fully aware of the importance of achieving customer satisfaction. Involving the reception staff in an evaluation of how the physical layout could be improved might help resolve one of the restraining forces. A detailed proposal for additional capital expenditure to replace old equipment might be made to the group finance director. Whatever initiatives are taken, the forcefield analysis allows these to be focused on the key forces with a view to enhancing the successful implementation of the original decision to move towards a zero defect situation.

STATISTICAL PROCESS CONTROL

The last technique introduced in this chapter is one which helps close the loop of the decision-making process. As discussed earlier, it is important as part of this process for an organisation to have methods and systems in place which periodically monitor and assess performance from a number of perspectives. Not only does this allow management to assess the impact of decisions that have already been taken, it provides them with a perspective on any developing situations which may require decisions at some stage in the future. One method that is useful in a variety of situations is that of statistical process control (SPC), also known as control charts (*see also* Chapter 7). This will be illustrated with a further scenario.

The hotel group has recently set up a system to collect customer feedback on a regular basis. Part of this process involves sending a short questionnaire to people who have used any of the hotels in the group in the last month. The questionnaire seeks the opinions of these people on a number of topics: the service received, perceptions of value for money, the quality of the restaurant service, and so on. One question posed asks whether the person would use any of the group's hotels in the future should the occasion arise. Naturally, the group is keen to encourage customers to return to the hotel. The group has set a target that no more than 4 per cent of customers surveyed should respond that they would not use the group's hotels again (because of poor-quality service, too high prices or whatever).

The group organises these surveys on a monthly basis to a randomly selected sample of last month's customers. Typically around 500 customer responses are received in each survey. Clearly the basics of a potentially useful monitoring system exist in this situation. There is a ready mechanism for monitoring progress towards the 4 per cent target and for identifying any worsening trends in this aspect of company performance. The principles of SPC are illustrated in Fig 13.18. On the vertical axis the variable is shown in which management has an interest: the percentage of customers who would not use the group's hotels again. On this axis management can establish a target or expected value for the variable, here 4 per cent. Using principles that will be discussed below, upper and lower expected limits to this variable can be pre-calculated. Within these limits management concludes that the variable is still within reasonable limits of the target value. Outside these limits management would conclude that the variable now differs from the target set. Such monitoring will take place over a period where the variable is repeatedly measured and its current value assessed against the target value.

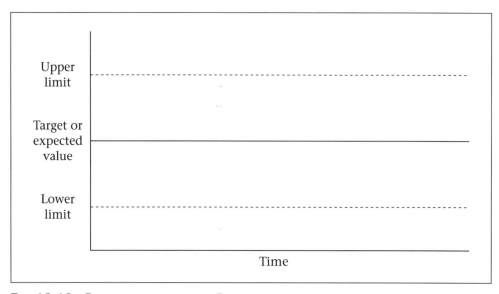

FIG 13.18 CONTROL CHART

However, there does appear to be a slight difficulty in this process, which relates to the fact that the results in any one month will represent only a sample of customers and not all customers. For example, suppose management finds that last month 5 per cent of customers surveyed indicated they would not use the group's hotels again. Should the group conclude that customer attitudes – and possibly hotel performance – have worsened and are unacceptably higher than the target of 4 per cent? After all, it is based on only some customers. Perhaps a different sample of 500 customer responses would indicate a different result.

This scenario illustrates what is known as 'sampling variation', which is a common problem for any organisation engaged in market research, opinion polls or customer satisfaction surveys. Sampling variation relates to the difference in results that might be expected simply by taking different samples of customers (or whatever is being measured). The subject area itself is a very technical one and the complete technical background required cannot be provided here. However, it is possible to introduce the general principles. At the heart of SPC lies what is known as the sampling distribution. All the group's customers last month can be defined as the statistical population (perhaps several thousand), and then it becomes clear that it would be possible to take many different samples of 500 customers from this population. Each sample would provide a result in terms of the percentage who would not use the group again. Some of these sample results would be the same, some would differ (simply because there are different combinations of customers in the sample from the population).

It is possible to construct a frequency diagram showing the sample results and the frequency of these results; then, according to statistical theory, a distribution like that shown in Fig 13.19 would be obtained. This figure shows what is known as the sampling distribution which takes a typical symmetrical shape (known as the Normal distribution). In the middle of this distribution is the result that would be obtained if all customers (the population) were asked. Most sample results (even though they are based on only 500 customer responses) will be similar to the population result. Relatively few sample results would be very different from the result

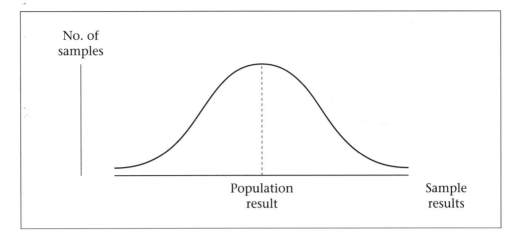

FIG 13.19 SAMPLING DISTRIBUTION: DISTRIBUTION OF SAMPLE RESULTS

obtained from asking the full customer population. In fact statistical theory allows for a further stage in predicting what these differences would be. Figure 13.20 shows the principles.

Using what is known as a standard error to measure variability, statistical theory predicts that 95 per cent of all sample results, where there is a normal distribution, will occur within 2 standard errors (SEs) of the population result, while 99.7 per cent will occur within 3 SEs. This implies that, although it is only a sample result, it is possible to quantify how close it is likely to be to the population result.

The implications are straightforward. It is possible to treat the target figure of 4 per cent as the desired population result (i.e. no more than 4 per cent of all customers saying they would not use the group's hotels again). It is possible then to compare

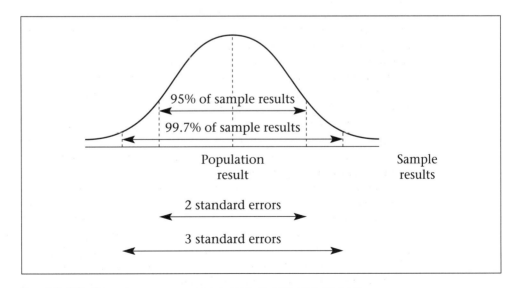

FIG 13.20 SAMPLING VARIATION AND STANDARD ERROR

the result from any one sample of 500 customer responses against this target figure and use the 2SE and 3SE values as a measure. Put simply, if the target is being achieved, then it can be anticipated (with 95 per cent confidence) that any sample of customer responses would be within 2SEs of 4 per cent, and with 99.7 per cent confidence that they would be within 3SEs of 4 per cent. But suppose we took a sample and found that the sample result was not within these 3SE limits? What would this imply? It would imply that the current population result was unlikely to be 4 per cent: that is, it would imply that the target of 4 per cent set by the group is not being met.

The standard error can be calculated by using the following formula:

$$\sqrt{\frac{P(100 - P)}{n}}$$

where P is the assumed population percentage and n is the sample size. Here we would have:

$$\sqrt{\frac{4(100 - 4)}{500}}$$

$$\sqrt{\frac{4(96)}{500}}$$

= 0.876 per cent

and 2SEs would then be:

2(0.876) = 1.75 per cent

and 3SEs 2.63 per cent.

This now provides a method for checking whether, based on a sample result of 500 customer responses, the group is meeting its target of 4 per cent or not. As long as the sample result is within 1.75 of the target (that is between 2.25 per cent and 5.75 per cent) it can be assumed that the target is being met. On the other hand, if the sample result is outside the 3SE limit (that is, outside the range 1.37 per cent to 6.63 per cent) then it is possible to be 99.7 per cent confident that the target is not being achieved. If it lies between 2SEs and 3SEs away from the target, a position can be adopted of seeing this result as warning that the target might not be being met. In the terminology of SPC the 2SE limit is known as a warning limit (warning that, if the sample result has exceeded this figure, then there would be a danger of not meeting the target) and the 3SE figure as an action limit indicating that management action is needed, since, based on the sample result, the target is not being met. This can be shown in diagram form (*see* Fig 13.21).

This is a straightforward method for monitoring the target value based on samples taken every month. The sample result can be plotted on the control chart. If the result is within the warning limits then it is possible to reach the conclusion that the target of 4 per cent is being met. If the result is outside the action limits then it can be concluded that the target is not being met and there is a need to take action accordingly. If the result is between the warning and action limits, then it can be concluded that there are grounds for suspecting the target is not being met, although it is not possible as yet to be positive about this. It is possible, under such circumstances, to arrange for another sample to be taken. Over time there would be a plot of the sample results. Not only would it be possible to monitor each month's

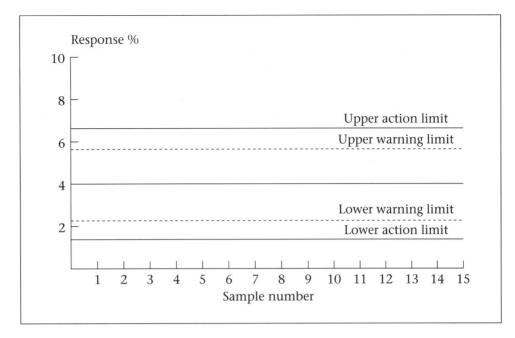

FIG 13.21 CONTROL CHART WITH ACTION AND WARNING LIMITS

result against the target; it would also be possible to observe any developing trends in the sample results. Figure 13.22 shows the principles.

The results of the last six months' samples are plotted. None of them breaches

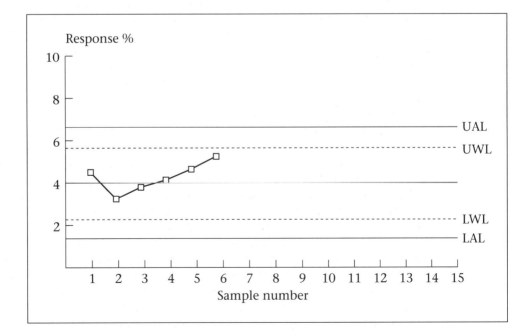

FIG 13.22 CONTROL CHART FOR SIX SUCCESSIVE SAMPLES

the warning limits so, on an individual basis, none of them is cause for concern. However, it should be noted that the last five months together show a definite upward trend in the sample results. It looks as if there is a slowly worsening attitude among samples of customers and this might be investigated before the next sample is taken.

SUMMARY

■ Decision making forms an important part of any manager's workload, no matter at what level of management the individual operates and what the type or business of the organisation. Indeed, it could be argued that decision making and problem solving are at the heart of a manager's role in any organisation.

■ The business environment in which such management decision making takes place is becoming increasingly complex, making the task of decision making that much more difficult. At the same time, and for many of the same reasons, the strategic and financial consequences of inappropriate decisions for an organisation are becoming greater.

■ The types of decision situation faced will naturally vary considerably from one organisation to another and from one manager to another. While decision making approaches must be tailored to fit the particular circumstances, many decision situations have common aspects.

■ There is no panacea that can be offered to a decision maker providing a foolproof and guaranteed method for decision making. However, adopting a logical and rational approach to a decision situation can be particularly productive. In any decision situation it will be worthwhile considering the wider decision-making process that applies and evaluating the various stages of this process that must be addressed for the particular situation under consideration. Similarly, in the task of generating potential alternative solutions for a decision situation and assessing those alternatives against the declared decision objectives, the use of a number of commonly used business models can be productive, although the output from such models must be seen as only part of the information-gathering process involved in decision making.

■ Such models are particularly valuable in decision situations where incomplete or inadequate information is available, where a number of alternatives are typically available and where uncertainty exists.

■ A number of these models have been introduced in this chapter, but it must also be said that the last two or three decades have seen a veritable explosion of such models being developed and used. The subject area known as management science has provided many of these model developments and a number of texts are detailed in the references for further reading which introduce additional models of potential use to the decision maker.

REVIEW AND DISCUSSION QUESTIONS

1 From a management perspective what is the difference between decision making and problem solving?

2 Consider an organisation with which you are familiar. What is the organisation's attitude to risk? How does this affect its decision-making process?

3 As a manager facing some decision situation which has areas of uncertainty associated with it, is it possible to quantify such areas of uncertainty?

4 What are the key differences between management decision making and personal decision making?

5 Discuss how time affects the various stages of the decision-making process.

6 Consider the various decision support models introduced in this chapter. What factors would discourage managers from utilising the information derived from such models in the decision-making process?

7 'Decision making is the most important task for any manager.' Discuss this statement.

8 A manager in an organisation has been offered a considerable promotion. However, the promotion would involve moving to another part of the country.
   a Using the decision-making process model, consider how the manager would try to reach an appropriate decision.
   b Draw a decision tree representing the decision situation.
   c Assume the manager has decided to take the promotion. Draw a force-field diagram to assess the critical factors which will affect the 'success' of the move.

CASE STUDY: JAGUAR CARS

A Jaguar car.
Instantly recognisable almost anywhere in the world.

Jaguar has had a very chequered history over the last few decades. In the early 1980s the company came close to disappearing, with reducing market share, decreasing financial viability, outdated technology and working practices, and major product quality problems. With the introduction of new management it was able – painfully – to turn itself around and achieved improvements in efficiency, quality and profitability. Towards the end of the decade a worldwide recession emerged and the company again hit problems. In 1989 the company was bought by Ford Motor Company for around US$2.5 billion, with the new owners then having to find a further $700 million to help keep the company going in the short term.

Jaguar starkly illustrates the difficulties involved in decision making in today's environment. On the face of it the company had tremendous potential. On the other hand it faced a number of major short-term problems. These included:

• the company was operating at a loss. It was estimated that in 1992 it actually lost $18 000 on each car sold;
• in motor industry terms it was very small, even when compared with its competitors in the luxury car market. Mercedes Benz, for example, has annual sales almost 20 times those of Jaguar;
• it was operating at below breakeven output. Breakeven annual sales were estimated at 35 000. In 1993 Jaguar expected to produce and sell only 29 000 cars;
• worldwide there had been a dramatic collapse in the market for luxury cars;
• the company's cars had significant quality problems, particularly in relation to its major competitors, with, for example, a Jaguar car experiencing 75 per cent more defects than a Mercedes;
• many of the company's cars were relatively old models. However, the development costs of a new model were likely to run into the hundreds of millions of £s. In addition, such development would take considerable time.

The new management of Jaguar faced an array of interlinked problems as well as considerable uncertainty about markets, demand, customer loyalty and competitors' strategy. They were also constrained by the desire to keep Jaguar as a unique product and not simply another variety of Ford car. A number of decisions were taken to try to move the company forward. These included:

• immediate improvements in operating efficiency. Assembly man-hours per car, for example, was reduced by almost 40 per cent in a two-year period, with a further 50 per cent reduction planned;
• significant quality improvements, with defects down by over 70 per cent on the XJ6 model alone;
• a major cost-reduction programme leading to a reduction in the workforce of almost 50 per cent;
• the introduction of, and development of, new models, but with decisions related to different timescales. In the short term the company decided to introduce a redesigned version of the XJ6 – which was relatively quick and low-cost option – and longer term to invest in the design and the production of a totally new car aimed at the business executive market.

The decisions faced by the company's management were clearly a mixture of the strategic and the operational. At the operational level decisions had to be taken about how best to improve the company's immediate position. These needed to be taken quickly and needed to have an immediate impact on the company's performance. While such decisions can be taken relatively easily – relating to quality, productivity and operating costs – implementing such decisions effectively can be more problematic given issues of staff morale and uncertainty, and there is clearly considerable scope for some of the problem-solving techniques introduced in this chapter.

At the same time a number of key strategic decisions were needed to try to ensure the company's long-term future. Such decisions related to the size of the company's customer base, the range of models available, its pricing policy and the location of its production base. Over time a series of related decisions emerged, and the sequential decision models introduced in this chapter clearly have a lot of potential in such a situation. As a short-term measure the company launched a redesigned version of the XJ6. In 1996 the company launched the XK8 sports car. The X200 executive saloon is planned for launch in 1998 with further plans for the production of a family saloon the X200. As with all management decision making only time will tell whether such decisions are strategically effective. ∎

REFERENCES FOR FURTHER READING

Ackoff, R L (1978) *The Art of Problem Solving*, Wiley.

Coles, S and Rowley, J (1995) 'Revisiting decision trees', *Management Decisions*, 33(8), pp 46–50.

Drucker, P (1992) *Management*, Oxford: Butterworth-Heinemann.

Hicks, M J (1991) *Problem Solving in Business and Management*, London: Chapman & Hall.

Islei, G *et al.* (1991) 'Modelling strategic decision making and performance measurements at ICI pharmaceuticals', *Interfaces*, 21(6), pp 4–22.

Juran, J M and Gryna, F M (1993) *Quality Planning and Analysis*, 3rd edn, McGraw-Hill.

Moore, P G and Thomas, H (1988) *The Anatomy of Decisions*, Harmondsworth: Penguin.

Richardson, C (1991) 'Staffing the front office', *Operational Research Insight*, 4(2), pp 19–22.

Wisniewski, M (1996) *Foundation Quantitative Methods for Business*, London: Pitman Publishing.

Wisniewski, M (1997) *Quantitative Methods for Decision Makers*, 2nd edn, London: Pitman Publishing.

Wisniewski, M and Dacre, T (1990) *Mathematical Programming: Optimization Models for Business and Management Decision Making*, Maidenhead: Mc Graw-Hill.

14 OPERATIONS MANAGEMENT

Ruth Boaden

OBJECTIVES

The objectives of this chapter are to:

◆ describe a framework for the analysis of operations management as one of the managerial roles within an organisation. It uses the analogy of operations as a transformation process, changing inputs into outputs

◆ to consider the past, present and future context of the transformation process within the organisation

◆ to show how the process may be classified and the impact of different types of process on the role of the manager

◆ to demonstrate how the outputs from the process may be measured and to consider the relevance of new ways of measuring

◆ to examine the impact of the external environment on operations, with particular reference to the customer and the international context

INTRODUCTION

The structure of the chapter reflects the theoretical basis around which it is built: that of operations being a transformation process where input resources are transformed into outputs. Following consideration of the past history and present organisational context of the process, future trends and means of classification are discussed. The role of the operations manager is also considered. Current and developing ways of measuring output are presented within the context of wider changes affecting operations. Finally, the relationship between operations and the customer is analysed, and some comment made on international trends and differences.

OPERATIONS MANAGEMENT AS A TRANSFORMATION PROCESS

Any organisation, whether it be a manufacturer, retailer, educational establishment, hospital or even government agency, exists to satisfy the needs of its customers or consumers, i.e. those who are the recipients of what is produced or the services carried out by the organisation (*see* Fig 14.1).

So within the context of an organisation, what are 'operations'? An operation may be defined as:

> *'a process, method or series of acts especially of a practical nature.'*
> (Collins, 1986)

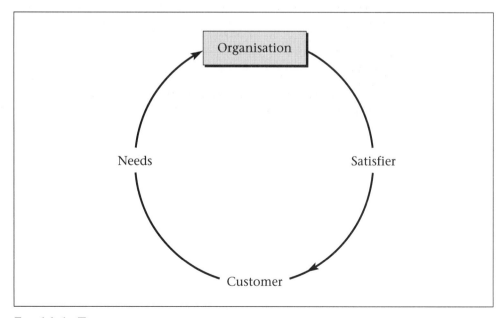

FIG **14.1** THE CLOSED LOOP OF CUSTOMER SATISFACTION
Source: Muhlemann *et al.*, 1992.

In general, operations simply harness resources in order to produce something or to provide a service – they are part of every kind of organised activity within the organisation. It is argued by some authors that operations management is an integral part of any managerial role (*see* Fig 14.2).

- **A manufacturing company conducts operations in a mill, a foundry, or a factory**

- **Banks operate from offices and branches**

- **Restaurant operations take place on chopping blocks, serving tables and takeaway counters**

- **Builders operate in offices where proposals are prepared and on construction sites**

- **University operations take place in lecture theatres, research laboratories, seminar rooms, and on the sports field**

FIG 14.2 OPERATIONS

Source: Adapted from Schonberger and Knod (1994). Reprinted by permission of Richard D Irwin Inc, Burr Ridge, Illinois.

More specifically, 'operations' can refer to a department or functional area within an organisation where certain resources are transformed into products or services by adding value to them. 'Operations managers' therefore have to 'manage' this process in some way.

There are two definitions of operations management which highlight the key features. Schroeder (1993) defines the key terms as:

> *'Operations managers are responsible for producing the supply of goods or services in organisations. Operations managers make decisions regarding the operations function and the transformation systems used. Operations management is the study of decision making in the operations function.'*

Harris (1989) uses a simpler definition which highlights all the key features of the task:

> *'operations management is the management of a system which provides goods or services to or for a customer, and involves the design, planning and control of the system.'*

Many authors view operations management as a transformation process, and this helps to highlight some of the key features of the task (*see* Fig 14.3).

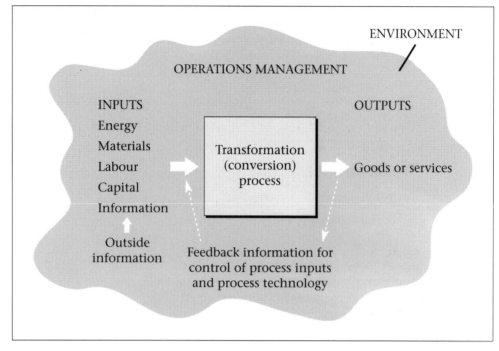

FIG 14.3 THE TRANSFORMATION PROCESS

Examples of various operations classified in this way are shown in Fig 14.4.

OPERATION	INPUTS	OUTPUTS
Bank	cashiers, staff, computer equipment, facilities, energy	financial services (loans, deposits)
Restaurant	cooks, waiting staff, food, equipment, facilities, energy	meals, entertainment, satisfied customers
Hospital	doctors, nurses, staff, equipment, facilities, energy	health services, healthy patients
University	staff, equipment, facilities, energy, knowledge	educated students, research
Airline	planes, facilities, pilots, flight attendants, engineers, labour, energy	transportation from one area to another

FIG 14.4 EXAMPLES OF OPERATIONS CLASSIFIED AS TRANSFORMATION PROCESSES

Source: Developed from Schroeder, R G (1993) *Operations Management*, 4th edn, © Copyright The McGraw-Hill Companies, Inc 1993. Reproduced with permission of McGraw-Hill, Inc.

It is useful to make a distinction between *transformed* and *transforming* resources: those which are treated or transformed in a certain way and those that act upon the transformed resources (*see* Fig 14.5).

FIG **14.5** TRANSFORMED AND TRANSFORMING RESOURCES
Source: Slack *et al.* (1998).

One of the transformed resources is usually dominant in an operation – a bank deals with materials and customers, but is primarily concerned with processing information. Manufacturing is primarily concerned with processing material, but information is also very important. Classification of operations according to their predominant transformed resource is shown in Fig 14.6.

In terms of the transforming resources, facilities may be high or low tech, but are still important for any type of organisation. Staff will have various degrees of skill depending on the operation, but reliability will be important in all cases. The role of staff in service operations is relatively more important than manufacturing because of the greater labour intensity of the transformation process.

The interface between the transformation process and the environment is particularly important – both the environment within the organisation and the external environment must be considered. The relationship of operations to the environment is shown in Fig 14.7. Some of the aspects of these interfaces will be discussed in more detail when the role of the customer in operations is described.

PREDOMINANTLY MATERIALS PROCESSORS	PREDOMINANTLY INFORMATION PROCESSORS	PREDOMINANTLY CUSTOMER PROCESSORS
all manufacturers	accountant	hairdresser
retail operation	market research company	hotel
warehouse	university research unit	hospital
postal service	telecommunications company	theatre

FIG **14.6** OPERATIONS CLASSIFIED ACCORDING TO PRIMARY TRANSFORMED RESOURCE
Source: Developed from Slack *et al.* (1998).

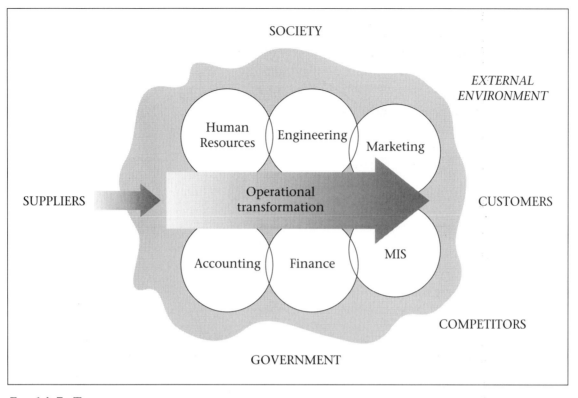

SOCIETY

EXTERNAL ENVIRONMENT

Human Resources

Engineering

Marketing

SUPPLIERS

Operational transformation

CUSTOMERS

Accounting

Finance

MIS

COMPETITORS

GOVERNMENT

FIG **14.7** THE RELATIONSHIP OF OPERATIONS TO THE ENVIRONMENT

Source: Schroeder, R G (1993) *Operations Management*, 4th edn, © Copyright The McGraw-Hill Companies, Inc 1993. Reproduced with permission of McGraw-Hill, Inc.

Operations is generally considered to be a functional area, like marketing etc, rather than a basic discipline area of study, like economics, sociology, systems concepts, etc. It has traditionally been emphasised more in manufacturing because it is the major part of the organisation – in service marketing it is often considered to be more important. In terms of relationships with other functions within the organisation, the relationship between the marketing and operations functions is often considered to be the most crucial, whatever the type of organisation. Muhlemann *et al.* (1992) detail the relationship by defining a 'closed loop' which summarises all the key tasks involved in identifying and satisfying consumer needs (*see* Fig 14.8). The marketing role therefore covers stages (i) and (v) of this loop – identifying and forecasting, and distribution.

However, this approach may be criticised by those who believe that operations can offer competitive advantage to an organisation (e.g. Wheelwright and Hayes, 1985) and that customers and operations should be working more closely together. Other authors (Hill, 1993) believe that marketing strategy actually drives operations strategy, following from the premise that customer requirements should drive the operations function. This is very much in line with the recent popularity of total quality approaches, which are identified by an increasing emphasis on putting the customer first, although this may be expressed in different ways (*see* Chapter 3).

In service organisations, the relationship between operations and marketing is closer than in manufacturing, and can be shown using the '3P' service model (*see* Fig 14.9).

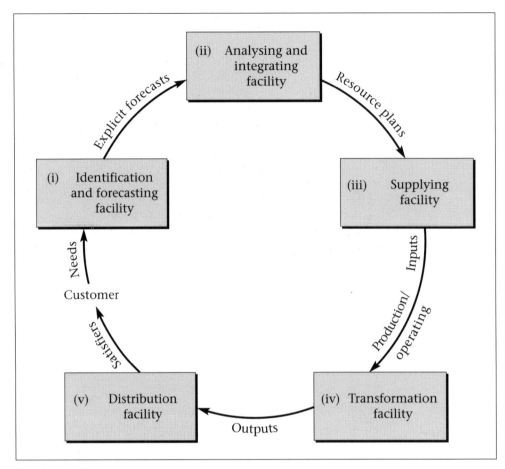

FIG 14.8 FROM CUSTOMER TO CUSTOMER – A CLOSED LOOP
Source: Muhlemann *et al.* (1992).

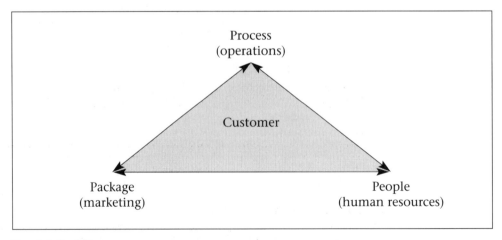

FIG 14.9 3P MODEL

The customer is at the centre in Fig 14.9, with the organisation concerned about the process of delivering the service, the people involved and the package (the way it is presented). These correspond to the organisational functions of operations management, marketing and human resources (the ones most often found in a service industry).

Another way of considering the role of operations within an organisation is to use the 'value chain' concept proposed by Porter (1989). A value chain is defined as the collection of activities used to design, produce, market, deliver and support its product. Customers, suppliers and the firm are broken down into discrete but related activities, with the value chain showing how value is created by the firm for its customers. Porter argues that competitive advantage is then gained when the value created exceeds the cost of creating it. 'Value' is what customers are willing to pay for, and is created within the firm by the activities shown in Fig 14.10.

It can be seen that operations is considered a primary activity, and the importance of its role will be shown later in the chapter. While 'logistics' is shown separately by Porter, it actually forms part of the broad definition of operations used within this chapter. Typical functions that might be included in such a broad definition of operations management include:

- **purchasing**

- **production**

- **logistics**

- **maintenance**

- **goods receiving**

- **dispatch**

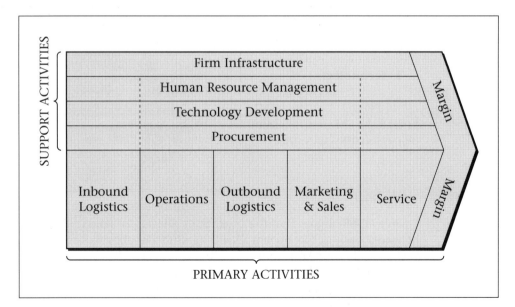

FIG 14.10 THE FIRM VALUE CHAIN

Source: Adapted and reprinted with the permission of The Free Press, a Division of Simon & Schuster, from *Competitive Advantage: Creating and Sustaining Superior Performance* by Michael E Porter. Copyright © 1985 by Michael E Porter.

THE TRANSFORMATION PROCESS

Past history

In one sense, operations management has existed as long as people have made things, although it was not recognised as such. Attention to 'production management' has been greatest in the past 200 years, and attention to operations management as a discipline only during the last 15 years or so. Operations management developed as a discipline because people realised that many different organisations were experiencing similar problems, and whether they were service, manufacturing or public sector organisations did not make a significant difference.

It is not possible to give a strict chronological account of the way in which the area has developed, but there are a number of major theoretical and practical contributions which have affected it (*see* Fig 14.11). A fuller account can be found in Fogarty *et al.* (1989) (*see also* Chapter 1).

- **The division of labour – Adam Smith and Charles Babbage**

- **Standardisation of parts**

- **The Industrial Revolution**

- **The scientific study of work – Frederick Taylor**

- **Human relations – the Hawthorne experiments**

- **Decision modelling**

- **Technology**

FIG **14.11** MAJOR CONTRIBUTIONS TO THE THEORETICAL DEVELOPMENT OF OPERATIONS MANAGEMENT

Division of labour

George (1968) argues that the concept of division of labour (*see also* Chapter 8) can be traced back to the ancient Greeks (Plato's *The Republic*), where it was recognised that specialisation of labour on a single task can result in greater productivity and efficiency than assigning a number of tasks to one worker. This was also discussed by Adam Smith, author of the classic *The Wealth of Nations* (1776), who noted that output is increased by specialisation of labour. Workers become increasingly expert at one task, there is an avoidance of lost time due to changing to other jobs, and tools and machines can be added to improve efficiency. Charles Babbage (1832) noted that specialisation of labour makes it possible to pay wages only for the specific skills required. Division of labour is now being reviewed because of its effect on worker morale, turnover, job boredom and performance, but it has been the foundation of many operations management techniques and methods of organising production systems.

Standardisation of parts

Manufacturing parts so that they are as interchangeable as possible is now commonplace within our society – for example, light bulbs of different wattage and shape but all with the same fitting. This was not, however, the case in the past, and designing parts in this way is one of the major features of operations management which enabled increasing efficiency and specialisation of labour.

The Industrial Revolution

The Industrial Revolution took place during the late 1700s and early 1800s and was the time when machine power was substituted for human power. It was made possible by inventions such as the steam engine (invented by James Watt in 1764) and electricity. The demand for manufactured goods generated by the First World War (1914–18) aided the development of 'mass production' where very large quantities of goods were made using relatively high levels of automation. Society now appears to have shifted to a 'post-industrial' period where manufacturing is not the primary source of income for many countries, and services form the basis of the economy.

Scientific study of work

This method determines the best method of working using scientific principle: observing present work methods, developing an improved method through scientific measurement and analysis, training workers in the new method, and continuing feedback and management of the work process. Taylor (1911) was the originator of these ideas and they gained widespread acceptance, although they have been criticised for being misapplied and used by management simply to 'speed up' workers without giving full consideration to their total range of needs. The scientific method is now seen by many as a means of exploiting workers and in opposition to newer methods of working which seek to take human needs into account.

Human relations

Motivation and the human element in the design of work are vital, and were highlighted by the Hawthorne experiments which indicated that worker motivation – along with the physical and technical environment – is crucial in improving productivity. The proponents of scientific management were forced as a result of these experiments to moderate their methods which had placed an overemphasis on the technical elements of work design, and the concept of job enrichment was developed (Hackman *et al.*, 1975).

Decision models

Many of the traditional texts on production management concentrate almost entirely on the use of mathematical models to represent a production system, in order to find optimal solutions within certain constraints. Examples of these models include the economic order quantity model used for inventory management and linear programming. Such models are still an important part of operations management, but their limitations are now more clearly acknowledged, particularly in terms of their disregard for the human elements of operations, and the limited range of assumptions on which many of the models had to be based in order to make them workable.

Technology

The application of computer technology has revolutionised operations management, with computers being used for many planning and controlling tasks such as inventory management, production scheduling and costing. Computers have been used for a number of years within the manufacturing process itself, and this is still an important application. The advent of information technology in particular, where computer technology is used to store and process information, has been of particular significance within operations (Underwood, 1994). Computer technology has also had a dramatic effect on service operations, with retailing systems, office systems and even medical diagnostic systems now being widely used.

PRESENT ORGANISATIONAL CONTEXT

Operations management plays an important role in any type of organisation, but different emphasis is placed on operations in manufacturing and service organisations. The differences and similarities between these types of organisation are important for operations managers, since they need to understand clearly the nature of the organisation in which they are working, and the relative importance of various aspects of operations management.

Operations can be classified in various ways. One useful classification is from Wild (1989) who identifies four different types:

- **Manufacture**: where the physical output differs from the input; there is a change in the **form** utility of resources; *making something* – examples include car manufacture, food manufacture.

- **Transport**: where the customer, or something belonging to the customer, is moved, without any change in physical resources; there is a change in **place** utility; *moving something or someone* – examples include trains, distribution companies.

- **Supply**: where the ownership of goods is changed without a change in form; there is a change in **possession** utility; *providing some physical goods* – examples include retailing, petrol stations.

- **Service**: where the customer, or something belonging to the customer, is treated in some way; there is a change in **state** utility; *something happens to someone or something* – examples include dentists, the fire service.

It is not, however, always appropriate to assign an organisation solely to one category – most organisations have aspects of all the above to varying degrees – but it is usual to be able to assign a primary category to an organisation, and this will have implications for operations management. The concept of the operations tetrahedron (Armistead and Killeya, 1984) highlights this but is of little practical relevance.

It can be useful to distinguish between organisations according to the degree to which their transformation processes produce *goods*, i.e. tangible entities, or *services*, i.e. intangible entities. A good is physical in nature, and can be stored, transformed and transported. A service is produced and consumed more or less simultaneously, but cannot be stored or transported (*see* Fig 14.12).

Primarily goods producers:

mines, chemical factories, oil refineries, farms, with little or no customer contact and not offering services as part of their marketing package

Mixed production organisations:

most manufacturing companies, insurance companies and fast food outlets. All offer both goods and services. Manufacturing organisations often sell warranties and provide repair and after-sales service

Primarily service producers:

dentists, management consultants, banks, educational institutions. Any tangible good provided in connection with the service is incidental

Fig 14.12 Goods or services

It can be argued that it is not appropriate to distinguish at all between manufacturing and service, but that there is simply a continuum of organisations with some having more emphasis on goods than others. However, most academics still maintain the distinction for the purposes of analysis, and the UK government continues to issue economic statistics based on these classifications.

Even within service organisations there are difficulties of classification, and the operations management implications vary. Schmenner (1986) has proposed the classification in Fig 14.13 which is widely accepted. Degree of labour intensity refers to the ratio of capital to labour.

Schmenner goes on to discuss the implications of this classification for managerial roles, and the points he makes can be summarised as in Fig 14.14.

		DEGREE OF CONSUMER/SERVICE INTERACTION AND CUSTOMISATION	
		Low	**High**
DEGREE OF LABOUR INTENSITY	High	MASS SERVICE e.g. retailing, banking, education	PROFESSIONAL SERVICE e.g. doctors, lawyers, accountants
	Low	SERVICE FACTORY e.g. airlines, truck transportation, hotels, leisure resorts	SERVICE SHOP e.g. hospitals, repair services

FIG 14.13 THE SERVICE PROCESS MATRIX

CLASSIFICATION	CHALLENGES
Low labour intensity	capital expenditure technology development managing demand to avoid peaks and promote off-peaks scheduling service delivery
High labour intensity	hiring staff training staff developing and controlling methods of working scheduling workers controlling a large number of dispersed locations managing growth
Low interaction/customisation	marketing attention to physical surroundings managing a rigid organisation structure
High interaction/customisation	managing cost increases maintaining quality dealing with customer participation in the process managing the advancement of staff managing a flat organisation gaining employee loyalty

FIG 14.14 CHALLENGES FOR MANAGERS IN SERVICE ORGANISATIONS

The major characteristics of services and their implications for operations management can be summarised as follows:

- intangible output
- variable, non-standard output
- a service is perishable
- high customer contact
- customer participation
- cannot be mass-produced
- high personal judgement used by employees
- labour intensity
- decentralised facilities, near to the customer
- demand varies greatly over a short period.

Intangible output

This describes the uniqueness of services more than any other aspect:

> *'It's wrong to say that services are just like products except for their intangibility. That's like saying apples are just like oranges except for their 'appleness' – intangibility is a state. No amount of money can buy an experience (going to the cinema), time (consulting) or process (dry cleaning). A service is rendered and experienced.'*
>
> (Shostack, 1977)

Variable, non-standard output

The extent of this will depend on the exact type of service provided, as shown by Schmenner (1986), and in particular the degree of labour intensity, which makes quality control difficult. Quality is difficult to predict, both for the organisation and the customer, and the reputation of the organisation is an important factor. Quality of service depends to a large extent, however, on the expectations of the consumer.

A service is perishable

A service itself is consumed instantly, e.g. using a hotel room or an airline seat, and cannot be stored, although consumers may enjoy the *benefit* for a long while afterwards, e.g. a heart transplant.

This has a major impact on capacity planning, which is a key aspect of operations management. Periods of slack demand cannot be used to build stock to meet high demand in other periods, so capacity has to be varied. The large numbers of checkouts in supermarkets, not all of which are used at slack times, is an example of this. It is, however, expensive to build in extra capacity which may only be used at certain times, and it is not possible to hire employees at very short notice to cope with extra demand, so they may have to appear as a constant overhead rather than being varied with demand.

High customer contact

Although this varies with the nature of the service (Schmenner, 1986), in general service organisations have a higher degree of customer contact than manufacturers; nevertheless this is changing even for manufacturing organisations. The customer may not be physically in contact with the provider, especially where technology is used, e.g. a telephone enquiry line, but in any case employee interaction is critical. In some cases, organisations move 'messy' parts of the service process to places where they cannot be seen by the customer – sometimes referred to as back-room operations. This then allows the organisation to focus more on employee/customer interaction at the crucial point. Other organisations are proud to show all the parts of the operation to the customer, e.g. McDonald's where all the kitchen operations are deliberately made visible.

Customer participation

The extent of customer participation depends on the type of service, and there may be a formal or informal relationship between the organisation and customer. It is a crucial factor in determination of quality and timeliness.

Cannot be mass-produced

This does not apply within the service factory quadrant of Schmenner's matrix, and considerable benefits have been gained by service organisations applying mass production principles to providing a service. It is perhaps in this quadrant that operations management has had the greatest impact on service organisations. However, the customised nature of many services, such as medical treatment and legal advice, makes these types of service organisations very difficult to manage effectively.

High personal judgement used by employees

This is particularly so in professional services, e.g. lawyers, hairdressers, which have a reputation for being the most difficult to manage. It applies to services which cannot be mass-produced and are often relatively labour intensive.

Labour intensity

This has implications for productivity (the ratio of output to input resources): service organisations nearly always have lower overall productivity than manufacturing organisations, who have a relatively large capital input. Where service organisations have substituted equipment for people (e.g. automatic cash dispensers in banks instead of going to the counter to obtain cash) there have been productivity improvements. People and equipment are not, however, always in opposition, and may complement each other.

Decentralised facilities, near to the customer

This is especially important where physical contact with the customer is involved, and service location is critical to revenue for many organisations. It is not possible to 'ship' services, because they have to be produced at the point of customer contact. In order to minimise variation between large numbers of locations, there is a trend towards uniformity – e.g. McDonald's – where all branches look very similar and common procedures are used, with central common training.

Demand varies greatly over a short period

Relative to manufacturing organisations, demand varies more often in service companies, with more of a random pattern (e.g. emergency services), and stocks cannot be made to help out. Some organisations try and alter demand (e.g. cheap off-peak offers), manage supply by building flexibility into operations (e.g. more checkouts open at busy times) or in some cases ignoring variations (accepting that there will be longer queues at lunch time). This third option is becoming less easy to justify as consumers are offered more choice and appear to be becoming more particular about service quality. The USA is an example of a society where service quality is now a crucial determinant of market position.

FUTURE TRENDS

Production management was important when the Western world was an 'industrial society', but the rise of service organisations and the decline of manufacturing have caused some people to question the relevance of operations. However, there are a number of reasons why operations management is still considered to be important.

The resurgence of interest in operations during the 1980s was fuelled by the decline in the international competitiveness of Western industry, whose markets were taken over by foreign products and competition. The rate of productivity growth was also falling behind other countries, especially those in the Far East, and this was seen as being the province (and the fault) of the operations function. Whatever the 'solution' may be to the economic problems of the West (if, indeed, there is a single solution), increased investment, more research and development, and changes in the approaches used to manage people all have to be put into action by operations managers and therefore affect the operations function.

Some have not only seen operations as the key to future economic prosperity, but also a means of securing competitive advantage. Wheelwright and Hayes (1985) proposed that operations can play one of four roles within an organisation (*see* Fig 14.15).

While there is still debate about whether these stages are entirely valid, and it is sometimes difficult to decide which stage individual organisations are at, the classification does illustrate clearly the variety of roles which operations can play. It is clear that weak operations will affect the competitive position of the organisation, and as operations has become more closely linked to other parts of the organisation, so its role in competitive positioning has become more important. At one time a good product, superior marketing or a technology which was difficult to imitate could make up for weak operations management. The role of operations is, however, different now:

> *'Superior operations management blends with superior design, marketing, accounting, supplier relations, human resource management and business strategy as an essential component of success. Weak operations management, on the other hand, tends to coincide with many other management weaknesses.'* (Schonberger and Knod, 1994)

433

Stage 1 Internally Neutral

Key characteristics:

- minimising any negative impact that operations might have on the business, i.e. keeping things going without 'rocking the boat'
- operations are flexible and reactive
- top management has little direct involvement
- aim is to guard against damaging problems
- operations managers are firefighters with no strategic involvement
- technology bought from outside, at little risk

Stage 2 Externally Neutral

Key characteristics:

- operations may be as good as anyone else in the industry, i.e. following industry practice
- basis for decisions is resource allocation: investment is forthcoming, but reluctantly and only in order to keep up
- operations is not seen as a source of competitive strength, although the effect of competition is recognised

Stage 3 Internally Supportive

Key characteristics:

- operations decisions made in order to support business strategy
- top management takes an active role in directing operations
- a clear operations strategy exists
- investment screened to be in line with strategy
- technology developed as a response to strategy, rather than just looking at what others are doing

Stage 4 Externally Supportive

Key characteristics:

- operations is a competitive force within the business
- new ways of managing operations are developed
- functional management works well together
- proprietary equipment and processes are developed
- top management involved in integrating all functions together to make a flexible organisation

FIG 14.15 STAGES OF OPERATIONS' EFFECTIVENESS

General trends which have affected operations include:

- **customer-directed operations**
- **continuous improvement**
- **total involvement**
- **integration with other functions**
- **globalisation of operations**

Customer-directed operations implies the external orientation of operations in order to meet customer requirements. Internal customer concepts are also important – 'customer' meaning the next process as well as the final user. The trend to increased subcontracting and more focused units makes the implementation of this concept more difficult, since it may be less easy for the organisation to control external suppliers and contractors than it would be to manage its own internal units.

Continuous improvement is directed towards meeting the customer's needs, with the notion that standards are no longer fixed. The Japanese influence (*see* Ishikawa, 1985) has been very important here, although many of the concepts are now widely applied in Western organisations (*see* Chapter 7).

The mechanism for achieving continuous improvement is essentially *total involvement*; teamwork and other co-operative arrangements are used to facilitate this. This is one of the biggest changes for many organisations since it requires changes in the way people think and work within the organisation, i.e. a culture change (Chapter 9).

Cross-functional operations are increasingly important, especially when new systems for manufacture or management are implemented. The recent emphasis on business process improvement also introduces a greater degree of *integration* (Harrington, 1991). However, the trend towards less self-contained manufacturing sites may make things more difficult to integrate.

Organisations and markets are more *global* since developments in technology have made such expansion possible. Organisations tend to operate in more but smaller locations. The increased use of mergers as a means of company growth has spawned large organisations without a single cultural identity.

Within the organisation it is argued that operations has an important role, and although this may be hotly debated by other functional areas, the argument proposed by Slack (1983) is based on facts rather than emotion. The case can be developed as follows.

OPERATIONS . . .

- concerns the management of most of the people within the organisation: either production workers or service personnel, and often represents 70–80 per cent of the total workforce;

- has responsibility for the effective use of the organisation's assets, both fixed assets and inventory (current assets), and therefore for the management of most of the organisation's funds;

- is responsible for most of the organisation's expenditure, and has the largest budget allocation of any one function;

- is a pervasive activity (i.e. interacts with everything else);

- is the area in the organisation where many social and technological changes are taking place.

The role of an operations manager can be illustrated by the following two case studies which give accounts of what an operations manager does.

CASE STUDY: OPERATIONS MANAGEMENT AT UNITED BISCUITS

Andrew Hawley was sponsored by United Biscuits during his studies for his degree in Business, and his early work experience with the company confirmed his interest in manufacturing operations: 'Where else could you be managing fifty people from the outset, in your early twenties? The satisfaction comes from being responsible for the performance of the plant and staff, seeing immediate results and – above all – from beating targets!'

Andrew had various roles in his first five years with the company; initially he was responsible for the day-to-day supervision of a factory, then he became a deputy factory manager of a small specialised plant, before moving to headquarters, where he is now responsible for aspects of operational and strategic planning.

'It is certainly a change being in a team of just six people after helping to manage a factory and I now face a whole new set of challenges. My hands-on experience of production has been invaluable for my current position. Without it, I wouldn't be able to decide on production systems and procedures three or more years in advance of implementation. The work is very diverse. Sometimes I am working to identify potential problems so that preventative measures can be implemented, and at other times I am involved in logistics projects aimed at integrat-

ing UB companies all over Europe, which will make enormous savings for the group. Many people have misconceptions about manufacturing and production management, they think that it is just about "doing" and is less stimulating and intellectually demanding than other disciplines. Nothing could be further from the truth in my opinion.

'It has been my job at United Biscuits to ensure that all products leave our plant manufactured to our very demanding specifications. This involes not only responsibility for the process and the people, important though they are, but also for clear communication and involvement with all of the other business functions to ensure that the business unit is run optimally. It is especially important to understand how production must be involved with the fundamental issues of cost, service, quality and innovation and to be able to create and manage change. Managers in the manufacturing role also have an important part to play in developing the business strategy, notably in co-ordination with the Marketing Department. In a real sense, when you're involved with manufacturing, every other discipline in the company is backing you, because you are the one that is producing exactly what millions of people are buying in the shops every day. This is, after all, what the company is there for in the first place!'

Source: Slack *et al.* (1998), *Operations Management*, Financial Times Pitman Publishing.

CASE STUDY: OPERATIONS MANAGEMENT AT A THEME PARK

Alan Randell, the manager at Thorpe Park, Chertsey, arrives by 9 am, signs on, by radio, with Operations Control, and then calculates today's budgeted attendance – based on historic trading and present marketing initiatives. His estimate of 8000 was surpassed by the eventual attendance of 10 000. He then confirmed states of operations and ride-readiness. The maintenance staff arrive at 6.30 am and the cleaning department at 7.30 am. At 9 am, all cast members (staff) have to be signed in and surveyed for their costume, hair length and entertainment presence. After checking with the admissions supervisor over kiosk state-of-readiness he decided to open 15 minutes early, at 9.15 am. By 9.30, there were already 436 parents and children inside.

After monitoring the turnstiles – he has entry operations responsibility as well as executive responsibility – he walks over the bridge.

'I saw Harley, the costumed character. Harley gave me five. It's a case of getting and delivering a level of adrenaline, happiness and smiles. I then went to see Snoopy's aerobics show. I'm looking to maintain Snoopy for the season. Then, the duty manager briefed me on cleanliness by Octopus Garden.'

There's almost 600 'cast', with 100 having a radio, so everything that's happening in the park comes over and is known about immediately, whether it's inside No Way Out (the giant backwards turbo-booster ride in pitch blackness), over the Flying Fish by Pot Bellies or on Miss Hippo's Jungle Safari.

'Back in my office I use the computer, which tells me how many fun-seekers are in the park, what time-segment they each arrived in, how that compares with yesterday and the same day last week – or any day in the last four years – and how much each of them paid, how they paid, when they paid ...'

Thorpe Park are dedicated to a family market and a parent-friendliness profile, so the manager constantly monitors rides and adjusts cast levels to control queue lineage and foot-flow.

'So far today I've increased to three the waterbuses from Customs House. We've also had one nose-bleed, a hand hurt on a fence and someone's been sick. After lunch – with this hot bright sunshine – I will be watching closely our key rides, the smash splashers, our wet wet wets: The Depth Charge, Thunder River and Logger's Leap. They'll be the hardest hit when the restaurants and food franchises' trade levels off. And at the Fantasy Reef pool, I'll want to make sure the balance of younger children with older is acceptable, so we'll have extra monitors.'

Source: Developed from an interview by John Hind, *Observer*, 8 June 1997. Reprinted with permission.

THE PROCESS ITSELF

How can it be classified

Operations management is about managing the transformation process, but there are a number of ways in which the process can be classified and these will affect the nature of the task. The classifications presented in this section are mainly applicable to manufacturing, but the concepts also affect service, especially when layout is considered. Process choice is important since it has implications for the way the system operates and is not quick or cheap to change.

There are five major types of process:

- project
- jobbing, unit or one-off
- batch
- line
- continuous

These are sometimes combined into three main categories: job/project, batch/inter-mittent and flow/mass. The exact terminology used will depend on the author of the book concerned, and to some extent whether the book is of US or European origin.

PROJECT

This type of process is used to produce a one-off item, e.g. a new building or film, or for a one-off service, e.g. a consultancy assignment. There is a sequence of opera-tions, but they are not usually repeated. The task is usually done at the customer's site (although not exclusively).

The major operations management task is to plan, sequence, co-ordinate and control the tasks leading to completion of the whole project – this is called project management. The process is usually relatively high cost with difficulty in automa-tion because of the lack of repeatability.

JOBBING, UNIT OR ONE-OFF

This type of process is used for one-off or small order requirements, with the prod-uct being of a smaller nature than for a project process, e.g. a purpose-built piece of equipment, designer dress, handmade shoes, bespoke computer system. The prod-uct is usually made in house and then transported to the customer, and commissioned before acceptance.

BATCH

This process is used when similar items are required in larger volumes than for a job-bing process, and the products are produced in batches at intermittent intervals. The essential characteristic is that to provide another product/service the process has to be stopped and reset; the same equipment is used for a number of different products. Examples include car components, white goods, casting, a computer bureau that uses the same equipment for work from a number of different clients. General pur-pose equipment and highly skilled labour are used: this gives high flexibility but low efficiency, with problems in controlling inventories, schedules and quality.

This is the type of process on which most production management texts have traditionally concentrated, and for which most methods have been developed. This is realistic since the majority of production is of this type, and probably a lot of service too.

LINE

In this process a linear sequence of operations is used to make the product or ser-vice, with equipment dedicated to that product or small range of products. The process is essentially repetitive where each product passes through the same sequence of operations. Examples include motor vehicle manufacturing, food preparation in McDonald's and some bank operations, e.g. cheque processing. The process is sometimes called 'mass' production, to distinguish it from continuous production. Line processes are very efficient but inflexible, as car makers have discovered to their cost; customers are demanding more variety in products but manufacturers have found it difficult to satisfy this demand because their processes were established for large runs of similar products. The main sources of efficiency are the substitution of capital for labour wherever possible and highly specified labour tasks with a high degree of repetition.

CONTINUOUS

This is a variation of a line process, where several basic materials are processed through successive stages into one final product. It is usually more automated and standardised than a line process. The best example is petrochemicals, but other examples include beer, paper and electricity production. The start-up cost of these processes is generally very high, so they tend to be run continuously, or as near as possible, with little or no labour intervention. This process is not used in services, because there is no labour content.

There are many detailed accounts of the various characteristics of the different classification of operations. Figure 14.16 summarises some of the key aspects as they affect the operations management task.

	JOB/PROJECT	BATCH/ INTERMITTENT	MASS/LINE
Product aspects			
product flow	none	jumbled	sequenced
product variety	very high	high	low
volume	single unit	medium	high
Labour aspects			
skills	high	high	low
task type	non-routine	non-routine	repetitive
Type of capital			
investment	low	medium	high
inventory	medium	high	low
equipment	general purpose	general purpose	special purpose
Operations objectives			
flexibility	high	medium	low
cost	high	medium	low
quality	more variable	more variable	consistent
delivery	low	medium	high

FIG 14.16 SUMMARY OF PROCESS TYPE AND MAJOR OPERATIONAL CHARACTERISTICS
Source: Developed from Hill (1991). Reprinted with permission.

THE ROLE OF THE OPERATIONS MANAGER

There are many frameworks which attempt to describe what an operations manager does. The one to be presented here is based on that developed by Schroeder and has been selected because it is based around the concept that operations management is primarily a decision-making role. There are others who argue that operations is an integral part of any managerial role (e.g. Schonberger and Knod, 1994) and that to some extent, every employee is a 'manager', at least of the immediate workplace (Scott Myers, 1991) – including those who actually make the product or provide the service, first-line supervisors, department heads, general managers as well as technical experts. However, a narrower definition is more common, and relates to those situated within the operations function itself. The involvement with day-to-day operations depends to a large extent on the level of the operations manager within the organisation, with lower-level managers having more detailed involvement. Job titles may include the following, and can relate to lower-level supervisory roles right up to senior management and director positions:

- Materials manager
- Purchasing manager
- Inventory manager
- Production control manager
- Quality manager
- Line manager
- Planning analyst

Operations managers make decisions in five main areas:

- **Quality:** managing quality issues, controlling quality and improving it.

- **Process:** selecting and designing the transformation process, selecting and using the appropriate technology, layout of facilities.

- **Capacity:** forecasting demand, making decisions about facility location, planning at top and detailed levels, including project planning.

- **Inventory:** planning appropriate levels of inventory and methods of control, linking inventory to production planning and scheduling.

- **People:** managing the workforce, designing and improving jobs.

The decisions made by an operations manager are both short, medium and long term and involve all aspects of a manager's role: planning, controlling, staffing, (Fogarty *et al.*, 1989). The scope of operations management decisions can be summarised in four categories (developed from Fogarty *et al.*, 1989) where the various dimensions of decision making are combined (*see* Fig 14.17).

A single decision may be made using criteria from any or all of the four areas, and it should be noted that they are interrelated, so that decisions made in one area will affect other areas. An overall plan, strategy and direction are needed in

TIME PERIOD AFFECTED	RESOURCE MANAGED	DECISION AREA AFFECTED	MANAGEMENT FUNCTION
long range	facilities	capacity	planning
medium range	equipment	materials	execution
short range	materials	quality	control
present	labour	process	organisation
	information	personnel	staffing
	capital		
	energy		

FIG 14.17 DIMENSIONS OF OPERATIONS DECISION MAKING

order to determine the direction of the organisation – the overall goals can then be detailed to determine actions and decisions needed in each functional area, including operations management.

Fogarty says that typical operations management decisions include:

- a plant manager deciding the number of people of different skills that will be needed to meet the schedule for the coming year;

- a restaurant manager deciding the number of cooks, waiters and other staff that will be needed on each shift during the coming week, and then scheduling individuals to work those shifts;

- an analyst in a bank studying the processing of customer's cancelled cheques, searching for methods of reducing bottlenecks in the operation, reducing the flowthrough time and increasing productivity;

- a manager of a goods receiving department studying methods of scheduling arrivals, assigning incoming trucks to unloading bays, unloading trucks, processing the necessary data, moving the items received to their proper location and eventually to their point of use.

The skills required for an operations manager are common with those of any manager, although there are a number of particular factors which are important. Most operations managers have a relatively high level of quantitative skill, which is useful in utilising the decision-making models which are a part of much operations management. A high level of interpersonal skill is also required, owing to the number of people involved. Many education systems in the West do not permit a wide enough range of interpersonal and behavioural skills to be developed if a high level of 'technical' education is pursued, with the result that many operations managers are criticised for being technically capable but not managerially proficient. Attempts are now being made to address this at all levels of the education system.

Some of the typical tasks undertaken by an operations manager include:

- **management of a cost centre;**
- **efficiency in the short and long term;**

441

- management of technology;
- control of subsystems within the whole;
- responsibility for work and money flow;
- characterised by tangible outputs;
- managing complexity.

Management of a cost centre

An operations manager is responsible for a large proportion of the organisation's assets, and therefore controls a relatively large budget. While this does not necessarily require detailed accounting skills, a good understanding of financial matters is an asset.

Efficiency in the short and long term

Day-to-day activities have to be well controlled, but an operations manager also has to have a long-term view, and must consider long-term trends too. The danger is to be only short-term oriented, because that is the most pressing consideration. The operations manager's task has been described as follows:

'the task is problem oriented . . . pressure is also a distinctive feature'.

Management of technology

The operations manager may have to manage technology both within the product itself and within the process. It is increasingly difficult for operations managers to keep up to date with technological advances in any detail, and so they should attempt to understand the level of technology employed and its purpose, rather than the details of individual technologies which should be left to technical experts. Maintaining this balance and avoiding the temptation to get drawn into detailed technical issues are often difficult.

Control of subsystems within the whole

Operations managers will have a number of different groups reporting to them and may be responsible to several different functions. A balance between the potentially conflicting demands of the various groups is needed, making sure they all contribute effectively to the whole. The danger is that the performance of one subsystem will be optimised at the expense of the others.

Responsible for money and work flow

Maintaining the balance between spending money and carrying out productive work is one of the major issues for operations managers. Figure 14.18 shows that money is spent until the goods have been produced, and it is only at that point that the organisation may begin to get money in (assuming a standard manufacturing process, not a project environment). In order to satisfy monthly accounting targets, operations are often put under pressure to 'get things out' at the end of the

MONEY FLOW	CURRENT ASSETS	WORK AND MATERIALS FLOW
OUT	raw materials and components	materials/components bought from outside
OUT	work in progress (WIP)	labour and other materials/components added
OUT	finished goods	more labour and materials/components added
IN		finished goods/services sold (cash sales)
IN (eventually)		finished goods/services sold (credit sales)
IN		payment made for credit sales

FIG 14.18 MONEY, WORK AND MATERIAL FLOW

month so that money can come in, although this may not be optimal in terms of efficiency within the operations function. The link between commercial rules, negotiated by the accounting function, and the operation of the process is not always clearly defined.

Characterised by tangible outputs

Even in the case of services, this will be true to some extent. Operations management is the management of the transformation process, which always has some form of output and which usually has at least some physical element. Because of the relative ease of measurement of the 'quality' or other features of the output, the short-term aspects of the operations management task are often given too high a priority. Coupled with the fact that operations is not always incorporated into corporate strategy, although it is argued that it should be (Hill, 1993; Skinner, 1969), there is a tendency simply to optimise the physical aspects of short-term performance.

Managing complexity

While this is true of any managerial task, the challenge for operations managers does not arise from the individual tasks involved, which of themselves can be quite tedious, but from combining the large number of these to make something which works well and is effective for the organisation as a whole. This task is well summarised by Schonberger and Knod (1994):

'Effective operations management blends the interests of customer, employee, and manager, along with those of the public, shareholders, and other stakeholders. Diverse resources, changing technologies, and hard-to-predict demands add to the challenge. Human ingenuity, diligence, and the right management tools, are required to blend all the interests properly.'

A typical day in the life of an operations manager is given in the following case study.

CASE STUDY: A DAY IN THE LIFE OF AN OPERATIONS MANAGER

Sue Jones is the operations manager for the UK plant of Estech Ltd – a medium-sized company that manufactures and repairs marine seismic equipment used by oil companies engaged in offshore oil exploration. The main activity is the manufacture and repair of hydrophonic cables towed by seismic survey ships. Each cable is made up of sections and costs about £500 000. Repair and technical support arrangements are vital given the hostile nature of the marine environment.

The plant is divided into two main areas, cable manufacture and repair, and technical manufacture and repair. Each area has a manager who is responsible to Sue, who currently has 40 people working for her. She is directly responsible to the managing director for all aspects of production, repairs, logistics, quality, site facilities and research and development.

8 am In the factory
The main factory starts at 7.30 am and Sue walks round the plant for half an hour talking to people, including John Butler, the filling shop supervisor. The previous day there were problems with one of the machines and Sue wants to check progress.

8.30 am Sue's office
Jim Edwards, the quality manager, appears at the office door to report that problems with the delivery of a key component have been sorted. Five minutes later it is the site facilities manager who calls. Sue operates an 'open door' policy and consciously sets this time aside for 'mopping up' problems from the previous day.

9 am Cable and repair manager's office
Sue joins the daily meeting of the production team. During the night Sue received a telephone call from the MD who had in turn received a call from the leader of a seismic survey team on board a survey ship off the coast of Nigeria. He had damaged three of his six cables in a collision and is anxious to get the damaged sections of cable repaired. This morning's meeting has to consider the feasibility of getting the damaged sections repaired within the next two weeks as the MD promised. Sue's task is to assess the situation with all those directly involved and with them arrive at a decision.

Not only do the team have to consider what is technically possible, they have to think through the consequences of rescheduling work. Fortunately two of the jobs being done this week are routine ones put into the schedule because there was a gap between two high-priority jobs. After much discussion the consensus is that the Nigerian job can be fitted in. Staff are going to have to reschedule their work and there will have to be some overtime, but the client is going to get what he wants.

9.45 am Sue's office
The next hour and a half are devoted to work on ongoing projects. These include negotiating the technical requirements of a major new potential customer, the development of a new product and the evaluation of a new supplier.

11 am Reception
Sue meets two visitors from a potential new customer. After a tour of the plant she joins them

in a meeting with the cable repair manager and two technicians.

1 pm Canteen
Lunch and an opportunity to talk to two new members of staff about their training course.

2 pm Sue's office
She makes some phone calls and prepares some faxes, as well as holding a meeting with the management accounts manager. The board has requested that the monthly production report should be available seven days after the month end rather than 14 days as at present. The meeting is to explore what needs to be done in order to meet the request. Once this meeting is over, Sue checks her 'things to do list'. The human resource manager has requested a job specification for a new technical post which has to be ready the following day.

4 pm The factory
The job specification is still not complete. Sue is back on the shop floor to check progress on the Nigerian job. All the schedule revisions have been sorted out and work will start in two days' time when the damaged cables arrive back in the UK.

4.15 pm Sue's office
Sue takes stock of the day. The job specification is still incomplete. She checks the 'things to do list' again. She has an appointment with the R&D manager at 5.00 pm. There are some minor administrative tasks that can be put off to the end of the day so Sue decides to finish the job specification immediately.

5 pm R&D manager's office
At the meeting, Dr Broadley, the R&D manager, is anxious that a new piece of equipment be purchased to facilitate his work on an enhancement to one of the company's major products. Sue agrees to take the matter up with the MD.

5.15 pm MD's office
Sue goes to see the MD and they review the day's events, particularly their success in fitting in the repair job for Nigeria, and the R&D manager's request for new equipment. They agree to investigate this further.

5.30 pm Sue's office
Sue dictates three letters and a couple of memos for the following day, sorts out the few remaining items left on her desk ready for tomorrow, and locks up and leaves.

Source: Developed from Waters, D (1996) *Operations Management*, Addison Wesley Longman.

THE OUTPUTS

Productivity as a performance measure

Measuring performance is one of the most important aspects of operations management, and one which has received a great deal of attention during the past few years. In order to make any improvements to the functioning of the transformation process, there must be methods for measuring its current effectiveness. This section considers the 'traditional' measures of performance, and the following section discusses more recent developments.

Productivity is the broadest and most common measure of operations management performance, and basically assesses how resources are utilised and managed to achieve a set of desired results. Productivity is defined as the ratio of output to input:

$$\frac{\text{output}}{\text{input}} = \frac{\text{results achieved}}{\text{resources consumed}}$$

An increase in productivity can therefore result from *either* an increase in output *or* a decrease in input. However, the problems of measuring output and input in the same units, and the debate about whether the resulting ratio has any real meaning, has led to productivity being considered in relative terms, i.e. considering *changes* in the ratio, comparing results in one period with those in another. A productivity index is often used, in which one period is given a value of 100 and then subsequent periods compared to the base.

Productivity has been a popular measure for many years, primarily because it is directly linked to profit, and has therefore attracted a good deal of senior management attention. If a percentage increase in sales is compared with an equivalent percentage increase in productivity, there is a very different effect on profit (*see* Fig 14.19).

While this analysis fails to indicate the relative amount of effort required to achieve the same percentage change in sales and productivity, it does demonstrate the link between productivity and profit which has for so long attracted the attention of senior managers.

There are three levels at which productivity may be measured:

- **national** – where the productivity of a nation or group of nations is measured. International comparisons are then made, and the resulting debates often lead to blame being allocated to various groups such as stockholders, operations managers, research managers;

- **industry** – where the productivity of particular sectors within the economy is measured. Most governments issue statistics on the relative performance of both manufacturing and service industries – often expressed as output per employee per hour. Such statistics are useful for individual firms to compare their performance to the industry average, although relative change is probably more important than absolute measures.

- **organisational** – where the productivity of a particular organisation is measured. This may be expressed in terms of:

	BEFORE CHANGES	AFTER 10% SALES INCREASE	AFTER 10% INCREASE IN PRODUCTIVITY
Sales	£100	£110	£100
Variable costs	£70	£77	£63
Fixed costs	£20	£20	£20
Profit	£10	£13 (+30%)	£17 (+70%)

FIG 14.19 IMPACT OF CHANGES IN SALES AND PRODUCTIVITY

TFP = total factor productivity

$$= \frac{\text{output}}{\text{labour + capital + materials}} \quad \text{(all measured in cost terms)}$$

Partial productivity measures relate the value of output to the value of one of the inputs:

$$\text{e.g. labour productivity} = \frac{\text{output (£ value)}}{\text{labour hours (or costs)}}$$

Labour productivity has been the most common measure, especially in manufacturing, but it oversimplifies the basis on which operations should be assessed and is misleading. It was used because it is relatively easy to calculate, because labour was a significant factor of production when productivity was first conceived, and because labour cost was seen as more inherently variable than material or capital. However, the relatively low proportion of total cost represented by labour cost in most manufacturing organisations today makes this measure unrepresentative. This relative proportion of costs attributable to 'staff' in various industries is shown in Fig 14.20 and it should be borne in mind that this will include indirect labour too (that allocated to overhead rather than that which varies with the volume of business being done).

An alternative measure of performance that has been developed more recently is added value:

$$\text{Added value = sales revenue – material and outside service costs}$$

$$\text{Added Value Index (AVI)} = \frac{\text{total employment costs}}{\text{added value}}$$

This is particularly useful for measuring managerial performance, since it is less affected by factors external to the manager's control (e.g. inflation) than is profit, and focuses on employee productivity which is a major managerial task.

	STAFF	TECHNOLOGY, FACILITIES & EQUIPMENT	MATERIALS/ BOUGHT-IN SERVICES
Hospital	45%	35%	20%
Car manufacturing plant	25%	15%	60%
Bus company	52%	40%	8%
Supermarket	10%	25%	65%

FIG 14.20 COMPOSITION OF TOTAL COST

FACTOR	SUBSECTORS
External	government regulation business competition customer demand *Generally not as influential as people think: there is still a lot of scope for improvement*
Capacity & inventory	capacity planning inventory management purchasing *Excess capacity often gives adverse productivity, and inventory can be a two-edged sword – too little leads to lost sales, reduced volume, and too much leads to higher capital*
Product	value engineering product diversity R&D *Too many new products reduce focus on new processes, and spread operations too thinly*
Process	layout process flow automation process selection *Process type and layout must be matched to the market; substituting capital for labour is still effective, where processes are basically manual or labour intensive*
Workforce	unionisation goals and rewards supervision organisation structure job design training selection and placement *Receiving a lot of attention, should be viewed as an integrated task, like the management of all other resources*
Quality	quality improvements *Error prevention and right-first-time programmes can improve productivity; measuring quality, e.g. costs, is very important, and necessary prior to an effective productivity improvement programme*

FIG **14.21** FACTORS THAT AFFECT PRODUCTIVITY

Measuring productivity is not enough: the factors which affect it must be understood, since they are the things that are under managerial control. Figure 14.21 summarises the main factors that affect productivity at the organisational level.

Undertaking a productivity improvement programme is one way to address the issue of performance improvement. Often companies have trouble getting started on productivity improvement because they do not have measures of productivity, commitment to change or feedback on results achieved. It should be borne in mind that any improvements in productivity should be made within the context of the organisation as a whole, and after consideration of how productivity improvement affects other performance objectives such as increased flexibility and reduced leadtime.

Steps that might be taken to instigate a productivity improvement programme are as follows (*see also* Fig 14.22):

- develop productivity measures at all levels of the organisation:
  - develop by managers, with staff assistance;
  - some units will need more than one measure;

- set goals for productivity improvement in terms of the measures stated:
  - realistic and time-dependent goals are needed;

- develop plans to meet the goals:
  - how will the goals be met?

- implement the plan:
  - easier if those doing it have been involved in formulating the plan;

Honeywell used the following questions to start a company-wide productivity improvement programme:

- What is our competitor's productivity?

- How do our competitors achieve productivity?

- Is there a universal productivity measure?

- How labour intensive should we be?

- Can the productivity of creative work be quantified?

- Who is in charge of productivity improvement?

- Where can a manager get help when he/she has a productivity improvement problem?

- What is the minimally acceptable productivity rate for a division/department/employee?

- How should productivity improvement be woven into annual planning?

FIG 14.22 STARTING A PRODUCTIVITY IMPROVEMENT PROGRAMME

- measure results:
  - data collection;
  - periodic assessment of results;
  - corrective action or revision of goals may be necessary.

The new way of measurement

The limits of productivity as a measure of operations performance, coupled with the trends in organisations and the environment which have led to a greater focus on customer needs, have led to new ways of operations performance evaluation being developed (*see* Chapter 7). Productivity is no longer seen as a single measure, although it may be used in conjunction with others. It is now generally accepted that the main criteria to be used for evaluating operations management are:

- **cost** (of the transformation process);
- **quality** (of product or service);
- **delivery** (to customer), sometimes divided into delivery speed and delivery dependability;
- **flexibility** (of process).

Many of the trade-offs which are regarded as an inherent part of operations management are related to these factors. These factors lead to five major performance objectives (Slack *et al.*, 1998):

doing things RIGHT → the QUALITY advantage

doing things FAST → the SPEED advantage

doing things ON TIME → the DEPENDABILITY advantage

CHANGING what you do → the FLEXIBILITY advantage

doing things CHEAP → the COST advantage

An organisation may want to achieve all or one of these, although generally it is not possible to develop action plans which support all of them simultaneously.

Quality

Quality is fundamental and visible, and leads to internal benefits such as reduced cost (because less time is spent in correcting mistakes and putting confusion right) and increased dependability (because people have more time to concentrate on being good at their job, and therefore become more reliable at doing it). (*See* Fig 14.23.)

Speed

This is to do with how long customers have to wait to receive products or services (*see* Fig 14.24). Increased speed reduces inventories (stock) since less material is needed for buffering, and also reduces risks; there is less reliance on forecasting, with more opportunity to make what the customer actually wants.

In a hospital?
- patients receive the most appropriate treatment
- treatment is carried out in the correct manner
- patients are consulted and informed
- staff are friendly and helpful

In a car manufacturing plant?
- all parts made to specification
- all assembly to specification
- product is reliable
- product is attractive

In a bus company?
- buses are clean and tidy
- buses are quiet and fume free
- timetable is accurate and easy to understand
- staff are friendly and helpful

In a supermarket?
- goods are in good condition
- store is clean and tidy
- decor is appropriate and attractive
- staff are friendly and helpful

FIG **14.23** WHAT DOES QUALITY MEAN?
Source: Developed from Slack *et al.* (1998).

In a hospital?
- time between requiring and receiving treatment
- time for test results to be returned

In a car manufacturing plant?
- time between deals requesting a vehicle and getting it
- time to deliver spares to service centres

In a bus company?
- time between customer setting out and reaching destination

In a supermarket?
- time taken for total transaction from selecting goods to leaving store
- availability of goods (are they on the shelf?)

FIG **14.24** WHAT DOES SPEED MEAN?
Source: Developed from Slack *et al.* (1998).

Dependability

This is concerned with doing things in time for customers to receive their product or service when they were promised (*see* Fig 14.25). Dependability saves time: less time has to be spent on sorting out problems and therefore there is more time to spend on direct productive work. It also saves money, where other resources have to be diverted to make up for problems, and gives stability in the operations; a level of trust is built up where things are reliable, and this will be lost when dependability is reduced.

451

In a hospital?
- proportion of appointment cancelled
- keeping to appointment times
- test results returned as promised

In a car manufacturing plant?
- on-time delivery of vehicles to dealers
- on-time delivery of spares to service centres

In a bus company?
- keeping to the published timetable at all points on the route
- availability of seats for passengers

In a supermarket?
- predictability of opening hours
- proportion of goods out of stock
- keeping to 'reasonable' queuing times
- availability of parking

FIG 14.25 WHAT DOES DEPENDABILITY MEAN?

Source: Developed from Slack *et al.* (1998).

Flexibility

This is to do with being able to change the operation in some way – what it does, how it does it or when it does it. There are four main types of flexibility:

- **product/service:** different products or services;
- **mix:** a wide range of products/services;
- **volume:** different quantities of products/services;
- **delivery:** different delivery times.

Further details about flexibility can be found in Slack (1989). Examples of flexibility in various types of operation are shown in Fig 14.26.

Flexibility has a number of internal benefits. It speeds up responses, for example when emergencies arise in a hospital; it saves time in changing over from one task to another; and maintains dependability where resources can easily be swapped to other tasks in order to fulfil overall promises.

Cost

This is still the major objective for many organisations, who believe that they compete primarily on cost, although often customers do have other considerations. Cost is incurred in three main areas:

TYPE OF FLEXIBILITY	HOSPITAL	CAR MANUFACT- URING PLANT	BUS COMPANY	SUPERMARKET
Product/ service	introduction of new types of treatment	introduction of new models	introduction of new routes	introduction of new goods or promotions
Mix	range of available treatments	range of product options	number of locations served	range of goods stocked
Volume	ability to adjust number of patients treated	ability to adjust number of vehicles manufactured	ability to adjust frequency of services	ability to adjust number of customers served
Delivery	ability to reschedule appointments	ability to reschedule manufacturing priorities	ability to reschedule trips	ability to obtain out of stock items

FIG 14.26 EXAMPLES OF FLEXIBILITY

Source: Developed from Slack *et al.* (1998).

- staff costs;
- technology, facilities and equipment costs;
- material costs and bought-in services.

The breakdown of total cost is, however, very different in different types of organisation, as shown in Fig 14.20. All the other objectives act on costs, via the internal effects described earlier, so cost improvement can be obtained from improving the other objectives.

Trade-off of performance objectives

If the relative importance of each performance objective is to be considered, then the possibility of trade-offs between objectives must also be considered. The conventional view is that improvement in one aspect of performance can *only* be achieved at the expense of performance in another area:

> *'Most managers will readily admit that there are compromises or trade-offs to be made in designing an airplane or truck. In the case of an airplane, trade-offs would involve matters such as cruising speed,*

take-off and landing distances, initial cost, maintenance, fuel con-sumption, passenger comfort and cargo or passenger capacity. For instance, no one can design a 500 passenger plane that can land on an aircraft carrier and also break the sound barrier. Much the same thing is true in manufacturing.'   (Skinner, 1969)

This has, however, been challenged by organisations which give the 'best of both worlds'. For example, quality and cost used to be seen in opposition, so that improved quality could only be had at greater cost, whereas now it is recognised that improved quality may actually reduce cost.

Constraints on improvement may be technical or attitudinal. For example, if the attitude about quality changes from: 'screen the bad products out' to 'stop the mistakes being made in the first place', then the quality/cost trade-off becomes irrelevant. This has happened in many of the 'world-class' organisations.

The long-term aim of operations managers has to be to change those things within the operation that cause performance of one aspect to deteriorate as the other improves, i.e. to change the constraints on the operation in total, rather than merely altering one aspect. Weak companies appear to embody the trade-off mentality in the way they operate, and suffer as a result. Companies attempting to improve develop immunity to some of the trade-offs, many having started with eliminating the cost/quality trade-off. 'World-class' companies aim for improvement in all areas and have largely eliminated trade-off obstacles.

THE EXTERNAL ENVIRONMENT

Operations management and the customer

Customers are important for any organisation, and it has already been shown that interaction between the operations function and the customer has increased in the past few years, and is likely to continue to do so. It is therefore important to consider the points at which the customer influences operations performance.

It has already been shown that the customer will have needs which should be met by the organisation. However, the needs of the customers themselves may have a number of components:

- **a statement of recognised need;**
- **an expectation of the way in which that need should be met;**
- **an idea of the benefits of having that need met.**

It can therefore be seen that 'customer requirements' are not simply concerned with the product or service provided, but also the way in which the operation is carried out and the expected effect on the customer. This is of particular importance for operations managers.

Customers have a direct influence on performance objectives through critical success factors: the key things by which the customer decides whether the organisation and its products are suitable for its needs. The link between these is shown in Fig 14.27.

While it is difficult to generalise about customer needs, it has been shown that in broad terms customers appear to have the requirements shown in Fig 14.28.

CRITICAL SUCCESS FACTORS	PERFORMANCE OBJECTIVES
If customers value things . . .	*then the operation will need to be good at these things . . .*
price →	cost
quality →	quality
fast delivery →	speed
reliable delivery →	dependability
innovative products and services →	flexibility of product/service
wide range of products and services →	flexibility of product/service mix
the ability to change timing or quantity of products or services →	flexibility of volume and/or delivery

FIG 14.27 CRITICAL SUCCESS FACTORS AND PERFORMANCE OBJECTIVES
Source: Developed from Slack *et al.* (1998).

HIGH	LOW
quality	costs
flexibility: to change volume, specification, delivery	lead times: and getting shorter all the time for new products and processing ongoing demands
levels of service	variability: most customers prefer no variability at all

FIG 14.28 CUSTOMER REQUIREMENTS
Source: Developed from Schonberger and Knod (1994). Reprinted by permission of Richard D Irwin Inc, Burr Ridge, Illinois.

These do not represent trade-offs; most customers do not want better quality at the expense of lower costs – they want better quality *and* lower cost! Not just that, they want continuous improvement in all aspects.

However, it is also important to be able to distinguish between critical success factors – not all are equally important for all customers. One way of doing this is through order-winning and order-qualifying criteria (Hill, 1993):

- **order-winning criteria**: those things which significantly contribute to getting an order against competitors in the same market. They are the most important in terms of defining competitive position – raising performance in an order-winning factor will either result in more business or improve the chances of gaining more business.

455

	PRODUCT GROUP 1	PRODUCT GROUP 2
Products	standard electronic medical equipment	electronic measuring devices
Customers	hospitals/clinics	other medical equipment companies
Product specification	not high-tech, but with periodic updates	most types are high performance
Product range	narrow – 4 variants	very wide with some customisation
Design changes	infrequent	continual
Delivery	fast – from stock	on-time delivery important
Quality	means reliability	means performance
Demand	predictable	unpredictable
Volume per product type	high	medium to low
Profit margins	low to medium	medium to very high
Critical success factors	↓	↓
Order winners	*price* *product reliability*	*product specification* *product range*
Order qualifiers	*delivery speed* *product performance* *quality*	*on-time delivery* *delivery speed* *price*
Less important	*product range*	
	↓	↓
Internal performance objectives	*cost* *quality*	*product/service flexibility* *mix flexibility* *dependability*

Fig 14.29 Comparison of critical success factors and performance objectives
Source: Developed from Slack *et al*. (1998).

456

- **order-qualifying criteria**: the aspects of performance that have to be above a certain level in order for the product/service even to be considered by the customer. They get the product into the market, or onto the customer's list.

Figure 14.29 shows the characteristics of two product groups produced by the same company, the way in which they differ, and the impact this has on order-qualifying and order-winning criteria.

Another way in which the customer indirectly influences operations is through the pattern of demand which enables the organisation to decide whether to make to order or make to stock. The decision will be related to the type of process employed, but not always directly. This is a key decision for every organisation, with advantages depending on the product and the market.

A make-to-order organisation responds to a customer order before starting manufacture. However, it may manufacture kits or subassemblies before customer orders are received, in order to be able to deliver within an acceptable leadtime.

A make-to-stock organisation does not assign orders to individual customers during the production process.

Figure 14.30 shows the impact of these two options on performance objectives and the major problems.

Customer interaction with the operations function will also depend on the type of process being employed. Figure 14.31 shows the nature of customer and supplier relationships for different classifications of operations.

CHARACTERISTICS	MAKE-TO-STOCK	MAKE-TO-ORDER
Product	producer specified low variety inexpensive	customer specified high variety expensive
Objectives	balance inventory, capacity and service	manage delivery leadtimes and capacity
Main operations problems	forecasting planning production control of inventory	delivery promises delivery leadtime

FIG 14.30 CHARACTERISTICS OF MAKE-TO-STOCK AND MAKE-TO-ORDER ENVIRONMENTS
Source: Developed from Schroeder, R G (1993) *Operations Management*, 4th edn, © Copyright The McGraw-Hill Companies, Inc 1993. Reproduced with permission of McGraw-Hill, Inc.

While the general principles concerning improvement of relationships with both suppliers and customers are valid for all organisations, it can be seen that operations will have a very different relationship with external agents depending on the nature of the process employed within the organisation.

		TYPICAL PROCESS CHARACTERISTICS			
		Project	**Jobbing ⟷ Batch ⟷ Line**		**Continuous**
CUSTOMERS	**Nature of sales**	one-off tenders	one-off tenders	defined prices with discounts	well established
	Degree of interaction	small	small	highly organised	long-term and highly organised
SUPPLIERS	**Relationships**	variable	informal	formal	long-term contracts
	Degree of interaction	variable	small	highly organised	highly organised

Fig 14.31 Process characteristics, customers and suppliers
Source: Developed from Hill (1991). Reprinted with permission.

INTERNATIONAL DIFFERENCES

Operations management is the same in principle wherever it is practised. However, there are differences in emphasis in different parts of the world which are argued to have implications for differences in productivity and organisational performance, especially between the West and the Far East. There is also an ongoing debate about the extent to which the national culture affects the decision-making role of the operations manager, and the methods which may be employed.

The global nature of business is now widely accepted, and yet its implications for operations have not always been thought through. Schroeder (1993) distinguishes between three types of international firms:

- **Global** – marketing a similar product throughout the world, with a world-wide scale of operations.
- **Multinational** – marketing and producing products in various countries, suited to local tastes. It is usually organised with separate divisions or independent foreign subsidiaries in each country.
- **Export** – ships product to various countries from a domestic facility. It may use agents for marketing abroad.

Schroeder argues that each type of firm still has a place, since they can compete on different things. A global firm is well placed to gain economies of scale and compete primarily on price. A multinational firm can differentiate its products for the relevant local markets, as well as differentiating service, quality, responsiveness to customer demands or other factors that may have local importance.

The main issues to consider in developing an understanding of international operations strategy are as follows:

- **Location of operations to form an international network.** This is a cost issue, but also has to take into account cultural issues and legal considerations, as well as potential markets.

- **Management of the network across national boundaries.** Technology has had a beneficial effect on this, but there are still issues to be considered.

- **Development of different operations practices within different countries.** This seems to be inevitable, however central the control of the organisation is. The social, political, demographic and economic environments all have a significant effect on the development of these practices.

- **Transfer of practices from one country to another.** This is a key issue for the West at present, as people try to implement Japanese-style practices within their own organisations. Many companies have found that the practices are applicable, but that they need some modification. The more similar the cultural and economic context, the easier it appears to be to transfer operations practices successfully.

There are a set of common principles which appear to be followed by the leading 'world-class' manufacturers in Japan, Germany and the USA. All these principles relate to the operations function. Authors differ as to the exact wording of these principles, although Schroeder (1993) broadly summarises them as follows:

- **Put the customer first.** This has to be followed by everyone, not just the salesforce.

- **Be quality conscious.** Quality has to be thought into every product, and every aspect of performance seen through the customer's eyes.

- **Involve employees.** This means seeking consensus and input from everyone, and the development of mutual trust and respect.

- **Practise just-in-time production.** This means striving to reduce waste in all forms, including inventory, space, errors and overhead.

- **Emphasise appropriate technology.** This includes technological innovation but also the use of technology where appropriate.

- **Emphasise the long term.** Where the short-term interests of shareholders are promoted at the expense of long-term investment, organisations struggle on a world-class scale.

- **Be action oriented.** World-class companies are relatively small and decentralised, with relatively flat organisation structures.

SUMMARY

■ This chapter shows that operations management may be considered to be a transformation process where inputs are transformed into outputs. This is a good basis for analysis of the influences on and functioning of operations.

■ Operations management has developed from and been influenced by a variety of factors from a number of academic disciplines.

■ The relationship between the operations function and other functions within the organisation depends on the type of organisation, i.e. the extent to which an organisation produces goods or services. This will also affect the nature of the operations management task, in particular the emphasis placed on various factors of operations management.

■ The major trends affecting operations include an increased emphasis on the customer, continuous improvement, involvement of everyone in the organisation, integration with other organisational functions and globalisation of organisations.

■ The operations process may be classified according to volume and type of product or service produced, and this will have an impact on the role of the manager.

■ The outputs from the process may be measured using a traditional ratio of input to output resources, but this is limited in applicability. New ways of measuring focus on the effectiveness of the five operations performance measures: quality, cost, delivery speed, delivery dependability and flexibility.

■ Customers and their requirements are increasingly important in determining how operations are managed, and it is important for the organisation to develop an understanding of the needs of the customer and the way in which they judge the suitability of an organisation, product or service.

■ The international context has also become increasingly important, particularly with the increased market share gained by Japanese manufactured goods, and merger and acquisition activity. Although it is not clear whether operations techniques are fully transferable across national boundaries; it seems that national culture may affect their implementation.

REVIEW AND DISCUSSION QUESTIONS

1   What is operations management and what is meant by the transformation process in an organisation?

2   How do the characteristics of services differ from those of products?

3   How does the operations manager carry out his or her role?

4   How can the performance of the transformation process be measured?

5   Why are both customers and the external environment important in operations management?

CASE STUDY: THE GROWTH OF OPERATIONS MANAGEMENT

Operations management has been around ever since people started working together to achieve common goals, but it has grown most rapidly since the Industrial Revolution. At the turn of the twentieth century, people began to look beyond the technology and consider the way it was managed. They found that:

- the productivity of an organisation depends on both the technology available and how well this technology is managed;

- good managers use a variety of knowledge and skills in their decision making, and do not rely on intuition and guesswork.

These findings stimulated the growth of operations management, particularly in the United States. Largely because of this, American companies soon dominated many areas of business. IBM was the world's largest computer manufacturer, General Motors was the largest car maker, ESSO was the largest oil company, American Express was the leading credit card, McDonald's served billions of hamburgers.

But by the 1970s these leading companies seemed to become complacent and did not take advantage of new opportunities. American car manufacturers ignored early demands for smaller, more economical cars, and imported cars soon took a major share of their market. IBM ignored personal computers and continued to work with the shrinking mainframe market. In 1960, seven of the world's 10 largest banks were American, but by 1991 Citicorp – ranked number eight – was the only US bank in the top 10. PanAm and TWA were the world's leading airlines, but neither survived massive reorganisations of the industry.

By the 1980s Japanese companies were leaders in operations management. They concentrated on high quality, customer service and high productivity – and soon dominated industries like motor cycles, consumer electronics, photocopiers, cameras, machine tools, steel, computer chips, shipping, cars and banking. The Japanese share of world car production rose from 3 per cent in 1960 to over 30 per cent in 1990.

Japanese companies did not use any magical formula to achieve their success, but they used sound operations management. Toyota spent 20 years developing a just-in-time system which kept production lines busy but virtually eliminated stocks of raw materials. Hewlett-Packard spent five years improving the quality of their goods to meet the high standards demanded by their customers. The result was a tripling of market share and profit, combined with a halving of manufacturing costs.

More evidence that the Japanese success comes from good management appears when they take over existing factories. In 1977 Motorola employed 1000 hourly paid employees and produced about 1000 television sets a day at their Quasar plant in Chicago. Later that year Matsushita bought the plant. Within two years they cut the indirect staff from 600 to 300, reduced assembly repairs by 95 per cent, reduced annual warranty costs from $16 million to $2 million, doubled the production rate to 2000 sets a day, yet still kept the same 1000 hourly paid staff.

Other countries have learnt from Japan's economic success and are now following their lead, particularly the Pacific Rim countries of South Korea, Taiwan, Singapore and Hong Kong. The economies of India, China and several other countries are developing quickly. At the same time companies in America and Europe are improving their own operations to regain their competitive edge. This has led to a dramatic increase in world trade and international competition. Such competition can only be met by using good operations management. By emphasising operations management an organisation can compete – ignoring operations will inevitably lead to failure. ∎

Source: Developed from Walters, D (1996) *Operations Management*, Addison Wesley Longman.

REFERENCES

Armisted, C G and Killeya, J C (1984) 'Transfer of concepts between manufacture and service', *International Journal of Operations and Production Management*, Vol 3, No 3.

Babbage, Charles (1832) *On the Economy of Machinery and Manufacturers*, London: Charles Knight.

Forgarty, D W, Hoffmann, T R and Stonebraker, P W (1989) *Production and Operations Management*, Cincinnati, Ohio: South-Western Publishing.

George, C S Jr (1968) *The History of Management Thought*, Englewood Cliffs, New Jersey: Prentice-Hall.

Hackman, J R *et al.* (1975) 'A new strategy for job enrichment', *California Management Review*, Summer 1975, pp 57–71.

Harrington, H J (1991) *Business Process Improvement*, New York: McGraw-Hill.

Harris, N D (1989) *Service Operations Management*, London: Cassell.

Hill, T J (1991) *Production/Operations Management*, 2nd edn, London: Prentice-Hall.

Hill, T J (1993) *Manufacturing Strategy*, 2nd edn, Basingstoke: Macmillan.

Ishikawa, K (1985) *What is Total Quality Control? The Japanese Way*, translated by D J Lu, Englewood Cliffs, New Jersey: Prentice-Hall.

Muhlemann, A, Oakland, J and Lockyer, K (1992) *Production and Operations Management*, 6th edn, London: Pitman Publishing.

Porter, M (1985) *Competitive Advantage*, New York: Free Press.

Schmenner, R W (1986) 'How can service businesses survive and prosper?', *Sloan Management Review*, Spring 1986, pp 21–32.

Schonberger, R J and Knod, E M (1994) *Operations Management: Continuous Improvement*, 5th Edition, Burr Ridge, Illinios: Richard D Irwin.

Schroeder, R G (1993) *Operations Management*, 4th edn, New York: McGraw-Hill.

Scott Myers, M (1991) *Every Employee a Manager*, 3rd edn, San Diego: University Associates.

Shostack, G L (1977) 'Breaking free from product marketing', *Journal of Marketing*, April.

Skinner, W (1969) 'Manufacturing – the missing link in corporate strategy', *Havard Business Review*, May–June, pp 136–45.

Slack, N (1983) 'Operations Management and curriculum design', *Management Education and Development*, Vol 14, No 1, pp 19–32.

Slack, N (1989) 'Focus on Flexibility', in R Wild (ed) *International Handbook of Production/Operations Management*, London: Cassell.

Slack, N, Chambers, S, Harland, C, Harrison, A and Johnston, R (1998) *Operations Management*, 2nd edn London: Financial Times Pitman Publishing.

Smith, A (1776) *An Inquiry into the Nature and Causes of the Wealth of Nations*, London: A Strahn and T Caddell.

Taylor, F W (1911) *The Principles of Scientific Management*, New York: Harper.

Underwood, L (1994) *Intelligent Manufacturing*, Wokingham: Addison-Wesley with the Economist Intelligence Unit.

Waters, D (1996) *Operations Management*, Addison-Wesley Longman.

Wheelwright, S C and Hayes, R H (1985) 'Competing through manufacturing', *Harvard Business Review*, January–February, pp 99–109.

Wild, R (1989) *Production and Operations Management*, 4th Edition, London: Cassell.

Wren, D A (1972) *The Evolution of Management Thought*, New York: Ronald Press.

FURTHER READING

Murdick, R G, Rendern, B and Russell, R S (1990) *Service Operations Management*, Needham Heights, Massachusetts: Allyn & Bacon.

Schonberger, R J and Knod, E M (1994) *Operations Management: Continuous Improvement*, 5th edn, Burr Ridge, Illinois: Richard D Irwin.

Schroeder, R G (1993) *Operations Management*, 4th edn, New York: McGraw-Hill.

Slack, N (1991) *The Manufacturing Advantage*, London: Mercury Books.

Slack, N, Chambers, S, Harland, C, Harrison, A and Johnston, R (1998) *Operations Management*, 2nd Edition London: Financial Times Pitman Publishing.

INFORMATION SYSTEMS MANAGEMENT

Mike Harry

OBJECTIVES

The objectives of this chapter are to:

◆ identify the different forms of information used in organisations and businesses

◆ establish an understanding of the systems relationship between the concepts of management, control and information

◆ use the understanding of this relationship to identify the role of the management information system in organisation and businesses

◆ identify and critically assess the management implications of specific forms of computer-based information systems

CASE STUDY: CHALLENGE CONTRACT CATERERS

In the 1990s the staff who served in the kitchens of Unitary Comprehensive School found themselves faced with redundancy. Long before this happened, there had been rumours about 'privatisation' and 'putting out to contract' all catering for institutions under county council control. Those council employees potentially affected ranged from the caterers at County Hall, in schools, at fire and police stations, and at an odd mixture of road depots, training centres and colleges.

The first reliable confirmation of these rumours came when all county council caterers received a note with their wage payment slips. It appeared that they were being made redundant, but that they were free to reapply for other jobs or to bid as contractors. A leaflet accompanying the wage slip gave details of existing catering contractors who might employ redundant staff, and also hinted that staff themselves could form companies which could bid for work.

For Alison Gray the redundancies were a particular blow. She had just moved into the area following a previous redundancy from a job in the financial sector. She had taken up a job as a part-time catering manager at Unitary Comprehensive to supplement her income as she tried to get back on her feet by setting up a new business of her own. The catering management job was not well paid, but it had the advantage of leaving sufficient time in the day for working on her new business ideas.

A meeting was held in the assembly hall of Unitary Comprehensive to protest against the redundancies. It was attended by catering staff from all over the county. There was a desultory attempt by the employees and their trade union to organise action against the redundancies. Alison recognised from her previous business experience that the actions decided on at the meeting would fail. The county council management and their consultants had all the advantages of knowing what was really going on. They anticipated most of the potential moves of the protesters. A few of these, including Alison, concluded that further action was futile after a meeting with teachers and parents' representatives two days later. In the school car park after the meeting, and then in a nearby pub, they decided on a new approach to the problem.

The new approach involved looking beyond the redundancies. The group discussions moved away from a focus on the unfairness of what had happened and theories about what conspiracies had been at work. Instead, they decided that they would challenge what they saw as a manoeuvre by the county council and form their own company which would bid for catering contracts. Given the challenge, they decided to call themselves Challenge Contract Caterers. The choice of the word 'challenge' was an ironic reference to the use of the same word in the public relations leaflet which the county council had included with the redundancy notices. It had referred to the 'challenge' which the council faced in making its services more 'competitive'.

Forming their own company was a peculiar mixture of the obvious and the obscure. Legal and accountancy aspects of the company formation required specialist knowledge and skills which none of the group had. For these they consulted lawyers and accountants. Fortunately, most of the costs incurred were available through a government scheme to encourage new business enterprises.

Details of what the company would do, and how it would do it, presented fewer problems. Alison and all of her colleagues realised that they were the experts when it came to understanding what a catering contract implied in terms of the job to be done and the resources needed. They realised that many of these resources would require an amount of investment capital well beyond their reach, but fortunately Alison's experience in the financial world was a help. She remembered reading reports in the financial press of large-scale catering organisations which were anxious to get into areas such as school and local government via franchising operations.

When the group investigated various potential franchising operations, they found that they had to be careful. What one company described as 'a revolution in industrial catering' amounted to no more than poorer quality product in a different package, backed up by a new advertising campaign. After many meetings and decisions, however, Challenge Contract Caterers fixed a potential franchising contract with a company, and put in their bid for the first round of tenders offered by the county council.

They were especially pleased at not only being successful, but with getting the contract for a group of schools in the area which included Unitary Comprehensive itself. They were also surprised to find that their successful bid made them locally famous. They were featured in a local newspaper in a way that was a mixed blessing. The 'mums go into business' angle of the newspaper article did not project the kind of professional image that Alison felt they needed, but the principle that 'no publicity is bad publicity' seemed also to bring advantages.

ISSUES IN INFORMATION SYSTEMS MANAGEMENT

The Challenge Contract Caterers case has been provided to raise two important issues:

- **What views can be taken of the nature of information?**

- **How does the view taken of information affect its management?**

The important conclusions demonstrated by analysing these issues are that:

- **information is a rich concept;**

- **managing information cannot be divorced from the whole management process.**

The richness of information as a concept

Challenge Contract Caterers might seem different from what could have been expected under the heading of 'information systems management'. A case involving the problems associated with managing a large computer system or the database of a large organisation might have been seen as more appropriate. Such a view would have chosen the stock control and logistics for a large retail chain, or the national computerisation of the social security system as an information system worth managing.

There is a common false assumption behind such a view. To assume that a large database is a more relevant example for the subject of information systems management than the activities of a small group of self-employed people implies that the complexity of an organisation can be equated to its size. According to this

465

view, a multi-million pound business must be more complex than a small number of people working together.

Even a simple non-business example can show that the equating of complexity with size is false. The plumbing system of a house takes up more space than a human being, weighs more and contains more energy. But it is easier to make water automatically come out of a tap than to make an individual human being give out sympathy, money or secret personal information, and much less easy to get a human plumber out on Christmas Eve.

The quality that makes human beings more complex than water systems is *richness*. Richness is not determined by size but by the *variety* of components contained in a particular whole and the degree of complexity of their interaction. This chapter will certainly cover important information systems management issues in the context of large organisations as well as small ones, but Challenge Contract Caterers will have achieved one of its purposes if it breaks the equation of complexity with size.

To show the richness of information as a concept, this chapter will consider in more detail some of the different views that can be taken of it, regardless of the size of organisation involved. In Challenge Contract Caterers, as well as many other organisations big and small, information might been seen as:

- data organised into a particular *structure*;

- the output of a *process* applied to other information or data;

- a means of *communication* between a sender and a receiver;

- a form of *knowledge*;

- a source of *clarification* and *reduction of uncertainty*;

- a possession which gives *power*;

- something of *interest*;

- *intuition*, with no immediately obvious logical source.

Next, consider each of these views, both in the specific context of Challenge Contract Caterers and in a wider choice of large and small organisations.

Examples of information as data organised into a particular *structure* can be seen in any business document. An entry such as 'Quantity 10, Price £23.50' contains the same individual characters and figures as 'Quantity 23, Price £10.50', but the information represented is different in each case. The particular structure used to organise data gives it an overall meaning called 'information'. The study of the concept of a database, later in this chapter, will show that a major property of a database management system is the ability to assemble data in the particular structure required by the user to produce necessary information.

Information is the output of a *process* applied to other information or data. The previous invoice example would also need to contain information about cost. This is easily obtained by multiplying the quantity and price, but such a trivial example is just one instance of the whole concept of data processing. From this viewpoint an information system can be seen as a kind of information factory that uses raw material called data and transforms it to produce a product called information. This chapter considers some of the different forms of transformation an information system has to carry out. The important implication for management, however, is that management itself is a customer for the product of this information factory. Throughout this chapter the management role in the design and operation of information systems will be emphasised.

Information implies *communication* between a sender and a receiver. Unread, unused or unknown information is a managerial nonsense: words have to be spoken, documents sent and electronic data transmitted. It is also important to remember that a glance or a nod can be informative. At Challenge Contract Caterers, Alison Gray and her colleagues had little or no initial information about their future becauses communication was confined to rumours. Once their payslips turned up, they suddenly were people who had information, however unwelcome. This chapter will show how an information system needs to deal with the communication of both hard and soft information.

Information as a form of *knowledge* is implied by phrases such as 'to know' and 'being informed'. In Challenge Contract Caterers, Alison Gray *knew* about franchising and other aspects of business, and she used this information as an aid to managing the setting up and operation of the company. Issues such as this will be explored further under intelligent and expert systems and the concept of a knowledge base.

The concept of information as a means of *clarification* and *reduction of uncertainty* follows from the view of it as a form of knowledge. Knowing about a whole range of factors enabled Challenge Contract Caterers to take hold of a business opportunity and be clear about their goals and the means of achieving them. The information involved covered a range from people's tastes in meals to company law. Again, this issue will be relevant to the study of expert systems and knowledge bases, but it introduces the more general concept of information as a reducer of risk.

Information as a source of *power* played its part in the Challenge Contract Caterers case, as it does in all organisations. It was not just the legal position of the county council that made it successful at getting its own way, since protests and pressure can make politicians change their minds. What increased the council's power was knowing what was going on long before the potential protesters. Similarly, Alison's knowledge of business and finance gave Challenge Contract Caterers power in relation to competing caterers. When considering the relationship between *how* particular information systems are implemented, and *what* they can or do achieve, good information management requires a recognition of the role of management policy and values. This theme will be frequently repeated and built on during the rest of this chapter.

Information as a source of *interest* could be illustrated with any example of vicarious gossip. In Challenge Contract Caterers this could have been someone saying: 'I see they got the catering contract then.' However, if information is a reducer of uncertainty and a source of power, it is also likely to be of interest to management. An important reason for anything but ephemeral interest in information is that we learn something from it that we can use in the future. The gossip who observed the success of Challenge Contract Caterers could have been on the first stage of finding out why, and learning how contracts might be won in the future. This chapter will show how the concept of learning can be integrated with a wider view of the relationship between management and information.

Information as *intuition*, with no immediately obvious logical source, can be used to question many of the views of information we have considered so far. 'Body language', 'it's not what you know but who you know', 'how come you are so clever and me so rich', are quotes and phrases from a view of management which regards all formal views of systems as ignoring what really goes on in management with a human component. Could Alison Gray really ascribe her success to pure reason? Yet all the time perhaps she felt Challenge Contract Caterers would work out well. The aim in this chapter will be to set the concept of an information system in a rich context of control and management.

Management and information systems management

Managing information technology is a major component of modern information systems management. However, most of the issues discussed so far do not come from the technology itself because information systems management is more than the management of:

- formal systems;
- information technology.

Neither of these assertions denies the importance of formal information systems or information technology. Instead, it should be realised that information management, like all other forms of management, requires a range of human and technical skills. The use of the following important management information systems terms therefore needs to be explained:

- information
- control
- management
- system

with the aim of revealing the management implications of the relationship between them.

INFORMATION, CONTROL AND MANAGEMENT SYSTEMS

Figure 15.1 shows the relationship between information, control and management systems. In terms of hierarchical structure, an information system can be seen as a subsystem of a control system, and a control system as a subsystem of a management system. To explain this relationship further, the meaning of the word system needs to be explored, followed by an explanation of the particular examples of management, control and information.

For the application of systems thinking to a broad range of subjects try Beishon and Peters (1981). For a detailed treatment of its application to information systems try Harry (1997).

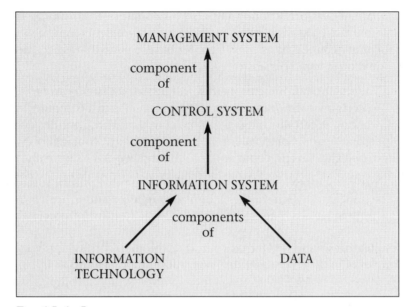

FIG 15.1 INFORMATION, CONTROL AND MANAGEMENT SYSTEMS

Properties of systems

Anything called a system in this chapter will be:

- An assembly of two or more *components*. Thus a computer system might consist of a keyboard, screen, a tower containing the disk drives and central processor, and a printer. If an organisation such as Challenge Contract Caterers is viewed as a system, it would include human, financial and material components, as well as equipment. Components may be physical or concrete. Thus equipment is concrete, information or money are abstract.

- The components will be *connected* together in some fixed set of relationships called a *structure*. The components of a computer system have to be connected up correctly for it to be a system rather than a chaotic heap. Similarly, the very word organisation implies appropriate forms of relationships between people, facilities, equipment and resources. The connections, like the components, may be abstract. Thus membership of an organisation, or the association of information with an individual, is a logical rather than a physical connection.

- The components within this structure will *interact*. Once the components of a computer system are correctly connected together they are able to send electrical signals to each other. Once someone becomes a member of an organisation, they communicate with other people, use equipment and interact in many ways.

- The interaction of the components will result in the system carrying out various *transformation processes*. A computer system will transform input data on, say, hours worked by employees into output information such as wages to be

469

paid. Transformations may also be concrete or abstract. Thus Challenge Contract Caterers physically transforms ingredients into meals; but when the county council transforms a tender bid into one that is accepted, the transformation is logical or abstract.

- The result of all these properties will be that a system can be viewed as a *whole* with its own *identity* and *emergent properties*. Once a computer system is up and working it can do things as a whole system which are not achievable by the separate parts. For Challenge Contract Caterers, 'cooking' only happens when ingredients, ovens, cooks and information about a recipe come together.

- The particular view of the system thus presented will be someone's *concept*. A school pupil, shareholder, county councillor and a health inspector are all likely to have different views of Challenge Contract Caterers as a system.

These features will be referred to and developed as they apply to the particular examples of management, control and information systems as in Fig 15.1.

Management and control

The following definition of management from Harry (1990) can be used as a starting point:

> *'Management is an activity which aims to achieve something desirable to those who manage.'*

How might this apply to the Challenge Contract Caterers case? Alison Gray and her supporters wanted to gain a contract in order to fulfil their ambitions. The county council wanted to reduce its expenditure and provide catering facilities. So both of these groups had something desirable they aimed to achieve.

These examples of 'something desirable' can be used to establish the concept of control as an essential component of management. Control is often taken to imply a particular management style. It may be used with another concept, hierarchy, to signify a rigid, authoritarian approach to management. Such a use of the two terms implies a stereotype 'boss' who 'controls' by 'giving orders'. In this chapter control refers to a concept and not a particular management style.

This distinction between a concept of something, and how it is done, can be expressed as the difference between the *whats* and the *hows*. The 'what' is the concept and the 'how' is the particular way it is implemented. In Challenge Contract Caterers those involved had ideas about what they wanted to achieve: a new lifestyle for Alison or reduced financial costs for the county council. How these were achieved might have been in several different ways. Alison could have continued the fight to retain the jobs; the county council could have tried breaking union agreements and reducing employees' pay. For both parties, these particular ways did not seem to be a good choice. How they eventually chose was different, but what they achieved came close to what they wanted. Alison found a new source of occupation and income; the county council reduced their financial costs.

The stereotypical view of control is restrictive because it fails to recognise the choice of ways of exerting control. The concept of control therefore needs further explanation, to show why it is the link between the concepts of information and management.

The main components of a control system

A standard model of a control system (Schoderbek *et al.*, 1990) has the following components:

- **Defined goals**, regarded as 'something desirable to those who manage'. Goals may be hard and soft. The county council's goal of reducing the number of people employed could be defined in terms of specific figures. Hard goals are those which can be assessed by objective criteria in this way. If Challenge Contract Caterers' goals included producing attractive meals, such a goal would not be objectively definable: it would depend on taste and a subjective interpretation of 'attractive'. Soft goals are those whose interpretation and definition depend on the values, *Weltanschauung* or world view of those concerned.

- **A transformation process** which is capable of achieving the defined goals. This is the same systems concept we covered above, with processes being both concrete and abstract. From a management viewpoint, their output should conform as closely as possible to the system's goals.

- **Environmental disturbances**, which may interfere with the workings of a transformation process and divert it from its goals, are not part of the control system. They are, however, the reason for its existence. Changes in the numbers of pupils requiring school meals, or the enthusiasm of contractor response to invitations to tender, will affect what modification of inputs management will make to the particular process being controlled. More meals would require more cooking facilities, less tenders might require better publicity for council contracts.

- **A sensor** which will enable the controller to register the outputs of the transformation process. The controller is a concept; in practice it could be a particular person, a group or a piece of equipment. Thus it might be a caterer noting a stock level, a clerical worker recording the values of tenders or a thermometer showing the temperature of an oven.

- **Feedback** which communicates the values of the outputs registered by the sensor. If we seek to control it is not sufficient to observe, the observations have to be communicated to those who need them to make control decisions.

- A process, called the **comparator**, which compares the values of the outputs from the transformation process with the goals we wished to achieve. Thus stock levels will be compared with reorder levels to see if a new order should be placed or tenders compared with a committee's view of what is competitive. In these examples, reorder stock level and the value of a competitive tender are goals.

- **An actuator/effector** which will adjust the inputs to the transformation process with the aim of bringing its outputs back towards the goals. Thus stock may be reordered or not, a tender may be accepted or further tenders may be invited.

The terms in bold are the components of the model of a control system illustrated in Fig 15.2. This model has its origins in engineering and cybernetics, but we are interested in its role of connecting management and information systems. If we did not make the distinction between the concept and the implementation of control, there would be the danger of assuming that controlling systems which included human beings was no different from controlling a central heating system or a bathroom shower. (Both of these last two examples are commonly used in textbooks to illustrate control systems.) In this chapter no such assumption is made. A cook and a council committee are both examples of control systems comparators and actuators, but we would not necessarily want a county council committee to cook our dinner.

The information system as a component of the control system

An important feature of Fig 15.2 can now be noted. The loop that runs from the sensor to the actuator/effector consists of components that are all dealing with information. This feature represents one of the important links the control system makes between the wider management system and the information system. Looking further into the control model shows that three types of information are needed for any working of a control system:

- information about the state of the process being controlled at any particular time, and its behaviour over a period. This will come from the sensor monitoring the process outputs;

- information about environmental disturbances;

- information about the goals which the process being controlled should attempt to achieve.

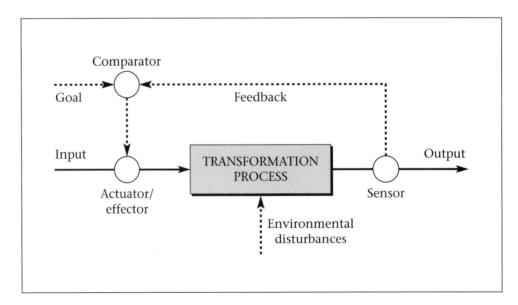

FIG 15.2 CONTROL SYSTEM

Generally, all of the components of the control system which are concerned with the input, processing, storage and output of information can be seen as making up a subsystem of the control system itself. Since the transformation processes of this subsystem are exclusively concerned with information, it can be sensibly called an information system.

There is one important feature missing from this view. Figure 15.2 tells nothing about where the information about goals comes from. A complete view of an information system must also therefore include the process of *goal setting*. Figure 15.3 shows how this is done.

Goal setting can be explained by viewing a control system as a hierarchy. When seeking to control a process, like in the examples above such as holding stock or selecting a tender, those in control must refer to goals like trying to maintain stock within certain levels, or trying to balance tender price and quality of service. However, the needs of catering customers and their numbers can change, or the county council may have to meet new financial and service conditions. Generally, changes in the environment of the organisation which is being managed will require modification of its goals.

This modification of goals, or goal setting, is itself a control process which seeks to control the control system modelled in Fig 15.2. The way it does this involves a similar sequence or loop for sensor to actuator as before. Figure 15.3 therefore shows that a complete control system is a hierarchy of two components or subsystems:

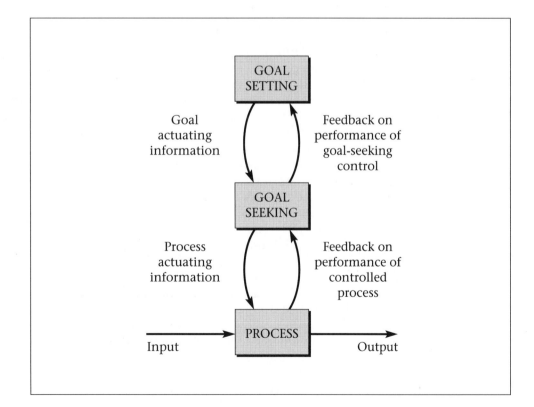

FIG 15.3 GOAL SETTING

- **Goal-seeking** control, which attempts to control a particular process, like stockholding or negotiating tenders in the examples above.

- **Goal-setting** control, which sets and modifies the goals used by goal-seeking control in response to changes in the environment. In the previous examples this resulted in decisions about desired stock levels or price and service quality.

Examples of goal-seeking and goal-setting functions in business organisations are shown in Fig 15.4. The terminology used is that of Harry (1997).

Forms of goal setting in the control hierarchy

The need for a goal-setting control component in the whole control system adds to the role described so far for the information system. Goal-setting control requires:

- The ability to *store* information received as feedback on the behaviour of the goal-seeking component of the control system.

- The ability to *analyse* this information and *learn* from it.

- Access to information about the *Weltanschauung* or world view of management which will enable goal setting to select goals which reflect the norms and values of management.

Referring back to some Challenge Contract Caterers' examples will help illustrate these three points.

The ability to store information can be seen to be necessary if we consider the setting of goals in the context of deciding how to maintain catering stock within certain levels, or selecting tenders which balance price and quality of service.

Which items, and at what stock levels, Challenge Contract Caterers seek to maintain will be a reflection of how anxious they are to promote particular items on the menu. Is a particular item especially profitable? Does it reflect the county council's health policy about diet? Do contractors deliver the services the council wants? What does the council *learn* from past experience of promoting services through allocating them to various contractors?

The answers to questions such as these will enable the management of an organisation to set its goals. Answers will only be possible if past experience is *stored information* available to the learning process; a record is needed of successes, mistakes and their outcome if learning is to happen.

But storage alone is not enough. Learning implies the ability to reflect and *analyse* the experience which is recorded. Raw data on the numbers and contents of meals eaten over a period only becomes information after such actions as comparing costs, calculating trends and looking at the whole picture presented by the data.

Even when data has been stored and analysed in this way, however, something else is needed if goals are to be set or modified. Analysis of stored data on meals will tell about such things as changing costs or popularity of menus. What it will not tell is whether the principal goal is profit maximisation at all costs, say, or a healthy food image. Such choices can only be made on the basis of a management policy, which will in turn reflect the values and norms which come from the *Weltanschauung* or world view of the organisation itself.

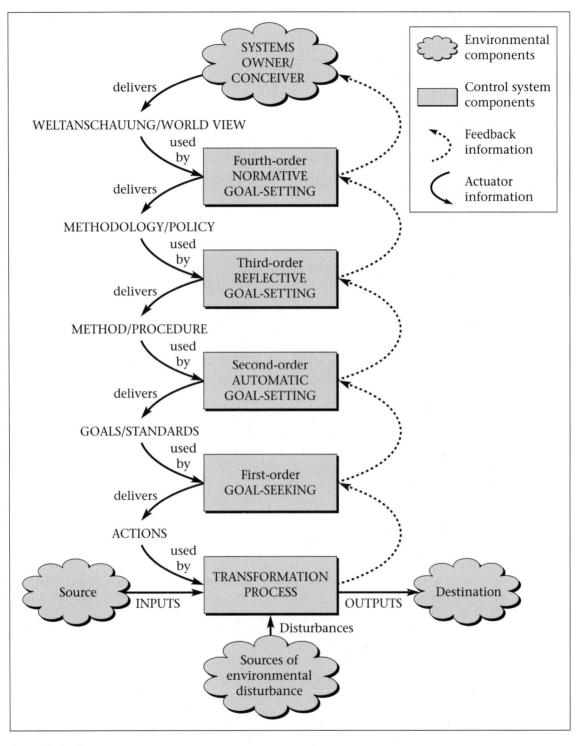

FIG 15.4 GOAL-SEEKING AND GOAL-SETTING FUNCTIONS

Goal setting therefore requires the information system to deal with a mix of hard information on such things as costs or sales, and soft, normative information about policy or values. Whether the physical implementation of the information system in any organisation explicitly recognises the normative component or not, does not prevent it being present. Failure to recognise that all goals reflect certain values does not prevent them from doing so.

A good model of an information system should therefore explain the relationship between the different forms of information that it has to deal with and the role that they play. Figure 15.4 represents one attempt to do this. The model distinguishes three components in the complete process of goal setting:

- **normative;**

- **reflective;**

- **automatic.**

It was shown above that there is a *normative* component in goal setting because goals reflect values. Whether this reflection is conscious or it occurs by default, a normative component is nevertheless present in the goal-setting process. The previous example showed that goals expressed in terms of a catering menu reflected norms about profit and healthy eating.

The *reflective* component in goal setting seeks to produce a method or procedure which can be used to set goals conforming to normative values. Thus if the norm of 'healthy food' means reducing saturated fat content, then reflective goal setting will deliver a method for assessing it.

Once the method has been set, *automatic* testing and calculation can be used to produce a decision about which food combinations on a menu conform to the established norms.

From this review of information, control and management systems, the following conclusions can be drawn:

- The information system of an organisation is more than the formal computing and paperwork system. All forms of information which are used to set goals and help management achieve them should be the concern of information management.

- Ignoring the existence of relevant information on the basis that it is hard to quantify or computerise will merely mean that it continues to play a role in an unmanaged way. Since all forms of information interact through the control system, unmanaged information will distort the workings of the formal system.

DATA PROCESSING AND DATABASE MANAGEMENT

The implications of the principles established for the design, development and operation of computer-based data processing and databases, when working as part of the wider information system, can now be examined in detail.

Designing and developing information systems

The relationships shown in Fig 15.4 have important practical implications for the design and implementation of computer-based information systems.

Figure 15.4 shows the information system as a translator of management *values* or *Weltanschauung* into specific goals expressing what the organisation seeks to achieve through its operations. There is no such thing as 'the' information system. For each organisation, the particular information system which it uses, including the computer-based technological component, will reflect the values of the wider management system. This relationship may not be formalised, but as noted above, 'ignoring the existence of relevant information on the basis that it is hard to quantify or computerise will merely mean that it continues to play a role in an unmanaged way'. In such cases of neglect, the values will be those of accepting accident, anarchy or blind politics as a means of implementing management goals.

If the information system is consciously to reflect the values of management, it should be designed top-down. The term 'top-down' should be understood in terms of the concept of systems hierarchy. The top of this hierarchy is not senior management or the 'bosses', but the whole organisation and its needs. The phrase 'top-down' therefore refers to the concept of using the norms of the whole organisation as a basis for establishing goals and thereby defining the role of the information system in the context of Fig 15.4.

Designing the details of a computerised information system can therefore only follow the establishment of its organisational context. In Challenge Contract Caterers, the council could only decide on the design of a system for accepting tenders after it had decided its political position on subcontracting. The details of *how* catering should be provided could only follow a decision on *what* values the process should reflect.

A modern view, such as Olle *et al.* (1988), sees four major stages in information systems development:

- **information systems planning** – determining the information requirements of the organisation and its business objectives. Also checking any existing information strategy and objectives;

- **business analysis** – analysing the business activities that may be covered by the information systems development process, and the properties of any existing information system;

- **systems design** – the 'prescriptive or definitive activity' which identifies the components of the system to be constructed and describes what they must do;

- **construction design** – how the system design of the previous stage is to be constructed.

Approaches following a version of this sequence are top-down because they establish what the business or organisation does and its information needs first. Only then does the detailed design and construction of the computer-based information system take place. Note also that these last two stages follow the top-down sequence of '*what* they must do' preceding '*how* the system is to be constructed'.

477

Scheduling the information system

The discussion of sensing and feedback above showed that the statement 'information about the behaviour of the process being controlled and its state at any particular time' implies that the sensor in a control system can monitor both *static* and *dynamic* properties of the process being controlled. For example, checking stock levels will not only reveal what is in stock at any time but also how stock levels move over a period. Similarly with checking the financial position of an organisation, the sensor could give the financial assets and liabilities at a particular point in time. Over a period it could also show their net movement. The balance sheet and the profit and loss account are thus examples of the static and dynamic properties of a controlled process.

Another feature of control was the feedback loop. This raises another important issue about sensing outputs: how frequently should the sensing and feedback take place? Our previous example of the balance sheet and profit and loss account illustrates this point. A worried shareholder might wish that accounts for shaky companies came out every month. Busy self-employed people can find the annual task of producing formal accounts, just to satisfy the Companies Act, comes round frequently enough.

In practice, information management must find a balance between:

- **real-time systems**, which continually sense the outputs from controlled processes;

- **batch-processing systems**, which store the information about the outputs from a process over a period of time. Only at the end of this period will it complete the feedback, comparison and actuation loop to modify the inputs to the controlled process.

The particular way in which this balance is made will depend on costs. Figure 15.5 illustrates the principle. One set of costs is associated with the operation of the information system itself. These tend to be higher for systems which operate high-frequency or continuous feedback. The other set of costs is associated with the increase in error or

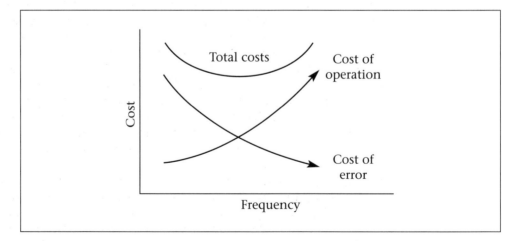

FIG 15.5 COSTS AND INFORMATION SYSTEMS MANAGEMENT

bad management decisions which comes with older, dated information. This tends to be associated with low update frequency batch-processing systems. The relationship between frequency of feedback and the total costs of operating the system will have a minimum, representing the balance between the two cost types.

In practice it is very unlikely that an exact minimum cost frequency could be calculated. It is possible, however, to use the principles illustrated by Fig 15.5 to identify which costs need to be assessed before making management judgements about the kind of information technology needed to support an information system. Some examples will illustrate this.

The first examples are concerned with computer-based information systems with a need for very frequent or near continuous feedback. As shown, these will be expensive to operate. Real-time systems are the extreme example of this. Every time there is any change in the business process being controlled, information about the change is immediately taken up by the computer system and processed. Common examples of real-time systems are:

- airline and hotel chain booking systems;
- banking and financial trading systems;
- large-scale electronic point of sale (EPOS) retailing/stock control systems.

These systems all require recorded information to be up to date. A booking system that could only tell whether there were any seats on a plane flight last week would be business suicide. Similarly, records of vacancies in hotels, the price of stocks and shares or the availability of goods from a central warehouse all require information on the state of the organisation as it is *now*.

Such systems are expensive to operate because the control loop joining the sensor with the rest of the information system is in continuous operation. In practice such systems are likely to be based on a telecommunications network which can immediately transmit data on enquiries, bookings, sales, etc to a computer system that continuously updates records. This also implies elaborate security and back-up to ensure that the system cannot be switched off, as well as paid human operators to ensure it remains in continuous operation.

The expense of a real-time system is justified by the need to avoid the high cost of potential error. In Fig 15.5 organisations requiring real-time systems are those whose cost of error is at high levels for all but the highest frequencies. This pushes the total cost curve minimum position towards high frequencies.

Many businesses do not require such up-to-date information. The costs of information being old are not so important. If employees are paid weekly on the basis of hours worked, it does not matter if there is no available running total during the week. All we need is to collect the daily hours data during the week and process it as a batch. Similarly with many monthly business accounts, documented records of sales are kept as they occur, but updating the account and issuing statements is only required at the month end.

Figure 15.5 implies that batch processing is more likely where the cost of error associated with aged information falls away rapidly at all but the lowest frequencies. Provided that we vet potential customers for creditworthiness, little is gained by operating a weekly rather than a monthly accounting system. The total cost curve for batch processing will therefore be one where the rapid decline of error costs with increased feedback frequency makes the minimum total cost correspond to low frequency feedback. This low frequency can often mean that only simple information technology is needed. The system may either be manual or contracted to a computer agency.

Exploiting the information resource

One view of information considered above was of data as the structured building material of information. This stock of material can be described as a *database*. This can be managed by software to produce the information needed by the user. Such a system for controlling a database is called a database management system (DBMS).

To understand the relationship between the data stored and the information produced by a DBMS, consider the following:

- What do the terms *file* and *record* mean in the context of contemporary computer-based information systems?

- If the two terms mean something different, how can this difference be shown to be important in terms of its implications for information management?

The first question can be answered by distinguishing the *physical* and *logical* views of data and information. These terms closely relate to our distinction between 'whats' and 'hows'. A logical view of information or data is concerned with what it is, and a physical view with how it is recorded, accessed or transmitted.

In everyday use a file is seen as a source of information about a number of people or things, presented as a series of records. Records and files are often seen in physical terms. Thus a file might be a box with the records as individual cards inside. In a computer system the records might be areas of magnetic patterns on a disk. However implemented, the physical view sees the connection between records in a file, and of data in the record, as physically connected on the recording.

Traditional computer-based systems take a physical view of records and files. The result has been that computer-based files and records have been subject to the same restrictions of access as individual filing cabinets in separate departmental offices. Thus the sales file is seen as a set of documents in the sales department, the personnel file as a set of documents in the personnel department, and the parts file is out at the moment because the production manager has just borrowed it.

Modern computer-based applications of database management no longer require us to think in these terms. Instead, the data used by a DBMS can be seen as a *resource* that can be 'mined' by the system, and the phrase 'data mining' is sometimes used to refer to how new information can be extracted by analysing a database.

Harry (1997) uses the analogy of two types of coffee machines to explain the difference between DBMS and traditional file-based processing. The first kind of coffee machine has separate columns containing plastic cups already filled with the ingredients. The second kind of coffee machine does not have ready mixed combinations: instead, it mixes ingredients to order.

Manual filing systems are like the first type of machine in that the data 'ingredients' are stored ready mixed. Thus the personnel file will have all the data about name, age, address, status, tax coding, etc, arranged together to form a record on a card.

For a DBMS, what is physically recorded is not data structured into records, but individual items of data. When the user asks for a record, the data items making up the record are assembled by the DBMS. This means that neither the computer nor its recording devices actually contains the records in their physical form, any more than our second type of coffee machine contains the various drinks. Instead, a database contains the *potential* to produce any kind of information 'drink', in the form of a record of data items assembled by the DBMS.

Figures 15.6 and 15.7 show these two views of accessing and processing data. Figure 15.7 shows that a database system has two main components:

- **the database;**

- **the database management system.**

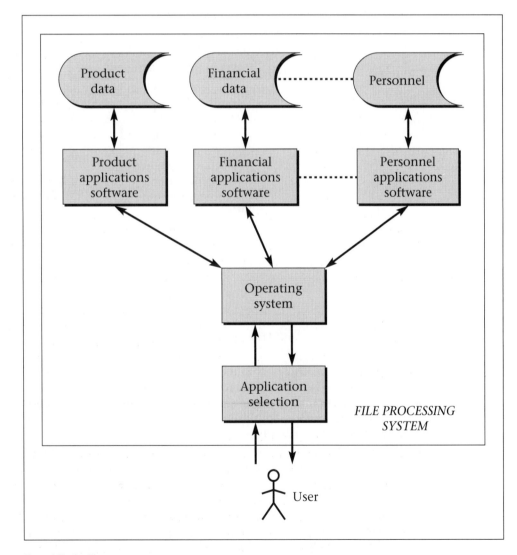

FIG 15.6 FILE PROCESSING SYSTEM

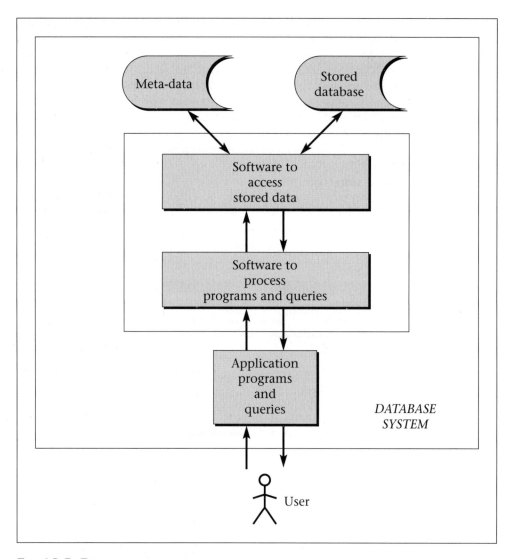

FIG 15.7 DATABASE SYSTEM

The database consists of stored data and meta-data, which defines the character-istics of the stored data. The database management system is the software that can assemble the data into the form required by the user, rather like the second kind of coffee machine could assemble white/black coffee with/without sugar, etc.

A DBMS makes it much easier to support the different information needs of the different functions of management, without special programming. The older file-based view meant that data was physically stored in a way that made it easy to meet the needs of the particular department that used the file. Thus order process-ing would store data about a particular customer in terms of who they were and what they had purchased in a particular month so that the computer program could process them to produce monthly accounts. If the marketing department wanted sales analysed by, say, classifying products sales against post codes, the reply might have been 'we need to write a special program'.

For current computer systems practice, this last example is misleading. It implied that the restrictions of the old physical file-based system are now past. In fact, the managers of many current computer systems still regard a request for non-routine output as 'special' or 'difficult'. A true DBMS presents no such problem, and the 'difficulties' could well be the result of information technology specialists defending their empires.

The software used by the DBMS can take different forms depending on the type of user. There are now several common forms of high-level software which are designed to help non-technical users query and process a database. The term 'high level' can be understood as a systemic concept. High-level software communicates in terms of 'whats' rather than 'hows'. In particular, declarative or fourth generation languages (4GLs) enable the user to state what they want from the database using English-like statements. Figure 15.8 gives an example of this, but even easier

COMMAND	DESCRIPTION
SQL Data Definition Language	
CREATE TABLE	Creates a table and defines its columns and other properties.
CREATE VIEW	Defines a view of one or more tables or other views.
ALTER TABLE	Adds a column to, or redefines a column in, an existing table.
DROP	Deletes a cluster, table, view or index from the database.
SQL Data Manipulation Language	
INSERT	Adds new rows to a table or view.
SELECT	Performs a query and selects rows and columns from one or more tables or views.
UPDATE	Changes the value of fields in a table or view.
SQL Data Control Language	
GRANT	Grants access to objects stored in database.
COMMIT	Makes database transactions irreversible.
LOCK TABLE	Locks a table and thus permits shared access to the table by multiple users while simultaneously preserving the table's integrity.
REVOKE	Revokes database privileges or table access privileges from users.

FIG 15.8 EXAMPLES OF ENGLISH-LIKE STATEMENTS USED FOR PROCESSING 4GL DATABASES

forms of software use graphics on the computer screen, icons, menus, or some combination of them.

The use of a DBMS has important implications for information management:

- The principles for defining the contents of a database and the process of constructing it should reflect the needs of the wider management system. This
  means that any method for development of a database system will include
  initial stages that analyse the needs of the business or organisation. This confirms the statements about information systems development above.

- The management structure which controls the setup and use of the database
  should reflect user need rather than computer specialist convenience.

The view of the control system in Fig 15.4 as the link between management and information shows why a database management system has more potential in management
terms than the older physical file-based systems. It was shown that information used
for goal-seeking control needs also to be stored and analysed by higher-order control to
set these goals. If this process of analysis requires specially developed computer programs, then all the higher-order functions of management, such as marketing, would
represent a special, expensive problem for the information system. In practice, a
modern DBMS should make this concern an irrelevance; whether it does or not, is an
information management not a technical issue.

MANAGEMENT INFORMATION SYSTEMS, DECISION SUPPORT SYSTEMS AND EXECUTIVE INFORMATION SYSTEMS

The terms management information system (MIS), decision support system (DSS)
and executive information system (EIS) frequently occur in books about information systems, and they are usually considered as different forms of information
system. Davis and Olson (1985) and Laudon and Laudon (1995) are examples of
popular texts which do this. This section will consider what features are supposed
to distinguish these three types of information system, and use the management,
control and information systems relationship to show that they are interrelated,
overlap and form component functions of the whole information system. It will
also show that they are neither new concepts nor 'conceptually very different' as
asserted in Laudon and Laudon (1995).

Management information systems (MIS)

The term management information system (MIS) is generally used to refer to the
information system which deals with the control of so-called 'routine', 'structured'
or 'day-to-day' operations. In many popular texts, as those above, the distinction
between the MIS and DSS or EIS is made in terms of a classical view of the management hierarchy. Figure 15.9 illustrates a version of this view.

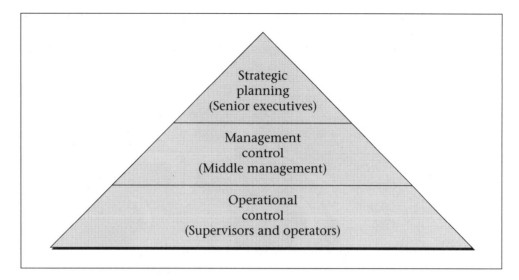

FIG 15.9 CLASSICAL VIEW OF MANAGEMENT FUNCTIONS

Whatever its relevance or usefulness, Fig 15.9 is neither a systems view of management nor of the concept of hierarchy (Harry, 1997). It represents management functions in terms of who does them, or how they are carried out (*see also* Chapter 1). It usually does this in terms of people's job titles, like 'operator' or 'senior executive'. In contrast, the systems view considers what functions are, regardless of how they are implemented, and hierarchy as levels of conceptual aggregation.

Figure 15.10 shows a view of MIS which conforms to the classical view of management hierarchy and the role of information systems within it. Its functions may be summarised as follows:

- **Reporting on summaries of basic transactions and exceptions from plan.** In control systems terms: feedback on deviations from the process goals.

- **Using simple analytical tools.** This implies that the MIS will use standard programs which merely require the user to answer set questions such as 'how many hours worked?' or 'what is the stock level?'

- **Solving structured, repetitive problems.** This implies that the 'lower-order' employees of the hierarchy of Fig 15.9 process information without the need to make decisions which affect management or strategic functions.

- **Producing routine reports.** In terms of control systems hierarchy, this implies batch processing of stored feedback, with the implication that this material may be used for goal setting. The term 'routine' could falsely suggest that the advent of a crisis in an organisation has never led to a special request from such 'routine' functions as sales-order processing for special reports, like an immediate analysis of some defaulting customer's account. In fact most forms of MIS take this in their stride if working with a modern database system as above.

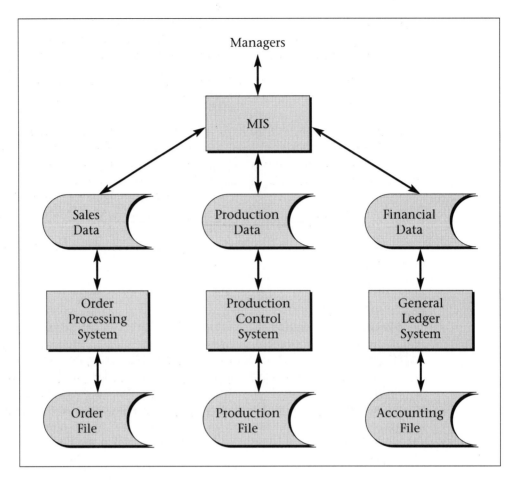

FIG 15.10 MIS

Note also that a conventional picture of MIS, such as that in Fig 15.10, gives no indication of how the system might be modified or even redesigned. Conventional views of information systems would see this as the separate specialist task of a function like 'systems analysis and design', which would manage the systems development issues discussed above.

Decision support systems (DSS)

While the MIS controls routine operations using structured data-processing methods, the DSS is seen as supporting decisions on 'less routine issues' and solving 'semi-structured' problems. The main features of DSS compared with MIS can be presented as:

- Modelling the potential effects of management decisions on the organisation in order to help select possible opportunities and find solutions to problems. This contrasts with MIS's concern with routine, structured procedures.

- Use of multi-purpose, analytical software such as spreadsheets, statistical packages and computer simulation. This contrasts with MIS's use of specific task-oriented software such as payroll or customer accounting.

- A higher degree of interaction between the software and the user, including the exploration of 'what if' questions and hypothesis testing.

In control systems terms, the DSS represents computer-based support for goal set-ting. It may be at the automatic goal-setting level, like using a discounted cash flow model to investigate the effects of discount rate on project viability. It could be at a higher reflective goal-setting level, like a cost accounting analysis of the effects of different stock valuation methods. Although the feedback from using DSS would be relevant to normative goal setting, the process of deciding norms is still an exclu-sively human province.

Generally, the potential for DSS can be seen by referring to the goal-setting func-tions in Fig 15.4.

Executive information systems (EIS)

An EIS is seen as a tool supporting 'senior executives', who are conceived as concen-trating on the strategic planning functions of the organisation, as in Fig 15.9. Strategy is principally concerned with the future of the organisation in terms of changing markets, economies, legislation, social norms and other components of the environment. Davis and Olson (1985) assert a continuing view that such 'external information dominates an EIS'. Typical information accessed and processed by an EIS would cover:

- **competitors;**

- **business and industrial legislation;**

- **regional, national and international economic statistics;**

- **markets and trends.**

EIS also sees the executive working in a particular organisational context, using par-ticular abilities and catered for by software which can provide:

- **graphics analysis and presentation**: 'the busy executive' requiring sum-maries of the essential features of data;

- **communications and electronic mail**: 'the mobile executive' who spends much working time outside the organisation;

- **decision support**: 'a captain of industry' making decisions like other man-agers, hence DSS is relevant here too. Similar tools to DSS, but applied to higher-level data.

In Fig 15.4 control systems terms, EIS supports processing information about disturbances from the environment. 'Senior executives' may also form part of the role of systems owner/conceiver. The focus of a database for external information is consistent with this. A software selection linked to a supposed work and life style is less convincing. What is particularly 'executive' about the need for concise graphical summary and presentation, or being mobile and needing communications software? Many sales reps have similar needs. Perhaps the promotion of EIS owes as much to persuasive computer salesmanship.

This purpose of this criticism is to consider whether a holistic, systems view of an information system should be viewed as different components, used by different forms of management, doing different things. This issue is considered next.

A systems view of information systems

In most organisations one person is unlikely to be involved in every kind of management activity. Some specialisation is usually needed. This means that everyone, not just 'managers', will use selected information. For example, marketing is more likely to want an analysis of sales figures than an update on tax changes governing the operation of payroll. In this situation, selection which focuses on particular parts of the database as an information resource makes practical sense.

There are, however, dangers to this approach of distinguishing between MIS, DSS or EIS on the basis of job description or the software used:

- It reverts to dividing the database so that it is not seen as an organisational resource but the separate property of departments. Labels like 'sales data' or 'financial data' then imply that data about a sale is not also data for marketing analysis, about a change in the financial position of the organisation, the workload placed on personnel in the order processing department and warehouse, etc, as in a systems view.

- Such a movement away from a systems view of management fails to make the distinction between whats and hows. It therefore ignores, for example, that a salesperson who makes a delivery date promise is making a production decision, or that an accountant who fixes a credit policy is making a public relations decision.

- The confusion of conceptual control hierarchy with the labels/job description of Fig 15.9 confuses whats and hows. Thus in Laudon and Laudon (1993), 'senior executives' are those concerned with high-level, strategic thoughts and decisions about the long-term future of the company, and 'management' are people who worry about whether the objectives set for them by higher management are being fulfilled. Actual organisations are not like this. Lower- and middle-ranking managers often worry about and contribute to strategic decisions through meetings which feed information back into the whole management information system. Also, senior executives are often involved in actuating low-level decisions when a local crisis requires them to get into 'firefighting operations'.

- The fragmentation of an information system provides no process for learning by the whole system, since this needs the integration of all its processes at all levels of control.

These conclusions are not intended to criticise MIS, DSS and EIS destructively, but to focus on what they are, what they do and their role in the whole organisation.

INTELLIGENT AND EXPERT SYSTEMS

Forsyth (1989) defined an expert system as 'a piece of software that causes TV producers to lose all sense of proportion'. This section will consider how expert systems and other advanced developments work, and what they can actually do.

Artificial intelligence or *AI* is the generic term which is used for various forms of information technology which attempt to emulate human behaviour such as reasoning, communication or sensory perception. Important examples are:

- **expert systems;**
- **fuzzy logic;**
- **image recognition;**
- **speech recognition;**
- **neural networks.**

Expert systems and fuzzy logic

Virtually all of the devices which have been described as 'computers' during the last 50 years work by using a program to control the processing of data. Thus in business, data on personnel working hours can be processed using a financial software package to produce a payroll, statistical packages can be used to analyse sales data for marketing, and so on. What all these applications do is:

- **Calculate**: the computer program subjects the input data to various calculation procedures to produce output in the form of results. Thus in our previous examples, working hours might be used to calculate pay, or sales data to calculate a percentage.

- **Assume existence of relevant formula**: calculations are only possible if a formula exists to govern them. Thus a payroll calculation would need to know the formula relating wage rates, tax and national insurance in order to be possible.

- **Have access to correct data**: a formula can only be used to carry out a calculation if the input data is available. Also, the data needs to be correct if the result is also to be correct: else 'garbage in, garbage out'. Thus the reliability of a sales analysis depends on the sales data used.

There are many situations in management where it is not possible to make calculations using a known and accepted formula on reliable data. It is not automatically possible to use a formula to know the cause of failure by an industrial process or to determine how a company should respond to a lawsuit. For such situations the layperson relies on the knowledge and experience of people who are often called 'experts'. Expert systems are an attempt to apply computer systems to supporting what humans do in such situations. In contrast to the three conditions above, expert systems:

- **Diagnose**: instead of calculating a result, they consider possible answers and give judgements as to which are likely. Thus an expert system might be used to diagnose why a product failed in a market rather than calculate a percentage.

- **Do not assume the existence of a single correct formula**: there is no established theory that explains all possible market failures. Expert systems have to work in terms of the possible inferences, given the evidence available.

- **Work with fuzzy data**: diagnosis has to be carried out on the facts available, and all these may not be clear or reliable. Thus in most marketing analysis it is not possible to have all the information about each sale, and even when people are interviewed they do not always know or say what they mean. It is even more difficult to speculate why things did not happen.

To deal with such conditions an expert system works differently from conventional computer systems. The essence of such a computer system is a program controlling the processing data to produce output or results, as was shown above. In an expert system, as in Fig 15.11, an *inference engine* uses the resources of a *knowledge base* to produce output in the form of diagnosis.

For a computer system to work as a component of an expert system, particular theoretical frameworks have to be used. Since computers are digital, all that they do is built on a complex combination of yes/no or 0/1. Human beings do not think in this way: 'Was the product successful?', 'Well it *seemed* to be, but we're not sure if the sales were affected by the weather.' If computer-based information systems are to work successfully with the wider management system of which they are a part, the human component must be accommodated. *Fuzzy logic* is a mathematical framework which attempts to describe the analysis and decision making that goes on when humans try to deal with concepts like '*seemed* to be' or 'not quite sure'. Sometimes described as 'possibilistic logic', it was invented by Zadeh (1965). No technique can manufacture certainty out of uncertainty, or remove the judgement required when dealing with it, but fuzzy logic does provide the framework needed by any attempt at a diagnostic system.

Image and speech recognition

Image recognition refers to the many combinations of hardware and software that can enable a computer system to record and reproduce images. This is necessary if information is seen as more than just words and numbers. If the software can also identify what the image is, identify and classify its properties in relation to other images, then such a system may be described as 'intelligent'. Thus a database of

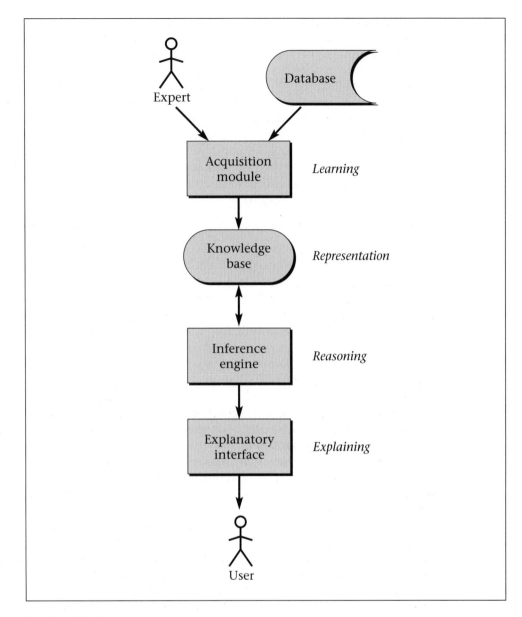

FIG 15.11 EXPERT SYSTEM

employees which can record pictures of individuals, as well as their personal details, is now quite common. An intelligent system could also match different photographs of that individual to the official record.

Photographs and sound recording existed well before computers. When these abilities were computerised, initial concentration was on images because the written word could substitute the spoken. Hence computer-based wordprocessing extended the abilities of the typewriter. Like the typewriter, however, wordprocessing depended on the keyboard to transcribe human use of words into machine use. Given that speech is not the transmission of individual letters, and that the QWERTY keyboard was deliberately designed to be hard to use, the ability to speak directly to a computer system could enable a better integration of the machine and human components of an information system. *Speech recognition* is the attempt to do this.

Speech recognition can work at increasing levels of complexity. At the simplest level the computer system can recognise particular words. A more sophisticated system might distinguish between speakers of the same word. A further level comes when the system can understand the meaning of words in combination, like phrases or sentences. The highest level is where the system recognises equivalents.

An example of these distinctions would be a cash machine system which tried to work in response to a spoken request for money. The simplest system might ask how much money you wanted and could recognise individual words like 'fifty' or 'twenty-five'. The next level of complexity would be where the machine could distinguish between two people speaking the same words. The system might be more useful if it could understand combinations of words. Thus 'withdraw fifty' could be distinguished from 'have I got fifty?' At the highest level the machine would understand that 'give me fifty', 'I'd like fifty', or 'fifty pounds please', were equivalents.

This final level of speech recognition begins to demand a machine that not only recognises speech, but starts to understand language. Even if it had not come across the particular format of a question like 'can you give me fifty pounds please?', it would be able to communicate with the user to find out what the new request meant. To do this, the machine would have to start *learning from experience*. It might do this by using its recognition of a questioning tone in the voice, the use of the word 'please', and knowing what 'fifty pounds' meant, to guess at a meaning of the new phrase. The particular form of questions by the machine would then be governed by the responses of the user and what it recognised and understood. The machine would then be learning rather as humans do.

Neural networks

Neural networks represent a way of computing that tries to work in the human way just described. A conventional computer-based expert system would try to capture experience at image recognition or speech understanding by using the two components we discussed above: a list of rules or knowledge base, and ways of concluding inferences from these rules, or inference engine. When trying to recognise a face or understand language, however, there are no obvious rules that make it easier for a computer to do this than a human being. Thus how might a computer be made to understand the meaning of the word 'game'? Deciding a set of rules that was anywhere near complete would be very difficult; yet humans use words easily from childhood. Similarly with images: I look out of the window and see six trees which I can distinguish from all the other features, including an excavator and a hen. A child could do the same; but what rules would you give to a computer to enable it to do this?

Neural networks do not work by storing up increasingly complex combinations of rules. Instead, they store the results of individual experiences in a network of interconnections which form one whole experience. Thus I decide that something is a tree because my senses' experience of it sufficiently matches the whole of my past experience of trees, rather than because my brain uses a 'computer program' from its store of rules to test out the data coming from my senses. Every time someone has such an experience, however, the totality of the experience of a tree may be modified, like the first time a tree is seen with copper leaves rather than green leaves.

From this futuristic survey, the following information management conclusions can be drawn:

- Expert systems and other forms of so-called machine intelligence are already useful for some management information systems which can work on the basis of diagnostic rules. Examples of these are in technical, legal and administrative areas where what is required can be translated into how its occurrence can be tested.

- Attempts to make machines emulate human management behaviour in dealing with more complex forms of information, like those which deal with interpretation, interest, power or intuition, may be covered by neural networks in the future, but at the moment this future is unclear. Integration of human and computer systems as in Fig 15.4 is still required.

THE CONTINUING INFORMATION REVOLUTION?

Words often become devalued by frequent use. About 500 years ago the word 'naughty' was a description that might have been given to someone who deserved to be hanged. These days, 'naughty' is used by TV adverts to cover the idea of eating chocolate in the bath.

Given the continuing tendency to devalue words by exaggeration, should there be caution when the developments in information technology of the last three decades of the twentieth century are described as a 'revolution'? The answer lies in the previous distinction of whats and hows.

When faced with something new, people often try to relate it to something that they already know, as a first step to understanding. Examples of this can be seen in the names used by previous revolutionary technologies. Many of the words used to describe the steam engine and the railway came from the pre-industrial era, such as 'carriage' or 'track'. The locomotive that pulled the carriages was thought of as an iron horse, and it is no coincidence that for nearly 100 years the iron horse continued to *pull* the carriages just as the horse itself had done. Only in the last half of the twentieth century has a recognition of *what* the motive power of a railway train does broken away from *how* the horse did it before. The sources of motion in modern trains may be at the front, the back or underneath the vehicles they propel. They can push as well as pull, and can work as efficiently backwards as they do forwards. The danger of using old hows to understand new ways of doing things is that the whats are obscured and potential new hows are therefore also hidden. As long as the railway locomotive was tied to the hows of the horse, new ways of implementing the what of motive power were inhibited.

Examples of this carrying over of old ideas are easy to find in information technology. One important example would be that of graphical user interfaces or GUIs. These aim to make computers accessible to people who are not computer specialists by presenting them with a screen made up of little symbols or so-called icons. These icons represent objects or actions which the user can control using a pointing device such as a mouse. (An Apple computer or a PC which uses Microsoft Windows are examples of this.)

GUIs seem to be very friendly and helpful. To see what is recorded in a file, the user points the mouse at an icon that looks like a folder that might be used in a traditional paper-based filing cabinet system. When the button on the mouse is clicked, the contents of the file appear on the screen. If the file and its contents are no longer relevant, they are scrapped by clicking on an icon that looks like a wastepaper basket.

Although this imagery (icon = Greek word for an image) is helpful for a user who wants to interpret the new technology in terms of the old, it is very misleading about what actually happens.

Clicking on an icon to supposedly withdraw a 'file' from the 'filing cabinet' is nonsense. Withdrawing an actual paper file from a real-life filing cabinet means that the cabinet no longer contains the file. The sort of conversation that might take place in the office would be: 'Where's the file?' 'I don't know: some one has it out at the moment.'

On a computer-based system, calling the file up onto the screen actually calls up a *copy*. The original information is still there, recorded on the computer disk. If the computer in question is just one of many PCs on a network, every user can have a copy whenever they like, regardless of what all the other users are doing. The icon-based GUI concept of a 'file' or 'folder' in a 'filing cabinet' is therefore very misleading. Everybody who wants one can have a copy of what is in the file, and the file itself is still safely in the cabinet.

It is also worth noting how misleading the images of files, folders and filing cabinets are in their implications for data security. If someone steals a folder from a filing cabinet, a quick check will show that it is missing and that theft has occurred. 'Removing' a folder from an electronic filing cabinet leaves no such gap.

The icon of a wastepaper basket or dustbin is not quite so misleading if looked at very carefully, but it can still be misleading for the non-specialist user in terms of the image it tries to convey. If a document is in the wastepaper basket, the tears in the paper or the screwing up mean that it is not the document that it was. For many non-specialist computer users, the image of a dustbin or wastepaper basket implies the end of the document concerned. A dustbin or wastepaper basket conjures up words like 'delete' or 'reject'. They effectively mean goodbye to the information concerned.

In fact, when a mouse is used to point to the icon of a dustbin, the file is not physically deleted at all. It is not even moved into a 'waste basket'. Instead, the system marks the space used to record the file as available the next time space is needed for new files. As long as no attempt has been made to record new data, the 'deleted' file remains perfectly recorded on disk and can be recovered. There have been several examples in the late 1980s of business fraudsters who have deleted files on disk just as the taxman or VAT inspectors were arriving, only to find that the damning evidence could still be recovered.

To appreciate how far new technology can be a *revolution* therefore requires a distinction of whats and hows. In so far as new technology is used to provide new hows for old whats, the revolution is merely one of degree: like faster calculation or more efficient storage. But if new technology means new whats, then it can be revolutionary indeed.

Thus if potentially unlimited copies of a 'file' can be accessed by users on a computer network without removal of the original data, the concept of access to information is something new compared to the old physical access to a filing cabinet. If networking of computer systems and telecommunications mean that an Australian and a Norwegian can have the same near-instant access to that data, the concept of the location of information is completely changed. It is the breakdown of the old physical restrictions, like the location of information, that are the real revolution, not just faster ways of doing what we did before.

There are therefore two ways of answering the question as to whether developments in computer-based information systems amount to a revolution. If a revolution implies new ways of doing old things, then recent developments in computing do not amount to a revolution. Indeed, modern systems will still require such traditional components as printed sheets of paper, handwritten signatures and sticky labels. If, however, the whole that emerges from the combination and interaction of the new with the old is considered, the word revolution is justified. The principal areas where this is likely are:

- **Communications and networking**: these are the physical means of implementing the systems principle of connecting parts into a whole which will have its own new emergent properties. Thus whatever the attempts by politicians to retain or remove boundaries, there is a *de facto* world information system for many types of information, as in the Internet.

- **The database concept**: since information is a property that emerges when data items are brought together, arithmetic growth of data stored leads to geometric growth of potential information available if data can be combined and manipulated in just about any way needed by the user.

- **Greater ranges of input technology**. Computer systems that cover the five human senses, and more, extend information well beyond what can be typed on a keyboard.

- **Artificial intelligence**: the ability to learn pushes the computer into a role in the higher information and control levels of decision making and goal setting (*see* Fig 15.4).

However, good and bad motivation, honesty and cheating, successful and failed communication, etc will still have the same effects as in the past, and will call for skills in human management.

COMMUNICATION AND THE INTERNET

The Internet began life as an American defence project which connected together people, computers and military facilities. The Internet had an important defensive property designed into it. In the event of war, destruction of even large parts of it would not prevent the remaining parts from continuing to work.

The existence of this robust communication system subsequently attracted other users, including the international academic community. The Internet was a good way for anyone with global interests to communicate. The kind of information that could be communicated was widened in the 1980s by the improvement in the ability of computer systems to process and communicate visual information.

Thus the end of the Cold War found the world with an international, robust communication system that enabled anyone with access to it to exchange printed, visual, aural or any other kind of information which was processable by computers and information technology. At this point, the Internet emerged as a subject in popular media which made many people who were not much interested in information systems realise that we apparently lived in an information age. In the early 1990s there was much talk of the 'Information Superhighway' and it is now hard to find a major organisation which is not 'on the Internet'. There appears to have been an explosion in information of all sorts available to anyone anywhere. Some of this seems very useful, some very trivial and some uncensored and quite unpleasant. The world is supposedly shrinking into a single cyber-community.

To make management sense of the popular stereotypes, we should first check what the Internet does. Its chief uses include:

- **remote log-in from one computer to another;**
- **remote access to files and software on other computers;**
- **file and software transfer;**
- **electronic mail (E-mail);**
- **newsgroup formation and access;**
- **news distribution;**
- **the World Wide Web (WWW).**

A facility known as *Telnet* enables one computer to log into another and use it as if it were a terminal attached to the remote computer. This means that a relatively humble PC can be part of a much larger and more powerful computer system to which it is remotely connected, with access to its data files and the operation of its software. Thus someone working at home could use their firm's computer system much as if they were working at the office.

FTP (File Transfer Protocol) is a facility that enables the copying of files from one computer to another across the Internet. The files may be data files like a public archive or library, but they could also be applications software. Again, connection to the Internet brings information and computing power to the user way beyond what might be available from an isolated, separate machine or a single organisational network.

E-mail and newsgroup facilities enable one-to-one and one-to-many communication across the Internet. Besides simple written messages, most E-mail enables users to attach files and other forms of information to their communications. Newsgroup facilities act like a public noticeboard to which subscribers can attach either original messages or replies to others.

Perhaps the most famous feature of the Internet is the *World Wide Web*. The first important feature of the Web is the continuous connection of large computer systems called *hosts* to the Internet, so that information held on them can be accessed at any time. The second important feature lies in the way that the information is stored. Like any other computer, host computers may store text, visual material, sound files, etc, but it is the use of the concept of *hypertext* that enables links to be made between one information component and another. With appropriate software the user can search through the connections made by these links. Thus a name on one document can be a link to some other document which has information related to that name. Since visual and sound information is included, a word could lead to a picture or video or a picture could lead to a sound. Build on to this complexity the fact that any information on any host can be linked to any other information on any other host, and the richness of the Web as an information source is apparent. The Web itself becomes one huge hypertext document.

It is very important to realise that the Internet is a *system* with all the properties that that implies. Like any other system it has its abstract as well as its concrete components. Anyone who has decided to become connected to the Internet finds that they don't just need to buy a modem to physically connect their computer to the telephone line. Connection also requires the appropriate software which is able to use the appropriate *protocols*. Thus the 'http://www' to be found at the start of a Web address is a coding to indicate that the communication is intended to make a link with information on the Web rather than one of the other facilities on the Internet. Thus connection has to be made logically as well as physically.

Like any other system also, description of the structure, processes or other properties of the Internet will be a reflection of the values and actions of the particular user concerned. The user is a component of the system who interacts with it, and it is the results of this interaction that determines the behaviour and output of the whole. Any view of the Internet that sees it as a set thing which delivers particular certainties to a passive user is a misconception.

What are the implications of the Internet for management? At this stage in its development these are likely to be:

- **distortion of physical geography;**
- **globalisation of information;**
- **reduction of systems lags;**
- **re-evaluation of information technology.**

Distortion of physical geography is the shrinking effect that the Internet has on distance. The Internet can make a manager as close to information and people halfway around the world as those in the same town. Phones, radios and TVs have already been doing this, but phones are mainly audio, one-to-one machines, and radios and TVs are not interactive. The Internet covers a combination of everything that these other forms of information technology can do, plus other new things such as the communication of software.

The Internet generally, and the Web in particular, are leading to a *globalisation of information*. A simple example will illustrate this. Someone in Britain wanted to buy a small amount of US Treasury bills. On consulting a UK stockbroker they were informed that this is both a complex and expensive business, and that anyway it is only worthwhile for amounts above $35 000. An easy visit to the US Treasury site on the Web revealed, however, that small amounts of stock can be easily bought at little expense, and that furthermore an application form for the stock can be directly downloaded on to the enquirer's computer. Applying the lesson of this experience to professional, business and management activity generally implies that protecting knowledge-based competitive advantage will become more difficult in the future.

Reduction of systems lags refers to the role of the information system as a component of control as illustrated in Fig 15.4. The widespread and continuous connection that now exists between most of the major world information systems in business, economics and finance means that the world never sleeps and that much information–spreading is near instantaneous. Consequently managers as operators of control systems can pick up and respond to environmental disturbances much more quickly than in the past. Whether this leads to more or less stability in markets is a complex point we cannot cover here, but it can be said that it leads to more extremes, in the sense that it magnifies existing tendencies.

But the most important impact of the Internet on management is likely to be the *re-evaluation of information technology*. If, as above, connection to the Internet puts the user at a terminal which has access to all the other computers and data on the Internet, then that user is effectively using a *global computer*. If the wide variety of forms in which this information can be accessed is also included such as text, live voice, audio, video, E-mail, newsgroups and software, then the present forms of information technology are likely to become quickly redundant. It would be very surprising to find by the year 2010 that TVs, computers, telephones and radios were still completely separate bits of equipment as they are today. Instead, new forms of information technology (the 'hows') are likely to combine many of the logical roles (the 'whats') of existing information systems.

SUMMARY

- The effects of developments in modern information technology on management require a rethinking of the implications of words like information and system, as well as the word management itself. New technology not only affects how management operates to achieve existing goals; it also opens up new potential for what management can hope to achieve.

- The key to understanding the effect of information technology on management is a recognition of the key role of the concept of *control* as the important connection between what management seeks to achieve, and what the information system must deliver.

- An analysis of this requirement shows that information is more than the output of the workings of computers and technology. A true information system also recognises the role of human beings and the organisational environment.

- A balanced view of the role of the information system in management must also recognise that a supposed 'revolution' resulting from information technology developments is not always as new as it might first appear.

■ A focus on what management does is more important than transient concern with information technology.

REVIEW AND DISCUSSION QUESTIONS

1   This chapter has discussed the richness of information as a concept. Take the list of data structure, process, communication, etc on p 466 as a starting point. Select a familiar or documented organisation. What examples can be found which illustrate the views listed? Are there other aspects of information which build on its richness as a concept?

2   What effects does the presence of human beings have on the concept of control when it is applied to the management of organisations?

3   What different uses are made of the word *file* in different business situations?

4   Are senior managers or directors principally concerned with strategy, rather than operations? Choose a familiar organisation, consider how it works, and discuss this issue.

5   What can machines do better than human beings? What can human beings do better than machines?

6   Can computer systems perform tasks without human support?

7   Given the information technology developments of the last decade of the twentieth century, what additional forms of information do organisations now most urgently need?

8   Is it sensible to talk of information being 'on' the Internet?

CASE HISTORIES

The Data Protection Act 1984 contains the statement 'Data is information.' This particular piece of legislation, and its subsequent operation, is a good case study of the pitfalls which can come from confusing data and information, and confusing whats and hows. Information is information, whether it is electronically recorded or otherwise. The social and political pressures which led to the United Kingdom setting up the Act had more to do with wider, non-technological issues than actual cases of computer system abuse. This is a good example of Fig 15.4.

An attempt by the London Stock Exchange to computerise share dealing, called TAURUS, was finally abandoned in 1993. The reasons for its abandonment were mostly concerned with the difficulty of finding a way to reconcile the needs of different users. This illustrates the limitations of information technology if unsupported by sufficient management and organisational skills. No amount of 'computer revolution' could have solved this problem. How is CREST now making out?

Microsoft® Windows™ is a product which was well established at the time, in late 1993, when the major world computer hardware producer IBM was undergoing wide-ranging internal reorganisational changes to respond to a drop in

►

demand for mainframe computers. Microsoft and IBM had both benefited in the past from the establishment of the personal computer. This is now the very form of hardware which appears to be destroying the mainframe as a product. Is the triumph of dispersed, user accessible microcomputers over centralised mainframe systems part of a general move towards downsizing?

Information is becoming more than the processing of words and numbers. Consider the role of visual and pictorial information as a commercial product, as on the Web. ∎

REFERENCES FOR FURTHER READING

Beishon, R J and Peters, G (eds) (1981) *Systems Behaviour*, 3rd edn, London: Harper & Row.

Bowers, D S (1993) *From Data to Database*, 2nd edn, London: Chapman & Hall.

Davis, G B and Olson, M H (1985) *Management Information Systems*, 2nd edn, New York: McGraw-Hill.

Forsyth, R (ed) (1989) *Expert Systems*, 2nd edn, London: Chapman & Hall.

Harry, M J S (1990) *Information and Management Systems*, London: Pitman Publishing.

Harry, M J S (1997) *Information Systems in Business*, 2nd edn, London: Pitman Publishing.

Laudon, C L and Laudon, J P (1995) *Business Information Systems*, Fort Worth: Dryden Press.

Olle, T W, Hagelstein, J, Macdonald, I G, Rolland, C, Sol, H G, Van Assche, F J M and Verrijn-Stuart, A A (1988) *Information Systems Methodologies*, Harlow: Addison-Wesley.

Schoderbeck, P P, Schoderbeck, C G and Kefalas, A G (1990) *Management Systems*, Homewood: BPI Irwin.

Sprague, R H and McNurlin, B C (1993) *Information Systems Management in Practice*, Prentice-Hall.

Veryard, R (1984) *Pragmatic Data Analysis*, Blackwell Scientific.

Winston, H W (1984) *Artificial Intelligence*, Addison-Wesley.

Zadeh, L (1965) 'Fuzzy Sets', *Information and Control*, 8, 338–52.

FINANCIAL MANAGEMENT

Leslie Chadwick

OBJECTIVES

The purpose of this chapter is to provide management, particularly non-financial managers/executives, with an understanding of the areas of accounting and finance so as to enable them to fulfil their strategic role more effectively. It is not the aim of the chapter to convert the reader into an accountant or to become too involved in the 'number-crunching' aspects of the subject.

It is important that management gains a reasonable understanding of accounting and finance, which it is hoped will help them to appreciate the data which is generated and its limitations.

The objectives of the chapter are to:

◆ describe briefly the areas of activity covered by financial accounting, cost and management accounting, financial management and auditing

◆ illustrate how the net profit before tax is computed and appropriated, i.e. shared out

◆ provide an understanding of the balance sheet information, in particular, capital employed and what it consists of, and the employment of capital, e.g. fixed assets and working capital

◆ understand what a cash flow statement includes to help explain why cash movements have occurred

◆ spell out some of the ways in which 'creative accounting' can affect the reported figures in the organisation's accounts

◆ look at accounting ratios which cover profitability, liquidity, efficiency, capital structure and investment, and understand what they are describing and possible reasons for fluctuations

◆ show how to calculate particular ratios   ▶

- ◆ appreciate that there are different ways of incorporating overheads in product costs

- ◆ provide an understanding of the principles of budgetary control

- ◆ demonstrate how a cash budget is prepared, and its purpose

- ◆ explain briefly what is involved in the preparation of capital budgets for both income and expenditure

- ◆ describe the duties of the external auditor relating to capital expenditure

- ◆ recognise the dangers to an organisation which can result from the behavioural aspects of budgeting

- ◆ show how standard costing helps to control both price and quantity via variance analysis

- ◆ provide an appreciation of what financial management involves, e.g. sources of finance, leasing, gearing, the cost of capital and capital investment appraisal

- ◆ briefly explain the following methods of capital investment appraisal: payback, average rate of return, net present value method, internal rate of return, discounted payback

INTRODUCTION

From a review of Fig 16.1, it can be observed that there are three distinct but related subject areas, which are:

- **financial accounting which incorporates financial management;**
- **cost and management accounting;**
- **auditing, both internal and external;**

and that all three areas depend upon the same pool of data.

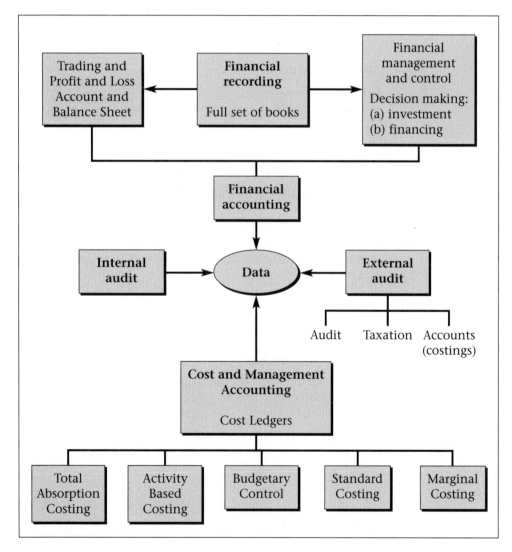

FIG 16.1 ACCOUNTING AND FINANCE

It should be noted that the responsibility for these activities will devolve to one or a number of persons depending on the size of the organisation. For example, in a small company one qualified or semi-qualified accountant could be responsible for everything.

FINANCIAL ACCOUNTING

Financial accounting involves the design and management of the recording system, manual or computerised, for cash and bank balances, receipts and payments, and various assets and liabilities. In addition to the production of internal accounts, another principal output is to be found in the company's annual report, published for external reporting purposes, which includes:

- **a profit and loss account;**
- **a balance sheet;**
- **a directors' report;**
- **a cash flow statement;**
- **a financial analysis consisting of appropriate ratios and statistics.**

How do we compute the profit and loss?

Figure 16.2 shows a specimen trading and profit and loss account, prepared for internal reporting purposes. This will be used to illustrate how certain figures have been arrived at.

Some authorities may just refer to what is in Fig 16.2 as the profit and loss account, or P & L, or call it the income statement.

The way in which the profit or loss is computed is governed by the application of accounting concepts and accounting policies. *The figures which appear in Fig 16.2 will have been computed along the following lines:*

Sales

The sales figure will include all cash and credit sales for the period covered by the accounts, irrespective of whether or not the cash has been received from the sales on credit. This is known as 'the realisation concept'. Any amounts which are owing from credit customers at the end of the period will be shown as 'debtors' or 'accounts receivable' in the balance sheet. Note that in the UK, for a company registered for VAT, the sales figure excludes VAT.

Cost of sales

This is computed by adding the opening stocks to the stock purchased during the period (the purchases), and then deducting the closing stock.

The opening stock of finished products, work-in-progress, raw materials and fuels could be described as 'the previous period's deferred expense'. This is an example of 'the matching concept'. The stock will be accounted for as an expense in the period

	19X7	Trading Account:	19X8	
£000	£000		£000	£000
	8 000	Sales		9 800
	4 420	*Less* Cost of sales		5 712
	3 580	*GROSS PROFIT*		4 088
		Profit & Loss Account:		
	56	*Add* Other income and discounts receivable		64
	3 636			4 152
		Less Expenses (such as motor expenses, stationery, office salaries, directors' remuneration, interest on loans & debentures, bank interest and charges, and adjustment to the provision for bad and		
	1 603	doubtful debts, depreciation of fixed assets etc.)		1 702
	2 033	*NET PROFIT BEFORE TAX*		2 450
		Appropriations:		
	265	*Less* Taxation		310
	1 768	*Net profit after tax*		2 140
	200	*Less* Transfers to general reserve		300
	1 568			1 840
		Less Ordinary share dividends:		
300		Interim paid	300	
900	1 200	Final proposed dividend	1 200	1 500
	368	*Retained*		340
		Add Profit & Loss A/c: undistributed profits		
	4 892	balance brought forward		5 260
	5 260			5 600

FIG 16.2 LE CAYLAR PLC: TRADING AND PROFIT AND LOSS ACCOUNT FOR THE YEAR ENDED 30 JUNE 19X8

in which it is sold. Until it is sold it will be carried forward to the next accounting period as the closing stock.

The purchases figure is computed in the same way as the sales figure, i.e. it consists of all of the purchases for the accounting period, both cash and credit, even though certain of the suppliers of goods/materials on credit have not yet been paid. Amounts which are still owing to suppliers at the end of the period will be shown as 'creditors' or 'accounts payable' in the balance sheet.

The opening and closing stocks of work-in-progress will, in addition to the material costs, include the labour cost plus a share of the overhead costs (overheads, such as rent of factory, insurance of machinery, etc). The principle which governs the way in which the stocks of finished goods and work-in-progress are valued is 'consistency'. However, companies can and do change their accounting policies. If they do change them, they must disclose the fact in their annual report and accounts which are prepared for external reporting purposes.

Gross profit

The gross profit is the difference between the sales figure and the cost price of the sales. It is sometimes referred to as the 'mark up' when expressed as a percentage of sales or cost.

Other income

Other income received, such as rent received from letting some of the premises, is accounted for per period. Thus if the accounting period is 12 months, and the property is let for the whole of that period, all the rent receivable for that period should be included even if it has not yet been received. Any amount of rent receivable owing would be carried forward as a current asset, i.e. as a rental debtor.

Discounts receivable

These are not discounts for bulk orders, they are discounts which are given by the suppliers of the goods and services received on credit, i.e. from creditors, for prompt payment of amounts owing to them.

Expenses

The various expenses will be for the accounting period. Any amounts owing which are applicable to the period will be included and then shown as an accrual in the current liabilities section of the balance sheet. In the case where an expense includes an amount which has been paid in advance for the next accounting period, the amount of the prepayment will not be included as an expense for the current accounting period. It will, however, be carried forward to the next accounting period as a current asset in the balance sheet. It will then be charged as an expense in the next accounting period.

Provision for bad and doubtful debts

This is a slice of the profits which ought not/cannot be taken as profits, because it represents the value of sales included in the earlier recorded sales figure which are expected to be bad or doubtful. Note that in the UK, for tax purposes, a specific provision is allowable for tax relief; a general provision, i.e. a percentage of debtors, is not allowable for tax relief.

Depreciation

Depreciation of fixed assets, i.e. those assets such as plant and machinery, fixtures and fittings and equipment that are bought to be used in the business over several years and not for resale, are depreciated to spread their cost over the useful life of the asset concerned. They are depreciated according to the method which is stated in the company's depreciation accounting policy which for example could read 'plant and machinery is depreciated according to the useful life less the anticipated residual value', or 'on a straight line basis, based upon the useful life of the asset'.

Interest payments

The figure here is made up of all the interest payments for the period under review made by the company on borrowings in the form of:

- **bank loans;**
- **overdrafts;**
- **debenture interest** (see sources of finance for more information about debentures).

Directors' remuneration

Includes all the salaries, fees, bonuses, etc, due or paid to directors for the period in question. It can be particularly interesting to note how information about this is shown in the annual reports of companies.

Net profit before tax

A more accurate description of this figure would be gross profit, plus other income less all expenses, including any adjustment to the provision for bad and doubtful debts, depreciation, interest payable (other than dividends) and directors' remuneration. A knowledge of what the net profit before tax figure represents is important and useful when looking at financial analysis regarding profitability ratios.

The profit and loss appropriation account

This shows how the net profit before tax is shared between taxation, dividends for shareholders (both for ordinary shareholders and preference shareholders), transfers to reserves and 'ploughed back' as retained earnings. The retained earnings (undistributed profits) for the period will be added to the cumulative balance brought forward from the last period and shown in the balance sheet as a reserve under the heading of retained earnings, undistributed profits or profit and loss account balance. This problem of having a number of names to describe the same item happens time and time again within accounting terminology and is something that the reader should be aware of.

Materiality

Before looking at the next item on the agenda, it is important to know about another concept which on occasions may conflict with other concepts because of the way in which it is applied. It is the concept of 'materiality' and dictates that where, for example, a fixed asset has such a low value it may be charged to the profit and loss account as an expense of the period in which it was purchased.

However, what is significant in terms of value is dependent on the judgement of whoever has to make that decision. Thus, the same expense or income item even in the same company could be treated differently by different individuals. Finally, it should be noted that the application of concepts such as materiality is affected by the taxation system, e.g. is the item a repair and renewal and chargeable as an expense in the profit and loss account, or is it a fixed asset that needs to be written off over a number of years?

What is a balance sheet?

A balance sheet is *not* an account, it is simply a statement of assets and liabilities extracted from the accounting records at a particular moment in time. It has been likened to a snapshot taken at a moment frozen in time, portraying the financial health of the organisation. This means that if another balance sheet is prepared within a few days, or a week or a month, the position could have changed dramatically. A balance sheet today, a picture of health, a balance sheet tomorrow, a picture of woe.

Assets are cash and bank balances or items which have been purchased (on cash or credit) such as machinery, stocks of raw materials and investments, or amounts owing to the company, e.g. by customers who have been sold products or services on credit. A quick definition of assets is 'what the company owns'.

Capital and liabilities, in the form of share capital, loans and amounts owing by the company to suppliers, represent a claim on the company. In brief, capital and liabilities are 'what the company owes'.

Why is capital shown as an amount owing? The answer to this is quite logical. Capital represents an investment in the company by shareholders and loan creditors. It is therefore an amount which is owing by the company to them. In the event of being wound up, the company, if it has sufficient funds, will repay all its debts including the share capital.

From a review of the balance sheet in Fig 16.3, it should be clear that the capital employed section shows where the financing has come from, e.g. share capital, reserves, etc, and the employment of capital section shows how this has been used, e.g. to buy fixed assets and current assets. It also shows, in the calculation of working capital, that current assets are partly financed by the current liabilities, e.g. creditors.

Capital employed

SHARE CAPITAL

- **Authorised share capital.** The description which appears on the balance sheet is a statement included for information purposes only. The authorised share capital is the maximum amount of shares which the company can issue, as directed by its Memorandum and Articles of Association (the document which governs its constitution, e.g. it defines the rights of shareholders).

- **Issued ordinary share capital.** The ordinary shares usually have voting rights assigned to them. They are described in a number of ways, for example:

  - **£1 ordinary shares.** This is their 'face' or 'par' value, any amount received in excess of this 'nominal' value of £1 is called the 'share premium'.

19X7			19X8	
		Authorised share capital		
		£50m £1 ordinary shares		
£000	£000		£000	£000
		CAPITAL EMPLOYED:		
		Issued share capital		
	20 000	20 m £1 ordinary shares (fully paid)		20 000
		Reserves		
2 500		Share premium	2 500	
4 400		General reserve	4 700	
5 260	12 160	P & L A/c (undistributed profits)	5 600	12 800
	32 160	Ordinary shareholders' funds		32 800
		Long-term debt		
4 000		Long-term loan (10%)	4 000	
nil	4 000	8% debentures	12 000	16 000
	36 160			48 800
		THE EMPLOYMENT OF CAPITAL		
	23 000	Fixed assets (net of depreciation)		31 000
		Working capital: (A) – (B)		
		Current assets		
9 400		Stocks	12 188	
		Debtors (after deducting provision for		
6 200		bad & doubtful debts)	8 640	
400		Prepayments	450	
2 100		Bank balances	2 600	
16		Cash in hand	22	
18 116			(A) 23 900	
		Less current liabilities (due within 12 months)		
3 556		Creditors	4 300	
235		Accrued expenses	290	
265		Taxation owing	310	
900		Proposed dividend	1 200	
4 956	13 160		(B) 6 100	17 800
	36 160			48 800

FIG 16.3 LE CAYLAR PLC: BALANCE SHEET AS AT 30 JUNE 19X8

– **Fully or partly paid.** Where the full amount on shares has not been received, including any share premium, this is described as 'money on call' or 'calls'. The call for further cash will be made as per the terms of the share offer. The holders of ordinary shares, in addition to attracting capital gains (or losses) on their shares, will also receive a dividend.

PREFERENCE SHARE CAPITAL

These are usually:

- **fixed interest bearing in terms of their dividends,** e.g. 6 per cent preference shares;

- **cumulative** (unless otherwise stated), which means that if their dividend is in arrears it will be carried forward to be paid in the future;

- **redeemable** at some future date;

- **non-voting shares,** unless their dividend is in arrear.

Note that there are no preference shares in Le Caylar plc's balance sheet.

RESERVES

Some of the reserves which you may come across are:

- **Share premium account.** As indicated earlier, you may recall that this is the amount by which the share price exceeds the par value (also called face value or nominal value). For example, if ordinary shares with a par value of £1 each are issued at £2.60 each, the balance sheet will show the number of ordinary shares issued valued at £1 each as ordinary share capital, and the number of shares issued multiplied by £1.60 each as share premium in the reserves section. The uses to which the share premium may be put are restricted in the UK to those specified by company law.

- **Capital reserve.** This may have arisen on the revaluation of freehold property or on the acquisition of a subsidiary company. (There was no capital reserve in Fig 16.3.)

- **General reserve.** This is the cumulative amount of profits which have been appropriated in the past (in the profit and loss appropriation account). The transfers are made at the discretion of the directors, probably because the profits represented by the transfers have been reinvested long term within the business, e.g. buying fixed assets, and cannot therefore be regarded as freely distributable as dividends to shareholders.

- **Profit and loss account balance (or retained earnings or undistributed profits)** are the cumulation of all the remaining profits which have been 'ploughed back' and reinvested in the business. The amount which is 'ploughed back' each year is shown in the profit and loss appropriation account. It is the net profit after tax, less tax, less transfers to reserves and less dividends for the period which have been paid or proposed.

- **Long-term debt or long-term liabilities.** Items which appear under this heading represent loan capital from banks or other financial institutions, or debentures:

  - **loans** may be secured or unsecured with fixed or variable rates of interest. Many types are now on the market, e.g. some loans even allow repayment holidays;
  - **debentures** are a specialised type of loan (usually secured by a charge on the assets) and repayable between certain future dates. Trustees are usually appointed to protect the interests of the debenture holders.

Employment of capital

FIXED ASSETS

These are the assets which are purchased to be used in the business and are not intended for resale, e.g. freehold land and buildings, plant, machinery, equipment, fixtures and fittings and motor vehicles. They are shown at their historic cost (or revaluation) less depreciation computed in accordance with the company's depreciation accounting policy. You may be a little confused with the way in which fixed assets appear. This should not be a problem: they tend to be shown at their original cost (or revaluation if there has been one) less the cumulative depreciation to date, i.e.:

cost of fixed asset
  less
cumulative depreciation to date
  =
net (or net book value)

INVESTMENTS

This asset can be made up of the investments made by the company in the shares of other companies or government stocks. They are usually shown at their cost, with a note of their valuation at the balance sheet date. (Figure 16.3 did not have any investments.)

WORKING CAPITAL

WC = CA – CL, meaning working capital is the difference between the current assets and the current liabilities, e.g. £17 800 in 19X8.

- **Current assets** are made up of:

  - **stocks** of raw materials, work-in-progress and finished goods;
  - **debtors** (amounts owing from sales to customers on credit) less any provision for bad and doubtful debts, if any, to value the debtors at a more realistic figure;
  - **prepayments**, which are amounts paid for various goods and services which will benefit the next or future accounting periods, e.g. rent, insurance, advertising, etc paid in advance;
  - **bank balances;**
  - **cash in hand** (including petty cash balances).

- **Current liabilities** consist of:
  - **creditors** for goods and services which have been supplied to the company on credit, i.e. amounts owing to suppliers;
  - **accruals**: expenses included in the profit and loss for the period, but which have not yet been paid, e.g. invoices for the servicing of company vehicles, stationery, accountancy fees, etc;
  - **taxation**: the amount owing to the tax authorities;
  - **proposed dividends**: the dividend which has yet to be paid to the shareholders for the period in question. Where companies pay an 'interim dividend', this figure will represent the amount of the 'final dividend'.

There are many other items which could appear, e.g. assets such as 'patents' and 'trademarks' and liabilities such as 'convertible loan stock' (loans that can at some future date be converted into ordinary shares). There is, however, a limit to what can be illustrated in a book of this type.

Cash flow statements

The format for the cash flow statement which is currently used in the UK is prescribed by a financial reporting standard (FRS 1). The cash flow statement, sometimes also described as a 'funds flow statement', gives an indication of the reasons why cash movements have happened during the accounting period under review.

A typical cash flow statement will include:

- **net cash flow from operating activities**;

- **returns on investments, and the servicing of finance**, e.g. dividends paid and received, interest paid;

- **taxation**;

- **investing activities**, e.g. the purchase and sale of fixed assets and investments;

- **financing**, e.g. funds from an issue of share capital, loans received or repaid.

Creative accounting

However, it should be appreciated that accounting is not an exact science and that it does have several limitations, some of which are as follows:

- The information included in the profit and loss account and balance sheet has been arrived at by individuals employing their own personal interpretations/judgement of the accounting principles and concepts. They may have also been prepared with the taxation aspects in mind.

- 'Window dressing' may also have taken place to show a position which is not typical of that which existed throughout the period. For example, because of a purge on collecting debtors, the debtors figure may be much lower than the level which existed throughout the period. 'Window dressing' can and does affect the ratios which are calculated, in many instances quite significantly. Other examples of window dressing are running down stocks, changing accounting policies, revaluations, etc.

● 'Off balance sheet financing'. Many companies nowadays have many fixed assets which do not appear on their balance sheets. This is because they either rent or lease certain fixed assets, e.g. machinery, office equipment, etc. This makes it very difficult when it comes to inter-firm comparisons using ratio analysis.

FINANCIAL ANALYSIS

A study of the various ratios over time for one's own organisation with those of other organisations and/or industry figures can provide management with much 'food for thought'. They can help indicate areas of activity which need investigation and provoke questions.

There are very many ratios, books full in fact, thus it is impossible to cover all of them here. Using Figs 16.2 and 16.3 of Le Caylar plc, a number of the ratios, which the non-financial manager/director/executive may find useful, are illustrated below (all amounts in £000).

Profitability

GROSS PROFIT TO SALES PERCENTAGE

	19X7	19X8
$\dfrac{\text{Gross profit}}{\text{Sales}} \times 100$	$\dfrac{3\,580}{8\,000} \times 100$	$\dfrac{4\,088}{9\,800} \times 100$
	$= 44.75\%$	41.71%

This shows the company's average mark-up on the selling price. The reason for the fall in 19X8 could be that the margins are being cut to reach sales targets and increase market share or certain lines are being sold off at well below the average mark-up.

NET PROFIT BEFORE TAX TO SALES PERCENTAGE

	19X7	19X8
$\dfrac{\text{Net profit before tax}}{\text{Sales}} \times 100$	$\dfrac{2\,033}{8\,000} \times 100$	$\dfrac{2\,450}{9\,800} \times 100$
	$= 25.41\%$	25%

One way of looking at this is to show how it explains the profit generated for each £1 of sales. Both years generate around 25p for every £1 of sales made. Movements in this percentage are caused by fluctuations in gross profit, expenses, depreciation, directors' fees, interest payments, etc. It can be said that it provides an indication of

513

what is happening to overheads. From these figures, it looks as though the company has managed to control its overheads more effectively. Despite a dip in the gross profit percentage, the net profit percentage is almost the same, even though the company has operated at a higher level of activity.

NET PROFIT BEFORE INTEREST AND TAX AS A PERCENTAGE OF THE CAPITAL EMPLOYED (RETURN ON INVESTMENT)

	19X7	19X8	
Net profit before tax	2 033	2 450	
Add Interest on loan (10%)	400	400	
Interest on debentures	–	960	(Full year assumed)
	£2 433	£3 810	

19X7	19X8
$\dfrac{2\ 433}{36\ 160} \times 100 = 6.73\%$	$\dfrac{3\ 810}{48\ 800} \times 100 = 7.81\%$

This is a very good measure for looking at the productivity of the capital employed. It looks at the net profit before interest and tax (NPBIT) as a percentage of the capital invested, irrespective of where that capital came from, e.g. share capital, reserves, loans, etc. It therefore gives an **overall return** on the capital employed.

Although the return is improving for the Le Caylar plc, it is less than the cost of the new borrowing. The debentures are at 8 per cent. One possible explanation was that the company was fighting for survival at a time of difficult trading conditions/recession. It is to be hoped that the new investment, indicated by the increase in fixed assets, will benefit future trading periods.

The interest calculations are computed by referring to the information given in Fig 16.3, the balance sheet.

Liquidity

To compute some of the liquidity ratios for both years more information is needed for 19X6, which is:

	19X6
Stocks	8 600
Debtors	5 200
Creditors	2 944

CURRENT RATIO
The current ratio is the ratio of current assets to current liabilities, and measures the company's ability to pay its debts as the debts become due:

19X7	19X8
$\dfrac{18\ 116}{4\ 956} = 3.66$	$\dfrac{23\ 900}{6\ 100} = 3.92$

For every £1 owing the company had £3.66 cover in 19X7 and £3.92 cover in 19X8. The increase looks as though it could be caused by the significant increases in stocks and debtors which tie up more capital. This could also provide another reason for the poor performance in the productivity of the capital employed, i.e. the return on investment.

ACID TEST

The acid test is computed as above, but excludes stocks as they are not classed as being as liquid as other current assets. It may also be described as the ratio of liquid assets to current liabilities:

19X7	19X8
$\dfrac{8\,716}{4\,956} = 1.76$	$\dfrac{11\,712}{6\,100} = 1.92$

The rule of thumb for this ratio is one to one, but in practice companies do tend to manage on less. An acid test of around 0.85 is not untypical. The company had cover of £1.76 in 19X7 and £1.92 in 19X8 for every pound that is owed. In the words of the Boston Matrix, it would no doubt be classified as a 'cash cow': not much growth in turnover but with a lot of cash. It does have a lot of capital tied up in debtors and large amounts in the bank.

Efficiency ratios

AVERAGE COLLECTION PERIOD

The average collection period shows how long it takes to collect the amounts owing from debtors. It can be computed as follows:

$$\frac{\text{Average debtors} \;\;(\text{i.e. opening plus closing debtors divided by two})}{\text{Sales}} \times 365 \text{ days}$$

19X7	19X8
$\dfrac{5\,700}{8\,000} \times 365 = 260 \text{ days}$	$\dfrac{7\,420}{9\,800} \times 365 = 276 \text{ days}$

It would appear that the company's credit control is very poor and getting worse, and that they are allowing their debtors far too long a time in which to pay them. Periods of around 45 days or 60 days are quite typical of certain industries and 90 days is not uncommon. Again, because of adverse trading conditions and increased competition they may have been forced into giving more than generous credit terms.

AVERAGE CREDIT PERIOD

The average credit period shows how long it takes to pay the suppliers of purchases on credit. This would be computed in the same way as the average collection period, if possible using the following calculation:

$$\frac{\text{Average creditors} \;(\text{i.e. opening plus closing creditors divided by two})}{\text{Purchases on credit}} \times 365 \text{ days}$$

At this point it should be noted that information about the amount of sales or purchases on credit is not always available. If that is the case, just use the total sales figure or total purchases figure.

RATE OF STOCK TURNOVER (OR 'STOCKTURN')

Here the computation uses the 'cost of sales' if available; if not the sales figure may be used. It represents how many times the average stock held is sold in a given period and can also be converted to give the average time that it remains in stock before being sold. One way of calculating it is:

$$\frac{\text{Average stock}}{\text{Cost of sales}} \times 365$$

19X7	19X8
$\dfrac{9\,000}{4\,420} \times 365 = 743$ days	$\dfrac{10\,794}{5\,712} \times 365 = 690$ days

Holding stocks for long periods is expensive in terms of the amount of capital tied up, interest payments and other holding costs. The company needs to make a very careful review of their stock control area; stocks would appear to be tied up for periods which are far too long. Certain companies have been known to carry on producing stock even though their market for certain products is in decline!

Capital structure

GEARING

Gearing (leverage) is an indication of the relationship between the long-term debt and the equity (equity defined as ordinary share capital plus the reserves). One way of expressing this relationship is:

$$\frac{\text{Long-term debt}}{\text{Equity + Long-term debt}} \times 100$$

19X7	19X8
$\dfrac{4\,000}{36\,160} \times 100 = 11.06\%$	$\dfrac{16\,000}{48\,800} \times 100 = 32.79\%$

In 19X7 the company could be described as 'low geared', i.e. it has a low proportion of long-term debt (sometimes just called 'debt'). The debentures issued in 19X8 have caused the company to become more highly geared. In times of poor trading conditions it is the more highly geared companies that are at risk because of their obligations to make loan repayments and pay interest at regular intervals on their debentures/long-term loans. Note that what is high or low gearing will depend upon the industry/type of business concerned. Gearing has been described as 'using debt to increase the wealth of ordinary shareholders', i.e. if the project concerned generates profit, after the payment of the interest on the long-term debt, any excess belongs to the ordinary shareholders.

Investment

EARNINGS/SHAREHOLDERS' EQUITY (RETURN ON EQUITY)

This is computed as follows:

$$\frac{\text{Net profit after tax (less preference dividend, if any)}}{\text{Equity (i.e. the ordinary shareholders' funds)}} \times 100$$

19X7	19X8
$\frac{1\,768}{32\,160} \times 100 = 5.50\%$	$\frac{2\,140}{32\,800} \times 100 = 6.52\%$

This provides an indication of the return that is being earned on behalf of the ordinary shareholders. There has been a slight improvement. It would be hoped that this will grow in the future as a result of the higher gearing and the increased investment in fixed assets.

EARNINGS PER SHARE (EPS)

The amount which each ordinary share is producing is calculated as follows:

$$\frac{\text{Net profit after tax (less any preference dividend, if any)}}{\text{Number of ordinary shares}}$$

19X7	19X8
$\frac{1\,768}{20\,000}$ 8.84 pence per share	$\frac{2\,140}{20\,000}$ 10.7 pence per share

This would have to be compared with a 'yardstick' such as the earnings per share of the industry average or various competitors.

COST AND MANAGEMENT ACCOUNTING

Cost and management accounting is involved with satisfying the information needs of management. It is there to assist management with their decision making, e.g. planning the organisation's economic performance, controlling costs and improving profitability. However, it should be noted that the information provided by the management accounting function is just one component part of the decision-making jigsaw. There are other factors to take into account, e.g. non-financial factors such as ease of maintenance, servicing arrangements, importing problems, standardisation, etc. One of the most difficult problems which the management accountant has to deal with, is how to account for overheads. Overheads comprise the indirect expenditure, i.e. expenditure which does not directly form part of the product or service.

There are three approaches which can be followed. These can be described briefly as:

- **Total absorption costing.** This method shares the production overheads up between departments/locations (cost centres), and then charges them to the products via a predetermined rate per direct labour hour or machine hour or some other basis (absorption rate/recovery rate), the aim being to recover the overhead expenditure in the product costs.

- **Activity based costing.** This is in effect a more sophisticated total absorption costing method. The overheads are shared up according to 'cost drivers'. A cost driver is the activity which causes the cost to be incurred, for example the number of setups, the number of purchase orders, etc.

- **Marginal costing.** Only the variable overheads, those which vary directly with the production of the product, are included in the product costs. The fixed costs are not included in the product costs and are treated as 'period costs', i.e. they are written off as an expense of the period to which they belong.

The bulk of what is reviewed here regarding management accounting is budgeting, plus a little standard costing.

In order for management to control costs, budgets and standards must be set for each element of cost, i.e. materials, labour and overheads.

Standard costing and budgetary control are modern techniques which measure actual costs against predetermined standards/budgets. By analysis of the variances between actual and standard/budget they provide management with a means of continuous control so that they can take appropriate remedial action, as indicated in Fig 16.4. The same principle may also be applied to sales and other sources of income.

The variance reports mentioned would be designed to highlight variances which are adverse and of significant value plus an explanation as to why the variance has occurred.

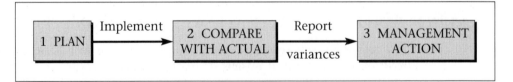

FIG 16.4 THE THREE PHASES OF PREDETERMINED COST CONTROL SYSTEMS

BUDGETARY CONTROL

Definitions

CIMA (The Chartered Institute of Management Accountants) in the UK defines budgetary control and a budget as follows:

> **Budgetary control is 'The establishment of budgets relating the responsibilities of executives to the requirements of a policy, and the continuous comparison of actual with budgeted results, either to secure by individual action the objective of that policy or to provide a basis for its revision.'**
>
> **A budget is 'A plan expressed in money. It is prepared and approved prior to the budget period and may show income, expenditure and the capital to be employed. May be drawn up showing incremental effects on former budgeted or actual figures, or be compiled by zero-based budgeting.'**

Some of the key words of budgeting which are included in the two definitions give a very good insight into the principles on which budgeting is founded. These are as follows.

Prepared in advance of the period

At the outset it must be appreciated that budgets are only estimates based on the best available information at the time of their preparation. Usually this involves updating what is known about the past, e.g. making use of the payroll analysis, the materials used analysis and the machine utilisation analysis, etc, updated by what is known about the future and involving various meetings and discussions.

To ensure that the budget is ready for implementation by the due date, a budget preparation timetable will be drawn up specifying dates for submitting drafts/revisions, meetings, etc. For all those involved there has to be effective co-ordination, co-operation and clear communication if the figures produced are to be realistic and reasonable. Usually the accountant will be responsible for co-ordinating the budget preparation process. The final budget, 'the master budget', is really a summary of all the other budgets and usually consists of a cash budget and a budgeted profit and loss account and balance sheet. However, it should be noted that the cost of the budgeting system should not be greater than the benefits.

Responsibilities of executives

Budgeting by its nature necessitates the authorisation and delegation of budget activities between individual managers and other personnel. This principle is known as 'control by responsibility', i.e. it makes an individual responsible for the whole or part of a particular budget, as illustrated in Fig 16.5. It is designed so that the targets set can be achieved: if the machine groups achieve their targets the production department concerned achieve theirs, and so on.

519

PRODUCTION BUDGET	RESPONSIBLE OFFICIAL
Company	Production director
Division	Divisional manager
Department	Departmental manager
Machine group	Supervisor or machine group leader

FIG 16.5 BUDGETING RESPONSIBILITIES

The setting of targets must where possible involve representation from the workforce if the relevant targets are to be fair, attainable and acceptable. Participation of managers plus workforce representatives, e.g. supervisors and trade union representatives, in target setting and in the budget preparation process can make or break the budget in terms of its acceptance by the personnel involved, e.g. production workers and sales staff. 'We don't do it that way in our organisation' is not a good enough reason for not having some form of participation. However, to make it work does take some careful thought and it may not be as easy as it sounds.

It is also important to have knowledge of the other functional areas of the business. This should help break down barriers, overcome prejudices and lead to an appreciation of each other's point of view. Functions ideally should work together in harmony (*see* Fig 16.6), not in isolation (*see* Fig 16.7).

Requirements of a policy

Policy is the means by which objectives are achieved. Budgeting provides a formal planning framework and forces managers to plan ahead. They need therefore to have a clear understanding of what their company's objectives are, e.g. profit targets and sales targets, in order to be able to formulate the policies which they hope will achieve them. All too often certain managers follow their own personal objectives or their own perceptions of what they consider their company's objectives to be. Hence the need for clearly communicated objectives and policies. Budgeting provides a sense of direction.

Continuous comparison

The comparison of actual performance against the budget and reporting the variances at regular intervals provides an 'early warning system' of things which are not going according to plan. Those variances which need to be looked at will be highlighted on the reports so that management can take corrective action. This highlighting of significant variances is known as 'management by exception'. It enables managers to get to the heart of the matter and spend their valuable time and energy on those items which really do need their attention. This frequent comparison system is the control element of budgeting, i.e. performance evaluation. Budgeting, in effect provides a 'benchmark' against which performance can be assessed.

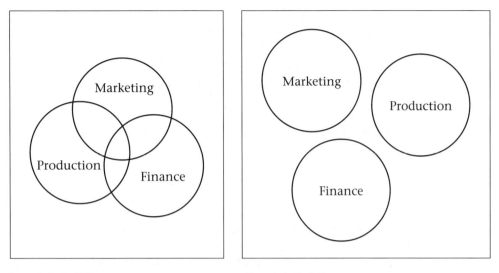

FIG 16.6 WORKING TOGETHER   FIG 16.7 WORKING IN ISOLATION

Source: Chadwick, L, *The Essence of Financial Accounting*, Prentice-Hall, 1996.

Policy revision

There is always a danger of adhering to the budgets (which as mentioned earlier are only estimates) too stringently and following the perception that 'the budget should be achieved at all costs'. For control purposes the budgets used should be flexible, i.e. computed for the actual levels of activity (output) which have been attained. Information provided by the system may lead to a revision of policy. The budget will have been computed using certain basic assumptions about the business environment; if these change, then the budgets/policies may also have to change.

Financial or quantitative statements

Budgets are interrelated, for example the sales budget determines the production requirements, the production budget dictates the amount of raw materials required and the labour budget, and so on. Thus, when the budget preparation process commences, budgets first tend to be drawn up in terms of quantity only. After a series of consultations/meetings to ensure the figures match, they are then costed. One of the prime considerations which has to be looked at before the budgeting process begins at all is the 'principal budget factor' (or limiting factor or key factor). It places a constraint, i.e. a limit, on what a company can or cannot do. For example, if the principal budget factor is the availability of certain raw materials, i.e. the company can only obtain a specific quantity in the forthcoming period, this in turn restricts the production of products using the material in question, which in turn limits the sales.

The 'principal budget factor', however, is not unchangeable. Management can by its actions reduce its effect or eliminate it altogether. For example, management action where the supply of raw materials is limited could include one or more of the following:

521

- improve production methods to reduce waste;

- amend product designs to use less of the raw materials in question;

- use a substitute raw material;

- buy some of the components which use the raw material from external suppliers;

- search for new suppliers.

Planning

To be successful in business, planning for the future is essential. Budgeting demands that planning backed by co-ordination, co-operation and clear communication take place at:

- **the stage of setting objectives and formulating policy,** e.g. discussions about how to achieve the objectives;

- **the budget preparation stage,** e.g. in order to keep to the budget timetable and to set sensible targets;

- **the control stage,** e.g. the way in which information is to be reported and acted upon. It is not intended to be a recriminatory post-mortem;

- **the monitoring stage,** e.g. monitoring the environment to detect changes in basic assumptions, reviewing and revising to cope with changing circumstances.

Cash budgets

Cash budgets (also called the cash flow forecast) attempt to predict what the cash and bank balances will be for a specified period, e.g. usually between three and 12 months. The movement of cash is recorded when it is expected to come in or go out. This involves taking into account the average period of credit granted to customers, i.e. debtors, or that allowed by suppliers, i.e. creditors. It does not matter about the period covered by the expenditure, e.g. rent paid or dividends paid. What does matter is the date on which the rent or dividend is expected to be paid in cash. Certain items which affect the measurement of the profit or loss in the P & L account do not affect the cash budget, for example:

- **depreciation** is a non-cash item: the money moves when the fixed asset is paid for;

- **stocks** of raw materials, work-in-progress and finished products;

- **accrued expenses,** i.e. expenses belonging to the period but still outstanding at the end of the period;

- **prepaid expenses:** any cash involved for these will have all gone through the cash budget and no adjustment will be made, as the cash has already moved;

- **provisions for bad debts** are non-cash items;

- **taxation owing** which will be paid in the future;

- **transfers to reserves:** no cash moves, it is just an appropriation of profits;

- **proposed dividends.**

The purpose of the cash budget is to:

- make sure that cash is **available as and when needed;**

- **highlight shortages** so that early action can be taken, e.g. internal action to delay certain payments, put back certain investment plans or hold discussions with the bank;

- **highlight surpluses** in order to put them to work, e.g. investing them short term, switching to a bank account which provides a better return. This is what is known as the 'treasury function'.

It can be observed from the cash graph in Fig 16.8 that position 'A' indicates a period of around four months when the company has surplus funds. Simply to leave it in a bank current account would be considered poor financial management, i.e. the balance could be earning a better return elsewhere. The critical position identified by area 'B' arises when the bank balance falls below the agreed overdraft limit. Because this position has been estimated and identified well before it is anticipated to happen, there is time enough for management to decide on the appropriate form of action. It could be possible to take internal action without having to apply to the bank for an increase in the overdraft limit.

A very brief specimen layout of a cash budget is provided in Fig 16.9. The analysis provided could, however, be much more detailed.

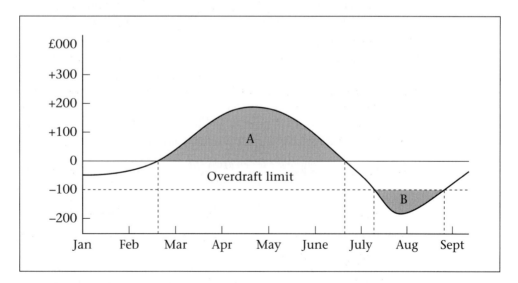

FIG 16.8 THE CASH GRAPH

| 19X7 | INFLOWS | | OUTFLOWS | | | | | |
	Opening balance	Sales	Purchases	Labour costs	Overheads (rent, etc.)	Dividends and tax paid	Fixed assets	Closing balance
Jan								
Feb								
Mar								
Apr								

FIG 16.9 A CASH BUDGET

CAPITAL BUDGETS

The capital budget (*see* Fig 16.10) spells out the organisation's future requirements in terms of:

(a) **fixed assets**, e.g. buildings, plant and machinery, equipment;

(b) **working capital**, e.g. an increase in inventory holdings such as raw materials;

(c) **investment in securities**, e.g. shares in UK companies;

(d) **redemption of preference shares and debentures**;

(e) **repayment of loans**;

(f) **forms of finance to be used and their timing**.

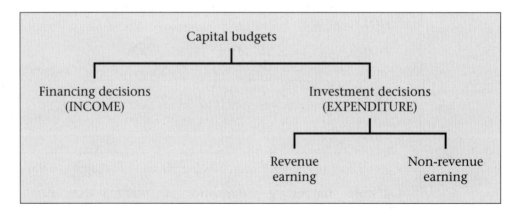

FIG 16.10 CAPITAL BUDGETS

Source: Chadwick, L and Pike, R, *Management and Control of Capital in Industry*, CIMA, 1982.

The capital budget will be subdivided into short-term and long-term plans. These plans will need to be carefully monitored and action taken to combat the effects of changes in the perceived environment. (Capital investment appraisal is covered later on in this chapter.)

Capital budgets: finance

The planned requirements in terms of expenditure must be financed from internal or external sources. Although the financing decision is closely related to the investment decision, it is in fact a quite independent decision. The capital budget relating to the financing requirements will be drawn up to cover:

- **the amount** required to cover the budgeted expenditure;

- **the timing** of the expenditure. In this respect, the cash budget is a very important tool as it indicates when the cash is needed;

- **the type of finance** to be used, e.g. debt, equity, internal financing.

It is most important to keep a watchful eye on what is happening in the capital markets. The possibility of the refinancing of existing borrowings should not be ignored. Refinancing could well save an undertaking (be it in the public or private sector) a great deal of money. It is imperative that alternative courses of providing fixed assets are considered, such as renting, hire purchase, leasing, sale and leaseback.

Capital budgets: investment

Management has the onerous task of seeing that all the personnel who should be involved with the preparation of capital budgets are in fact actively involved.

The preparation of the capital budgets for revenue-earning and non-revenue-earning investments could well be along the following lines.

TIMETABLE
A timetable will need to be drawn up and circulated in good time, giving dates for submission of proposals, meeting dates for consideration of proposals, and the final meeting date at which the budget should be approved.

CO-ORDINATION
The person responsible for co-ordinating all the budgets, usually the accountant, must ensure that all personnel concerned know what is expected of them. The co-ordinator should also make sure that appropriate data and information are made available to all those who are involved in the capital budgeting preparation process. Such information may include:

- **details of environmental change** (internal and external);

- **industry figures**, e.g. performance indicators, growth in sales;

- **the revenue implications of capital expenditure**, e.g. the recurring annual costs associated with a particular fixed asset;

- **the company's policy on credit, stock and replacement of fixed assets;**
- **grants available,** e.g from UK and EU sources;
- **taxation implications.**

In order to obtain the co-operation and participation of those involved, it is essential that there is clear and effective communication.

ASSESSING THE NEEDS
To a large extent, the needs in terms of plant, machinery, equipment and fixtures will be determined by the other, interrelated budgets.

SUBMITTING PROPOSALS
Departmental managers, knowing what is required of them, will need to formulate and submit their proposals. In the case of revenue-earning capital expenditure their needs will no doubt be based on:

- **matching** the needs of the other functional budgets;
- **replacement** of existing assets.

It is important for management to formulate a replacement policy for revenue- and non-revenue-earning capital expenditure: for instance executive cars could be replaced every three years, while certain machines could be replaced every five years. A replacement schedule may be drawn up containing details of the fixed assets which are to be replaced (e.g. estimated residual values) and their proposed replacements. The policy must be flexible and reviewed at regular intervals.

For non-revenue-earning capital expenditure the managers concerned should provide those who have the final say with satisfactory justification for the expenditure. Organisations spend a great deal of money on items that are non-revenue-earning, such as fixtures and fittings and office equipment.

SEARCH
When submissions have been received, a search should take place to reveal other alternatives which were not pointed out at the time of the original submission.

PRELIMINARY VETTING
The managers concerned will look carefully at all the proposals and obtain further information if necessary. They will then decide which proposals will go through to the next stage of the exercise. Rejecting some proposals at this stage will avoid wasting valuable time and effort later on.

EVALUATION
The evaluation of the revenue-earning capital budgets will take place, using, for example, capital investment appraisal. Various factors such as price, quality, reliability will have to be taken into account when assessing alternative non-revenue-earning capital expenditures.

PRESENTATION

The results of the evaluation will be presented to management in an appropriate format. Meetings may be arranged to discuss the proposals with the staff concerned.

SELECTION

After careful consideration of the information contained in the evaluation, plus any further information, management will meet to decide and approve the capital expenditure budget. This may be subdivided into short-term, medium-term and long-term capital budgets.

COMMUNICATION

The process does not end with selection. It is also important to inform the appropriate personnel of the decisions which have been reached, and to thank them for playing their part in the budgeting exercise. The budgets may be reviewed and revised several times before they are finally accepted and approved.

Capital allocation

When faced with the task of allocating capital expenditure between the various departments and cost centres, the following points should be taken into account:

- Is capital expenditure over the last few years a good guide to what will be expected next year? This approach tends to look backwards and not forwards and goes against the principles of sound budgeting. The information relating to past allocations is just one very small component part of the mass of information required. If historic capital expenditures were acceptable as a basis for fixing future allocations, this would encourage spending on unnecessary projects. Justification of projects is therefore of paramount importance.

- Across-the-board cuts in capital expenditure do not make any sense. This kind of compromise has the effect of cutting the essential as well as the not so essential projects.

- It is important that needs are assessed, expenditure justified and projects and alternatives considered and carefully appraised. A zero-base budgeting (ZBB) approach may be worth considering.

Zero-base budgeting

ZBB has been found to be particularly useful for non-revenue-earning capital projects and for service and support areas. It forces managers to justify and rank their programmes/projects. Top management can then screen and review the proposals and after careful consideration decide which ones will go ahead. It is claimed that ZBB promotes a much more efficient allocation of the scarce resources of an organisation.

Capital expenditure: the role of audit

It is the duty of the external auditor to verify:

- **the existence**
- **the ownership**
- **the basis of valuation**

of fixed assets and investments.

The external and internal (if any) auditors are particularly concerned with internal control systems governing the purchase of fixed assets. They will look most carefully to see that the purchase has been correctly authorised by the appropriate personnel. Their role also extends to preventing and/or detecting errors and fraud in this area and thereby reducing/eliminating losses.

Capital budgets: conclusions

Success in the area of capital budgets depends on a number of factors, some of the principal ones being as follows:

- It is essential for there to be adequate and effective co-ordination, co-operation and communication between all those who are involved in the budgeting process.

- Time should be devoted to a full and frank discussion of the proposals and alternatives.

- The process should involve the appropriate personnel concerned.

- Thought is needed to secure control over the capital budgets and authority should be laid down and clearly defined, for example the authority to order up to a certain value of materials and the authority to sign orders.

- All the personnel concerned should be educated regarding the benefits of budgeting and the way in which capital budgeting decisions are made within their organisation.

- As with other budgets, provision should be made for the monitoring and comparison of budgeted and actual results. Reasons for variances should be investigated and, where appropriate, remedial action should be taken.

- The plans should be flexible enough to alter as changes in the environment dictate.

- The interest of directors (and managers) in contracts should be established and taken into account.

- The internal and external auditors have a part to play in the control of capital expenditure. Their help in devising internal control systems should not be overlooked.

- Another approach that is worth looking at is zero-base budgeting, which challenges managers to rank and justify their proposals.

- Behavioural factors cannot and should not be ignored.

- It is important for the whole capital budgeting process to be planned and timetabled, so that it can be ready for implementation on time.

Behavioural aspects of budgeting

Behavioural factors can significantly influence the capital expenditure decision and budgeting in general.

SEATS OF POWER

Certain individuals and/or groups within an organisation may be able to exert considerable influence over the outcome of proposed capital expenditure. This could lead the organisation in a direction which conflicts with its corporate objectives. Eventually it could destroy itself by, for example, going overboard with the development of a new product. The power referred to may be by political access, i.e. access to top management, or by voting rights on committees.

EMPIRE BUILDERS

Empire builders within an organisation can involve it in unnecessary expenditure. Actions by such individuals and/or groups may fulfil their own personal objectives, but these may run contrary to the organisation's corporate objectives. The organisation in such cases could well find itself with a high proportion of surplus assets such as plant, equipment and buildings.

GATEKEEPERS

Gatekeepers are personnel who sit on important information flow junctions. They are in a position to regulate the flow of information, and so are in a position to determine what various levels of management may or may not see.

BEAT THE SYSTEM

Individuals or groups may be able to beat the system. They may even take a pride in doing so.

For example, a company places a limit of £10 000 on the ordering of capital equipment. Above this limit, additional authority is required. The personnel beating the system simply buy a machine for, say, £11 500 by making out two orders, one for say £9000 and the other for £2500. This does happen in the real world and efficient internal control systems and audit procedures are called for.

THE KNOW-ALL

Managers have been known to buy expensive equipment without realising that the equipment concerned would only work if certain additional equipment was also purchased. Had they discussed this with their subordinates, they might have avoided making such disastrous and expensive decisions. In one case, although the subordinates were not consulted they knew of the decision by their know-all manager to purchase a fixed asset. They all remained silent, even though they knew there would be problems, and were pleased when things went wrong! This highlights just how important participation is and that meetings to discuss investments in fixed assets can save a great deal of time and money.

STANDARD COSTS

Definition

A standard cost is an estimated cost, prepared in advance of production or supply, correlating a technical specification of materials and labour to the prices and wage rates estimated for a selected period, with the addition of an apportionment of the overhead expenses estimated for the same period within a prescribed set of working conditions.

The advantages of standard costing are:

- it provides management with regular and prompt reports on matters which are not proceeding according to plan or expectations, thus enabling corrective action to be taken;

- it ensures control of all factors, whether related to expenses or output, which affect production costs;

- it looks at both price and quantity variances when it reviews performance;

- Cost control is exercised in standard costing via variance analysis.

Figure 16.11 illustrates how standard costing fits into the cost control picture. This is a slightly more detailed version of Fig 16.4. The inclusion of the feedback loop is important and indicates that standards must also be monitored so that any necessary amendments can be made.

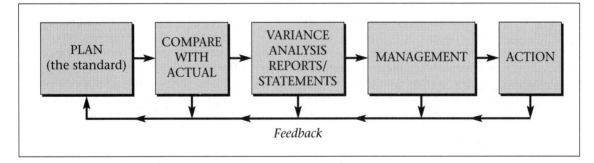

FIG 16.11 COST CONTROL USING STANDARD COSTING

Calculation of the variances

The cost (total) variance is the difference between the standard cost (for the actual level of activity) and the actual cost. This can be subdivided into two subvariances, as in Fig 16.12.

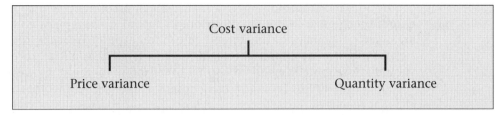

FIG 16.12 THE COST VARIANCE

	Labour or wages variance	Labour rate or wage rate variance	Labour efficiency variance
	£	£	£
Actual hours @ actual rate (1950 @ £4.20)	8190	8190	–
Standard hours @ standard rate (2000 @ £4)	8000	–	8000
Actual hours @ standard rate (1950 @ £4)	–	7800	7800
	£ 190 (A)	£ 390 (A)	£ 200 (F)

SUMMARY (PROOF)   £
Labour rate variance   390 (A)
Labour efficiency variance   200 (F)
= Labour cost variance   £190 (A)

(A) = Adverse (F) = Favourable

FIG 16.13 LABOUR VARIANCES

The labour variances (*see* Fig 16.13) are the labour rate variance and the labour efficiency variance. The materials variances are the material price variance and the material usage variance. The division into both price and quantity variances is an aid to control, e.g. if the labour force is taking longer to produce products than the time allowed this can be investigated/discussed with appropriate personnel.

It can be observed from the calculations in Fig 16.13 that both subvariances add back to the cost (total) variance. What really matters is the reporting side and the decision as to what form of corrective action will be taken.

FINANCIAL MANAGEMENT

Although financial management was shown as being part of the financial accounting side of the business in Fig 16.1, it has developed over the years into a specialist area in its own right. Whether or not the financial management function is carried out by a financial accountant or a management accountant will depend to a large extent on the size of the organisation. Financial management covers numerous areas such as sources of funds, cost of capital, capital structure, dividend policy, capital investment appraisal, etc. It is considered that all managers/executives should know something about capital investment appraisal. However, first there will be an attempt to provide a brief insight into some of the other areas of financial management.

Sources of finance

Managers, especially the financial management side of an organisation, are particularly involved with the raising of capital and the management of the financial structure.

Capital can be obtained from a multitude of places. The charges for capital will reflect the timespan concerned and the risk to the institution which is providing the finance. It must be remembered that in addition to paying the interest on certain types of finance, e.g. loans and debentures, there is also an obligation to repay the capital.

Finance is always available, but at a price. Matching the life over which finance is repayable with the life of the project or investment is worth considering and is certainly a commonsense approach. There are numerous sources of finance, but internal finance, e.g. selling surplus assets, improved credit control, etc, must not be overlooked.

In addition, a careful watch needs to be kept on what is available through government agencies and the EU. These sources change quite frequently, hence the need for regular monitoring.

The lease or buy decision

An alternative to outright purchase of a fixed asset is leasing. It enables firms to acquire various fixed assets, such as premises, plant, machinery, fixtures, equipment and motor vehicles. With a lease, the lessor retains ownership of the asset, although at the end of certain leases ownership passes or may pass to the lessee. The lessee agrees to meet certain conditions, e.g. to pay a rental at specified intervals, to keep the asset in good condition, to carry out regular maintenance and to insure the asset.

Leasing tends to be encouraged by tax implications, high interest rates and cash shortages. It frees an undertaking from having to find a large lump sum and the costs of acquiring and servicing such a sum.

It can be said that in relation to machinery and equipment, leasing provides a hedge against obsolescence. Leases are negotiated for a number of years, at the end of which the asset in question may be returned and another asset leased. This enables the undertaking concerned to keep pace with developments in new technology without being burdened with machinery and equipment which are out of date.

Capital structure and gearing

Capital structure and gearing were discussed briefly in connection with financial analysis earlier on in this chapter. The term capital structure is generally used to describe a concern's more permanent and/or long-term financing, e.g. ordinary shares, preference shares, long-term debt and reserves. However, the capital structure is not just an array of long-term financing, it also gives rise to a particular set of risks and costs.

Gearing (known as leverage in the USA) refers to the relationship between interest-bearing capital, e.g. preference shares, debentures and long-term loans, and the ordinary shareholders' interests, i.e. issued and paid-up ordinary share capital plus reserves. If the proportion of interest-bearing capital to ordinary share capital is high the company is described as being highly geared. If the position is vice versa the company is classed as low geared. However, to state with authority whether or not a company is high or low geared one must look at the gearing ratios for the particular industry in which the company operates.

There is a greater possibility of increasing the return on net worth and the stake of the ordinary shareholder if the company is highly geared and trading conditions are favourable. Conversely, when trading conditions are poor a highly geared company stands to make low returns because of the obligation to pay interest. It is this obligation to pay interest and in certain cases to repay the capital within a specified period, e.g. on a long-term loan, that increases the risk to the company. The interest (e.g. on debentures) must be paid whether or not the company makes a profit.

The cost of capital

The cost of capital is one of accounting theory's most controversial topics. It is an area which cannot be ignored because all capital does have both a cost and an opportunity cost. When selecting a discount rate for capital investment appraisal purposes, many authorities favour the use of the cost of capital figure. However, there are a number of different cost of capital figures which could be used. A full discussion of this subject is outside the scope of this chapter. Investors are only likely to invest in a business if the return is commensurate with the risk involved. ROI (return on investment) has been said to be the real name of the business game.

CAPITAL INVESTMENT APPRAISAL

The planning, control and investment of capital projects

The planning, control and investment of capital involve attempting to answer numerous questions, many of which are open ended, subjective and not easily defined. Some of the key questions are:

- **Which source of funds should be used for financing a particular investment?** This involves considering factors such as the cost of capital, the term (e.g. long term or short term), repayment arrangements, legal aspects and matching.

- **What is the cost of capital?** In determining this it will also be necessary to establish which cost of capital figure should be used (e.g. weighted average cost).

- **What should be the return on capital employed?** It is very difficult to define an adequate return and the amount anticipated will vary between firms and industries. ROI (return on investment) is very important from the viewpoint of the providers and users of the funds.

- **In the area of capital investment appraisal, which discount rate should be used?** A number of alternatives could be selected and deemed appropriate, e.g. the cost of capital or anticipated returns on projects commensurate with the risk involved.

- **In deciding on an investment of capital, how will the risks involved in the project be assessed and taken into account in the computations?** This very broad area is the subject of constant debate and features regularly in the financial press. Uncertainty may be handled by probability approaches to likely results, to give the best and worst and most likely outcomes.

- **Why should the company opt for a particular capital structure?** Following on from this, one could also ask which capital structure would be most appropriate for the company now and in the future.

- **How much working capital should a firm have?** Cash flow and profitability do not go hand in hand. It is vital to a business's long-term survival to be able to pay debts as the debts need to be settled.

The essential elements of a system for planning and evaluating capital investments are illustrated in Fig 16.14, and are as follows:

- **Objectives.** All projects should be in line with the objectives and/or the policy of the company concerned. In particular, the company's objectives relating to the required return on capital employed should be clearly stated and understood.

- **Data collection and analysis.** Data has to be collected, classified, analysed and presented in a form appropriate to the needs and understanding of the user. A key decision that has to be made is the method/s by which the investment is to be appraised, e.g. discounted cash flow.

- **The management information system.** The provision of relevant and appropriate information to management can most certainly enhance the decision-making process. An effective management information system is therefore a prerequisite for efficient planning and control. The quality of the information will help determine the accuracy of forecasts relating to future performance. However, it is possible to provide management with too much information, and information overload tends to weigh them down. The quality of the information rather than its quantity is therefore closely linked to the quality of decision making.

- **Monitoring the external environment.** The external environment in which a firm operates is diverse and complex. It must be continuously monitored to

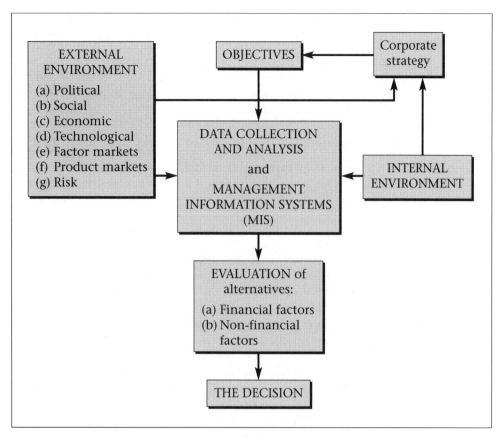

Fig 16.14 **The capital investment decision**

Source: Chadwick, L and Pike, R, *Management and Control of Capital in Industry*, CIMA, 1982.

reveal threats and opportunities which could, at a stroke, change the whole nature of the firm's capital investment programme, e.g. political instability in the country of a major customer.

- **The internal environment.** A firm cannot ignore its own internal environment and analysis will indicate strengths and weaknesses, e.g. in industrial relations, idle capacity, etc. The acceptance by workers of new plant or new processes can be of prime importance.

- **Evaluation.** In addition to the financial factors which have to be examined, management must also take various non-financial factors into account, e.g. availability of spare parts, flexibility, standardisation, etc.

A decision to go ahead with an investment does not end the story. The investment should be carefully monitored, and changes in the environment cannot be ignored. Companies must be able to adjust rapidly to meet enforced changes in circumstances if they are to survive and prosper.

The real value of a business is the sum of the value of its *existing* assets plus the value of its *future* investment opportunities. Existing assets represent prior investment decisions, the consequences of which (in terms of profits and cash flows) are still with us. Future investment opportunities represent the scope a business possesses for making profitable investment decisions in the future. The investment potential will vary from firm to firm and industry to industry and will depend, to a large extent, on:

- **management's ability to generate, select and execute investment projects;**
- **its capacity to raise funds to finance investments;**
- **corporate strategy.**

The problem of data

The key to good investment decision making rests in the quality of information on which an investment project is evaluated. The actual method of appraisal is of only secondary importance compared with the vital issue of the reliability of underlying estimates and assumptions. At best the data is often a reasoned estimate; at worst it may be little more than a guess. It is of little benefit to introduce sophisticated appraisal techniques unless the degree of accuracy they suggest is matched by the quality of data supporting the analysis.

The methods described in this chapter all depend on the predetermination of the cash flows. Thus one should always be aware that the cash flows used in capital investment appraisal are only estimates. The cash flows which are to be used should be relevant/incremental cash flows, i.e. if the expense or revenue arises as a result of the project going ahead, it is a relevant cash flow. If the expense or revenue would happen whether or not the project goes ahead, it is irrelevant, e.g. certain fixed costs. Also, as with cash budgets, depreciation is a non-cash item and so is not included in the cash flows.

EVALUATION METHODS

Methods which do not take the time value of money into account

PAYBACK

This method calculates how long it takes the cash flows generated by a specific project to recover the initial cost of the investment. Those who use this method of evaluation prefer projects which repay the cost of the initial investment in the shortest time. In estimating cash flows, the earlier cash flows are likely to be more accurate than the later ones.

AVERAGE RATE OF RETURN (UNADJUSTED RATE OF RETURN)

This return on investment method expresses the average cash flow per year as a percentage of the initial investment. Although it is simple to calculate it must be pointed out that it does ignore the timing of the cash flows, i.e. it averages the cash flows over the life of the project, when in fact they could fluctuate quite significantly from year to year and within each individual year.

Methods which do take account of the time value of money

Both the payback and average of rate of return methods suffer because they ignore the time value of money. The timing of the cash flows, i.e. the year in which the money comes in or goes out, can have a dramatic impact on a project. The time value of money means that £1 tomorrow will be worth less than £1 today. Thus cash flows which are to be received in the future are not worth as much as they are now. The following methods are preferable because they do take into account the time value of money.

NET PRESENT VALUE METHOD

To find the net present value (NPV), each of the cash flows is multiplied by the appropriate discount factor using discount tables, e.g. the present value of £1 table. These are then added up and the initial investment deducted. If the resulting figure, the NPV, is positive the project is worthy of consideration; if the NPV is negative the project should be rejected because it is not a wealth-creating opportunity. Note that when using this method, if all the cash flows are identical, the present value of an annuity of £1 table could be used and would save calculation time. Note also, however, that the selection of the discount rate is at the discretion of the selector.

PROFITABILITY INDEX

This is the present value of the cash flows divided by the initial cost of the project and is useful for comparing two dissimilar projects (i.e. projects with different investment requirements).

INTERNAL RATE OF RETURN (IRR) OR YIELD METHOD

The internal rate of return is the discount rate which will produce an NPV of nil, i.e. the cash flows discounted less the initial cost of the machine/equipment/project = nil. Therefore projects with an IRR greater than the cost of capital are worthy of consideration.

DISCOUNTED PAYBACK

This method simply calculates the payback using the discounted cash flows.

Taxation aspects

Taxation allowances must be included in the cash flows for the period which benefits from those allowances. Tax payments must be included in the cash flows for the period in which they are to be paid over. Thus, care needs to be exercised in taking the tax factor into account by considering the various time lags, e.g. the tax on the income from year 1 could be paid in year 2, and so on.

Non-quantitative aspects

Frequently, the cost or benefits arising from a particular investment decision are difficult if not impossible to quantify. Yet non-quantitative aspects should not be ignored. There is a real danger of accountants being so preoccupied with the financial aspects of capital investment appraisal that they may tend to ignore other important factors. Such non-financial factors include:

- **efficiency of servicing;**
- **reliability;**
- **risks associated with buying from overseas;**
- **desire for technical superiority;**
- **flexibility.**

SUMMARY

■ In financial accounting the profit and loss account and balance sheet were reviewed together with the terminology associated with them, e.g. prepayments, depreciation, assets and liabilities, and the way in which the figures are arrived at. In addition, their limitations were highlighted, e.g. the way in which 'creative accounting' can affect the figures.

■ Financial analysis was also introduced via a number of ratios, e.g. profitability and liquidity ratios, and some possible explanations for movements in them were provided.

■ The management accounting area covered budgetary control and an introduction to standard costing. In budgeting the key words should act as a reminder of the principles of good budgeting practice. They were:
  - preparation in advance;
  - control by responsibility;
  - setting targets;
  - participation;
  - policy, objectives and planning;
  - continuous comparison and 'management by exception';
  - budgets are interrelated;
  - monitoring, reviewing and revising.

■ An introduction was also provided to the way in which cash budgets are prepared and the 'treasury function', and capital budgets relating to both financing decisions and investment decisions, including zero-base budgeting (ZBB) and the role of audit. The final component of the budgeting portion of the chapter is a reminder to all management that the behavioural aspects of budgeting cannot and should not be ignored.

■ From the study of the standard costing area it should be noted that variances are caused by price movements, e.g. material prices, labour rates, or quantity variances, e.g. material usage, labour efficiency.

■ In the financial management area brief mention was made of the sources of finance, the lease or buy decision, capital structure and gearing and the cost of capital.

■ Capital investment appraisal was discussed briefly and the influences on the capital investment decision, the methods of evaluation and the problems associated with the data used. The final section highlighted the fact that financial data is just one part of the decision-making jigsaw, and that there are a number of non-financial factors which are also worthy of consideration.

REVIEW AND DISCUSSION QUESTIONS

1 How is the cost of sales figure arrived at?

2 How is the gross profit calculated?

3 What is the purpose of depreciation?

4 How is the net profit before tax arrived at?

5 Why can 'materiality' affect the net profit or loss figure?

6 What differences are there between ordinary shares and preference shares?

7 Explain what the reserves section of a balance sheet may consist of.

8 Describe how the capital invested in a company may be represented under the heading in a balance sheet of employment of capital.

9 At what value are fixed assets shown in a balance sheet?

10 How can 'creative accounting' affect the figures shown in the profit and loss account and balance sheet?

11 If the acid test ratio is 0.85 does the company have liquidity problems?

12 Explain briefly how production overheads are dealt with in total absorption costing and marginal costing.

13 Explain the importance to budgeting of:
   • the budget preparation timetable;
   • control by responsibility;
   • management by exception;
   • behavioural aspects;
   • participation.

14 What is the purpose of a cash budget?

15 Explain what factors/considerations the capital budget relating to the financing requirements will take into account.

16 Explain what the capital expenditure budget will take into account during its preparation stage.

17 Explain briefly the importance of the following to capital expenditure budgeting:
   - communication;
   - education;
   - authority;
   - monitoring.

18 How does cost control using standard costing work?

19 What are the dangers of high gearing?

20 In relation to capital investment appraisal, explain briefly the following:
   - the 'time value of money';
   - the external environment;
   - the net present value method;
   - non-financial factors.

21 Obtain copies of the annual published accounts of three companies who operate in the same industry.

   (a) Compare their directors' reports and accounting policies.

   (b) Compare their profit and loss accounts, balance sheets and cash flows.

   (c) Compare the statistics, financial ratios, etc and comment on the variations.

   (d) Make a list of why it is difficult to compare the three companies, e.g. consider 'off balance sheet financing' and the variations in their published statistics, etc.

   (e) Find out how capital investment appraisal is performed within an organisation with which you are familiar.

22 Discuss how three companies with identical products, identical income and identical expenditure could all end up computing different net profit before tax figures.

23 'A balance sheet can never show how much a company is really worth.' Discuss.

24 Why is it so difficult to compare the financial performance of one company with another, even in the same industry?

25 Discuss why participation is such an important part of the budget preparation process.

26 Discuss how the capital budgeting process for investments in new machinery or equipment should be carried out.

CASE STUDY: MPs SLAM OPERA BOARD'S CATALOGUE OF ERRORS

Rarely can a House of Commons report have been so conclusive, so damning: 'The current board should dissolve itself, and the chief executive should resign, with immediate effect.'

This is not some specious financial company at the receiving end of the sharp tongue of Gerald Kaufman and the culture, media and sport committee he chairs. It is the Royal Opera House, Covent Garden, perhaps the most prestigious cultural institution in the land and the one receiving the highest annual subsidy – £15m a year – from the Arts Council of England.

Mr Kaufman's committee can choose its targets for investigation. It lighted on Covent Garden, partly because it has received so much taxpayers' money – £98m over the past five years – but mainly because it seemed to be getting ever deeper into management and financial difficulties.

In May, its chief executive, Genista McIntosh, resigned after only four months, while in July only an immediate loan of £2m from two stalwart Covent Garden Friends, Vivien Duffield and Lord Sainsbury, saved the Royal Opera from sudden insolvency.

In the same month, the Royal Opera House embarked on a two-and-a-half year exile while its Covent Garden home was rebuilt at a cost of £214m, with £78.5m of the money coming from lottery funding. It quickly became apparent that the financial costs of life on the road were going to exceed budgets: this week the extra expense of closure was put at £32m, as against the £22m estimate. Mr Kaufman was ready to pounce.

Virtually no one escapes criticism in his committee's report, which was unanimous. The speedy and secretive arrival of Mary Allen, who switched from running the Arts Council to take over from Ms MacIntosh, gets short shrift.

'Given her experience of public office, Ms Allen's conduct fell seriously below the standards to be expected of the principal officer of a public body, whose loyalty should first and foremost be to the organisation which employs her.'

Ms Allen's Arts Council boss, Lord Chadlington (the former Peter Gummer), who preceded her to Covent Garden as chairman, is equally castigated, even though he arrived at the ROH after the organisational and financial plans for the closure had been concocted.

'Lord Chadlington should have appointed a new finance director with greater urgency, instead of permitting a year to elapse.'

The previous management regime, headed by Sir Jeremy Isaacs, along with his board, is also put in the stocks: 'The failures of the board in 1995 are responsible in considerable measure for the House's current crisis.'

So it goes on, through a catalogue of errors – from inadequate financial controls (with no monthly balance sheets) to over-optimistic forecasts of revenues while the Royal Opera and the Royal Ballet were on the road.

The report proposes two options. The first is privatisation, which would involve the loss of Arts Council subsidy 'forthwith'.

The second is a wholesale clear-out at the top. 'Should the board and the chief executive decline to accept the committee's recommendation that they resign, we recommend that the secretary of state make clear to the Arts Council that he expects them to cease payment of grant-in-aid to the Royal Opera House.'

The Kaufman committee has no power, but its damning report will be hard for Chris Smith, the culture secretary, to ignore. He might not want to do so. Last month he asked Sir Richard Eyre, former director of the National Theatre, to undertake a comprehensive review of opera provision in London. Everything is suddenly up for grabs. ∎

Source: *Financial Times*, 4 December 1997. Reprinted with permission.

REFERENCES FOR FURTHER READING

Chadwick, L (1996) *Essence of Financial Accounting*, 2nd edn, London and New York: Prentice-Hall.

Chadwick, L (1997) *Essence of Management Accounting*, 2nd edn, London and New York: Prentice-Hall.

Chadwick, L and Kirby, D (1995) *Financial Management*, Elements of Business Series, London: Routledge.

Chadwick, L (1998) *Myths and Realities of Management Accounting and Finance*, London: Financial Times Pitman Publishing.

MANAGEMENT ISSUES

BUSINESS ETHICS AND CORPORATE RESPONSIBILITY

Richard Welford

OBJECTIVES

The objectives of this chapter are to:

◆ argue that all corporate decisions are linked to a set of business ethics

◆ analyse how far the structures and procedures which define the ethos of an organisation can predict the prospects for corporate performance

◆ consider the importance of public interest and the relationship of an organisation with stakeholders

◆ explain the ethical responsibilities of corporations

◆ outline the internal and external factors which influence a corporation's ethical stance and internal values

INTRODUCTION

Corporate responsibility is a relatively new line of study among students and managers, but its roots undoubtedly go back to some of the key philosophical debates over ethics, values, equity and equality. The emergence of business ethics and responsible action on the corporate agenda is, however, more a function of the growing awareness of the social, political and environmental impact of the modern industrial enterprise. Many of the shifts in political attitudes towards firms, for example, reflect serious abuse by specific companies and specific business leaders. The misappropriation of pension funds, repression of workers in the Third World, environmental incidents, and even the bribery and corruption associated with deals to gain large government contracts are all issues which have hit the headlines over the last few years.

The starting point in this chapter is to argue that all corporate decisions are linked to a set of business ethics, and that by considering the structures and procedures which define the ethics of an organisation we ought to be able to say something about the prospects and preconditions for corporate performance. However, the systematic treatment of business ethics has been neglected in most advanced economies. Within the social sciences we have seen the study of political economy, for example, replaced by economic science and positive economics, and this has placed an emphasis on theories of optimisation rather than wider corporate and social responsibility at the firm level. Western economies, in particular, have developed along particular paths with an emphasis on industrial growth, efficiency (defined in narrow monetary terms) and performance (usually defined by profits and increases in share prices). The politics associated with Thatcherism and Reaganomics led to the common cry that 'there is no alternative' and to the development of a narrow, profit-centred corporate ethic.

There are those who suggest, however, that social responsibility and environmental considerations can no longer be ignored in the context of an ethical (and indeed efficient) approach to doing business. Hartley (1993), for example, suggests that the interests of a firm are actually best served by scrupulous attention to the public interest and by seeking a trusting relationship with the various stakeholders with which a firm is involved. In the process, society is also best served because the firm is forced to consider a whole range of competing objectives and to move away from activities which are derived from short-term performance indicators. These various stakeholders which the firm must consider are its customers, suppliers, employees, shareholders, the financial institutions, local communities and government. The stakeholder concept stresses the idea that a company has responsibilities to all these groups (even though they will have unequal amounts of power) and will be involved in balancing the often competing demands put upon it. A company's ethical stance will therefore be influenced both by internal values and by pressures exerted on it from external sources. Such pressures have grown as stakeholders have become more interested in the activities of business and as information availability and communications technology have increased.

BUSINESS ETHICS

The starting point must therefore be to provide some sort of definition of business ethics. This is difficult because it will depend on both the values of individuals working in the organisation and particularly on the culture created by the individual ethics of senior management, and on any codes of conduct which formally exist within the organisation or standards adopted from external agencies. We do not observe one single ethical code in all parts of society, but different codes in different places and at different times, and this is replicated within any organisation. We can, however, distinguish between 'personal value systems' which individuals will bring to the workplace and a 'formal business code' which may exist in some businesses through an explicit set of rules (Burke *et al.*, 1993). Perhaps more importantly, we ought to think about the 'actual value system', which is the moral climate experienced by staff in their daily business lives and which will determine the behaviour of the organisation as a whole, and a 'necessary value system', which is the minimum level of ethics (often equated with legal requirements) which has to exist for the organisation to survive.

In a pluralistic society, social, cultural and organisational power structures will tend to interact with these value systems. Such interaction may bring about a consensus or norm in certain areas of business activity, but it may also result in conflict where the ultimate outcome will depend crucially on the balance of power. One of the phenomena we have seen in the last few years is a shift of some of that power towards the consumer and the general public, and this has renewed the interest in business ethics and corporate responsibility.

Ethics tend also to be culturally specific. In some societies what may be considered as unethical by others may be considered as completely normal. Take the case of child labour for example. In the West we view the idea of 14 year olds working full time as intolerable. But in many parts of Asia, for example, there is no choice between work and education. If 14 year olds do not work then they are left to beg on the streets.

Another issue which causes problems for those advocating stronger codes of business ethics is that not all desirable ethics are mutually consistent. In those circumstances, judgements have to be made based on valuing different ethical actions. This too is a significant source of conflict. Again, outcomes will be determined by power structures and dominant ideologies will tend to arise. Such ideologies are nevertheless often a product of compromise and may not necessarily be first best solutions.

The study of business ethics is not new. In the nineteenth century, utilitarian reformers highlighted the need for ethical principles to be part of the free enterprise system. Currently, the literature on business ethics and on ethics generally is vital and growing. A key issue, however, is that there are many dilemmas where major principles, held to be moral imperatives, can in some circumstances be incompatible. There must therefore exist some sort of hierarchy which places more emphasis on one principle than another. What we are clearly observing today is the movement of social and environmental considerations up that hierarchy, for example.

Ultimately, it is organisation which dictates the hierarchy of different principles. The various levels of organisation, from whole economic and political systems via institutions and organisations to individual relationships, suggest particular hierarchies of principles (Donaldson, 1989). These hierarchies obviously shift over time and between different economic and political systems. They can be influenced, although that, in turn, will depend on power relationships. Many principles of business ethics might be considered somewhat abstract. A key issue, therefore, is how commonly accepted principles (such as improved environmental performance at the organisation level) can be translated into practice. This has to be done via codes (legal and self-regulating), education, communication and information. But these vehicles for change are themselves open to manipulation by those with power and the best principles are not always translated into best practice.

When ethical outcomes are discussed, words such as moral, ethical, good, efficient, rational, effective, fair, best and improved all come to mean different things in different circumstances. The meanings, connotations and overtones of words and phrases are often deployed in the conflicts and struggles for supremacy. The language of management is rich in emotive and ideological content, and therefore what organisations and managers say they are doing must be treated with healthy scepticism. What they are actually doing assessed against clearly defined principles and measures is much more important. Hence in communicating their message about social and corporate responsibility, organisations must be open and honest and not be tempted along the road of self-gratification and overstatement which is so often observed.

According to Donaldson (1989) there has been a relative neglect of the systematic handling of values in business which has been self-conscious. The consequences of the neglect can be seen both in anxiety about industrial performance in the West and a rise of concern about moral or ethical issues. A patchy awareness of the problem is to be seen in the sporadic (and at times piecemeal) nature of attempts by governments to regulate industry. This is well illustrated by the uneven growth in environmental legislation in the West and the continued growth of *ad hoc* codes of conduct in this area.

All organisations operate an ethical code, whether they know it or not. This may not be at all times consistent, but it is based on codes of conduct embedded in company culture and through the actions and decisions of senior management. Those codes will also be influenced by society's norms and in the business world by institutions and practices which stress the need to create wealth measured in quantitative financial terms. For any business which wishes to survive or avoid hostile takeover, the system necessarily pushes profits to the top of the corporate agenda and pushes other issues down the agenda.

Moreover, there is no business practice, action or statement that cannot have an ethical dimension. Businesses serve a variety of purposes for different stakeholders. Therefore we might argue that as a necessary condition, business activities are justifiable only in so far as they can be shown to meet the legitimate requirements of stakeholders. However, these requirements can be, and often are, in conflict and can change over time. In identifying requirements and reconciling them we have major problems. Moreover, we have suggested that the principles, ideals and moral values on which stakeholders' requirements are based can be in themselves contradictory. The traditional way of resolving these issues is for the organisation to assume primacy over individuals, allowing it to pursue objectives dictated by senior management subject to financial constraints imposed by owners and lenders. Thus organisations often adopt their own identity and culture and often exist outside the democratic framework. But we must realise that business ought to be a means and not an end, and it is a means for satisfying the requirements of all who have a legitimate claim.

548

It might be argued that any philosophy or course of action that doesn't take the public interest into consideration is intolerable in today's society (Hartley, 1993). Today's firms face more critical scrutiny from stakeholders and operate in a setting which is becoming more regulatory and litigious. The notion of public trust is also becoming more important. A clear measure of how far we have come towards a more responsive and responsible business climate is indicated by the fact that if a firm violates public trust then it is likely to be surpassed by its competitors, who will be eager to please customers by addressing their wants more accurately. Moreover, while the overwhelming majority of business dealings are non-controversial, any abuses increasingly receive considerable publicity, harming the image of business. Once a company's image has been damaged, it often takes a long time to reverse that damage.

In order to remain economically active, organisations need to learn from their mistakes or from those of other organisations. They need to take care to avoid situations and actions that might harm their relationship with their various stakeholders. In the worst of all cases, where an organisation faces a catastrophe, suddenly and without warning, its whole market image and business strategy can be destroyed. Examples of such events are increasingly commonplace. For example, in the case of Union Carbide, when one of its chemical plants in Bhopal, India leaked 40 tons of toxic chemicals, the event had (and continues to have) a profound effect on the reputation of that company. Although the company quickly rushed aid to the victims, it was bitterly condemned for complacency and the loose controls that permitted the accident to happen in the first place.

Environmental considerations are only one of many issues which might be included under the umbrella of business ethics. They nevertheless constitute an issue which has grown in importance. As a result of the many accidents and growing environmental damage caused by organisations, there have been increasing demands from consumers for firms to operate more ethically in this area. The consumer movement has fundamentally shaped and contributed to the significant increase in legislation and regulation at all levels of government. This has been aimed at preventing abuses in the marketplace and in the environment, and therefore environmental management strategies are increasingly commonplace in leading organisations around the world. To date, however, environmental considerations have not been given enough attention within the framework of business ethics, because dominant ideologies are being shaped more by short-term financial considerations than by the need to do business in a sustainable way. However, we must recognise that there will be spatial differences in ideologies and ethics, and before we proceed we ought to examine international and cross-cultural issues.

INTERNATIONAL AND CULTURAL DIFFERENCES

Ethics might be viewed as a subset of culture, and where cultural differences exist across boarders there are likely to be differences in ethics which are culturally defined. 'Culture difference' is a term frequently used to explain behavioural and other differences when doing business in foreign countries. However, it is a concept which has received scant attention and although most people would have ideas about the generic implications of different cultures, whether or not they really understand the specific features is more questionable.

Kroeber and Kluckhohn (1952) provide the following definition of culture:

'Culture consists of patterns, explicit and implicit, of and for behaviour acquired and transmitted by symbols, constituting the distinctive achievement of human groups, including their embodiments in artifacts: the essential core of culture consists of traditional (i.e. historically derived and selected) ideas and especially their attached values; culture systems may, on the one hand, be considered as products of action, on the other as conditioning elements of further action.'

This somewhat complex definition brings with it a number of important distinguishable factors:

- Culture is not innate, but learned. In other words, people are not born with an understanding of culture. It is something acquired through the socialisation process.

- It is shared, communicated and transmitted by members of a social set and defines the boundaries between different groups. This point is linked with the first, since it is through reinforcement within a social group that culture is learned.

- Various elements of culture are interrelated. Attitudes and beliefs may, in turn, be related to religious and/or ethical ideologies, and ethics and ideologies may be adopted which match attitudes and beliefs resulting from experience and socialisation.

Corporate responsibility and business ethics are very much interrelated and the behaviour of the organisation with respect to these issues will be dependent on shared cultures within social groups, the organisation of the business (which itself will tend to have a corporate culture) and countries (or regions). We must also recognise, however, that culture changes over time; this explains some of the swings towards and away from issues of corporate responsibility which we have seen over the past four decades. Such change can be gradual or extremely swift. Changes in the treatment of and attitudes towards women and their abilities in the workplace is something which we have seen develop gradually. However, we have seen rapid changes in attitudes surrounding sexuality as a result of HIV and a rapid awareness of the problems caused by CFCs following discoveries of holes in the ozone layer.

Differing ethics across national boundaries will be fundamentally related to values and attitudes. Values are often considered to be the standards by which things may be judged and serve to shape people's (and organisations') beliefs and attitudes (Welford and Prescott, 1994). This is probably the most elusive element of culture, as values and attitudes only become apparent through communication and interaction. Ethics, which will be part of these values, will therefore often have to be discovered, and where there are additional barriers to understanding (e.g. different languages, legal frameworks and customs) such discovery is very difficult. However, not to attempt to identify the values and ethics of a business means that a trading partner may well find itself in trouble if such values and ethics are not congruent.

Culture, therefore, helps us to define not only individual attitudes and behaviours (including those of managers) but also business norms. It is difficult to isolate the business culture in a country from that appertaining to the people and their society. Both feed off each other and similar patterns can be observed between the systems and networks at both an individual and commercial level. However, we must remember that ethics and attitudes held by an organisation will not simply be the sum of all individual ethics within it. That would be to ignore the differing amounts of power which various stakeholders have to influence corporate culture. Equally, the politics and economic policies of a country cannot really be isolated from the framework within which the organisation operates, and organisations often find it useful to change their corporate priorities (and therefore ethics) when political power shifts externally.

Conducting international trade therefore requires organisations to manage across cultures, within a wider array of ethical considerations and where the notion of corporate responsibility may be very different indeed. Mole (1990) defines culture as 'the way we do things round here', recognising that people and organisations in different countries, as a result of their specific cultural backgrounds, behave differently, and that to analyse the situation any further is extremely difficult. Therefore, operating across borders requires respect and a basic understanding of political, economic, legal, professional and ethical norms. At the management level, business cultures and those pertaining to the individual interact to dictate the behaviour of managers within the work organisation. Failure to adapt to approaches to the nuances of behaviour and attitudes in different countries can cause expensive mistakes.

As business becomes increasingly internationalised, there is therefore an increasing likelihood of encountering business partners from very different cultures, who subscribe to radically different ethical systems. The fact that there are different management cultures with different value systems means that there are no easy solutions to ethical dilemmas in international business. Many would argue that the simplest and most practical approach to ethical problems is to adopt moral relativism. In its simplest form, this means adopting local values and ethics when doing business in any particular location. This may be acceptable when it is the Western business executive who must be prepared to forgo alcohol in countries where it is shunned. However, it might also mean going along with the practice of bribery in countries where this is the norm, indeed it could even be argued that bribery is not so insidious in these countries as it is in the West, since it is regarded as quite a normal way to supplement rather low wages.

However, there is a serious problem with adopting a stance based on cultural relativism. If it is desirable for Westerners abroad to adopt the prevailing norms in the countries in which they do business, then the same might have to apply in the reverse situation. In other words, immigrant workers, for example, would be expected to adopt Western norms of behaviour, dress and customs. There would be no room for the Jewish sabbath or regular prayer breaks for Muslims. But such a stance would run counter to ideals of religious (and other) freedoms which are inherently bound up with respecting the individual (Chryssides and Kaler, 1993).

CODES OF CONDUCT AND STANDARDS

Although there has been an increasing amount of regulation covering a range of social and environmental issues, there is still more emphasis put on market-based and voluntary measures. Coupled with this, previous deregulation measures, introduced by more right-wing governments to appease industry, have continued to result in more emphasis being put on voluntary codes of conduct and standards.

The design and definition of voluntary codes and standards are therefore important to consider.

Codes of conduct defined within an organisation or imported from elsewhere in the form of standards are usually associated with practical sets of rules and guidelines. They tend to be expressions of mixtures of technical, prudential and moral imperatives. They influence behaviour and therefore ethical outcomes. However, standards which are externally driven are typically expressed in a form that is well protected from discussion, expressing aims in a matter-of-fact language (Donaldson, 1989). In turn, therefore, a standard carries with it a dominant ideology which, because it is standardised, has a multiplier effect and increasing weight if the standard becomes a norm.

The adoption of codes of conduct and standards within any organisation necessarily raises a number of questions. The most obvious one concerns the type of sub-culture which a code brings with it. Does it represent a piecemeal attempt to placate demands from pressure groups and consumers, or is it a more serious attempt at ethical behaviour, for example? We ought also to ask how effective the codes are in promoting what they stand for. Taken together these questions provide a measure of the extent to which the standards are genuine and operational, rather than cynical and self-deluding.

Codes of conduct which become accepted across firms in an industry or even across industries are very powerful, and we often see them written into contracts between organisations. We might be inclined to think that a code promoting some sort of social commitment or environmental improvement is a huge step forward and that organisations which follow others in adopting such standards should be congratulated. But rather more analysis of the content and purpose of such a code is necessary before we can reach an answer to that question. Without suggesting that codes may be bad, we must nevertheless consider whether, in fact, some codes push employees and customers into a set of values which verge on indoctrination. Stakeholders in those sorts of situations come to possess what Marxists see as false consciousness. In addition, the fact that a code of conduct is widely accepted does not guarantee that the values within it are not restricted or inconsistent.

There is very little research on the generation, operation, monitoring and amendment of codes of conduct. However, it is argued forcefully by Donaldson (1989) that because codes tend to be expressions of mixtures of technical, prudential and moral imperatives, and because they tend to vary in the extent to which they are or can be enforced, they cannot be regarded as the major vehicles for identifying and encouraging the practices which will raise the level of values in business and industry. Moreover, codes and standards are defined outside of the normal democratic framework which determines laws. They are constructed by agencies (often professional bodies or representatives of senior management in industry) with their own motivations, values and interests. On this subject Donaldson and Waller (1980) point to a statement of Bernard Shaw when he asserted that professions can be conspiracies against the laity, and their codes, it may be added, are widely held to be primarily aimed at the protection of the members of the profession, rather than the public. Much the same accusation might be levelled against industry standards. Moreover, the matter of the development of codes and standards is bound up with the matter of enforcement. Codes which are not enforced or fail to deliver their expected outcomes, for whatever reason, might be thought of as little more than cynical expressions of pious hopes.

552

Much of what has been discussed here can be illustrated by reference to the Responsible Care Programme, which in itself provides a standard for firms operating in the chemical industry to adopt. It is a voluntary code where performance is measured in terms of continuous improvement. Responsible Care is unique to the chemical industry and originated in Canada in 1984. Launched in 1989 in the UK by the Chemical Industries Association (CIA), the cornerstone of the system is commitment. Chief executives of member companies are invited to sign a set of guiding principles pledging their company to make health, safety and environmental performance an integral part of overall business policy. Adherence to the principles and objectives of Responsible Care is a condition of membership of the Chemical Industries Association (CIA). All employees and company contractors have to be made aware of these principles. The guiding principles also require companies to:

- **conform to statutory regulations;**

- **operate to the best practices of the industry;**

- **assess the actual and potential health, safety and environmental impacts of their activities and products;**

- **work closely with the authorities and the community in achieving the required levels of performance;**

- **be open about activities and give relevant information to interested parties.**

A company operating the Responsible Care Programme is required to have a clear corporate policy and the communication of this is seen as vital. The key principle being used in the Responsible Care Programme is self-assessment. However, the CIA does assess the effectiveness of the programme across all firms by collecting indicators of performance from them. Companies are encouraged to submit six classes of data to the Association. Individual company data are not published, but a national aggregate figure is published annually. This shows industry trends and enables individual companies to assess their own placing accordingly. The six indicators of performance are:

- **environmental protection spending;**

- **safety and health** (lost time, accidents for employees and contractors);

- **waste and emissions:**
  – discharges of 'red list' substances;
  – waste disposal;
  – an environmental index of five key discharges by site;

- **distribution** (all incidents);

- **energy consumption** (total on-site);

- **all complaints.**

A key element of the Responsible Care system is the sharing of information and participation of employees and the local community. Local Responsible Care 'cells' operate for the exchange of information and experience between firms. Employee involvement is also welcomed and the CIA has established training programmes which set targets for appraisal. Firms are encouraged to have community liaison groups and initiatives recognising the continuing need to forge improved relationships with the public.

However, in its 1993 report on the Responsible Care Programme (ENDS, 1993), the CIA was implicitly forced to admit that the programme was not functioning in accordance with its aims. The main reason for this is that sites claiming to adhere to the Responsible Care standard were simply not adhering to its principles. Over the three-year reporting period only 57 per cent of firms made returns for all three years, and only 74 per cent made any returns at all. Even more importantly, the third indicator of performance deals with waste and emissions, where firms are supposed to report an environmental index by site designed to give a composite picture of gaseous, liquid and solid releases. Only one-third of the total firms supposed to be operating Responsible Care reported this data in full, and of those who reported the index, over 30 per cent reported a worsening environmental impact. In 1997, although these statistics showed some improvement, it was still the case that many companies claiming to operate a Responsible Care programme were still not adhering to all its principles.

Codes of conduct are therefore nothing if they are not adhered to, and voluntary approaches often slip down a list of priorities when other pressing issues arise. While some chemical companies are clearly committed to improving their health, safety and environmental performance, it seems that not all are adhering to the spirit of Responsible Care. Indeed, while some make efforts to follow the guidelines of the programme, many more treat Responsible Care as a smokescreen. Many of those managers in the chemical industry who appear confident of their procedures to improve environmental performance are certainly either suffering from the false consciousness which was suggested earlier, or are making much more cynical attempts to hide their environmental impact in an attempt to hang on to market share and profitability.

THE CONTRIBUTION OF ETHICS TO MANAGEMENT STRATEGIES

Ethics refers to standards of right conduct. Unfortunately, there is often incomplete agreement as to what constitutes ethical behaviour. In the case of illegal and exploitative activities, there is not much dispute. But many practices fall into a grey area, where opinions may differ as to what is ethical and what is unethical and unacceptable. One possible example of environmental strategies which fall into that grey area relates to the eco-labelling of products and claims associated with the environmental friendliness of a product. There are examples of firms using tactics to persuade people to buy, often misleading customers into thinking they are getting a product which will not harm the environment, and exaggerating advertising claims. Unfortunately, some business firms have decided to 'walk on the edge' of ethical practices (Hartley, 1993). This is a dangerous strategy because the dividing line will be different for everybody. Moreover, what society once tolerated as acceptable behaviour is rapidly becoming unacceptable, and organisations which choose to position themselves so close to criticism will end up battling with time. To a large extent business ethics are firmly on the agenda in the late 1990s. Society expects, and is now demanding, much more ethical conduct, whereas it had previously regarded questionable practices with apathy or ignorance.

It is now no longer justifiable to see business ethics as directly connected with the law and 'necessary value systems' are inappropriate. The relationship between ethical conduct and the law is sometimes confusing. Naïve businesses might rationalise that actions within the law are therefore ethical and perfectly justifiable. But an 'if it's legal, it's ethical' attitude disregards the fact that the law codifies only that part of ethics which society feels so strongly about that it is willing to support it with physical force (Westing, 1968).

Many organisations assume that the more strictly one interprets ethical behaviour, the more profits suffer. Certainly, the muted sales efforts that may result from toning down product claims or refusing to buy raw materials which result in the exploitation of indigenous populations may hurt profits. Yet a strong argument can also be made that scrupulously honest and ethical behaviour is better for business and for profits. Well-satisfied customers tend to bring repeat business, and it is therefore desirable to develop trusting relationships with not only customers but also personnel, suppliers and the other stakeholders with which an organisation deals. Ethical conduct is not incompatible with profitability but it does change time scales. It is more compatible with maximising profits in the long run, even though in the shorter term disregard of these ethical principles may yield more profits.

It is perhaps useful at this point to turn to some particular areas where the issue of corporate responsibility is seen as being important. Let us consider the following four issues:

- **profits and growth;**

- **the dominance of competition;**

- **expediency and indifference;**

- **dominant ideology and business strategy.**

Profits and growth

In most organisations, career development and higher salaries depend on achieving greater sales and profits. This is true not only for individual employees and executives but for departments, divisions and the entire organisation. The value that stockholders and investors, creditors and suppliers place on a firm depends to a large extent on growth. In turn, the dominant measure of growth is increasing sales and profits. The better the growth rate, the more money is available for further expansion by investors and creditors at attractive rates. Suppliers and customers are more eager to do business. Top-quality personnel and executives are also more easily attracted.

In particular, the dominant drive would seem to be towards profits and profit maximisation. This is justified by economists such as Friedman (1963) who argues that 'few trends could so thoroughly undermine the very foundations of our free society as the acceptance by corporate officials of no social responsibility other than to make as much money for their stockholders as possible'. Friedman's view and that of many others simply neglects the responsibility that all actors in society have to benefit society in terms which are wider than the narrowly based performance measures which he adopts.

The emphasis on quantitative measures of performance and on growth, in particular, has some potential negative consequences. It tends to push social issues down the corporate agenda. An emphasis on growth becomes all pervading, and social and environmental objectives (which may or may not exist) are compromised. Moreover, with a dominant growth strategy, people are not measured on the basis of their moral contribution to the business enterprise. Hence, they become caught up in a system which is characterised by an ethic foreign to and often lower than the ethics of human beings (Holloway and Hancock, 1968). That tends to devalue the role of the worker and of those involved further down the supply chain. It is little wonder, therefore, when it comes to the consideration of the effect that the production and processing of raw materials might have on indigenous Third World populations, that very little weight is attached to the needs and aspirations of these peoples.

According to Bloom *et al.* (1994), in a wide-ranging survey of European directors, companies are perceived, by their leaders, as always needing to act within a social as well as an economic context because of the range of stakeholder pressures. All shareholders, suppliers, employees, clients, creditors, local communities, etc have legitimate interests in the future of the company, and this influences decision making and planning. As a result, many directors implicitly wish to take a longer-term perspective on their activities but are hindered from doing so because of the shorter-term demands of shareholders and stock markets.

Many senior managers come to realise, however, that profit maximisation measures are not the only measure of success in a company, and nor should they be the central aim or starting point of business strategy. Profit comes as the product of success, and success, in turn, depends on creating an organisation where all the interlocking elements work well together and function appropriately. For example, paying workers the lowest possible wage, making them work in poor conditions and treating them in a patronising way are more likely to lead to conflict rather than co-operation. Such conflict will lower productivity and profits. Moreover, a strategy producing maximum profit today may not be consistent with maximum profit tomorrow. That will depend on the investment strategy of a firm and that, in turn, requires managers to create a durable company which can survive competing pressures from all its stakeholders.

Because of the nature of capital markets, however, Bloom *et al.* (1994) report that many British directors are caught in a trap. In the UK about 80 per cent of company shares are quoted on the stock market, compared with under 50 per cent in Germany and less than 20 per cent in Italy. Because of pressure for dividends from shareholders and the threat of hostile takeover if profits (and therefore share prices) fall, managers do not have the breadth of movement to think about longer-term issues. Shareholders therefore have a very important role to play in allowing firms to operate on the social dimension. They are just one stakeholder, but their ownership of shares, and therefore the ownership of part of the company, often means that their position is firmly at the top of the pile of stakeholders. This, perhaps, requires us to think carefully about what ownership really means. Shareholders provide money to firms for reasons which they choose. But they can get out of their commitment to the company a lot more quickly and easily than an employee or a supplier can. Some see shareholding as rather more analogous with horseracing than anything else. When you back a horse in a race, you put money on that horse hoping for some sort of return if it does well. But you do not own a bit of the horse. If you did own the horse, it would require much more of a commitment than simply providing the money and sitting back. If the horse was flogged and abused in order to win a race, then the owner would be accountable for its ill-treatment. In the corporate sense, therefore, we must not only consider the rights of ownership but also the responsibilities and obligations of ownership, which are often forgotten.

That is not, however, to devalue economic performance. Often economic performance, motivation and commitment are the basis of a company's capacity to perform in a social dimension. For larger companies the need to operate on a social scale is increased because of the magnitude of their decisions. Whereas small firms will have little impact on social structures around them, a large firm deciding to lay off large parts of its workforce, for example, will have a much bigger influence. Moreover, companies operating on an international scale (particularly those which are essentially transnational) will have an enormous social impact. They will have a complicated network of stakeholders to deal with, including governments, international agencies, workers and customers with very different cultures and often powerful pressure groups.

The dominance of competition

An intensely competitive environment, especially if coupled with a firm's inability to differentiate products substantially or to cement segments of the market, will tend to motivate unethical behaviour (Hartley, 1993). The actions of one or a few firms in a fiercely competitive industry may generate a follow-the-leader situation, requiring the more ethical competitors to choose lower profits or lower ethics. Moreover, in a fiercely competitive environment the objective of the firm is dominated by the need to increase market share, to stay one step ahead of competitors, and therefore to adopt isolationist and independent strategies. To succeed in the marketplace businesses feel the need to cut costs, to downgrade other objectives which might be perceived as expensive, and to cut corners where possible.

That is not to suggest that competition is bad, but that its dominance does mitigate against the opportunities which can be brought about through co-operation. Moreover, wider social issues are often overlooked because they are perceived as adding to costs with any benefits being somewhat intangible. The blind belief that competition is always in some way superior to other models means that alternative arrangements such as co-operative strategies, public sector monopolies, not-for-profit organisations and local purchase and trading schemes are often devalued. Yet these alternatives often provide for outcomes which may be ethically, socially and environmentally superior.

Expediency and indifference

The attitude of expediency and indifference to customers' best interests accounts for both complacency and unethical practices. These attitudes, whether permeating an entire firm or affecting only a few individuals, are hardly conducive to repeat business and customer loyalty. They are more prevalent in firms with many small customers and in those firms where repeat business is relatively unimportant. To take an example, such attitudes also have an impact on environmental issues. They tend to mean that corners are cut and due care is not taken to protect the environment. They tend to increase the unnecessary use of resources and generate excessive waste, and to mitigate against the adoption of systems and procedures which can prevent accidents and environmental damage. Moreover, indifference and apathy tend to mitigate against accepting the responsibility which every individual and every organisation has in protecting the environment now and into the future.

Welford (1994) demonstrates that in the context of environmental issues, managers often have higher environmental ethics for themselves and their families than they do within the workplace. Whereas they are often complacent within the workforce, they see environmental improvement more generally as important to their own quality of life. This clear contradiction represents a 'free-rider problem'. Whereas they want to see environmental improvement they are unwilling to adjust their own behaviour in their workplace to achieve that, relying only on other people making the changes required to improve overall environmental performance. Such indifference to the real importance of everyone working together is explained by an unwillingness to spend the time and effort considering what improvements managers might make themselves. Other priorities (often associated with profitability) are allowed to provide the excuse for inaction.

Dominant ideology and business strategy

Significant evidence exists that management trends which become popular exert a strong influence on the ongoing techniques of corporate management. New concepts which are successfully implemented in certain organisations become accepted, become dominant and even when they are inappropriate become the norm (Mintzberg, 1979). DiMaggio and Powell (1983) offer three explanations for this phenomenon. First, organisations will submit to both formal and informal pressures from other organisations on which they depend. Secondly, when faced with uncertainty organisations may model themselves on organisations which have seemed to be successful and adopt the sorts of techniques which they see being introduced. Thirdly, normative pressures which stem from a degree of professionalism among management can cause the adoption of 'fashionable' management techniques. Universities, training institutions, standard setters and professional associations are all vehicles for the development of normative rules. These are precisely the trends we are seeing in contemporary approaches to corporate responsibility, which are often piecemeal and sporadic. This piecemeal approach is becoming the accepted ideology because it is being adopted by leading firms, espoused by academics and legitimised by standard setters and policy makers.

The attitudes, values and actions of senior management will tend to form the culture in any organisation. In particular, the chief executive will tend to be very important in influencing the behaviour of the next tier of executives, and down the line to the shopfloor employees. We know that senior managers will tend to have a contagious influence, and too often they will have a vested interest more associated in short-term performance than in acting ethically. Acting ethically and in a socially responsible manner therefore often requires culture change from the top down, but if the chief executive is not keen to drive such change then we must ask ourselves who will?

Related to the top executive's influence over a company is the often mechanistic management systems and structures which so often exist in the most inflexible organisations. These are in place because they are easy to control, but such structures will often stifle creativity. Moreover, any discussion relating to values will be second to structure, and this will too often define the firm's immediate interests in terms of short-term performance. Customer and employee safety, integrity and environmental protection will be secondary considerations.

While senior management itself may not be directly involved in unethical practices, it often promotes such behaviour by strongly insisting on short-term profit maximisation and performance goals. When these goals are difficult to achieve and not achieving them can be met with severe penalties, the climate is set for undesirable conduct: deceptive advertising, overselling, adulterated products, inappropriate waste management practices, negligence towards environmental standards and other unethical behaviour. A clear alternative to the mechanistic, management-dominated approach is to encourage the participation of the workforce and make them feel valued. This, in turn, encourages commitment to the organisation and better work practices, and avoids problems associated with apathy and indifference (Welford, 1992).

STRUCTURAL BARRIERS TO ETHICAL BUSINESS AND CORPORATE RESPONSIBILITY

The very nature of the contemporary capitalist structure which stresses competition, the maximisation of profits and the reduction of costs acts as a fundamental barrier to the adoption of ethical practices in business. In many markets, particularly where oligopolistic structures exist, we often see strategies which are based on tacit collusion where firms will follow dominant market leaders. It is often perceived that unless such a strategy is adopted, firms will be at a competitive disadvantage and their viability may even be threatened. Therefore what becomes accepted business practice, by dominant firms, tends to permeate a whole industry, so that the dominant ideologies associated with the most profitable companies perpetuate themselves and set the tone for business strategies. In these circumstances it is market share and financial performance which come to dominate other measures of the success of the company.

On the other hand, in times when demand falls or when any firm finds itself in a very competitive situation, financial indicators remain dominant and cost cutting often prevails. However, we know that in two major catastrophes, Bhopal and the Alaskan oil spill, cost cutting severely affected safety measures and contributed greatly to the gravity of the problem and the consequent handling of it (Hartley, 1993). Whatever the market structure, therefore, success is measured first and foremost on principles of financial management and wider ethical considerations are sidelined. The overemphasis on money, dictated by the economic system, therefore represents a barrier to the adoption of real corporate responsibility.

According to Donaldson (1989), however, the most serious barriers to improvement are not in the nature of people or business and industry, but are attitudinal. There is therefore a need to change attitudes via a change in the culture of an organisation. Central here is a commitment towards improved ethics. Many studies have demonstrated the ease with which the commitment of employees can be gained through methods associated with behavioural science (Luthans, 1985). While such techniques are sometimes criticised as being potentially manipulative, we must recognise that they hold great potential for increasing ethical behaviour.

We are, however, not seeking a bolt-on morality (so common with codes of conduct and standards), but a genuine attempt at introducing real ethical improvements.

This inevitably leads us on to considering whether current bureaucratic structures in society and industry are conducive to the introduction of systems which promote ethical behaviour. The stunted development of any consideration of alternative forms of bureaucracy provides us with a major challenge for the future. There is a need for more innovation and imagination on the part of management. Co-operative and participative forms of industrial organisation have, for example, often been seen as appropriate only to alternative small artisan operations, or have been a last-resort attempt at rescuing businesses which are due to close for commercial reasons. Ethical concerns challenge us to look more closely at developments associated with industrial democracy and alternative industrial arrangements. The bureaucratic habits of hierarchy and the narrow distribution of power may not, in the end, be conducive to a sustainable future.

Operational barriers to ethical business and corporate responsibility

Businesses are also prevented from acting in a more responsible way by ideologies relating to product responsibility, promotional activities and international trade which are based on custom and practice rather than any real evaluation of ethical considerations. There is an accepted code of conduct in each of these areas which, once again, stresses short-term performance, perceives change as being costly, and fundamentally devalues the rights of individual human beings. It is worth examining each of these issues in turn.

Product responsibility

The traditional view of a product is that once it is sold the responsibility for its safe use and disposal passes to the consumer. That cut-off point means that firms often do not consider the wider impacts caused by the use and disposal of their product. More forward-looking companies are now accepting that the product which they produce is fundamentally their responsibility from cradle to grave, and the most advanced companies have introduced product stewardship procedures to ensure that a product is used correctly and disposed of in an environmentally friendly way. However, this approach is yet to be found throughout industry, where the dominant ideology seems to stress the idea that property rights imply responsibility, so that as soon as such rights are transferred through the sale of the product, the company no longer has a duty of care against environmental damage.

Promotional activities

Promotional activities are designed to increase sales and are judged on the basis of so doing. Too many experiences of marketing strategies, to date, have been associated with exaggeration and deception. There is often a temptation in marketing departments to overemphasise a product's attributes. Unfortunately, moderation is not always practised. Mild exaggerations often multiply and become outright deception. With many products, false claims can be recognised by customers, who refuse to buy the product again. But where such claims cannot be easily substantiated false claims are harder to detect. Nevertheless pressure groups and competitors are always willing to expose unreasonable claims and that damages not only product sales but also the reputation of the firm. Advertising statements, if well presented and attractive, should induce customers to purchase the product. But if the expectations generated by advertisements are not realised, there will be no repeat business. Repeat business is the very thing most firms seek: a continuity of business, which means loyal and satisfied customers.

International trade

Many firms today do business worldwide and source their raw materials from a range of countries. Although this presents great opportunities, it also poses some problems, some ethical dilemmas and many opportunities for abuse. Unethical practices have a critical effect on the image of companies at home and abroad. Union Carbide's acceptance of lower operating standards in its Third World operations led to the Bhopal accident. The lesson to be learned is that standards and controls must be even more rigidly applied in countries where workers and managers may be less competent than they are in more economically and educationally advanced countries. A major ethical question also revolves around the sourcing of raw materials from parts of the world where indigenous populations are adversely affected. The drive for low-cost inputs leads to the exploitation of such people and the abuse of their land, and attacks their fundamental right to lead their lives as they would wish.

CORPORATE RESPONSIBILITY AND INDUSTRIAL DEMOCRACY

So, it is commonly claimed that there is an inevitable trade-off between profit and ethics or morals, and that the ultimate constraint to improved ethical behaviour is the need to show an acceptable rate of return on investment. The counter claim is that behaving responsibly is good business and that taking an honest and ethical approach to industrial activities will lead to satisfied customers and repeat business. The problem with both of these arguments is twofold. First, they implicitly assume that we can measure ethics and thereby characterise the 'ethical firm' or provide lists of good or bad practices. The notion of the ethical firm is not only difficult to describe but attempting to do so is also fruitless. Secondly, both arguments implicitly assume an underlying business structure where the primary outcome is profitability, even though alternative models might be more applicable.

There is a need to look towards alternative ideas and alternative structures. Many of these actually require quite marginal changes but can bring about much improved outcomes. For example, there are key procedures associated with reforms in the workplace which firms can adopt which will push them along the path of more ethical behaviour. This revolves around issues of industrial democracy and respecting the values of everybody associated with an organisation. More open procedures and less hierarchical bureaucracy in decision making could be developed within organisations. This, in turn, needs to be linked to an ethical awareness-raising campaign both within and external to the firm, helping to raise the overall ethical profile.

561

The debate surrounding bureaucracy is too wide to go through here, but one of the most important points, and of direct relevance to the contemporary business scenario, is expounded by Argyris (1964). Argyris argues that firms typically place individuals in positions of passivity and dependency that are at odds with the needs of mature individuals. Bennis (1972) and Burns and Stalker (1963) go further in suggesting that bureaucracies are too inflexible to be able to adapt to changes in increasingly volatile and discriminating markets. Traditional bureaucracies reserve decision making to the top of the organisation and decisions are subsequently handed down. Because of the narrow constituency involved in the decision-making process, they may not only be suboptimal decisions but may be severely at odds with the values of a workforce. Bureaucracies hold within themselves methods of controlling and channelling information. Those with power in the bureaucracy will go to great lengths to ensure conformity to internal codes, and they have a great range of sanctions available to them for persuasion and enforcement. We have already argued that such codes may be at odds with more ethical behaviour. Flatter hierarchies, participative decision making and increased self-determination by workers seem to be initial obvious steps to be taken to begin to resolve such problems.

If increased industrial democracy better enables firms to act in ethical ways, and if the many advocates of participative arrangements (e.g. Welford, 1989) are right in suggesting that participation improves productivity and performance, then we need to consider why we have seen no manifestation of this form of industrial organisation. Any movement towards some form of corporate democracy is taking place slowly and in a piecemeal fashion. But it might be accelerated if legislation which more freely permits different styles of participation and democratic processes were to be introduced, thus doing away with the restrictive structure of authority and responsibility required by law which often inhibits moves in this direction.

SUMMARY

■ Companies are faced with a challenge of integrating ethical considerations into their production and marketing plans. There is always an incentive, however, for profit-maximising firms seeking short-term rewards to opt out of their ethical obligations towards corporate responsibility. What is required, therefore, is a thorough re-examination of business ethics within any organisation and a change in ideology towards an acceptance by industry of its moral and social responsibilities.

■ Perhaps one of the most important lessons which firms are beginning to learn relates to the desirability of seeking an honest and trusting relationship with customers (as well as with their other stakeholders). Such an ethical relationship requires concern for customer satisfaction, widely defined, and fair dealings. Objectives should be written in ethical terms and stress loyalty and repeat business. Such a philosophy and attitude must permeate an organisation. It can easily be short-circuited if a general climate of opportunism and severe financial performance pressures prevail.

■ An honest and trusting relationship should not be sought with consumers or final users alone. It should characterise the relationship between sales representatives and their clients, which suggests no exaggeration or misrepresentation, greater efforts at understanding customers' needs, and better servicing. It may even mean forgoing a sales opportunity when a customer's best interest may be better served by another product or at another time. The trusting relationship suggests repudiating any adversarial stance with employees, with suppliers and, beyond this, with all the communities in which a firm does business. Firms need to throw away ideologies based on financial performance alone and consider their corporate relationship with society. Such a relationship requires sound ethical conduct. It should foster a good reputation and public image.

■ It has been argued that the competitive nature of markets is often a barrier to responsible corporate performance and creates isolationist strategies. Unethical and unilateral actions may result in an initial competitive advantage, but may hurt a firm's overall image and reputation in the longer term. To have a coherent social strategy, firms need a consistent set of business ethics and need to measure their performance using a range of longer-term indicators. The notion of stakeholder accountability also reminds us that it is really not possible to separate ethical considerations from other issues such as the treatment of women and minority groups, the treatment of animals and the protection of indigenous populations. A set of ethics alone will not necessarily lead to better business practices, however. What we also require is a fundamental re-examination of dominant ideologies in the business world and culture change which is capable of challenging accepted wisdoms.

■ The rise of organised pressure groups and interest groups makes it doubly important that managers consider the arguments of all stakeholders in a decision's outcome. Since these groups publicly promote their causes in a single-minded way and do not therefore have the competing objectives so often faced by management, they have an advantage over the traditional company in the strong message which they can convey. Decisions taken in isolation by an elite group are therefore far more likely to result in suboptimal outcomes.

■ The main thrust of the argument in this chapter, however, is that the major issues and arguments surrounding business ethics and social and corporate responsibility are not so much substantive but more associated with procedures and received 'wisdom' associated with structures and hierarchies. It has been argued that these barriers to improved ethics can be removed through the removal of such traditional structures. We need to think carefully about putting a new emphasis on stakeholder accountability and a move towards new democratic forms of organisation within the workplace. There is nothing in the nature of people or businesses which makes adjustment towards ethical behaviour impossible. Vested interests held by those in power do have to be addressed, however, and this is one of the major challenges which we must overcome.

REVIEW AND DISCUSSION QUESTIONS

1 What is the link between corporate responsibility and business ethics?

2 Is it enough for business ethics to be defined so as to meet the legitimate needs of stakeholders?

3 How do differences in cultures often found in different countries make the role of the manager more difficult?

4 Do you consider that codes of conduct and standards simplify ethical dilemmas or simply reinforce accepted ideology (which may actually be unethical)?

5 What do you consider are the biggest barriers to improving corporate responsibility?

6 Is it always unethical to offer bribes when doing business internationally?

CASE STUDY: SHELL TO FACE SHAREHOLDER VOTE ON ETHICS   FT

Shell Transport & Trading, the UK arm of the Anglo-Dutch oil group, is facing a potentially embarrassing battle with some institutional shareholders over a resolution they have put down for the annual meeting in May. A group of shareholders holding just under 1 per cent of the company is calling on it to improve accountability by establishing new procedures for dealing with environmental and human rights issues. Pirc, the corporate governance consultant advising the shareholders, says the Shell resolution is the first of its kind in the UK. In the US, public companies regularly face resolutions from shareholders about environmental and social concerns.

The Shell shareholder group includes 18 public and private pension funds, five religious institutions, an academic fund, and individuals from a pressure group called the Ecumenical Committee on Corporate Responsibility. They say Shell's reputation has been damaged by controversies such as the aborted plan to sink the Brent Spar oil storage rig at sea and its environmental and human rights record in Nigeria. Their statement supporting the resolution says: 'Shareholders have a responsibility as owners to ensure that companies have structures and policies in place to enable them to operate to the highest standards, and that companies should disclose to shareholders progress made in achieving improvements in performance. We believe that this resolution will help Shell accomplish these goals.'

In particular, the group wants a named member of Shell's committee of managing directors to take charge of environmental and corporate responsibility policies. It also wants Shell to agree to an external audit of these policies, and to publish a report to shareholders before the end of this year on its operations in Nigeria, which have been the focus of pressure group campaigning for several years.

Shell has denied allegations from pressure groups that it has contributed to pollution of the environment in the Niger Delta region and has assisted the Nigerian government's alleged persecution of the region's Ogoni tribe. Shell Transport & Trading, a UK quoted company, and Royal Dutch Petroleum, quoted in the Netherlands, own the Royal Dutch/Shell group on a 40:60 basis. The company confirmed that the resolution had been lodged and that shareholders would be voting on it at the annual general meeting. 'We are considering our response to it at the moment,' the company said, adding that the issues in the resolution were being covered by a company review of its Statement of General Business Principles, which deals with environmental issues. ■

Source: Financial Times, 24 February 1997. Reprinted with permission.

REFERENCES FOR FURTHER READING

Argyris, C (1964) *Integrating the Individual and the Organization*, New York: John Wiley.

Bennis, W (1972) 'A funny thing happened on the way to the future', in J Thomas and W Bennis (eds) *The Management of Change and Conflict*, Harmondsworth: Penguin Books.

Bloom, H, Calori, R and de Woot, P (1994) *Euromanagement: A new style for the global market*, London: Kogan Page.

Burke, T, Maddock, S and Rose, A (1993) *How Ethical is British Business?*, Research Working Paper, Series 2, Number 1, University of Westminster.

Burns, T and Stalker, G (1963) *The Management of Innovation*, London: Tavistock Press.

Chryssides, G D and Kaler, J H (1993) *An Introduction to Business Ethics*, London: Chapman & Hall.

DiMaggio, P J and Powell, W (1983) 'The Iron Cage Revisited: Institutional Isomorphism and Collective Rational in Organisational Fields', *American Sociological Review*, 48, 147–60.

Donaldson, J (1989) *Key Issues in Business Ethics*, San Diego: Academic Press.

Donaldson, J and Waller, M (1980) 'Ethics and Organisation', *Journal of Management Studies*, 17, 1.

ENDS (1993) 'Jury Still Out on Responsible Care', *Industry Report no 55*, ENDS 222, July.

Friedman, M (1963) *Capitalism and Freedom*, Chicago: Phoenix Books, University of Chicago Press.

Hartley, R F (1993) *Business Ethics: Violations of the Public Trust*, New York: John Wiley.

Holloway, R J and Hancock, R S (1968) *Marketing in a Changing Environment*, New York: John Wiley.

Kroeber, L and Kluckhohn, L (1952), *Culture*, New York: Vintage Books.

Luthans, F (1985) *Organizational Behaviour*, 4th edn, New York: McGraw-Hill.

Mintzberg, H (1979) *The Structuring of Organizations*, New York: Prentice-Hall.

Mole, J (1990) *Mind your Manners: Culture Clash in the Single European Market*, London: The Industrial Society.

Welford, R J (1989) 'Growth and the Performance Participation Nexus: the Case of UK Producer Cooperatives', *Economic Analysis and Workers' Management*, 23.

Welford, R J (1992) 'Linking Quality and the Environment: A Strategy for the Implementation of Environmental Management Systems', *Business Strategy and the Environment*, 1, 1.

Welford, R J (1994) 'Barriers to the improvement of environmental performance', in R J Welford (ed) *Cases in Environmental Management and Business Strategy*, London: Pitman Publishing.

Welford, R J and Prescott, C E (1994) *European Business: An Issue Based Approach*, London: Pitman Publishing.

Westing, J H (1968) 'Some Thoughts on the Nature of Ethics in Marketing', in R Mayer (ed) *Marketing Systems*, 1967 Winter Conference Proceedings, Chicago: Marketing Association.

ENVIRONMENTAL ISSUES AND ENVIRONMENTAL MANAGEMENT

Richard Welford

OBJECTIVES

The objectives of this chapter are to:

◆ explain why there has been a growth in public sector awareness of environmental issues

◆ analyse the pressures which environmental issues place on industry

◆ consider the effects of different industrial sectors on the environment

◆ discuss what constitutes an environmentally friendly product or operation

◆ outline management strategies to improve an organisation's environmental performance

INTRODUCTION

Over the last 20 years there has been a growing interest in the environment, or more specifically in the damage being done to the environment worldwide. In Europe the process of integration has brought the transnational nature of the environmental problem to the forefront. The hole in the ozone layer and global warming are the result of not one country's action but that of many. Acid rain, which is polluting rivers and lakes and damaging forests, often emanates from one country and is deposited in another.

The effects of different industrial sectors on the environment vary enormously. At one end of the spectrum we might put the oil companies whose very business is environmentally damaging, and at the other end we might put retailers and the service sector who have less of a direct impact on the environment, although, in most cases, they could still make environmental improvements through recycling and improved transportation policies. There is still much confusion both for consumers and companies about what constitutes an environmentally friendly product or operation, and the 'green revolution' to date has provided few answers, although many misrepresentations, particularly in the area of product marketing, have been exposed.

At the root of some of the environmental problems we face is the growth in consumerism and materialism. The notion that 'the consumer is king' may drive the market mechanism, but the overemphasis placed on the satisfaction on customers' wants in the developed economies of the world has had a profound effect on our planet's ability to sustain life and on biodiversity. It is generally accepted that the world cannot go on using the resources of the planet at the present rate. But there is a 'free-rider problem' at work. Everyone thinks that there should be something done, but many people just assume that everyone else will do it, and since their individual impact is minute it will not matter to the environment.

Everything which consumers, companies and other institutions do will have some impact on the environment, but the emphasis in this chapter is placed on the strategies which organisations can follow to improve their environmental performance. Even substances which in their final form are environmentally benign may have been unfriendly in their manufacture, especially if that manufacture was energy greedy. They may have been produced using non-renewable resources and may also pose problems after they have been used and come to be disposed of. If we take what is commonly called a cradle-to-the-grave view of products, where we examine their environmental impact through their life cycle from raw material usage to disposal, then there are few, if any, products which will not have some negative impact on the environment. The key question is, therefore, not how we completely eliminate environmental damage, but how we reduce it over time, and how we achieve a state of balance such that the amount of environmental damage done is repairable and therefore sustainable.

Industry, particularly in the developed world, must increasingly take into account the costs of the effect of its operations on the environment, rather than regarding the planet as a free resource. In the past, few companies have counted the costs of the pollution which they discharged into the atmosphere, and the debate has now turned to legislation aimed at forcing companies to comply with certain standards and taxing firms which pollute. The so-called 'polluter pays' principle is now central to legislation in the developed countries. The implication here is clearly that prices will rise for consumers as organisations experience increased costs associated with environmental improvements. Less energy consumption and more efficient use of resources are obvious targets for improvement and should not conflict with industry's aims, since their attainment can actually reduce costs. Many materials are already recycled and a thriving, and at times profitable, recycling industry has been established across Europe.

Many of the products now considered to be environmentally hazardous were at the time of their discovery regarded as an invaluable resource. The best example of this has been the use of chlorofluorocarbons in refrigerators, which have since been found to be a major ozone-depleting agent. Predicting a product's long-term impact on the environment is a difficult process and, until recently, has rarely been done. This will change as firms are forced to consider cradle-to-grave management of their products, and as we increasingly give the benefit of doubt to the welfare of the planet. Moreover, industry has a responsibility to ensure that its products are less harmful to the environment and there is a need to push along a very steep environmental learning curve.

Many governments across Europe have been implementing increasingly stringent environmental legislation. At the level of the European Union the Fifth Environmental Action Programme sees much to be achieved via the provision of information about products and processes available to the public. However, a common problem is that the statutory bodies which do exist with responsibility for monitoring the environmental performance of organisations have limited resources and powers in most cases. Organisations themselves have often, in the past, been shown to be ignorant of current environmental legislation, particularly with regard to European Union environmental directives and legislation on issues such as waste disposal, air pollution and water quality. However, such ignorance is not an excuse for non-compliance. Moreover, non-compliance which can be attributed to negligence cannot only result in fines but also occasionally in imprisonment for company directors.

In the USA the Environmental Protection Agency (EPA) is an independent environmental body with significant power. In 1980 the US Congress passed the Comprehensive Environmental Response, Compensation and Liability Act, better known as Superfund. Under the provisions of the Act, companies must report potentially toxic spills and releases greater than a clearly defined minimum. Violations of this are criminal offences with penalties of up to one year in jail and fines of up to $10 000. Superfund also deals with uncontrolled hazardous waste sites, where previous or present owners and operators of a site must help pay for whatever remedial action is necessary. If the previous firm has gone out of business the EPA has often managed to obtain funds from companies which sent the waste there for treatment or disposal in the first instance. In the UK, by contrast, local authority regulators and Pollution Inspectors all adopt an approach of constructive engagement with companies rather than fining them in the first instance for pollution violations.

The rapid growth of public environmental awareness in recent years has placed new pressures on industry. These pressures can take many forms as individuals collectively exercise their environmental conscience as customers, employees, investors, voters, neighbours and fellow citizens. However, whether it is due to intellectual fatigue with environmental issues, a lack of conviction that an individual's own actions will have an impact or a reluctance to reduce private consumption for public welfare, many individuals seemingly prefer to pass their responsibilities on to those parties that they feel can make a significant impact. The two major parties that the public perceive can make a difference are government and industry. Given an inherent public reluctance to reduce their own levels of consumption, it is apparent that government and industry must respond in order to protect the environment effectively.

USING THE PRICE MECHANISM TO ALLEVIATE POLLUTION

The use of the market mechanism to distribute goods and services in the West, with its consequent stress on property rights, has contributed to the environmental degradation which we have experienced. Much of the environment (particularly the air and atmosphere) is treated as a free good since no individual owns it and there are no assigned property rights to it. Firms and consumers have therefore made excessive uses of environmental resources both as an input and as a source of output (or sink). This is illustrated in Fig 18.1.

Suppose that a firm produces a good and in the process of doing so it pollutes the air around it. Traditionally, and ignoring legislation which might or might not exist, the firm can do this freely since no one owns the air. Assume that the demand for the product is D_1 and the production and marketing costs of the firm imply that it is willing to sell along a supply curve given by S_1. Essentially, S_1 is drawn based on only the private costs of the firm, that is, those which it must pay in a monetary form. But the pollution imposed on the local community imposes a cost on them and on society as a whole. If the firm was required to internalise those costs, either by paying a tax to pollute based on an estimate of the social cost that that pollution imposed (the tax might subsequently be used to clean up the

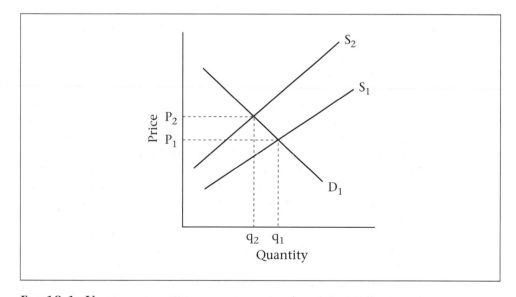

FIG 18.1 USING THE MARKET MECHANISM TO DEAL WITH ENVIRONMENTAL DAMAGE

pollution), or by the use of legislation banning the pollution meaning that the firm would have to invest in a new non-polluting process, then its own costs would rise. The firm's willingness to supply at any particular price would be reduced and S_1 would shift backwards to S_2. The equilibrium in the market would shift from P_1q_1 to P_2q_2. Thus less of the good would be produced and at a higher price.

The premise on which most developed countries' environmental legislation has largely been based is the 'polluter pays' principle. In other words, this is a notion that public money should not be used in clearing up or avoiding pollution but, as described above, that polluters themselves should face those costs. From a welfare point of view the difference between a firm compensating a local community for the pollution it creates and the community paying the firm not to pollute is purely distributional. But from an ethical perspective it is often argued that the 'polluter pays' principle is superior.

We might extend the sort of analysis described by Fig 18.1 to the economy as a whole. Since most processes will impose at least some negative impact on the environment, the fact that the environment has not been properly costed and treated as a free good over time has meant that we have produced too many goods. Moreover, we might hypothesise that mass-production techniques which have enabled firms to produce more and more goods and to charge lower prices have been particularly damaging.

Sustainable development

The belief which lies behind the concept of sustainable development is that there is a trade-off between continuous economic growth and the sustainability of the environment. Over time growth causes pollution and atmospheric damage. The concept of sustainable development stresses the interdependence between economic growth and environmental quality. It is possible to make development and environmental protection compatible by following sustainable strategies and by not developing the particular areas of economic activity that are most damaging to the environment.

The Brundtland Report, commissioned by the United Nations to examine long-term environmental strategies, argued that economic development and environmental protection could be made compatible, but that this would require quite radical changes in economic practices throughout the world. They defined sustainable development as 'development that meets the needs of the present without compromising the ability of future generations to meet their own needs'. In other words, mass consumption is not possible indefinitely, and if society today acts as if all non-renewable resources are plentiful, eventually there will be nothing left for the future. But more importantly than that, mass consumption may cause such irreparable damage that humans may not even be able to live on the planet in the future.

The challenge that faces the economic system is how to continue to fulfil its vital role within modern society while working towards sustainability. Complying with the principles of sustainability cannot be achieved overnight. However, both for entire economies and for individual businesses, there is hope that it can be achieved within the time scales which appear to be necessary if environmental catastrophe is to be avoided.

According to Welford (1993), sustainable development is made up of three closely connected issues and associated conditions:

- **Environment.** The environment must be valued as an integral part of the economic process and not treated as a free good. The environmental stock has to be protected, which implies minimal use of non-renewable resources and minimal emission of pollutants. The ecosystem has to be protected so the loss of plant and animal species has to be avoided.

- **Equity.** One of the biggest threats facing the world is that the developing countries want to grow rapidly to achieve the same standards of living as those in the West. That in itself would cause a major environmental disaster if it were modelled on the same sort of growth as experienced in post-war Europe. There therefore needs to be a greater degree of equity and the key issue of poverty has to be addressed. But it seems hypocritical for the West to tell the Third World that it cannot attain the same standards of living and consumption.

- **Futurity.** Sustainable development requires that society, businesses and individuals operate on a different time scale than currently operates in the economy. While companies commonly operate under competitive pressures to achieve short-run gains, long-term environmental protection is often compromised. To ensure that longer-term, inter-generational considerations are observed, longer planning horizons need to be adopted and business policy needs to be proactive rather than reactive.

The Brundtland Report concludes that these three conditions are not being met. The industrialised world has already used much of the planet's ecological capital and many of the development paths of the industrialised nations are clearly unsustainable. Non-renewable resources are being depleted, while renewable resources such as soil, water and the atmosphere are being degraded. This has been caused by economic development, but in time will undermine the very foundations of that development.

The Brundtland Report calls for development which is environmentally and socially sustainable rather than the current situation of unplanned, undifferentiated growth. This means reconsidering the current measures of growth, such as gross national product (GNP), which fail to take account of environmental debits such as pollution or the depletion of the natural capital stock. While concern about the depletion of materials and energy resources has diminished since the 1970s, there is nevertheless concern surrounding the environment's capacity to act as a sink for waste. For example, bringing developing countries' energy use up to the level of the developing world's would mean an increase in consumption by a factor of five. Using present energy generation methods the planet could not cope with the impact of sulphur dioxide and carbon dioxide emissions and the consequential acidification and global warming of the environment.

One major obstacle preventing sustainability from being achieved is the overall level of consumption. However, Western consumers are apparently reluctant to reduce significantly their own levels of consumption. While governments are increasingly adopting economic instruments such as taxes, subsidies and product labelling schemes to reduce and channel consumption toward more environmentally friendly alternatives, industry itself must be encouraged further to increase environmental efficiency.

Sustainability challenges industry to produce higher levels of output while using lower levels of inputs and generating less waste. The problem that remains is that while relative environmental impact per unit of output has fallen, increases in the absolute level of output, and hence environmental impact, have more than offset any gains in relative environmental efficiency. However, if we examine the ways in which environmental efficiency has been improved, then we can begin to understand some of the key practical elements with which sustainability may be better promoted.

CORPORATE RESPONSES TO SUSTAINABLE DEVELOPMENT

Organisations are faced with a challenge of integrating environmental considerations into their production and marketing plans. There is always an incentive, however, for profit-maximising firms seeking short-term rewards to opt out and become a free-rider (assuming that everyone else will be environmentally conscious such that their own pollution will become negligible). However, European Union environmental legislation is increasingly plugging the gaps which allow this to happen, and firms attempting to hide their illegal pollution are now subject to severe penalties. In many cases individual company directors can also be prosecuted for negligence which leads to environmental damage. Even before then, businesses should recognise that it is not only ethical to be environmentally friendly, but with the growth of consumer awareness in the environmental area, it will also be good business.

Organisations clearly have a role to play in the development of substitutes for non-renewable resources and innovations which reduce waste and use energy more efficiently. They also have a role in processing those materials in a way which brings about environmental improvements. For many products (e.g. cars and washing machines), the major area of environmental damage occurs in their usage. Organisations often have the opportunity of reducing this damage at the design stage, and when new products are being developed there is a whole new opportunity for considering both the use and disposal of the product.

Given the internal and external demands to improve the environmental performance of an organisation, those organisations that achieve high standards of environmental performance will benefit in a number of ways. In order to realise this competitive advantage, organisations must seek to develop management strategies which will improve their environmental performance and address the environmental demands placed on them by government, the EU and stakeholders. By incorporating the increasingly important environmental dimension into the decision-making processes of the organisation, managers can seek to reduce costs and exploit the opportunities offered by increased public environmental concern within a dynamic marketplace. Such a strategy must be proactive and honest. It may also involve a degree of education and campaigning such as that undertaken by The Body Shop. But more than anything, it must be ethical.

The general principles of such a strategy are embodied within the International Chamber of Commerce Business Charter for Sustainable Development. The key elements to this strategy are embodied in 16 'Principles for Enviromental Management'. Organisations are encouraged to endorse the following aims:

1 **Corporate priority** – To recognise environmental management as among the highest corporate priorities and as a key determinant to sustainable development; to establish policies, programmes and practices for conducting operations in an environmentally sound manner.

2 **Integrated management** – To integrate these policies, programmes and practices fully into each business as an essential element of management in all its functions.

3 **Process of improvement** – To continue to improve corporate policies, programmes and environmental performance, taking into account technical developments, scientific understanding, consumer needs and community expectations, with legal regulations as a starting point; and to apply the same environmental criteria internationally.

4 **Employee education** – To educate, train and motivate employees to conduct their activities in an environmentally responsible manner.

5 **Prior assessment** – To assess environmental impacts before starting a new activity or project and before decommissioning a facility or leaving a site.

6 **Products and services** – To develop and provide products and services that have no undue environmental impact and are safe in their intended use, that are efficient in their consumption of energy and natural resources, and that can be recycled, re-used or disposed of safely.

7 **Customer advice** – To advise, and where relevant educate, customers, distributors and the public in the safe use, transportation, storage and disposal of products provided; and to apply similar considerations to the provision of services.

8 **Facilities and operations** – To develop, design and operate facilities and conduct activities taking into consideration the efficient use of energy and raw materials, the sustainable use of renewable resources, the minimisation of adverse environmental impact and waste generation, and the safe and responsible disposal of residual wastes.

9 **Research** – To conduct or support research on the environmental impacts of raw materials, products, processes, emissions and wastes associated with the enterprise and on the means of minimising such adverse impacts.

10 **Precautionary approach** – To modify the manufacture, marketing or use of products or services to the conduct of activities, consistent with scientific and technical understanding, to prevent serious or irreversible environmental degradation.

11 **Contractors and suppliers** – To promote the adoption of these principles by contractors acting on behalf of the enterprise, encouraging and, where appropriate, requiring improvements in their practices to make them consistent with those of the enterprise; and to encourage the wider adoption of these principles by suppliers.

12 **Emergency preparedness** – To develop and maintain, where appropriate hazards exist, emergency preparedness plans in conjunction with the emergency services, relevant authorities and the local community, recognising potential cross-boundary impacts.

13 **Transfer of technology** – To contribute to the transfer of environmentally sound technology and management methods throughout the industrial and public sectors.

14 **Contributing to the common effort** – To contribute to the development of public policy and to business, governmental and inter-governmental programmes and educational initiatives that will enhance environmental awareness and protection.

15 **Openness to concerns** – To foster openness and dialogue with employees and the public, anticipating and responding to their concerns about the potential hazards and impacts of operations, products, wastes or services, including those of transboundary or global significance.

16 **Compliance and reporting** – To measure environmental performance; to conduct regular environmental audits and assessments of compliance with company requirements and these principles; and periodically to provide appropriate information to the board of directors, shareholders, employees, the authorities and the public.

THE EUROPEAN INTEGRATION PROCESS AND ENVIRONMENTAL MANAGEMENT

The original Treaty of Rome was concerned with stimulating economic growth and contained no specific reference to the environment. Since then, however, EU environmental policy has developed in line with general concern in Europe and the deteriorating environmental position in which Europe finds itself. By 1990, 160 pieces of environmental legislation had been passed covering pollution of the air and water, noise pollution, chemicals, waste, environmental impact assessment, the prevention of industrial accidents and wildlife protection.

However, few member states have been able to enforce EU legislation fully. Denmark is probably the only country with a consistently good record and the southern European countries have consistently bad records. Once again, this highlights the emphasis often given to economic growth rather than environmental protection, with the primary aim of countries such as Spain and Portugal being the attainment of similar living standards to the rest of the Union.

The Single European Act gave environmental policy a boost stating that there is not only a need for such legislation but that the laws should meet three key objectives:

- **preservation, protection and improvement of the quality of the environment;**
- **protection of human health;**
- **prudent and rational use of natural resources.**

These objectives must be met by applying four principles:

- **prevention of harm to the environment;**
- **control of pollution at source;**

- **the polluter should pay;**

- **integration of environmental considerations into other European Union policies** (all EU policies are now required to take the environment into account).

The Internal Market Programme has added a new note of urgency to environmental problems. The relationship between economic growth and the environment has returned to centre stage. Clearly, there exists a major opportunity with industrial and legislative restructuring to put into place the appropriate financial and regulatory mechanisms that would make the internal market environmentally sustainable. The extent to which this happens will be seen over time, but the Single European Act also provides the necessary constitutional basis for a forceful environmental response. Perhaps the strongest part of this is the requirement that policy makers should make environmental considerations a component of all the European Union's other policies.

In 1992 the European Union's Fifth Environmental Action Programme was introduced. The First Environmental Action Programme in 1973 set out a number of principles which have formed the basis of environmental action in the EU ever since. The aims are set out in Fig 18.2.

The main activities of the EU in the environmental policy arena, until 1987, were centred on the application of nearly 200 command and control directives in areas as diverse as lead in petrol and aircraft noise. More recently, realising that environmental policy is of little use unless enforced, EU environmental policy has given increased emphasis to the improved enforcement of existing legislation. Emphasis has also shifted from the use of traditional command and control instruments in environmental policy to the application of economic market-based instruments such as the proposed carbon tax, and voluntary initiatives such as the eco-labelling and eco-management and audit schemes (*see* below). The aim of such measures is to encourage change in all sectors of industry and society, in a more general way than can be achieved through the use of tightly defined legislative instruments. Economic instruments and voluntary measures are seen as complementing rather than substituting for the more traditional application of command and control measures.

The EU view of the future of environmental policy and its interface with industrial development is clear. With over 400 million inhabitants, the European Union is the largest trading bloc in the world, and is therefore in a critical position to take the lead in moving towards sustainability. The Commission accepts that tighter environmental policy will have an impact on the costs of industry; however, a high level of environmental protection has increasingly become not only a policy objective of its own but also a precondition of industrial expansion. In this respect, a new impetus towards a better integration of policies aiming at consolidating industrial competitiveness and at achieving a high level of protection of the environment is necessary in order to make the two objectives fully mutually supportive.

These views are given more substance within the Fifth Environmental Action Programme. While this programme sets out the likely developments of EU environmental policy in a general sense, a number of specific measures relating to industry are included. Perhaps most importantly, the commitment of the EU to strengthen environmental policy is underlined. The EU shares the view that urgent action is needed for environmental protection, and that many of the great environmental

1 Prevention is better than cure.

2 Environmental effects should be taken into account at the earliest possible stage in decision making.

3 Exploitation of nature and natural resources which causes significant damage to the ecological balance must be avoided. The natural environment can only absorb pollution to a limited extent. Nature is an asset which may be used but not abused.

4 Scientific knowledge should be improved to enable action to be taken.

5 The 'polluter pays' principle: the polluter should pay for preventing and eliminating environmental nuisance.

6 Activities in one member state should not cause environmental deterioration in another.

7 Environmental policies of member states must take account of the interests of developing countries.

8 The EU and member states should act together in international organisations and also in promoting international environmental policy.

9 Education of citizens is necessary as the protection of the environment is a matter for everyone.

10 The principle of action at the appropriate level: for each type of pollution it is necessary to establish the level of action which is best suited for achieving the protection required, be it local, regional, national, EU-wide or international.

11 National environmental policies must be coordinated within the EU without impinging on progress at the national level. It is intended that implementation of the action programme and gathering of environmental information by the proposed European Environment Agency will secure this.

FIG 18.2 EU's ENVIRONMENTAL PRINCIPLES

Source: Official Journal of the European Communities: C112 20.12.73.

struggles will be won or lost in the next ten years. Further, it states that achieving sustainability will demand practical and political commitment over an extended period and that the EU as the largest trading bloc in the world must exercise its responsibility and commit itself to that goal.

For industries and companies that are facing a rising tide of environmental legislation, it is essential that attempts are made to find out about and then positively address the legislative pressures which they are under. However, the Fifth Environmental Action Programme focuses on the improved enforcement of existing legislation rather than the adoption of new legislation. To some extent this should allow industry to take stock of the rapid increase in environmental legislation that has taken place in recent years and to focus on achieving compliance with existing legislation. Despite the stated objective to concentrate on the effective implementation of existing policy, there are many pieces of environmental legislation in the EU policy pipeline which are awaiting final adoption. Many of these measures have fundamental implications for business, and it therefore remains essential to track forthcoming legislation.

Furthermore, the Maastricht Treaty and the Fifth Environmental Action Programme require that environmental policy should be fully incorporated into all other European Union policies. Therefore, while it may become easier to track the development of policies which are explicitly environmental, it will become more difficult to monitor the development of environmental policy throughout the activities of the Commission as a whole. The European Environment Agency now collects data and monitors compliance throughout the European Union, and disseminates information to all interested parties. It is being proactive in encouraging all firms (including smaller enterprises) to take environmantal issues more seriously.

The strategic significance of the EU's views cannot be overstated. By taking a long-term EU-wide perspective and accepting that industrial competitiveness is enhanced by tight environmental legislation, the policy framework within which all European organisations must participate will reflect these views. Some organisations, some regions and some nations will benefit. If the views of the EU are correct, the economic prospects of the European Union as a whole will benefit and the environment will certainly benefit. However, at the organisation level realising these benefits will not be automatic, and strategic planning and proactive responses to the changing policy climate are imperative if success is to be secured. Information must be gathered, its implications assessed and the necessary action taken in a systematic and integrated way.

Tackling environmental problems always requires a concerted and co-operative effort, and in the EU success will depend on the extent to which member states are politically committed to the environmental philosophy and the extent to which they are willing to co-operate. The balancing of the economic growth/environment trade-off is likely to determine the Europe-wide success of any policies. But there also need to be concerted and co-operative political motivations. There will be those who will therefore argue that the attainment of an effective and concerted environmental policy in Europe will require political and economic union. However, since the EU and national governments legislate over environmental protection and police offenders, significant environmental improvement will only be attained with the co-operation and commitment of producers. There is therefore a need for firms to institute environmental management practices and it is to this issue that the rest of the chapter is devoted.

ENVIRONMENTAL MANAGEMENT STRATEGIES

Most organisations have realised that environmental issues need to be addressed for a number of reasons, including consumer pressure, potential cost savings, legislation and ethics. Larger companies are, in turn, putting pressure on supply chains, insisting that their smaller suppliers also respond to environmental issues. There is therefore growing interest in the area of environmental management. Environmental considerations are likely to be a source of quite profound changes in business practices. With this in mind there are a number of questions which organisations should ask themselves:

- Is the organisation meeting its existing environmental commitments?

- Is the organisation adhering to environmental legislation, and what will be the impact on it as environmental legislation becomes more stringent?

- Is concern for the environment integral to each of the organisation's operations?

- Do managers and workers see environmental improvement as a goal and in what ways are personnel being encouraged to be more involved?

- Does the organisation have the capacity to evaluate the environmental impact of its processes and products, including packaging and distribution channels?

- Are there new product opportunities which the organisation could exploit which would have less negative environmental impact?

- How vulnerable is the organisation to environmental changes such as climate change?

- What financial and organisational constraints are there which might prevent environmental improvement taking place?

- How are the organisation's competitors placed in terms of environmental accountability, and can the environmental performance of the organisation be turned to a competitive advantage?

- Does the organisation have a systematic approach to management which can be used to integrate environmental issues?

The answers to these questions provide the organisation with the basis of a strategic plan for the environment. An environmental policy can be developed from these questions and it can be circulated to the organisation's personnel, suppliers and vendors, and the public. The environmental policy sets out the context for future action. There is no single model and the policy will reflect an organisation's structure, location, industrial sector and business culture. If such a document is published then it is important that it is adhered to, thereby providing an all-important environmental ethos around which the organisation must operate.

All aspects of an organisation's operations, from accounting and purchasing, to product design, manufacture, sales, marketing, distribution and the use and disposal of the product, will have an impact on the environment and the environmental policy should reflect a recognition of this. The policy needs to be comprehensive and detailed, but it should not contain statements or targets which the organisation cannot hope to achieve. This will do more harm than good if exposed. The content of any policy will vary and be influenced by the activities of the particular organisation. However, there are some general principles which can be applied to the content of the policy statement:

- Adopt and aim to apply the principles of 'sustainable development', which meet the needs of the present without compromising the abilities of future generations to meet their own needs.

- Strive to adopt the highest available environmental standards in all site locations and all countries, and meet or exceed all applicable regulations.

- Adopt a total 'cradle-to-grave' environmental assessment and accept responsibility for all products and services, the raw materials used and the disposal of the product after use.

- Aim to minimise the use of all materials, supplies and energy, and wherever possible use renewable or recyclable materials and components.

- Minimise waste produced in all parts of the business, aim for waste-free processes, and where waste is produced avoid the use of terminal waste treatment, dealing with it, as far as possible, at source.

- Render any unavoidable wastes harmless and dispose of them in a way which has the least impact on the environment.

- Expect high environmental standards from all parties involved in the business, including suppliers, contractors and vendors, and put pressure on these groups to improve their environmental performance in line with your own.

- Be committed to improving relations with the local community and the public at large and where necessary introduce education and liaison programmes.

- Adopt an environmentally sound transport strategy and assess the general infrastructure of the organisation.

- Assess, on a continuous basis, the environmental impact of all operations and procedures via an environmental audit.

- Assist in developing solutions to environmental problems and support the development of external environmental initiatives.

- Preserve nature, protect ecological habitats and create conservation schemes.

- Accept strict liability for environmental damage, not blaming others for environmental damage, accidents and incidents.

Environmental policies should identify key performance areas and form a sound basis for setting corporate objectives. They need to be detailed enough to demonstrate that the organisation's commitment goes beyond lip-service. A clearly defined environmental policy should be implementable, practical and relate to the areas in which the organisation wishes to improve its environmental performance.

In particular, when designing an environmental policy the organisation needs to think hard about how it is going to quantify its objectives and measure its environmental performance.

For a policy to be implemented, personnel with special responsibilities for environmental performance will have to be found. Many organisations in Europe have found that the best way to achieve this, in the short run, is to appoint a main board environment director. This person will be there to champion the environment and will need some very important personal skills as well as legitimacy. Such legitimacy is often achieved by the publication of the organisation's environmental policy.

There are three very clear roles which an environmental director can take on:

1 **Taking a strategic view:** promoting minimal environmental impact from products and processes and developing an integrated and comprehensive approach.

2 **Raising the profile of the environment:** co-ordinating educational effort within the organisation, developing partnerships with customers, other organisations (particularly suppliers), environmental pressure groups, legislators, the EU and national government.

3 **Putting policy into practice:** the establishment of monitoring systems and environmental audits, the establishment of environmental improvement plans, involving all personnel and making them accountable and responsible for the environmental performance of their business, and taking anticipatory action which is central to good environmental performance.

The initial stage in the implementation of an environmental approach at organisation level must be for the organisation to establish exactly how well or how badly it is performing environmentally. An increasingly common way of achieving this is to conduct an environmental audit.

ENVIRONMENTAL AUDITING

The first environmental audits can be traced back to the USA, where corporations adopted this methodology during the 1970s in response to their domestic liability laws. Such audits are now common among European businesses. Many banks and other financial institutions are insisting on companies undertaking environmental audits in order to reduce future environmental liabilities (Welford, 1996). Environmental audits are usually carried out by teams which include lawyers, economists, engineers, scientists and environmental generalists drawn from industry, government and consultancy.

Environmental auditing is a check both on the environmental performance of an organisation and on the performance of the management system (*see* below) which should be designed to bring about improvements in that performance. In the first instance the organisation needs to establish a baseline against which to measure future audits, commonly referred to as the environmental review. The environmental review follows many of the procedures of an audit as laid out below. However, strictly speaking an audit measures the attainment or non-attainment of some target objectives, whereas the environmental review simply provides an initial assessment of the environmental performance of the organisation.

The environmental audit consists of a regular, independent, systematic, documented and objective evaluation of the environmental performance of an organisation. It should measure how well organisations, management and equipment are performing with the aim of helping management to safeguard the environment. It also provides management information which can be used in the control of environmental practices and in assessing compliance with organisation policies which include meeting regulatory requirements. It should be stressed, however, that within the task of environmental management there is a role for everyone in the organisation.

The overall aim of environmental auditing is to help safeguard the environment and minimise the risks to human health. Although auditing alone cannot achieve that, it is a powerful managerial tool. The key objectives of the environmental audit are:

- to determine the extent to which environmental management systems in an organisation are performing adequately;

- to verify compliance with local, national and European environmental and health and safety legislation;

- to verify compliance with an organisation's own stated corporate policy;

- to develop and promulgate internal procedures needed to achieve the organisation's environmental objectives;

- to minimise human exposure to risks from the environment and ensure adequate health and safety provision;

- to identify and assess risk resulting from environmental failure;

- to assess the impact on the local environment of a particular plant or process by means of air, water and soil sampling;

- to advise an organisation on environmental improvements it can make.

There are a number of benefits to organisations in undertaking an environmental audit. These include assurances that legislation is being adhered to and the consequent prevention of fines and litigation, an improved public image which can be built into a public relations campaign, a reduction in costs (particularly in the area of energy usage and waste minimisation), an improvement in environmental awareness at all levels of the organisation, and an improvement in overall quality. On the other hand, there are some potential disbenefits of the audit. These include the initial costs of the audit and the cost of compliance with it, and the temporary disruption of plant operations. It is also vital that management sees that the recommendations of the environmental auditor are adhered to, otherwise an audit report could be incriminating in a court case or insurance claim.

All environmental audits involve gathering information, analysing that information, making objective judgements based on evidence and a knowledge of the industry and of relevant environmental legislation and standards. There is also the need to report the results of the audit to senior management with recommendations and possible strategies for the implementation of the findings. This all requires considerable preparatory work as well as follow-up time in order that the findings are accurate and comprehensive. Ideally, therefore, there need to be three clear stages to an audit (*see* Fig 18.3).

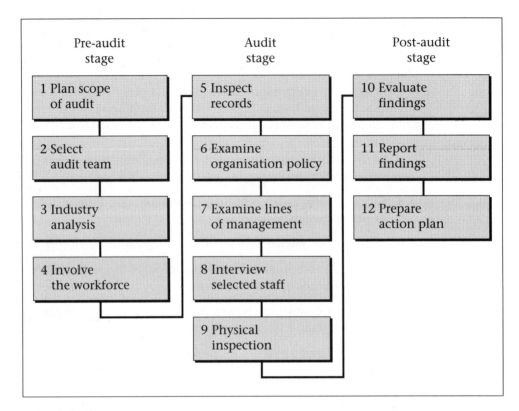

FIG 18.3 STAGES OF AN ENVIRONMENTAL AUDIT

Environmental audit stages

The first, pre-audit stage, will aim to minimise the time spent at the site and to maximise the audit team's productivity. It will involve:

1 Planning the nature and scope of the audit and providing a framework for setting goals and objectives, developing strategies for their achievement and specifying accountability for accomplishing the work and scheduling the audit process.

2 Selecting members of the audit team and allocating resources to the strategies and policies determined in the previous step. The audit team will consist of people chosen for their expertise, not only in environmental matters but also having knowledge of the industry in which the organisation operates. An assignment of audit responsibilities should be made according to the competencies and experience of the team.

3 Getting to know the industry and organisation to be audited. A useful strategy here is to use pre-survey questionnaires submitted to management in order for the audit team to familiarise themselves with the type of installation, the site and the location. It will also focus the minds of management on what will be required of them during the audit.

4 Questionnaires may also be sent to a representative sample of the workforce (to be filled out in confidence), asking about key issues such as communications, planning, health and safety, and working conditions.

The second stage is the on-site audit itself. This will include:

5 An inspection of records kept by the organisation, certificates of compliance, discharge consents, waste licences, etc.

6 Examination of inspection and maintenance programmes and the organisation's own policy on what to do in the event of spills and other accidents. Auditors will have to assess the soundness of the facility's internal controls and assess the risks associated with the failure of those controls. Such controls will include management procedures and the equipment and engineering controls that affect environmental performance.

7 Examining lines of management and responsibility, competence of personnel and systems of authorisation. There needs to be a working understanding of the facility's internal management system and of its effectiveness.

8 A confidential interview of selected staff at all levels of operation with a view to collecting information, particularly in the area of the effectiveness of systems and waste management.

9 A physical inspection of the plant, working practices, office management systems and surrounding areas, including a check on safety equipment, verifying the organisation's own sampling and monitoring procedures, investigating energy management systems, and where necessary taking samples of waste, liquids, soil, air and noise.

The final stage of the audit will involve:

10 Confirming that there is sufficient evidence on which to base and justify a set of findings and evaluating the audit information and observations. Such evaluation will involve the audit team meeting to discuss all facets of the environmental audit.

11 Reporting the audit findings in written form and in discussion with the management of the audited organisation. This entails a formal review of the audit findings to avoid misinterpretation, and discussion about how to improve the environmental performance of the organisation based on the audit report. Management is thus provided with information about compliance status and recommendations regarding action which should be taken.

12 It will often result in the development of an action plan to address deficiencies. It will include assigning responsibilities for corrective action, determining potential solutions and establishing timetables. Recommendations for the next audit may also be made.

The environmental audit is more likely to be successful if the general ethos of the organisation is supportive to the success of the programme and the welfare of the organisation. To this extent it is useful to consider some key characteristics which will provide the foundation for a successful programme. These factors will include:

- comprehensive support for the programme throughout management and particularly by senior management;

- acceptance that an auditing programme is for the benefit of management rather than a tool of individual performance assessment and is a function which, in time, will improve management effectiveness;

- the recognition that useful information will come out of the audit programme and that information needs to be shared and acted upon;

- the commitment to considering the comments and suggestions at each level of the organisation's management and workforce and encouraging responsible participation;

- a commitment to establishing systems for managing and following up on results;

- clearly defined roles and responsibilities and clear operational systems;

- the recognition of an integrated approach where the auditing system is linked to a wider management system.

Much stress needs to be placed on the idea that audits should be seen by management as a positive help rather than a threatening or hostile exercise (Welford, 1992). The organisation must create a culture, led by its top team, which recognises the positive benefits of the audit and sees it as good day-to-day management practice. Management must feel that they own the audit and even though some external expertise may be used, it is an activity which is promoted and driven internally rather than externally.

In the Netherlands the concept of environmental auditing has been known since 1984, although Dutch subsidiaries of American-owned firms had used the technique before then. The Confederation of Dutch Industries promotes environmental management within organisations, encouraging interaction between government and industry and providing guidelines. Environmental auditing in the Netherlands is largely confined to the largest of industries, but the Dutch expect that good practice by large, successful firms will be emulated by small and medium-sized organisations.

In Norway, factories are required to establish and maintain an internal environmental control system, supervised by a government agency. Environmental auditing is not legally required but a number of organisations practise environmental auditing on a voluntary basis. Within the Norwegian company Norsk Hydro every major installation is audited once every two years, lasting between three and five days in each case.

In the UK, the CBI has published a set of environmental auditing guidelines. These stress the practicalities of undertaking an environmental audit and stress the need to implement audit recommendations and continue monitoring processes.

The number of companies operating audit programmes in the European Union will grow whether or not environmental auditing legislation is implemented (Clement, 1991). Demands from groups such as environmentalists or local communities will lead to pressure on organisations not only to undertake environmental audits but also to disclose the results of those audits. The increase in auditing activity is also likely to lead to more standardisation of auditing practice and environmental standards. However, without the development of an overall integrated environmental management system, environmental auditing will be a mere palliative.

THE EU ECO-MANAGEMENT AND AUDIT SCHEME

While the primary stance of the Environment Directorate of the EU has always been to encourage organisations to improve standards of environmental performance without waiting for regulation, there is nevertheless a growing amount of European environmental legislation and directives. Moreover, the EU has been keen to establish common environmental standards and systems for environmental reporting. One such system is embedded in the eco-management and audit scheme Regulation.

At the end of 1991 the European Commission approved a proposal for a Council Regulation to establish a European Union eco-management and audit scheme (EMAS) which would be open for voluntary participation by industrial companies. The Regulation was published in March 1992. The EMAS provides a framework for companies to think ahead, assess their own environmental impacts and commit themselves to a policy of reducing them. It also encourages firms to keep the public informed by regularly making statements and reporting progress. At the present time EMAS is voluntary and administered by individual member states, but many expect the system to become compulsory for larger firms in time and the Council has retained the right to introduce compulsory registration. Member states themselves also have the right to adopt a compulsory registration system for certain industrial categories if they feel this is beneficial.

The objective of the scheme is to promote improvements in the environmental performance of industry by encouraging companies to:

- establish and implement environmental protection schemes;
- carry out regular, systematic and objective evaluations of the environmental performance of these systems;
- provide information about environmental performance to the public.

The purpose of the scheme is not to confirm compliance with legislative requirements (although this must be achieved), nor is it aimed at awarding best practice or performance. The scheme aims to recognise efforts to improve environmental performance over time, given a baseline established by an environmental review of the firm. The scheme highlights the need for a continuous cycle of improvement.

In order to join EMAS a firm has to adopt and adhere to the cycle depicted in Fig 18.4. Essentially this requires the firm to:

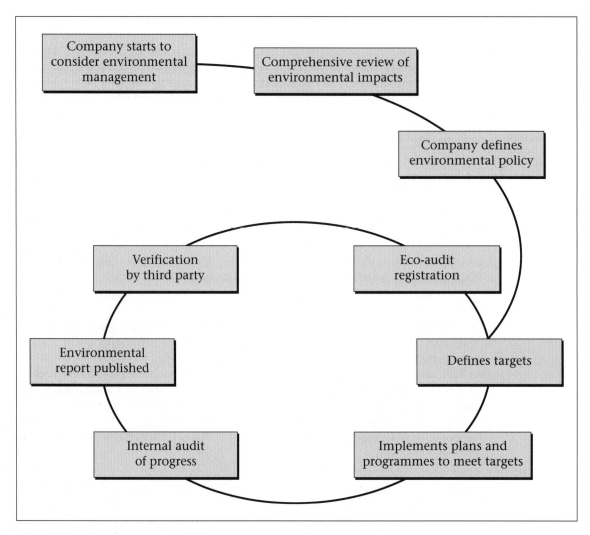

FIG 18.4 THE EUROPEAN EMAS CYCLE

- define an environmental policy, based on an overall review of the environmental impacts of its activities;

- set targets for achievement within a set time;

- put into place plans and systems to achieve these targets and include provisions for the constant monitoring of these;

- periodically audit to assess progress;

- report the audit findings to the public and have these findings verified by a third party;

- set new targets for further progress and repeat the procedure.

There is a need to establish systems based on the environmental review which:

- assess and manage the environmental impact of activities;
- manage the use of energy, raw materials and water;
- minimise waste;
- consider the selection and design of products and processes;
- prevent accidents;
- include staff in consultation and provide motivation and training;
- inform and involve the public.

Essentially, the audit assesses this system and evaluates performance in relation to the environmental review and the operation of the system as defined and documented. The results of the audit have to be considered by senior management and any necessary revisions to the company policy, objectives, targets, action plans and systems made.

All of these steps can be internal to the company if there is sufficient expertise available to perform the various tasks adequately. Indeed, the intention of EMAS is that the discipline of having to follow these steps should help the company better manage its own environmental performance. However, there are also important external aspects to the scheme.

EMAS requires that an external environmental statement is prepared based on the findings of the audit or initial review. Validation of this statement must be made by external accredited environmental verifiers. The validation will confirm that the statement has covered all of the environmental issues relevant to the site in enough detail and that the information presented is reliable. The validation process involves the examination of relevant documentation, including information about the site, its activities, a description of the environmental management system, and details and findings of the environmental review or audit. This would normally be followed by an inspection visit to the site and preparation of a verifier's report.

In order to join EMAS a company has to be able to demonstrate that this sequence of events has taken place, and that sensible targets have been set towards which the firm should make progress. The approved independent and accredited environmental verifier (AEV) will have checked that the audit process was carried out properly and that the environmental report is a true and fair view of the company's environmental performance. Application can subsequently be made for inclusion in the eco-management and audit register of companies. In order to continue to be registered companies have to continue the EMAS cycle and maintain commitment to improving environmental performance. Any lapse will result in the removal of a company's name from the register.

PRODUCT STEWARDSHIP AND ECO-LABELLING

Product design managers are increasingly examining ways in which the total life cycle of a product can be managed to ensure that potential environmental damage is minimised. In other words, they are looking to create an enclosed resource loop where waste is recycled and even the product itself is recycled at the end of its use.

Natural ecosystems operate in a similar fashion so that the waste from one process feeds into another as a nutrient. Traditional environmentally damaging production and consumption work more in a linear way such that inputs and outputs are not connected and possible environmental improvements are missed. One alternative is cradle-to-grave management where organisations have to recognise their wider responsibility and manage the entire life cycle of their products.

Many organisations are recognising their responsibility in this area in terms of what has been termed 'product stewardship'. This involves:

- examining the design of a product and considering how efficient it is;

- considering the energy sources, raw materials and components used in the product and deciding whether they might be substituted by alternatives which are more environmentally friendly;

- examining the production process itself and considering whether a more energy-efficient and less polluting process innovation might be found;

- re-examining the disposal of the product and the waste from its production in terms of recycling and returning the used materials to the production cycle after use;

- reconsidering the after-sales service and packaging of the product and ensuring that adequate information is provided for its safe and energy-efficient use and environmentally friendly disposal of waste caused by consumption of the product.

It is relatively easy for organisations to target their internal systems and make changes to improve the environment. The part of cradle-to-grave management which is probably hardest to achieve is the return of materials from the consumer-waste stream. For example, only 2 per cent of consumer-used plastic is recycled in the EU, owing to a lack of an effective collection infrastructure combined with underdeveloped markets for recycled plastics. One solution is for companies to take action and to construct their own recycling infrastructure. Many environmentalists would like to see the re-introduction of deposits on glass bottles, for example.

Over time eco-labelling schemes have been devised in a number of countries in an attempt to promote the use of production methods which are less harmful to the environment. The first such scheme was introduced in the Federal Republic of Germany in 1978. Canada, Japan and Norway established their own schemes in 1989. The schemes were also introduced to prevent spurious environmental claims. Germany's Blue Angel eco-labelling scheme is probably the world's best established programme. Launched in 1978 by the German government, it now has almost 4000 products carrying the label. The organisers of the scheme claim that 80 per cent of German households are aware of the scheme and it receives widespread support from manufacturers. Like the EU scheme the label is not restricted to domestic-made goods. The Japanese multinational Konica was the first company to win a Blue Angel label for use on a photocopier, for example. Many firms are aware that they cannot be without the Blue Angel award because the public sector and many large German companies will make every attempt to buy only products which carry the label.

The objectives of the EU's eco-labelling Regulation, agreed at the end of 1991, are to promote products with a reduced environmental impact during their entire life cycles and to provide better information to consumers on the environmental impacts of products. These must not be achieved at the expense of compromising product or workers' safety, or significantly affecting the properties which make the product fit for use. The EU scheme is designed to reduce confusion by providing an authoritative and independent label to identify those goods with the lowest environmental impact in a particular product group. That is not to suggest that those products are environmentally benign, but simply that their environmental performance is superior to products in the same group which do not have a label. The scheme should also encourage the production and sale of more environmentally responsible products and so alleviate the impact of consumption on the environment.

The label should affect all businesses along a supply chain even if some suppliers cannot use the label themselves. This is because suppliers will have to provide detailed information about their own components and their manufacturing process, in order that the suppliers of the end product can apply to use the eco-label, on the basis of a life-cycle assessment. Thus, in time, the label may become a minimum standard, specified by an increasing number of buyers who practise green procurement policies.

All products, excluding food, drink and pharmaceuticals, are potentially eligible for an eco-label if they meet these objectives and are in conformity with the EU's health, safety and environmental requirements. Products comprising substances or preparations classified as 'dangerous' under EU legislation will also be barred from receiving an eco-label, along with any product manufactured by a process likely to cause significant direct harm to humans or the environment.

The EU scheme issued as a Regulation applies directly to all member states and is EU-wide. It is a voluntary scheme and self-financing. It assesses individual products and their manufacturing processes so that a multi-product organisation will have to make multiple applications if it wishes all of its products to have eco-labels. The criteria for the award of an eco-label is ever tightening, so that on application for the renewal of an eco-label producers cannot assume that just because their environmental performance has remained unchanged it will be awarded the label again.

Judgement of the products must be made on the basis of a cradle-to-grave analysis or life-cycle assessment (LCA). The assessment matrix in Fig 18.5 must be used in setting criteria for the award of an eco-label. This will require account to be taken, where relevant, of a product group's soil, water, air and noise pollution impacts, waste generation, energy and resource consumption and effects on ecosystems. These impacts must be assessed in the pre-production, production, distribution, use and disposal stages. The criteria established for the award of an eco-label within a product group must be precise, clear and objective so that they can be applied consistently by the national bodies which award the eco-labels.

National competent bodies who are independent and neutral award the eco-labels for products. They are made up of representatives from industry, government, environmental pressure groups and consumer groups, and the body has to reflect the full range of social interests. These bodies act as a kind of jury and assess the environmental performance of the product by reference to the agreed general principles and specific environmental criteria for each product group.

The use of an eco-label is not necessarily open to any product. The first step is to get a particular product group accepted as suitable for the award of a label. It may be the case that a particularly polluting group of products (e.g. cars) will not be open to such an award. Requests for the establishment of new product groups may come from consumers or industry itself and are addressed to the competent body in the member state. The competent body, if it so wishes, can ask the Commission

Environmental Fields	Product life cycle				
	Pre-production	Production	Distribution	Utilisation	Disposal
Waste relevance					
Soil pollution and degradation					
Water contamination					
Air contamination					
Noise					
Consumption of energy					
Consumption of natural resources					
Effects on ecosystems					

FIG 18.5 EU ECO-LABELLING SCHEME INDICATIVE ASSESSMENT MATRIX

to submit a proposal to its regulatory committee. In any event the Commission will consult with interest groups and take advice from a range of sources. If it is decided that a particular product group will be open to the award of an eco-label, then this will be announced in the *Official Journal of the European Communities*. This process is outlined in Fig 18.6.

Following applications from manufacturers or importers of a particular product for the award of an eco-label, the national competent body has to notify the Commission of its decision relating to the award of an eco-label, enclosing full and summary results of the assessment. The Commission will then notify other member states and they usually have 30 days to make reasoned objections to the recommendations. If there are no objections the award proceeds and a contract to use the label for a specified period is drawn up. Lists of products able to use the eco-label are published. In the case of any objections and disagreement the Commission, acting through its advisory or regulatory body of national experts, will make the final decision. This procedure is summarised in Fig 18.7. Companies applying for an eco-label have to pay a fee to cover administration costs and a fee is also charged for the use of the label if awarded. Companies which succeed with their applications can only use the eco-label in advertising the specific products for which it was awarded.

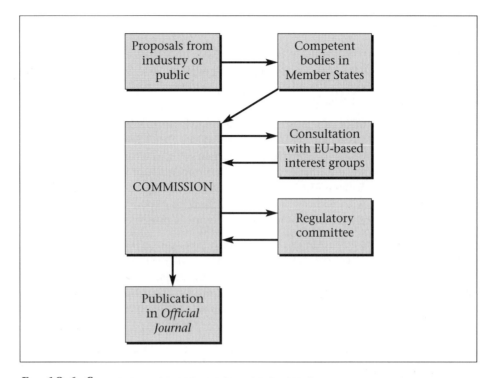

FIG 18.6 SELECTION OF NEW PRODUCT GROUPS

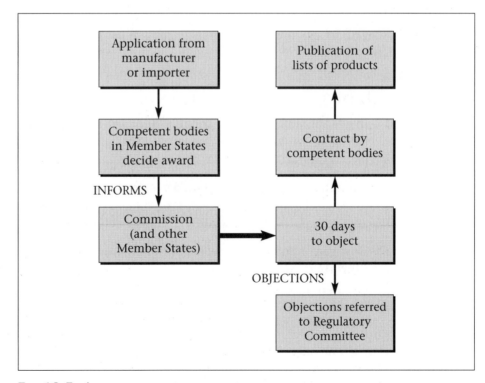

FIG 18.7 AWARD OF AN ECO-LABEL TO INDIVIDUAL PRODUCTS

SUMMARY

■ Governments will increasingly seek to make the polluter pay and one consequence of this is that some industries and products may simply disappear. But ultimately, the success of environmental improvement will be determined largely by the responsiveness of business.

■ That is not to suggest that legislation is a bad thing. Indeed it can act as the impetus to an organisation thinking about instituting proper environmental management. In addition, increasing legislation and government expenditure to increase environmentally related expenditure might be seen as a win–win situation. It stimulates the economy without leading to the pollution problems often associated with growth. Moreover, a shift in expenditure from the military to promoting security on the environmental front is possible.

■ The environmental revolution has been gathering momentum and speed since the 1960s and has developed rapidly in the 1980s and 1990s. Environmental considerations are likely to form an integral part of commercial normality and indeed competitiveness in the future. Definitions of business success are likely to include the assumption of zero negative impact on the environment at the very least.

■ A competitive advantage can be achieved not merely by keeping abreast of environmental developments, but also by initiating change within an organisation and responding with new environmentally friendly products and production processes.

■ Indeed, growing consumer awareness and environmental pressure groups are likely to ensure that organisations which do not take action on the environmental front will lose market share. With increased competition as a result of European integration, environmental management will provide organisations with a competitive edge.

REVIEW AND DISCUSSION QUESTIONS

1 In general, how can an organisation turn an expensive environmental management policy into a competitive advantage?

2 How would economic theory suggest that a pollution problem is tackled?

3 Is a sustainable development model of economic development possible?

4 In what ways does European integration help to control pollution? What sort of steps are being taken in the EU?

5 How can industry be encouraged to institute environmental management systems?

6 To what extent will new EU voluntary standards become the norm for European business?

CASE STUDY: THE BODY SHOP INTERNATIONAL

BACKGROUND

The Body Shop was founded in March 1976 when Anita Roddick opened her first shop in Brighton. Before 1976, working for the United Nations, she had travelled around the world and met people from a number of different cultures. Observing how people treated their skins and hair, she learned that certain things cleansed, polished and protected the skin without having to be formulated into a cream or shampoo. When she started The Body Shop, Anita Roddick aimed to utilise these raw ingredients such as plants, herbs and roots in products which would be acceptable to consumers. Only six years later she was described by the International Chamber of Commerce as 'the inventor of sustainable retailing' (Williams and Goliike, 1982).

The first shop was basic and at first sold only 15 lines. They were packed in different sizes to fill up the shelves and to give the customer an opportunity to try a product without buying a large bottle – a principle which remains today. A refill service operated which allowed customers to refill their empty bottles instead of throwing them away. Although this was clearly an environmentally friendly strategy, it was also initially implemented to cut down the costs of packaging.

Today, The Body Shop's principal activities are to formulate, manufacture and retail products which are primarily associated with cleansing, polishing and protecting the skin and hair. The underlying aims are to conduct that business ethically, with a minimum of hype, and to promote health rather than glamour. Naturally based, close-to-source ingredients are used wherever possible and ingredients and final products are not tested on animals (Wheeler, 1992). Packaging is kept to a minimum and refill services are offered in all shops. Packaging, in the form of plastic bottles, can be returned to shops and is recycled into accessories.

The Body Shop's full range now contains almost 400 products. The organisation trades in over 40 countries and employs around 6000 people, either directly or in franchises. Senior management in the organisation is committed to the encouragement of positive change. The aim is to establish a new work ethic that will enable business to thrive without causing adverse damage to the environment, at both the local and global level. There is an emphasis placed on not selling products which have an adverse effect on sustainability; that is, those which consume a disproportionate amount of energy during manufacture or disposal, generate excessive wastes, use ingredients from threatened habitats, which are obtained by cruelty, or which adversely affect other countries, especially in the developing countries.

Environmental strategies are at the centre of The Body Shop's approach to business. Moreover, the organisation has been so successful in raising the profile of the environment both within and external to the business that it is endlessly cited as being the leading business, worldwide, in this field. Even though the organisation itself would argue that there is still more to be achieved, this case study examines the practices and systems which have enabled The Body Shop to reach this leading position.

COMMITMENT AND POLICY

One of the most apparent characteristics of The Body Shop is its commitment to environmental and social excellence. This is often attributed to Anita Roddick herself; while many of the principles are hers, the truth is that commitment exists not only at board level but throughout the whole organisation. Everybody is encouraged to contribute to environmental improvement. The ultimate aim of The Body Shop is to include environmental issues in every area of its operations but, at the same time, the organisation rejects environmental opportunism which has often paralleled the green marketing strategies of more cynical firms.

At first, The Body Shop did not commit itself to a formal strategy or programme of environmental improvements. Action was taken when

▶

environmental problems were identified. This approach tended to increase employee involvement and reduce bureaucracy. However, with the continued growth of the organisation, it has been necessary to move to a more systematic approach, setting targets and planning for environmental improvement.

The overriding factor for The Body Shop is the perception of a moral obligation to drive towards sustainability in business (Roddick, 1991). It is impossible to measure progress towards this ideal without a detailed policy statement followed by a systematic process of data gathering and public reporting. Hence, auditing activities are considered absolutely essential to the company's long-term mission to become a truly sustainable operation. In other words, it aims to replace as many of the planet's resources as are utilised. That fundamental aim translates into a wish to play a full part in handing on a safer and more equitable world to future generations. The fundamental basis of this goal is a commitment to the broader concept of sustainable development. It is the strong belief of The Body Shop that the moral burden of achieving sustainability in business should become the principal driving force behind business in the future.

ENVIRONMENTAL MANAGEMENT AND ENVIRONMENTAL AUDITING

The only real way to achieve environmental improvement is to take a systematic approach to achieving its aims through an appropriate management structure and periodically to assess or audit progress, measuring the extent to which targets and basic objectives are being met. For that reason environmental auditing has a very high profile at The Body Shop. On the main site, it involves all staff and managers in continuous data collection, frequent reviews of priorities and targets (on a department-by-department basis) and an annual process of public reporting of results. The process extends to all retail outlets in the UK, and during 1993/94 it was being replicated in all overseas franchise operations.

In parallel with the necessity for environmental auditing, there is a need to put in place management systems capable of achieving targets and adhering to environmental policy. The Body Shop maintains a very decentralised system of environmental management. A corporate team of ethical audit specialists acts as a central resource for networks of environmental 'advisers' and co-ordinators in headquarters departments, subsidiaries, retail outlets and international markets. Environmental advisers and co-ordinators are usually part-time, fulfilling their role in environmental communications and auditing alongside normal duties.

The Body Shop carries out its environmental auditing in line with the EU eco-management and audit scheme, publishing three reports entitled *The Green Books* which lay out its annual report to the public on its environmental performance. Early on it was decided that the most important areas of environmental concern at The Body Shop were energy efficiency, waste management and product life-cycle assessment. Although the retail outlets fell outside the scope of this auditing procedure, other assessments have been or are being conducted in these areas. All UK shops, for example, were given an 'eco-audit' checklist covering their most important environmental issues. This was supplemented by training programmes on environmental improvement for shop environmental advisers (SEAs).

In 1996 The Body Shop carried out and published a full social audit of its activities. The approach was to assess the environmental, social and animal protection performance of the company, by reference to the opinions and perceptions of a range of stakeholders. This move widened the environmental auditing methodology previously adopted by The Body Shop and included a range of social issues. This is fully consistent with the moves towards incorporating wider aspects of sustainable development into the organisation and is now being replicated by a number of other companies.

REFERENCES FOR FURTHER READING

Clement, K (1991) 'Environmental Auditing for Industry: A European Perspective', *European Environment*, Vol 1, Part 3, June, pp 1–4.

Roddick, A (1991) 'In Search of the Sustainable Business', *Ecodecision, 7*.

Welford, R J (1992) 'A guide to Environmental Auditing', Supplement to *European Environment.*

Welford, R J (1993) 'Breaking the Link between Quality and the Environment', *Business Strategy and the Environment*, 2, 4.

Welford, R J (1996) *Corporate Environmental Management: Stystems and Strategies*, London: Earthscan.

Wheeler, D (1992) 'Environmental Management as an Opportunity for Sustainability in Business – Economic Forces as a Constraint', *Business Strategy and the Environment*, 1, 4, 37–40.

Williams, J O and Goliike, U (1982) *From Ideas to Action, Business and Sustainable Development*, ICC Report on the Greening of Enterprise, London: International Chamber of Commerce.

MULTINATIONAL MANAGEMENT

Kate Prescott

OBJECTIVES

The objectives of this chapter are to:

◆ consider the differences between the management of business operations in a domestic setting and in a multinational setting

◆ explain the problems faced by organisations in foreign markets

◆ analyse the management strategies which enable foreign organisations to maximise their advantages in foreign markets

◆ compare the wide range of management practices in multinational organisations

◆ develop an understanding of the complex task of multinational management

INTRODUCTION

An obvious question to ask in relation to multinational management is: 'How does it differ from management of business operations in a domestic setting?' There are four key issues which must be addressed in order to provide an answer:

1 understanding and reacting to change in the global environment;

2 cross-cultural management;

3 managing flexibly and creatively in today's dynamic business setting;

4 drawing on the knowledge and skills of the worldwide management arena in order to develop 'best practice'.

This chapter seeks to address the implications of all four factors in order to provide an understanding of the complex task of multinational management. In addition, since one of the most significant changes in international business in recent years has been the rise in the incidence of international activity by small firms, discussion throughout the chapter will not be restricted to the challenges of multinational enterprises (MNEs). The managerial demands on small and medium-sized enterprises (SMEs) will also be discussed.

The process of international management does not take place in a vacuum; success depends on adapting to the diverse environments in which businesses operate. For managers this is a highly complex task, not least because human beings by their very nature often feel uncomfortable or dislocated when operating outside their own cultural domain.

Setting a context

The challenge of international management is fitting strategic development to a continually evolving marketplace. Before embarking on a discussion of what this means in practice, it is useful to establish some parameters and terminology which explain different stages of development and current trends in the strategic activities of international operators.

There are four basic strategies which firms may employ to enter and compete in the foreign market. The choice of type depends critically on the extent to which firms wish to focus on cost reduction or local responsiveness.

The four strategic options are:

INTERNATIONAL STRATEGY

Here firms transfer skills and advantages, usually developed domestically, to overseas markets where there is the potential to secure differential advantage. Product development tends to be centralised, and tight control and co-ordination come from the centre. In foreign markets, firms typically establish sales and marketing activities, and sometimes production.

This strategy is useful where firms are attempting to exploit their core competence internationally without pressures for local responsiveness and cost reduction. An example of such a firm is McDonald's. For them, the focus is on exploiting their brand and image. Customisation of products is not important (although elements of the product range are adapted from market to market) and duplication of business in different centres is not damaging to profitability as economies of scale are not critical to success.

MULTIDOMESTIC STRATEGY

With a multidomestic strategy, the focus is on maximising local responsiveness. Unlike international firms, these organisations extensively customise both their product and marketing strategy to suit the local needs of the market. This usually means not only local production and sales and marketing, but also local product development and R&D centres designed to support market-specific rather than international activity. A structure of this type typically gives rise to a high cost base, although this can be compensated for by adding value to local products through targeted differentiation and marketing.

A major problem facing multidomestic firms is control. With different divisions pursuing their own objectives, this can mean the creation of decentralised federations through which it is difficult to transfer skills and information.

GLOBAL STRATEGY

A global strategy is one in which firms exploit experience curve effects and economies of scale. Production, marketing and product development activities are concentrated in a smaller number of advantageous locations (e.g. low-cost production centres or regionally-based marketing centres). The extent of customisation tends to be limited, as this raises costs through duplication. Instead, firms exploit cost advantages, often competing aggressively on price.

This strategy is inappropriate where the demands for local responsiveness are high. Today, this option is therefore only really available to firms where there is an option to develop a common worldwide product, often only the preserve of industrial goods companies. For many consumer goods companies, there remains continued pressure to adapt to local market conditions, customising products and strategies.

TRANSNATIONAL STRATEGY

Today, the highly competitive nature of world markets means that firms are exploring strategies which allow them to reap the benefits of both cost minimisation and local responsiveness and to exploit competences which are developed in all business centres worldwide (Hedlund, 1986). While this is obviously the ideal, it is a far from straightforward approach to international development: rationalising the demands for cost minimisation (which dictate more centralised business operations and larger-scale operating units) with those for local responsiveness (which dictate customisation and duplication) is a highly complex task and one which demands a high level of flexibility.

The only way of achieving such a complex mix is to split businesses into a series of constituent functions which are variously centralised and decentralised. For example, a firm may choose to concentrate its R&D and production operations in a small number of regional sites (maybe one in the Americas, one in Europe and one in Asia Pacific) while at the same time dispersing sales and marketing activity to each target market to ensure maximum local responsiveness.

Some of the first moves made in this direction were by the Japanese in the early 1980s. Multinational giants such as Honda and Cannon fostered the idea of the *four headquarters system*. This involved their establishing major regional research, production and marketing centres in the three main areas of the global triad (America, Europe and Asia Pacific), each responsible for adapting business to regional needs. These were then supported by an all-embracing corporate headquarters which co-ordinated the transfer of competences and skills between regions as well as establishing global policy and corporate identity. Within each region, local adaptation is also made possible by the establishment of market-based sales and marketing centres. Today, there is evidence of transnational strategy (or at least elements of such an approach) across a wide range of producers, including Nestlé, Unilever, Caterpillar and Ford.

These four different approaches to international expansion incorporate a number of key issues which will be revisited later in the chapter:

1 Managing the diversity of global regions and markets.

2 Selecting appropriate strategies which take into consideration market and product characteristics. These include market entry strategies as well as those concerned with internalisation versus externalisation of business operations.

3 Centralisation versus decentralisation; standardisation versus adaptation.

4 Establishing strategies and structures which are flexible and responsive to change.

5 Learning and developing systems for best practice.

On the first of these issues, it is important to understand how international managers are reacting to change in the global environment, managing across different international cultures, and coping with commonality and diversity between markets.

THE CHANGING GLOBAL ENVIRONMENT

Regionalisation

'Regionalisation' has become an increasingly important feature of the global business environment since the Second World War, although the constructs on which regional integration are based (principally free trade) are far from new. Adam Smith, writing in the eighteenth century, noted that the greatest economic benefits accrue from free trade, the 'invisible hand' of government trade policy serving only to distort the process of industrial specialisation which allows countries to utilise their resources to best effect. In 1947, as countries moved to forge greater global co-operation in an effort to put the adverse experiences of the Second World War behind them, the General Agreement on Tariffs and Trade was formed (GATT) with the intention of reducing/removing tariffs and quotas between countries on a unilateral basis.

GATT AND FREE TRADE

Through the 11 multilateral rounds on tariff negotiation to date, the achievements of GATT have been considerable, extending in the last (Uruguay) round to concerns of trade in services on a global basis. However, many critics now argue that the role of GATT has been undermined, as international business flows in the modern world have grown more complex, and trade policies and protectionist measures have become more concerned with non-tariff barriers which are less easy to detect and far harder to control.

TRADING BLOCS

Compounding the problems of GATT has been the development of regional trading blocs, the Single European Market being the most publicised and far reaching. Although the more recent signing of the North American Free Trade Agreement (NAFTA) including the USA, Canada and Mexico, and ongoing talks concerning greater unification of Asia Pacific countries, demonstrates the importance of regionalisation in the global 'triad' (the three leading regions of the developed world). The most notable feature of trading blocs is that they promote free trade on the 'inside' (between participating member states), although external protectionism can be (and often is) a central tenet of supporting government policy. It is only necessary to look to the accusations by the Japanese and Americans of the Europeans creating an impenetrable 'fortress', or the efforts of the USA to reduce Japan's trade surplus with the USA and the concomitant threat of increased protectionism, to understand that many of the trade deals currently being forged are between the triad members – the Americas, the Asia Pacific region and Europe. This has led to a re-emergence of 'bilateral bargaining' in trade negotiations, which GATT was so anxious to eradicate in the post-war era (Welford and Prescott, 1996).

The desire for countries to affiliate themselves in large economic groupings stems from the belief that large, unrestricted markets lead to intensified competition and thus provide an impetus for improved efficiency. While the term 'efficiency' is often used loosely, here it specifically refers to both static effects (those arising from immediate cost-saving strategies) and dynamic effects (those accruing from better innovation and product development). From the perspective of the European Union, poor economic performance throughout the 1970s and 1980s was seen to stem from the inability of firms to operate freely on a pan-European scale, restricting competition and efficiency, and thus putting European firms at a disadvantage *vis-à-vis* their global rivals, from America and Japan in particular.

PROTECTIONISM

The magnitude of change within the Single European Market inevitably raised concern among American and Japanese industrialists, not least because the external trade measures being proposed smacked of renewed protectionism through such means as anti-dumping measures (penalties against firms adjudged to be selling goods in export markets 'below cost'); rules of origin (which dictate that the country of origin must be the country where the last major transformation took place, effectively eliminating firms moving goods through countries with unrestricted trade links with the target market); local content rules (which stipulate that, in certain industries, goods sold locally have to contain a certain proportion of components produced in the target market); and voluntary agreements (which act in the same way as quotas, although they are set by the exporting rather than the importing nation, usually on the grounds of goodwill).

However, rather than restricting global competition, these measures have, arguably, compounded competition as firms have sought to bypass the non-tariff barriers through foreign direct investment. This latter point gives credence to the belief that the scope of GATT was not sufficient to control 'trade' on a global scale. Whereas in the early stages of global development firms tended only to consider exporting as the available route for foreign market development, in more recent times firms have extended their world activities through a variety of strategic methods. In 1996 GATT was replaced by the World Trade Organisation (WTO) whose remit has been extended beyond just trade agreements and into the realms of global business flows.

THE MANAGERIAL CHALLENGE

The questions being asked of managers operating in countries within trading blocs appear clear: embrace the advantages being offered by free trade and extend business activities throughout the internal free market. However, this belies the fact that in many industries the marketplace is global, not regional. Concentrating on the extended domestic market (the artificially created internal market) overshadows the importance of establishing a strong global presence. This wider thinking can be summed up in the words of one UK manager asked about his attitude towards the European Single Market:

> *'We should not get together in an incestuous huddle and ignore the opportunities provided by the rest of the world.'*
>
> (Buckley, Pass and Prescott, 1992)

Relying solely on the advantages of regionalisation and attempting to avoid the hurdles of renewed global protectionism are likely to produce few rewards. Managers have to be aware that to be successful globally means taking advantage of the benefits stemming from regionalisation (the impetus for efficiency and technological development) and harnessing the benefits to exploit wider global markets.

This is as applicable to small firms as to their larger counterparts. Taking the example of the UK, managers are well advised first to consider expansion into markets which are 'close to home'. In a geographic sense, this would mean markets such as Belgium, the Netherlands, France and Germany. However, as the experience of many small firms has demonstrated, while such countries are 'close' in spatial terms to the UK, culturally they are far more distant than the United States, Canada, South Africa and Australia, where old colonial links mean a great deal of cultural similarity and a far more familiar operating environment. Consequently, 'cultural distance' may persuade firms to look beyond the extended European market at an early stage in their internationalisation.

Technological development

CHANGE AND DEMANDS ON PRODUCT DEVELOPMENT

While it was once possible for firms to develop a new technology, protect it with patents and exploit the monopoly advantages of the uniqueness of the products developed from the technology, in today's dynamic global environment this is no longer the case. Indeed, Porter (1990) argues that firms attempting to follow this strategy are likely to lag behind in terms of world development as they rest on their laurels from past technological development rather than attempting to produce a continuous stream of new products.

Part of the reasoning behind Porter's argument stems from the rapid rate of change in technology in the modern world and thus the shortening of technological life cycles. This has two important implications: first, product development processes need to be improved to speed up the introduction of new products into the market; second, in order that such a rapid introduction of new products can be managed efficiently, managers must adopt new production techniques so that major plant refitting does not become commonplace.

The car industry provides a good example of these management demands in practice. Japanese car manufacturers, whose encroachment on the global car industry was dramatic to say the least, concerned themselves with just these challenges. They developed design techniques which allowed them to introduce new models at a more rapid rate than their Western counterparts (47 months in 1989 compared with 60 months for their American competitors) and introduced flexible working practices which permitted a large number of models to be produced at the same time. Much of this was achieved via manufacturing modularisation, which means that most of the components which go to make up a Japanese car are in-sourced from external suppliers:

> *'Modular manufacturing involves designing and assembling the entire car as a series of sub-assemblies or modules. New modules can be developed directly to replace an existing one, allowing cars to be changed easily.'*
>
> (*The Economist*, 29 July 1989)

In this way the Japanese are able to combine the benefits of rapid new technology introduction and production efficiency (through scale economies).

TECHNOLOGY AS A FACILITATOR

So far, it has been suggested that technology change is a 'hurdle' which managers must overcome to keep abreast of the competition. Technology change has also, however, served to facilitate internationalisation of firms by making communication, information handling and distribution easier and more efficient (Hill, 1997).

The introduction of the microprocessor, satellite and cable technology has speeded up global communication and made it possible for very large volumes of information to be gathered and transmitted. Containerised shipping and air-freight have also had a profound effect in terms of physical product distribution, commercial jet travel 'shrinking the globe' in terms of ease of travel to far-flung destinations (Dicken, 1992).

Such changes have all reduced the real costs of communication and transportation, which means that it is now possible to co-ordinate and manage a global organisation with subsidiaries based in the far-flung corners of the world. No longer do various subsidiaries operate as discrete, stand-alone entities divided from their parent firm by geographical distance. They may now form an integral whole, joined by modern communication and systems designed to share and develop information on a global basis.

On the one hand, such developments have served to facilitate global business developments; on the other, they have posed serious challenges in terms of effective management and business development. They have raised the importance of integration and co-ordination, but have often resulted in 'information overload' at a head office level, to the extent that many managers have recognised that, in order to avoid the organisation becoming a bureaucratic monolith beset by problems of red tape and X-inefficiency (so often associated with large organisations), new management and organisational structures are essential to combat the information challenges of the modern era. These will be discussed in more detail later in the chapter.

RESEARCH AND DEVELOPMENT

Research and development (R&D) tends to be treated as a single term when, in reality, these constitute two separate managerial functions. Research refers to the creation of new technologies or product innovations whereas development relates to the process of turning the technologies into products for the marketplace. The importance of this distinction can be clearly seen when considering the success of Japanese firms in the global marketplace. In the early post-Second World War years of Japan's economic development, the country was concerned with licensing Western technologies as a way of improving the country's technological base. However, rather than simply replicating the technology and selling it back to the West, the Japanese focused on the process of 'development', refining and improving the technologies to better 'fit' market demands. More recently, Japanese firms, supported by government programmes, have extended their activities into the area of primary research – which, arguably, gives them the potential to improve their technological position in world marketplaces. It is essential, therefore, that research activities take place in conjunction with global market considerations and that technologies are tailored to meet market demand.

In line with the above, new product ideas and technologies have generally emanated from those countries with the strongest demand conditions and the largest consumer markets. In the post-war period this meant that many major product developments originated in the USA. With the rise of the Asia Pacific region and recovery of West European markets after the war, this is no longer the case. In 1990, for example, Japan spent 3 per cent of GDP on R&D, Germany 2.7 per cent and the USA 1.8 per cent. Other countries too are developing strong research centres in certain industries, which means that developments can now emerge from any number of world markets. For this reason many firms have recognised the importance of internationalising their R&D activities, setting up facilities in centres of global excellence and using local market demand conditions as the impetus for new ideas. This trend will be fully explored later.

MANAGERIAL CHALLENGES

For MNEs with 'deep pocket advantages' (that is, extensive resources for investment), the message is clear. Invest in programmes for continual product development and improvement, and manufacturing/business systems which facilitate international business activity and flexibility. This does not mean a 'scattergun' approach to investment, but requires careful decision making about the most appropriate areas for investment at any one time. Modern technologies, which are highly complex, require significant amounts of money for research and development. Choosing the direction of research is therefore critical and can be something of a lottery. Governments in many of the developed markets of the world have reacted to this

Japan	USA	EC
Software engineering	Automation	Information technology
New materials	Computing	New materials
Biotechnology	Advanced materials	Biotechnology
Biomaterials	Medical technology	Energy
	Thin layer technology	

FIG 19.1 EMERGING AREAS OF TECHNOLOGY
Source: European Commission, 1988.

problem and have highlighted key areas of technological development which they consider to be the important growth areas today and into the next millennium. The main areas highlighted by American, Japanese, and European governments are outlined in Fig 19.1.

Encouragement of development in these critical areas is also backed by government research funding. In the EU, this includes ESPRIT (European Strategic Programme for Research and Development in Information Technology), RACE (Research and Development in Advanced Communication Technology for Europe), BRITE (Basic Research in Industrial Technology for Europe) and EURAM (European Research in Advanced Materials). Many of the grants targeted through these programmes are available to firms prepared to engage in joint activities with competitors. They are therefore not only designed to promote new technologies but also technology transfer for the improvement of the wider European technology base. Managers are therefore well advised to be aware of potential grants and be prepared to liaise with other industry players.

For smaller firms, with fewer resources to dedicate to technological development, the challenges are more severe. Failure to keep abreast of technology may ultimately result in their demise, but investment in R&D may be considered too high risk. Nevertheless, as there is no documented proof that large firms are more successful innovators than small firms, there is no size limit on firms allowed to bid for government support. Alternatively, small firms may be best served by concentrating their efforts on product development, refining technologies for specific market niches or licensing in technologies with market potential.

Political change

The opening up of Communist countries to Western businesses and the adoption of capitalist principles by many previously centrally-planned economies has extended business opportunities on a global scale. The rush is on for developed country multinationals to establish a presence in the newly emerging markets, be it via joint venture or foreign direct investment. China, India, the Czech Republic, former East Germany, Brazil and a whole host of other emerging markets have become the playground for international operators seeking long-term growth and development.

Although many of these regions are far from ensuring long-term political stability, their liberalisation, deregulation and genuine openness to companies from developed countries (and their technologies) has changed the orientation of many businesses. Even where opportunities may not result in short-term profit, the search for first-mover advantages and the belief that countries such as these will offer up vast consumer markets in the future make them attractive to today's investors.

MANAGEMENT CHALLENGES

Entering these new countries and servicing the needs of customers poses a number of serious challenges to international firms:

- Dealing with new cultures, many of which are still dominated by communist ideals and work practices that can make the establishment of efficient business systems difficult. Employees who fail to understand the importance of productivity; partner companies for whom the concept of marketing is alien; bureaucratic rules; black-market economies; and corruption all need to be understood and catered for.

- Co-operative business solutions are often the only means of entry, either to reduce risk, or to secure access where governments place restrictions on foreign ownership. Some companies therefore need to develop new internal skills to manage co-operative rather than competitive business operations.

- Changing the balance of world business operations. Emerging markets in the East (particularly India and China), with their large populations and extensive natural resources, mean a further shift in economic activity towards the Asia Pacific region. This will inevitably change the balance of world business and force companies to reassess their own international balance and coverage.

International money markets

The move towards monetary union in the Single European Market, although beset by problems as a result of national sovereign concerns (that is, the continuing belief by member state governments that monetary policy should remain the concern of the nation state and not the European bureaucrats), has received a lot of support from European managers. The main reason for this is that a common currency in Europe will allow firms to plan with greater certainty, as European business transactions will be removed from the uncertainties of exchange rate fluctuations.

In recent years, flexible exchange rates have come to characterise international business transactions. This means that the value of any currency for international traders is the price at which the currency is traded in the open market. Consequently, international business traders are subject to adverse changes in domestic and foreign economic conditions which have an important impact on the price competitiveness of goods traded abroad. Consider, for example, the effect of the high interest rates imposed on UK firms and individuals in the late 1980s. The result was to raise the demand for sterling, as it was considered to be an appreciating asset. Greater demand for the currency meant that the price for sterling rose, making British goods more expensive in foreign markets, thus reducing their competitive potential. With exchange rate fluctuations difficult to predict, there is always the risk that between agreement of terms for exporting contracts and final payment, exchange rate movements eradicate profits.

For small firms, usually dealing in fewer overseas markets and thus spreading their risk more thinly, adverse movements in exchange rates can be critical. Risks can, however, be minimised through 'insurance'; forward exchange protection provided by banks (at a price) can eliminate the risk and ensure that the final payment matches the agreed price at the time the contract was signed. For larger firms, establishing overseas facilities may prove a more favourable alternative. This means that contracts are written in the foreign country (and currency), and only converted into the domestic currency when exchange rates are favourable.

A fixed exchange rate (sought through the European Exchange Rate Mechanism) and ultimately a single European currency would eradicate such problems for European firms, further facilitating the potential to operate unhindered in a wider European market. Many economists believe that European firms will only reap the full benefits of economic union when a single currency has been established – putting them on a par with their American and Japanese counterparts who are able to conduct business in large domestic markets in a single currency.

CROSS-CULTURAL MANAGEMENT

The terms 'culture' and 'cultural difference' are used liberally by international managers, although the reality of what these concepts mean in practice is likely to be far less widely understood. As soon as any organisation begins to sell its products and services outside its own domestic market, it will be exposed to a different cultural environment with its own distinct norms and behaviours. Ultimately, cultural sensitivity can mean the difference between success and failure. Ricks and Mahajan's (1984) analysis of 'blunders' in international marketing examines a number of cases where firms (even leading multinational players) have failed to fully understand local market nuances, with disastrous results. For example, General Motors' promotional campaign in Belgium centred on a slogan 'Body by Fischer' which in translation read 'Corpse by Fischer'; the same company launched a brand of car in Puerto Rico called the 'Nova', which in the local language sounded like 'no va' – it does not go; Goodyear Tyre and Rubber Company made illegal claims of superiority about their products in West Germany, because they did not take account of local legal requirements; and General Mills allegedly targeted their advertising in the UK towards children, which was considered unethical. Mistakes of this kind can prove costly and may also damage the reputation of the firm in the marketplace. Taking cultural management seriously is therefore a prerequisite in doing business abroad if a firm wants to ensure long-term growth and survival.

Defining and categorising culture

One of the most notable studies of the relationship between national cultures and values in the workplace was undertaken by Geert Hofstede between 1967 and 1973. Based on research of 116,000 business personnel from over 17 countries, he identified 11 clusters of countries along four key dimensions. (Hofstede, 1983.)

- **Power distance**: focuses on how society deals with inequalities between people in physical and educational terms – countries with a high score (between 0 and 100) are those which feature broad differences between individuals in terms of power and wealth.

- **Uncertainty avoidance**: This index relates to the extent to which countries establish formal rules and fixed patterns of life (such as career structures).

- **Individualism:** At the high end of the scale are those societies where ties between individuals are very loose, as opposed to those societies where individuals are born into 'collectives' which support and foster development in return for loyalty.

- **Masculinity:** The more 'masculine' a society, the more it values assertiveness and materialism. Less concern is shown for quality of life. 'Femininity' relates to caring and concern for people.

Figure 19.2 highlights the relative positions on a four-dimensional matrix for a range of countries. It clearly demonstrates that there are broad differences along the four dimensions between the highlighted countries, differences which need to be taken into account when managing across borders. For instance, the UK displays low scores for both power distance and uncertainty avoidance, an average

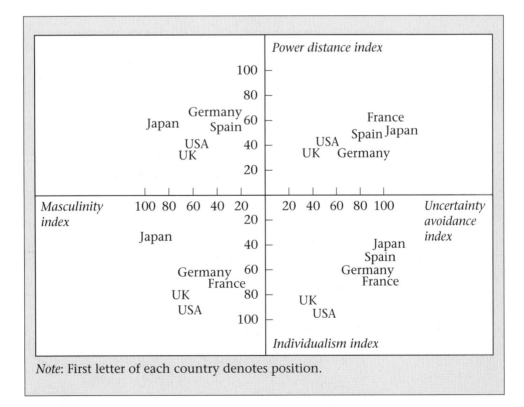

Note: First letter of each country denotes position.

FIG 19.2 CROSS-CULTURAL COMPARISONS

score on the masculinity index and a high score for individualism. This suggests a society in which negotiation figures large in decision making (low power distance), rules are flexible and adaptable (low uncertainty avoidance), and great store is placed on personal development, and success and entrepreneurship (high individualism and medium masculinity). This compares with a country like France, where society is based on a pyramidal hierarchy held together by tight rules and unity of command, or Germany, where personal command is largely unnecessary as rules settle everything.

More recently, Hofstede has also added a fifth dimension to his research: **time frame**. Here he distinguishes between long-term and short-term orientation of business. Long-term orientation relates to such values as thrift and perseverance, while short-term values include respect for personal tradition, social obligations and 'saving face'. Generally, East Asian cultures show the most long-term orientation, while European and American cultures figure quite low in the rankings.

Research of this nature has provided managers with insights into different business behaviours and practices around the world, preparing them for the challenges of management in terms of:

- understanding business practices and ways of viewing business development;

- understanding business structures and organisation from a cultural perspective;

- understanding what motivates people in terms of their career and personal aspirations.

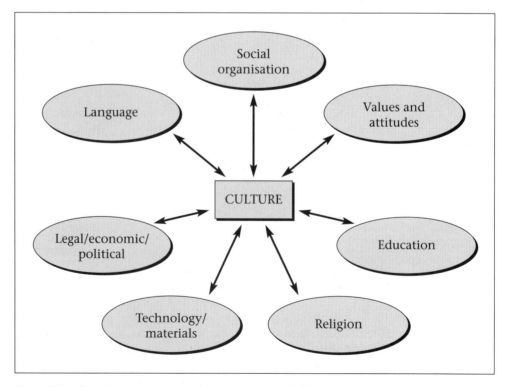

FIG 19.3 ELEMENTS OF CULTURE

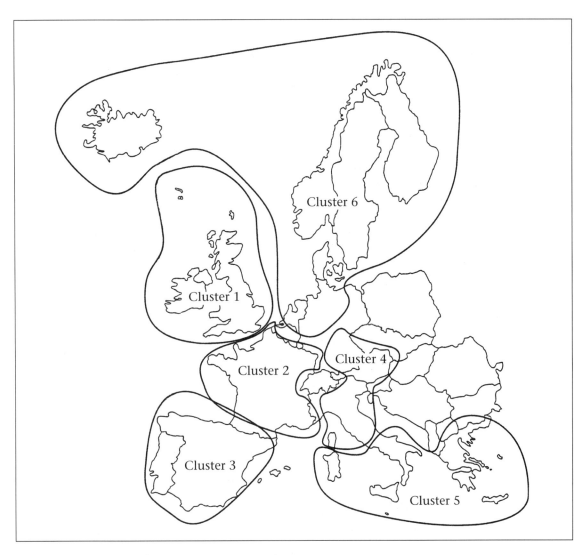

FIG **19.4** EUROPEAN 'CULTURAL CLUSTERS'

Source: Vandermerwe (1993).

It may be argued, however, that Hofstede's four dimensions (now five dimensions) provide an oversimplistic view of cultural difference between the markets of the world and fail to give much insight into the workings of society as a whole. Here, other alternatives need to be considered. The model depicted in Fig 19.3, which suggests a number of cultural elements for analysis, provides an alternative which extends understanding beyond the business world to customers and markets.

Cultural analysis of this nature allows managers to identify commonalities and differences between countries, and thus to develop clusters of countries for targeting sales and marketing activity. Examples of such clustering are provided in Fig 19.4. This is based on work undertaken by Vandermerwe (1993) on similarities and

609

differences between demographics, economic variables and life-style characteristics of the member states of the EU. Interestingly, her findings show that clusters are not necessarily based on geographic boundaries. She also goes on to suggest that other 'clusters' need to be considered by European managers:

1 mass clusters with common consumer needs;

2 niche clusters where consumers have similar but not identical needs;

3 local and specialised clusters.

The management challenge, then, is not simply to be aware of the individual cultural elements of each society, but in understanding and managing the extent and nature of diversity between different cultures.

Managing diversity

Nations and societies are not the same: each has features which make them unique and distinct from both their immediate and distant neighbours. This diversity poses a serious challenge to international managers, who not only have to understand different needs, wants and buyer behaviours in different clusters, but also have to integrate this diversity into an holistic strategy.

It has been argued (Bloom, Calori and de Woot, 1994) that Europeans are better than their international counterparts at dealing with diversity. Because business in Europe has been developed across a wide array of diverse national cultures, mechanisms for integrating diversity have been central to competitive success. This compares with the Japanese who developed their businesses in a highly homogeneous market and with the Americans who have sought to integrate diverse cultures into a uniquely identifiable and all-embracing 'American' norm. As a result, it is not surprising that American and Japanese management models typically highlight diversity as a problem, while Europeans consider it a way of life.

This kind of thinking has led to distinct differences in approach to international strategic development across the world. Porter (1991) suggested:

> *'One of the things that Europe 1992 integration will do is hasten the process by which larger European companies move from confederations of subsidiaries to become truly integrated, world-wide competitors. For each product line, there will be a clear home base, with some or many outside the home country. European companies have tended to do well in businesses that are essentially a collection of national markets but not so well in the truly global arena.'*

In other words, Europeans' tendency to deal with diversity by focusing on differentiation and local market adaptation, while attractive in the past, is less desirable in the European (and global) markets of the 1990s, where greater commonality between regions and potential for more standardisation and integration of business practices is not only possible, but desirable.

Brian Goldthorp, Director of Personnel at Trafalgar House confirms this line of thinking:

'But the reverse side of the coin is that when we look at parts of the world where these pressures of diversity are not as overwhelming as they are in Europe, we continue to concentrate on dealing with differentiation, so Europeans are less successful there. American and Japanese corporations show the reciprocal traits. They are enormously good where there are products and strategies of an undifferentiated kind.'

(Bloom, Calori and de Woot, 1994, p 41)

Aside from advantages of local responsiveness, other benefits accrue from a differentiated approach to strategic management across cultures: an ability to work successfully in other cultures and adapt to the nuances and norms of different societies. Japanese managers often find this difficult as a result of their 'sheltered' development in a homogeneous society. The literature is now awash with examples of the serious problems experienced by Japanese companies attempting to introduce Japanese management practices into the West. Their approach is to persuade people that the Japanese way is the best, even if some of the practices run counter to local cultural norms and practices. Americans, on the other hand, tend to be more dogmatic: they impose structures and rules, and demand change from local employees.

The message seems to be that managers need to extend their 'toolkit'. They need to be made aware of the different strategic options available to them so they can devise the most appropriate fit between strategy and diverse market structure. This may mean shifting towards a more transnational strategy – balancing differentiation (local adaptation) and standardisation (centralisation into larger units), simply looking for parts of the business where change of this kind is appropriate, or consolidating the chosen approach (global or multidomestic) to suit the needs of the product market.

Cultural change

All of the above takes place against a backdrop of change. Culture, whether national or business-based, is a dynamic phenomenon: norms and practices are continually adjusting and changing. However, there is little agreement on whether such change is bringing markets closer together, or breaking them apart into smaller niche segments.

Some industry observers argue that culture is becoming increasingly homogeneous on a global scale. Certain global products have become widely accepted, partly because they appeal to large, cultural subgroups which show a degree of standardisation on a global scale. Coca-Cola, Levi Jeans and Reebock training shoes, McDonald's Hamburgers and Swatch watches have broad appeal to the youth 'subculture'. Products of this kind suggest that there is scope for global standardisation, although in all these cases the way in which the product is managed at a local level shows a degree of differentiation on a market-by-market basis as a result of local country cultural conditions. Such adaptation may include:

- product/servicing adaptation to cater for different needs and wants and competitor activity;

- adaptation of promotion and advertising such that the message is relevant to local customers and meets with local legislation and standards;

- adaptation of channel decisions due to different buying behaviour;

- adaptation of recruitment policies in line with local educational systems and standards;

- adaptation of pay and remuneration to ensure staff motivation;

- adaptation of price to fit with local conditions.

Others point to the way in which cultural groups are becoming more distinct from each other:

> *'In Coca-Cola we're seeing a dichotomy taking place in business today. Some of the customers of the Coca-Cola system in Europe, such as large international companies, are becoming more European. Many of them want one programme for Europe.*
>
> *On the other hand, the consumer is becoming more local, in our view. We are advertising Coca-Cola in Barcelona today in two languages – Spanish and Catalan. It is a recent phenomenon and we see it taking place in Scotland, Wales, the French regions, the German Lander... People are becoming more culturally attuned with their localities and marketeers have to recognise it and be prepared to deal with it.'*
>
> (Ralph Cooper, President of Coca-Cola's European Community Group
> Bloom, Calori and de Woot, 1994, p 50)

It is clear that Levitt's (1983) prediction that intensified competition and techno-logical development would lead companies to operate globally, ignoring 'superficial' national differences, is unlikely ever to apply to all firms in all indus-tries across the world.

While we may be seeing the emergence of a 'global village' in terms of our aware-ness of our neighbours, this does not automatically suggest that neighbours will seek to become like each other. With evidence apparently to prove both sides of the debate, the only conclusion can be: 'it depends'. While, from a management point of view, this is far from satisfying, as it provides few guidelines and prescrip-tions, it is important to consider the strategic management challenge as one which incorporates a review of individual markets, products and timeframes (Halliburton and Hünerberg, 1987).

MATCHING STRATEGIES TO THE INTERNATIONAL ENVIRONMENT

International firms have at their disposal a wide range of strategic options from which to draw. At a generic level, firms may choose between exporting, licensing and other contractual arrangements and foreign direct investment, although at an operational level each of these alternatives offers up a wide range of strategic alter-natives. It is beyond the scope of this chapter to explore fully the nature of these alternatives (refer to the further reading). What is important, however, is under-standing some of the key differences and managerial considerations.

Understanding decision-making criteria

To return to the argument outlined above: the dynamic and diverse global business environment of today makes it difficult to prescribe generic solutions to management challenges. Much depends on the nature of the market, the product and the firm itself. Failure to make pragmatic decisions about the best 'fit' of strategy to market conditions is likely to result in managers missing the best opportunities for exploiting their advantages in foreign markets. This involves managers considering a wide array of both internal and external factors and choosing the most appropriate strategy in each instance. External factors include:

- **Host market factors** – size, growth, competitive conditions, distribution, infra structure;

- **Host market environment** – political, economic and socio-cultural conditions;

- **Host market production factors** – availability, quality and costs of inputs;

- **Domestic market factors** – competitive conditions, growth, government policies and internal factors;

while internal factors include:

- **Product factors** – product technology, differentiation, service provision and potential for global standardisation;

- **Company resources** – management, capital and technology, and overall commitment to international business.

Assessing the most appropriate means of entering and servicing the market along each of these dimensions is likely to result in a number of different options being appropriate for a variety of reasons. Managers therefore have to decide on a final strategy based on (a) their overall objectives for growth and development, and (b) the weighting of factors in their own industry's competitive development.

For instance, the firm has to decide on both the long-term and short-term objectives for entering a particular market. If, for instance, the company's objective is merely to sell off excess capacity in overseas markets, it is unlikely that foreign investment will prove attractive. If, on the other hand, the company is looking to establish a committed presence in the market, then it may wish to invest significant resources in establishing a strong market presence. In terms of weighting factors, in some industries certain factors emerge as being more critical than others. Take, for example, the retail financial service industry: with many markets being mature and in a state of overcapacity, foreign direct investment, attractive in terms of local presence and closeness to customers, is both expensive and limited in its potential to secure significant market penetration. Gaining access to established distribution networks through alliances (or possibly takeover of existing organisations) is the priority, and thus distribution conditions should be highly weighted in making the final decision.

It is clear from this very brief overview that the decision-making challenge facing international managers, with regard to market entry, is highly complex, requiring high levels of research and detailed analysis. More often than not, however, firms base their decisions on imperfect information, as information is either too expensive to gather or not available, or decisions need to be made quickly if firms are to take advantage of available opportunities. For many managers, then, the reality of international decision making is strategic adjustment – considering changes in operational modes, which mean either shifts between generic modes of market servicing, or inter-mode shifts, such as from exporting via a sales representative to exporting via a wholly-owned subsidiary. These decisions are usually made in line with the ongoing experience of the firm, the learning curve, wherein additional knowledge about the market and the product's experience in that market gives better information on which to base strategic decisions.

Consequently, foreign market servicing decisions are dynamic. Continual assessment and reassessment is essential if firms are to adjust to changes in both internal and external conditions.

Exploiting compensating advantages

Firms entering foreign markets are often at a disadvantage *vis-à-vis* indigenous companies as a result of their lack of understanding of the local market. The pioneering work of Hymer (1960), which is often considered to be the foundation of current international business theory, proposed that market entrants require some form of compensating advantage to compete successfully with local firms, which possess innate strengths. Such advantage may include proprietary technology (raising the emphasis of technology development and management), preferential access to capital, superior marketing skills, absolute cost advantages, economies of scale, or product differentiation.

Firms exporting to the foreign market are usually at a disadvantage compared to local organisations because of their distance from the market. This has two effects: it makes it difficult to monitor market conditions; but, perhaps more importantly, it also raises doubts in the mind of the consumer about the firm's ability to deliver on time and to provide appropriate service and back-up. Local agents and distributors can act as a surrogate presence in the market, alleviating these problems, although the question for consumers remains, 'Why should I buy from a foreign firm when a local organisation can equally satisfy my needs?' Managers must, therefore, concern themselves with positioning the product (through differentiation) and promoting it in such a way that there are perceived advantages in purchasing a foreign alternative.

Firms undertaking licensing and other contractual arrangements avoid the problems of 'foreignness', because local firms act as representatives in the local market. Indeed, as products are produced locally, consumers may be unaware of the fact that the technology or brand belongs to a foreign firm. The main concern with licensing (and joint ventures) is that the agreement will give rise to a competitor. Because the firm is imparting knowledge and/or expertise to a third party, there is the possibility that the company's comparative advantage will be eroded through transfer and this will subsequently be used against the firm on termination of the contract. Patents and trademarks may provide a degree of protection. Alternatively firms may consider providing partners with a 'secret ingredient' supplied to the third party through a tied purchase agreement, where the licensee or joint venture partner is contracted to obtain certain components from the licensor. Some antitrust authorities, however, rule against such agreements as they see them as being anticompetitive.

Within licensing and other contractual arrangements, therefore, the key managerial decision is not so much what returns will be produced in the short term, but the long-term implications of technology transfer. If the firm's compensating advantage is its proprietary technology, sharing technological information should usually be avoided.

Foreign direct investment gives firms the ability to establish a local persona and compete on a more equal level with indigenous firms. Indeed, many of the long-established multinational enterprises in global markets have carved out a global rather than home-country persona which gives them complete acceptability in foreign markets.

The issue of government procurement requires some attention in relation to foreign direct investment. In some industries, governments are the major purchasers of goods and services (for instance the defence industry and pharmaceuticals). There is a natural tendency for governments to purchase goods and services from local firms to the exclusion of foreign organisations, regardless of price and quality differentials, because of the benefits of lower transport and trading costs, better after-sales service and quicker delivery. There are also social benefits in terms of supporting employment, assisting ailing industries, bolstering new emerging sectors and ensuring profits are earned locally. Firms operating in these industries, therefore, have little choice but to locate activities in the target market. Failure to do so is likely to result in their exclusion from public procurement contracts and an inability to penetrate the market.

Internalisation versus externalisation

Taking the three generic modes, it is possible to suggest that exporting and foreign direct investment differ from licensing in that production is internalised, that is, carried out by the firm itself. In the case of licensing and other contractual relationships, however, production (and possibly other complementary functions) are 'externalised' and are carried out by a third party. In many ways, however, this is an oversimplistic way of categorising strategies, as it only relates to the nature of the production process and ignores other business functions such as sales and marketing, and distribution. Taking this wider perspective, it is possible to suggest various forms of exporting via intermediaries which also include elements of externalisation, and licensing which involves the supply of critical components to the licensee firm and involves a degree of internalisation. What is important, therefore, is not an attempt to categorise various strategic alternatives, but an understanding of the managerial challenge in terms of balancing advantages from internalisation and externalisation (that is, undertaking business activities within the firm or relying on third parties conducting various value chain activities).

Critical to the management consideration in this respect is the concept of control. Internalisation of activities implies full control over business functions. This is often believed to be a source of advantage as it gives managers free choice over strategies and operational decision making, which can be hard to achieve when working with a third party. Nevertheless, firms have to trade off the additional costs incurred in gaining control, both in terms of ownership of business facilities and the ongoing costs associated with day-to-day management of a full range of business functions, against the benefits of ownership.

615

This assumes that success is critically dependent on control, which may not always be the case. Take the example of a firm exporting via a host country distributor. In an effort to ensure that the foreign intermediary maximises business on the exporter's behalf, the firm may set targets and quotas, offer rewards for meeting specified sales volumes, or impose sanctions if targets are not met. In this way, the firm may seek to 'control' the intermediary. Alternatively, the firm may choose to co-operate with the intermediary, providing additional support, such as sales and service training, and providing targeted promotional literature.

Research by the Industrial Marketing and Purchasing Group (Valla, 1986) supports the idea that co-operation in such circumstances is preferable to control, with better results stemming from investing more human resources into the operation, basing staff from the supplier organisation in the target market to assist the intermediary, demonstrating positive commitment and encouraging the agent to work harder on the principal's behalf. Similarly, encouraging personnel to become involved with their counterparts in the customer organisation at various functional levels strengthens the bond between supplier and final customer, and raises the level of trust and understanding. Here, bilateral relations between supplier and intermediary are extended to 'tripartite' relations, where the manufacturer is also in direct contact with the final customer, working in conjunction with the intermediary.

The success of Japanese firms in the car industry provides a further example of co-operation rather than control. Rather than integrate backwards and 'internalise' component manufacture, Japanese firms prefer to establish close working relationships with their suppliers, a co-operative solution rather than an attempt to derive full control. The success of this kind of practice has led Western car manufacturers to follow suit, the industry now being characterised by car assemblers (the leading manufacturers) extending their power through close business linkages rather than ownership of diverse business functions.

What ownership does afford, however, is internalisation of information and more direct lines of communication between the market and the decision-making locus of the organisation. In this respect, intermediaries may be seen as either facilitators or bottlenecks for information gathering. Where working relationships are good, the third party organisation is more likely to collect and pass on critical information, although there is a limit to the amount of time and attention they are able or prepared to dedicate to such a function for one manufacturer, which may only contribute a small part of their total business portfolio. This has led, in many instances, to firms establishing sales and marketing offices in foreign markets, not only for the purpose of handling contracts in the overseas market, but in order to have an operation 'on the ground' able to monitor changes in market conditions and demand patterns. This points to the splitting up, in locational terms, of various business functions in the value chain.

CENTRALISATION VERSUS DECENTRALISATION

It is also possible to distinguish between the three generic modes of foreign market servicing in terms of the location of business activities. Licensing and foreign direct investment involve manufacturing in the host country, while exporting involves manufacturing in the domestic market or another manufacturing base outside the target market. Once again, however, this oversimplification ignores the tendency for firms to internationalise different parts of the business rather than all elements of the value chain.

The critical managerial decision here is between centralisation and decentralisation. Centralisation assumes that advantages accrue from conducting business in large-scale centres where economies of scale can be achieved in a variety of business functions. Decentralisation, on the other hand, assumes that greater advantages arise from conducting business in the host market, where adaptation to the local environment and greater decision-making flexibility through local autonomy permits a higher degree of local sensitivity.

Within the European Union, many of the cost-saving benefits ascribed to unification are seen to come from economies of scale, which suggests centralisation is the key challenge. This need not, however, mean single-site production locations. Plant economies can be achieved through specialisation, individual manufacturing units concentrating on single products, or on a narrow range of the company's portfolio, which allows the removal of effort duplication and thus greater plant efficiency. With the barriers between markets opening up as a result of the Single European Market, this kind of business reorganisation is becoming attractive. McCains, the Canadian frozen food manufacturer, has followed this approach in its European operations, and the UK Pharmaceutical firm, Glaxo, has taken advantage of the liberalisation of the American market through the NAFTA agreement to reorganise production in its Mexican, US and Canadian plants on a product-specific basis.

A trend may, however, be observed in terms of decentralisation of sales and marketing activities. While cost-saving and plant economies may be attractive in production, closeness to the market and local responsiveness dominate in sales and distribution. Management can no longer consider the business as an amalgam of functions. These need to be unbundled and decisions made separately concerning their centralisation or decentralisation, if a balance is to be struck between the advantages offered by both approaches.

This means looking beyond simple taxonomies and classifications, and finding creative solutions to problems. Take the case of Lucas Girling, part of the Lucas Engineering Group, manufacturing motor braking systems. As closeness to customers is paramount (because of the co-operative alliances established in the car industry), the company has little choice but to manufacture in close proximity to the major car assemblers. At face value, this dilutes the potential for economies of scale, necessitating their establishing many global production centres, with a degree of duplication of effort. However, through the adoption of 'flexible specialisation' and computer-aided manufacturing, their plants are small (employing between 40 and 50 employees) and capable of batch-sized production. Thus, even with decentralisation, they are able to achieve adaptability and efficiency.

STANDARDISATION VERSUS ADAPTATION

Standardisation of products also gives the potential for economies of scale. However, global standardisation is not possible for many products, as they need to be adapted to cater for local market conditions and, in particular, for that country's cultural nuances. Where product adaptation is necessary, the attraction of centralised production diminishes, as the downtime in production required to change machinery over from one product to another can be outweighed by the benefits of establishing dedicated manufacturing facilities in the target market.

The decision to standardise or adapt involves a trade-off between the costs and benefits to the firm. In essence, managers have to decide whether the cost savings from producing on a large-scale basis outweigh the profits resulting from local market adaptation (which may involve the establishment of local manufacturing plants). This decision is determined by a number of factors:

- **The nature of the product:** it is generally agreed that industrial products are easier to standardise than consumer products, the latter being greatly influenced by cultural tastes;

- **Legal requirements:** product, packaging and labelling standards which often differ markedly on a country-by-country basis;

- **Physical conditions:** such as climate, living conditions and income;

- **Competition:** which will dictate market positioning and differentiation.

What also emerges is that the standardisation versus adaptation issue impinges on the decision to centralise or decentralise manufacturing and, taken together, these two issues combine to explain the overall strategic orientation discussed above: international, multidomestic, multinational and transnational.

Business organisation

Business organisation is seldom something which is planned: typically it evolves as an organisation grows and diversifies. Structures emerge out of strategic decisions regarding the nature of products and services, and the geographic coverage of the firm in the international marketplace. Through this evolutionary process, there are four different types of organisational structure the firm may employ: an international division structure, a product division structure, a geographic division structure and a matrix structure. Each of these is depicted in Fig 19.5.

INTERNATIONAL DIVISION STRUCTURE

Firms expanding abroad for the first time tend to establish an export office or an international division, staffed, in the first instance, by a small number of personnel, responsible for all international business dealings (i.e. all products in all markets). As the scale and scope of international activity grows, the export focus of this division may change to one which supports international production effort. This production may be organised on a country-by-country basis (a full range of the portfolio being produced in each target market) or a product basis (different products being produced in different centres). Davis (1992) reports that 60 per cent of all firms that have internationalised have first adopted this structure.

There are a number of problems associated with this kind of structure. First, it creates conflict between national and international decision making. It is not uncommon for the international division to have less say in corporate policy making, even when it contributes more to the overall business, simply because it was 'added-on' at a later stage in the company's development. Second, it is difficult for the head of the international division to rationalise the demands of different countries and/or products. Third, it does not provide opportunities for co-ordination between domestic and international activities. This can make global product development difficult to achieve and global production planning, based on

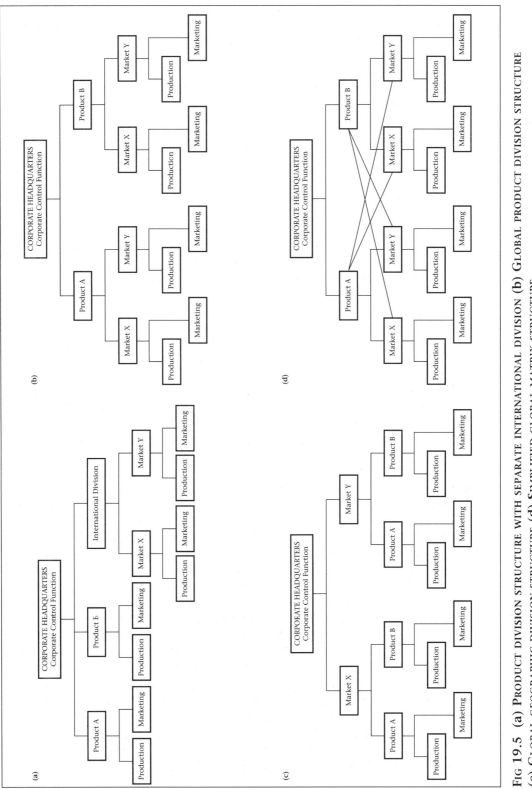

FIG 19.5 (a) PRODUCT DIVISION STRUCTURE WITH SEPARATE INTERNATIONAL DIVISION (b) GLOBAL PRODUCT DIVISION STRUCTURE (c) GLOBAL GEOGRAPHIC DIVISION STRUCTURE (d) SIMPLIFIED GLOBAL MATRIX STRUCTURE

experience curve and locational economies, hard to manage. As a result of these limitations, firms expanding internationally often shift to one of the international division structures outlined below.

PRODUCT DIVISION STRUCTURE

This is usually adopted by companies which have a diverse product portfolio. The headquarters is responsible for supporting and managing each product on a world-wide basis in terms of design, value adding, sales and promotion. The great advantage of this kind of structure is that it allows a company to focus on global efficiencies within disparate product divisions: locating production in low-cost centres and generating efficiency through product focus. The main disadvantage of such an option is that it can hamper the ability of the firm to be responsive at a national level.

GEOGRAPHIC DIVISION STRUCTURE

The focus here is on adapting to differences between countries and geographic regions. Different divisions are set up in geographic centres and decision making is regionally rather than internationally centralised. This structure tends to be used where companies have a low degree of diversification but are intent on maximising advantages from local adaptation. Geographic areas are often self-contained, with their own R&D, production, and sales and marketing. The main advantage of this approach is the ability to maximise local responsiveness, although this may be traded-off against a higher cost structure, as duplication is commonplace.

GLOBAL MATRIX STRUCTURE

The above description suggests that a geographic division structure better suits a multidomestic focus, while a global product division structure is appropriate for firms pursuing global or international strategies. But what is appropriate for firms attempting to pursue a transnational strategy? The global matrix structure offers the potential to derive the benefits from both the geographic and product division structures outlined above. The theory suggests that decision making is organised along two dimensions – product and market, based on a process of co-operation, consultation and compromise.

While, in theory at least, the matrix structure looks to offer distinct advantages, in practice these advantages are far from easy to realise. Consensus decision making is hard to achieve, particularly as there is inherent conflict between local adaptation and the generation of scale economies. Attempts to reach consensus can severely slow down the decision making process and limit the degree to which the firm is responsive to the dynamics of the market.

As a result, 'matrix' organisations of the 1990s have emerged from attempts to evolve flexibility rather than from wholesale adoption of new structures. The matrix structure involves the establishment of networks, the splitting up of businesses into constituent functions (production versus marketing versus R&D) and the establishment of interfunction/intercountry project groups.

Recent research on managing the multinational enterprise points to the development of global 'heterarchies' characterised by multiple centres of control (functional, geographic or product based) co-ordinated through normative means: 'Corporate culture, management ethics, style and similar concepts become critical in understanding why a heterarchy does not break down into anarchy'. (Hedlund and Rolander, 1990, pp 25–6). A multinational company might therefore have various 'headquarters' around the world: an administrative HQ in their domestic market; a financial centre in London; an R&D centre in Germany (a centre of excellence for technological development); and manufacturing headquarters in the three triad regions – the Americas, Asia Pacific and Europe. Certain Japanese multinationals, such as Canon and Honda, have developed what has been termed 'the four headquarters system', which involves establishing regional headquarters in Japan, Asia, the USA and Europe. The aim is to satisfy local requirements while at the same time exploiting the strengths of being a worldwide producer.

The main advantage of the heterarchy is its flexibility. It allows managers to concentrate on different functional areas of the business independently (and perhaps at different times) and permits a high degree of diversity in strategic development, giving subsidiaries scope to develop local business operations in a way which is appropriate to local conditions. Flexibility also extends to the development of co-operative agreements with other organisations which may be decided at a functional rather than corporate level. The obvious question, though, is how does this highly diverse and geographically dispersed organisation integrate? The answer lies in the sharing of information between the various parts, now possible with modern technology, which means that experiences of one division in one part of the world can be shared and drawn on by divisions elsewhere. The domestic head office, therefore, becomes a conduit for information transfer and a co-ordinating mechanism for the company's objectives and overall direction. No longer is it a decision-making machine; it is a facilitator for a global business network.

Organising for technological development

With technology change featuring so largely in the emerging global business environment, the challenge of managing technological development deserves some comment. Up until relatively recently, many multinational firms took the decision to centralise their global R&D activities for a variety of reasons. First, there was the need to control the development of new technologies on which the company's future competitiveness might rest. Second, there were economies of scale in R&D where very large amounts of resources can be concentrated into single centres with no duplication of effort. Finally, there was the fear that foreign research departments might be a source of leakage of ideas and knowledge.

Changes in the global environment and the carving up of the world market into three leading global centres, many yielding 'centres of excellence' in research in particular industries, has changed the thinking of technology managers in many multinational firms. Decentralisation of R&D functions has begun to feature in the strategies of global firms as they seek to derive maximum advantage from a global organisation. The following outline of various types of R&D organisational development, derived by Barlett and Ghoshal (1990), explains this thinking.

- **Centre for global**: This is the approach typically followed by multinationals (outlined above). While there are advantages in terms of control and scale economies, this approach runs the risk of being insensitive to local market demands in the leading markets of the world.

- **Local for local**: This approach suggests conducting research in all target markets in order that the technologies which are developed match with local market demands. While beneficial in terms of local adaptation, the approach implicitly involves duplication of effort and a tendency for subsidiaries to 'reinvent the wheel' in an attempt to maintain the local autonomy.

- **Locally leveraged**: Under this arrangement managers can take the most creative and innovative developments from the various subsidiaries and share them with other subsidiaries worldwide. The main disadvantage here is that there are frequently impediments to transferring products from one market to another – particularly cultural differences and local market demand conditions.

- **Globally linked**: The final approach (promoted by Bartlett and Goshal as the optimum solution to the technology development challenge) involves the establishment of flexible linkages between research teams from various global centres. Structures of this kind allow companies to exploit synergies in technology development at the same time as exploiting local leverage advantages. The major drawback to this approach is the cost of co-ordination and the complexities of managing the linkages on an ongoing basis.

None of the approaches, therefore, emerges as adeptly suited to the changing global environment. Each has its advantages and disadvantages. This points to managers developing flexible systems which allow them to maximise a variety of advantages from the different approaches, while at the same time minimising the costs and managerial complexities. This may mean having major centres for R&D in a number of key global locations, with a series of local R&D support offices acting more as idea-generating centres rather than capital-intensive research laboratories.

International strategic development of small firms

The literature on business start-up has typically suggested that companies should concentrate their activities on securing a defensible domestic position before exploring international opportunities. The belief is that small firms should start in a national region, roll out to the national market, and then cherry pick opportunities in the international arena. But how appropriate is such a prescription for a small firm in the 1990s which has developed an innovative technology and whose marketplace is a niche which extends beyond national borders?

Today, many global industries sport the features of a global oligopoly: at one end of the scale, a small number of large multinationals (often no more than one from each developed nation) competing globally on differentiation rather than price; and, at the other, a large number of small specialist niche players satisfying the needs of small customer groups. With intense competition, these niches are tending to get smaller and smaller, and firms are therefore forced to target their activities more closely towards ever more specialised customer groups. This often means that national marketplaces are not of a sufficient scale to support the activities of small, specialist firms, which are therefore forced to internationalise, often early on in their development cycle.

These firms, lacking the financial resources to consider large-scale investment, are forced to explore creative solutions to their international expansion and development. This often leads them to work co-operatively, either with distributors or partner–manufacturers, or to establish small-scale offices (often staffed by only one person) in key markets where it is essential to have eyes and ears to the ground).

While many of the problems of standardisation versus adaptation, internalisation versus externalisation and co-ordination remain the same for small organisations, they face a series of other challenges:

- cash flow management, which has implications if adding resources to support international expansion;

- financial management and the high risk of non-payment – whereas large firms can cross-subsidise, small firms are vulnerable and therefore have to seek protection through the purchase of, often expensive, insurance products;

- strategic vision and international capabilities – with a small workforce, much depends on the vision and ability of the chief executive.

It is arguable, therefore, that small-firm managers need to be better prepared than their large-firm counterparts. For them, survival may rest on their successfully exploiting opportunities in a diverse array of markets worldwide, which stretches their resources and demands very high levels of cultural sensitivity and diversity integration.

Business co-operation

One of the issues highlighted above was the importance of flexibility in strategy development. Firms need to be able to react quickly to changes in the marketplace and emerging trends in business development. It is possible to argue here that firms with extensive fixed assets may find themselves at a disadvantage. Take, for example, a firm which has integrated backwards and internalised its sources of supply. Although this means guaranteed inputs into the production process, it limits the extent to which the organisation can shop around for the cheapest components and materials, or those incorporating the latest technological breakthroughs. In other words, it limits the extent to which the firm can react to developments in the market. The alternative position, buying on the open market may, however, be equally unsatisfactory: there is no control over the flow of supply or the price of the inputs. The solution being sought by many firms is to consider co-operation rather than internalisation. Similar trends are also being witnessed further down the channel when working with distributors and retailers.

Co-operation is not, however, restricted to relationships within the organisation's value chain. More and more organisations are combining their resources to solve common strategic problems, be it in the area of product development and R&D, or production, business development or marketing. Such relationships with other organisations not only mean sharing knowledge and skills, but also the ability to switch allegiances and the nature of alliances when market conditions change.

Technological collaboration

The recent trend towards greater co-operation in business may be partly adduced to rapid changes in technological developments, as outlined above. With shortening technology life cycles, and therefore the marketable 'life' of products, managers are increasingly looking to lower costs of R&D and to ensure rapid returns on their investment in the marketplace. The latter is often achieved through rapid internationalisation of new product developments, whereas the former is increasingly causing firms to share the costs and risks of technological development with other competitors in the industry. This trend has been further reinforced by the rising costs of R&D, which in some developed markets have outpaced rates of inflation by as much as 10 per cent. In some sectors, therefore, even the largest multinational enterprises are finding it difficult to fund major research initiatives on their own. This is spawning a large number of industry linkages and co-operative arrangements for the development of new primary technologies.

At face value, this may appear to be tantamount to 'collusion', diluting the impact of free trade and restricting competition. However, the position in the value chain of many of these collaborative linkages suggests otherwise. As the research process is distinct from the marketing of products, firms may collaborate on upstream activities but compete aggressively in the marketplace. A further feature of such collaboration is the setting of industry standards. In the consumer electronics industry, for example, firms will not have forgotten the case of the video cassette recorder, where the VHS technology introduced by Matsushita 'cannibalised' the Betamax technology and led to Matsushita controlling approximately 45 per cent of the world VCR market in 1983. With this in mind, Philips entered into an alliance with Matsushita in 1992 to manufacture and market the digital compact cassette (DCC) which Philips had developed. They hoped that the global power of the joint company would eliminate market competition provided by Sony's 'mini-compact disc' technology, the sharing of the risk and the pooling of global resources giving them extensive global spread through which such an international standard could be set.

Collaboration and market entry

Linkages between firms are not, however, restricted to technology development. Intensified competition brought about by free trade initiatives means that many mature, developed markets can be difficult to enter. Strategic alliances between firms can serve as a useful means of securing market access as well as bypassing the cultural difficulties of being a foreign firm operating on alien soil. Furthermore, entering into an alliance with a partner in this way can be an effective way of sidestepping head-to-head competition. It also provides firms with an important means of learning about the foreign market. The significance of the learning curve in international business activity cannot be overstated. When operating in a foreign market for the first time, foreign firms are often at a disadvantage *vis-à-vis* local indigenous firms as a result of their lack of understanding about local cultures and business practices. By entering into an alliance with a local player, there is a form of 'quasi-internalisation' of market knowledge and development, critical information being passed from the local organisation to the international entrant.

Many Western firms have used the joint venture route as an important means of securing a strong foothold in the Japanese market. Typically Japan is seen as a 'black box' to Western managers, its culture and business practices differing markedly from those pertaining to Western nations. Lowering the risk of failure through joint ventures and using the strategy as a pre-emptive stage in developing wholly-owned manufacturing facilities in the Japanese market, has been a popular development route for Western firms attempting to consolidate their activities in Japan.

Collaboration and vertical integration

Alliances have also become popular between manufacturers and their suppliers. This may arguably result from the well-publicised success of Japanese firms, which have developed very strong co-operative links with their suppliers, although the rapid technology change must also play a part. In order to ensure that suppliers and manufacturers are continuing to move in the same direction, joint research programmes can facilitate component development and ensure an automatic 'match' between the demands of the producer and the products of the supplier. Once again, the car industry provides a good example of this in practice. Component suppliers are no longer seen as being separate from the automobile production process; they are involved throughout the research, development and commercialisation process in order that the elements of the final vehicle fit the standards and specifications outlined by the car designers and manufacturers.

Industry networks

Emerging from the various forms of co-operation and alliance are a number of complex industry networks where firms are linked together through both formal and informal contracts. Figure 19.6 outlines the nature and scope of such a complex network in the information technology sector. It clearly shows that there are very few firms in the industry which remain insular as regards the process of co-operation. The number of alliances between firms also gives rise to the notion that many of them are 'project based', that is, entered in order to develop a solution to a specific problem. This contradicts the traditional view of joint ventures which implies long-term commitment and co-operation, and highlights the changing nature of modern-day alliances, which tend to be more fluid and flexible. The main implication here is that firms which remain on the outside are likely to be left out of the technological changes, market developments and vertical business agreements which are now characteristic of many industrial sectors. They are thus likely to fall behind their competitors and find it difficult to stay abreast of the dynamic changes taking place. Failure to embrace the challenges posed by industrial co-operation may therefore cost companies dearly.

Managerial challenges

Joint ventures may prove as attractive to small firms as to their larger rivals. However, the risk for small firms is being taken over by the more powerful partner. Small organisations dealing in innovative products are a rich source of new technology introduction for larger firms, joint ventures serving as a pre-emptive stage in acquiring the technology (and the firm).

For all firms, successful joint ventures usually necessitate a shift in company 'culture'. Companies generally grow on the basis of their ability to compete and to develop strategies allowing them to gain a strong market position at the expense of leading rivals. However, as the global market environment is becoming increasingly

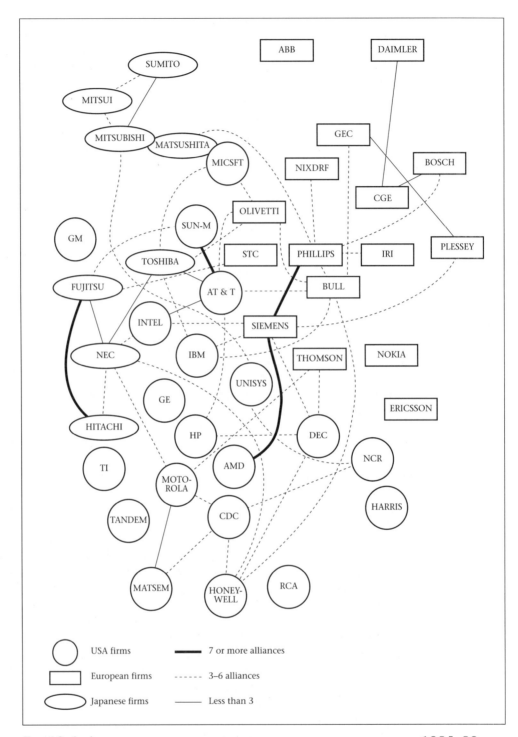

FIG 19.6 ALLIANCES IN THE INFORMATION TECHNOLOGY SECTOR 1985–89
Source: Freeman, C and Hagerdoorn, J (1992). Reprinted by kind permission of the authors.

competitive in terms of market entry and development as well as technological innovation, success in some business sectors is becoming more and more reliant on striking a balance between competition and co-operation, rather than simple organic expansion. Nevertheless, it must be stressed that joint ventures are not a 'quick fix' for firms attempting to develop their international activities. While many firms have found that entering markets through established distribution networks of competitor firms can provide rapid access to markets and easy assimilation of cultural differences, the longevity of joint ventures is thrown into question by the documented high failure rates resulting from the difficulties of managing joint operations on an ongoing basis (Doz, Prahalad and Hamel, 1990). Conflict between partners is common in joint alliances due to a number of factors:

- the ongoing desire to sub-optimise – this can result in a failure to share information or overpricing for managerial/component inputs;

- resource imbalances resulting in a failure by one party to dedicate managerial time or finance to the activity;

- exchange rate fluctuations resulting in lowering of expected returns by one party;

- conflicting strategic objectives and hidden agendas – all too often firms enter into joint ventures for reasons which they do not publicise to their partner; this inevitably results in a lack of trust and in failure of the venture;

- the relative strategic importance of the venture leading to conflict over control of the operation.

It is clear, then, that failure to embrace the challenges posed by co-operation will ultimately result in the demise of the venture. Indeed, some industry observers now suggest that project-based alliances are preferable to the pursuit of long-term business alliances, which tend to be fraught with problems, not least because flexibility can be hard to achieve, since it means constantly re-evaluating expectations and outcomes:

> *'Purely contractual agreements offer little flexibility, unless they are constantly renegotiated, a cumbersome and often irritating process. Contracts, though, by limiting the partners' commitment, can be terminated at a relatively low cost. Flexibility may thus be achieved through belonging to a network of companies, engaging in flexible short-term contracts, provided these companies know each other well enough to limit transaction costs.'*
>
> (Doz, Hamel and Prahalad, 1990, pp 140–1)

The trend in business seems to be so much in this direction that Handy (1994, pp 38–9) has concluded:

> *'When intelligence is the primary asset, the organisation becomes more like a collection of project groups, some fairly permanent, some temporary, some in alliance with other parties.'*

BEST PRACTICE MANAGEMENT

Boyacigiller and Adler (1995) point to an interesting limitation in the understanding of multinational management: management, as an academic subject, is biased towards the cultural understanding of the American way of doing things. The economic power of the USA through the 1950s and 1960s led to the development of models and theories which can be considered peculiarly American in nature. As international activity spread to the multinational enterprises of Europe and Japan, new and equally culturally-bound theories of business developed.

It is only in the last decade or so that theorists and businesses alike have begun to learn from their international neighbours that there are many ways of doing business and the key is not to try to persuade the world that a particular way is best, but rather that an amalgam of different elements, all delivering 'best practice', must be the ultimate goal.

In the early 1980s there was a wave of interest in Japanese management practices in the West, the key question asked being: 'What makes the Japanese so successful?' This led to an exploration of the various facets of Japanese management and questions regarding the transferability of these facets to non-Japanese business. In many ways, this hunger for knowledge was unsurprising. In 1987 Japan produced over 10 per cent of world GDP, compared with a figure of only 2 per cent 20 years earlier. Japan's share of world exports has risen from 7 per cent in 1962 to 16 per cent in 1990, and in 1989 the outflow of Japanese FDI totalled $67.5 billion (up from an average of $3.6 billion throughout the 1970s). The question for Western firms is to what extent can this formula be copied or, indeed, should it be copied as a means of attaining global success?

Japanese management practices

> 'We are going to win and the industrial West is going to lose out: there's nothing much you can do about it, because the reasons for failure are within yourself ... for you, the essence of management is getting the ideas out of the heads of the bosses into the hands of labour ... for us, the core of management is precisely the act of mobilising and pulling together the intellectual resources of all employees ... only by drawing the combined brainpower of all employees can a firm face up to the turbulence and constraints of today's environment.'
>
> (Konosuke Matsushita, *The Economist*, 6 March 1993)

This quotation from a top Japanese executive demonstrates that Japan's success may be partly attributable to a totally different managerial ethos, which is an integral part of the local business culture. This immediately casts doubt over the ability of Western firms simply to replicate Japanese working practices in Western organisations. Nevertheless, it is possible to distinguish between the 'hard' production techniques which can be copied relatively easily, and the 'soft', more intangible cultural framework in which the Japanese economy operates.

Production techniques utilised so successfully in Japan are not unique. Many of them were introduced into Japan with US aid packages and technology transfer deals after the Second World War, particularly the quality control philosophy and associated business methodologies. They were enthusiastically implemented by Japanese managers after being adapted to suit the Japanese cultural preference for group and team working – the concept of *'wa'* which is about belonging, co-operation, harmony and achievement.

Oliver and Wilkinson (1992) identify four groupings of factors characteristic of Japanese industry:

1 Manufacturing methods (including total quality control, quality circles, in-process controls such as statistical process control, just-in-time delivery and management systems and continuous improvement – Kaizan).

2 Organisational structures and systems (including management accounting, which does not simply inform but forces improvements, research and development, led by powerful susha – project leaders) and flatter organisational structures.

3 Personnel practices (including lifetime employment, longer working hours and commitment to consultation and improvement).

4 Wider social, political and economic conditions (incorporating enterprise unions, buyer-seller relationships, government support, and economic structures, including an integral banking system).

Manufacturing methods

The first of these areas constitutes the most tangible elements of the Japanese business system. The practices focus on quality and efficiency and, as such, have the potential to enhance competitiveness. It is these, more than the other factors highlighted, which have been transferred to the West. Figure 19.7 outlines the nature and scope of the most commonly-utilised business practices.

Organisation structures

The main distinguishing feature of Japanese organisations is their flat structure, which promotes a hands-on management ethos and management by consensus. This 'bottom-up' approach to management reflects the belief that workers have the potential to improve the quality of their work. This consensus mentality and team approach to business is reflected in little salary differentials between the top and bottom of the organisation.

Nevertheless, while teams are used to solve problems and aid company efficiency, this is not at the expense of personal leadership and individual champions of industry. Many leading Japanese companies have attained their position in world markets as a result of strong leadership.

Management accounting procedures also differ radically from those typically found in Western organisations. They are extremely product focused and involve activity-based costing programmes rather than 'cost plus'. This gives organisations greater flexibility to adapt to changes in the business environment and reflect a

MANUFACTURING TECHNIQUE	OVERVIEW
Total Quality Control	The de-specialising of the business function. Responsibility for quality remains in its 'natural' place, namely where production is performed. It incorporates all business functions with the aim being customer satisfaction, both internal to the organisation (downstream business units) and external to the company (intermediaries and final customers).
Quality Circles	These are small groups, usually between five and ten people, who meet voluntarily to try to find ways to improve quality and productivity. Members are trained in statistical analysis and problem-solving techniques.
Statistical Process Control (SPC)	This system is used to assist in the control of production processes in order to achieve less variation in output and to ensure quality. SPC involves operators periodically sampling their own production, not with a view to accepting or rejecting it, but in order to produce a chart of how the process itself is behaving. In addition to reducing scrap and reworking costs, minimising variation in components can significantly improve product performance.
Just-in-time (JIT) Production	'The JIT idea is simple: produce and deliver finished goods in time to be sold, sub-assemblies just in time to be assembled into finished goods, fabricated parts just in time to go into the sub-assemblies and purchase materials just in time to be transformed into fabricated parts.' (Schonberger, 1982.) The system requires predictable and planned demand, or production flexibility, to cater for changes in demand.
Kanban Production System	This system involves containers for holding stock and cards for initiating production. This means that the amount of stock in the system can be varied by altering the number of cards in the system. In this way materials are pulled through the production process according to the demand for final assembly rather than pushed through by an inflexible production plan.
Flexible Working	In Japanese firms this includes team working (or cellular manufacturing). This is facilitated by multiskilled workers, who can be rotated between jobs. The system simplifies workflow, allowing workers to be moved to alleviate bottlenecks and ensure a continuous flow of production.

FIG 19.7 JAPANESE MANUFACTURING TECHNIQUES

market-driven rather than profit-driven view of organisational development. This approach is part of the reason why Japanese firms tend to have a longer-term view of business development, planning being based on the development of market share rather than on quick returns on capital, which can often preclude new investment and development.

However, it is possible to over-emphasise the long-termism of the Japanese economy:

> *'A far-sighted Japan and a myopic America make a tidy contrast, but one with little basis in fact. By and large, Japanese managers are at least as much obsessed with short-term results as their American counterparts ... They have arrived where they are today not by rigidly adhering to pre-determined long-range strategies, but by paying scrupulous attention to performance on a monthly or even weekly basis – performance measured not against a three- or five-year plan, but against budget, against return on sales, against competitor performance.'*
>
> (Kenichi Ohmae, *McKinsey Quarterly*, Spring 1982, pp 2–3)

It is therefore the difference in approach to measuring profits rather than profit concerns themselves which distinguish between Japanese and Western firms. Whereas Western firms tend to concentrate on return on investment (ROI), Japanese organisations concentrate on return on sales (ROS).

A final area of interest is the links developed between manufacturing companies and their suppliers. As already outlined earlier in the chapter, co-operation, either formal (through joint development agreements) or informal (through shared communication and assistance), can be regarded as quasi-internalisation of up-stream business functions. The Japanese have developed very sophisticated mechanisms for co-operating with contractors and suppliers, to the extent that they have even supported FDI programmes for their 'partner' organisations to service their business needs in overseas markets.

Personnel practices

Japanese personnel practices rely on co-operation, not mere compliance. The concept of 'collectivism' starts in the family and extends to the business organisation, where mutual dependence and loyalty are central features. Within such groups there is a strict hierarchy, based on seniority, where those lower down the organisation (or family) have a duty to their elders, which must be repaid through diligence and loyalty. Seniority is also the basis for promotion.

Loyalty gives rise to a sense of belonging, and concern over the future welfare of the group, which results in a committed and motivated workforce, working for the good of the company (group) rather than the individual. Loyalty also leads to lifetime employment, as workers and managers feel tied to common goals rather than individual development and career progression.

The best Japanese companies are highly dependent on the contribution of their skilled, flexible workforce. Core workers are protected and nurtured because they are viewed as a critical resource. They face tough selection and induction procedures and ongoing training, but in return they enjoy secure contracts and attractive remuneration packages. Nevertheless, profit-linked bonus schemes can result in broad differentials in pay between boom and slump periods.

Wider economic and political considerations

The term 'Japan Inc' was coined in response to the coherence and interrelatedness of Japan's economic effort. Western organisations, which for many years believed that Japan was closed to Western business, have used this term to describe the highly protectionist nature of the Japanese economy, wherein the Ministry of Trade and Industry (MITI) have carved out comfortable cartel-like markets devoid of the threat of Western competition. The reality, however, is far more complex.

First, it is important to allay the myth that the Japanese market is devoid of competition. Domestic competition among Japanese firms is highly aggressive and, while many industries are characteristically oligopolistic in nature (tending to lead to oligopolistic-style strategies), this has more to do with the Keiretsu groups, which are broad-based conglomerates stemming from the activities of large and wealthy industrial families. Companies within these groups arc highly interrelated through a complex array of cross-shareholdings and directorships. Each Keiretsu involves a number of disparate industries, including manufacturing organisations, banking institutions, trading companies and service firms. There is therefore great potential for synergy within Keiretsu groups, as skills and resources can be drawn from a wide pool of industrial and commercial activity. The 22 existing groups account for a substantial proportion of the economy, are extremely influential and constitute the international face of Japan.

However, this is not the full picture. Outside the Keiretsu groups, the economy boasts a very high proportion of small firms and family firms which make up half of the employment in Japan. They enjoy long-term relationships with the Keiretsu groups, although they are vulnerable and tend to suffer in periods of economic downturn. As these firms are sub-contractors and suppliers to the major economic groups, they are a significant feature of the total Japanese business system. For example, in the late 1980s Toyota manufactured approximately 4.5 million cars with 65 000 workers. General Motors, on the other hand, needed 750 000 employees to produce 8 million cars. The difference may be explained by the value of the car produced by the suppliers – one quarter for General Motors but one half for Toyota.

A key feature of the Keiretsu group is the integral nature of the banking sector. With banks being part of the conglomerate, tied into the successes of the group, Japanese firms tend to enjoy more favourable banking rates than their economic counterparts overseas. In addition, the Keiretsus have strong links with powerful state bureaucracies which involve joint decision making and consultation. This gives the main economic groups a leading voice in industrial policy and development, which ensures political policy takes into account the needs of industry and commerce.

Western business practices

Figure 19.8 provides a summary of key Japanese principles and a comparison with Western business practices.

For the sake of convenience the above comparison treats 'Western business practice' as a single common entity. It has already been suggested earlier in this chapter, however, that there are distinct differences in culture between the developed markets of the West. How, then, can such an agglomerative analysis provide a useful foundation for understanding business practices? The answer to this lies in the focus of analysis. What is being discussed here is corporate culture and business practice, which shows a higher degree of commonality between Western nations than social and economic culture. Nevertheless, differences between nations do exist and where these are deemed important they are given due regard.

JAPANESE STYLE	WESTERN STYLE
Organisational principles	
1 The firm viewed as a collective body; total devotion of the individual to the firm i.e. joining the firm, not hiring by contract.	1 Functionalist organisation of individuals as specialists.
2 Human-centred, not functionalist-centred organisation.	2 Co-operative work system based on division of labour; subdivision and standardisation of jobs.
3 Stress on co-operative teamwork.	3 Pyramid-shaped bureaucracy.
4 Indeterminate job description and job standing (authority and responsibility); generalist orientated.	4 Clearly defined job description and job standing (authority and responsibility).
5 Japanese-style adaptation of modern bureaucracy.	5 Employment of contract ('give and take' commercial exchange).
Decision making and Communication	
1 Collective decision making (bottom-up consensus-type decision making as seen in the *ringi* system).	1 Top-down decision making and one-way orders (no consideration given to opinions at the lower echelons.
2 Verbal and non-verbal communication (*nemawashi* or behind-the-scenes manoeuvres; information transmitted by implicit understanding, gut decision).	2 Autocratic authority at the top; expanded power of the bureaucracy.
3 Collective work performance system (common-room system; total membership participation and planning).	3 Individual responsibility and competition (fair-play principles).
4 Exemption from responsibility (seat of authority is obscure; no one takes responsibility).	4 Strong owner consciousness (the company President is also a hired hand).
5 Separation of ownership and management (no real power in officers' meetings and general stockholders' meetings).	5 Local armament by lawyers (legal specialists).
6 Japan Inc (collusive relationships of government, business and labour).	*(Continued overleaf)*

FIG 19.8 JAPANESE-STYLE VS. WESTERN-STYLE MANAGEMENT

JAPANESE STYLE	WESTERN STYLE
Personnel system/labour management	
1 Life-long employment (no layoffs but there is flexibility by means of part-time and temporary employees).	1 Employment of people only at times when needed; layoffs in bad times.
2 Seniority-based promotion system (evaluations for promotions are quite comprehensive; they stress not just work results but incentive and effort, as well as reflecting capability).	2 Wages and job compensation according to competency (efficiency system) with no relationship to age and seniority.
3 Seniority wage system (stress is placed not just on compensation for labour but on overall exhibition of ability); stress on fringe and welfare benefits.	3 Seniority system at times of promotion and layoffs.
4 Extensive employee training and education.	4 Labour unions are functionally organised by craft and job type; unions safeguard the individual's life and rights.
5 Enterprise labour unions; co-operation between labour and management.	5 Much tension between labour–management relations.
Human relations and values	
1 Groupism (the group comes first; value placed on the group; the individual is devoted heart and soul to the group) and mutual dependence.	1 Individualism (ultimate value placed on the individual; devotion and loyalty to the group are weak).
2 Concurrence of the firm's goal and the individual's life goal (devotion to the group; prestige, sense of security; morale pursuant to participation; co-prosperity idea; love of company spirit).	2 To the individual the firm is nothing more than a means to obtain wages and to the firm the individual is like a piece of machinery, a tool.
3 Stress on harmony in human relations (emphasis on feelings and motives, warm human relations, mutual consent of all members and linking of hearts).	3 Human relations in the workplace are simply artificial relations for work purposes; relations cease outside of the company.
4 Egalitarianism in substance (little chance for class discrimination; small earning differentials).	4 Egalitarian in form (strong class consciousness, competition for equal opportunity).
5 Strong desire for the elevation of quality and efficiency.	5 Purpose of life resides in the family and leisure; strong community consciousness.

FIG 19.8 CONTINUED

Based on Hafiz Mirza (1984), 'Can – should – Japanese management practices be exported overseas?', *The Business Graduate*, January.

Individualism

The benefits of individualism have been well proven in Western organisations. The notion of entrepreneurial spirit is not only welcomed, it is actively encouraged, as the tendency for individuals to compete against each other frequently gives rise to the development of new ideas. In the commercial organisation this means new products and technologies. This supports the notion that individualism promotes benefits for society.

Nevertheless, individualism has its drawbacks. First, it tends to promote mobility between organisations, as employees attempt to build impressive work records and move up the management ladder at a faster rate than their peers. This produces managers with broad general management experience but limited knowledge and understanding of the workings of an individual company. Nevertheless, mobility can mean that Western managers are exposed to a wide array of differing business practices as they move between organisations. This mirrors the situation in Japan, to some extent, although here mobility tends to be controlled within organisations by senior managers rather than at the personal level.

Second, it dilutes continuity in management, with new personnel frequently replacing old and constantly moving business departments in a different direction. This can be unsettling to the workforce and overall morale, with concomitant adverse effects on productivity.

Finally, individualism may make it difficult to build co-operation, both within and outside the company. With co-operation between business departments and between organisations becoming an increasingly important feature of global business activity, there is a case for concern regarding Western managers' ability to adapt from a competitive to a co-operative mentality.

Communication and employee involvement

Traditionally, employee involvement in Western business management has been limited, with organisations demonstrating classic hierarchical structures, decisions being made at a senior level and executed by the workforce. Interestingly, the Social Chapter of the Single European Market initiative is attempting to redress this balance and create a more harmonious relationship between managers and workers. The UK has been vehement in its criticism of this proposal, partly because it is seen as rejuvenation of union activity through the 'back-door'. The Conservative Government of the 1980s worked hard to dilute the power of UK trade unions in an effort to eradicate union interference in working practices, which frequently led to industrial action and lost output. Their criticisms, however, appear to have missed the point. Employee involvement is not so much about empowering the workforce to take action against management as to provide an environment in which employees are encouraged to take a greater interest in the long-term success of the organisation.

Germany provides a direct corollary to the UK case. It has broadly adopted the concept of 'co-determination' where, in companies of more than 2000 employees, the law dictates that 50 per cent of representation on supervisory boards must come from employees other than management. In the early stages of introduction there was a great deal of management scepticism, not least because worker representatives have to be given access to full company information, including objectives and strategic direction. An indirect benefit of worker participation is its ability to protect firms from hostile takeovers.

In the USA, slow take-up of employee involvement programmes is partly due to union resistance. Rather than favour teamwork programmes, certain unions have seen them as a covert means of 'union-busting' by changing the nature of employee interaction. Interestingly, the programmes of employee involvement being implemented in the USA are beginning to diverge from those in Japan:

> *'In American-style teamwork, for example, workers not only gain a more direct voice in shop floor operations – as in Japan. They also take over managerial duties, such as work and vacation scheduling, ordering materials, and hiring new members.'*
>
> (*Business Week*, 10 July 1989)

In essence, US systems are building on Japanese principles in such a way that they fit with local cultural conditions. By empowering employees in this way, companies are combining the benefits of co-operation and teamwork with individualism and entrepreneurship.

Training and development

As the demands on firms are changing and increasingly requiring more flexible manufacturing and work practices, teamwork and multiskilling are essential if firms are to remain competitive. This means training the workforce in a variety of skills so that they can react quickly to changes in models and production runs. Harnessing the knowledge and expertise of in-house managers can reduce the cost of such training considerably. SP Tyres in Birmingham, a company which has introduced teamwork and flexible manufacturing, has an extensive and very cost effective training programme:

> *'This is because most of it is done relatively inexpensively in-house by multi-disciplinary teams, led by senior managers. These teams take responsibility for training other members of staff, often in areas outside their occupational expertise.'*
>
> (*Financial Times*, 3 January 1990)

Wider education and training issues are also of relevance. Japan's educational system stresses life-long learning programmes which provide for ongoing training once individuals have left the formal education system. In the West, it is the German education system which is held up as an example of good practice. A key feature of the system is the close relationship between business organisations and educational institutions, and the high propensity of organisations to make in-house provision for training their employees. This runs the gamut from the extensive apprenticeship system to management training programmes, supported by University and Polytechnic staff but conducted in the workplace. The main benefit of such industry/education co-operation is that it allows individuals to be trained in the necessary skills for their career/job role as well as meeting the skills training needs of the organisation, while also creating company loyalty. Moves in other countries to encourage greater co-operation between industry and education are testament to the benefits which can be derived. Failure of managers to consider the educational needs of their workforce is likely to result in long-term problems for the organisation, as the skills required of workers are continually changing in response to developments in technology and global economic conditions.

Western short-termism

Western short-termism has often been accused of being the root cause of failings in Western competitiveness. Indeed, a study on the competitiveness of British industry (Buckley, Pass and Prescott, 1992) concluded that the short-term mentality of many British businesses restricted investment and development in such a way that full exploitation of advantages was not possible. The UK stock market was frequently cited as a major contributory factor in this short-term mentality, with firms being constantly judged on their share performance rather than on their long-term potential. The other major contributory factor is obviously Western business culture, which, as outlined above, tends to measure company performance in terms of ROI rather than more market and growth-led dimensions. With this being the generally-accepted basis of comparison, it is hard to envisage how it may be turned around without major government and stock-market influence.

In many ways the plethora of articles on 'Japanese success' were misleading. Many implicitly assumed that everything about Japanese management was better than anything the West could offer. This belied the fact that America still boasted a larger number of multinational companies and the UK remained the second-largest foreign direct investor in the world economy.

The Japanese have never been too proud to learn from their Western counterparts and this is perhaps the key lesson, not the idea that Japanese management practices are inherently 'better'. Japanese management is a continually-developing phenomena which often draws on Western input. Peters's and Waterman's *In Search of Excellence* (1982) described the practices employed by the most successful US Corporations and sold 50 000 copies within two days of the Japanese translation being published, and Ohmae (1983) reported Japanese managers remarking on similarities between their companies and the 'excellent' ones in the USA.

The message for firms, therefore, is to pursue good business practice, regardless of its source. The Japanese do not have a monopoly over 'best practice' and, while they have developed successful mechanisms for management, each firm has to adopt policies which fit both with its national and corporate culture. Some Western firms have claimed that techniques which are seemingly 'Japanese' were introduced without the influence of Japan. Vauxhall UK claims that some changes, such as single-table union bargaining, were at least as strongly influenced by practices in the company's US plant as by Japan, and Northumbria Water suggests that their business turnaround was based on a wide array of influences, Japanese management practices being only one (*Financial Times*, 20 September 1991). Even the Nissan business operation in the UK is not solely based on Japanese-style techniques, being a combination of 'the best of Japanese and British strengths to create a harmonious and productive working environment' (*The Guardian*, 8 September 1987).

It should be stressed that the Japanese business system cannot be replicated in another country. Subtle ambiguities of culture and different ways of thinking (which mean many things cannot be precisely defined) and acceptance of constant dynamism, as distinct from seeking an end to a process, underpin the concept of constant improvement (Fry, 1991). Rather, Japanese success should act as a catalyst to other nations to pursue the development of 'lean organisations' with the capability for global competitiveness.

Perhaps Western firms should take a lead from companies such as IBM which, for many years, pursued strategies which have now been labelled 'Japanese'. The 'IBM way' was described by Bassett (1986) as 'exactly the opposite of the Japanese method', as the company culture was based on individualism rather than collectivism. Nevertheless, efficiency and quality are key elements of company strategy and there are perhaps grounds to suggest 'Japanese and American management is 95 per cent the same and differs in all important respects' (Takeo Fujisawa, co-founder of the Honda Motor Company). Differences lie in approach rather than practice.

SUMMARY

- This chapter has outlined many of the complexities of multinational management, which essentially centre on managing organisations in a diverse and dynamic global environment.

- Readers should now understand something of the importance of managing in an ever-changing global environment, be aware of the decision-making challenges facing managers with regard to developing strategies which cater both for environmental change and cultural diversity, and have some knowledge of varying business practices employed by firms around the globe – practices which are now converging and merging to make international firms more efficient and effective in their global operations.

- It should be apparent that management of multinational and international firms requires continual change and adaptation. The economic world is not static and thus, in order to remain competitive, managers must constantly look for new strategies and business practices which allow such changes to be turned into opportunities rather than threats. Resting on the laurels of past business success or simply attempting to capitalise on monopolistic technologies is not sufficient to carry firms into the future.

- Innovating organisational structures and strategies is just as important as developing new products and technologies such that the 'winners' in the new global order will be those firms adept at managing change, rather than those intent on managing fixed resources.

REVIEW AND DISCUSSION QUESTIONS

1 With environmental change serving as a key exogenous factor in organisational decision making, how can managers develop business systems which allow them to prepare for, and adapt to, such change?

2 How may managers ensure that they do not lose their competitive advantage by deciding to 'externalise' key parts of the value chain?

3 The literature on international business is awash with examples of failed joint ventures between firms. How then can the increased trend towards joint venture activity be justified?

4 Consider why firms are beginning to reject hierarchical organisational structures in favour of flatter, functional-centred business systems?

5 To what extent can Japanese management practices be transferred to Western firms?

6 Are Western management practices 'inferior' to those employed by the Japanese?

CASE STUDY: BRITISH TELECOM

INTRODUCTION

In 1984 British Telecom (now BT), the then state monopoly for telephone services and systems in the UK, was privatised. Part of the underlying motivation for this privatisation was to enhance telecommunications services in the UK and provide for a more competitive marketplace through the enhancement of efficiency in the provision of lines and equipment to UK customers. At this point, BT's international activities were constrained to its participation in global telecommunications networks managing incoming and outgoing telephone calls from other countries.

The impetus for competition engendered by privatisation rapidly led to BT reassessing its strategy and it was not long before the company publicly announced its intention to become a leading player in the global telecommunications industry. The strategies employed in this global expansion span a variety of alternative approaches, which are indicative of a growing awareness that to be competitive in the industry necessitates becoming an integral member of the newly emerging global 'network' of telecommunications companies.

These changes also took place against a backdrop of dramatic change in the telecommunications industry. The development of new technologies was opening up new opportunities and areas of development which extended far beyond the fixed line networks once associated with national (and international) telecommunications, and liberalisation of the industry across the globe was eradicating the 'monopoly' status of many countries' leading players.

CHANGES IN THE GLOBAL ENVIRONMENT OF TELECOMMUNICATIONS

The telecommunications industry is in the throes of massive change. Privatisation and liberalisation are key features of many developed markets as governments are keen to promote competition and thus improve business efficiency and technological development. State monopolies continue to be broken up, and firms eager to expand their operations are increasingly looking to foreign markets as the source of new opportunities. Indeed, in the European Union a new agenda for telecommunications has been introduced outlining a timetable for liberalisation which, in line with Competition Policy objectives, is viewed as a critical element of improved competitiveness for EU-based firms. Even countries such as Germany, which have made a conscious decision to retain state ownership of their 'flagship' company, have found it essential to liberalise their domestic markets and open up their borders to competition.

New technologies and services are also providing a catalyst for change. Mobile telephones (based on cellular technology), satellite communications, interactive computerised technology and radio-based communication systems are all adding a new dynamic to a marketplace in which new opportunities are emerging as firms are able to develop innovative solutions to the telecommunications needs of their customers.

One of the largest markets to open up in recent years is that of the business world where the global spread of multinational companies is producing a market for tailor-made communications packages for companies eager to integrate the various parts of their diverse and highly dispersed organisations. This has further fuelled the process of internationalisation and has led companies to consider the organisational and managerial requirements of moving from domestic-based companies (often protected monopolies) to international service providers:

'Faced with intrusion into their own national backyards the movement abroad is being led by AT&T, BT, Cable and Wireless and US Sprint. As they attempt to meet the demand for end-to-end service delivery from multinational customers and increase revenue by entering high growth markets overseas, the new wisdom is to think global and act local.'

(*Financial Times*, 7 October 1991 p xxi)

▶

The last statement in the above quotation sets the tone for the kinds of business arrangement being demanded by major telecommunications customers – local representation and an ability to work closely with customers to develop services which cater for their specific needs and demands. As a result, it is perhaps no surprise that much of the early foreign expansion by many European firms was centred on America, the home of many of the world's largest multinational companies. Nevertheless, more recently expansion across Europe and into Japan and the Far East has continued apace. Figure C.1 outlines

Year	Number of deals	Value (US$m)
1985	5	399
1986	7	132
1987	7	63
1988	11	116
1989	50	2 694
1990	67	16 539

FIG C.1 CROSS-BORDER ACQUISITIONS IN THE TELECOMMUNICATIONS INDUSTRY
Source: Booz, Allen and Hamilton.

the extent of takeover activity in the telecommunications industry up to 1990 – a clear indication of the growing rate of international expansion by the world's leading players.

Strategic alliances are also becoming an important aspect of the industry, where firms are seeking to strengthen their position in the global market by joining forces with firms in other markets with well-developed networks and customer franchises. Deutsche Telecom, France Telecom and Sprint agreed terms for an alliance which gives them the capability to offer worldwide services to business customers. 'Unisource', an alliance between PTT Telecom Netherlands, Sweden's Telia and Swiss Telecom, was established to link activities of major service providers on a European scale, and was later joined by Spanish Telefonica to further strengthen cross-border coverage. It is also likely that AT&T of the

USA will join the alliance to provide a transatlantic arm to the business, which will place it in the same league as Deutsche Telecom, France Telecom and Sprint Alliance.

BRITISH TELECOM'S INTERNATIONAL DEVELOPMENT

Today, British Telecom is the second largest telecommunications operator in Europe (following Deutsche Telecom) and the sixth largest in the world. For many European companies it is viewed as a model for its conversion from a publicly run utility to an extremely profitable commercial enterprise. Part of this achievement stems from the dramatic downsizing of the organisation with the implementation of 'Project Royal Sovereign', which involved it in reducing its workforce by 25 000. Although its international operations were limited in terms of their contribution to company turnover (3 per cent in 1991), the development of international business activities means that BT is likely to derive a growing proportion of its business from foreign countries in the future.

Figure C.2 outlines the number of cross-border deals entered into by BT up to 1991. Less than a decade on from the company's privatisation in 1984 it was apparent that the company had taken on the challenge of becoming an international player.

The Figure includes a number of activities which have since been divested or closed. Based on rather limited success in the telecommunications equipment sector (particularly in Canada), BT refocussed its global efforts on the global telecommunications services market, where it believed it could most effectively translate its strengths developed over many years in the UK services market.

The BT Syncordia operation, launched in September 1991, was perhaps the most interesting of its ventures to date. The company is a specialist organisation for marketing the global network for outsourcing of data, image and voice networks to multinational companies. The company is based in Atlanta, Georgia, with the intention of accessing the largest private networking market in the world.

Company	Activity	% held	Date acquired or established	Cost £m	Status
CTG	Canada-based distributor of IT products	100	1986	not disclosed	sold
Mitel	Canadian telecoms manufacturer	51	1986	156	sold
Dialcom	US-based message handling	100	1986	not disclosed	merged with BT N America
IAL	US-based global airport and telecom services	100	1986	not disclosed	continuing
GibTel	Gibraltar telecom services	50	1988	not disclosed	continuing
Voicecom	US voice messaging	28	1988	not disclosed	continuing
Belize Telecom	Telecom services	25	1988	not disclosed	continuing
Metrocast	US paging	80	1988	16	closed
McCaw	US cellular	22	1989	907	continuing
Tymnet	US data communications	100	1989	231	merged with BT N America
Syncordia	US-based global telecommunications	100	1991	not disclosed	continuing

FIG C.2 BT's MAIN OVERSEAS INVESTMENTS
Source: Company Reports; *Financial Times*, November 1991.

BT management believed that a company dedicated to servicing the needs of multinational corporations would demand a culture and style different from that pertaining in their domestic operations, which centre on servicing the needs of private individuals. By establishing the company as an 'outpost' of BT, it was believed that this could be achieved. The company's aim is to target the world's largest 1500 companies and offer a single point of contact.

Nevertheless, BT's original idea was to create a consortium of leading telecommunication suppliers and it has made continual attempts to attract powerful partners, including Deutsche Telecom and Nippon Telephone in Japan. Its aim is to consolidate its business in Europe and Asia as well as to strengthen its financial base and world credibility. In 1992, however,

Deutsche Telecom backed out of the deal and set up a competing venture with France Telecom, called Eunetcom. The link with Nippon Telephone remains unresolved. The Ministry of Post and Telecommunications in Japan is concerned that if Nippon Telephone joined BT Syncordia this would bring it into direct competition with KDD, Japan's main international operator. BT, on the other hand, argues that as the joint venture would need to lease circuits from KDD, it would become a customer rather than a competitor. While the debate continues, Nippon Telephone has agreed to assist in establishing BT's customer support centre in Tokyo and 11 Nippon employees continue to work at the Syncordia headquarters in Atlanta.

Later in 1994 BT also announced an alliance with MCI of America. The two companies

▶

agreed to create a strategic global alliance through the formation of a joint venture company in which over $1 billion would be invested. This combined the two companies' international enhanced voice and data services for multinational companies over an advanced intelligent global network including global network services, frame relay, flexible bandwidth and network outsourcing. BT held approximately 75 per cent of the equity in the company, with three directors on the board. Furthermore, BT agreed on a 20 per cent investment in MCI. The underlying aim was for MCI to be responsible for distribution in North, South and Central America; BT in the rest of the world.

The partnership considerably strengthened BT's position in the North American market and was a long-sought partnership for a company intent on developing strong global links to support its international ambitions and a global image. It may be seen as part of the company's 'grand strategy' of using strategic and *ad hoc* alliances as a way of developing its capacity for delivering global network solutions. In 1996, it was announced that the ties between the two companies would be deepened further through a formal merger, BT purchasing the remaining 80 per cent of MCI. The planned management structure was evenly balanced, with Sir Iain Vallance, the BT chairman, and Bert C Roberts Jr, the MCI chairman, serving as co-chairmen, and BT's chief executive, Sir Peter Bonfield, becoming chief executive of the new company, 'Concert'. However, this plan was thrown into doubt in October 1997 when WorldCom made a surprise $30 billion bid for MCI. This move, which may or may not jeopardise the activities of the BT–MCI 'Concert' joint venture, certainly demonstrates the awareness of telecommunications companies that global growth is essential to long-term success. While the alliances highlighted here concern other leading telecommunication service companies, BT has also entered into agreements with information technology suppliers. For example, it has signed a deal with Olivetti as a way of extending its European field services capability. Under this agreement BT Europe retains responsibility for customer service, whether delivered directly by BT-employed staff or through Olivetti's field engineers.

This raises a further feature of BT's global operations. Local representation is viewed as a key aspect of securing business contracts, particularly in the light of clients' demands for close working relationships and customised solutions to telecommunications problems. Syncordia's service centre in Tokyo is an example of this kind of activity. Centres of this nature (which also feature in Europe and the USA) demonstrate commitment to the market for customers and assist in extending the company's global image.

CONCLUDING COMMENTS

As telecommunications markets open up, firms need to move quickly to take advantage of the newly emerging opportunities. Ian Vallance, chief executive officer of BT, has suggested:

> 'The PTTs can't survive indefinitely, and we reckon that ultimately there will only be a handful of global players in telecom, including a couple from the United States, a Japanese group and maybe one or two from Europe. We aim to be among them … having been through the painful period of liberalisation and privatisation which the rest of the world outside America has still to go through, we are corporately equipped to take the lead.'

While BT Syncordia is currently closely aligned with its parent company, heavily reliant on the technical, marketing and financial backing of BT, it is likely that, as it expands its business operations in a rather different cultural vein to its master, it will take on a rather different persona.

REFERENCES FOR FURTHER READING

Bartlett, C A and Ghoshal, S (1990) 'Managing innovation in the transnational corporation', in Bartlett, C A, Doz, Y and Hedlund, G (eds) *Managing the Global Firm*, London: Routledge.

Bartlett, C A, Doz, Y and Hedlund, G (1990) *Managing the Global Firm*, London: Routledge.

Bassett, P (1986) *Strike Free: New Industrial Relations in Britain*, Bashingstoke: Macmillan.

Beamish, P W J, Killing, P, Lecraw, D J and Crookell, H (1991) *International Management: Text and Cases*, Homewood, Ill: Irwin.

Bloom, H, Calori, R and de Woot, P (1994) *Euromanagement: A New Style for the Global Market*, London: Kogan Page.

Boyacigiller, N A and Adler, N J (1995) 'The parochial dinosaur: organisational science in a global context', in Jackson, T (ed) *Cross Cultural Management*, Oxford: Butterworth-Heinemann.

Buckley, P J, Pass, C and Prescott, K (1992) *Servicing International Markets: Competitive Strategies of Firms*, Oxford: Blackwell.

Davis, S M (1992) 'Managing and organising multinational corporations, 1979', reprinted in Bartlett, C A and Ghoshal, S (eds) *Transnational Management*, Homewood, Ill: Irwin.

Dicken, P (1992) *Global Shift: The Internationalisation of Economic Activity*, 2nd edn, London: Paul Chapman.

Doz, Y, Prahalad, C K and Hamel, G (1990) 'Control, change and flexibility: the dilemma of international collaboration', in Bartlett, C A, Doz, Y and Hedlund, G (eds) *Managing the Global Firm*, London: Routledge.

The Economist (1993) 'The Japanese Economy – from Miracle to Mid-life Crisis', 6 March.

Fry, E (1991) 'Subtlety and the Art of Japanese Management', *Business Credit*, October.

Graham, J (1988) 'Japanisation as Mythology', *Industrial Relations Journal*, Vol 19, No 1.

Halliburton, C and Hünerberg, R (1987) 'The globalisation dispute in marketing', *European Journal of Marketing*, Vol 5, No 4, pp 243–9.

Handy, C (1994) *The Empty Raincoat: Making Sense of the Future*, Arrow.

Hedlund, G (1986) 'The hypermodern MNC – a heterarchy?', *Human Resource Management*, Spring, Vol 25, No1.

Hedlund, G and Rolander, D (1990) 'Action in Heterarchies: new approaches to managing the MNC', in Bartlett, C A, Doz, Y and Hedlund, G (eds) *Managing the Global Firm*, Routledge.

Hill, C W L (1997) *International Business: Competing in the Global Marketplace*, Irwin.

Hofstede, G (1983) 'The Cultural Relativity of Organisational Practices and Theories', *Journal of International Business Studies*, Fall, pp 75–89.

Hymer, S (1960) *The International Operations of National Firms: A Study of Direct Investment* doctoral dissertation, Massachusetts Institute of Technology.

Levitt, T (1983) 'The globalisation of markets', *Harvard Business Review*, May/June, pp 92–102.

Mirza, H (1984) 'Can – Should – Japanese Management Practices be Exported Overseas?', *The Business Graduate*, January.

Ohmae, K (1982) *The Mind of the Strategist: Art of Japanese Business*, Harmandsworth: Penguin.

Oliver, A and Wilkinson, S (1992) *The Japanisation of British Industry: New developments in the 1990s*, 2nd edn, Oxford: Blackwell.

Peters, T and Waterman, R (1982) *In Search of Excellence*, New York: Harper and Row.

Porter, M E (1990) *Competitive Advantage of Nations*, London: Macmillan.

Porter, M E (1991) 'Towards a dynamic theory of strategy', *Strategic Managmeent Journal*, Vol 12, No 2, pp 95–112.

Ricks, D A and Mahajan, A (1984) 'Blunders in International Marketing', *Long Range Planning*, February, pp 78–85.

Schonberger, R (1982) *Japanese Manufacturing Techniques*, New York: The Free Press.

Valla, J P (1986) 'Industrial firms in European markets: the French approach to Europe', in Turnbull, P W and Valla, J P (eds) *Strategies for International Industrial Marketing*, New York: Croom Helm.

Vandermerwe, S (1993) A framework for constructing Euro-networks', *European Management Journal*, Vol 11, No 1, March.

Vernon, R and Wells, L T Jr (1991) *The Manager in the International Economy*, 6th edn, Prentice-Hall.

Welford, R and Prescott, K (1996) *European Business: an issue based approach*, London: Pitman Publishing.

Young, S, Hamill, J, Wheeler, C and Davies, R (1989) *International Market Entry and Development: Strategies and Management*, Harvester Wheatsheaf.

MANAGEMENT IN PERSPECTIVE

Tim Hannagan

OBJECTIVES

The objectives of this chapter are to:

◆ discuss the universality of the role of managers

◆ summarise the skills required in management

◆ analyse the development of careers in management

◆ compare and contrast management in the UK, USA, Germany, France and Japan

◆ consider the results of flatter management structures as organisations face the challenges of their business environment

◆ develop consideration of management ideas in the context of the need for managers to take advantage of changing circumstances

INTRODUCTION

The management role is as old as history, although it only became the subject of serious study in the late nineteenth century. The organisation of the building of the pyramids in the years before 2000 BC, the exploits of generals such as Alexander the Great around 300 BC, and the development of great civilisations and empires all over the world through history required management at all levels. The extent to which management is universal and involves generic skills is a point of argument and discussion. Is managing a commercial organisation that different from managing one in the public sector? Is managing a football team very different from managing a hospital or university? There is no doubting the views of Socrates, who suggested by his usual method of asking questions that successful businesspeople and generals perform much the same functions (Fig 20.1).

Socrates went further to argue that 'the management of private concerns differs only in point of number from that of public affairs. In other respects they are much alike, and particularly in this, that neither can be carried on without men, and the men employed in private and public transactions are the same.'

The management role has always involved decision making, choice, supervision and control, and has always been much more than a purely operational function. In the future as in the past it will include the need to forecast and plan, to organise, to command and co-ordinate. The role does not mean following instructions without question or carrying out routine tasks as is the case in an operational job; it does mean taking decisions between different courses of action. A manager has been described as a person who decides what needs to be done and who arranges for someone to do it, and clearly a managerial job offers opportunities for making choices in what is done, how it is done and when it is done. All of this is within the context of an organisation, its corporate and ethical structure and its external environment.

It is possible to 'measure' a management job by the length of time the manager is left to work on his or her own before the work is checked for quality. This 'time–space discretion' may be a few hours for a supervisor or foreman, to a few days for junior and middle managers, to weeks or months for senior managers. Generally speaking, the more choices a manager has, the further up the management hierarchy he or she has climbed. A junior manager has a limited area of choice and limited means to manoeuvre, but the management function can be said to have clearly entered a job at the moment when a significant amount of decision making and choice enters the role.

Promotion in an organisation normally means an increase in the management function, so that decision making and choice become an increasing part of the job. The move from 'player' to 'manager' requires a considerable adjustment, one which people find difficult to make. The brilliant salesperson, for example, may not be a good sales manager: his or her expertise is in the process of selling and not in the organising, controlling and decision making required to be a manager. At the next stage, top managers are concerned much more with planning and organising and will spend relatively little time supervising, while middle managers may spend fairly even amounts of time on planning, organising, directing and controlling. Again the change in role will involve an adjustment which may be hard to make.

The so-called 'Peter principle' can come into play as people are promoted. This suggests that people tend to be promoted to their level of incompetence, that is,

NICOMACHIDES: Isn't it like the Athenians? They have not chosen me after all the hard work I have done since I was called up, in the command of company or regiment, though I have been so often wounded in action. They have chosen Antisthenes, who has never served in a marching regiment nor distinguished himself in the cavalry and understands nothing but money making.

SOCRATES: Isn't that a recommendation, suppose he proves capable of supplying the men's needs?

NICOMACHIDES: Why merchants also are capable of making money, but that doesn't make them fit to command any army?

SOCRATES: But Antisthenes also is eager for victory, and that is a good point in a general. Whenever he has been a choir-master, you know, his choir has always won.

NICOMACHIDES: No doubt, but there is no analogy between handling of a choir and of an army.

SOCRATES: But you see, though Antisthenes knows nothing about music or choir training, he showed himself capable of finding the best experts in those activities. And therefore if he finds out and prefers the best men in warfare as in choir training, it is likely he will be victorious in that too; and probably he will be more ready to spend money on winning a battle with the whole state than on winning a choral competition with his tribe.

NICOMACHIDES: Do you mean, Socrates, that the man who succeeds with a chorus will also succeed with an army?

SOCRATES: I mean that, whatever a man controls, if he knows what he wants and can get it he will be a good controller, whether he controls a chorus, an estate, a city or an army.

NICOMACHIDES: I would never have thought to hear you say that a good business man would make a good general.

SOCRATES: For the good business man, through his knowledge that nothing profits or pays like a victory in the field, and nothing is so utterly unprofitable and entails such heavy loss as a defeat, will be eager to seek and avoid what leads to defeat, prompt to engage the enemy if he sees he is strong enough to win; and above all, will avoid an engagement when he is not ready.

FIG 20.1 SOCRATES
Source: Adapted from Adair (1989).

just above the point at which they can cope, to a point where they can no longer cope. Luckily this is not always the case, but it is essential for managers to discover the level at which they are confident in their ability and can be a success. This is not an easy process, because ambition and higher salaries will encourage managers to seek promotion perhaps to a point where they are no longer successful. At the same time, senior managers may promote more junior managers because of their performance at that level.

Organisations have introduced training and development programmes to prepare managers for more senior levels and to attempt to assess their suitability for promotion. The armed services have had this procedure in place for many years in order to decide who should become an officer and then be promoted at every level. This type of process establishes a structured management career, which is reflected in many large companies but is becoming rarer as managers take more responsibility for their own development.

MANAGEMENT SKILLS

Managers need a diversity of skills because of the complexity of the job. These should include conceptual skills which involve planning and thinking. Managers require the ability to see the organisation as a whole and the relationship of its various parts. They need to understand how their particular department fits into the total organisation. As managers are promoted, the ability to think strategically becomes more important. For example, the software company Microsoft reflects and is perhaps dependent on the strategic decisions of Bill Gates, the founder and chairman. He is able to spread his ideas throughout the whole giant organisation via electronic mail. This includes the decision to move into the superhighway of communication and information technology. The senior vice-president for US sales and marketing has been quoted as saying: 'Each part of the company has a life of its own, but Bill is the glue that holds it all together' (Brenton Schlewder, 1990).

As managers are promoted into more senior positions, they must develop conceptual and strategic skills or their performance will be poor and they will effectively have reached their level of incompetence.

Managers are responsible for organising and controlling people. The ability to work with people is an essential skill for a manager. People management skills are demonstrated by the way a manager is able to motivate, co-ordinate and communicate with other people. This not only involves distributing work and resolving conflicts, but also coaching and encouraging people. Managers have to relate to a wide range of people, employers, colleagues, more senior managers, customers, suppliers, members of the community. They need to have social skills to enable them to be comfortable in a range of situations, to represent the organisation confidently and to focus people's efforts on the objectives of the organisation. Excellent companies encourage teamwork and a high level of motivation in order to provide for the needs of customers.

Technical skill is the understanding of proficiency in the performance of specific tasks, whether they are concerned with product engineering, marketing or finance. These skills include specialised knowledge, analytic ability and competence in processes and procedures applied to solving problems. Such skills are more important for junior and middle managers than for senior management, where human and conceptual skills are more important. However, most managers have to prove themselves in a technical area before they are given the opportunity to exhibit their conceptual and human skills.

MANAGEMENT CAREERS

Management careers tend to evolve through a series of stages. These can either be seen as a fairly straightforward move from exploration, through establishment and maintenance to decline, or as a more complex process of transition which occurs every five or seven years. Individual careers do not, of course, necessarily follow either of these patterns exactly, but these patterns do help in understanding where managers are in their careers and what shape the future may be.

The first stage is one of exploration, which occurs at the beginning of a career and is characterised by self-analysis and the exploration of the different types of available jobs. This is a stage which most people experience in their late teens and into their 20s. They may hold part-time jobs while at school or college which help them understand about work and the type of job they may want or want to avoid if possible. The first full-time job is often not the one people settle into these days (in contrast to the pre-1940s) and there may be some experimentation with various jobs before a career begins to be established.

A career can be seen as a sequence of work experiences which accumulate over a person's working life more or less successfully. The second stage is when the career path is established. This is typically when people are aged between the middle 20s and middle 30s. Jobs may now establish a pattern where the experiences of the exploration stage are put into practice and each job is sought as a progression on the previous one. Promotion is sought in the same company or in different companies and a career pattern begins to develop.

The third stage in career evolution is the maintenance stage, where the established career pattern is maintained and nurtured. The manager's career may stabilise at this stage, grow or even stagnate. It is particularly at this point that careers may reach a plateau where there is little further development. The last stage is the decline stage which usually occurs near retirement, when people may not be able to maintain prior performance levels because of a loss of interest or difficulty in keeping their job skills up to date. The maintenance stage may occur at any age from the mid-30s or 40s onwards, while decline may set in during the 40s, 50s or not until the 60s.

The career plateau occurs when a person becomes stuck in a particular job where the likelihood of promotion or major development is very low. It may arise because of a level of ability or bad luck or poor assessment by superiors, but most people will experience it in one way or another. There is a tendency for there to be far more candidates for higher-level positions than there are positions available, so that as managers rise up the hierarchical pyramid, even highly successful managers eventually reach a career plateau. This is at least the case in terms of promotion and with flatter organisations the number of promotional steps has declined in most organisations. At the same time companies can no longer afford to keep large numbers of 'plateaued' managers, with the consequence that redundancy and early retirement become a feature of management careers (*see* Fig 20.2).

In practice, managers may reach their career plateau at any time because a promotion may prove to be the last at junior, middle or senior management level. Pay levels may reflect this situation as well, so that real pay reaches a maximum as the plateau is reached. It is important for managers to recognise that they have reached this stage and to make the most of it. The plateau can be made much more

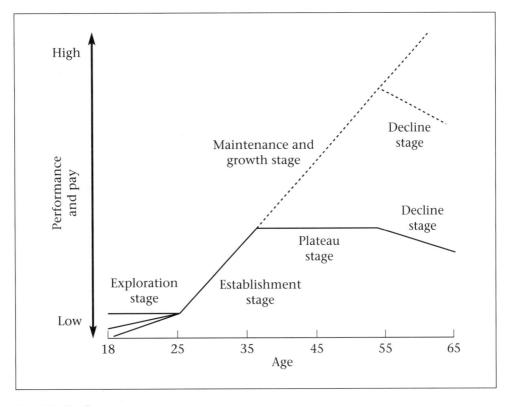

FIG 20.2 CAREER STAGES

interesting if sideways moves and changes in job roles are possible, or fresh opportunities may open up by changing jobs or taking on new developments.

The Lewison model of career evolution (Lewison *et al.*, 1978) suggests that adult
life involves a series of transitions in a fairly predictable sequence every five to
seven years (*see* Fig 20.3).

The plateau in their career which managers may reach in their 40s or 50s can lead
to the mid-life crisis or the age 50 transition, and perhaps a relatively early decline.
Some managers move from one job to another in an attempt to find an area of
growth, while others attempt to maintain their interest in a role in which they have
become expert. They have to accept that younger managers may overtake them and
that they are not going to reach the top of their career path. Lewison's model may
act as a guide to pitfalls and opportunities ahead, and to some extent these stages
are 'proved' by the exceptional cases which are highlighted in pop music and film
careers. A pop group may compress all these stages into a few short years so that
they reach the top of the charts and their highest pay levels in their 20s. They then
reach a brief plateau and a quick decline from which they may never recover. The
more talented groups 're-create' themselves for new audiences every few years,
while others move into different areas of the entertainment industry.

It is obviously necessary for all managers to analyse their career aims and objectives, to be clear about their own abilities and shortcomings, to be realistic about
the opportunities that are available and accept the fact that no one is as interested
in an individual's career as that particular person can be. For an ambitious

- **Age 17–22**   **Early adult transition** – assertion of independence, breaking away from family ties. Those who prolong parental ties may underperform in their careers

- **Age 22–28**   **Entering the adult world** – a preoccupation with entering the adult world, education completed and career selection begins

- **Age 28–33**   **Age 30 transition** – review of career and life progress and feeling of last chance to change career

- **Age 33–40**   **Settling down** – job and career advancement takes precedence

- **Age 40–45**   **Mid-life transition** – another period of review, possible mid-life crisis

- **Age 45–50**   **Entering middle adulthood** – consolidation of period of review, with a possible sense of fulfilment

- **Age 50–55**   **Age 50 transition** – possible crisis or review of previous periods of transition

- **Age 55–60**   **Combination of middle adulthood** – relatively stable, with preparation for retirement

- **Age 60–65**   **Late adult transition** – retirement with review and reflection on career

- **Age 65+**   **Late adulthood** – evaluation and summing up

FIG 20.3 LEWISON MODEL OF CAREER EVOLUTION

manager, a career needs to be planned so that the correct steps can be taken at the right moments, but these plans are unlikely to succeed without a realistic analysis of what opportunities exist and what talents are on offer.

MANAGEMENT DEVELOPMENT

The 1987 British Institute of Management (now the Institute of Management) and Confederation of British Industry report on *The Making of British Managers* started from the premise of widespread recognition that effective management is a key factor in economic growth. It also considered that British managers lacked the development, education and training opportunities of their competitors:

'One of the most important resources possessed by the nation is its managerial skills. Ideas can only be turned into wealth when combined with effective management. The ability to create more wealth is vital if the growing expectations of society are to be met. Those services which spend the wealth must also be well managed to ensure the maximum benefit from the resources available.'

The report found that about 2.75 million people were in managerial roles in Great Britain, that is, over 10 per cent of the working population. This proportion has grown since 1987 with the rise in the number of people required to manage other people, physical resources, financial resources and ideas, and the fall in the number of low-skilled jobs. The report found that about 1.1 million people were in senior and middle management positions, with approximately 90 000 people entering management each year. The great majority of these were found to have no formal management education and training. Compared to the UK's major competitors, it was felt that Britain had very limited systems for management development, and France, Germany, Japan and the USA, for example, were thought to have superior methods for developing managers to match their educational patterns and their particular culture.

It was considered that the largest companies, such as Shell, Unilever and ICI, had recognised the need for a management development process in the 1920s and 1930s, but in many other companies this meant providing a variety of experiences to a relatively small number of trainees. By the 1950s management training programmes had become more structured and many large companies went on the 'milk round' to universities in order to recruit trainees. The need for training became more generally recognised with the Industrial Training Act of 1964 and several of the Industrial Training Boards initiated specific management training programmes. At the same time, higher education became more involved after the Robbins Report in 1963. This recommended that postgraduate management schools should be established in addition to the development already taking place in the universities. As a result of this, the London and Manchester Business Schools were founded in 1965.

There had been developments in management training before the 1960s, but the 1960s was the period during which these developments began to take off. For example, the British Institute of Management had introduced a certificate and diploma following its formation in 1947 and these developed into the Diploma in Management Studies (DMS) in the 1960s. By 1987, 23 universities provided undergraduate degrees in management while 41 polytechnics and colleges of further and higher education provided undergraduate and 70 provided postgraduate courses.

One of the significant points raised by the BIM and CBI report was the difference between the demand for management education and training by employers and the demand by individuals. From the employers' point of view, their interest was in managers obtaining skills rather than qualifications. Some employers were found to be opposed to qualifications because they made managers potentially more mobile. Individuals, on the other hand, wanted to obtain qualifications and skills in order to increase their opportunities on the management job market. Employers believed that the most important factors contributing to creating an effective manager were innate ability and job experience, but it was accepted that education and training further increased managerial effectiveness. It was also recognised that few managers obtain experience outside a single function, so that education and training have a very important part to play in broadening a manager's perspective.

Employers believed that it was impossible and inappropriate to attempt to make management into a profession similar to accountancy and law, but making a managerial career more similar to the professions was seen to be beneficial. It was considered to be important for managers to acquire specific competencies appropriate to each stage of their career. This approach has led to the development of various schemes in order to enhance management training since 1987. The UK 'Charter Group Initiative' was an attempt to encourage organisations to provide their staff with the opportunity to obtain the best management practice in business skills and professionalism in management. This would be developed by the creation of a formal, professional qualification to be achieved in stages in order to provide an individually planned programme. It would blend on-the-job development and experience combined with appropriate inputs of formal training and coaching. This would lead to the recognition of Chartered Managers who would not only be graduate recruits but also current managers and employees:

> *'the demographic trends in the UK are such that the future competitiveness of British business will be strongly dependent on continuous development of the skills and professionalism of the existing workforce.'*
> (Charter Group Initiative, *Prospectus*, 1987)

There was no doubt about the crusading spirit at the time. Lord Young (the President of the Board of Trade) spoke of this at the National Economic Development Council's 25th Anniversary on 29 April 1987:

> *'Let us make no mistake about it. People are the most important resource this country has; in the end the only resource. North Sea oil will pass. The main thing going for us is our people.'*

He pointed out that the pool of skilled and enterprising people was too small, that everyone was fishing in the same pool and that it was not well stocked. The lead for this change had to come from the top, the chief executive and the board. He threw out a challenge:

> *'I want to find 100 leading companies to start the crusade. And then 100 more. Give us the benefit of your experience. I would like Chief Executives to make the following pledge: that their company recognises the professionalism and enterprise of their managers at all levels as a key to their business success. That they will develop the talents of their managers as an essential part of their business strategy.'*

In fact, support for this initiative came from companies such as British Airways, British Aerospace, British Gas, British Petroleum, British Railways, British Telecom, Cadbury Schweppes, Ford Motor Company, GKN, Grand Metropolitan, IBM UK, ICI, Jaguar, Marks & Spencer, National Freight Consortium, National Westminster Bank, Rank Xerox, Rio Tinto Zinc, J Sainsbury, Shell UK, Unilever and Woolworth Holdings. This was a roll call of top British companies across the spectrum of employers who could be expected to promote the initiative successfully over the following few years. The immediate aim was to achieve a 'critical mass' of 100–200 organisations similarly committed to the Charter Group objectives.

At the time it was recognised that while the government had done much to create a business environment conducive to enterprise, the primary responsibility for developing business skills and management professionalism lay with business itself. The business leaders supported the view that success in the fast-moving, diverse and increasingly global business arena of the future depended more than ever on the proficiency, motivation, creativity and enterprise of the people engaged in it. The facts were that only 20 per cent of managers had degrees or professional qualifications of any sort, compared to 63 per cent in (West) Germany and 85 per cent in the USA. At the same time, 20 per cent of the largest British companies had made no provision at all for management training in 1986. There was felt to be little argument about the diagnosis of the problem, as set out in Fig 20.4.

The solution was to establish a Management Charter to embody the principles and undertakings which leading exponents of good management practice would expect to achieve or better in the development of their staff, particularly with regard to proficiency in business skills and the professionalism of management. A professional qualification would be established, the Chartered Manager, with an emphasis on the individually planned blending of on-the-job development and experience combined with relevant, timely inputs of formal training or coaching. The aim was to develop an accredited qualification of Chartered Manager which would be as widely recognised as Chartered Accountant or Chartered Engineer.

The process would be for chief executives to recognise that investment in management training was as important as investment in research, product development or capital. They would make a commitment to integrate learning and work in a continuous development process aimed at helping each individual to realise his or her maximum potential within the organisation. They would use a system of regular performance appraisal and development planning to guide this process, to identify improved performance, skills and professionalism, and to relate such attainment to appropriate advancement and rewards. They would provide facilities and support for learning and self-development, fostering the common purpose to improve the organisation through development of its individual members.

In 1988 it was estimated by the British Institute of Management that 35 000 managers required training beyond a basic level every year, and 17 500 required more advanced training, while about 12 300 managers in fact received training. This gap was not the result of a lack of opportunity because there were hundreds of courses available, many tailored to the exact requirements of companies and run on an in-company basis. These courses were at all levels and open to individuals with a variety of backgrounds. They were most frequently on management skills, human resource management and in specialist areas. They varied between courses leading to a Certificate, Diploma or MBA, and those covering particular management skills topics such as 'how to succeed in selling' and 'techniques of time management'. Leadership and team-building courses at this time were making increasing use of outward bound centres and activity-based exercises, while distance learning had become popular. The Master in Business Administration (MBA) was increasingly seen as the most important qualification for those who wanted to advance in management. This was based on the North American model where the MBA was perceived to have a major impact on improving career prospects.

A survey of 258 chief executives, carried out for the *Sunday Times* in 1997, found that British managers do not have the skills to obtain the full potential from their businesses. It suggested that they lack vision and are too concerned with cost-cutting rather than building their businesses. The majority of the chief executives thought that the business, social and economic environment in Britian had created a culture in which cost-cutting was the driving force for managers, instead of the

- Modern management practice and the associated business skills are evolving with increasing rapidity under the influence of advancing technology and market pressures. To be most effective the process of 'investing' in the development of management professionalism and business skills must be market (i.e. business) led, with government and education making a vital, but nevertheless supporting, contribution.

- This 'investment' in management and business proficiency must be a continuous, career-long process – the product of continuous constructive interaction between the aspirations and commitment of the individual and the business objectives of the employer.

- In varying degrees – and deep down into an organisation – the successful workforce of the future will need to combine professional and business/management skills with functional expertise. Management development in the sense now envisaged is not seen as the preserve of a limited elite being groomed for the boardroom, but a widely practised aspect of professionalism as relevant to the engineer, the accountant, the marketer or operations staff.

- At its best the expertise and professionalism of British management is world class, but this standard of attainment is disturbingly rare. Much of British business claims to acknowledge the value of the human resource, but:
  - fails to recognise the importance of attracting the most talented, creative and dynamic people from schools, colleges and universities;
  - fails to provide a reward system which motivates and encourages initiative and enterprise;
  - fails to provide the means of developing and realising the full potential of each member of the organisation;
  - feels little or no responsibility for establishing positive, collaborative links with schools and higher education establishments aimed at exciting young people with an appreciation of what a business/industrial career has to offer and contributing to the quality and relevance of the teaching.

- In catching up with those international competitors who have been investing more widely and intensively in the development of management professionalism and business skills, we have the opportunity to gear our new approach specifically to the characteristics and needs of the business environment of the future.

FIG 20.4 THE CHARTER GROUP INITIATIVE

development of the skills needed to manage growth and innovation. They considered leadership and vision to be by far the most important skills, while they thought that managers were better versed in technical and financial skills. They (80 per cent) did think, however, that management quality had improved over the last ten years, 54 per cent thought it was good and 40 per cent thought it was average. Only 2 per cent thought that British management quality was excellent, while 4 per cent thought it was poor. On the other hand, American managers were regarded as the model for Britain to follow.

THE MAKING OF MANAGERS

The MSC, NEDC and BIM Report on *The Making of Managers* (The Handy Report) published in 1987 provided international comparisons with the *The Making of British Managers*. It was a major survey of differences in management customs and practices between some of the leading economies and now provides an 'historical' perspective for understanding both the variety of approaches to management that exist today and also in judging the degree of convergence that has taken place (*see* Chapter 19).

International investment in the middle and late 1990s, such as that by Japanese and Korean companies in the UK, resulted in the increasing movement of managers between countries. This, linked with developments in communications through improved technology, such as the Internet and the world wide web, has brought management concepts in different countries closer together. At the same time, the rise of new burgeoning economies and the break-up of old empires, such as that of the Soviet Union, has created a sharp learning curve for managers in these countries and a fresh challenge for managers in international companies.

Management in the United States

The American manager has for many years viewed education as a good investment in the future and the Handy Report found that in 1987 a quarter of all undergraduates at American universities were majoring in business or management and a quarter of all postgraduates were studying for the MBA. Large firms were providing opportunities for training and education and many had their own training centres.

Most American managers in the larger companies in fact start their careers with a degree in some subject and this was topped up with formal business and management study. Demonstrated ability counted for more than academic credentials, but there was a belief that the two were connected. It is believed in the USA that an increasingly well-educated management will give American corporations the flexibility which they will need to survive and to grow.

It can be argued that the 'frontier mentality' of North American history has produced a culture where every man and woman is thought of as being responsible for their own destiny in life. Any limits to personal achievement are thought to be self-imposed. This culture encourages mobility, both functional and geographical. There is little sympathy for the unsuccessful unless they are clearly unfortunate, and money is important, both as a measure of achievement and the means to it. There is a belief that the future could and should be an improvement on the past and that in the end, organisation, hard work and money can solve any problem.

These generalisations help to identify the particular qualities of American managers. In a survey of vice-presidents and corporate specialists, carried out by Korn Ferry International, a composite picture was drawn of the senior American executive:

> *'Our typical respondent is a 51-year-old white male. He is married, has never been divorced and has three children. He received a BA from a State University and, although many of his colleagues did not attend graduate school, he went on to earn an MBA from a large and prestigious private institution. He believes that his education provided him with the general knowledge and technical skills required.'*
>
> (Summarised in *The Making of Managers*)

The survey showed that integrity was seen as the most important element in a successful business career; concern for results and a desire for responsibility were also necessary attributes. Likeability and appearance were not felt to be important, nor was formal business training. However, general education was considered to have a significant impact on career development. Hard work was considered to be the single most important factor in success, with ambition and luck playing a part. While the 'typical respondent' was in general management, he and most of his colleagues would have started in a functional department such as accounts, product development or marketing.

In 1987, the strength of US management was seen to be built on an infrastructure of early education in business. This was reinforced by a respect and a desire for learning and self-improvement. The philosophy of the corporations was that the individual is responsible for his or her development with, in most cases, the active support and encouragement of the organisation. The so-called 'Handy Report' identified that few corporations guaranteed lifetime careers, a development which became increasingly apparent in the UK in the 1990s. In contrast to the United States, the report also identified that the then West Germany had what now appears to be an equally old-fashioned view of management training to that held in the UK. Most of the courses and training in West Germany were found to be job related and company specific, with the emphasis on reinforcing company loyalty rather than individual development.

Management in Germany

The 'Handy Report' found that (West) Germany had a respect and admiration for the well-trained professional in contrast to the gifted amateur, as well as encouraging a broadly based and rounded general education. A knowledge and understanding of the work to be done was a prerequisite for advancement, with study at the higher levels being both relevant as well as broad and a large percentage of senior managers having doctorates in a relevant field of study. The German manager was expected to be well educated before joining the company and then to follow a period of 'apprenticeship' in a functional area, being judged solely on performance. As a result, it was found to be rare to have managerial responsibility before the age of 30 in a large German firm.

The report identified the fact that German management is essentially functional management, and therefore great significance was placed on vocational training for a particular job. It followed from this that it was important for potential managers to study for the appropriate degree at university. Internal management development and training was found to be prevalent in large companies, but depended in practice very much on the views of a manager's supervisor. The prevailing view was that a superior must have sovereignty over his or her staff and would, therefore, decide on the amount and level of management training. There was a much greater likelihood of training in a large company than in a medium-sized or small company.

The education of managers in Germany was felt to reflect two aspects of opinion, between which there lies some tension. On the one hand there was a respect and admiration for the scientific, professional manager rather than the intuitive, 'gifted amateur' manager. On the other hand, the idea of a broadly based, rounded education for as many people as possible was felt to be evident in the breadth of study required through school education and the length of university education. While graduates were the norm in big corporations, training tended to be internal and company focused, with only the more forward-looking companies encouraging self-development programmes to widen the horizons of their managers.

> *'The West Germans themselves see little need to change an approach which has served them so well and worry only that a possible shortage of new managers at the end of the century (due to the fall in the birthrate and the greater number of managers then due to retire) may force them to shorten the period of preparation before entry.'*
>
> *(The Making of Managers)*

The integration of East and West Germany and the economic recession of the early 1990s created new problems for German companies. The need to develop and update East German management in order to maintain a competitive edge provided a challenge to the German economy throughout the 1990s.

Management in France

The 1987 report on *The Making of Managers* argued that France has traditionally relied on a small number of highly educated individuals produced by the *Grandes Ecoles* of engineering and business to provide large companies with the core of their 'cadres' of management. It has been recognised for a long time that a small, highly educated elite is not enough and every organisation has, by law, to spend a minimum of 0.5 per cent of their wage bill on further training. More recent changes have included an increased enthusiasm for industry as a provider of wealth and jobs, against a background of widely felt antipathy to industry. A change in this position was noted in the 'Handy Report'. It was found that engineers occupied the highest number of top management posts in France, although they were in competition with other specialists such as economists, lawyers and graduates from business schools.

There has been considerable enthusiasm for American management methods, indicated by the value placed on American business qualifications (such as the MBA) and the creation of many business schools. At the same time there has been an increasing emphasis on professionalism with more attention paid to personal qualities, good leadership and communication skills. It was recognised that there were a number of issues facing managers in the future. These included:

- changes brought about by new technology;

- social pressures created by an increasingly well-qualified workforce demanding more autonomy and participation;

- an increasing number of women in managerial roles;

- a move towards more flexible models of organisation which allow more personal initiative and the development of human potential;

- the need for better management of innovation and quality;

- the growing importance of the international dimension.

Management in Japan

The 1987 report found that it is recognised in Japan that without many natural resources the country's main asset is people, so the country has to work to live and has to work more effectively than others in order to live well. It was obvious then to everyone, and particularly to parents and corporations, that it was sensible to invest as much as possible into the development of people. In 1987 94 per cent of the population remained in school until the age of 18, so that Japan has a uniformly well-educated workforce with the best university graduates providing the raw material for future managers, and a preference for long-term planning so that the future can be arranged in an appropriate way.

The report found that potential managers were expected to be well educated, although not necessarily in a vocational area. The management development process was one of progressive job rotation supplemented by reviews and assessment and a variety of forms of study, ranging from in-company courses to self-development correspondence courses. The process might take as long as 14 years, usually in one organisation because of the assumption of a lifelong career in that organisation. By this procedure, the company built up a group of managers who were versatile, well educated and well trained in the company politics and procedures.

Medium and small companies did not have such intensive or extensive training programmes and their managers relied on individual enlightenment and a range of external training courses. The small and medium enterprise section employed 80 per cent of the workforce and, as with large companies, there was an engrained habit of study and the pursuit of learning.

> *'The Japanese do not have a secret formula for management development. There is nothing which is not done elsewhere, somewhere. The Japanese, however, do it seriously and deliberately. Companies believe that their managers are their assets. These assets cannot easily be replaced or removed so they must be developed. They believe that careful thought and study can solve most problems, with the consequence that thinking and study are worth cultivating. Whatever else changes in Japan these attitudes and beliefs are unlikely to change.'* (The Making of Managers)

The success of the Japanese economy in the post-1945 period can be ascribed to factors such as those listed in Fig 20.5.

- A fiercely competitive and initially overprotected domestic market.

- An economy rebuilt with American assistance after 1945.

- An initial comparative advantage in labour costs.

- A relatively very small defence expenditure in terms of GNP.

- The opportunity to choose the best licensing technology as a result of being a relatively late developer.

- A lack of national resources, which generated a 'war economy' mentality.

- A very effective education system.

- Government/industry relations encouraging management education and productivity.

- The nature of Japanese enterprise, and long-term planning.

- The ability of Japanese management.

FIG 20.5 FACTORS IN THE SUCCESS OF THE JAPANESE ECONOMY SINCE 1945

Another of these success factors is the importance given to long-term planning, which is supported by the importance given to the long-term continuity of organisations. Company managers and workers are seen as having a higher priority than shareholders, so that short-term profit is not a driving force in the organisation. Since the publication of the Handy Report, the Japanese economy has been affected by increasing competition from other Far Eastern countries such as South Korea, Taiwan and China, and has shared with them the problems faced by the Pacific Rim economies in the late 1990s. Long-term continuity of employment is no longer guaranteed in the way it used to be and short-term profit has become more important.

Large Japanese firms have in the past tended to have similar characteristics:

- internal labour markets;

- enterprise (single company) unions;

- security wage and promotion systems;

- lifetime employment;

- long-term planning perspectives;

- bottom-up consensus decision making;

- extensive on-the-job training;

- range of company incentives.

There has been little emphasis on postgraduate business degrees and professional associations because the priority has been on the enterprise affiliation. Also, for some time there has been a great contrast between these large organisations and the small and medium-sized sector, where there are a myriad of subcontractors and suppliers operating in a much less stable and long-term environment. This large, contrasting sector means that any generalisations on Japanese management have to be qualified in terms of a discussion about large companies.

Management in the UK

The Handy Report showed that there is no single universal way of educating and training managers in the developed countries of the world. It concluded that it was important for a country to check the system best suited to its culture. The two surveys, *The Making of British Managers* and *The Making of Managers*, suggest that the UK has not developed any widely used, clearly understood method for educating and training its managers. In fact, this training was found to be considered an individual affair to some extent. Individuals certainly regarded their managerial career as their own property, rather than that of their employers. *The Making of British Managers* found that the decision to undertake courses leading to qualifications was overwhelmingly taken personally, while the decision to undertake courses not leading to qualifications was evenly split between individuals and their employers. The interest in qualifications was found to be universal, apart from those employed in large organisations with a strong reputation for training.

Individuals anticipated greater managerial mobility between companies in the future, and wanted 'portable credentials' which recognised not only formal management education and training, but also accumulated managerial experience. It was felt that qualification courses could lead to improved on-the-job performance and to promotion, and those who joined programmes in educational institutions expressed a high level of satisfaction with the outcome as reflected in their career progression.

The Making of British Managers recommended a Diploma in Business Administration among a range of ideas to expand management education and training. This would be a foundation course to act as an entry qualification for a management career for young people. In practice, the Diploma in Management Studies has developed as the entry-level qualification, creating a structure through the CMS and DMS, to an MBA. The Open University Business School, for example, has expanded rapidly since 1988 in order to meet the demand for these qualifications.

The Management Charter Initiative was an attempt to meet the need for a programme which would recognise accumulated managerial experience as well as formal education and training. After an enthusiastic start in the late 1980s, its development has been slow. From 1995 onwards, its purposes have to some extent been taken over by the introduction of National Vocational Qualifications in management. These NVQs do assess prior experience and learning (APEL) as well as providing for progressive levels of qualifications. This process is drawing in business qualifications and professional qualifications in order to provide an assessment framework that enables both recognition and progression to take place. Professional institutes associated with particular management functions are stronger in the UK than in its major competitor countries and form an important element of the training process. Generally, however, the comparison between Britain and other countries in these two major reports is not favourable. Subsequent surveys, articles and reports do not suggest that this situation has greatly changed. This was recognised by the government-supported National Education and Training Targets in 1992 in order to provide objectives for foundation and lifetime learning targets through to the end of the century.

These targets can be seen as an element in the overall attempt by the government to raise education and training standards and participation. The years between 1989 and 1994 saw a large increase in the number of school leavers progressing on to higher education. This was marked in the 1992 Further and Higher Education Act by granting university status to the polytechnics. At the same time, growth in further education was encouraged between 1993 and 1996 by the incorporation of colleges of further education and sixth form colleges and by an injection of government funds.

These policies, supported through the Training and Enterprise Councils (TECs) and other organisations, have been an attempt to bring Britain's workforce up to the same general educational level as the population in other advanced industrial countries. It applies not only to present and future students in education in terms of foundation learning, but also to present and future employees in terms of life-time learning. By the year 2000 the aim is for 80 per cent of young people to reach NVQ 2 or GCSE level, with 50 per cent reaching NVQ 3 or GCE Advanced Level, that is, the equivalent of graduating from high school in American terms. Also by the end of the century, the objective was for 50 per cent of the workforce to have been trained to at least this level. By the time the Adam Smith Institute Report *20-20 Vision: Targets for Britain's Future* was produced in 1994, these targets were felt to be modest in order for Britain to keep up with other advanced countries. Since 1995–96 both the Further and Higher Education sectors have faced reductions in funding in comparison to the demand for student places and targets have proved difficult to achieve. The 'Lifelong Learning' initiative introduced in 1998 was another attempt to improve UK education and training. The objectives included the expansion of further and higher education numbers by half a million by the year 2002, launch of a University of Industry (UFI) by 1999 and establishment of Individual Learning Accounts. The ILAs have the aim of widening participation in education and training, while the UFI was designed as an open-all-hours one-stop shop for training based on a freephone service giving information and advice on a range of lifelong learning courses at convenient places near where people live. The UFI has been described as the first college to be built in cyberspace!

FLATTER MANAGEMENT

In the late 1980s and through the 1990s many companies have shed management layers and created a 'flat' or 'flatter' organisation. The objective was to create a leaner, more flexible organisation which could cope with the challenges of change and increased competition. These changes brought new problems. In 1991 the British Institute of Management (BIM) examined the experiences and views of a wide range of British managers. Most companies felt that they faced a range of increasing challenges:

- **the rate of change is speeding up;**
- **customers are becoming more demanding;**
- **more markets are becoming global;**
- **environmental and social pressures are increasing.**

661

Nine out of ten of the organisations surveyed by BIM were cutting management layers in response to changes to the business environment. Many were found to be turning to the flat organisation as an alternative to the conventional hierarchical structure in an attempt to maximise the use of staff. The philosophy of the flat organisation is based on breaking down the tiers of the hierarchy and ensuring that more staff have a broader base of skills, eliminating the need for many specialisms. Rewards are based on outcomes and value added, rather than work.

The BIM report revealed a gap between the perceptions which senior managers had of how their staff coped with the changes and the reality of those trying to implement them. Middle and junior managers felt that they were receiving conflicting signals, for example by being under pressure both to improve customer satisfaction and to achieve staff reductions and cost savings. At the same time managers were being asked to do more with less. When a layer of management is taken out, previous workloads and responsibilities are often simply passed on to those who remain without a systematic reassessment of priorities and resources. It was found that extra training was seldom provided so that managers were expected to work harder without being equipped to work smarter.

At the same time many organisations were found to be clinging to traditional boundaries and practices, despite the awareness of the need to change. For example,

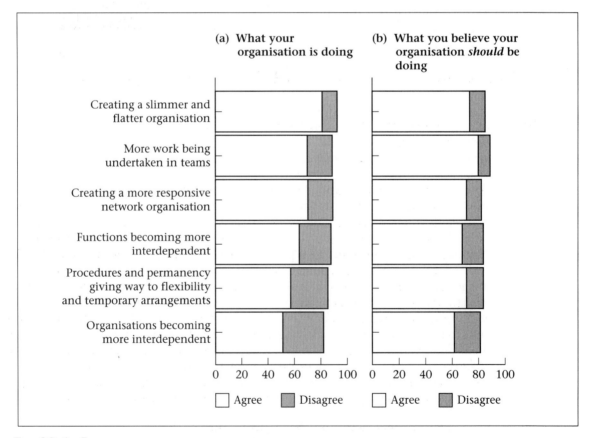

FIG 20.6 CHANGES WHICH WILL ALLOW ORGANISATIONS TO RESPOND BETTER TO CHALLENGES IN THE BUSINESS ENVIRONMENT

Source: Coulson and Coe (1991). Reproduced with permission of the Institute of Management.

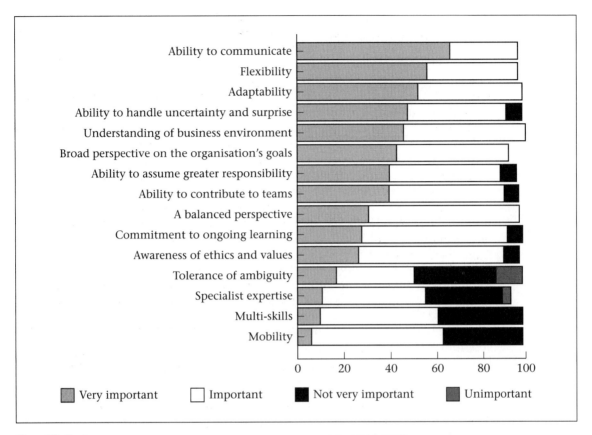

FIG 20.7 IMPORTANCE OF PARTICULAR MANAGEMENT QUALITIES
Source: Coulson and Coe (1991). Reproduced with permission of the Institute of Management.

90 per cent of managers agreed that issues and problems no longer correspond with traditional functional boundaries, while 73 per cent thought that functional specialists and departments must be maintained. There was a wide recognition that managers required new skills, although little help was provided for them to acquire these. In fact, 95 per cent of respondents agreed that 'managers need to be equipped with new skills', and 97 per cent 'that management development will become increasingly important'. Figure 20.6 shows the changes that managers thought were important to enable their organisations to respond better to challenges in the business environment.

In most areas managers believed that their organisations should be doing more than they were in terms of teamwork, networking, flexibility and ensuring the interdependence of both functions and organisations. Only in creating slimmer and flatter organisations was there a view that the organisation might do a little less. At the same time, the qualities managers were felt to need supported and were complementary to these views. It was considered that future managers should possess:

- **a broad perspective on the organisation's goals;**
- **flexibility;**
- **adaptability;**

- the ability to communicate;
- an understanding of the business environment;
- a balanced perspective.

Nine out of ten of the respondents believed that managers would need to be:

- able to assume greater responsibility;

- able to contribute to teams;

- aware of ethics and values;

- able to handle uncertainty and surprise.

As Fig 20.7 shows, there was strong agreement about the importance of qualities such as good communications skills, flexibility and adaptability, whereas tolerance of ambiguity and specialist expertise were felt to be less important.

The report exposed contradictions in the views of respondents about flatter and leaner organisations. While most respondents thought that they should be moving to a flexible network organisation with a breaking down of functional barriers, only 10 per cent thought that the multi-skilling implied by this process was very important. While two-thirds of respondents felt that developing human potential was very important to managing change, only one-quarter were committed to ongoing learning as a very important management quality. In fact it can be argued that what is required to promote success is a highly skilled and adaptable workforce, whose skills are continually updated in order to respond to the even faster pace of change. The BIM report asked the question.

> *'How many of the German or Japanese competitors of the UK compa-*
> *nies participating in the survey will be making this mistake?'*

Similar problems were exposed in terms of teamworking skills and the importance of vision and mission to an organisation. More work was seen to be in teams, but the ability to work in teams was seen as very important by only 36 per cent of respondents. More training and support were needed in this area, as they were in terms of vision and mission, where to be effective the mission had to be compelling, shared and realistic. As organisations flatten their hierarchical pyramids the report identified that managers were not necessarily being equipped with the skills to work in the new managerial environment.

In *20-20 Vision: Targets for Britain's Future*, produced by the Adam Smith Institute in 1994, the author Dr Madson Pirie stated:

> *'Retraining should be a feature of British life, part of the economic*
> *background. Employers should be encouraged, and should be given*
> *incentives, to find courses which enable adult workers to acquire*
> *new skills and competences.'*

The expansion of higher and further education in the UK during the 1990s and the development of National Vocational Qualifications, along with many other initiatives (such as Investors in People and Lifelong Learning), are clearly moves in the right direction and many companies have become involved in the process. Philips Components, which manufactures cathodes, has been quoted as declaring that:

'The continental manufacturing industry can be scathing of British education – they think our people aren't properly equipped to do their jobs. NVQs give us the chance to redress this imbalance. We can recognise skills staff already have. They are the means to prove we do have a world class workforce.'

(*Getting Started: Using NVQs in Engineering for Employers*, NCVQ, 1994)

Frizzell Financial Services had re-engineered its company by 1995 in order to provide a customer-led organisation which involved over 80 per cent of its management staff in competence-based training at NVQ levels 3 to 5 (i.e. degree level). The competence levels aimed at by the NVQ process can perhaps be seen most clearly in engineering (*see* Fig 20.8).

Levels 4 and 5 equate to the main management levels of training, where responsibility for the work of other employees and the allocation of resources becomes important. These moves are an attempt to produce a new breed of managers in Britain, capable of understanding what constitutes value in the eyes of customers and delivering that value at an economic cost. Organisations of every kind, public and private, manufacturing and service, have been developing decision making closer to the customer and are developing managers capable of meeting this challenge. The 'Customer Service NVQ' has established level 4 as requiring the competence to 'solve problems on behalf of customers' and to take action to deliver solutions, while level 5 demands the competence to 'initiate and evaluate change to improve service to customers'.

JOB LEVEL	SCOPE OF RESPONSIBILITIES	NVQ LEVEL
Operators	Routine and predictable activities.	1
Operators with higher skills	Some complex and non-routine activities. Some individual responsibility or autonomy. Working in groups or a team.	2
Craftsmen and technicians	Range of varied activities, mainly complex and non-routine. Guidance or supervision of others is usually involved.	3
Technician engineers	Broad range of complex, technical or professional activities. Responsibility for others and for allocation of resources.	4
Professional engineers, scientists and technologists	Substantial personal autonomy and responsibility for others, allocation of resources, analysis, diagnosis, planning, evaluation.	5

FIG 20.8 NVQ COMPETENCE LEVELS IN ENGINEERING

Management ideas

Management ideas and techniques come in and out of fashion, and writers such as Pascale (1991) have agreed that management ideas have acquired the 'velocity of fads' in the post-1945 period. This has been attributed to the rise of so-called professional management, based on the premise that a set of generic concepts underpinned management everywhere. At the same time there was the view that there were instant solutions to management problems and these have been packaged in the form of conferences and workshops, books and software offering a mass market of managerial techniques. In these there is the suggestion that a day spent on 'time management' will completely alter the ability of a manager to organise working time and improve productivity; the attendance at a conference on 'selling techniques' with 2000 other potential super salespeople will enable managers to sell 'ice-cream to Eskimos'; listening to cassette tapes and following the instructions of computer discs will increase 'brain power' sufficiently to enable managers greatly to increase their potential advancement.

> *'Today the bewildering array of fads pose more serious diversions and distractions from the complex task of running a company. Too many modern managers are like compulsive dieters, trying the latest craze for a few days, then moving relentlessly on.'*
>
> (Byrne, 1986)

The search for panaceas to management problems may arise from increasing competition or from individual needs. Competition may encourage the adoption of new ideas before they are well tested. Organisations may be forced by a fear of competition to experiment with a variety of solutions in order to obtain a competitive advantage. This is obviously likely to be particularly the case in periods of recession, but may occur at any time in a particular sector. The 'solutions' may be imitated quite widely and even institutionalised through government support. Support for quality management, for example, has moved through quality circles, team building, the Management Charter, Investors in People, benchmarking and so on.

Management programmes to do with people – 'putting people first', 'participatory management', 'customer service through staff development' – whether customers or employees, have been constantly replenished and refurbished. Peters and Waterman found that excellent companies changed service-incentive programmes at least once a year in order to keep them fresh. The companies did not expect their programmes to last long:

> *'No one device . . . even in the best institutions – is likely to be effective indefinitely.'*　(Peters and Waterman, 1982)

Individuals may view a new idea a method of enhancing their careers. A new idea needs a 'champion' who promotes its adoption within a company and this enables an individual to be a star. For a time the champion becomes an expert to whom other managers have to turn for understanding of the new technique or system. The introduction of a new technique can provide a defence against the accusation that management is not up to date and trying every available method of meeting competition. Also, new ideas may be seen as offering relatively quick solutions to different problems. As managers are promoted from their specialist function, they may look for 'quick-fix' ideas and techniques as a way of exerting an immediate influence.

The whole process can be seen as a superficial approach to deep-seated problems. While it may be sensible to look for up-to-date ideas as hooks on which to hang long-term solutions, it may not be sensible to believe that most problems can be easily solved. A study of the management of change shows that while people's behaviour may be altered fairly quickly, for a time at least, changing their attitudes will take much longer. For example, a customer-care programme can encourage employees to smile and to answer consumer questions promptly and positively, but if attitudes have not changed this may be a thin veneer which disappears once things begin to go wrong. This does not mean that the programme should not be introduced, but it does mean that it needs to be considered as a long-term programme.

> *'A review of the more popular "new" management ideas of the 1980s shows that many of them represent new wine in old bottles. The total number of bottles remain the same, but each is refilled with new contents.'*
> (Huczynski, 1993)

Huczynski argues that a management idea which addresses an individual's own needs is likely to have the greatest impact. This suggests that management ideas should be packaged on this basis. For example, quality management was popular in the 1980s, packaged in terms of the idea of quality circles because it integrated elements of group leadership, teamworking, problem solving, delegating and so on (*see* Fig 20.9).

A further perspective on management ideas can be obtained by comparing short courses, such as those on time management, against MBA-type programmes. The former type of course may be perceived as too relevant, while the latter may be

INNER SELF	OUTER SELF	INTER-PERSON	GROUP	ORGANISATION
Self-confidence	Rapid reading	Delegating Communicating		
Stress management	Writing skills	Appraising	Group leadership	Quality management
Learning styles	Assertiveness Problem solving Decision making Goal setting	Motivating Interpersonal skills Negotiating	Running meetings Team working	Searching for excellence Customer care Managing change

Most impact ◄─────────────────────────► *Least impact*

FIG 20.9 **MANAGEMENT IDEAS CLASSIFIED BY PERSONAL IMPACT**
Source: Based on Huczynski, A A, (1993). *Management Gurus*, Routledge. Reprinted with permission.

perceived as threatening because MBA-type programmes are based on research and the objective assessment of management performance. This could expose managerial weaknesses and undermine a manager's positive image. In practice, organisations which provide short courses often focus on individual managers and emphasise success in order to promote a feeling of well-being. The development of this positive feeling may be more important than the actual content of the course.

It can be argued that the whole search for management principles is not designed to maximise profit but to legitimise the manager's role. Mant (1979) argues that managerial literature went beyond the description and categorisation of management tasks and engaged in manufacturing:

> *'a mythology about executive work, sedulously nourished by the management consultants, business school professors and so on. Executives like the myth and are prepared to pay good money to have it reinforced.'*

The myth concerned rational, scientific decision making and relied on creating a theory of management which underpinned the practice of management. In fact, of course, there are a number of theories of management, some of which contradict each other (*see* Chapter 1). These can be summarised in a slightly different form which suggests that there are four main views of management (based on Watson, 1986):

- **Management as science**: successful managers are those who have learned the appropriate body of knowledge and have developed an ability to apply acquired skills and technique. This view has been supported by scientific management and classical administrative theory.

- **Management as art**: successful managers are those born with appropriate intuition, intelligence and personality which they develop through the practice of leadership. Leadership skill can be developed although not taught.

- **Management as politics**: successful managers are those who can work out the unwritten laws of life in the organisational jungle and are able to play the game so that they win. Managers are involved in power struggles and in competition for scarce resources with fellow managers.

- **Management as magic**: successful managers are those who recognise that nobody really knows what is going on and who persuade others of their own powers by calling up the appropriate gods and by engaging in the expected rituals. Charismatic leadership can be seen in this context.

Experienced managers know that successfully playing the role may involve all four of these approaches. Intuition will play a part, as will information, and persuasion, charisma and personality. Intelligence is important and communication as well as an understanding of other people, the games they play and their attitudes and prejudices. It helps to acquire skills in running meetings, in negotiating, in finance and personnel policies, and it is important to be aware of techniques of selling and marketing for creating popular products and services. Successful managers learn from successes and failures and never stop learning, and see themselves as serving others, supporting them as well as leading them in order to achieve certain objectives.

In an article in 1994 Sir Geoffrey Chandler argued that:

'Drivers have licences, doctors seven years' training and the Hippocratic Oath, business-men the seat of their pants. And pants can be very successful. The history of business and industry is starred with self-made figures whose lack of formal education, abundant determination and acute intuition are part of the folklore.'

The article continues by pointing out that driving and medicine are of course dangerous to others, while business too can make or break the lives of individuals and communities. Yet the UK tends to allow business to be amateur without universal standards of competence and training. In France, Germany and Japan, on the other hand, there are much higher levels of qualifications and training of both management and workforce. In the USA the belief in self-development has gone hand in hand with a belief in education as a route to success. The Wharton School of Business was founded in 1881, Harvard in 1908, while the London Business School opened in 1965.

'Just as a driving licence doesn't make a good driver, so an MBA doesn't make a good manager.' (Sir Geoffrey Chandler, 1994)

Analysis needs to be balanced by intuition and by an understanding of people. A manager does not need to have heard of Theory X and Theory Y to know that people respond better to persuasion and encouragement than coercion, but if a manager does not have this intuitive understanding, training in the theories of management and in the practical experiences of managers can lead to a rational understanding of the most successful methods.

With organisational restructuring, the career expectations of managers have changed dramatically. The connection between how well a manager performs and job security has been shaken. There has been a shift from managers being secure in their jobs if they did not make mistakes, to job security based on performance measurement, to losing a job irrespective of performance because of organisational requirements. In the past, middle managers in particular were reasonably paid, had job security and could expect a slow but steady rise in pay even if they had reached their career plateau. This is no longer the case. Faith in the orderly, single-company career path has been lost.

Managers have now to take control of their own careers to an extent unknown in the past. They have to become entrepreneurial about their own careers, and entrepreneurial managers have to create a product or service of value. Instead of seeing career development as moving up a hierarchy, entrepreneurial managers see progress in their careers as the territory grows below them, as the demand for their services grows, as their pay increases. These managers may become traditional entrepreneurs in developing their own business or modem entrepreneurs developing their own 'consultancy' based on their skills and ideas, but they all have to make sure that they obtain the training and experiences they need in order to remain 'employable' and 'in demand':

'Hereafter, the employee will assume full responsibility for his own career – for keeping his qualifications up-to-date, for getting himself moved to the next position at the right time, for putting away funds for retirement, and, most daunting of all, for achieving job satisfac-

*tion. The company, while making no promises, will endeavour to pro-
vide a conducive environment, economic exigencies permitting.'*

(Kiechael, 1987)

In many cases, managers have been able to move out of companies and then be re-employed by them as independent advisers or consultants. These developments are threatening for many people but hold out considerable benefits for those managers able to take advantage of the situation. 'The future ain't what it used to be', and the economic environment, international competition and the global environment have all changed. The major challenge from a management perspective is to create a situation where managers welcome change and are in a position to take advantage of it.

SUMMARY

- This chapter places management and careers in management in context. It discusses how far it is possible to see management as a transferable skill which can be applied with success to a variety of circumstances, so that a manager has the ability to manage any type of organisation.

- The career paths of managers can be viewed in different ways, but tend to follow a fairly distinct pattern from an exploratory stage through to retirement. Major reports in the UK have highlighted the way managers are trained and developed through their career.

- Comparisons can be drawn between management in the UK, the USA, Germany, France and Japan. In all these countries the role of the manager has to a greater or lesser extent been affected by company re-engineering and the move to 'flatter organisations'. Management ideas can be considered in terms of organisational as well as personal needs, and the management role can be seen as constantly evolving in response to change.

REVIEW AND DISCUSSION QUESTIONS

1 Is it possible for a manager to manage any type of organisation successfully, or is it necessary to have knowledge and experience of the area to be managed?

2 What are the most important skills a manager requires?

3 Do management careers follow a pattern because of organisational, individual or other factors?

4 How do British managers compare to managers in other countries in terms of their development and training?

5 What qualities are required for managers to cope with the development of flatter organisations?

6 Of what use are management ideas and concepts in the practice of management?

CASE STUDY: LOSS OF FAITH IN MANAGERS

FT

When we asked 140 MBA students at the London Business School to describe their career ambitions, only six aspired to management positions in established corporations. Most hoped to derive professional satisfaction by constantly broadening and deepening their personal portfolio of skills, and by contributing to society in meaningful ways. As managers in established companies, they felt, they could neither develop personally nor contribute to social and economic progress.

It is easy for corporate executives to write these students off as arrogant or naive. Easy but dangerous. Managers must confront the reality that the best and the brightest from other professional schools, universities and technical programmes are not joining established companies. This inability to attract and retain talented young people is only one symptom of a more profound challenge to managers of large corporations – society has lost faith in them.

The evidence of lost faith is overwhelming. Corporate executives fare poorly in polls of public trust. We admire football players for their multi-million pound contracts, but vilify managers who prosper from performance-based incentives. The best selling Dilbert series argues that management positions exist as places where the least competent employees can do the least harm.

This crisis of faith in management has serious implications, not only for business, but for society as a whole. Unless the tide is turned firms will not replenish their management ranks with talented young people; executives will find themselves increasingly hemmed in by regulations designed to limit their influence; and managers will lose faith in themselves. These trends could hobble the large businesses that now represent society's main engine of economic progress.

From its beginnings in the nineteenth century, management has stood out as the ungainly stepchild among the professions. The goal of law is justice, the goal of medicine health. Management, in contrast, lacks a clear idea. Professionals in other fields may fall short of their lofty goals, but at least they have ideals to fall short of. Some argue that managers create wealth for society, but this goal too easily blurs into personal greed, so losing social legitimacy and inspirational power. Moreover, few managers of large companies are seen to be generating new economic value. In contrast to entrepreneurs who are lionised for creating wealth and institutions *de novo*, managers of ongoing concerns are viewed as mere rentiers, living off their companies' past legacy like dissolute heirs squandering the family fortune.

Bill Gates becomes a cult hero by creating Microsoft, while Michael Eisner wins at best grudging recognition for transforming Disney from a tired theme park in the US to a global creative powerhouse. The spate of recent restructuring, layoffs and divestment has further eroded confidence in managers. Through repeated bouts of restructuring many managers have elevated efficiency to the corporation's highest goal. While they are a necessary means, operational efficiencies rarely succeed as a goal to attract, impassion and retain motivated employees.

Moreover, employees in contracting companies see few attractive opportunities for professional development. Nor, in an age of layoffs and downsizing, do employees trust companies to manage their careers for them.

The first step in reversing this growing crisis of faith is to recognise that corporations and their managers act as the primary engine of social and economic progress. Progress requires innovative combinations of resources, technologies and knowledge to create new products and services. Innovation requires human will and creativity to impose change on the world. While individual entrepreneurs often provide the initial creative spark, large organisations are generally necessary to stoke the flame. Apple computers started in a garage, but the Macintosh was produced by an established company, as were the Walkman, synthetic fabrics and AZT. Placing societal progress at the heart of the company's vision and purpose is not a

▶

public relations gimmick. Rather the ideal of progress underpins the success of the companies we most admire. The precise vision of progress varies across companies, with different companies aspiring to change the world through technological innovation (Honda, Merck, Sony, 3M), social activism (The Body Shop, Ben & Jerry's) and empowering the underdog (Mary Kay Cosmetics, Ikea, Wal Mart). These visions of progress infuse organisations with a sense of purpose that allows them to attract, motivate and retain committed employees.

Inertia is the enemy of progress. Past insights ossify into clichés, processes lapse into routines and commitments become ties that bind companies to the same course of action. Perhaps the most vital and fulfilling element of a manager's job is to prevent inertia. To seize the promise of the future, managers must constantly overcome the burdens of the past.

A manager's role, therefore, is not to toil long and hard to make the inevitable happen. His or her job is to make happen what otherwise would not happen. ■

Source: *Financial Times*, 6 June 1997. Reprinted with permission.

REFERENCES FOR FURTHER READING

Adair, John (1989) *Leaders*, Guildford: Talbot Adair Press.

Byrne, J A (1986) 'Business Fads: What's In and What's Out', *Business Week*, 20 January.

Chandler, Sir Geoffrey (1994) 'The Business of Book-Learning', *Management Today*, November.

Charter Group Initiative (1987) *Prospectus*, London: National Economic Development Council.

Confederation of British Industry (1992) *World Class Targets*, London: CBI.

Constable, J and McCormick, R (1987) *The Making of British Managers*, London: British Institute of Management and Confederation of British Industry.

Coulson, Colin and Coe, Trudy (1991) *The Flatter Organisation: Philosophy and Practice*, Corby: Institute of Management.

Further Education Unit (1994) *Tackling Targets*, London: FEU.

Handy, Charles (1987) *The Making of Managers*, London: Manpower Services Commission, National Economic Development Council, British Institute of Management.

Huczynski, Andrzej A (1993) *Management Gurus*, London and New York: Routledge.

Kiechael III, Walter (1987) 'Your New Employment Contract', *Fortune*, 6 July.

Lewison, Daniel J, Darrow, Charlotte N, Kein, Edward B, Lewison, Maria H and McKee, Braxton (1978) *The Seasons of a Man's Life*, New York: Knopf.

Mant, Alistair (1979) *The Rise and Fall of the British Manager*, London: Pan.

National Council for Vocational Qualifications (1994) *Getting Started: Using NVQs in Engineering for Employees*, London: NCVQ.

Pascale, Richard Tanner (1991) *Managing on the Edge*, Harmondsworth: Penguin.

Peters, T and Waterman, R (1982) *In Search of Excellence*, New York: Harper & Row.

Pirie, Dr Madson (1994) *20-20 Vision: Targets for Britain's Future*, London: Adam Smith Institute.

Schlewder, Brenton (1990) 'How Bill Gates Keeps the Magic Going', *Fortune*, 18 June.

Smith, David (1997) 'Managers Lack Proper Skills', *Sunday Times*, 14 September.

Sumantra, Ghoshal and Sull, Donald (1997) *Financial Times*, 6 June.

Watson, T J (1986) *Management, Organisation and Employment Strategy*, London: Routledge.

INDEX